DUMFRIES & GALLOWAY COLLEGE

Heathhall Dumfries DG1 3QZ • Tel. (01387) 243826 / 261261

LEARNING RESOURCES CENTRE

This book is due for return on or before date shown below

2 WEEK LOAN

Fifth Edition

Basic Construction Materials

THEODORE W. MAROTTA

Professor of Civil Engineering Technology
Hudson Valley Community College

CHARLES A. HERUBIN, P.E.

Professor of Civil Engineering Technology
Hudson Valley Community College

Prentice Hall

Upper Saddle River, New Jersey   Columbus, Ohio

Library of Congress Cataloging-in-Publication Data

Marotta, Theodore W.

   Basic construction materials / Theodore W.

Marotta, Charles A. Herubin.—5th ed.

     p. cm.

   Includes index.

   ISBN 0-13-570169-4

   1. Building materials. I. Herubin, Charles A.

II. Title.

TA403.M295   1997

624.1′8—dc20   96-27571

                              CIP

Cover Art: © Chuck Mason/International Stock
Acquisitions Editor: Ed Francis
Production Editor: Julie Peters
Production Manager: Laura A. Messerly
Editorial/Production Supervision: WordCrafters Editorial Services, Inc.
Cover Designer: Scott Rattray
Marketing Manager: Danny Hoyt

This book was set in Times Roman by Carlisle Communications and was printed and bound by R.R. Donnelley & Sons Company. The cover was printed by Phoenix Color Corp.

© 1997 by Prentice-Hall, Inc.
Simon & Schuster/A Viacom Company
Upper Saddle River, New Jersey 07458

Earlier editions, entitled *Basic Construction Materials: Methods and Testing,* © 1993, 1987, 1981, 1977 by Prentice-Hall, Inc.

Printed in the United States of America

10 9 8 7 6 5 4 3 2 1

ISBN 0-13-570169-4

Prentice-Hall International (UK) Limited, *London*
Prentice-Hall of Australia Pty. Limited, *Sydney*
Prentice-Hall of Canada, Inc., *Toronto*
Prentice-Hall Hispanoamericana, S. A., *Mexico*
Prentice-Hall of India Private Limited, *New Delhi*
Prentice-Hall of Japan, Inc., *Tokyo*
Simon & Schuster Asia Pte. Ltd., *Singapore*
Editora Prentice-Hall do Brasil, Ltda., *Rio de Janeiro*

■ Preface

This book covers a few basic materials of the many used in construction. These are discussed thoroughly in order to provide preparation for further courses in construction methods, specification writing, or design methods, or for entering the construction industry. Therefore, we have increased the number of review questions at the end of each chapter, adding metric problems as well as increasing the number of usable industry reference standards.

The materials selected for the book are:

aggregates	masonry
asphalt, asphalt concrete	iron, steel
Portland cement concrete	wood

These are the materials most widely used in construction and are the ones over which people in the construction industry have the most control. Shaping them to final size, protecting them from the elements, and fitting them together are accomplished in the field to a greater extent with these materials than with most others.

The format of the book consists of text material as well as industry standards from the American Concrete Institute and the American Society for Testing Materials. Because the construction industry is undergoing metrication, that is, the process of changing over to the metric system of weights and measurements, the appendix also includes valuable metric information.

We appreciate the continued assistance of the technical and manufacturer's associations whose publications provided much valuable information for this book. Comments and assistance from our teaching and construction industry colleagues, as well as from our students, have been very helpful and are gratefully acknowledged. We would also like to acknowledge the support and assistance afforded us by the editorial staff at Prentice Hall.

T.W.M.
C.A.H.

■ Contents

3 ASPHALT 83

4   PORTLAND CEMENT CONCRETE   145

1

Introduction

Every construction project is intended to result in a finished product which will perform certain functions in conformance with, and sometimes in spite of, the effects of nature. Whether or not satisfactory results are achieved depends upon the materials selected and how they are used. They must perform under specific conditions of usage. The designer, the builder, and the user must all understand construction materials to produce the finished facility and to use it to best advantage. Knowledge of design procedures, construction methods, and maintenance practices is needed. Underlying all these qualifications is a knowledge of materials. In order to be completely satisfactory, each material used must perform its function well over a sufficiently long time, and both original cost and maintenance expense must be reasonable.

THE CONSTRUCTION PROCESS

The construction process begins when a person or organization, hereafter called the *owner*, decides to improve the land with permanent or semipermanent additions. The next step is to hire a *designer*, either an engineer or an architect, to design the construction project. The designer's organization prepares *plans* called working drawings showing details and how the finished construction will look. The plans explain briefly what materials are to be used. *Specifications* are prepared explaining in greater detail what materials to use, the characteristics the materials must have, and what methods of inspection and testing the owner's representative will use to check those characteristics.

Basic materials, such as wood, asphalt and stone, and manufactured products, such as plywood sheets, cast iron pipe, and concrete blocks, must all be specified. Combinations of materials are commonplace, such as trusses consisting of glued laminated timber members in combination with steel members, cast iron pipe with portland cement lining, concrete beams reinforced with prestressed steel wire, or window and frame units containing glass, several kinds of metal, and plastic all in one *assembly*.

An assembly is either fully built at the factory (*shop assembled*) or partially completed in the factory and assembled in the field (*jobsite assembled*). Some of the types of work performed in the field are also manufacturing processes. The mixing and placing of concrete and the cutting and welding of steel are in this category.

A *builder* or contractor is chosen to perform the construction and enters into a contract with the owner to provide a finished product completed in accordance with the plans and specifications. The owner is represented during the construction stage by an agent, usually the designer, who administers the contract impartially, by approving or rejecting materials and workmanship, by approving final construction, and by determining the amount of payment due. *Inspectors* are present at the jobsite to inspect the work in progress and perform field tests as part of construction supervision. Laboratory testing may be performed by an *independent testing laboratory*. The testing laboratory reports whether or not materials comply with specifications.

The builder uses materials in his operation which do not become part of the finished construction and are not controlled by the designer. Examples are temporary sheeting to hold back the sides of an excavation, and removable forms to hold concrete in the desired shape until it cures. The builder, like the designer, must select, inspect, and test materials best suited for the purpose from among those available.

Those who supply materials and partially or fully assembled components to be used in construction are called *suppliers*. Included are manufacturers, quarries, sawmills, and others.

NEED FOR MATERIALS WITH VARIOUS QUALITIES

The construction industry requires materials for a vast range of uses. The qualities these materials possess are as varied as the strength and flexibility required of an elevator cable or the warm, wood grain appearance and smooth finish of a birch or maple cabinet. (See Figure 1–1.)

The construction of a simple building such as a house requires selection of materials to perform the following tasks:

1. Footing
   a. Distribute the weight of the building to the soil
   b. Resist cracking despite uneven soil settlement
   c. Resist corrosive attack from soil and water
2. Basement floor
   a. Provide a smooth surface
   b. Resist wear
   c. Resist cracking despite upward water pressure or uneven soil settlement
   d. Keep moisture out
   e. Resist corrosive attack from soil and water

3. Basement walls

   a. Support the rest of the building

   b. Resist lateral side pressure from the earth

   c. Keep moisture out

   d. Resist corrosive attack from soil and water

4. Other floors and ceilings

   a. Provide a smooth surface

   b. Resist wear

   c. Support furniture and people without sagging excessively or breaking

   d. Provide a satisfactory appearance

   e. Clean easily

   f. Insulate against noise transmission

5. Outside walls

   a. Support floors and roof

   b. Resist lateral wind pressure

   c. Provide a satisfactory appearance inside and out

   d. Insulate against noise and heat transmission

   e. Keep moisture out

6. Partitions

   a. Support floors and roof

   b. Provide a satisfactory appearance

   c. Insulate against noise transmission

7. Roof

   a. Keep moisture out

   b. Support snow and other weights

   c. Resist wind pressure and wind uplift

   d. Provide a satisfactory appearance

   e. Insulate against noise and heat transmission

The types of materials used in smaller buildings have become somewhat standardized. However, new materials are constantly being proposed, and the use of the better ones results in lowered costs or improved living conditions. Their development and proper use require an understanding of materials.

A building is used to illustrate the points that a construction project includes many components that must perform various functions and that new materials must be constantly analyzed. However, the same is true of any other construction project. A project such as paving a street or laying a pipeline requires more kinds of material to perform more differing functions than the casual observer would ever guess. New materials are continually available in these fields also.

(a)

(b)

(c)

4

(e)

(d)

FIGURE 1–1 Materials for various types of construction: (a) asphalt concrete pavement; (b) concrete bridge (*Courtesy Portland Cement Association*); (c) steel towers; (d) wood floor pattern (*Courtesy Wood Mosaic*); (e) wood framing (*Courtesy Weyerhaeuser*)

As man's desires expand, the need is created for materials with new qualities. In order to explore space, lightweight materials were needed that could resist heat of a higher degree than ever before. Necessary qualities may be obtained by developing special treatments for common materials or by developing entirely new materials. For example, treatments have been developed to make wood highly fire resistant. The development of steel allowed the construction of bridges with longer spans than had been possible with wood.

SELECTING MATERIALS

We constantly encounter man-made objects built of materials carefully selected to be the most satisfactory ones for that particular use. Any satisfactory choice always requires a knowledge of construction materials and an adequate selection procedure.

A construction project originates in the mind of the owner. The owner may be a city administrator determined to build a sewer system and a plant for treating sewage; a landowner who wants to build an office building and lease office space; or a government body planning to build a dam or bridge. The owner is concerned with the cost of the project and the service it will provide.

A designer is selected who, among other things, is responsible for selection of all construction materials to achieve the desired performance within the budget cost. He considers the service each component must perform, appearance, original cost, maintenance expense, and useful life expectancy. Maintenance includes such operations as cleaning, preventing and repairing corrosion damage, and repairing or replacing damaged material.

Original cost and maintenance expense must be weighed together against useful life expectancy. Original cost and maintenance expense must also be balanced against each other. Often a low first cost means high maintenance expense and vice versa. However, this is not always so. Expensive material may be expensive to maintain. Even though it is the total cost that must be considered, it is important to remember that the original cost must be paid during construction and immediately thereafter, while the maintenance expense is paid through the life of the facility.

The designer may select the material or assembly he wants, or prepare specifications describing the performance required and let the builder do the selecting within the requirements of the specifications subject to the approval of the person supervising construction.

If the designer specifies exactly what materials and assemblies are to be incorporated into the project, he knows, either from past experience or from investigation, that they will be satisfactory. He avoids the risk of using something new or unfamiliar. He also misses the opportunity of using something that is more economical or performs better. Specifications prepared this way are called *material specifications*.

If the designer specifies performance in terms of appearance, strength, corrosion resistance, and other features, he has the benefit of the builder's experience in selecting the most economical materials. Specifications prepared this way are called *performance specifications*. They must be very carefully written to prevent any inferior products from satisfying the specification requirements; and the builder's selections must be carefully investigated to be sure they are acceptable according to the specifications. Both types of specification and various combinations of the two types are used. Each type is suitable for certain cases.

The process of selection includes the following steps:

1. Analysis of the problem (performance required, useful life required, allowable cost and maintenance expense);
2. Comparison of available materials or products with the criteria of step 1;
3. Design or selection of type of material, size, shape, finish, method of preserving, and method of fastening in place.

PROPERTIES OF MATERIALS

Thermal Expansion

All building materials change size with a change in temperature, becoming smaller when colder and larger when hotter. A piece of material, if heated uniformly, expands, with each unit length becoming a certain percentage longer. This elongation takes place in all directions and is somewhat different for each material. In order to predict amounts of expansion and contraction to be expected, a *coefficient of expansion* is determined for each material. It is a decimal representing the increase in length per unit length per degree increase in temperature. The coefficient varies somewhat at different temperatures but is nearly constant for the range of temperatures involved in most cases so that one coefficient can be used for each material.

The coefficient of expansion for iron is 0.0000067 in. per in. per °F or 0.0000121 cm per cm per °C. Each in. of length, width, or thickness becomes 1.0000067 in. if the temperature is increased 1°F and increases an additional 0.0000067 in. for each additional °F increase. As the temperature decreases, the dimensions decrease at the same rate. Figure 1–2 shows the coefficients of expansion for some common building materials.

Materials to be used together in an assembly must have approximately the same coefficients of expansion, or else some provision must be made for their different expansions. The use of steel reinforcement in concrete is a good example of combining materials with approximately the same linear coefficients of thermal expansion. Long structural members may expand and contract so much that expansion room must be provided at the ends.

EXAMPLE

Calculate the change in length of a 350-ft steel pipe that will be exposed to temperatures ranging from 55 to 200°F.

$$\delta = \alpha L(\Delta T)$$

where: δ = the total change in length (in., ft)
α = the linear coefficient of thermal expansion
L = the original length
ΔT = the change in temperature (°F) (°C)
$\delta = (0.0000065)(12 \times 350)(200 - 55)$
$\delta = 3.959$ in.

FIGURE 1–2 Coefficients of expansion

Material	Coefficient of Linear Expansion	
	per °F	per °C
Asphalt	0.00034*	0.00061*
Portland cement concrete	Assumed to be 0.0000055 but varies from 0.000004 to 0.000007	Assumed to be 0.0000099 but varies from 0.000007 to 0.000013
Gray cast iron	0.0000059	0.0000106
Wrought iron	0.0000067	0.0000121
Structural steel	0.0000065	0.0000117
Stainless steel	0.0000055 to 0.0000096	0.0000099 to 0.0000173
	Parallel to grain	
Wood	0.000001 to 0.000003	0.000002 to 0.000005
	Perpendicular to grain	
	0.000015 to 0.000035	0.000027 to 0.000063
Mineral aggregate	0.000003 to 0.000007	0.000005 to 0.000013

*Coefficient of volumetric expansion; coefficient of linear expansion is not useful.

Calculate the change in length of a 120-m steel pipe that will be exposed to temperatures ranging from 12 to 95°C.

$$\delta = (0.0000117)120(95-12)$$
$$\delta = 0.1165m$$

Thermal Conductivity

A building used by people must be kept warmer than the surrounding air in cold climates and cooler than the surrounding air in hot climates. Heat flows to a cooler area much like water flows to a lower level. The flow continues until outside and inside temperatures are equal. Heat movement takes place by conduction through any solid object separating areas of different temperatures.

It costs money to heat or cool a building, and the movement of heat in the wrong direction is expensive. The rate of movement varies with the material through which the heat passes. For large areas such as walls and roofs this rate is an important consideration. The rate is measured as thermal conductivity (U) in British thermal units (Btu) of heat transmitted per square foot of cross section per hour per °F difference in temperature between the two sides of the material.

Insulation, which is material with a very low U, is used to line large surfaces to lessen the rate of heat flow. The U of a material varies directly with its density. Dead air spaces in a material are effective in reducing the U factor. The best insulation, expanded plastic foam, consists of bubbles with the proportion of solid material less than 1 percent of the volume and the rest consisting of air or gas. Insulation is also made of fibers, ground particles, or other porous material. However, some structural materials have a low U factor and therefore serve as insulation also. Wood and certain types of lightweight concrete are two such materials that are covered in this book.

The resistance that construction materials offer to the flow of heat is called *thermal resistance* and is designated by the letter R. Most of the materials used in construction have been tested and assigned R values based upon the material's thickness as commonly used, or an R value rating per inch of material. For example, an expanded polystyrene extruded panel with a cut surface and a density of 1.8 pcf has an R value of 4.0; therefore, a 4-in.-thick panel would have a total R value of 16. Concrete masonry units are rated on overall thickness of the unit; therefore, an 8-in., 3-core unit has an R value of 1.11 for its 8-in. thickness. The calculations for heat loss and cooling loads of large buildings are normally completed by mechanical engineers who work with the architect to furnish a complete heating, ventilating, and air conditioning (HVAC) system for the structure.

Strength and Stress

All construction materials must resist force. A *force* is a push or pull that has a value and a direction. The pull of gravity is responsible for most of the forces dealt with in construction. However, there are other causes such as wind and water currents.

A force exerted on the surface of an object is assumed to spread uniformly over the internal area of the object. (See Figure 1–3.) A force does actually spread within the material, but not uniformly. *Stress* is force per unit area over which the force acts. It is obtained by dividing the force by the area on which it acts and is expressed as pounds per square inch (psi) or kips per square inch (Ksi). A kip is equivalent to 1000 lb.

Strength of a material, in general terms, is the ability to resist a force. That ability depends on the size and shape of the object as well as on the material of which it is made. An object with a large area is able to resist more force than an object of the same material but with a smaller resisting area.

In order that strength may be considered as a property of the material, it is necessary to relate strength to the material itself regardless of its size or shape. Therefore, the *strength* of a material in technical terms is equal to the stress that the material can resist. Strength has the same units as stress, that is, psi, Ksi, or MPa.

The useful strength of a material is equal to the stress at failure. Failure takes place when an object can no longer serve its purpose. The material may fail by breaking or by excessive deformation. *Deformation* means a change in the outside dimensions of an object caused by a force. The amount of deformation depends on the size and shape of the object as well as on the material of which it is made. As in the case of strength it is desirable to relate deformation to the material itself regardless of its size or shape.

The term *strain* means the total change in dimension divided by the original dimension. Strain is the effect caused by stress. Strain is a ratio and therefore has no units. The amount of deformation and the original length must be measured in the same units to provide a correct ratio. They are usually measured in inches.

Strain can be shown by stretching a rubber band or compressing or twisting a piece of rubber hose. A sample of rubber subjected to a compressive force becomes substantially shorter and a little wider. One subjected to a tensile stress becomes substantially

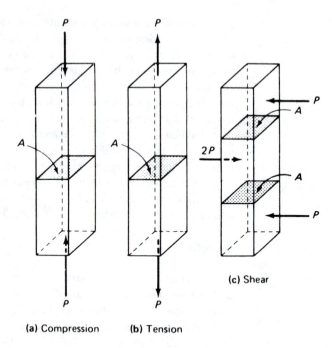

(a) Compression   (b) Tension   (c) Shear

FIGURE 1-3 Illustration of stresses

In each case average stress $= \dfrac{P}{A}$

longer and a little narrower. The deformation and original length considered in computing strain are the ones in the direction of the stress.

EXAMPLE

A metal bar with a rectangular cross section 1.5 in. by 2 in. breaks at a tensile load of 125,000 lb. Calculate the stress in the bar at failure.

$$s = \frac{P}{A}$$

where: s = the average computed stress (psi, Ksi)
      P = the external applied load (lb, kips)
      A = the cross-sectional area (sq in., sq ft)

$$s = \frac{125,000}{1.5 \times 2} = 41,667 \text{ psi}$$

The calculated stress may be converted directly to megapascals (MPa)

$$s = 41,667 \text{ psi} \times 0.00689476 = 287.28 \text{ MPa}$$

or the problem can be solved using metric values

1.5 in. × 0.0254 = 0.0381 m
2.0 in. × 0.0254 = 0.0508 m
125,000 lb × 4.44822 = 556,027 N

$$s = \frac{556\,027 \text{ N}}{0.0381 \text{ m} \times 0.0508 \text{ m}} = 287.29 \text{ MPa}$$

If a lower force stretches the bar so far that it is no longer useful, its failure strength equals the stress found by dividing the lower force by the area of the original cross section. The deformation that can be allowed in the bar depends on what it is used for. Therefore, failure depends upon the purpose for which the material is used. Failure could conceivably take place at a lower stress in one case with a particular material than in another case with the same material. Beams supporting a warehouse roof where appearance is not important can withstand any stress that does not break them; but if the beams support a plaster ceiling, they fail at a stress that causes sufficient deflection to crack the plaster.

Through experience and the performance of tests, the stress that causes failure can be determined for various materials and uses. A knowledge of this stress is useful for designing purposes. However, nothing is designed to be stressed to the point where it is ready to fail. Instead, a lower stress called the *allowable stress* is selected, and this is the maximum stress allowed.

There are several reasons for not designing material to be stressed close to the failure stress:

1. The actual force (and therefore stress) on a structure may exceed expectations.
2. True failure stress may be somewhat less than that determined experimentally.
3. The simplified procedures used in design predict approximate stresses which may be exceeded somewhat in actuality.
4. Materials may be weakened by rusting (steel), rotting (wood), or spalling (concrete).

The failure stress is greater than the allowable stress by a factor called the *safety factor*. If failure stress is twice the value of the allowable stress, the safety factor is two. The safety factor equals the failure stress divided by the allowable stress.

Usually failure stress is determined experimentally. A safety factor and an allowable stress are selected by a committee of experts and the allowable stresses are published. Some organizations that publish allowable stresses are the American Institute of Steel Construction, the American Concrete Institute, and the National Forest Products Association. Designers select kinds of material and sizes and shapes of members to support loads that subject the member to stresses that are equal to or less than the allowable. Economy requires that the actual stress be near the allowable; if it is not, the material is being used inefficiently because less material would be adequate. The actual stress is called the *working stress*.

Important factors considered in deciding on a safety factor are:

1. How exactly loads can be predicted and calculated,
2. How exactly acting stresses can be calculated,
3. How exactly failure stresses can be determined,
4. How consistently the material conforms to the experimental strength,
5. How serious the consequences of a failure are,
6. How much warning the material gives before failing, and
7. How much the material is likely to deteriorate under the conditions of use.

There are three kinds of stresses and corresponding strengths—compressive, tensile, and shearing. They depend on the position of the forces with respect to the object. The three are illustrated in Figure 1–3.

Stress is determined by dividing the acting force by the original area upon which it acts. It is this area that resists displacement. Tensile and compressive stresses act on the cross-sectional area perpendicular to the direction of the force. Shear stresses act on the cross-sectional area parallel to the direction of the force. The force is not uniformly distributed across the area, but in computing tensile and compressive stresses it is assumed to be uniform with satisfactory accuracy.

Shearing stress acts unequally over an area, and the stress at the location of highest stress must be considered. The action of shearing stresses is complex compared to that of the axial stresses, tension and compression.

Since the cross sections are changed in size by forces, they influence the stresses. If a force remains constant, the actual stress changes when the cross section changes. It is customary to compute stress on the basis of the area as it is before any force is applied. Computations are easier this way and in all practical applications the area of interest is the original area, since any problem relating size to strength will be solved on the basis of original size, not a size distorted by a force.

Materials differ in their response to stress. A *ductile* material can be drawn into a thin, long wire by a tensile force. A *malleable* material can be flattened into a thin, wide sheet by a compressive force. A *brittle* material breaks with very little deformation. It appears to fail suddenly because there is no noticeable deformation to serve as a warning.

In this discussion, forces have been assumed to be applied once for a brief period of time. Ordinary tests made to determine strength consist of subjecting a sample of the material to a force that increases steadily until the material breaks. These tests take a few minutes and indicate static stress at failure. However, in a structure, forces may be applied for extended periods of time, they may be applied and removed many times, and they may be applied suddenly with impact or shock.

A material, even if brittle, deforms slowly when a force is applied to it for an extended period of years, even though the force is too small to cause failure in a short time. This deformation is called *creep*. The creep may be great enough to constitute failure.

Although a force of a certain amount may not cause breaking no matter how long it is applied, it may be large enough to cause breaking if it is applied and removed many times (tens of thousands of times), even if over a shorter time. For example, structural members of a bridge are subjected to application and removal of stress each time a vehicle crosses. Failure from this cause is called *fatigue,* and it occurs with very little deformation.

Because there is so little deformation, there is no warning and the break seems to be sudden. However, it begins as a tiny crack and becomes larger over many cycles until the structure fails by breaking. The smaller the stress, the more times it must be repeated to cause failure. There is a stress below which the material will not fail at any number of cycles, called the *endurance limit.* Any stress above this limit will cause failure if repeated enough times.

Specimens tested for endurance are generally subjected to bending first one way and then the opposite way. This reversal of stress produces failure at fewer cycles than the simple application and removal of force. The endurance limit found this way may be less than half the static stress at failure.

Toughness is the capacity of a material to absorb energy while a force is applied to it. Energy is expended by a force acting over a distance and is absorbed by a material being forced to deform through a distance. Toughness is the product of stress and strain up to the point of fracture. It is computed by determining the area under the stress-strain curve (see Figure 1–4), which is equivalent to multiplying the average stress by the total strain (force times distance). The result is called the *modulus of toughness.* Strength and ductility are both involved. The toughness of a material indicates its ability to withstand a sudden force, known as an *impact load* or *shock load.*

Resilience is the ability of a material to recover its original size and shape after being deformed by an impact load. The *modulus of resilience* is the product of stress and strain up to the elastic limit. It is a measure of the useful toughness, since beyond the elastic limit permanent deformation ordinarily renders the material unfit for further use. It is computed by determining the area under the stress-strain curve from zero to the elastic limit.

Modulus of Elasticity

Strain is directly proportional to the stress that causes it over a considerable range for many materials. At stresses higher than this range, each additional increment of stress causes greater strain than the previous increment of stress. The stress at which strain just begins to increase at a rate greater than in the proportional range is the *proportional limit.* An example is shown in Figure 1–4a. Stress in lb per sq in. is a very large number compared to the resulting strain for almost all construction materials.

The constant value of stress divided by strain is called the *modulus of elasticity* or *Young's modulus.* The relationship is expressed as modulus of elasticity equals stress divided by strain or $E = s/\epsilon$. Since ϵ is a ratio with no units, E has units of lb per sq in. the same as s although E is not a stress. The modulus of elasticity indicates the stiffness or resistance to movement of a material. A stiff material deforms less under a given stress than does a material of less stiffness. A metal wire is very stiff compared to a rubber band of the same size and the E of the metal wire is a much higher value. The modulus of elasticity is a characteristic which is different for each material. For example, A36 steel has a modulus of elasticity of 30×10^6 psi, gray cast iron's modulus is 15×10^6 psi, and concrete's modulus of elasticity is about 3×10^6 psi with variations related to the concrete's compressive strength value.

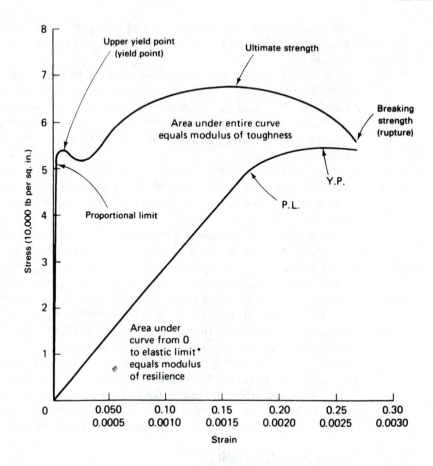

*Elastic limit is difficult to determine and is usually assumed to be at the proportional limit. This is very nearly correct and is accurate enough for ordinary use.

(a) Stress-strain diagram for ductile steel: upper curve (upper scale) shows relationship up to breaking point; lower curve (lower scale) shows curve with greater accuracy up to the yield point.

FIGURE 1-4 Stress-strain diagrams

Some materials do not have a range of constant relationship between stress and strain. The stress-strain relationship for this type of material is shown in Figure 1-4b. As stress is increased in a test specimen of this type of material, the strain increases at an increasing rate. There is no modulus of elasticity for such materials because there is no range of constant relationship between stress and strain. However, an E value is so convenient for design that an approximate value is sometimes used. Any ratio of stress-strain selected as the E value is correct at only one stress or possibly two. However, a ratio may be chosen which is reasonably close throughout the range of stresses that is encountered in use. This ratio is used for design. Methods used to determine approximate E ratios are shown in Figure 1-5.

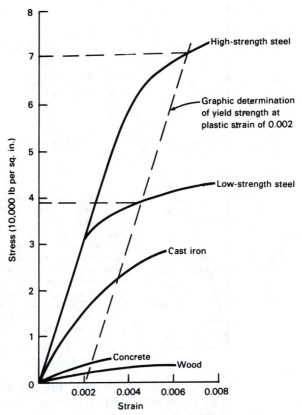

(b) Relative shapes of stress-strain diagrams for different materials.

FIGURE 1–4 (Continued)

Any of the values in the equation $E = s/\epsilon$ can be determined if the other two are known. The modulus of elasticity has been determined by extensive testing for all commonly used construction materials, and the usual design problem is to find either stress or strain. In experimental work a sample is tested under increasing stress with the strain being measured. Both are recorded at suitable intervals and the values used to plot their relationship. The complete test method is ASTM E8 standard methods of tension testing of metallic materials and is often referred to as a *static-tensile test*.

The modulus E applies to compressive or tensile stresses and for most materials is very nearly the same in compression and tension. The relationship of shearing stress to shearing strain is designated E_s (the modulus of rigidity) and is a lower value.

EXAMPLE

Calculate the change in length of a 50-ft steel rod subjected to a tensile load of 12,000 psi.

$$E = \frac{s}{\epsilon}$$

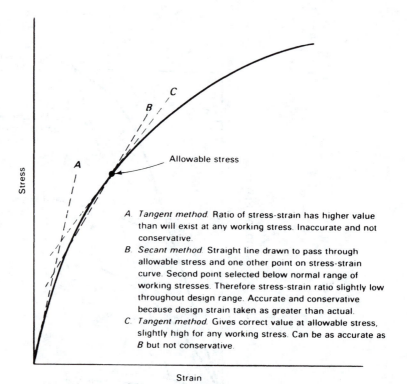

A. *Tangent method.* Ratio of stress-strain has higher value than will exist at any working stress. Inaccurate and not conservative.

B. *Secant method.* Straight line drawn to pass through allowable stress and one other point on stress-strain curve. Second point selected below normal range of working stresses. Therefore stress-strain ratio slightly low throughout design range. Accurate and conservative because design strain taken as greater than actual.

C. *Tangent method.* Gives correct value at allowable stress, slightly high for any working stress. Can be as accurate as B but not conservative.

FIGURE 1–5 Typical stress-strain diagram for material without a range of constant s/ϵ values, showing methods of determining a usable modulus of elasticity

where E = the modulus of elasticity (psi)

s = the average computed stress (psi)

ϵ = the strain (in./in.)

$$30{,}000{,}000 \text{ psi} = \frac{12{,}000 \text{ psi}}{\epsilon}$$

where ϵ = 0.0004 in./in.

$$\epsilon = \frac{\delta}{L}$$

δ = total deformation or change in length (in.)

L = original length (in.)

$$\delta = \epsilon L$$

where δ = 0.0004 in./in. (50 ft $\times$ 12 in.)

δ = 0.24 in.

Elastic and Plastic Properties

Elasticity is the property of a material that enables it to return to its original size and shape after a force is removed. Elasticity is not judged by the amount of strain caused by a given stress, but by the completeness with which the material returns to its original size and shape when the force is removed. A metal wire does not stretch nearly as far as the same size rubber band under the same force. However, it is just as elastic within its elastic range because it returns to its original size and shape when the force is removed just as the rubber band does.

Plasticity is the property that enables a material changed in size or shape by a force to retain the new size and shape when the force is removed. Many materials are completely elastic (i.e., return exactly to original size and shape upon removal of a force) throughout a range of stress from zero to a stress called the *elastic limit.* At stresses greater than the elastic limit, the material takes a *permanent set* or a plastic deformation which remains when the force is removed. When a material is stressed beyond the elastic limit, the total strain is made up of recoverable elastic strain and permanent plastic strain.

Elastic strain takes place first, followed by the plastic strain; that is, as stress is increased starting from zero, the strain is entirely elastic until the elastic limit is reached, and then any additional strain is entirely plastic as stress greater than the elastic limit is imposed. For an elastic material, the total strain may be elastic or it may be elastic plus plastic, but it may not be plastic only. For each type of material, the elastic limit has a value in lb per sq in. It is the stress above which plastic deformation takes place and below which elastic deformation takes place. The elastic limit cannot be easily identified. Because it is at approximately the same location as the proportional limit, it may be taken as the same point for all but experimental work.

Yield point is the lowest stress at which an increase in strain occurs with no increase in stress. It is therefore at a point of zero slope in the stress-strain curve. In Figure 1–4a, the yield point is shown. Yield point is an important stress for steel (see Chapter 5). However, some steels have no yield point. As stress increases beyond the elastic limit, plastic deformation becomes unacceptable at some point and is considered failure for these steels. The stress at which the excessive plastic deformation is reached is the *yield strength.* Figure 1–4b shows a graphic determination of steel yield strengths with a plastic (permanent) strain of 0.002 considered failure. The term *yield stress* includes yield point or yield strength.

Materials of construction behave differently at high and low temperatures. Like many familiar objects, they are stronger and more brittle at low temperatures and weaker and more pliable (ductile) at high temperatures. The transformation is not noticeable in materials such as steel, wood, and concrete unless the change in temperature is quite extreme.

SOURCES OF INFORMATION

To use materials properly, it is necessary to understand the natural characteristics of the basic materials, the variations in these characteristics made possible through special techniques, and the ways in which materials can be used in combination with one another.

FIGURE 1-6 Wood, concrete, and steel selected for their distinct properties combine to create this unique bridge (*Courtesy APA—The Engineered Wood Association*)

(See Figure 1–6.) This information is obtained from past performance of materials in use and from experimental investigation and tests performed on materials. Much of the information is published in technical reports or in advertising material prepared by suppliers. Some sources of information are described here.

Sweets Catalog File is a compilation of technical advertising literature published by suppliers. The file includes approximately a dozen categories, with each supplier's literature included in the appropriate category. Literature from about 2000 suppliers describing many thousands of products is included. Each supplier pays the publisher of *Sweets Catalog File,* the F. W. Dodge Company, a fee for the inclusion of its literature, and the file is available for nominal cost to designers who have a sufficient volume of business to justify receiving it.

Groups of suppliers producing the same product often set up *manufacturers' associations* to promote the use of their product. The association, which is financed by the suppliers, is a separate organization functioning to increase the usage of the product. The association does not sell the product or represent any one of the associated suppliers.

A manufacturers' association seeks to increase sales by finding new and better ways to use the product and by utilizing advertising campaigns. It conducts research and provides the latest findings to designers and builders, often at no charge. It provides technical assistance to designers and builders by means of published material including standard specifications and by personal visits from staff members to the office or jobsite to assist in solving unusual problems. It is to the association's advantage that its product be used successfully so that it will be used again. Some well-known manufacturers' associations are the Portland Cement Association (PCA), National Clay Pipe Institute (NCPI), American Iron and Steel Institute (AISI), the Asphalt Institute, National Sand and Gravel Association (NSGA), American Plywood Association (APA), and National Ready Mix Concrete Association (NRMCA).

The *American Society for Testing and Materials* (ASTM) is an organization engaged in the standardization of specifications and testing methods and in the improvement of materials. It is made up of suppliers, designers, builders, and others interested in engineering materials. The organization publishes the ASTM Standards containing more than 8600 standard specifications and testing methods covering design, manufacture, construction, and maintenance for practically every type of construction material. The ASTM Standards consist of 68 volumes, each covering one field of interest and each under the jurisdiction of a standing committee which continually reviews and improves standards.

Each committee has members representing suppliers and users. New standards and revised standards are published as tentative for a time so that criticisms can be considered before adoption of them is final. The ASTM Standards may be purchased one standard at a time; by section, each of which includes several related parts of the 68 volumes; or as a complete set.

The *American Standards Association* (ASA) develops national industrial standards through the work of committees representing manufacturers, technical organizations, and government departments. The final standards are determined in much the same way as the standards of ASTM. The ASA also adopts the standards of other organizations and has adopted many of the ASTM standards.

There are many other national organizations with memberships and purposes similar to those of ASTM or ASA, but with narrower interests. These organizations develop standard specifications, inspection methods, and test procedures and also adopt ASTM or ASA standards. Some of these organizations are the American Association of State Highway and Transportation Officials (AASHTO), American Institute of Steel Construction (AISC), and American Concrete Institute (ACI).

Underwriters Laboratories (UL) is a nonprofit organization which investigates and tests materials, products, equipment, construction methods, and construction systems in its laboratories. A supplier may have its product tested for a fee, and, if approved, it will be included in the UL approved list and the UL seal of approval may be displayed on the product. This approval is widely recognized as a safeguard against hazards to life and property, and specifications often require UL approval. The UL is particularly well known for evaluation of fire resistance of building components.

Professional organizations such as the American Society of Civil Engineers (ASCE) and the American Institute of Architects (AIA) devote much of their effort to improving design and construction practices. Valuable information concerning materials is published in their magazines and technical reports.

INSPECTION AND TESTING

Inspection means examining a product or observing an operation to determine whether or not it is satisfactory. The inspection may include scaling the dimensions, weighing, tapping with a hammer, sifting through the fingers, or scratching with a knife, as well as many other operations, some of which could conceivably be called tests. However, the results of the inspection and minor tests are not generally measurable. Often an inspection raises questions which are then resolved by testing.

A *test* consists of applying some measurable influence to the material and measuring the effect on the material. A common type of test consists of subjecting a sample of material to a measured force which is increased steadily until the material breaks or is deformed beyond a specified amount. This type of test measures the strength of the material directly by determining how strong the test specimen is. Some tests predict one characteristic by measuring another. For example, the resistance of aggregate to the destructive influence of freezing and thawing weather is predicted by soaking the aggregate in sodium sulfate or magnesium sulfate, drying in an oven, and determining the weight loss.

Inspection and tests can be categorized according to purpose as follows:

1. *Acceptance:* Inspection and tests performed to determine whether or not a material or product meets specific requirements in order to decide whether or not to accept or reject the material or product. A manufacturer performs such inspections and tests on raw materials he intends to use. A builder performs these inspections and tests on manufactured products and raw materials that he intends to use; and the owner's representative performs them on the builder's finished product.

2. *Control:* Inspection and tests performed periodically on selected samples to ensure that the product is acceptable. A supplier or manufacturer monitors his own operation by periodic checks of his product. The builder may check his product similarly. If control measures show the product to be below standards, the reason is determined and corrective measures taken.

3. *Research and development:* Inspection and tests performed to determine the characteristics of new products and also to determine the usefulness of particular inspection procedures and tests to judge characteristics or predict behavior of materials. A reputable manufacturing company tests a new product extensively before putting it on the market. Before adopting a new, simpler type of inspection or test procedure for acceptance or control, a highway department compares results obtained from the new procedure with results from the old procedure over a large range of conditions and over an extended period of time.

Tests for acceptance or control must usually be performed quickly. For reasons of economy, the tests cannot interfere with the manufacturing process. For the same reason, tests at a construction site cannot unduly delay the construction work. Since these tests are performed so many times, their cost is an important factor. Therefore, quick, inexpensive tests proven to be good indicators of actual performance are used extensively for these purposes. The type of test used in development of a product must give more exact results and is generally more time consuming and requires more expensive equipment.

An example will illustrate inspection and testing for the different purposes. A company making building blocks of concrete tries to reduce cost by using an industrial waste material as an aggregate. The proposed aggregate is examined and tested extensively before being used. It is then used in various combinations to make batches of concrete blocks which are compared with each other by inspection and testing. The combination that proves to be most satisfactory is used to manufacture blocks.

While blocks are in production, a continuous program is carried on to check the finished blocks by inspection and tests. A certain percentage of the blocks are checked as a matter of routine to determine whether or not the quality changes. If there are indications of a change in quality the cause of the change is determined and action taken to return to production of uniform quality.

The builder who purchases the block or the owner's representative then inspects and tests a certain percentage of the blocks before accepting them. Each block is inspected for damage before being put into place in the structure. A final inspection is given to the entire project as a whole when it is completed.

Tests performed on samples of material from the same source do not yield exactly the same results for each sample. There are two reasons for this:

1. No material is perfectly homogeneous. There are slight differences in the composition of any substance from one point to another. In addition, there are always minute flaws which, though unimportant in a large mass of material, have a great effect if one is included in a small sample to be tested. Thus, one sample is not completely representative of the whole.

2. The testing methods, although performed according to standard procedures, cannot be duplicated exactly each time.

Some tests give nearly the same results when performed by different operators. These tests are said to have a high degree of *repeatability*. Tests have varying degrees of repeatability, which should be taken into account when interpreting the results. An indication of degree of repeatability is included in some test procedures. A supplier can be required to meet very exacting specifications if a test method is available that provides very accurate results. If there is no such method, more accuracy can be obtained by taking the average of several tests. If it is not feasible to do this, the specifications must be written to permit more variation in the product.

Variations in test results can be kept small by selecting large enough samples, by employing proper procedures for random sample selection, and by running enough tests to get a meaningful average and eliminating those results that are erroneous because of a faulty sample or faulty test performance.

A certain minimum size sample or minimum number of samples is needed to be truly representative of the whole. The more variable a material is, the larger or more numerous the samples must be. The less precise the test methods are, or the lower the correlation between test results and the property actually being investigated, the greater the number of times the test must be run.

The size and number of samples should be determined on a statistical basis. Size and number must be large enough to include all the characteristics to be tested, the least common characteristic once and the more common ones in their proper proportion. Many testing procedures include minimum sizes or numbers of samples to accomplish this.

STANDARDS

The designer or builder may desire any number of properties in the material he is going to use. He must be able to specify the degree of each property in terms that he and the supplier understand, and he and the supplier must have some mutually acceptable means of determining whether or not the materials possess each property in sufficient amounts. The supplier must be able to prove to the buyer that the material possesses the properties desired to the degree desired.

In unusual cases a measurement or test may be devised for one specific application. Fortunately, this is not usually necessary. Standard measuring and testing methods are available and so are standard definitions of terms. Both buyer and supplier understand what is meant when standard terminology is used or reference is made to standard specifications, and both can use the same reproducible methods to determine whether or not the materials possess the required properties in sufficient quantity.

When standard specifications and standard testing methods are available, it makes no more sense to devise special, nonstandard specifications or test methods than it does to measure lengths with a yardstick or meter stick of nonstandard size. Material specifications consist largely of explanations of what properties a material must possess and the allowable limits for those properties.

A *testing method* is a specification explaining how to perform a test and how to measure the results. When the material is tested, if it possesses all the required properties to a sufficient degree, it is said to meet the standards or meet the specifications.

Inspections often require measurements. A measurement may be as simple as determining the diameter of a piece of pipe by measuring it with a 6-ft rule to be sure it is of the size specified, or it may involve a more time-consuming and accurate measurement such as the determination of the percentage of air entrained in portland cement concrete.

A measurement may consist of determining the size of a crack in the end of a piece of wood by measuring it with a carpenter's rule. The piece of wood is considered to lose a certain percentage of its strength according to the size of the crack, and it must be discarded if it has a crack larger than a certain size. However, there are three types of cracks and each is measured in a different way. Therefore, the cracks must be measured according to standard specifications if all pieces are to be graded on an equitable basis. Tests can be effective only if they measure the appropriate characteristic the same way each time so that the results can be evaluated according to their relationship to past results. For the same reason, inspection should be performed in an identical way each time as much as possible.

REVIEW QUESTIONS

1. Prepare an organizational chart depicting the construction process. Identify the parties involved, their functions, responsibilities, and connections with each other.

2. Explain the functions of independent testing laboratories in the construction industry.

3. Why must a builder/contractor understand materials?

4. Explain how the material used for a basement floor and the material used for a roof must be different.

5. As a research project, make a list of the kinds of materials used in (a) a water distribution system, (b) a city street pavement, (c) a sewage collection system, and (d) a roofing system.

6. Discuss the advantages of material specifications versus performance specifications. Research an actual project specification and identify the types of specification formats used and the reasons they were used.

7. A mechanical device rests in a level position on two supports, each 42 in. high, at 60°F. The support at one end is gray cast iron; at the other end, structural steel. What is the greatest amount the device can be out of level due to differences in expansion if the temperature rises to 165°F?

8. Calculate the change in length of a 100-ft-long steel bridge girder that will be exposed to a temperature range of −25 to 110°F.

9. What is the stress in a steel rod with cross section of 2.4 sq in. if it is subjected to a tension of 120,000 lb? In a concrete cylinder 6 in. in diameter subjected to a compressive force of 122,700 lb?

10. Calculate the stress in a 65-ft steel cable that has a total deformation of 0.33 in.

11. Calculate the total deformation in a 15-ft, 2-sq-in. steel bar hanger that supports an 18-ton load.

12. A material is expected to fail at 50,000 psi. A safety factor of 2 is to be used. What is the allowable stress?

13. Calculate the compressive stress in a 6-in.-diameter by 12-in.-high concrete test specimen if the total deformation under load is 0.015. Calculate the total load on the test cylinder.

14. A material may fail by breaking or deforming excessively. Which is the case for creep? For fatigue? For impact failure?

15. What purpose do specifying organizations such as ASTM and ACI serve in the construction industry and why are they important?

16. What is the purpose of manufacturers' associations and how do they accomplish their purpose?

17. What is the difference between inspection and testing?

18. Calculate the stress at failure of a concrete test cylinder with a measured diameter of 152.4 mm and a recorded load of 371 426 N.

19. Calculate the stress at failure of a 50-mm mortar cube that failed at 35 586 N.

20. Calculate the change in length of a 110-m-long steel pipe exposed to temperatures ranging from 5 to 90°C.

2

Aggregates

Aggregates are particles of random shape. They are found in nature as sand, gravel, stones, or rock that can be crushed into particles. They may also be byproducts or waste material from an industrial process or mining operation. The term *aggregates* generally refers to mineral particles which have rock as their origin unless otherwise specified. These include sand, gravel, field stone, boulders, and crushed rock, since all are derived from rock by the forces of nature or, in the case of crushed rock, by a manufacturing process. *Rock* includes any large solid mass of mineral matter which is part of the earth's crust. Some other materials used as aggregates are blast-furnace slag, boiler slag, building rubble, refuse incinerator residue, and mine refuse.

Aggregate sizes vary from several inches to the size of the smallest grain of sand. In special cases aggregate larger than several inches may be used. Particles smaller than the size of a grain of sand are considered as impurities even if they are of mineral composition. Depending on the amount of impurities and the use to be made of the aggregate, these impurities may be tolerated or removed. In some cases these small particles are deliberately mixed with aggregate and are then considered as an additive.

The road building industry is the greatest consumer of aggregates. Aggregates are used as bases or cushions between the soil and traffic wheels or between the soil and pavement, and are also used in bituminous pavement and portland cement concrete pavement. They are used as leveling and supporting bases between the soil and all types of structures. They are used as *ballast* which is the base for railroad tracks. They are used as protective and decorative coatings on roofs and floors. Another major use of aggregates is to filter water, which requires holding back suspended solids while allowing water to pass through.

There is not always a clear distinction between aggregate and the engineering material, soil, which also comes originally from rock. Some naturally occurring sand and gravel soils are usable as aggregate without processing. Most aggregate is soil that has been processed. Soil which remains in place and serves as the ultimate foundation of all construction is not considered as aggregate, no matter what its composition.

DEFINITIONS

Terms related to concrete aggregates are defined in ASTM C125, Terms Relating to Concrete and Concrete Aggregates. Many of the definitions are applicable to any type of aggregate and are given here to facilitate the discussions in this chapter.

coarse aggregate*: (1) Aggregate predominantly retained on the No. 4 (4.76-mm) sieve; or (2) that portion of an aggregate retained on the No. 4 (4.76-mm) sieve.

fine aggregate*: (1) Aggregate passing the $\frac{3}{8}$-in. sieve and almost entirely passing the No. 4 (4.76-mm) sieve and predominantly retained on the No. 200 (74-micron) sieve; or (2) that portion of an aggregate passing the No. 4 (4.76-mm) sieve and retained on the No. 200 (74-micron) sieve.

gravel*: (1) Granular material predominantly retained on the No. 4 (4.76-mm) sieve and resulting from natural disintegration and abrasion of rock or processing of weakly bound conglomerate; or (2) that portion of an aggregate retained on the No. 4 (4.76-mm) sieve and resulting from natural disintegration and abrasion of rock or processing of weakly bound conglomerate.

sand*: (1) Granular material passing the $\frac{3}{8}$-in. sieve and almost entirely passing the No. 4 (4.76-mm) sieve and predominantly retained on the No. 200 (74-micron) sieve, and resulting from natural disintegration and abrasion of rock or processing of completely friable sandstone; or (2) that portion of an aggregate passing the No. 4 (4.76-mm) sieve and predominantly retained on the No. 200 (74-micron) sieve, and resulting from natural disintegration and abrasion of rock or processing of completely friable sandstone.

bank gravel**: Gravel found in natural deposits, usually more or less intermixed with fine material, such as sand or clay, or combinations thereof; gravelly clay, gravelly sand, clayey gravel, and sandy gravel indicate the varying proportions of the materials in the mixture.

crushed gravel: The product resulting from the artificial crushing of gravel with substantially all fragments having at least one face resulting from fracture.

crushed stone: The product resulting from the artificial crushing of rocks, boulders, or large cobblestones, substantially all faces of which have resulted from the crushing operation.

**Note:* The definitions are alternatives to be applied under differing circumstances. Definition (1) is applied to an entire aggregate, either in a natural condition or after processing. Definition (2) is applied to a portion of an aggregate. Requirements for properties and grading should be stated in the specifications.
**Definition from ASTM D8.

crushed rock***: The product resulting from the artificial crushing of all rock, all faces of which have resulted from the crushing operation or from blasting.

blast-furnace slag: The nonmetallic product, consisting essentially of silicates and aluminosilicates of lime and of other bases, which is developed in a molten condition simultaneously with iron in a blast furnace.

SOURCES

The earth's crust is solid rock called *bedrock,* and much of the crust is covered with soil particles originally derived from the bedrock. This soil is classified according to size, as gravel, sand, silt, and clay, with gravel being the largest and clay the smallest. Natural aggregates include sand, gravel, or larger stones, and bedrock reduced to particle size by manufacturing methods.

The sand and gravel occurring in nature were at one time broken from massive parent rock, transported by nature, and left in various types of deposits called sand or gravel banks. The processes that cause breaking, transporting, and depositing have operated continuously throughout the past and continue to operate now. (See Figure 2–1.)

Cracking of rock and eventual fracturing occurs mainly through expansion and contraction of the rock due to changing temperatures. The process is hastened if temperatures are sometimes low enough so that water within the cracks freezes and expands. The broken particles fall or roll short distances downhill under the force of gravity and may be carried farther by flowing water or the slowly flowing ice of a glacier. Many particles are broken loose originally by flowing water or glacial ice.

A freshly broken particle has a rough surface and an angular shape. The more it travels, the smoother its surface becomes and the more rounded its shape becomes. Rolling down a mountainside has a rounding effect. Sliding farther along, helped by rainwater runoff, and eventually tumbling along in a stream cause further rounding and smoothing. Being scraped along the ground first on one side and then on another while being carried in glacial ice has a particular effect on the shape and texture of aggregate particles. Glacial deposits consist of particles of widely varying sizes with some of the coarseness and angularity worn away. Many of the glacier-carried particles reach the streams of meltwater at the melting end of the glacier. They are then carried the same way with the same results as in any other stream. The deposits simply dropped by a glacier are called *till* and those carried farther by meltwater are called *outwash.* Outwash deposits are smoother, rounder, and more uniform in size than till.

The most perfectly rounded particles are those that are carried to the edge of a large body of water where they are washed back and forth incessantly by ocean or lake waves and become smooth and nearly spherical.

Rock particles, especially in dry climates or flat areas, may lie where they fall—next to a steep cliff, for example. Centuries of such deposition may provide sufficient quantities for commercial extraction and use of the aggregate which is rough-surfaced and of angular shape.

***Definition used in this book.

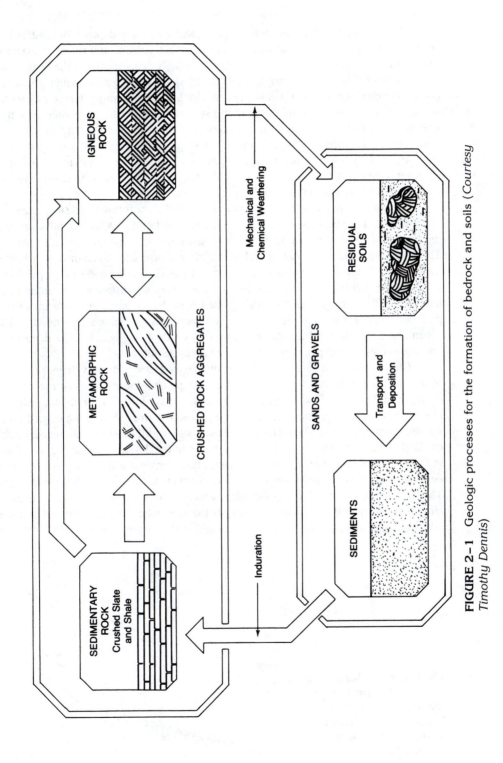

FIGURE 2-1 Geologic processes for the formation of bedrock and soils (*Courtesy Timothy Dennis*)

Many particles fall or roll into flowing water, and many deposits of sand and gravel are found in the beds of streams and rivers or where streams and rivers formerly were. The size of particles a stream carries is approximately proportional to the sixth power of the velocity of flow. The velocity depends on the slope, being greater with a greater slope, and on the quantity of water, being greater with a greater quantity. Greater quantities of water flow at certain times of the year and steeper slopes in some sections of a flowing stream cause faster flow in those sections regardless of the quantity of flow. These variations of quantity of flow and in-stream slope result in a wide variety of carrying capacities throughout a stream over a period of time. The result is a separation of aggregates into various size ranges along the length of the stream. In some cases gravel with remarkable uniformity of size is found in one location.

An example is a level, slow-flowing section of river following a steep section with swift current. The swift current carries large and small particles. When the water reaches the slow-flowing section, the large particles settle and the smaller ones are carried past. The result is a deposit of clean gravel of a fairly uniform size, containing no silt, clay, or trash. If the current continues to flow slower and slower, smaller and smaller particles will gradually be dropped in succession as the water flows downstream. The entire reach of the river is then an aggregate deposit graded from larger particles upstream to smaller particles downstream. (See Figure 2–2.) The very finest particles are carried to a lake or ocean and settle there where the movement of water is negligible. Lake deposits often contain too many fine particles to be good aggregate sources.

Glaciers are formed in high altitudes and pushed slowly down valleys by the weight of ice and snow piled up behind them. They scrape and gouge pieces of rock, large and small, from the sides of the valley and carry them slowly to the lower, melting edge of the glacier, where the larger particles are dropped and the smaller ones are carried away by the stream of meltwater. The melting edge moves downhill in winter and recedes uphill in the heat of summer. The flow of water is greater in the daytime than at night and greater in the summer than in winter. The variation in flow causes a wide variety of particle sizes deposited helter skelter as the stream changes channels and cuts through previous deposits. This area about the variable melting edge, which is known as a *moraine,* contains many large boulders, and the area downstream has the aggregate deposits expected in a stream.

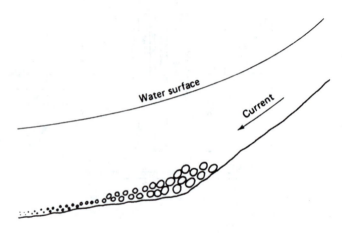

FIGURE 2–2 Section through river showing aggregates deposited because of reduction in water velocity due to flatter slope

Aggregates are obtained from beds of lakes and streams, but more often are obtained from deposits where they were formerly lakes or streams. Movements in the earth's crust result in relocation of streams and lakes, so that some former stream and lake beds are now on high ground with their aggregate deposits intact.

At several periods of time much of the northern hemisphere was covered by glaciers. These glaciers, behaving similarly to the valley glaciers described previously, but covering the width of a continent, left huge deposits of aggregate, and the streams of meltwater flowing from their southern extremities also deposited huge quantities. The glaciers have receded and the streams and rivers they caused have disappeared. The deposits they left provide many of the best gravel banks now to be found.

METHODS OF EXTRACTION AND PROCESSING

Aggregate is recovered from deposits laid down in geologic times and from deposits still being laid down. The deposits are found on the ground surface and below the surface of the ground or water. Some aggregate is suitable for a specific use just as extracted, and some must be processed before being used.

Underwater Sources

Aggregate is brought up from lake and river bottoms by barge-mounted dredges with a single scoop or an endless chain of scoops and by dragline. The disturbance to the bottom and the motion of the scoop or bucket through the water cause some of the undesirable fine particles and lightweight material to be washed away as the load is being brought up. Barges are loaded and transported to shore, where their cargoes of aggregate are unloaded and stockpiled (see Figure 2–3).

Aggregate is also pumped with pumps similar to those used for pumping concrete described in Chapter 4. Aggregate of sizes up to 6 in. and larger can be pumped and forced through a pipe to a barge or directly to the shore.

A knowledge of the characteristics of stream flow and deposition is required to locate the most likely places to find worthwhile aggregates. Samples of aggregates are brought to the surface and examined for desired characteristics before equipment is moved to a site to begin recovering them. Unsuitable material may have to be removed first to reach the kind of aggregate that is wanted.

The operating area is generally controlled by government regulations to prevent interference with the natural flow of water and to preserve navigation channels. Many times when channels or harbors must be deepened for ships, the aggregate brought up from the bottom has commercial value.

Land Sources

Aggregates are excavated from natural banks on land by bucket loaders, power shovels, draglines, and power scrapers. Unsuitable soil and vegetation, called *overburden,* must be removed to reach the deposits. Removal, which is accomplished with bulldozers and power scrapers, is called *stripping*. (See Figure 2–4).

(b)

(a)

FIGURE 2-3 Obtaining aggregate from underwater deposits: (a) dragline excavating from the bottom of a bay; (b) dredging from a river bottom with chain of scoops (*Courtesy Dravo Corporation*)

FIGURE 2–4 Track drills used in a quarry to drill the holes required to blast out bedrock for aggregate production (*Courtesy Callanan Industries, Inc.*)

The landform indicates what type of deposit is below the surface. Landforms are studied by means of aerial photographs or field trips, and the best locations are pinpointed. Holes are bored or test pits dug, samples are brought up, and examinations and tests are made to determine the suitability of the aggregates for the intended purpose.

The landforms containing natural deposits can be recognized by one who understands the processes of nature by which they were formed. Certain types of glacial deposits consist of much silt and clay or particles of a wide range of sizes, including large boulders. Neither type is as valuable as glacial outwash, which contains cleaner aggregates of more uniform size.

If crushed rock is to be used as aggregate, it must be blasted loose with explosives (see Figure 2–5) and then crushed by machinery to the size desired. Crushing provides a finished product of uniform size, and by proper blasting, crushing, and screening, the size can be controlled to suit the market. (See Figure 2–6.)

Particles of crushed rock have angular shapes and rough surfaces which are better suited for some uses than the more rounded shapes and smoother surfaces of naturally formed particles. These characteristics will be discussed later in this chapter. A rock formation has similar characteristics throughout so that when a good formation is found, a large supply of consistently good-quality aggregate is likely. This is usually not true of sand and gravel deposits which are likely to have inferior particles mixed with acceptable ones. A mixture is inevitable if particles were transported through a geological time period from many rock formations to form the sand or gravel deposits. As a result, bank sand and gravel are often of poorer quality than crushed rock, and additional processing is needed to remove unacceptable particles.

FIGURE 2–5 Blasting bedrock (*Courtesy Dravo Corporation*)

Bank run aggregate is of a particular size range in any one deposit, and the finished product is normally screened to obtain separation of sizes and may be crushed to a smaller size. However, if a size larger than most of the available bank run aggregate is needed, then crushed rock must be used. Generally, a crushed rock source has more versatility, and a natural bank is likely to be more economical for one particular type of aggregate. (See Figure 2–7.)

ROCK TYPES

The constituents of the more common, or more important, natural mineral aggregates derived from rock are described in ASTM C294 and briefly summarized here. (See Figure 2–8). Rock, from which most aggregate is derived, is of three types according to origin—igneous, sedimentary, and metamorphic. *Igneous rock* was at one time molten and cooled to its present form. *Sedimentary rock* at one time consisted of particles deposited as sediment by water, wind, or glacier. Most were deposited at the bottom of lakes or seas. The pressure of overlying deposits together with the presence of cementing materials combined to form rock. *Metamorphic rock* is either igneous or sedimentary rock that has been changed in texture, structure, and mineral composition, or in one or two of these characteristics, by intense geologic heat or pressure or both.

The natural mineral aggregates of whatever sizes and wherever found came from one of the three types of rock. Any given particle of aggregate may have been through the cycle of rock formation, breaking, transporting, and depositing more than one time.

FIGURE 2-6 Aggregate production requires rock crushers, screens, and conveyors to crush, size, and transport the material (*Courtesy Callanan Industries, Inc.*)

FIGURE 2-7 Bucket loader filling truck with crushed rock aggregate (*Courtesy Callanan Industries, Inc.*)

Igneous rock varies in texture from coarse grains to glasslike smoothness, depending on how quickly it cooled. Slower cooling creates a coarser texture. Some volcanic rock cooled as foam, resulting in very light weight because of the hollow bubbles.

Granite is a common, coarse-grained, light-colored igneous rock. *Gabbro* is a common, coarse-grained, dark-colored igneous rock. Both are much used in the construction industry. *Basalt* is a fine-grained equivalent of gabbro. *Diabase* is intermediate in grain size between gabbro and basalt. Diabase and basalt are known as *trap rock*.

FIGURE 2–8 Rock and mineral constituents in aggregates
(*Source:* Portland Cement Association)

Minerals	Igneous rocks	Metamorphic rocks
Silica	Granite	Marble
Quartz	Syenite	Metaquartzite
Opal	Diorite	Slate
Chalcedony	Gabbro	Phyllite
Tridymite	Peridotite	Schist
Cristobalite	Pegmatite	Amphibolite
Silicates	Volcanic glass	Hornfels
Feldspars	Obsidian	Gneiss
Ferromagnesian	Pumice	Serpentinite
Hornblende	Tuff	
Augite	Scoria	
Clay	Perlite	
Illites	Pitchstone	
Kaolins	Felsite	
Chlorites	Basalt	
Montmorillonites		
Mica	**Sedimentary rocks**	
Zeolite	Conglomerate	
Carbonate	Sandstone	
Calcite	Quartzite	
Dolomite	Graywacke	
Sulfate	Subgraywacke	
Gypsum	Arkose	
Anhydrite	Claystone, siltstone,	
Iron sulfide	argillite, and shale	
Pyrite	Carbonates	
Marcasite	Limestone	
Pyrrhotite	Dolomite	
Iron oxide	Marl	
Magnetite	Chalk	
Hematite	Chert	
Goethite		
Ilmenite		
Limonite		

Note: For brief descriptions, see Standard Descriptive Nomenclature of Constituents of Natural Mineral Aggregates (ASTM C294).

Trap rock provides excellent aggregate. Light-colored *pumice* and dark-colored *scoria* are two types of igneous rock filled with bubbles. They are used to produce lightweight aggregate.

Sedimentary rock generally shows stratification indicating the way it was laid down; it generally breaks more easily along the lines of stratification. Rock formed of gravel is called *conglomerate* and, if formed of sand, is either *sandstone* or *quartzite*. *Siltstone* and *claystone* are soft rock formed of silt or clay. *Shale* is hard claystone. All three break along planes or stratification to form flat particles. Therefore, they do not make the best aggregate, although shale is better because of its greater hardness.

Limestone (mainly calcium carbonate) and *dolomite* (mainly magnesium carbonate and calcium carbonate) were formed under salt water and are largely the remains of sea creatures. They do not break into flat particles. They are both rather soft but generally make satisfactory aggregates. *Chert,* which is formed from fine sand, is hard but often is not resistant to weathering.

It is difficult to generalize about metamorphic rock since the change, or metamorphosis, takes so many different forms. Metamorphic rock is dense but often forms platy particles. Generally, aggregate is hard and strong, but its platy shape is undesirable. *Marble* is a recrystalized limestone or dolomite. *Slate* is a harder form of shale. *Gneiss* is a very common metamorphic rock often derived from granite, but also derived from other rock. It is laminated but does not necessarily break along the laminations. *Schist* is more finely laminated than gneiss but of similar character. Granite, schist, and gneiss are often found together, separated from one another by gradual gradations.

It should be noted that gradations from one type of rock to another are common, and much rock does not fit into any definite category. Aggregate from a natural aggregate deposit may be of various kinds, and it is not then necessary to identify the parent rock types. Even when aggregate is to be obtained from a rock formation, identifying the rock types gives only a general indication of its characteristics which must be checked by testing samples. However, once characteristics are known for part of a geologic formation, only spot checks are necessary to verify characteristics of the entire formation since it was all formed over the same time by the same process.

PROPERTIES AND USES

The usefulness of aggregates to the engineering and construction fields depends on a variety of properties. Performance can be predicted from these properties, and, therefore, the selection of aggregate for a particular task is based on examination and tests. Rather than writing rigid specifications defining properties absolutely required, the specification writer must take into account the types of aggregate readily available and design the specifications to obtain the most suitable aggregate from local sources. A comparison of the specifications devised by various states for highway construction aggregate shows this to be the practice. States containing an abundance of high-quality natural aggregate have more demanding specifications.

Qualities that indicate the usefulness of aggregate particles to the construction industry are:

1. Weight.
2. Strength of the particles to resist weathering, especially repetitive freezing and thawing.
3. Strength as demonstrated by the ability of the mass to transmit a compressive force.
4. Strength as demonstrated by the ability of the individual particles to resist being broken, crushed, or pulled apart.
5. Strength of the particles to resist wear by rubbing or abrasion.
6. Adhesion or the ability to stick to a cementing agent.

7. Permeability of the mass, or the ability to allow water to flow through, without the loss of strength or the displacement of particles.

Weight is of primary importance for large-size stone called *riprap* placed along the edge of a body of water to protect the bank or shore from eroding; for a *blanket* of stones placed to prevent erosion of sloping ground; and for stone retaining walls held in place by wire baskets called *gabions*.

Resistance to weathering is necessary for long life of any aggregate unless it is used only indoors. The quality of resisting weathering is called *soundness*.

Strength of the mass is needed if the aggregate is to be used as a base to support the weight of a building, pipeline, or road, or if it is to be used in portland cement concrete or bituminous concrete. The strength of individual particles to resist being broken, crushed, or pulled apart is important when the aggregate is to be subjected to a load. Pressure on a particle can crush or break it, allowing movement of adjacent particles. Failure of too many particles causes enough movement to constitute failure. Aggregate particles embedded in portland cement are often subject to tension. Concrete pavement and other concrete structures are subject to tension, although not as severe as the compression they receive. The tension and compression must be carried through the aggregate particles as well as the cement paste.

Aggregate may be subject to rubbing and abrasion during processing and handling, and also in service. Aggregate may be chipped or ground by loading equipment, screening equipment, or conveyor belts. Aggregate having insufficient resistance to abrasion produces some additional small broken particles, and the original particles become somewhat smaller and more rounded. The result is that size, gradation, and shape are all changed from what was originally intended. Aggregate particles at the surface of all types of roadways are subject to abrasion from vehicle wheels. The particles throughout asphalt pavement are subject to abrasion because the pavement continuously shifts under the weight of traffic, causing the particles to rub each other.

If the aggregate is to be used in concrete, adhesion between the particles and the cementing agent (either portland cement or asphalt cement) is necessary. Although most aggregate adheres well enough, some requires removal of unsatisfactory material before use, and some is definitely not suitable for use in concrete.

A high degree of permeability is needed if the aggregate is used as a filter or drain, and a low permeability is necessary if the aggregate is used for anything else. *Permeability* is a measure of the ease with which water will flow through an aggregate's voids.

Miscellaneous Uses

Various sizes of stone are used for riprap to protect natural or man-made earthwork. The individual pieces must be large enough so that the force of the water will not move them. Along a reservoir shore or the water's edge at a dam, protective aggregate consisting of particles from baseball size to basketball size might be dumped in a belt extending from low water to high water along the waterline location. On the banks of swiftly flowing streams, it may be considered necessary to place much larger sizes, with each one being fitted into place much like a stone wall, but lying against the bank in a belt extending from low-water to high-water level. Broken rock of irregular slablike shapes is often used and put into place with a crane. The chief requirements for riprap are high weight and low cost. (See Figure 2–9.)

When the bank is too steep or the current too violent for riprap, gabions may be used to hold stones in place. A *gabion* is a basketlike container for stones that is made of heavy steel mesh, forming the shape of a block with level top and bottom and four vertical sides. Gabions are set in place and filled with stones the size of a fist or larger to act as riprap or to form a retaining wall to hold back an earth bank. They may be piled one on top of another as shown in Figure 2–10. Stones are placed by hand or with machinery. The gabions are wired to each other to form a continuous structure. However, the structure is flexible and adjusts without breaking to uneven soil settlement or undermining by water current. The stone-filled gabions are permeable so that soil water flows through readily without building up pressure behind a gabion wall. If stones are available nearby, there is little cost for production or transportation of materials. The finished gabion structure looks rustic, making it more suitable for some settings than concrete or steel work.

River and lake currents and tide movement are often diverted from their natural paths to control the deposition of waterborne particles—in order to fill a beach or to keep a ship docking area from being filled, for example. This is done by building long, narrow obstructions to guide the flow of water in a new direction that will deposit suspended material where it is wanted or remove deposits from where they are not wanted. These low wall-like structures are called *training walls, breakwaters, groins,* or *jetties.* They are built of loose stones piled into the shape of a low, wide wall or of gabion construction where greater forces must be resisted.

High unit weight and reasonably good resistance to weathering are all that are required of the material for the uses described so far. Even though some substances are

FIGURE 2–9 Riprap on stream bank (*photo by Richard S. Williams Jr., U.S. Geological Survey*)

FIGURE 2–10 Bekaert gabions partially in place in Northern California
(*Courtesy Terra Aqua Conservation*)

heavier and more weather resistant than natural stones, no other material approaches the advantages in low cost and ready availability in nearly every possible location. The useful life of the stones in any of these structures is very long, although in some cases abrasion, breakage, or washing away of stones can be expected to shorten life. Wire gabions should be inspected regularly for corrosion or wear. When replacement is needed, the entire structure is replaced, or a new one is built right over the original one.

Aggregate and Strength

Aggregate obviously cannot transmit a tensile force from one particle to another. Cementing agents, which are considered later in this chapter and in Chapters 3 and 4, combine with the particles to form a mass which can resist a small amount of tension. It may appear that particles transmit compressive forces from one to another. However, they do not. If particles with flat surfaces were piled vertically, as shown in Figure 2–11a, a compressive force could be transmitted through the pile just as it is in a structural column made of stone.

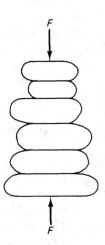

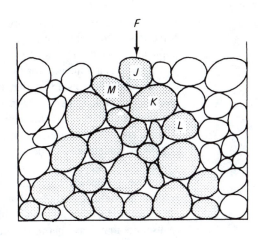

(a) Aggregate piled to transmit
a compressive force. This
is not a practical arrangement.

(b) Aggregate in a container.
A compressive force on
particle J is transmitted by
shear through the shaded
particles.

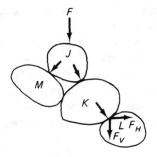

(c) Particle J pushes down and out on K and M
like a wedge. Particle K transmits part of the
force to L with horizontal and vertical components.

FIGURE 2-11 An "aggregate column" contrasted with a container of
aggregate which transmits force by shear

Aggregate cannot be piled in this way. It appears as shown in Figure 2-11b when
in use. Figure 2-11b illustrates a cross section through a container of aggregate with a
concentrated weight or force acting downward on one particle of aggregate. Because of
the random arrangement of particles, the concentrated load is necessarily transmitted to
more particles as the force is transmitted deeper into the container and thereby is spread
over most of the bottom of the container.

In order for the load to spread horizontally, there must be a horizontal force. The
vertical load from the top is transmitted through the points of contact, as indicated in

Figure 2–11c, over an ever larger area with ever smaller forces. The originally vertical force has a horizontal component at each point of contact below the point of original application. At the points of contact, if the surfaces are not perpendicular to the line of force, there is a tendency for the upper particle to slide across the lower particle or push the lower particle aside so that the lower one slides across the particle below it. The tendency to slide transversely is a shearing stress, and the strength to resist the sliding is the shearing strength of the aggregate. (See Figure 1–3.) This strength is the result of friction and interlocking between adjacent particles. Failure to resist the shearing stress results in some particles being forced closer together. Often other particles are pushed aside.

The surface of aggregate settles when particles are pushed closer together. The settlement could be considered as a strain caused by the imposed stress. Aggregate should be compacted so that all the significant settlement takes place before the aggregate is put to use. In that way, harmful settlement is eliminated. The only other way in which aggregate can settle is for particles to be crushed. They will not be crushed unless they are soft or very brittle. Soft or brittle particles should not be used.

Although aggregate particles can be crushed if a great enough force is exerted on them, in use, good aggregate will not hold still to be crushed; it will move before it can be crushed. Horizontal displacement takes place under a smaller force than is needed to crush or break the aggregate. Therefore, the controlling strength is shearing strength which is indicated by the load that can be carried without horizontal movement sufficient to be considered failure.

The tendency to move horizontally is resisted by friction and interlocking between particles. Both are illustrated in Figure 2–12. The friction that can be developed between two particles depends on the roughness or smoothness of the particle surfaces. The rougher the surface is, the more resistance there is to sliding. The resistance developed by interlocking depends on the shape of the particles and is greatest for angular particles such as crushed rock, and least for well-rounded particles such as beach sand.

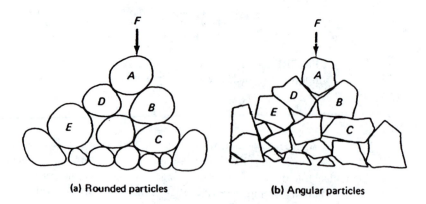

(a) Rounded particles

(b) Angular particles

Particles labeled *B* resist horizontal movement by friction.
Particles labeled *C, D,* and *E* resist by friction and interlocking.

FIGURE 2–12   Friction and interlocking

In Figure 2–12, particle *A* pushes down and to the right on particle *B*. Particle *A* cannot move downward without pushing particle *B* down or to the right. To go down or to the right, *B* must push *C* down or slide across it. In this example, *C* cannot be pushed down because it is held by particles under it. Particle *B* must overcome friction to slide over *C*. The force exerted by *A* on *B* may be enough to push *B* right over *C*. Theoretically, *C* could also push lower particles aside, but such a progression cannot continue without particles sliding over particles at some level.

Particle *D* is in a situation similar to particle *B,* but must move upward to overcome interlocking in order to move horizontally. A greater force is needed on *D* to push it up and over *E*. If the forces are great enough to cause horizontal movement at enough points of contact, the aggregate fails.

No force acts on a single particle, but some loads, such as the forces from the wheels of a vehicle, act on a small area at a time. Even wheel loads, however, act over a number of particles, which causes the actual transmittal of forces from particle to particle to be more complicated than indicated in Figure 2–11. Figure 2–11c shows a partial sketch of forces in one plane. The load is actually transmitted outward in all directions, forming an ever larger circle as it proceeds downward.

Figure 2–13 shows what an aggregate road looks like after failure. Overloading causes particles to be pushed aside and forced to ride up over adjacent particles.

Because of the way in which a concentrated force is spread out through a thickness of aggregate and converted to a lower pressure distributed over a larger area, aggregate is often used as a *base* to support a weight which is too heavy to be applied directly to the soil. A geotextile fabric placed between soil and aggregate prevents mixing the two, which would weaken the aggregate base. The aggregate base spreads the weight over a larger area of soil at a lower pressure. Generally, soil is not as strong as aggregate, but it consists of separate particles as aggregate does and so behaves in much the same way under a load. It fails in shear if overloaded. It is capable of settling more than aggregate and may also fail by settling excessively.

Aggregate is obtained from the best source and brought to the construction site, but the construction takes place on whatever soil is there. Therefore, the soil may be much weaker than available aggregate. Figure 2–14a shows how a concentrated wheel load is spread out over the soil by an aggregate base. Stress on the soil is reduced in proportion to the square of the depth of the aggregate base, because the area of the circle over which stress is spread is proportional to the square of the depth.

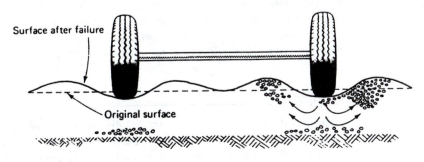

FIGURE 2–13 Aggregate failure under wheel loads

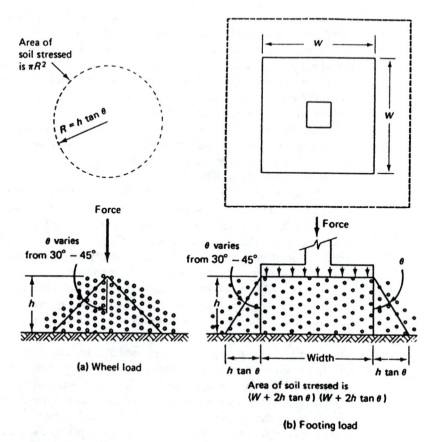

FIGURE 2–14 Wheel and footing loads transmitted to soil

The radius of the circle of pressure equals the depth of aggregate multiplied by the tangent of the angle θ shown in Figure 2–14a. With the load applied over an area small enough to be considered a point, the forces are distributed to the soil over a circular area with a radius of $h \tan \theta$. The area of the circle equals the radius squared multiplied by π. The mathematical equation ranges from $R = h \tan 30°$ to $R = h \tan 45°$, depending on the strength of the aggregate. Aggregate with greater shearing strength spreads the load over a greater area, and the angle θ in Figure 2–14a is greater. The forces are not distributed uniformly within this circle, but for ordinary cases the pressure may be considered uniform.

Example

A wheel load (force) of 3000 lb is applied directly to a crushed rock base 8 in. deep as illustrated in Figure 2–14a. Compute the pressure transmitted to the soil if the base material is of high quality, and angle θ can be considered to be 45°.

$$\text{Pressure} = \frac{\text{Force}}{\text{Area}} = \frac{\text{Force}}{\pi R^2}$$
$$\text{Area} = \pi(h \tan \theta)^2 = 3.14(\tfrac{8}{12} \times 1)^2$$
$$\text{Area} = 1.4 \text{ sq ft}$$
$$\text{Pressure} = \frac{3000 \text{ lb}}{1.4 \text{ sq ft}} = 2100 \text{ psf}$$

Figure 2–14b shows a concrete spread footing transmitting a structural column load through a crushed stone base to the soil. The pressure from the bottom of the footing spreads in all directions as it passes through the base to the soil. It may be assumed to spread in the shape of the footing (normally square or rectangular), becoming wider in all directions as the depth increases.

The highly concentrated load carried by the column is spread out within the footing until it is transmitted to the base over the entire bottom of the footing. The footing is one solid unit and does not transmit force in the same way as the aggregate particles. However, its purpose is the same. It reduces the pressure on the base as the base reduces the pressure on the soil. The footing could be built directly on soil. Whether or not to use a cushion of aggregate is decided by comparing the cost of a larger footing with the cost of the smaller footing plus the aggregate.

Example

A column load (force) of 33 kips acts on a 3'0" × 3'0" spread footing. Using Figure 2–14b, calculate the pressure on the soil if the depth of aggregate base is 8 in., and determine what depth of base is needed to reduce the pressure on the soil to 1.0 kip per sq ft. Assume angle θ is 40°. What is the maximum pressure on the aggregate?

$$\frac{\text{Pressure 8 in.}}{\text{below footing}} = \frac{\text{Force}}{\text{Area}} = \frac{\text{Force}}{(W + 2h \tan \theta)^2}$$
$$\text{Area} = (3 + 2 \times \tfrac{8}{12} \times 0.839)^2$$
$$\text{Area} = 17.0 \text{ sq ft}$$
$$\text{Pressure} = \frac{33 \text{ kips}}{17.0 \text{ sq ft}} = 1.94 \text{ Ksf}$$
$$\frac{\text{Area required for}}{1 \text{ Ksf pressure}} = \frac{\text{Force}}{\text{Pressure}}$$
$$\text{Area} = \frac{33 \text{ K}}{1 \text{ Ksf}} = 33 \text{ sq ft}$$
$$\text{Area} = (W + 2h \tan \theta)^2$$
$$33 = (3 + 2h \times 0.839)^2 = (1.678h + 3)^2$$
$$2.82h^2 + 10.07h - 24 = 0$$
$$h = \frac{-10.07 + \sqrt{(10.07)^2 - 4 \times 2.82(-24)}}{2 \times 2.82}$$
$$h = 1.63 \text{ or, say, 1 ft 8 in.}$$

$$\frac{\text{Maximum pressure}}{\text{(at bottom of footing)}} = \frac{\text{Force}}{\text{Area}}$$

$$\text{Pressure} = \frac{33}{3 \times 3} = 3.67 \text{ Ksf}$$

Loosely piled aggregate particles may be easily pushed aside. In other words, they lack shearing strength. (See Figure 2–15.) Aggregates have a loose arrangement or structure somewhat like Figure 2–15a after handling. They are normally compacted into a tighter structure to increase friction and interlocking before a permanent load is placed on them. The reasons for compacting aggregate base material are to reduce its compressibility and to increase its shear strength.

Vibrations jar the particles into a close structure more effectively than simply rolling with a heavy weight. This can be demonstrated by filling a box with sand or gravel and compacting it by applying weight with a roller or some other means which does not jar or vibrate the material. A small amount of compaction takes place. Then shake the box lightly or rap it on the sides, and a substantial lowering of the level of the material takes place caused by compaction due to vibration.

Compaction results in an increase in density, and the density or unit weight can be used as an indication of the strength of an aggregate base. In Figure 2–15, example b is denser than example a.

Another way to increase density is to mix a variety of sizes. The smaller particles occupy spaces that would be voids if all the particles were large. (See Figure 2–16.) If the sizes are equally represented throughout the entire range of sizes, the aggregate is *well graded.* The aggregate must be well graded to achieve the highest shearing strength. A very strong base can be built with aggregate having a wide range of sizes of proportions selected to achieve the greatest density, as in Figure 2–16b. It is customary to obtain a high strength with a mixture of coarse and fine aggregates, which achieves a strength close to that of the ideal mixture with substantial economy in the cost of handling and mixing materials. Aggregates are separated into standard sizes by screening, and each size

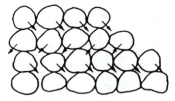

(a) Aggregate dumped and spread.
Strength due to friction only.
Particles readily move downward
and horizontally under a vertical
load as indicated by arrows.

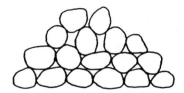

(b) Compacted aggregate.
Strength due to friction and
interlocking.
Particles are pushed downward
and horizontally as far as they
can go and are now stable.

FIGURE 2–15 Increases shear strength due to compaction

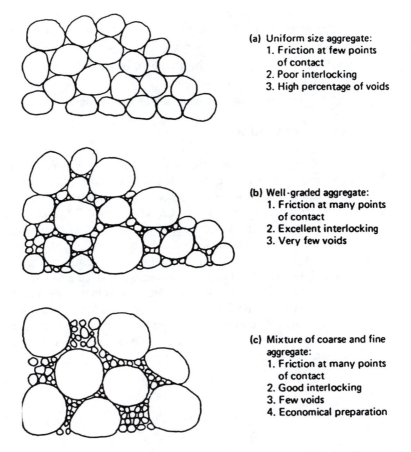

(a) Uniform size aggregate:
   1. Friction at few points of contact
   2. Poor interlocking
   3. High percentage of voids

(b) Well-graded aggregate:
   1. Friction at many points of contact
   2. Excellent interlocking
   3. Very few voids

(c) Mixture of coarse and fine aggregate:
   1. Friction at many points of contact
   2. Good interlocking
   3. Few voids
   4. Economical preparation

FIGURE 2-16 Increased density (and shearing strength) of well-graded aggregate

is stockpiled. If the mixed sizes were stockpiled, it would be difficult to prevent segregation in the stockpile. A desirable mixture is obtained by mixing two, and sometimes more, sizes of aggregate.

Factors which increase the shearing strength of aggregates are summarized here. All the factors, with the exception of the roughness of the particle surfaces, cause an increase in density. The amount of increase in density is an indication of the amount of strength gain to be expected.

1. A well-graded aggregate is stronger than one not well graded.

2. The larger the maximum size of aggregate is, the greater its strength. Larger particles provide greater interlocking, because particles must move upward for greater distances to override them.

3. The more flat, broken faces the particles have, the greater the strength developed through interlocking. Flat faces fit together more compactly with more contact

between faces than if the particles are rounded. This does not mean the particles themselves should be flat. Flat particles slide readily over each other and result in lack of strength.

4. Compaction, especially by vibration, increases the shearing strength of aggregate of any size, shape, and gradation.

5. Rough particle surfaces increase strength because of greater friction between them.

Pavement Base

Typical pavement construction consists of several layers or *courses* which reduce the pressure of concentrated wheel loads so that the underlying soil or *foundation* is not overloaded. (See Figure 2–17.) Wearing surfaces of asphalt mixtures and portland cement concrete are discussed in Chapters 3 and 4. The underlying soil may be that which is there naturally or may be hauled in to build a fill or embankment. It is not considered to be aggregate. It is strengthened by compaction with heavy construction equipment before a base or subbase is placed on it. Subbase material is usually unprocessed, run of bank material selected to meet specifications which have proven through performance to provide satisfactory material. Base material is more carefully selected.

In typical asphalt pavement, called *flexible* pavement, the base and subbase carry the load and distribute it to the soil under two thin layers of asphalt concrete. The concrete slab is the chief load-bearing element of portland cement concrete pavement, which is known as *rigid* pavement. (See Figure 2–17).

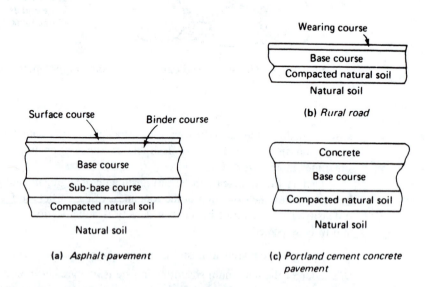

(a) *Asphalt pavement*

(b) *Rural road*

(c) *Portland cement concrete pavement*

The load spreads over an area that increases with depth. Therefore the unit stress is less at greater depths. The material is arranged to be weaker and less expensive at greater depths.

FIGURE 2–17 Typical pavement cross sections

The base under the rigid pavement slab spreads the load somewhat over the foundation, but is designed mainly to protect the pavement from the detrimental effects of too much moisture. These effects are frost action (heaving up against the slab when freezing and losing support by liquifying when thawing); standing water which lowers the strength of the base; and *pumping* which occurs when the pressure of passing traffic forces water out through pavement joints or at pavement edges, carrying small particles out with it. Eventually, a hollow space is formed under the pavement by the removal of particles.

Water does not accumulate if voids are large enough so the base drains freely and capillary water cannot rise into the base. A well-graded coarse aggregate with no appreciable amount of fines is needed. Water may also be kept out if the aggregate has all voids filled to make it watertight. A well-graded aggregate with sufficient fine material to fill the voids is needed for watertightness.

The base under the wearing surface is the chief load-bearing element of rural or secondary roads. (See Figure 2–17.) The asphalt surface course is there to resist traffic abrasion and protect the base from rain. Therefore, strength of the base aggregate to transfer the load to the foundation is of utmost importance. With a tight, water-repellant surface, aggregate must be well graded and compacted for strength but have enough open voids so that capillary water will not rise to be trapped under the surface course. Often the base is strengthened by mixing in just enough asphalt cement to coat the particles so they stick together but leave the voids open.

A base course with no surfacing must resist traffic and rain as well as support the load and transfer it satisfactorily to the foundation. The aggregate must be tightly bound for strength and watertightness, but should allow the rise of capillary moisture to replace moisture lost to the air. A lightly traveled road does not need a protective covering over a properly constructed base.

Freezing of water in the base or subbase does not cause much expansion. If water is drawn up by capillary action to replace the water removed by freezing and it in turn freezes, larger masses of ice called *ice lenses* are formed. These cause disruptive heaving of the surface. Coarse soils have such large voids that water cannot rise by capillarity. Fine soils with sufficient clay allow capillary water to rise very high, but movement is so slow that the quantity of water rising is insufficient to form ice lenses. The voids of silt-sized particles are small enough to permit a capillary rise of several feet in quantities sufficient to form ice lenses. Aggregate sizes must be such that voids are either too large or too small to form ice lenses.

Springtime thawing of ice lenses results in a quantity of water being held under the surface course by frozen soil below it which keeps it from draining. This removes the solid support of the base causing the surface to break up under traffic.

The seepage of rainwater through the base carries fine particles out of the base suspended in the water. The more the particles are carried out, the faster the water flows and the larger the particles it carries are, weakening the base more and more.

Water rises by capillarity in all aggregate unless the voids are too large. Since a small amount of moisture gives added strength in cohesion to the base, it is desirable for capillary water to rise in sufficient quantity to replace evaporated water. If there is no surface over the base, capillarity should be encouraged. If the base is sealed by a watertight surface, the capillary water will accumulate under the surface course, weakening it by depriving it of solid support from the base. Therefore, large size aggregate with large voids is used.

Road and airplane runway bases, whether covered with pavement or not, are subject to moving loads and are exposed to weather and running water—conditions which do not ordinarily affect aggregate bases for pipelines or footings. The moving traffic loads push horizontally. When accelerating or decelerating, tires change the vehicle velocity by pushing (backward to accelerate, forward to decelerate) against the surface below them. (See Figure 2–18.) The vibration of traffic movement assists in loosening the bond and pushing particles to the sides. Freezing and thawing of the moisture in the aggregate, rainwater seepage downward, and movement of capillary water upward all tend to loosen the aggregate bond and remove fine particles, which further loosens and weakens the bond between particles.

Aggregate bases subject only to static loads and protected from weather and moving water need not meet the rigid standards required of pavement bases. Often the gradation of such bases is not critical. The gradation of base material for roads and airplane runways is more important in order to achieve maximum contact between particles and maximum watertightness.

Sufficient fine material must be used to ensure filling the voids without separating the larger particles from contact with each other. The larger particles are the load-bearing structure, and the fine particles hold or bind the coarser ones by preventing movement between them. The fine material is called *binder.* Base material may be a mixture of several sizes of processed aggregate or a mixture of soil and aggregate. The most efficient procedure is to mix the proper quantity and sizes of aggregate with the natural soil occurring on the site of the road or runway to produce suitable base material. Sometimes only a small percentage of aggregate is needed, and sometimes the soil is not usable at all so that the entire base must be aggregate. However, it is desirable to use the maximum amount of soil from as close to the finished construction as possible.

Stabilizing Aggregate

Aggregate strength can be improved by the addition of measured quantities of clay, which is a soil with very fine particles having properties unlike any of the larger soil particles. One of these properties is *cohesion* or the tendency to stick together. The strength due to cohesion is added to the shearing strength possessed by the aggregate. The clay, therefore,

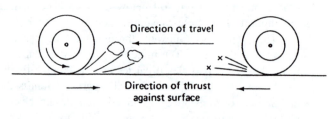

(a) Acceleration   (b) Deceleration or braking

FIGURE 2–18   Horizontal traffic loads on pavement

acts as a cement or paste. Other substances are also used for the same purpose. These include salts, lime, portland cement, and bituminous cement. The use of these other substances to increase strength is called *stabilization*. (See Figure 2–19.)

Calcium chloride and sodium chloride are the two salts mixed with aggregate to increase its strength. Coarse aggregate, fine aggregate, and binder must all be in the proper proportion, and the salt is mixed with them in quantities of 1 to $2\frac{1}{2}$ lb per sq yd of surface or 2 percent of the weight of aggregate. The salt, either calcium chloride or sodium chloride, is well mixed with the aggregate and the proper amount of moisture. The salt forms a brine with the water. This brine forms a film around each particle, which increases the strength of the aggregate in two ways.

The brine film is stronger in surface tension than ordinary moisture, and because of this it increases the cohesion of the particles. The brine film allows the particles to be forced closer together under compaction than they could be with ordinary moisture. It may be thought of as a better lubricant than plain water. Increased cohesion and increased density each cause an increase in strength.

Stabilizing with salt improves the roadway in two additional ways. These improvements result in greater strength, although in themselves they do not increase strength. Abrasion of the roadway surface by traffic causes fine particles to be lost as dust. The loss of these particles leaves voids which loosen larger particles, with the result that much of the aggregate is thrown to the sides of the road. In addition to damaging the road, the loss of the dust causes dust clouds, which are a nuisance and even a health hazard.

Brine does not evaporate as readily as untreated water, and therefore it holds fine particles in place much better despite abrasion by traffic, thereby lessening damage to the road and to nearby properties. Calcium chloride, in addition, is a hygroscopic substance, meaning that it absorbs moisture from the air. It therefore maintains a damp surface that prevents dusting.

Water percolating through aggregate removes some of the fine particles as it flows. The result is damage to the roadway similar to that caused by wheel abrasion on a dry

FIGURE 2–19 Road reclaimer/stabilizer cuts and blends up to a depth of 16 in. and can add stabilizing agents to the reclaimed material (*Courtesy CMI Corporation*)

roadway. Salt stabilization fills the voids with stationary moisture, closing the voids to the passage of water and preventing the washing through of fine particles.

Lime is also used to stabilize aggregate base material. The lime used is burned limestone in either of two forms—quicklime, which is calcium oxide containing magnesium oxide in an amount as high as 40 percent or as low as 0.5 percent ($CaO \cdot MgO$); or hydrated lime, which is quicklime combined with enough water to produce $Ca(OH)_2 \cdot MgO$ or $Ca(OH)_2 \cdot Mg(OH)_2$. Unburned limestone cannot be used. Hydrated lime is more stable and therefore easier to store than quicklime, which hardens upon contact with air.

Lime is mixed with the aggregate in quantities of 2 to 4 percent of the aggregate weight. Water is used to accomplish thorough mixing and to combine chemically with the lime to form the final product, which is limestone.

Lime stabilizes aggregate in two ways. It reacts with clay, causing the particles to combine to form larger particles, giving a better gradation to aggregate containing too much clay. The new, larger particles will not swell excessively when moist as some clay does. Lime also causes a solidifying of the mass by reacting chemically with silica and alumina in the clay and aggregate. Calcium silicates and calcium aluminates are formed. These are cementing agents which act to hold the particles together. These cementing agents are also contained in portland cement and cause its cementing ability. A pozzolan may be added to provide silica and alumina when the aggregate does not contain enough. These readily combine with the lime to form a cement. Pozzolans are discussed in Chapter 4.

Portland cement or asphalt cement may be added to aggregate base to increase its strength. Stabilization with these two materials is covered in Chapters 3 and 4. Stabilization is not the same as manufacturing portland cement concrete or asphalt concrete. It refers to the addition and mixing of a small amount of cement to improve the strength of aggregate.

Concrete is aggregate stabilized with portland cement paste or asphalt cement so that a different material is formed which is no longer made up of particles. The material formed is continuous and rigid in the case of portland cement concrete, and semirigid in the case of asphalt concrete. Concrete strength depends on the strength of the aggregates, the strength of the cementing agent, and the strength of the adhesion between the two.

Permeability and Filters

The best permeability is obtained by using aggregate as large as possible and as uniform in size as possible. Both properties cause large voids with the result that water flows through easily. These voids would have to be filled with smaller particles for the aggregate to achieve its highest strength. Therefore, good permeability and high strength cannot be obtained together.

A filter consists of aggregate designed and installed for the purpose of holding back particles larger than a certain size while letting water flow through with a minimum of interference. A filter works as shown in Figure 2–20 with each layer being held in place by larger particles and in turn holding back smaller particles. Size and gradation are of primary importance for a filter.

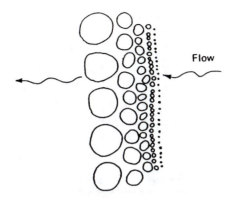

FIGURE 2-20 Filter particles positioned by flowing water

Size must be such that the voids, which are smaller than the filter particles, are also smaller than the particles to be held back. However, they must be as large as feasible to permit water to flow through readily.

The filter catches all particles larger than the voids. If the filter particles are of uniform gradation, the void size is also uniform and all particles above the void size will be caught. Because of this fact, a filter can be designed to hold particles larger than a certain size.

If the filter material is not uniform, some areas will allow particles of a certain size to go through and other areas will hold the same size particles. Where filter particles are too small, the filter becomes plugged, and where filter particles are too large, particles that should be caught are allowed to pass through.

In a properly designed filter, the filter material originally lets all particles below the void size flow through, gradually forming a layer of particles smaller than the filter particles and just too large to flow through the voids. This layer of particles, having smaller voids, catches smaller particles, and a layer of these smaller particles is formed. Layer after layer builds up until voids become so small that no particles flow through and water flow is somewhat restricted. Eventually, the filter is plugged. Several important types of filter are shown in Figure 2-21.

An underdrain system must be removed and replaced before it becomes completely plugged. A water well filter preventing sand from entering the well must be cleaned periodically by surging water back and forth through the filter. This removes fine particles by jarring them loose. They enter the well and are removed by pumping. This process is a major operation.

A filter for cleaning a drinking water supply requires cleaning daily or several times a day. It is a routine operation and is performed by forcing water backward rapidly through the filter, forcing out the finer layers which have built up. These are collected and disposed of as waste material.

A sewage filter requires occasional removal of a thin layer from the top as it becomes plugged, and eventual replacement after a sufficient thickness is removed. If the filter is below the ground surface as shown in Figure 2-21e and the sewage filtered is not

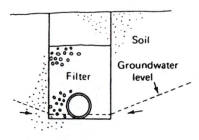

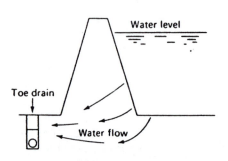

(a) *Underdrain*—lowers groundwater by
carrying it away through a perforated
pipe. The pipe is surrounded by a filter
to prevent small particles from entering
the pipe through the perforations,
settling in the pipe, and restricting pipe
flow.

(b) *Toe drain* – underdrain that intercepts
water seeping through and under an
earth dam. Its purpose is to prevent
undermining by piping which is the
removal of soil particles by the flowing
water until the dam is undermined.
The filter prevents piping by holding
the soil in place while allowing water
to pass.

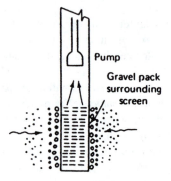

(c) *Gravel pack*—filter that prevents particles from entering the well as ground water flows
through the soil, through the screen, through the pump, and to a water system at the
surface.

FIGURE 2–21   Five types of filter

excessive, the filter operates indefinitely without maintenance because the sewage
particles are consumed by microbes.

Filters may be divided into two categories. One type holds a mass of soil in place
so that water can flow through the soil and then through the filter without carrying
particles of soil with it. Mineral aggregates are always used for this type. The first three
examples in Figure 2–21 are of this type. Another type of filter removes suspended
particles from water as it flows through. Drinking water is cleaned this way before use,
and waste water is cleaned this way before being returned to the ground or to a body of
water. The last two examples in Figure 2–21 are of this type. Sand is used for this type
filter, but so are many other materials including coal, charcoal, and diatomaceous earth.

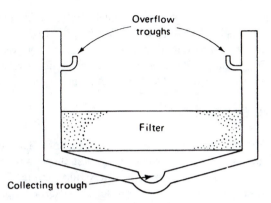

(d) *Water filter* — holds particles as water seeps downward through filter to collecting trough. When filter becomes nearly plugged, a small amount of water is pumped rapidly upward through the filter, overflowing into the troughs and carrying the filtered particles out with it. The particles that collect over many hours are removed in a few minutes.

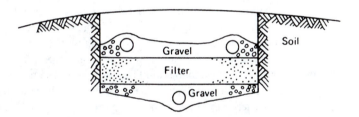

(e) *Sand filter* — sewage, with most of the solids removed by settling, flows through the upper pipes, into the filter through perforations, through the filter, and through perforations into the lower pipes which carry it to a stream or lake. The particles caught in the filter are organic and are consumed by bacteria. If properly designed, the filter will last indefinitely without cleaning.

FIGURE 2-21   (Continued)

TESTS

The behavior of aggregates in use depends on the interrelationship of many properties. Many of these properties have been identified and defined. Standard tests have been devised to evaluate the properties. Performance can be predicted from test results based on past performances.

Cost is of great importance when large quantities of aggregates are being selected. Aggregate is always available at low cost, but the cost rises significantly if the aggregate must be handled one additional time or transported a great distance. It is often preferable to use the best aggregate available nearby rather than to improve it by processing or to obtain better aggregate from a greater distance. It must sometimes be decided whether to accept aggregate of a satisfactory quality or to pay for more processing to obtain aggregate of a better quality. The value of a particular property is often a matter of engineering judgment. Aggregate routinely used in some areas might not be acceptable where better aggregate is readily available. Because of this there is no absolute value required for many of the properties and even ASTM standards do not specify exact requirements for acceptability.

Size and Gradation

Particle sizes are important for all applications. The concept of aggregate size is difficult to express, since the particles have odd shapes that cannot be measured easily and the shapes and sizes vary greatly in any one sample. The important features are *range of sizes,* or smallest and largest particles, and *gradation,* or distribution of sizes within the range covered. A few very large particles or a few very small particles do not ordinarily affect the performance of the mass of aggregate. Therefore, what is usually important is the range from the smallest particles that are contained in a significant amount to the largest particles that are contained in a significant amount.

A set of sieves fitting tightly one on top of the other is used to determine size and gradation of aggregate. A sample of the aggregate to be analyzed is placed in the top sieve, which has the largest holes. The second sieve has smaller holes, and each succeeding sieve has holes smaller than the sieve above it. At the bottom is a solid pan. The pan collects all particles smaller than the openings in the finest sieve, which is chosen to collect particles of the smallest significant size. (See Figure 2–22.)

The *nest* of sieves is shaken, and each particle settles as far as it can. If no particle remains on the top sieve, then the top sieve size represents one kind of maximum size for the sample. The absolute maximum particle size is somewhere between this top sieve size and the size of the next sieve. If even a few particles remain on the top sieve, it is not known how large the maximum size particles are. Usually it is not significant if only a small percentage remains on the top sieve.

Some particles fall through to the pan, and their size is not known either. If the lowest sieve has small enough holes to catch the smallest significant size, the size of particles in the pan is not important. However, an excessive quantity of material fine enough to reach the pan is of interest, just as an excessive quantity of aggregate larger than the largest sieve is of interest.

A sieve consists of a circular frame holding wires strung in such a way as to form square holes of a designated size. Particles are considered to be the size of the holes in the sieve on which they are caught. Whether or not flat particles and long, narrow ones go through a screen may depend on how they land on the screen while being shaken. Thus, chance may play a minor part in the number of particles retained on or passing a sieve. Statistically, results are the same over a large number of tests of the same material. Extremely flat or elongated particles, which could cause the greatest variations, are unacceptable in nearly all cases and so are not ordinarily tested by sieve analysis.

Some standard sieve sizes commonly used for aggregates in construction and actual dimensions of the sides of the square openings are listed in Figure 2–23. Nominal dimensions and permissible variations for openings in all standard sieves, as well as other specifications for their construction, are listed in ASTM E11, Standard Specifications for Wire-Cloth Sieves for Testing Purposes.

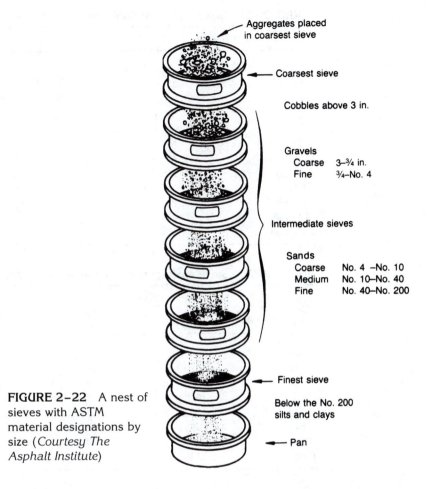

Aggregates placed
in coarsest sieve

Coarsest sieve

Cobbles above 3 in.

Gravels
Coarse   3–¾ in.
Fine   ¾–No. 4

Intermediate sieves

Sands
Coarse   No. 4 –No. 10
Medium   No. 10–No. 40
Fine   No. 40–No. 200

Finest sieve

Below the No. 200
silts and clays

Pan

FIGURE 2–22 A nest of sieves with ASTM material designations by size (*Courtesy The Asphalt Institute*)

Sizes designated in millimeters and inches or fractions of an inch indicate that clear openings between wires are squares with the given dimension as the length of the sides of the square. When the size is a number, such as No. 50, it means there are that number of holes in a lineal inch. The No. 50 sieve has a total of 50 openings per lineal inch or 2500 openings in a square inch. The openings are not $\frac{1}{50}$ of an inch in width because wire takes up much of the space. Therefore, these openings are smaller. Figure 2–23 shows the length of the sides of each square opening, in millimeters and inches.

The results of a sieve analysis are tabulated and percentages computed as shown in Figure 2–24. All relationships are by weight. The title "percent retained" refers to the percentage of the total that is retained on each sieve. The title "cumulative percent retained" refers to the percentage of the total that is larger than each sieve. It is, therefore, the sum of the percentage retained on the sieve being considered plus the percentage retained on each sieve coarser than the one being considered. The title "percent passing" means the percentage of the total weight that passes through the sieve under consideration. It is, therefore, the difference between 100 percent and the cumulative percentage

FIGURE 2–23 Sieve sizes commonly used in construction

Sieve Designation		Nominal Opening (in.)
75 mm	3 in.	3.0
37.5 mm	$1\frac{1}{2}$ in.	1.5
19.0 mm	$\frac{3}{4}$ in.	0.75
12.5 mm	$\frac{1}{2}$ in.	0.5
6.3 mm	$\frac{1}{4}$ in.	0.25
4.76 mm	No. 4	0.187
2.36 mm	No. 8	0.0937
1.18 mm	No. 16	0.0469
0.6 mm	No. 30	0.0234
0.3 mm	No. 50	0.0117
0.15 mm	No. 100	0.0059
0.074 mm	No. 200	0.0029

FIGURE 2–24 Sieve analysis results (coarse aggregate)

Sieve Size	Weight Retained (g)	Percent Retained	Cumulative Percent Retained	Percent Passing
4in.	0	0	0	100
3in.	540	11	11	89
$1\frac{1}{2}$in.	1090	21	32	68
$\frac{3}{4}$in.	1908	37	69	31
$\frac{1}{2}$in.	892	17	86	14
#4	495	10	96	4
Pan	211	4	100.0	0.0
Total	5136	100.0		

retained for that sieve. A small error should be expected. Usually some dust is lost when the sieves are shaken. There is a gain in weight if particles left in the sieves from previous tests are shaken loose. However, there should be none if proper procedures are followed.

The weight of the original sample before sieving should agree with the sample weight after sieving. When the material is being tested for acceptance purposes the difference between the two weights cannot differ by more than 0.3 percent based on the original dry-sample weight. The loss or gain due to sieving for general gradations is usually set at 2 percent and the total weight of the material after sieving is used as the divisor. The loss or gain of material due to sieving is usually a function of how clean the sieves were at the start of the test and how well the technician cleans each sieve during the test.

Example

Complete the sieve analysis calculations for the coarse aggregate data shown in Figure 2–24.

Step one: Calculate percent retained.

$$\text{Percent retained} = \frac{\text{Weight of material retained on sieve}}{\text{Total sample weight}} \times 100$$

$$\text{\% retained (4 in.)} = \frac{0}{5136} \times 100 = 0 = 0\%$$

$$\text{\% retained (3 in.)} = \frac{540}{5136} \times 100 = 10.5 = 11\%$$

$$\text{\% retained (1}\tfrac{1}{2}\text{ in.)} = \frac{1090}{5136} \times 100 = 21.2 = 21\%$$

$$\text{\% retained (}\tfrac{3}{4}\text{ in.)} = \frac{1908}{5136} \times 100 = 37.1 = 37\%$$

$$\text{\% retained (}\tfrac{1}{2}\text{ in.)} = \frac{892}{5136} \times 100 = 17.4 = 17\%$$

$$\text{\% retained (\#4)} = \frac{495}{5136} \times 100 = 9.6 = 10\%$$

$$\text{\% retained (pan)} = \frac{211}{5136} \times 100 = 4.1 = \underline{4\%}$$

$$100\%$$

The sum of the individual percents retained must equal 100 percent.

Step two: Calculate cumulative percent retained.

Cumulative percent retained (4 in.) = 0 = 0%

Cumulative percent retained (4 in., 3 in.) = 0 + 11% = 11%

Cumulative percent retained (4 in., 3 in., 1$\frac{1}{2}$ in.) = 0 + 11% + 21% = 32%

Cumulative percent retained (4 in., 3 in., 1$\frac{1}{2}$ in., $\frac{3}{4}$ in.) = 0 + 11% + 21% + 37% = 69%

Cumulative percent retained (4 in., 3 in., 1$\frac{1}{2}$ in., $\frac{3}{4}$ in., $\frac{1}{2}$ in.) = 0 + 11% + 21% + 37% + 17% = 86%

Cumulative percent retained (4 in., 3 in., 1$\frac{1}{2}$ in., $\frac{3}{4}$ in., $\frac{1}{2}$ in., #4) = 0% + 11% + 21% + 37% + 17% + 10% = 96%

Cumulative percent retained (4 in., 3 in., 1$\frac{1}{2}$ in., $\frac{3}{4}$ in., $\frac{1}{2}$ in., #4, pan) = 0% + 11% + 21% + 37% + 17% + 10% + 4 % = 100%

Step three: Calculate percent passing.

Percent passing = 100% − Cumulative percent retained

Percent passing (4 in.) = 100% − 0 = 100%

Percent passing (3 in.) = 100% − 11% = 89%

Percent passing (1$\frac{1}{2}$ in.) = 100% − 32% = 68%

Percent passing ($\frac{3}{4}$ in.) = 100% − 69% = 31%

Percent passing ($\frac{1}{2}$ in.) = 100% − 86% = 14%

Percent passing (#4) = 100% − 96% = 4%

Percent passing (pan) = 100% − 100% = 0%

Step four: Plot the percent passing versus sieve size on a gradation chart (Figure 2–25a).

ASTM C136, Sieve or Screen Analysis of Fine and Coarse Aggregates, describes standard procedures for performing a sieve analysis and specifies the amount of error

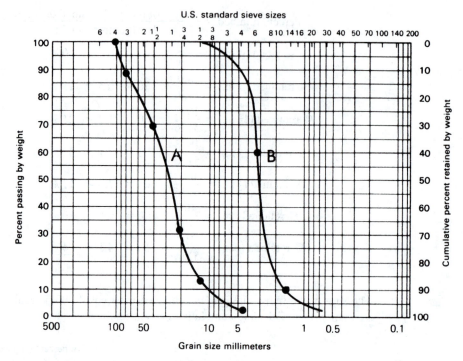

FIGURE 2-25 (A) Curve representing the example problem gradation; (B) typical gradation curve—uniform aggregate

allowed. A brief description of the proper procedure follows. A representative sample is placed in the top sieve after the entire nest including the pan has been put together. The cover is placed on top. The nest of sieves is shaken by hand or by mechanical shaker long enough so that additional shaking cannot appreciably change the quantities retained on each sieve. The quantity retained on each sieve is removed from the sieve, using a brush to collect particles caught in the wire mesh, and weighed. Each quantity weighed should be kept on a separate sheet of paper until the sum of individual weights has been compared with the total weight of the sample. Then, if there is a discrepancy, the individual quantities can be reweighed. Percentages should be reported to the nearest whole number.

It is customary in the aggregate industry to process and stockpile aggregates in several size ranges, designated either as fine and coarse or by the size of the largest sieve retaining an appreciable percentage of the total particles. There are several advantages in this type of handling rather than stockpiling aggregate of the entire range of sizes in one pile. Segregation is more difficult to prevent in a quantity with a wide range of sizes. Also, a mixture of any desired range and gradation can be prepared with the proper proportions from several stockpiles. Therefore, the supplier with aggregate separated according to size is prepared to supply whatever the market requires. The mixture proportions can even be adjusted slightly during a project when conditions require it.

Other ASTM standards deal with specialized types of sieve analysis. ASTM C117, Standard Method of Test for Materials Finer than No. 200 Sieve in Mineral Aggregate by Washing, provides a method for washing clay particles through the sieves when the clay is stuck together in chunks or adheres to larger particles. ASTM D451, Sieve Analysis of Granular Mineral Surfacing for Asphalt Roofing and Shingles; ASTM D452, Sieve Analysis of Nongranular Mineral Surfacing for Asphalt Roofing and Shingles; and ASTM D546, Sieve Analysis of Mineral Filler, set forth other specialized sieve analysis procedures. Mineral filler is very fine, dustlike aggregate used in bituminous concrete to fill voids between fine aggregate particles.

The results of a sieve analysis are often plotted on graph paper with sieve sizes on the horizontal axis as the abscissa and percent coarser (retained) and finer (passing) on the vertical axis as the ordinates. Sample plots are shown in Figure 2–25. The horizontal axis is divided according to a logarithmic scale because of the wide range of sizes to be plotted. The largest sieve openings may be several hundred times the size of the smallest sieve openings. The smaller sizes must be spaced far enough apart for clarity; but if the same scale is used for the larger sizes, an excessively long sheet of paper is needed. Linear scales are therefore not used. The semilogarithmic scale is much more satisfactory.

A graph of percent by weight versus sieve sizes is called a *gradation chart*. It is a better presentation in some ways than a tabulation. Size, range, and gradation can be seen on the graph. The range of sizes can be obtained from graph or tabulation with equal ease. However, finding the size and gradation may require the use of a gradation chart. There are several ways in which the size of aggregate is defined.

It has been found that the filtering performance of an aggregate can be predicted by the particle size that has a certain percentage by weight finer than its own size. This size is designated by the letter D with a subscript denoting the percentage finer. In Figure 2–25b, D_{15} is 2 mm and D_{85} is 4 mm.

The *effective size,* used to designate size of aggregate to be used as a filter for sewage or drinking water, is that diameter or size on the graph which has 10 percent of the total finer than its size. It is not necessarily a sieve size and cannot be found accurately without a gradation curve. In Figure 2–25b it is 1.4 mm. Sieve sizes may increase to the left as in Figure 2–25 or increase to the right as in Figure 2–26.

The *maximum size* of aggregate, when used in the design of portland cement concrete mixes, is taken for that purpose to be the size of the sieve next above the largest sieve that has 15 percent of the total sample coarser than it (cumulative percentage retained). Therefore, in Figure 2–24 the maximum aggregate size would be 3 in.

Fineness modulus is a value used in the design of portland cement concrete mixes to indicate the average size of fine aggregate. It may also be used to indicate the average size of coarse aggregate. It is determined by adding the cumulative percentages retained on specified sieves and dividing by 100. Specified sieves include 6 in., 3 in., $1\frac{1}{2}$ in., $\frac{3}{4}$ in., $\frac{3}{8}$ in., No. 4, No. 8, No. 16, No. 30, No. 50, and No. 100. The sample must be run through all these sieves, omitting those too large to retain any aggregate, but not any that are smaller than the smallest aggregate. Calculating the fineness modulus requires the inclusion of cumulative percentages retained on each sieve.

The fineness modulus should be determined to two decimal places. The whole number indicates the sieve on which an average size particle would be retained. To locate this sieve, count upward from the pan a number of sieves corresponding to the whole

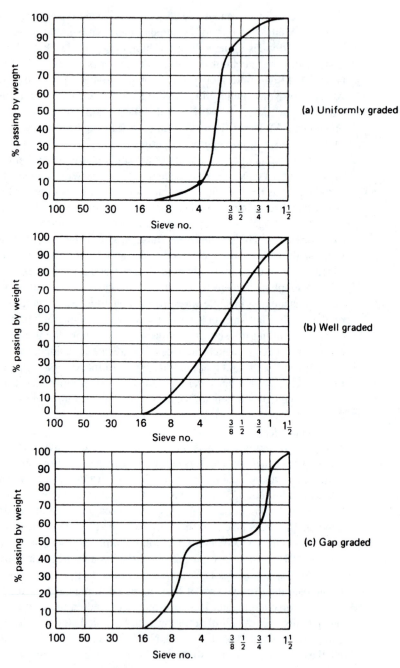

FIGURE 2-26 Three gradation types

number of the fineness modulus. The average size is further defined by considering it to be located between the designated sieve and the sieve above it a portion of the distance upward, as indicated by the decimal. The decimal 0.75 would locate the average size at 75 percent of the way up from the lower sieve toward the upper one.

Gradation, meaning the distribution of particle sizes within the total range of sizes, can be identified on a graph as well graded, uniform, or gap graded (sometimes called skip graded). *Well graded* means sizes within the entire range are in approximately equal amounts, although there will be very small amounts of the largest and smallest particles. *Uniform* gradation means that a large percentage of the particles are of approximately the same size. *Gap graded* or *skip graded* means that most particles are of a large size or a small size with very few particles of an intermediate size. Typical curves for the three types of gradation are shown in Figure 2–26.

The shape of the curve aids in identifying the type of gradation. A line nearly vertical indicates that a large quantity of material is retained on one or possibly two sieves. In Figure 2–26a, 85 percent of the particles are finer than the $\frac{3}{8}$-in. sieve, and only 10 percent are finer than the No. 4 sieve. Therefore, 75 percent of the material is caught on the No. 4 sieve. In other words, much of the aggregate is the same size, and the material is uniform.

A line with a constant slope, as in Figure 2–26b, changes the same amount in the vertical direction with each equal increment in the horizontal direction. This indicates that approximately the same quantity of material is retained on each successive sieve and therefore that the aggregate being tested is well graded.

A horizontal or nearly horizontal line, as in Figure 2–26c, indicates there is no change or little change in percent finer through several successive sieves. Therefore, no material or very little material is retained on these sieves, and there is a gap in the gradation. Aggregate can be processed or mixed to provide any of these gradations if desired. In nature aggregate seldom occurs in these ways, and gradation charts usually take less idealized shapes.

The gradation curve does not give a precise indication of uniformity, although if curves for two aggregates are plotted at the same scale, one could tell which is more uniform. The *uniformity coefficient* is a mathematical indication of how uniform the aggregate is. It is determined by dividing the diameter or size of the D_{60} by the diameter or size of the D_{10}. The smaller the answer, the more uniform in size the aggregate. The uniformity coefficient cannot be determined from a tabulation of sieve analysis results because the D_{60} and D_{10} are usually between sieve sizes, and a plot must be made to locate them.

Aggregate size and gradation are often specified by listing sieve sizes and a range of "percent passing" for each size. The sample being tested is sieved with the specified sieves and is acceptable if, for each sieve, the sample's percentage falls within the specified range. A plot of the upper and lower specified limits is called an *envelope*. An aggregate meets the specifications if its gradation curve plots entirely within the envelope. (See Figure 2–27.) A gradation curve is not needed but it shows the aggregate's relationship to the envelope in detail that cannot be obtained from a tabulation.

Another way to specify size and gradation is with a range for the effective size and a range for the uniformity coefficient.

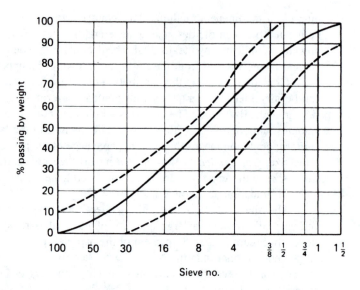

FIGURE 2-27 Gradation curve that fits within an envelope, thereby meeting the specification

Surface Area

The surface area of a quantity of aggregate is sometimes important. A ratio of surface area to volume or surface area to weight is determined and used for computations dealing with surface area. Of all possible particle shapes, a sphere has the lowest ratio of surface area to volume or weight. Particles that roughly approximate spheres in shape also have roughly the same surface to volume ratio as spheres, and all other shapes have greater ratios, with the ratio being greater as the particle differs more from a spherical shape. The following calculation shows the ratio of surface area to volume for a sphere:

$$\text{Surface area} = 4\pi r^2$$
$$\text{Volume} = \left(\frac{4\pi r^3}{3}\right)$$
$$\text{Ratio} = \frac{\text{Surface area}}{\text{Volume}} = \frac{4\pi r^2}{\left(\frac{4\pi r^3}{3}\right)} = \frac{3}{r}$$

The ratio is therefore 3 divided by the radius of the sphere. The ratio is greater for small particles than for large particles because the ratio becomes greater as the radius becomes smaller.

In waste water filters, organic matter is consumed by bacteria that live on aggregate surfaces. Consumption, and therefore the quantity of waste water that can be treated, is proportional to the numbers of bacteria which are proportional to the total surface of the particles. It is, therefore, advantageous to have a large total surface per volume of aggregate to support more bacteria.

It is also of importance if aggregate particles are to be bound together for strength. The design of an asphalt paving mix requires enough liquid asphalt to form a coat of a certain thickness completely over each particle. An estimate is made of the square feet of surface per pound of aggregate, and the proportion by weight of asphalt material to aggregate is determined according to the amount of surface to be coated. The particles are always bulky in shape for strength so that the surface area is small (slightly larger than for spheres), and the result is that a small quantity of asphalt material is sufficient to coat the particles.

Weight-Volume Relationships

The total volume of an aggregate consists of solid particles and the voids between the particles. The total volume is important because aggregate must be ordered to fill a certain volume. Aggregate for a filter must cover a certain number of square feet to a particular depth. Aggregate for a roadbed must be placed in a certain width and thickness for a specified number of miles.

The volume of solid matter is also of importance. The volume of one aggregate particle consists of a mass of solid material. However, all particles used as aggregates contain some holes or pores. The pores range in size from a large open crack that can hold small particles to holes that cannot be seen, but can absorb water. For some uses the volume of these pores is important and for some uses it is not.

Example

Calculate the solid volume and percent of voids in a fine aggregate if it has a specific gravity of 2.65 and a bulk unit weight of 111.3 pcf (1782.85 kg/m^3).

$$\text{Solid volume} = \frac{\text{Weight (lb)}}{\text{Specific gravity} \times \text{Unit weight of water}}$$

$$\text{SV} = \frac{111.3 \text{ lb}}{2.65 \times 62.4 \text{ lb per cu ft}} = 0.673 \text{ cu ft}$$

$$\text{\% Voids} = \frac{\text{Specific gravity} \times \text{Unit weight of water} - \text{Unit weight}}{\text{Specific gravity} \times \text{unit weight of water}} \times 100$$

$$= \frac{2.65 \times 62.4 \text{ lb/cu ft} - 111.3 \text{ lb/cu ft}}{2.65 \times 62.4 \text{ lb/cu ft}} \times 100$$

$$= 32.7\%$$

$$\text{Solid volume} = \frac{1782.85 \text{ kg}}{2.65 \times 1000 \text{ kg/m}^3} = 0.673 \text{ m}^3$$

$$\text{\% Voids} = \frac{2.65 \times 1000 \text{ kg/m}^3 - 1782.85 \text{ kg}}{2.65 \times 1000 \text{ kg/m}^3} \times 100$$

$$= 32.7\%$$

In asphalt concrete, a percentage of the volume of the pores is filled with liquid asphalt material. Therefore, the correct quantity of asphalt cement for the mix includes enough to coat the particles plus enough to partially fill the pores.

In portland cement concrete, the mixing water completely fills the pores in the aggregate. Lightweight aggregate, because of its very porous structure, may absorb so much water that there is not enough remaining to combine with the cement satisfactorily.

The volume of the pores in aggregate used as a base or as a filter is of little importance except that freezing and thawing cause the breaking of porous particles more so than of more solid particles. A few fine particles may enter the larger pores in coarse aggregate, but their total volume is negligible. In base material the voids between coarse aggregate particles are filled with fine aggregate. The volume of voids must be known to obtain the correct volume of fine aggregate but the volume of pores is not needed.

It is usually desirable to know the volume of aggregate in relationship to its weight. This is so because the quantity needed is determined according to the volume it must occupy, but that quantity is ordered and measured for payment by weight.

Various combinations are used to relate weight and volume, depending on how the aggregate is to be used. The possibilities include using total volume (solids and voids), volume of solids including pores, or volume of solids less volume of pores; and using wet weight, saturated, surface-dry weight, or oven-dry weight. These alternatives are illustrated in Figure 2–28.

1. The volume of aggregate may include solid matter, plus pores in the particles, plus voids. This is called *bulk volume* of aggregate.

2. The volume may include solid matter, plus pores in the particles but not voids. This is called the *saturated, surface-dry volume.*

3. The volume may include solid matter only, not pores or voids. This is called *solid volume.*

4. The weight may include solid matter, plus enough water to fill the pores, plus free water on the particle surface. This is called *wet weight.*

5. The weight may include solid matter, plus enough water to fill the pores. This is called *saturated, surface-dry weight.*

6. The weight may include solid matter only. This is called *oven-dry weight.*

If aggregate particles are soaked in water until all pores are filled and then removed and wiped dry, the pores will remain filled with water for a time. If that aggregate is placed into a calibrated container of water, the rise in water level indicates the saturated, surface-dry volume of aggregate because the volume added to the container of water consists of solids plus pores saturated with water.

If aggregate is dried in an oven until all moisture is driven from the particle pores and then placed into a calibrated container of water, the rise in water level indicates the solid volume because the volume added to the container of water consists only of solid material. Some time is needed for the water to enter the pores, and the solid volume cannot be determined at once. In soaking particles to fill their pores with water, a 24-hour soaking period is considered sufficient.

The simplest weight-volume relationship is expressed as unit weight of aggregate. The procedure for determining it is contained in ASTM C29, Unit Weight of Aggregate. The sample of aggregate is oven dried, and a cylindrical metal container of known volume is filled with it and weighed. The procedure for filling the container is specified

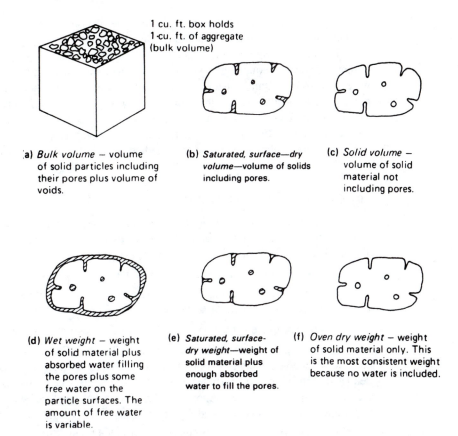

a) *Bulk volume* – volume of solid particles including their pores plus volume of voids.

(b) *Saturated, surface—dry volume*—volume of solids including pores.

(c) *Solid volume* – volume of solid material not including pores.

(d) *Wet weight* – weight of solid material plus absorbed water filling the pores plus some free water on the particle surfaces. The amount of free water is variable.

(e) *Saturated, surface-dry weight*—weight of solid material plus enough absorbed water to fill the pores.

(f) *Oven dry weight* – weight of solid material only. This is the most consistent weight because no water is included.

FIGURE 2–28 Kinds of volume and weight for aggregate particles

in detail to ensure consistent results. The container is filled in three equal layers, and each layer is compacted with 25 strokes of a rod of standard dimensions.

The oven-dry weight of aggregate divided by its bulk volume is its unit weight. This is not the same as unit weight of aggregate particles, which is the oven-dry weight divided by the actual volume of the particles not including voids.

Specific gravity (SG) of a substance is the ratio of the unit weight of that substance to the unit weight of water. The specific gravity of aggregate particles is useful in calculations, particularly those to convert weight of the irregularly shaped particles to saturated, surface-dry volume or to solid volume.

There are two kinds of specific gravity used with aggregate particles. *Bulk specific gravity* is based on oven-dry weight and saturated, surface-dry volume of the aggregate particles. Pores in the particles are considered part of the volume. *Apparent specific gravity* is based on oven-dry weight and solid volume of the particles. Either one of these can be considered as a true specific gravity, and each has its own use.

A type of specific gravity called *effective specific gravity* is used in the design of asphalt concrete. It is derived by dividing oven-dry weight by the weight of a volume of water equal to the solid volume plus the volume of pores that is not filled with asphalt cement when aggregate and cement are mixed.

Dividing the weight of a certain volume of any substance by the weight of the same volume of water is equivalent to dividing unit weight of the substance by unit weight of water, and so the result is specific gravity of the substance. Methods for determining bulk and apparent specific gravity and absorption for aggregate are contained in ASTM C127, Specific Gravity and Absorption of Coarse Aggregate, and ASTM C128, Specific Gravity and Absorption of Fine Aggregate. Bulk specific gravity is sometimes determined using saturated, surface-dry weight, and that method is included in these two ASTM standards.

The methods are briefly described here.

Specific Gravity of Coarse Aggregate

1. A representative sample of coarse aggregate weighing about 5 kg is dried by heating and weighed at intervals until two successive weighings show no loss of weight. The final weight is recorded as the oven-dry weight.

2. The oven-dried sample is soaked in water for 24 hours.

3. The aggregate is removed from the water and dried with a cloth until no film of water remains, but the particle surfaces are damp.

4. The aggregate is then weighed. The result is saturated, surface-dry weight in air.

5. The aggregate is submerged in water at $23 \pm 1.7°C$ ($73.4 \pm 3°F$) in a wire basket, and the submerged weight is obtained. The submerged weight of the basket must be deducted. The submerged particles displace a volume of water equal to their own volume including all pores because the pores are filled with water before being submerged. There is a weight loss when submerged which is equal to the weight of water displaced.

6. Oven-dry weight of aggregate in air divided by the difference between saturated, surface-dry weight in air and weight submerged equals bulk specific gravity. The weight loss in water is the weight of a quantity of water equal to the saturated, surface-dry volume of aggregate. Therefore, this calculation determines the ratio of weight of a volume of aggregate (solid matter plus pores) to the weight of an equal volume of water.

7. Oven-dry weight of aggregate in air divided by the difference between oven-dry weight of aggregate in air and weight submerged equals apparent specific gravity. In this case the weight loss in water is the weight of a quantity of water equal to the volume of solid matter of aggregate. Therefore, this calculation determines the ratio of weight of aggregate solid matter without pores to weight of an equal volume of water. It should be understood that oven-dry weight of solid matter alone is the same as oven-dry weight of solid matter plus pores since the empty pores have no weight.

The only difference between calculating bulk specific gravity and apparent specific gravity is that the saturated, surface-dry volume is used for bulk specific gravity and the volume of solid matter alone is used for apparent specific gravity. Using saturated, surface-dry particles means that saturated, surface-dry volume is the basis for determining the weight of an equal volume of water to find bulk specific gravity. Using oven-dry particles means that the solid volume is the basis for determining the weight of an equal volume of water to find apparent specific gravity.

8. Bulk specific gravity is based on oven-dry weight unless specified otherwise. It may be determined on a saturated, surface-dry basis by using the saturated, surface-dry (SSD) weight in air as aggregate weight rather than the oven-dry (OD) weight. This variation is covered in ASTM C127.

9. *Absorption,* which is the percentage of the weight of water needed to fill the pores compared to the oven-dry weight of aggregate, is computed by dividing the difference between SSD weight and OD weight in air by the OD weight in air.

Example

$$\text{Given: SSD weight in air} \quad 5480 \text{ g}$$
$$\text{Submerged weight} \quad 3450 \text{ g}$$
$$\text{OD weight} \quad 5290 \text{ g}$$

$$\text{Bulk SG} = \frac{\text{OD weight}}{\text{SSD weight} - \text{Submerged weight}} = \frac{5290}{5480 - 3450} = 2.61$$

$$\text{Apparent SG} = \frac{\text{OD weight}}{\text{OD weight} - \text{Submerged weight}} = \frac{5290}{5290 - 3450} = 2.88$$

$$\% \text{ Absorption} = \frac{\text{SSD weight} - \text{OD weight}}{\text{OD weight}} = \frac{5480 - 5290}{5290} \times 100$$
$$= 3.6\%$$

Specific Gravity of Fine Aggregate

1. A representative sample of fine aggregate weighing about 1000 g is dried to a constant weight, the oven-dry weight.

2. The oven-dried sample is soaked in water for 24 hours.

3. The wet aggregate is dried until it reaches a saturated, surface-dry condition. This condition cannot be easily recognized with small-sized aggregate. To determine the point at which it reaches this condition, the drying must be interrupted frequently to test it. The test consists of putting the aggregate into a standard metal mold shaped as the frustum of a cone and tamping it 25 times with a standard tamper. The cone is removed vertically and the fine aggregate retains the mold shape if sufficient moisture is on the particle surfaces to cause cohesion. The aggregate is considered saturated, surface-dry the first time the molded shape slumps upon removal of the mold.

4. A representative sample consisting of 500 g of aggregate (saturated, surface-dry weight) is put into a 500-cm^3 container, and the container is filled with water at 23 ± 1.7°C (73.4 ± 3°F).

5. The full container is weighed. The total weight consists of the sum of:

   a. known weight of flask,

   b. known weight of aggregate (SSD), and

   c. unknown weight of water.
   The weight of water can be determined by subtracting flask and aggregate weights from the total weight.

6. The entire contents is removed from the container, with additional rinsing as required to remove all particles, and the oven-dry weight of aggregate is determined.

7. The container is weighed full of water.

8. The foregoing procedures provide all the data needed to compute SG and absorption. Saturated, surface-dry volume of aggregate is used for bulk SG, and solid volume is used for apparent SG. Oven-dry weight of aggregate is used for either type of SG, and SSD weight may be used for bulk SG if so stated. Either SG equals oven-dry weight of aggregate divided by weight of container filled with water plus weight of aggregate in air, minus weight of container filled with aggregate and water. For bulk SG, the SSD weight of aggregate in air is used in the denominator, and for apparent SG the oven-dry weight of aggregate in air is used in the denominator. The procedure is illustrated in Figure 2–29.

9. Absorption is the weight of water needed to fill the particle holes, divided by the weight of solid matter and expressed as a percentage. It is computed by dividing SSD weight minus oven-dry weight by oven-dry weight.

Example

$$
\begin{aligned}
\text{Given: SSD weight} && 500 \text{ g} \\
\text{OD weight} && 492.6 \text{ g} \\
\text{Flask + Water weight} && 537.6 \text{ g} \\
\text{Flask + Water + Fine aggregate weight} && 846.2 \text{ g}
\end{aligned}
$$

$$
\begin{aligned}
\text{Bulk specific gravity} &= \frac{\text{OD weight}}{[(\text{Flask} + \text{Water}) + (\text{SSD wt})] - [\text{Flask} + \text{Water} + \text{Fine aggregate}]} \\
&= \frac{492.6}{[537.6 + 500] - [846.2]} = 2.57
\end{aligned}
$$

$$
\begin{aligned}
\text{Apparent specific gravity} &= \frac{\text{OD weight}}{[(\text{Flask} + \text{Water}) + (\text{OD weight})] - [\text{Flask} + \text{Water} + \text{Fine aggregate}]} \\
&= \frac{492.6}{[537.6 + 492.6] - [846.2]} = 2.68
\end{aligned}
$$

$$
\begin{aligned}
\% \text{ Absorption} &= \frac{\text{SSD weight} - \text{OD weight}}{\text{OD weight}} \times 100 \\
&= \frac{500 \text{ g} - 492.6 \text{ g}}{492.6 \text{ g}} \times 100 \\
&= 1.50\%
\end{aligned}
$$

Deleterious Matter

Excessive amounts of foreign material are detrimental in aggregate used for any purpose. What constitutes an excessive amount depends on the usage of the aggregate. Very little foreign matter can be permitted in aggregate for portland cement concrete, asphalt concrete, or filters. Permissible amounts are greater for aggregate used as a base.

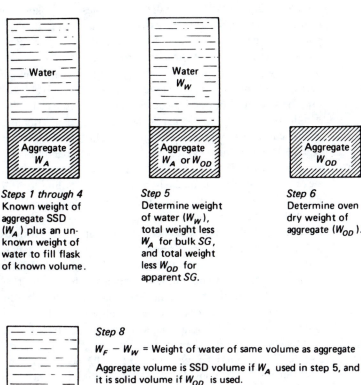

Steps 1 through 4
Known weight of aggregate SSD (W_A) plus an unknown weight of water to fill flask of known volume.

Step 5
Determine weight of water (W_W), total weight less W_A for bulk SG, and total weight less W_{OD} for apparent SG.

Step 6
Determine oven dry weight of aggregate (W_{OD}).

Step 8
$W_F - W_W$ = Weight of water of same volume as aggregate

Aggregate volume is SSD volume if W_A used in step 5, and it is solid volume if W_{OD} is used.

$$SG = \frac{W_{OD}}{W_F - W_W}$$

Bulk SG is obtained if W_A used in step 5, and apparent SG is obtained if W_{OD} is used.

Using the weights obtained through step 7 including weight of container (W_C)

Step 7
Determine weight of water to fill flask (W_F).

$$SG = \frac{W_{OD}}{W_C + W_F + W_A - (W_C + W_W + W_A)} = \frac{OD\ agg.\ wt}{wt\ water\ same\ vol.\ as\ agg.\ SSD}$$

FIGURE 2-29 Specific gravity of fine aggregate

ASTM C33 contains allowable limits for seven types of deleterious substances which must be controlled in aggregates to be used for portland cement concrete. Maximum permissible quantities are listed according to a percentage of the weight of the entire sample for fine aggregates and coarse aggregates. The seven categories are friable particles, material finer than No. 200 sieve, soft particles, coal and lignite, chert, organic impurities, and materials reactive with the alkalis in cement.

Friable particles are those which are easily crumbled such as clay lumps, weak sandstone, or oxidized ores. An excessive amount of these causes a change to a gradation with more fine particles when the friable ones are broken in use. The end result is similar to using an aggregate with excessive fine material in it. The method of testing for friable particles is described in ASTM C142, Test for Friable Particles in Aggregates. Friable particles are described as those that can be crushed between thumb and forefinger without using fingernails. Material is separated on sieves before the test, and after all friable particles are broken, each fraction is sieved on a sieve finer than the one it was retained on. The weight of crushed particles that goes through the finer sieves divided by the total weight of the test sample gives the percentage of friable particles. ASTM C33 limits friable particles to 3 percent for fine aggregates and 2 to 10 percent for coarse aggregates when either is to be used for portland cement concrete.

Material finer than No. 200 sieve is that material which passes through the No. 200 sieve in a washed sieve analysis performed according to ASTM C117, Test for Materials Finer than No. 200 Sieve in Mineral Aggregates by Washing. The material must be washed through the sieves because much of it may be stuck to larger particles. One reason the fine material is objectionable is that it coats larger particles. The coating is a hindrance to the adherence of portland cement paste or asphalt cement to the aggregates. In portland cement concrete, the fine material, whether loose or coating a particle, absorbs water before the water can combine with cement to form a paste.

ASTM C33 limits material finer than No. 200 sieve in fine aggregate to 3 percent for portland cement concrete subject to abrasion and 5 percent for other portland cement concrete, and in coarse aggregate to 1 percent for all concrete. If the finer material is stone dust which has a bulky shape, it is not as harmful as clay particles which have a flat shape, and these limits may be increased to 5 and 7 percent, respectively.

Fine material may be objectionable in filter material because it will either be washed through the filter or partially plug the filter, depending on the relative sizes of the fine material and the filter material. Plugging to any extent is always undesirable, as it lowers the quantity of water that can pass through the filter. Fine material flowing through is objectionable if it settles to the bottom and impedes the flow of water in a conduit following the filter or if the filter's purpose is to provide clear water.

Soft particles are those that are marked with a groove after being scratched on a freshly broken surface by a pointed brass rod under a force of 2 lb in accordance with ASTM C235, Test for Scratch Hardness of Coarse Aggregate Particles. The test is simple and suitable for field investigation of a possible aggregate source. Soft particles are detrimental when the aggregate is to be subject to abrasion, such as in a gravel road, bituminous concrete road, or portland cement concrete floor subject to steel wheel traffic. The main concern is that soft particles will be crushed or rubbed into powder, thereby interrupting the continuity of the aggregate structure by removing some of the aggregate particles that are needed either to transmit shear or to maintain a continuous surface. Therefore, soft particles are of little concern in fine aggregate. ASTM C33 limits soft particles in coarse aggregate to 5 percent for concrete in which surface hardness is important and has no limit for soft particles in fine aggregate.

Lightweight pieces are particles in coarse or fine aggregate that have an SG substantially less than that of the aggregate as a whole. They are objectionable for several reasons. They are often soft or weak. If they consist of coal or lignite, they cause unsightly pitting and black staining at the surface of a portland cement concrete structure and have an SG of about 2.0. Chert particles with an SG of 2.35 expand because of their porous particle structure and cause pitting in concrete.

The test for determining the percentage of lightweight pieces in aggregate is described in ASTM C123, Lightweight Pieces in Aggregate. It consists of placing the aggregate sample into a mixture of liquids proportioned to have an SG between that of the acceptable aggregate and that of the lightweight pieces. The SG of the liquid is designed according to the SG's of particles to be separated. The lightweight particles float and are skimmed or poured out. Zinc chloride in water may be used, or carbon tetrachloride or kerosene may be blended with a heavy liquid to produce the desired SG. ASTM C33 limits coal and lignite in fine and coarse aggregate to 0.5 percent when surface appearance of concrete is important and to 1 percent when surface appearance is not important. Chert is limited in coarse aggregate to 1 percent for concrete exposed to severe weather and 5 percent for concrete with mild exposure.

Organic impurities are nonmineral material of an organic type, mainly tannic acid, sometimes found in fine aggregate. Organic material hinders the hardening of portland cement paste and so must be limited in fine aggregate to be used in portland cement concrete. A method of testing for excessive organic impurities is contained in ASTM C40, Organic Impurities in Sands for Concrete. The principal value of the test is to furnish a warning that further tests are necessary before the aggregate can be approved.

The method consists of preparing a reference solution of standard brown color and comparing it with a solution containing a sample of the aggregate being tested. A measured quantity of the fine aggregate is mixed with a specified solution of sodium hydroxide in water. After 24 hours the solution containing aggregate is compared to the standard color solution. The more organic material there is in the aggregate, the darker the solution is. If it is darker than the standard color, it presumably contains excessive organic material.

Suspect aggregates should not be used for portland cement concrete unless it can be proven that mortar made from it is as strong or nearly as strong as mortar made from the same aggregate with the organic impurities washed out. The method for making this comparison is described in ASTM C87, Effect of Organic Impurities in Fine Aggregate on Strength of Mortar. Cubes of mortar are made from both washed and unwashed aggregate, and the average crushing strengths compared. The mortar made from the unwashed aggregate should be at least 95 percent as strong as the mortar made with clean aggregate. This test takes one week for the mortar cubes to cure, compared to one day for the simpler presumptive test.

Reactive aggregates are those which contain minerals which react with alkalis in portland cement, causing excessive expansion of mortar or concrete. The expansion causes disintegration which may not be apparent in use for several years. The reaction is either alkali-silica or alkali-carbonate, depending on the type of aggregate. The reaction takes place when mortar or concrete is subject to wetting, extended exposure to humid atmosphere, or contact with moist ground. It can be prevented by using cement with a low alkali content or with an additive which has been proven to prevent the harmful expansion. The additives either combine with alkalis while the cement paste is still in a semiliquid state, thus removing the alkalis, or prevent the reaction between the deleterious substance and the alkali. The alternative is to check aggregates for reactivity whenever it is suspected. The tests are difficult and usually time consuming, and no one test is entirely satisfactory for all cases. Often aggregates are accepted based on past experience in similar cases and in doubtful cases the aggregate is tested.

A standardized microscope examination which is useful to determine the quantity of reactive material in aggregate is described in ASTM C295, Petrographic Examination of Aggregates for Concrete. However, the actual results caused by the reactive substance are a better criterion than the quantity of reactive substance in the aggregate.

A chemical method, described in ASTM C289, Test for Potential Reactivity of Aggregates (Chemical Method), indicates the potential reactivity by the amount of reaction between a sodium hydroxide solution and the aggregate submerged in it. This test is not completely reliable but serves as an indicator before undertaking a longer test.

Another method, described in ASTM C227, Test for Potential Alkali Reactivity of Cement-Aggregate Combination (Mortar Bar Method), is to make mortar specimens and measure them for possible expansion while stored at uniform temperature and moisture over a period of at least 3 months and preferably 6 months. This method is recommended to detect only alkali-silica reactions, because carbonate aggregates of substantial reaction potential give very little indication of it during this test.

ASTM C342, Test for Potential Volume Change of Cement-Aggregate Combinations, describes a similar test to determine volume change of reactive aggregates in mortar specimens exposed to wide variations in temperature and moisture over a period of 1 year. This test applies particularly to certain cement-aggregate combinations found in parts of the central United States.

ASTM C586, Potential Alkali Reactivity of Carbonate Rocks for Concrete Aggregates (Rock Cylinder Method), indicates the potential alkali-carbonate reactivity between cement and limestone or dolomite. Small cylinders cut from aggregate are immersed in a sodium hydroxide solution, and change in length is determined over a period of about a year. The method is meant for research or screening of a possible source rather than to check conformance to specifications.

Miscellaneous Properties

Toughness, which means resistance to abrasion and impact, is indicated either by the Deval test described in ASTM D2, Abrasion of Rock by Use of the Deval Machine, and ASTM D289, Abrasion of Coarse Aggregate by Use of the Deval Machine; or by the Los Angeles abrasion test described in ASTM C131, Resistance to Abrasion of Small Size Coarse Aggregate by Use of the Los Angeles Machine, and ASTM C535, Resistance to Abrasion of Large Size Coarse Aggregate by Use of the Los Angeles Machine. ASTM D2 describes the Deval test for crushed rock, and ASTM D289 describes the Deval test for other aggregate. The two Los Angeles tests are for any coarse aggregate, one for smaller and one for larger sizes. The Los Angeles tests are of more recent origin. They can be run in less time and provide a greater range of results so that differences in toughness are more apparent.

Toughness is an important quality for aggregate subjected to mixing in a portland cement concrete mixer or an asphalt concrete pugmill (actions similar to that of the Deval and Los Angeles tests); to compaction with heavyweight or vibratory compaction equipment as roadbeds and asphalt pavement are; or to steel-wheeled or hard-rubber-tired traffic as some industrial floors are. In addition, the particles in gravel roads and asphalt concrete roads rub against each other throughout the lifetime of the road each time traffic passes by. All these processes can break and abrade particles, thus changing the design gradation and opening holes in the surface.

In the Deval test, aggregate is rotated 10,000 times in a cylinder with six steel spheres for ASTM D289 and no spheres for ASTM D2. Coarse aggregate of various sizes may be tested but none smaller than the No. 4 sieve. Material broken fine enough to pass the No. 12 sieve is expressed as a percentage of the total sample weight to indicate the susceptibility to abrasion and breakage.

In the Los Angeles test (see Figure 2–30), aggregate of the type to be used is combined with 12 steel spheres or fewer for smaller aggregates and rotated in a cylinder 500 times for small-size coarse aggregate and 1000 times for large-size coarse aggregate. A shelf inside the cylinder carries the aggregate and steel balls to a point near the top where they fall once each revolution. This fall plus the addition of more spheres for larger aggregates causes greater abrasion and breakage than in the Deval tests. Material broken

FIGURE 2–30 Los Angeles Abrasion Machine (*Courtesy The Asphalt Institute*)

fine enough to pass the No. 12 sieve is expressed as a percentage of the total sample weight to indicate the susceptibility to abrasion and breakage.

If the aggregate particles are all of equal toughness, the loss of weight in fine particles increases in direct proportion to the number of revolutions. If there are some very weak particles, they will be completely crushed in the early part of the test, while the tougher particles will continue to lose weight at a constant rate throughout the test. In this case there will be a rapid loss of weight at first, tapering off to a uniform rate of loss near the end.

A very tough aggregate with a small but significant percentage of very weak particles is not as valuable as an aggregate that is consistently moderately tough. Yet each type could produce the same results at the end of a test. A method of checking on the uniformity of toughness throughout the sample consists of comparing the weight of material passing the No. 12 sieve after one-fifth of the revolutions with the weight passing after all the revolutions. The ratio should be approximately one-fifth if the sample is of uniform toughness, and will be higher if the sample is not uniform.

Soundness of aggregates means resistance to disintegration under weathering including alternate heating and cooling, wetting and drying, and freezing and thawing. Expansion and contraction strains caused by temperature changes impose a stress on aggregate (as well as on any other material) which may eventually cause breaking. Chemical changes which slowly disintegrate some types of aggregate are brought about by atmospheric moisture which contains dissolved gases. Drying and rewetting renews the chemical attack, which is generally the dissolving of a constituent of the aggregate. By far the most destructive effect of weathering is caused by freezing and thawing. Pores in the particles become filled with water, which freezes and expands within the pores, exerting great pressure that tends to break the particle open at the pores.

ASTM C88, Soundness of Aggregates by Use of Sodium Sulfate or Magnesium Sulfate, provides a method for measuring soundness by immersing aggregate in a sodium sulfate or magnesium sulfate solution and removing and oven-drying it. Each cycle requires a day's time. This procedure causes an effect similar to weathering in that particles are broken away from the aggregate, but at an accelerated rate. It is believed that salt crystals accumulating in the aggregate pores exert an expanding pressure similar to that caused by the formation of ice. After the specified number of cycles, which varies with the intensity of weathering that must be resisted, the weight in material that passes a sieve is determined as an indication of the soundness of the aggregate. The sieve is slightly smaller than the size that retained all the aggregate originally for coarse aggregate and the same size as the one that retained all the aggregate for fine aggregate.

The procedure is designed to test resistance to the freeze-thaw cycle because this is the most destructive type of weathering, and aggregate with high resistance to freezing and thawing can resist any weather. An alternative test may be made by freezing and thawing the wet aggregate; but many cycles and a long period of time are necessary if the freezing and thawing during the useful life of the aggregate are to be simulated.

Hydrophilic aggregate is that aggregate which does not maintain adhesion to asphalt when it becomes wet. The word *hydrophilic* means "loves water." The implication is that hydrophilic aggregate prefers water to asphalt. Some silicious aggregates, for example, quartzite, are hydrophilic and therefore cannot be used satisfactorily with asphalt cement without special preparation of the asphalt cement. ASTM D1664, Coating and Stripping of Bitumen-Aggregate Mixtures, provides a method for testing aggregates for adhesion to asphalt. Aggregate is completely coated with the asphalt and submerged in water for 16 to 18 hours. The amount of asphalt coating that strips away from the aggregate is determined by a visual estimate of whether the aggregate surface left coated is more or less than 95 percent of the total surface.

Sampling

Aggregate tests and inspection must be performed on representative samples. Ideally, a representative sample is a small quantity with exactly the same characteristics as the entire quantity. Expressed practically, a representative sample closely reproduces those characteristics of the entire mass that is to be tested. Methods of taking samples must avoid *segregation* which is any separation of particles on the basis of some property. The most common segregation is by particle size, with smaller particles tending to become separated from larger ones. ASTM D75, Sampling Stone, Slag, Gravel, Sand and Stone Block for Use as Highway Materials, provides methods for proper sampling of aggregate.

Samples are required for:

1. Preliminary investigation of a possible source of supply, whether a rock formation, an aggregate deposit, or an industrial byproduct. The supplier makes this investigation before investing the money to extract and process aggregate.

2. Acceptance or rejection of a source of supply by the buyer. This is a preliminary determination. An inspection and tests are made for this purpose by a prospective buyer who intends to buy large quantities for one project or a series of projects. An example is a state public works department which approves or disapproves gravel or sand pits for state projects for the coming year or other period of time.

3. Acceptance or rejection by the buyer of specified material from the supplier. Inspection and tests are performed as a final check for conformance to the agreement at the time of delivery.

4. Control of removal and processing operations. The supplier assures himself that his product remains of consistent quality by testing it.

A natural deposit is investigated by making test holes and examining or testing their entire contents. A layered deposit with somewhat different characteristics in each layer requires a sample cutting through a large number of layers. Aggregate sources frequently include pockets or areas of nontypical aggregate. Separate samples may be needed from each of these pockets or areas whenever they are observed.

A representative sample from a stockpile that may be segregated requires one large sample made up of samples from top, middle, and bottom of the pile. A representative sample from a bin should be taken in several increments while aggregate is being discharged by intercepting the entire cross section of the stream of particles each time but not the very first or very last particles being discharged. A representative sample from a railroad car, truck, or barge should be taken from an appropriate number of flat-bottomed trenches dug completely across the width of the contained aggregate.

The samples collected in any of the ways noted are generally combined in appropriate proportions to make one large sample representing the entire quantity of aggregate. That is, the size of each separate sample has the same relationship to the size of the combined sample as the quantity of aggregate represented by each separate sample has to the entire quantity of aggregate. When variations in characteristics or amount of segregation are of importance, each uncombined sample is inspected and tested separately.

The combined samples are often too large to use and must be reduced in size for handling and testing without changing characteristics that are to be investigated. Sample size is reduced by quartering or by dividing in a sampler splitter. Either method provides a representative sample. The two methods are illustrated in Figure 2–31.

SPECIAL AGGREGATES

Lightweight aggregates are those that have a unit weight of no more than 70 lb per cu ft (1120 kg per m³) for fine aggregate, 55 lb per cu ft (880 kg per m³) for coarse aggregate, and 65 lb per cu ft (1040 kg per m³) for combined fine and coarse aggregate. These weight limitations and other specifications for lightweight aggregate for structural use are found in ASTM C330, Lightweight Aggregates for Structural Concrete, and ASTM C331, Lightweight Aggregates for Concrete Masonry Units. The purpose of using lightweight aggregate in concrete structures is usually to reduce the weight of upper parts of a structure so that the lower supporting parts (foundations, walls, columns, and beams) may be smaller and therefore cost less. Lightweight aggregates are also used in insulating concrete. Transportation costs are less for lightweight aggregates and for lightweight concrete or masonry products than for their traditional, heavier counterparts.

Three types of lightweight aggregate are used for concrete in which strength is of major importance. Volcanic rock such as pumice, scoria, or tuff, all of which contain numerous air bubbles, and man-made particles prepared by expanding blast-furnace slag, clay, diatomite, fly ash, perlite, shale, slate, or vermiculite, are used in portland cement concrete structural members or for concrete masonry units. In addition, cinders from the combustion of coal or coke are used for masonry units only.

As slag flows from a blast furnace in a molten stream at temperatures of 1400 to 1600°C, it is chilled with high-pressure water spray forced into the molten mass where it becomes steam as it cools the slag. The expanding steam causes bubbles so that the slag is frothy by the time it cools. The operation, which is completed in a few minutes, results in a hard mass of lightweight material called *expanded slag* or *foamed slag* which must be crushed into aggregate size.

Certain slags, shales, and slates when heated to about 2000°F expand to as much as seven times their original size because of the expansion of gas formed within them. The gas may be formed from minerals occurring naturally in the clay or rock or from a chemical that is added. The heating process, which usually takes place in a rotary kiln, must be rapid so that the gas expands with explosive force sufficient to expand the particle and create a series of discrete air cells. The expansion must take place when the particle is soft enough from the heat to be expanded by the gas rather than shattered. The aggregate may be reduced to proper size before heating to produce particles of the desired size or may be crushed and sorted to the desired size after expansion and cooling.

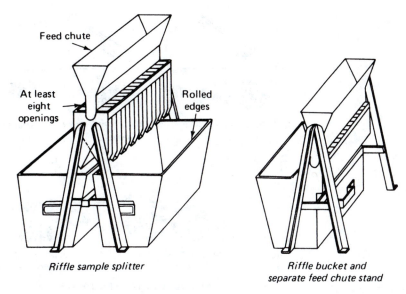

(a) Large riffle samplers for coarse aggregate

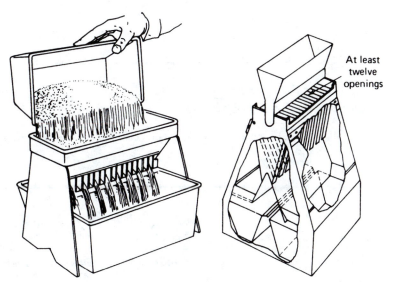

Note — May be constructed as either closed or open type. Closed type is preferred.

(b) Small riffle sampler for fine aggregate

FIGURE 2–31 Reducing sample size (*Courtesy American Society for Testing and Materials*)

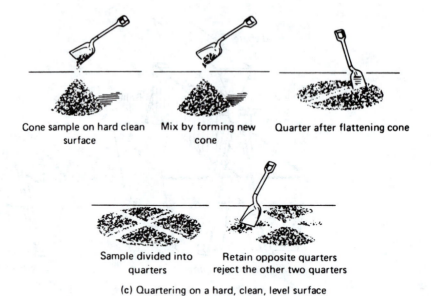

Cone sample on hard clean surface   Mix by forming new cone   Quarter after flattening cone

Sample divided into quarters   Retain opposite quarters reject the other two quarters

(c) Quartering on a hard, clean, level surface

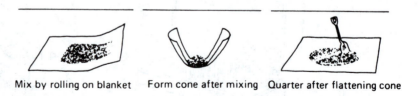

Mix by rolling on blanket   Form cone after mixing   Quarter after flattening cone

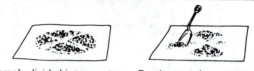

Sample divided into quarters   Retain opposite quarters, reject the other two quarters

(d) Quartering on a canvas blanket

FIGURE 2–31   (Continued)

Diatomite, which consists of the skeletons of tiny aquatic plants called diatoms, can be heated to the melting point to be used as a cinderlike, lightweight aggregate.

Fly ash consists of fine mineral particles produced by the burning of coal. It is useful in portland cement concrete as a substitute for cement. This use is discussed in Chapter 4. Fly ash to be used as an aggregate may be pelletized to form coarse aggregate or used as fine aggregate. It may be mixed with coal mine wastes for aggregate manufacture. In fact, the production of aggregates made of fly ash in combination with other materials for road bases, railroad ballast, and asphalt or portland cement concrete occupies many large industries.

Perlite is volcanic glass in spherical particles of concentric layers. It contains water which, if heated rapidly enough, becomes steam with enough force to shatter the spheres into particles and expand the particles.

Vermiculite includes a variety of water-bearing minerals derived from mica. These expand perpendicularly to the layers when steam is formed by rapid heating.

Cinders used as aggregates are fused into lumps by combustion of coal or coke and are not the softer ashes formed by lower-temperature combustion. Cinders contain some unburned material which is undesirable. Sulfur compounds found in cinders corrode steel, and cinders or concrete containing cinders should not be placed in contact with steel.

Manufactured sands are fine aggregates produced by the crushing and screening of quality rock. They are used as fine aggregates in areas where the natural sands are of poor quality or scarce.

Lightweight aggregate is sometimes incorporated into concrete primarily for heat insulation. Any of the aggregates used for lightweight concrete designed primarily for strength except cinders may also be used for insulating concrete. However, aggregates prepared by expanding natural minerals such as perlite and vermiculite are the lightest and generally the best insulators of all these. ASTM C332, Lightweight Aggregates for Insulating Concrete, specifies a maximum weight of 12 lb per cu ft (dry loose weight) for perlite and 10 lb per cu ft for vermiculite.

Lightweight aggregate may have a tendency to stain concrete surfaces because of iron compounds that are washed out by rain. ASTM C641, Staining Materials in Lightweight Concrete Aggregates, describes procedures for testing this tendency.

Heavy aggregates are those with higher specific gravities than that of aggregates in general use, although there is no definite line separating them from ordinary aggregates. They are used primarily to make heavy concrete. Heavy concrete is needed in special cases to resist the force of flowing water or to counterbalance a large weight, on a bascule bridge, for instance. Heavy aggregate is also used in nuclear-radiation-shielding concrete where greater density provides greater shielding. Natural minerals used are iron minerals with specific gravities as high as 4 to 5.5 and barium minerals with specific gravities up to 4.5. Steel punchings, iron shot, and a byproduct of the production of phosphorus called ferrophosphorus (SG of 5.7 to 6.5) are used as heavy aggregates.

Natural heavy mineral aggregates and ferrophosphorus are described in ASTM C638, Constituents of Aggregates for Radiation-Shielding Concrete, and general requirements are specified in ASTM C637, Aggregates for Radiation-Shielding Concrete.

Radiation shielding is also accomplished by the inclusion of natural boron minerals, or boron minerals heated to partial fusion, as aggregates in the concrete shield. These are also described in ASTM C638.

REVIEW QUESTIONS

1. How is bedrock reduced to aggregate particles in nature?

2. How could you differentiate between a gravel deposit of glacial till and one of glacial outwash?

3. A 2000-lb wheel load is to be supported by aggregate over soil that can withstand a pressure of 1000 lb per sq ft. What depth of aggregate is needed if $\theta = 40°$?

4. A pipe is to be installed under the ground on a bed of aggregate 6 in. thick. The entire weight on the aggregate from pipe and soil above the pipe is 1800 lb per lineal ft of pipe. What is the pressure on the soil if $\theta = 45°$? Assume the pipe load on the aggregate acts on a line.

5. What is the way in which all stabilizing techniques increase the strength of aggregate?

6. Explain why a filter should be made of uniformly graded aggregate.

7. Using the following data, determine the percent retained, cumulative percent retained, and percent passing for each sieve. Plot the gradation curve. Determine the effective size and uniformity coefficient if appropriate. Determine the fineness modulus and check ASTM C33 gradation requirements.

a.

Sieve Size (in.)	Weight Retained (g)
3	736
2	984
$1\frac{1}{2}$	1642
$\frac{3}{4}$	1030
$\frac{3}{8}$	625
Pan	96

b.

Sieve Size	Weight Retained (g)
No. 4	59.5
No. 8	86.5
No. 16	138.0
No. 30	127.8
No. 50	97.0
No. 100	66.8
Pan	6.3

c.

Sieve Size (in.)	Weight Retained (lb)
3	1.62
2	2.17
$1\frac{1}{2}$	3.62
$\frac{3}{4}$	2.27
$\frac{3}{8}$	1.38
Pan	0.21

d.

Sieve Size	Weight Retained (g)
No. 4	10.2
No. 8	81.6
No. 16	92.3
No. 30	122.8
No. 50	116.2
No. 100	46.3
Pan	19.1

8. How many cubic yards of aggregate must be ordered for a road base 16 in. thick and 2 miles long with a top width of 30 ft, if the side slopes are one on one, or 45°?

9. How many tons of coarse aggregate will be required to fill a trench 5 ft deep, 3 ft wide, and 300 ft long? The coarse aggregate unit weight equals 93.6 lb per cu ft.

10. A sample of coarse aggregate weighs 1072 g when oven dry, 1091 g when saturated surface dry, and 667.6 g submerged. Calculate the bulk specific gravity, apparent specific gravity, and absorption.

11. A sample of lightweight coarse aggregate weighs 532.3 g when oven dry, 615.7 g when saturated surface dry, and 191.3 g submerged. Calculate the bulk specific gravity, apparent specific gravity, and percent absorption.

12. A sample of fine aggregate weighs 501.2 g when SSD and 491.6 g when OD. The flask weighs 540.6 g when filled with water and 843.1 g when filled with the aggregate sample and water. Calculate the bulk specific gravity, apparent specific gravity, and percent absorption.

13. A sample of fine aggregate weighs 544 g when SSD and 530 g when OD. The flask weighs 654 g when filled with water and 985 g when filled with fine aggregate and water. Calculate the bulk specific gravity, apparent specific gravity, and absorption.

14. Calculate the solid volume and percent of voids of an aggregate that weighs 111.2 pcf and has a specific gravity of 2.62.

15. What is the difference in detrimental effects of clay lumps and clay particles in aggregate to be used for portland cement concrete?

16. Explain why a comparison is made between the percent of the sample passing the No. 12 sieve after one-fifth of the Los Angeles Abrasion test and the percent passing at the completion of the test.

17. What are the four situations in which aggregate must be sampled and tested?

18. Describe the structure of lightweight aggregate.

19. Research local Department of Transportation coarse and fine aggregate specifications for concrete. Compare them to the ASTM C33 requirements located in the appendix.

20. Calculate the solid volume and percent of voids of an aggregate that has a density of 1581 kg/m^3 and a specific gravity of 2.59.

21. Calculate the metric tons of gravel required to fill an excavated area 70 m by 50 m by 2 m deep if the gravel has a density of 1890 kg/m^3.

3

Asphalt

Bituminous materials are important construction materials. They are strong cements, durable, highly waterproof, and readily adhesive. Bituminous materials are also highly resistant to the action of most acids, alkalis, and salts. They will be found on all types of construction projects from buildings to highway and heavy construction. They are used in roofing systems, sealants and coatings, and in pavements. Asphalt and tar are bituminous materials. Asphalt is produced by the distillation of petroleum crude oil, and tar is produced by the destructive distillation of organic materials.

HISTORY

The use of asphalt by man can be traced back to approximately 6000 B.C. Asphalts were used as cements to hold stonework together in boat building and as waterproofing in pools and baths. Some asphalt was mixed with sand and used to pave streets and palace floors.

The Egyptians made use of asphalt in the mummification process and as a building material. The Greeks and Romans not only used asphalt as a building material but also used burning asphalt as a military weapon.

The asphalt used by these ancient civilizations was *natural asphalt* formed when crude petroleum oils rose to the earth's surface and formed pools (see Figure 3–1). The action of the sun and wind drove off the lighter oils and gases, leaving a heavy residue. The residue was asphalt with impurities such as water and soil present. Using crude distillation processes, cementing and waterproofing materials were obtained.

FIGURE 3–1 Formation of natural asphalt (*Courtesy Barber-Greene Co.*)

NATURAL ASPHALT

Many pools of natural asphalt still exist; the largest are the Bermudez deposit in Venezuela and the asphalt lake on the island of Trinidad. Sir Walter Raleigh obtained Trinidad asphalt to caulk his ships during a voyage to the New World. Until the development of distillation processes to produce asphalt from crude petroleum, the deposits were a major source of asphalt. In the United States, the LaBrea pits in Los Angeles, California, are of interest because of the fossil remains and skeletons of prehistoric animals found in the pits.

Rock asphalt is another natural asphalt of limited commercial value because of its low asphalt content. As early as 1802 crushed rock asphalt was being used in France to pave floor, bridge, and sidewalk surfaces. Rock asphalt was imported in 1838 to pave sidewalks in Philadelphia, Pennsylvania. *Rock asphalt* is asphalt impregnated in porous rock, while another form called gilsonite is found in veins. *Gilsonite* is a hard, brittle, and relatively pure asphalt which can be economically extracted from the earth for commercial purposes.

Even though natural asphalt does occur, the majority of asphalt used in construction today is obtained from petroleum crude. Depending upon its use, the asphalt can be produced in a variety of types and grades ranging from a hard, brittle material to a thin liquid. Approximately 70 percent of the asphalt produced is used in paving and related industries, 20 percent is used in the manufacture of roofing materials and systems such as built-up roofs, and the remaining 10 percent is used in miscellaneous areas such as metal coatings and waterproofing.

BITUMINOUS MATERIALS

The American Society for Testing and Materials defines bituminous asphalt and tar as follows:

bitumens: mixtures of hydrocarbons of natural or pyrogenous origin or combinations of both, frequently accompanied by their nonmetallic derivatives, which may be gaseous, liquid, semisolid, or solid, and which are completely soluble in carbon disulfide.

asphalt: a dark brown to black cementitious material, solid or semisolid in consistency, in which the predominating constituents are bitumens which occur in nature as such or are obtained as residue in refining petroleum.

tar: brown or black bituminous material, liquid or semisolid in consistency, in which the predominating constituents are bitumens obtained as condensates in the destructive distillation of coal, petroleum, oil shale, wood, or other organic materials, and which yields substantial quantities of pitch when distilled.

Tar

Asphalt should not be confused with coal tar because asphalt is readily soluble in most petroleum products and tar is resistant to petroleum-based solvents. Asphalt is composed almost entirely of bitumens while tar has a low bitumen content.

Tar is generally produced as a byproduct during the production of coke. While the coal is being heated, the gases generated are refined to produce road tars, roofing tars, waterproofing pitches, creosote oils, and various tar chemicals. The amount of coal tar produced by this distillation process will vary depending upon the coal, equipment, and temperature used. Coal tars generally have high specific gravities, viscosities, and good adhesive properties.

Asphalt

Petroleum asphalt is the basic paving material in use today, even though some countries still use relatively small amounts of natural asphalt and tars.

Petroleum crude oils are generally classified on the basis of their crude oil content.

1. Asphaltic base crude (almost entirely asphalt)
2. Paraffin base crude (contains paraffin but no asphalt)
3. Mixed base crude (contains both paraffin and asphalt)

The amount of asphalt obtained from a crude oil is based upon its American Petroleum Institute (API) gravity; the higher the gravity, the lower the asphalt content, and the lower the API crude gravity, the higher the asphalt content. A crude with an API gravity of 30 may produce about 20 to 26 percent asphalt, while a crude with an API gravity of 17 may produce 50 percent asphalt. The remaining products would be gasoline, kerosene, fuel oil, and lubricating oils.

The flow chart in Figure 3–2 illustrates the production of asphalt and other petroleum products from crude oil.

ASPHALT PRODUCTION

Asphalt Cements

Asphalt is produced from crude oil by distillation. The method preferred for the production of asphalt for paving construction is *fractional distillation*. The crude oil is heated and the lighter oils vaporize and are drawn off at their condensation temperature, leaving a residual material—asphalt cement.

To increase the production of the lighter constituents of crude oil such as fuels and lubricating oils, *destructive distillation* is employed. The crude oil is heated under

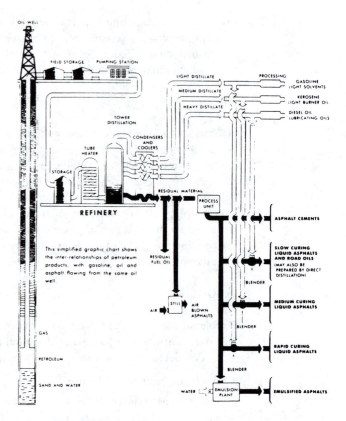

FIGURE 3-2 Petroleum asphalt flow chart (*Courtesy The Asphalt Institute*)

pressure to higher temperatures than used in fractional distillation. The resulting asphalt from this system is called "cracked" asphalt. The *cracked asphalts* are usually less durable and weather resistant and are not used in highway surface construction, but they are used in base construction where they are protected from weathering by the surface course.

In both processes the distillation may be stopped while the residue is still liquid or semisolid. The material is then called residual oil. When the resulting product is solid or semisolid, it is called *asphalt cement.*

Special properties may be imparted to asphalt by blowing air through the residual oil. The oil is at an elevated temperature, and the asphalt is oxidized. The asphalts produced are called *blown asphalts.*

One of the significant property changes is the raising of the asphalt's softening point. Since asphalt is a *thermoplastic* material, it softens as it is heated and hardens as it is cooled. The raising of the asphalt's softening point becomes an important property change. The degree of blowing will determine the changes in the asphalt's properties. Blown asphalts are generally not used as paving materials.

Blown asphalts are used mainly for roofing materials, automobile undercoatings, pipe coatings, and crack and joint sealers, and as undersealing asphalts to fill cavities under portland cement concrete pavements.

With the addition of catalysts during the blowing process, a material results which will remain soft at temperatures far below those at which asphalt becomes brittle. These *catalytically* blown asphalts have uses as canal liners because of their elasticity.

Liquid Asphalts

The asphalt cement produced by distillation will require heating to a liquid state before it can be used in construction. To eliminate the need to heat the asphalt to a liquid state, the cement can be modified into a cutback asphalt or emulsified asphalt. The *cutback asphalt* is produced by dissolving the cement in a solvent. The solvents are sometimes called distillate, diluent, or cutter stock. The solvent will evaporate after the completion of construction, leaving the asphalt cement to perform its function. If the asphalt is an *emulsion*—that is, suspended in water—when the water evaporates or the emulsion breaks, the asphalt cement will remain.

Asphalt Cutbacks   The cutback liquid asphalts are produced by cutting the asphalt cement with a petroleum solvent. The cutbacks are classified according to the relative speed of evaporation of the solvent and are split into three groups.

1. *Rapid-curing (RC):* asphalt cement and a volatile solvent in the gasoline or naphtha boiling point range.
2. *Medium-curing (MC):* asphalt cement and a solvent in the kerosene boiling point range.
3. *Slow-curing (SC):* asphalt cement and an oily solvent which has low volatility.

The liquid asphalt obtained by the addition of a solvent will vary in fluidity depending upon the asphalt cement, the volatility of the solvent, and the proportion of solvent to cement. Therefore, several grades of a cutback will be found in each classification.

The RC, MC, and SC designations define the cutbacks by class. Within each class the minimum kinematic viscosity in centistokes at 140°F denotes the grade of cutback asphalt. For example, the MC-3000 cutback has a minimum viscosity of 3000 centistokes and a maximum viscosity of 6000 centistokes. The *viscosity* of a fluid or semifluid is a measure of the material's resistance to continuous flow; therefore, the higher grade numbers designate the more viscous cutbacks.

To produce an RC-70, the refiner would blend approximately 40 percent solvent with 60 percent asphalt; to produce a more viscous grade, the RC-3000, a blend of approximately 15 percent solvent to 85 percent asphalt would be required.

Asphalt Emulsions   Emulsified asphalts are produced by separating the hot asphalt cement into minute globules and dispersing them in water that has been treated with an *emulsifying agent.* The asphalt is called the discontinuous phase and the water the continuous phase. The asphalt emulsion is processed in a *colloidal mill* which applies shearing stress to the asphalt and water as it passes between a stationary plate and a rotating plate. An inverted emulsion may be formed with the asphalt as the continuous phase and the water in minute globule size as the discontinuous phase. This inverted emulsion is usually produced with asphalt cement that has been cut with a small amount of an MC-type solvent.

If the asphalt globule has a negative charge, the emulsion produced is classified as *anionic*. When the asphalt globule has a positive charge, the emulsion is classified as *cationic*. Since anionic emulsified asphalts carry a negative charge, they work best with positive-charged aggregates such as limestone and dolomite. The cationic asphalt emulsion with its positive charge works best with silicious aggregates and with wet aggregates. The two types of emulsions cannot be mixed together.

By varying the materials and manufacturing processes, three emulsion grades are produced in either the anionic or the cationic state.

Grade	Anionic	Cationic
Rapid setting	RS	CRS
Medium setting	MS	CMS
Slow setting	SS	CSS

Since like charges repel, the asphalt globules are kept apart until the material comes in contact with aggregate particles and the charges are neutralized or the water evaporates. The process of the asphalt globules coming together in rapid- and medium-curing emulsions is called the *break* or *set*. The slow-setting emulsions depend primarily upon the evaporation of water to set.

The production of liquid asphalt products is based upon the cutting back or emulsifying of asphalt cement with the exception of slow-curing cutbacks. The slow-curing cutback may be produced by direct distillation if the residual material is of good quality and can be refined to meet an SC standard grade.

With the increasing realization that the world supply of petroleum is limited, highway engineers have begun research into using other materials that are plentiful and economical as substitutes for asphalt.

Sulfur has been used experimentally as a pavement binder because it is plentiful and economical, and it exhibits certain desirable properties when mixed with other engineering materials.

Sulfur extended asphalt (SEA) is a binder in which up to 50 percent of the asphalt is replaced with elemental sulfur. Between 15 and 20 percent of the sulfur is dissolved by the asphalt, and the remaining sulfur is dispersed as micron-sized particles in the binder. The blending of the sulfur into the asphalt requires high shear energy, such as that supplied by a colloidal mill.

The resulting SEA binder when combined with aggregates can be used as a road paving material. Current research indicates no detrimental effects upon the test pavements now in service.

Sand asphalt sulfur (SAS) is a blend of sand, asphalt, and sulfur, with the sulfur comprising 8 to 14 percent of the mix weight. SAS is used as a paving material. While hot, it can be cast in place like portland cement concrete or it can be placed by utilizing asphalt paving equipment. As the material cools, it develops strength, with the sulfur filling the voids and locking the sand particles together. This locking or keying of the sand particles allows the use of aggregates that would be unsuitable for a normal asphaltic concrete.

Plasticized sulfur (PS) is elemental sulfur combined with one or more chemical modifiers. The Federal Highway Administration (FHWA) is currently supporting research in the area of plasticized sulfurs with the ultimate goal of producing a pavement binder which will replace asphalt cements and possibly portland cements. The plasticized sulfur paving mixes are mixed and handled with conventional paving techniques and equipment. The material costs are about the same as asphalt pavements, but as material prices continue to rise, plasticized sulfurs may become the paving materials of the future.

ASPHALT TESTING

Thermoplastic materials such as asphalt are classified by their consistency at different temperatures. *Consistency* describes the fluidity or plasticity of an asphalt at a particular temperature. Since the characteristics and behaviors of thermoplastics vary with temperature, it is important that all tests be performed at standard test temperatures. If the test temperatures were different, it would be possible to evaluate two different asphalts and have the test results indicate that the asphalts tested were the same materials.

Various tests have been developed to predict asphalt's suitability to perform certain functions. Generally the tests performed on asphalt will measure consistency, durability, rate of hardening, serviceability, and ability to be effective in hostile environments.

Some of the tests are common to both solid and liquid asphalts while others are suitable for only solid or only liquid asphalts.

Asphalt Cements

Penetration Test   *Empirical tests* are those tests based upon experience over long periods of time with a particular test procedure. An empirical measure of asphalt consistency is the penetration test. The penetration test determines the relative hardness or consistency of an asphalt cement.

Based upon penetration ranges at 77°F, the 40–50 range is the hardest asphalt cement, and at room temperature a faint thumbprint may be left in a sample's surface. Cements harder than the 40–50 range can be produced for special uses. The softest cements are in the 200–300 range, and gentle finger pressure will indent the surface of a sample.

As illustrated in Figure 3–3, a sample of asphalt cement is placed in a sample tin which is immersed in a constant temperature bath at 77°F (25°C). The sample is placed on the penetrometer base where a needle weighted to 100 g is brought into contact with the sample surface. The needle is allowed to penetrate the sample for 5 s. The distance the needle penetrates into the sample is measured in units of 0.1 mm and is called the penetration. The penetration ranges are therefore the number of tenths of a millimeter the needle can penetrate a sample for it to be classified as a particular asphalt cement. The standard conditions for this test may be found in ASTM D5 and AASHTO T49.

Viscosity Test   The *viscosity* of a material is a measure of its resistance to flow. To provide control of asphalt cement consistencies at temperature ranges more closely

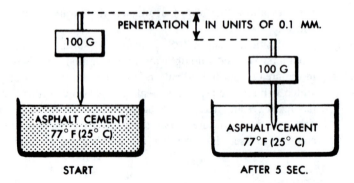

FIGURE 3-3   Standard penetration test (*Courtesy The Asphalt Institute*)

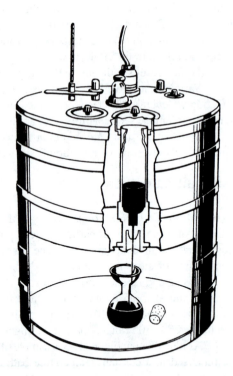

FIGURE 3-4   Saybolt Furol Viscosity test (*Courtesy The Asphalt Institute*)

associated with construction uses, the viscosity of asphalt cements is tested at 275 and 135°F. The viscosity of asphalt cements can be determined by either the Kinematic Viscosity test at 275°F, or the Saybolt Furol Viscosity test at 135°F.

The Saybolt Furol Viscosity test (Figure 3–4) requires the heating of a given sample of asphalt in a standard tube. The tube has a standard *orifice* or opening of prescribed shape and dimensions. The orifice has a stopper in place until the material reaches test temperature. When the material reaches test temperature, the stopper is removed and the material is allowed to flow into a flask. The time required in seconds for 60 ml of asphalt cement to flow through the orifice into the flask is determined. The time in seconds is the Saybolt Furol viscosity of the asphalt cement—(SSF) Seconds-Saybolt Furol.

The thicker or more viscous the material, the longer the time required for 60 ml of material to pass through the orifice and the higher the Saybolt Furol viscosity (SSF).

The viscosity of an asphalt cement may also be determined by using the kinematic viscosity apparatus shown in Figure 3–5. A thermostatically controlled constant temperature bath is used. The bath is filled with a suitable clear oil when tests are made at 275°F. The Zeitfuchs cross-arm viscometer tubes are suspended in the heated oil. The asphalt cement sample is poured into the large opening of the tube until it reaches the filling line, being careful not to exceed the line limit or the sample will pass through the tube before it has reached the proper test temperature. After the sample has been in the tube for the required time, a slight pressure is applied to the large opening or a vacuum to the small

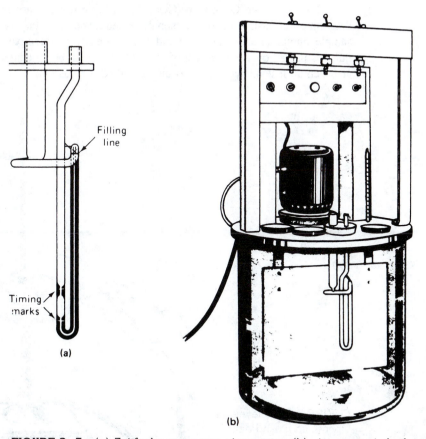

FIGURE 3–5 (a) Zeitfuchs cross-arm viscometer; (b) viscometer in bath (*Courtesy The Asphalt Institute*)

opening to start the sample flowing over the fill line. Once the sample passes over the siphon section of the tube, gravity causes the material to flow down the vertical section of the tube. The timer is started when the sample reaches the first mark and stopped when the material reaches the second mark. The tubes have previously been calibrated using standard oils of known viscosities. The calibration factor of the tube times the number of seconds required for the material to pass through the timing marks is the kinematic viscosity of the material in units of centistokes.

The numerical results of the Saybolt Furol Viscosity test are approximately one-half the results of the Kinematic Viscosity test. Care must be taken when cleaning the cross-arm tubes that have been calibrated since they are expensive.

Flash Point Test   The *Flash Point test* is a safety test. Since asphalt cements must be heated to be used in construction, the flash point of an asphalt tells the user the maximum temperature to which the material may be heated before an instantaneous flash will occur in the presence of an open flame. The flash point is usually well above the normal heating ranges of asphalt cements. While usually not specified, the fire point of an asphalt cement is the highest temperature at which the material will support combustion.

The Cleveland Open-Cup (COC) Flash Point test (Figure 3–6) is usually used to determine the flash point of an asphalt cement. The brass cup is filled with the proper sample amount of asphalt cement and heated at a specified temperature gain rate. A small flame is passed over the surface of the asphalt cement being heated, and the temperature at which an instantaneous flash occurs is called the flash point.

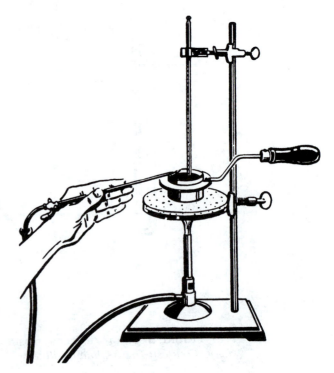

FIGURE 3–6 Cleveland Open-Cup Flash Point test (*Courtesy The Asphalt Institute*)

Another test used to determine the flash points of asphalt cements is the Pensky-Martens (PM) Point test (Figure 3–7). The PM test is a little different in that the sample is stirred continuously in the closed container. The PM method often gives lower values for the flash point of an asphalt cement than the COC method.

Thin-Film Oven Test   When asphalt is heated and then cooled, its consistency tends to increase. When asphalt is heated and exposed to air, as during the mixing process, the asphalt hardens. Since the material must be heated before it can be used, the *Thin-Film Oven (TFO) test* (Figure 3–8) is a procedure used to expose the asphalt to conditions which occur in heating operations. There should be no appreciable difference in consistency when the material is heated to 325°F and then cooled. Since asphalt coating thicknesses vary and temperature will vary, the test is only used as an indicator of probable behavior.

The test requires that a 50-cc sample of cement be placed in a 5.5-in.-diameter flat bottom pan with a $\frac{3}{8}$-in. depth. The film thickness is about $\frac{1}{8}$ in. The pan is placed on a shelf in a ventilated oven at 325°F for 5 hours. The shelf rotates the sample 5 revolutions per minute. After 5 hours have elapsed, the sample is then placed in a penetration sample tin. The penetration loss of the sample after the oven test is expressed as a percentage of the penetration of the material before being heated in the oven.

Ductility Test   In many applications, ductility is considered an important property of asphalt cements. The presence or absence of ductility is usually considered more significant than the degree of ductility. Asphalt cements possessing *ductility* are normally more adhesive than asphalt cements lacking ductility. However, some asphalt cements having a high degree of ductility are also more temperature susceptible. That is, their consistency will change more in response to a temperature change. In paving mixes, ductility and adhesion are important properties, while in crack filling and pavement undersealing, temperature susceptibility is the more important property.

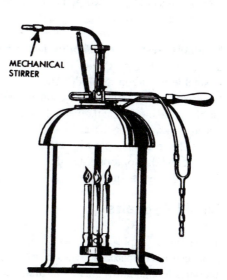

MECHANICAL
STIRRER

FIGURE 3–7   Pensky-Martens Flash Point test (*Courtesy The Asphalt Institute*)

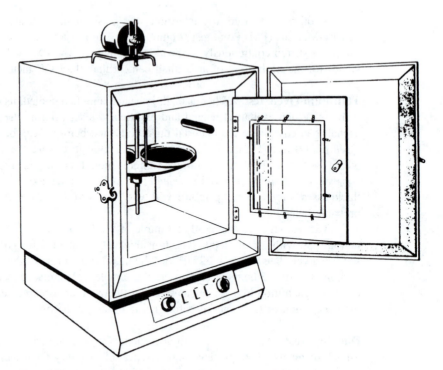

FIGURE 3–8 Thin-Film Oven test (*Courtesy The Asphalt Institute*)

Asphalt cement ductility is measured by an "extension" type test (Figure 3–9). Standard briquettes of asphalt are molded and brought to the standard test temperature of 77°F. One part of the specimen is pulled away from the other at 5 cm per minute until the thread connecting the two parts of the sample breaks. The ductility of the asphalt is the elongation in centimeters.

Solubility Test The *Solubility test* determines the purity of an asphalt cement. The active cementing portion of the sample is represented by that portion of the sample that is soluble in carbon disulfide. The inert matter such as salts, free carbon, or nonorganic materials is insoluble. Since asphalt cements are about as soluble in trichlorethylene, carbon tetrachloride, and other solvents as they are in carbon disulfide, they are often used because they are less hazardous.

The test is simple to perform. A 2-g sample of asphalt is dissolved in 100 ml of solvent and the solution filtered through an asbestos mat in a porcelain (Gooch) crucible. The residue on the mat is weighed and expressed as a percentage of the original sample.

Liquid Asphalts

Three types—rapid curing (RC), medium curing (MC), and slow curing (SC)—are produced in comparable grades based on kinematic viscosity ranges at 140°F. In the MC specification, an extra grade appears—the MC-30. It is used as a priming grade in some

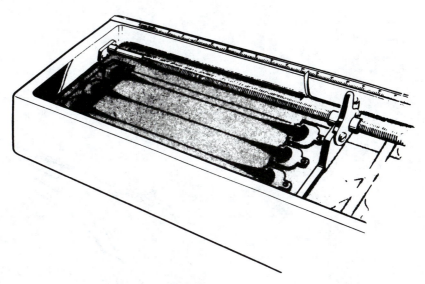

FIGURE 3-9 Ductility test (*Courtesy The Asphalt Institute*)

sections of the United States. Each grade of cutback is categorized by the *kinematic viscosity* or resistance to flow while in motion in centistokes and is designated by the lowest viscosity of that grade. Each grade includes a range from the designating value to a value of twice that amount. The most viscous grades of the three asphalts (RC-3000, MC-3000, SC-3000) are only moderately less viscous than the highest penetration grade (200–300) of asphalt cement. The least viscous grades (RC-70, MC-30, MC-70, SC-70) may be poured at room temperature. The consistency of these grades is approximately the same as heavy dairy cream.

Kinematic Viscosity Test   RC, MC, and SC liquid asphalts are classified into standard grades by the *Kinematic Viscosity test*. The basic test procedures are the same as for asphalt cements. Since the kinematic viscosity is determined at 140°F, water can be used as the medium in the constant temperature bath instead of oil. To prevent the volatiles from escaping, sample preparations are different. The full test particulars will be found in ASTM D2170 and AASHTO T201.

Flash Point Test   The purpose and significance of the *Flash Point test* (Figure 3–10) on asphalt cutbacks is the same as asphalt cements. The Cleveland Open-Cup test is used to determine the flash point of SC materials. Indirect heating is used to test for the flash point on RC and MC grades because of the volatile nature of the diluent in these grades. The Tag Open-Cup apparatus is used for this test. The cup is glass instead of metal, and the material is heated in a water bath rather than by direct flame.

Liquid asphalts are commonly used at temperatures above their flash points. The more volatile the diluent in the liquid asphalt, the more hazardous its use. Some rapid-curing cutbacks may flash at temperatures as low as 80°F. All of the cutbacks present some danger in use and should be handled properly.

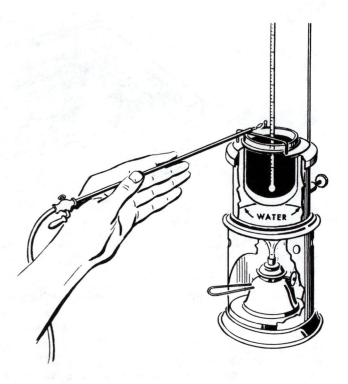

FIGURE 3–10 Tag
Open-Cup Flash Point
test (*Courtesy The
Asphalt Institute*)

Distillation Test   Since RC, MC, and, in some instances, SC grades of liquid asphalt are blends of asphalt cement and suitable diluents, properties of these materials are of importance in their application and performance.

The *Distillation test* (Figure 3–11) separates the asphalt cement and diluents to determine their quantities and for other testing. Two hundred ml of liquid asphalt is placed in a distillation flask connected to a water-cooled condenser tube. As the flask is heated, the diluent vaporizes and is liquified in the condenser tube which drains into a graduated cylinder. The volatility characteristics of the diluent are indicated by the quantity of condensate driven off at several specified temperatures. When 680°F is reached, the material remaining in the distillation flask is considered asphalt cement. For RC and MC cutbacks, penetration, ductility, and solubility properties of the residue are determined as described for asphalt cements.

For SC cutbacks, the amounts of distillate at various temperatures are of little importance; since they are mainly oily in nature, their rate of evaporation in service is quite slow. Therefore, only the total quantity of distillate driven off up to 680°F is measured. The residue is considered to be representative of the asphalt portion of the cutback, and its consistency is determined by the Kinematic Viscosity test.

Solubility of an SC cutback is determined using the material itself and not the residue from distillation.

Water Test   Asphaltic materials, except emulsified asphalts, are usually specified to be *water free,* or substantially so. Water present in the asphalt materials creates a hazardous

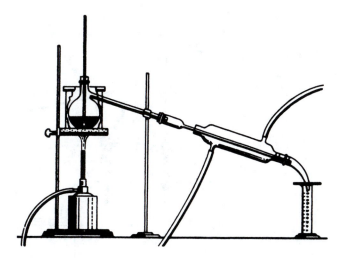

FIGURE 3–11
Distillation test for
cutback asphalts
(*Courtesy The Asphalt
Institute*)

condition by causing foaming when the materials are heated. To determine the amount of water present in liquid asphalt, if any, a sample of the material is mixed with xylol or high-boiling-range petroleum naphtha in a glass or metal still. A reflux condenser is attached to the still with its discharge into a graduated trap. When heat is applied to the still, any water in the liquid asphalt will collect in the trap. The percentage of water by volume is then determined.

Asphalt Emulsions

Specifications for emulsified asphalts are included in the ASTM Standards. Asphalt emulsions, which have a variety of viscosities, asphalt cement bases, and setting properties are available.

Saybolt Furol Viscosity Test   The consistency properties of anionic and cationic emulsions are measured by the Saybolt Furol Viscosity test. As a matter of testing convenience and to achieve suitable testing accuracy, two testing temperatures are used (77 and 122°F) depending on the viscosity characteristics of the specific type and grade of asphalt emulsion. The test procedure is basically the same as that used to test asphalt cements. The unit of measure is the poise.

Distillation Test   The *Distillation test* (Figure 3–12) is used to determine the relative proportions of asphalt cement and water in the asphalt emulsion. Some grades of emulsified asphalt also contain an oil distillate. The Distillation test provides information on the amount of this material in the emulsion. Also, the Distillation test provides an asphalt cement residue, on which additional tests (penetration, solubility, and ductility) may be made as previously described for asphalt cement.

The test procedure is substantially the same as that described for liquid asphalt. A 200-g sample of emulsion is distilled to 500°F. The principal difference in the emulsion distillation test is that the end point of distillation is 500°F rather than 680°F, and an iron

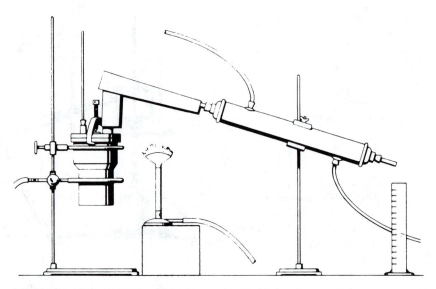

FIGURE 3–12 Distillation test for emulsified asphalts (*Courtesy The Asphalt Institute*)

or aluminum alloy still and ring burners are used instead of a glass flask and Bunsen burner. This equipment is designed to prevent trouble that may result from foaming of emulsified asphalt as it is being heated. The end point of distillation is carried to 500°F, and this temperature is held for 15 minutes in order to produce a smooth, homogeneous residue.

Settlement Test The *Settlement test* detects the tendency of asphalt globules to "settle out" during storage of emulsified asphalt. It provides the user with an element of protection against separation of asphalt and water in unstable emulsions that may be stored for a period of time.

A 500-ml sample is placed in each of two graduated cylinders, stoppered, and allowed to stand undisturbed for 5 days. Small samples are taken from the top and bottom parts of each cylinder. Each sample is placed in a beaker and weighed. The samples are then heated until water evaporates; residues are then weighed. The weights obtained provide the basis for determining the difference, if any, between asphalt cement content in the upper and lower portions of the graduated cylinder, thus providing a measure of settlement.

Sieve Test The *Sieve test* complements the Settlement test and has a somewhat similar purpose. It is used to determine quantitatively the percentage of asphalt cement present in the form of pieces, strings, or relatively large globules. Such nondispersed particles of asphalt might clog equipment and would tend to provide nonuniform coatings of asphalt on aggregate particles. This nonuniformity might not be detected by the Settlement test, which is of value in this regard only when there is a sufficient difference in the specific gravities of asphalt and water to allow settlement.

In the Sieve test, 1000 g of asphalt emulsion are poured through a U.S. standard No. 20 sieve. For anionic emulsified asphalts, the sieve and retained asphalt are then rinsed with a mild sodium oleate solution. For cationic emulsified asphalts, rinsing is with distilled water. After rinsing, the sieve and asphalt are dried in an oven, and the relative amount of asphalt retained on the sieve is determined.

Demulsibility Test   The *Demulsibility test* is used only for rapid- and medium-setting grades of anionic asphalt emulsions. It indicates the relative rate at which colloidal asphalt globules coalesce (or break) when spread in thin films on soil or aggregate particles.

Calcium chloride coagulates or flocculates the minute globules present in anionic emulsified asphalts. To make the test, a 100-g sample is thoroughly mixed with a calcium chloride solution. The mixture is then poured over a No. 14 sieve and washed. The degree of coalescence is determined from the amount of asphalt residue remaining on the sieve.

A high degree of demulsibility is required for the rapid-setting grade of anionic emulsified asphalt because it is expected to break almost immediately on contact with the aggregate surface. Therefore, a very weak calcium chloride solution is used for the Demulsibility test on these products. A somewhat more concentrated solution is used when testing medium-setting grades, as they are formulated to break more slowly.

Slow-setting grades often are used in mixes containing fine aggregates or in other applications where rapid coalescence of asphalt particles is undesirable. The Cement Mixing test is therefore used in lieu of the Demulsibility test as a control for the setting rate of these products.

Cement Mixing Test   The *Cement Mixing test* is performed by adding 100 ml of emulsion diluted to 55 percent residue with water to 50 g of high, early strength portland cement with stirring for thorough mixing. Additional water is stirred in. The mixture is then washed over a No. 14 sieve, and the percentage of coagulated material retained on the sieve is determined.

As noted, the Cement Mixing test is used instead of the Demulsibility test for slow-setting grades of emulsified asphalt. It is specified for both the anionic and cationic types to assure products substantially immune from rapid coalescence of asphalt particles in contact with fine-grained soils or aggregates.

Coating Ability and Water Resistance Test   This test determines the ability of an emulsified asphalt to:

1. coat an aggregate thoroughly,
2. withstand mixing action while remaining as a film on the aggregate, and
3. resist the washing action of water after mixing is completed.

The test is primarily intended to aid in identifying asphalt emulsions that are suitable for mixing with coarse-graded aggregate intended for job use. For specification purposes, the test is required only for cationic, medium-setting asphalt emulsions.

A 465-g air-dried sample of aggregate that is to be used on a project is mixed with 35 g of emulsified asphalt for 5 minutes. One-half of the mixture is removed from the pan and placed on absorbent paper, and the percentage of coated particles is determined.

The remaining mixture in the pan is carefully washed with a gentle spray of tap water and drained until the water runs clear. This mixture is then placed on absorbent paper and the percentage of coated aggregate particles determined.

This procedure is repeated for wet aggregate (9.3 ml of water mixed with the air-dried aggregate) before mixing with emulsified asphalt.

Particle Charge Test   The *Particle Charge test* (Figure 3–13) is an identification test for rapid- and medium-setting grades of cationic asphalt emulsions.

A positive electrode (anode) and a negative electrode (cathode) are immersed in a sample of emulsified asphalt and connected to a controlled direct-current electrical source. After 30 minutes, or after the current has dropped to 2 mA, the two electrodes are examined to determine which one has an asphalt deposit. An asphalt deposit on the cathode identifies a cationic emulsified asphalt.

pH Test   The *Acidity-Alkalinity (pH) test* is used only to determine and specify the degree of acidity for slow-setting grades of cationic asphalt emulsions. It is used in place of the Particle Charge test, which is used for rapid- and medium-setting grades of cationic asphalt emulsions.

A potentiometer, or pH meter, is used to make the test. A small sample of asphalt emulsion is placed in a beaker, and glass electrodes are inserted in the sample. The difference in potential is then measured in pH or millivolt units, which is an indication of the acidity of the sample.

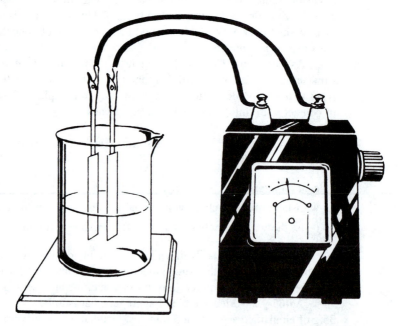

FIGURE 3–13   Particle Charge test (*Courtesy The Asphalt Institute*)

Oil Distillate Test   Rapid- and medium-setting grades of cationic asphalt emulsion, and some anionic asphalt emulsions, may include an oily distillate fraction, the maximum amount of which usually is limited by specifications. The amount of distillate is determined in the Distillation test (for emulsified asphalts) previously described. Distillate collected in the graduated cylinder includes both oil and water from the asphalt emulsion. Because these two materials separate in the graduated cylinder, the amounts of each can be determined.

Air-Blown Asphalts

Although similar in many respects to the normal paving grades of asphalt cement previously discussed, the blowing process provides materials that soften at higher temperatures than asphalt cements. Because the higher softening point is a most important and desirable property of blown asphalts, they are usually classified in terms of the Ring and Ball Softening Point test, rather than in terms of the Penetration test used for asphalt cements.

While blown asphalts are graded on the basis of the softening point, there are still Penetration test requirements at three temperatures. These requirements provide a degree of control over the temperature susceptibility, or the rate of consistency change with temperature, for these materials.

Tests included in the specifications will be discussed, except where they are the same as those discussed for asphalt cement.

Softening Point Test   The *Softening Point test* (Figure 3–14) is used as the basic measurement of consistency for grading blown asphalts.

Samples of asphalt loaded with steel balls are confined in brass rings suspended in a beaker of water or glycerine, 1 in. above a metal plate. The water, or glycerine, is then heated at a prescribed rate. As the asphalt softens, the balls and the asphalt gradually sink toward the plate. At the moment the asphalt touches the plate, the temperature of the water is determined, and this is designated as the Ring and Ball (RB) Softening Point of asphalt.

Penetration Test   The specifications indicate penetration requirements at temperatures of 32, 77, and 115°F. The Penetration test as made at 77°F was described and illustrated for asphalt cements; and, at this temperature, the test is the same for the blown asphalts. At 32 and 115°F, the differences are in the needle weight and the length of time the needle is permitted to bear on the surface of the asphalt. These differences are indicated in the specification tables.

Loss on Heating Test   The *Loss on Heating test* is generally similar to the Thin Film Oven test as described for asphalt cements. The only differences are in the dimensions of the asphalt sample. Whereas the asphalt sample in the TFO test is about $5\frac{1}{2}$ in. in diameter and $\frac{1}{8}$ in. deep, the sample for the Loss on Heating test is approximately $2\frac{1}{4}$ in. in diameter and 1 in. deep. In both tests the asphalt and container are placed on a rotating shelf in a ventilated oven and maintained at 325°F for a period of 5 hours. The shelf rotates at approximately five to six revolutions per minute.

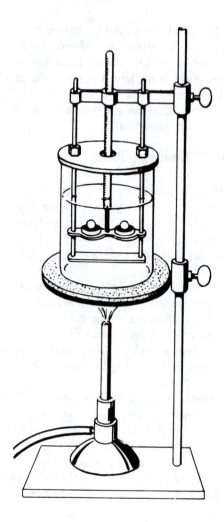

FIGURE 3–14
Softening Point test
(*Courtesy The Asphalt
Institute*)

As with the TFO test, the Loss on Heating test actually is not a test within itself. It is a procedure that is intended to subject the asphalt to hardening conditions similar to those expected in the application processes. A Penetration test usually is made on the asphalt after the Loss on Heating test for comparison with the penetration of the asphalt prior to the test.

EFFECTS OF TEMPERATURE AND VISCOSITY

As discussed previously, asphalt is a thermoplastic material that changes viscosity with changes in temperature. However, the precise relationship between temperature and viscosity (called temperature-viscosity curves or graphs—see Figure 3–15) for a particular penetration grade and type of asphalt from one refinery may not be identical with the same type and grade of asphalt from another refinery.

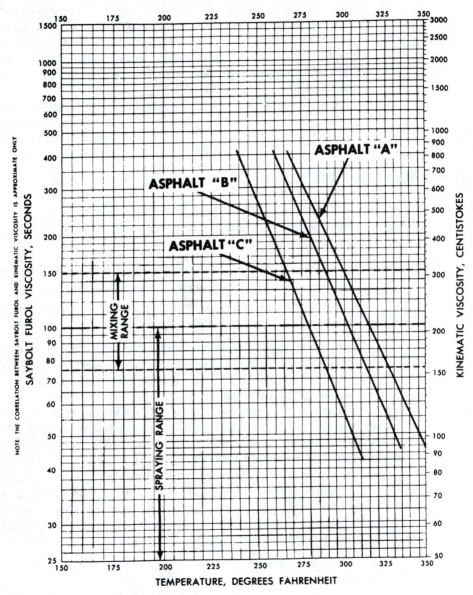

FIGURE 3–15 Viscosity vs. temperature for asphalts (*Courtesy The Asphalt Institute*)

Assume for a given mix that asphalt at a viscosity of 100 seconds-Saybolt Furol (SSF) will provide ideal mixing conditions. To obtain this viscosity, asphalt A must be mixed at 315°F, and asphalt C at 275°F. The difference in temperatures between asphalts A and C required to produce equal viscosity is 40°F. Therefore, unless temperatures were regulated to have the asphalt mixes at a temperature providing substantially equal viscosity for the asphalt cements, mixing and handling characteristics of mixes with these two asphalts would be different. This does not mean that there is a difference in quality between the two asphalts, only a difference in a physical property that must be taken into account when the asphalts are used.

Viscosity of asphalt during construction operations such as mixing and spraying is of prime importance. Therefore, the temperature-viscosity relationship for the asphalt being used should be known so the mixing and spraying temperatures can be regulated.

ASPHALT PAVEMENTS

The basic idea in building a road or parking area for all-weather use by vehicles is to prepare a suitable subgrade or foundation, provide necessary drainage, and construct a pavement that will:

1. Have sufficient total thickness and internal strength to carry expected traffic loads;

2. Prevent the penetration or internal accumulation of moisture; and

3. Have a top surface that is smooth and resistant to wear, distortion, skidding, and deterioration by weather and de-icing chemicals.

The subgrade ultimately carries all traffic loads. Therefore, the structural function of a pavement is to support a wheel load on the pavement surface and transfer and spread that load to the subgrade without overtaxing either the strength of the subgrade or the internal strength of the pavement itself.

Figure 3–16 shows wheel load, W, being transmitted to the pavement surface through the tire at an approximately uniform vertical pressure, P_0. The pavement then spreads the wheel load to the subgrade so that the maximum pressure on the subgrade is only P_1. By proper selection of pavement materials and with adequate pavement thickness, P_1 will be small enough to be easily supported by the subgrade.

Asphalt pavement is a general term applied to any pavement that has a surface constructed with asphalt. Normally, it consists of a surface course (layer) of mineral aggregate coated and cemented with asphalt and one or more supporting courses, which may be of the following types:

1. Asphalt base, consisting of asphalt-aggregate mixtures;

2. Crushed stone (rock), slag, or gravel;

3. Portland cement concrete; and

4. Old brick or stone block pavements.

Asphalt pavement structure consists of all courses above the prepared subgrade or foundation. The upper or top layer is the asphalt wearing surface. It may range from less than 1 in. to several inches in thickness, depending on a variety of design factors.

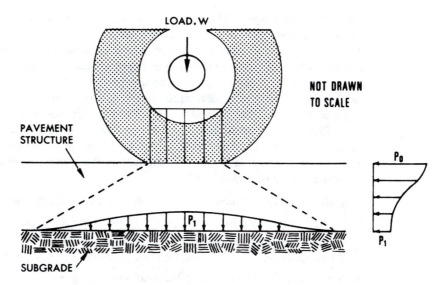

FIGURE 3–16 Spread of wheel load through pavement structure (*Courtesy The Asphalt Institute*)

While a variety of bases and subbases may be used in asphalt pavement structures, more commonly they consist of compacted granular materials (such as crushed rock, slag, gravel, sand, or a combination of these) or stabilized soil. One of the main advantages of asphalt pavements is that a variety of materials may be used; thus, economy is achieved by using locally available materials.

Generally, it is preferable to treat the granular material used in bases. The most common treatment is to mix asphalt with the granular material, thus producing an asphalt base. A 1-in. thickness of asphalt base is about equal in load-carrying performance to a 2- or 3-in. thickness of granular base materials not treated with asphalt.

Untreated bases and subbases have been widely used in the past. However, as modern traffic increases in weight and volume, these bases show performance limitations. Consequently, it is now common practice to limit use of untreated bases to pavements designed for lower volumes of traffic.

When the entire pavement structure above the subgrade consists of asphalt mixtures, it is called a *full-depth asphalt pavement*. This is generally considered the most modern and dependable type of pavement for present-day traffic.

Other materials sometimes used to treat or stabilize granular base and subbase materials or selected soils are portland cement, lime, coal tar, calcium chloride, or salt (sodium chloride).

DETERMINING REQUIRED PAVEMENT THICKNESS

A significant advance in highway engineering is the realization and demonstration that structural design of asphalt pavement is similar to the problem of designing any other complex engineering structure. When asphalt pavement was first being introduced, determining the proper thickness was a matter of guesswork, rule of thumb, and opinion based on experience. Almost the same situation once prevailed in determining the dimensions of masonry arches and iron and steel structures. However, these early techniques have long since yielded to engineering analysis. Similarly, based on comprehensive analysis of vast volumes of accumulated data, the structural design of asphalt pavements has now been developed into a reliable engineering procedure. Research aimed at further refinements and a fully rational design procedure is continuing.

There is no standard thickness for a pavement. However, the Asphalt Institute has published general guidelines to be used for parking areas and driveways. (See Figure 3–17.) Required total thickness is determined by engineering design procedure. Factors considered in the procedure are:

1. Traffic to be served initially and over the design service life of the pavement;
2. Strength and other pertinent properties of the prepared subgrade;
3. Strength and other influencing characteristics of the materials available or chosen for the layers or courses in the total asphalt pavement structure; and
4. Any special factors peculiar to the road being designed.

Traffic Analysis

The weight and volume of traffic a road is expected to carry initially and throughout its design service life influences the required thickness of asphalt pavement structure. Several methods have been developed to determine present and future traffic volumes. The information obtained is used for pavement design purposes. Necessary factors have been derived from road test data and from elaborate traffic counts on roads in service. However, in special situations, such as logging roads where the weight and frequency of the actual trucks are known, the designed pavement thickness is based specifically on the known factors.

Subgrade Evaluation

There are several methods for evaluation or estimating the strength and supporting power of a subgrade, including:

1. Loading tests in the field on the subgrade itself; for example, the Plate Bearing test uses large circular plates loaded to produce critical amounts of deformation on the subgrade in place.

2. Loading tests in a laboratory using representative samples of the subgrade soil. Some commonly used tests are (a) California Bearing Ratio (CBR) test, which is sometimes used on the subgrade in place in the field; (b) Hveem Stabilometer test; and (c) Triaxial test.

3. Evaluations based on classification of soil by identifying and testing the constituent particles of the soil. Four well-known classification systems are (a) American Association of State Highway and Transportation Officials (AASHTO) Classification System; (b) Unified Soil Classification System; (c) Corps of Engineers, U.S. Army; and (d) U.S. Federal Aviation Administration (FAA) method.

PAVEMENT THICKNESS FOR DRIVEWAYS FOR PASSENGER CARS

THICKNESS REQUIREMENTS IN INCHES

	FULL DEPTH ASPHALT CONCRETE		ASPHALT CONCRETE SURFACE		PLANT-MIX SURFACE USING LIQUID ASPHALT		ASPHALT SURFACE TREATMENT	
	Asphalt Concrete Surface	Asphalt Concrete Base[1]	Asphalt Concrete Surface	Crushed Rock Base[2]	Asphalt Plant-Mix Surface	Crushed Rock Base[2]	Asphalt Surface Treatment	Crushed Rock Base[2]
Gravelly or sandy soils, well drained	1	2–3	3	2	4.5*	2	1**	6–8
Average clay loam soils, not plastic	1	3–4	3	2–4	4.5*	2–4	1**	8–10
Soft clay soils, plastic when wet	1	4–5	3	4–6***	4.5*	4–6***	1**	10–12***

[1] Prime required on subgrade.
[2] Prime required on base.
* Must be spread and compacted in layers not exceeding 1½ inches in depth and the volatiles (petroleum solvents or water) allowed to evaporate before the next layer is placed. Also, a seal coat may be required as a final surfacing.
** Economical but relatively limited service life. Usually less than 1 inch thick.
*** Two inches of coarse sand or stone screenings recommended between subgrade and base as an insulation course.

FIGURE 3–17 Suggested pavement thickness for parking areas and driveways
(*Courtesy The Asphalt Institute*)

PAVEMENT THICKNESS FOR PARKING AREAS FOR PASSENGER CARS

| | THICKNESS REQUIREMENTS IN INCHES | | | | | | | |
| | FULL DEPTH ASPHALT CONCRETE | | ASPHALT CONCRETE SURFACE | | PLANT-MIX SURFACE USING LIQUID ASPHALT | | ASPHALT SURFACE TREATMENT | |
	Asphalt Concrete Surface	Asphalt Concrete Base[1]	Asphalt Concrete Surface	Crushed Rock Base[2]	Asphalt Plant-Mix Surface	Crushed Rock Base[2]	Asphalt Surface Treatment	Crushed Rock Base[2]
Gravelly or sandy soils, well drained	1	2–3	3	2	4.5*	2	1**	6–8
Average clay loam soils, not plastic	1	3–4	3	2–4	4.5*	2–4	1**	8–10
Soft clay soils, plastic when wet	1	4–5	3	4–6***	4.5*	4–6***	1**	10–12***

[1] Prime required on subgrade.
[2] Prime required on base.
* Must be spread and compacted in layers not exceeding 1½ inches in depth and the volatiles (petroleum solvents or water) allowed to evaporate before the next layer is placed. Also, a seal coat may be required as a final surfacing.
** Economical but relatively limited service life. Usually less than 1 inch thick.
*** Two inches of coarse sand or stone screenings recommended between subgrade and base as an insulation course.

FIGURE 3–17 (Continued)

PAVEMENT THICKNESS FOR PARKING AREAS FOR HEAVY TRUCKS

THICKNESS REQUIREMENTS IN INCHES

	FULL DEPTH ASPHALT CONCRETE		ASPHALT CONCRETE SURFACE		SURFACE TREATMENT ON PENTRATION MACADAM		PLANT-MIX SURFACE USING LIQUID ASPHALT	
	Asphalt Concrete Surface	Asphalt Concrete Base 1	Asphalt Concrete Surface	Crushed Rock Base 2	Asphalt Surface Treatment	Asphalt Penetration Macadam Base 1	Asphalt Plant-Mix Surface	Crushed Rock Base 2
Gravelly or sandy soils, well drained	1.5	3–5	4.5	0–4	1*	7–10	7**	2–4
Average clay loam soils, not plastic	1.5	5–6	4.5	4–6	1*	10–11.5	7**	4–6
Soft clay soils, plastic when wet	1.5	6–8	4.5	6–10***	1*	11.5–14.5	7**	6–10***

1 Prime required on subgrade.
2 Prime required on base.
* Usually less than 1 inch thick.
** Must be spread and compacted in layers not exceeding 1½ inches in depth and the volatiles (petroleum solvents or water) allowed to evaporate before the next layer is placed. Also, seal coat may be required as a final surfacing.
*** Two inches of coarse sand or stone screenings recommended between subgrade and base as an insulation course.

FIGURE 3–17 (Continued)

109

Asphalt Paving-Mix Design

The design of asphalt paving mixes, as with other engineering materials designs, is largely a matter of selecting and proportioning materials to obtain the desired qualities and properties in the finished construction. The overall objective for the design of asphalt paving mixes is to determine an economical blend and gradation of aggregates and asphalt that yields a mix having:

1. Sufficient asphalt to ensure a durable pavement;

2. Sufficient mix stability to satisfy the demands of traffic without distortion or displacement;

3. Sufficient voids in the total compacted mix to allow for a slight amount of additional compaction under traffic loading without flushing, bleeding, and loss of stability, yet low enough to keep out harmful air and moisture; and

4. Sufficient workability to permit efficient placement of the mix.

There are currently two methods used to design asphalt paving mixes and the selection and use of these mix design methods is principally a matter of engineering preference. Each of the methods has unique features and advantages for particular design problems.

The two methods are:

1. The Marshall method and

2. The Hveem method.

The complete test methods will be found in the Asphalt Institute Manual MS-2, *Mix Design Methods for Asphalt Concrete and Other Hot-Mix Types.*

The Superpave™ system of asphalt-aggregate mix design was developed as part of the Strategic Highway Research Program (SHRP). The goal of the research was to develop a performance-based specification for asphalt paving materials that would produce pavements with a minimum amount of rutting, fatigue cracking, and low-temperature cracking. The system takes into account environmental conditions, traffic levels, and pavement structures as part of the design procedures, and early field data indicates that the Superpave system works; however, the system is still tentative.

The Asphalt Institute publications—Performance Graded Asphalt Binder Specification and Testing Superpave Series No. 1 (SP-1) and Superpave Level 1 Mix Design Superpave Series No. 2 (SP-2)—contain current information on Superpave methods and test equipment.

TYPES OF ASPHALT PAVEMENT CONSTRUCTION

Plant Mix

Asphalt paving mixtures prepared in a central mixing plant are known as *plant mixes*. Asphalt concrete is considered the highest-quality type of plant mix. It consists of well-graded, high-quality aggregate and asphalt cement. The asphalt and aggregate are heated separately from 250 to 325°F, carefully measured and proportioned, and then mixed until the aggregate particles are coated with asphalt. Mixing is done in the pugmill unit of the mixing plant. The hot mixture, kept hot during transit, is hauled to the construction site, where it is spread on the roadway by an asphalt paving machine. The smooth layer from the paver is compacted by rollers to proper density before the asphalt cools.

Asphalt concrete is but one of a variety of hot-asphalt plant mixes. Other mixes, such as sand asphalt, sheet asphalt, and coarse-graded mixes, are prepared and placed in a similar manner. However, each has one common ingredient—asphalt cement.

Asphalt mixes containing liquid asphalt also may be prepared in central mixing plants. The aggregate may be partially dried and heated or mixed as it is withdrawn from the stockpile. These mixes are usually referred to as *cold mixes,* even though heated aggregate may have been used in the mixing process.

Asphalt mixtures made with emulsified asphalt and some cutback asphalts can be spread and compacted on the roadway while quite cool. Such mixtures are called *cold-laid asphalt plant mixes.* They are hauled and placed in normal warm-weather temperatures. To hasten evaporation of emulsification water or cutback solvents, these mixtures, after being placed on the roadway, are sometimes processed or worked back and forth laterally with a motor grader before being spread and compacted.

Mixed-in-Place (Road Mix)

Emulsified asphalt and many cutback asphalts are fluid enough to be sprayed onto and mixed into aggregate at moderate- to warm-weather temperatures. When this is done on the area to be paved, it is called *mixed-in-place construction.* Although *mixed-in-place* is the more general term, and is applicable whether the construction is on a roadway, parking area, or airfield, the term *road mix* is often used when construction is on a roadway.

Mixed-in-place construction can be used for surface, base, or subbase courses. As a surface or wearing course, it usually is satisfactory for light and medium traffic rather than heavy traffic. However, mixed-in-place layers covered by a high-quality asphalt plant-mix surface course make a pavement suitable for heavy traffic service. Advantages of mixing in place include:

1. Utilization of aggregate already on the roadbed or available from nearby sources and usable without extensive processing, and
2. Elimination of the need for a central mixing plant. Construction can be accomplished with a variety of machinery often more readily available, such as motor graders, rotary mixers with revolving tines, and traveling mixing plants.

Slurry Seal

A *slurry seal* is a thin asphalt overlay applied by a continuous process machine to worn pavements to seal them and provide a new wearing surface. Slurry seals are produced with emulsified asphalts. Aggregates used for slurry seals must be hard, angular, free of expansive clays, and uniformly graded from a particle size about the thickness of the

FIGURE 3–18   Continuous process slurry seal machine (*Courtesy Slurry Seal, Inc.*)

finished overlay down to No. 200. Crushed limestone or granite, slag, expanded clays, and other lightweight materials are typical aggregates used for slurry seals. The truck-mounted equipment (Figure 3–18) transports, proportions, mixes, and applies the slurry seal.

RECYCLED ASPHALT CONCRETE

Asphalt pavement recycling combines reclaimed pavement materials with new materials to produce asphalt mixtures that meet normal specification requirements. The most common methods of pavement removal include ripping and crushing and cold milling or planing of the existing pavement.

The materials produced by these methods are classified as reclaimed asphalt pavement (RAP) or reclaimed aggregate material (RAM). Because reclaimed aggregate material contains no asphalt, it is handled and processed using the same techniques as virgin aggregates. The reclaimed asphalt pavement contains aged asphalt, and therefore is subject to crushing limitations and stockpile height requirements no greater than 10 ft. Also, if possible, it must be protected from the weather. (See Figure 3–19.)

The use of RAP to produce new paving materials is based on the heat-transfer method. The virgin and RAM materials are superheated and fed into the pugmill where the RAP, new asphalt, and, if required, a recycling agent are introduced. The mixing process allows for some heat transfer to take place, and complete temperature equilibrium is usually reached sometime later, after the mix is discharged into trucks or a storage silo.

FIGURE 3–19 Milling machines remove asphalt concrete pavements to line and grade. The material removed will be recycled (RAP) (*Courtesy Astec Industries, Inc.*)

The amount of reclaimed asphalt pavement that can be used in the recycled mix depends on (1) the moisture content and stockpile temperature of the reclaimed material, (2) the required temperature of the recycled mix, and (3) the temperature of the superheated aggregate. If optimum conditions exist, as much as 40 percent of the new mixture can be reclaimed asphalt pavement (RAP). However, a RAP utilization of 20 to 30 percent is a realistic range for normal operations.

ASPHALT SPRAY APPLICATIONS

Many necessary and useful purposes are served when paving asphalt, temporarily in a fluid form, can be sprayed in uniform and controlled amounts onto a surface.

Surface Treatments and Seal Coats

A sprayed-on application of asphalt to a wearing surface, with or without a thin layer of covering aggregate, is called an *asphalt surface treatment*. By definition, such surface treatments are 1 in. or less in thickness. Sometimes these surface treatments are included in the original construction. More often they are applied to old pavements after a period of service and before surface deterioration from traffic wear and weathering proceeds too far.

The sprayed-on asphalt serves to improve or restore the waterproof condition of the old pavement surface. Also, it serves to arrest any scuffing or raveling of the wearing surface. The addition of a cover of aggregate over the sprayed-on asphalt restores and improves the skid resistance of the wearing surface.

Multiple-surface treatments consist of two or more alternate layers of sprayed-on asphalt and aggregate cover.

Surface treatments that have waterproofing or texture improvement, or both, as their main purpose are called *seal coats*.

Single- or multiple-surface treatments with aggregate cover also may be placed on granular-surfaced roads to upgrade them for traffic. The treatment eliminates dust, protects the road by shedding water, and provides a smoother riding surface. It is a useful, low-cost, all-weather improvement of a granular-surfaced road, but it has limited traffic capacity and should be used only where traffic is light or where the period of expected service is limited.

Tack Coats and Prime Coats

Each layer in an asphalt pavement should be bonded to the layer beneath. This is accomplished by spraying onto the surface of the underlying layer a thin coating of asphalt to bind the layers together. This thin spread of asphalt is called a *tack coat*. Tack coats are used to bond asphalt layers to a portland cement concrete base or old brick and stone pavements.

When an asphalt pavement or asphalt surface treatment is to be placed on a granular base, it is desirable to treat the top surface of the base by spraying on a liquid asphalt that will seep into or penetrate the base. This is called *priming,* and the treatment is called *prime coat.* Its purpose is to serve as a transition from the granular material to the asphalt layer and bind them together. A prime coat is different from a tack coat as to type and quantity of asphalt used. However, both are spray applications.

Penetration Macadam

Asphalt penetration macadam pavement consists of one or more layers of large-sized broken stone and rock chips interlocked by rolling. Fluid asphalt is sprayed onto each layer, and it seeps into or penetrates the layer to bind the stones together.

An asphalt surface treatment or asphalt mixture of some kind is usually put on the top of a penetration macadam pavement to serve as a wearing surface.

ASPHALT PLANTS

Asphalt paving mixes made with asphalt cement are prepared at an asphalt mixing plant. Here aggregates are blended, heated and dried, and mixed with asphalt cement to produce a hot-asphalt paving mixture. The mixing plant may be small and simple, or it may be large and complex, depending on the type and quantity of asphalt mixture being produced.

As shown in Figure 3–20, components of an asphalt plant are:

1. Cold aggregate storage,

2. Drying,

3. Screening,

4. Hot storage, and

5. Measuring and mixing.

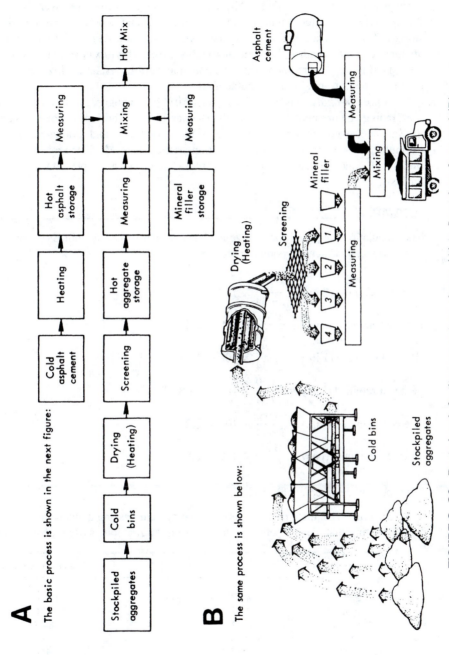

A

The basic process is shown in the next figure:

Stockpiled aggregates → Cold bins → Drying (Heating) → Screening → Hot aggregate storage → Measuring → Mixing

Cold asphalt cement → Heating → Hot asphalt storage → Measuring → Mixing → Hot Mix

Mineral filler storage → Measuring → Mixing

B

The same process is shown below:

Stockpiled aggregates

Cold bins

Drying (Heating)

Screening

Measuring

Mineral filler

Asphalt cement

Measuring

Mixing

FIGURE 3-20 Basic batch facility operations shown (A) in flow chart form and (B) schematically (*Courtesy The Asphalt Institute*)

115

Aggregate is removed from storage, or stockpiles, in controlled amounts and passed through a dryer where it is dried and heated. The aggregate then passes over a screening unit that separates the material into different size fractions and deposits them into bins for hot storage. The aggregate and mineral filler, when used, are then withdrawn in controlled amounts, combined with asphalt, and thoroughly mixed. This mix is hauled to the paving site.

During the production of asphaltic concrete, various tests are utilized to measure the quality of the hot mix being manufactured.

A *hot bin analysis* is the test used to verify that the aggregates in the hot bins meet the grading requirements for the asphalt concrete mix. Individual hot bin samples are drawn and sieved. The gradation data is then combined and evaluated, the Job Mix Formula (JMF) being used as the evaluation criteria. The JMF is the mix design used for the asphalt concrete being produced. Figure 3–21a shows a sample data sheet for hot bin analysis.

EXAMPLE

The calculations required for a sieve analysis are performed for bin 2 (Figure 3–21a).

Step one: Calculate percent retained.

$$\text{Percent retained (2 in.)} = \frac{0}{29.34} \times 100 = 0$$

$$\text{Percent retained (1}\tfrac{1}{2}\text{ in.)} = \frac{0.70}{29.34} \times 100 = 2.4$$

$$\text{Percent retained (1 in.)} = \frac{3.75}{29.34} \times 100 = 12.8$$

$$\text{Percent retained (}\tfrac{1}{2}\text{ in.)} = \frac{23.99}{29.34} \times 100 = 81.8$$

$$\text{Percent retained (}\tfrac{1}{4}\text{ in.)} = \frac{0.65}{29.34} \times 100 = 2.2$$

$$\text{Percent retained (pan)} = \frac{0.25}{29.34} \times 100 = 0.8$$

Total percent retained equals 100.

Step two: Calculate percent passing. The percent passing a given sieve is calculated by subtracting that sieve's percent retained from the previous sieve's percent passing.

Sieve Size			Percent Passing
2 in.	100–0	=	100.0
$1\tfrac{1}{2}$ in.	100–2.4	=	97.6
1 in.	97.6–12.8	=	84.8
$\tfrac{1}{2}$ in.	84.8–81.8	=	3.0
$\tfrac{1}{4}$ in.	3.0–2.2	=	0.8

The percent passing the last sieve in the series should equal the percent retained in the pan. The sieve analysis calculations are performed for the remainder of the bin samples.

HOT BIN ANALYSIS

PLANT __Vaughn Asphalt Products__   INSPECTOR __David Wemple__   DATE __5__/__12__/__80__

ITEM NO. __403.11__   MIX TYPE __1__   AGGREGATE TEMP. __250__ °F   BITUMEN TEMP. __325__ °F

Project __NYS Thruway TAA80-4B__

BIN BREAKDOWN

Sieve Sizes	No.2 Wt.	No.2 ret.%	No.2 pass%	No.1 Wt.	No.1 ret.%	No.1 pass%	No.1A Wt.	No.1A ret.%	No.1A pass%	No.1B Wt.	No.1B ret.%	No.1B pass%	FINES Wt.	FINES ret.%	FINES pass%	MIN. FILLER Wt.	MIN. FILLER ret.%	MIN. FILLER pass%
2"	00	0	100															
1½"	.70	2.4	97.6															
1"	3.75	12.8	84.8	0	0	100												
½"	23.99	81.8	3.0	3.31	15.2	84.8	0	0	100									
¼"	.65	2.2	.8	17.58	80.6	4.2	2.77	13.6	86.4				0	0	100			
1/8"				.63	2.9	1.3	16.87	82.9	3.5				2.7	.4	99.6			
20													327.2	53.9	45.7			
40													102.3	16.8	28.9			
80													79.0	13.0	15.9			
200													57.2	9.4	6.5			
PAN	.25	.8		.30	1.3		.70	3.5					38.9	6.5				
Totals	29.34			21.82			20.34						607.3					

COMBINED — GRADATION

BIN	lbs batched	% batched	2"	1-1/2"	1"	1/2"	1/4"	1/8"	20	40	80	200
2		30.5	30.5	29.8	25.9	.9	.2					
1		15.8	15.8	15.8	15.8	13.4	.7	.2				
1A		14.8	14.8	14.8	14.8	14.8	12.8	.5				
1B												
FINES		38.9	38.9	38.9	38.9	38.9	38.7	17.8	11.2	6.2	2.5	
Min. Filler												
TOTAL		100%	100%	99.3	95.4	68.0	52.6	39.4	17.8	11.2	6.2	2.5
JOB MIX LIMITS			100	92/100	81/93	65/77	49/63	35/49	17/31	9/23	6/14	4/8

Lbs. Bitumen Batched __300__

% BITUMEN __5.0__

JOB MIX LIMITS __4.6-5.4__

FIGURE 3-21a Sample data sheet—hot bin analysis (*Courtesy Soil and Material Testing, Inc.*)

PRODUCTION TESTS
BITUMINOUS CONCRETE DRUM MIX PLANT

Plant: __Vaughn Asphalt__   Location: __Castleton, N.Y.__   Region : __1__

Date: __7/5/95__   Mix Type: __6FS2__   RAP %: _____

Inspector: #12   % Mineral filler added:

Check test(s)   [X] Composite gradation   [X] Extraction gradation
Reeported on   [X] Composite moisture   [ ] Mix/Rap moisture
This form: [ ] Stockpile gradation   [X] Bitumen content

MOISTURE CONTENT

	Composite	Composite	Mix	Rap
Wt. Wet (A)	1524.6			
Wt. Dry (B)	1446.1			
Wt. H2O (A-B	78.5			
% Moisture $\frac{A-B}{B} \times 100$	5.43			

AC $\quad$ 93.85

TM $\quad \overline{1774.4} \times 100 = 5.29$ %AC

BITUMEN CONTENT

Wt. Sample (A)	1203.4	1197
Wt. Agg. (B)	1134.4	1126.8
Wt. Gain Filt (C)		
Wt. Bit (A − [B+C])	69	70.2
% Bitumen $\frac{A-[B+C]}{A} \times 100$	5.7	5.9
Corrected %Bit (%Bit − Mix Mois) JMF Range		

Sieve	(6:00 AM) Gradation			(7 AM) Gradation			(11:15) Gradation			
	Weight	% Ret.	% Pass	Weight	% Ret.	% Pass	Weight	% Ret.	% Pass	JMF RG
2"										
1-1/2"										
3/4"	0	0	100	0	0	100	0	0	100	100
1/2"	.09	.6	99.4	3.3	.3	99.7	7.4	.7	99.3	95–100
1/4"	4.32	28.8	70.6	331.6	29.2	70.5	302.5	26.8	72.5	65–72
1/8"	2.49	16.6	54	193.8	17.1	53.4	213.7	19	53.5	50–62
#20	2.73	18.2	35.8	263.2	23.2	30.2	272.8	24.2	29.3	24–38
#40	.91	6.1	29.7	77.7	6.8	23.4	73.1	6.5	22.8	17–27
#80	1.56	10.4	19.3	147.3	1.3	10.4	138	12.2	10.6	9–15
#200	2.53	16.9	2.4	74.9	6.6	3.8	77.5	6.9	3.7	3–6
#PAN	.38	2.5		42.6	3.8		41.8	3.7		
TOTAL	15.01			1134.4			1126.8			

FIGURE 3–21b Sample data sheet—cold-feed gradations, moisture contents, and extraction test on the asphalt concrete produced (*Courtesy Soil and Material Testing, Inc.*)

Step three: Calculate the combined gradation based on the bin draws and bin gradations. The partial combined gradation values are calculated by multiplying the percent batched, expressed as a decimal, times the percent passing each sieve in the bin series.

Bin 2 Sieve Size	Percent Batched		Percent Passing		Partial Combined Gradation
2 in.	0.305	×	100	=	30.5
$1\frac{1}{2}$ in.	0.305	×	97.6	=	29.8
1 in.	0.305	×	84.8	=	25.9
$\frac{1}{2}$ in.	0.305	×	3.0	=	0.9
$\frac{1}{4}$ in.	0.305	×	0.8	=	0.2

The partial combined gradation values are entered on the bin 2 line, and the procedure is used to calculate the partial combined gradation values for the 1, 1A, and fines bin.

Step four: The summation of the values entered on the data sheet in Step three are completed and checked against the job mix limits. The combined gradation value for the 2-in. aggregate equals 100 percent passing, and the job mix limit requirement is 100 percent. Therefore, the bin 2 aggregate is within specifications. This process is repeated for each aggregate size used in the asphalt concrete mix.

The *bitumen extraction test* is used to measure the asphalt content and percentages of materials finer than the No. 80 sieve of the hot mix during production. A sample of the mix is obtained, weighed, and placed in a centrifuge with a solvent. After repeated wash cycles, the sample is removed from the centrifuge, dried, and reweighed. The weight loss divided by the dry weight will give the percentage of asphalt in the original sample. A sample data sheet for this test is given in Figure 3–22.

The quality control technician will also be monitoring the temperatures of the asphalt cement and aggregates going into the pugmill as well as the mix temperature as it leaves the plant in trucks. The technician will also be checking scale accuracy and recording equipment and maintaining the daily records.

Types of Asphalt Plants

Asphalt plants are classified as *stationary* or *portable*—both *batch* and *continuous-mix type.* The stationary plant is permanently situated and is not normally dismantled and moved. The portable plant can be easily disassembled, moved by rail or highway, and reassembled with a minimum of time and energy.

In the batch-type mixing plant (Figure 3–23), different size fractions of hot aggregate in storage bins are withdrawn in desired amounts to make up one batch for mixing. The entire combination of aggregate is then dumped into a mixing chamber called a *pugmill.* The asphalt, which has also been weighed, is thoroughly mixed with the aggregate. After mixing, the material is emptied from the pugmill in one batch.

In the continuous-type mixing plant, aggregate and asphalt are withdrawn, combined, mixed, and discharged in one uninterrupted flow. The combining of materials is

SOIL & MATERIAL TESTING, INC.

MATERIALS BUREAU

BITUMINOUS CONCRETE PLANT EXTRACTION RESULTS

Region____6_____   Sample No._____

Plant _Vaughn Asphalt Products_____ Location__Saratoga, N.Y._____

This test represents ___1_____ days production of Item No. __403.13__

Mix Type ___3_____ Job Mix Formula No._____

Type of sample; Plant ___X_____ Paving _____.

Date Sampled __10/8/91_____ By _David Wemple_____

Weight of Sample __614.4_____ grams

Weight of Aggregate ____585.9_____ grams   % Bitumen Content ___4.86__

Weight of Bitumen _____28.5_____ grams   Job Mix Limits _4.5-5.3____

SIEVE ANALYSIS				
SIEVE	GRAMS RETAINED	% RETAINED	CUMULATIVE % PASSING	JOB MIX LIMITS
2"				
1-1/2"		.0	100	100
1"	17.6	3.0	97.0	95-100
1/2"	116.3	19.8	77.2	74-86
1/4"	126.8	21.6	55.6	51-65
1/8"	94.0	16.0	39.6	32-46
#20	146.4	25.0	14.6	15-29
#40	30.4	5.2	9.4	8-22
#80	19.8	3.4	6.0	4-12
#200	16.1	2.7	3.3	2-6
PAN 3.9+14.6 = 18.5		3.3		
TOTALS	585.9			

29.4 - 25.5 = 3.9(Filter Paper Correction)   Computed By D.Wemple

FIGURE 3–22 Sample data sheet—bituminous concrete plant extraction results (*Courtesy Soil and Material Testing, Inc.*)

generally done by volumetric measurements based on unit weight. Interlocked devices, feeding the aggregate and asphalt into one end of the pugmill mixer, automatically maintain the correct proportions. While being mixed, the materials are propelled by stirring paddles to the discharge end.

Figure 3–24 illustrates the operation of a dryer drum or continuous-type mixing plant. Aggregates with controlled gradations are placed in the cold feed bins (1). The mix

FIGURE 3-23 Asphalt concrete batch plant (*Courtesy Astec Industries, Inc.*)

design (JMF) determines the proportions of the aggregate drawn from the bins and moved to the drum mixer by the cold feed conveyor (2). The exact weight of the aggregate feed is monitored by the automatic weighing system (3), which is interlocked with the asphalt pump (5). The asphalt pump draws the correct quantity of asphalt cement from the storage tank (6) and feeds the asphalt into the drum mixer where the aggregates and asphalt are blended together (4). Dust escaping from the mixing system is captured in the dust collector (7). The completely mixed asphalt concrete is continuously fed into a surge storage silo (9) by the hot mix conveyor (8). The entire production system is controlled and monitored by the plant operator stationed in the control van (10).

Storage of Hot-Mix Asphalt

Should paving operations be temporarily interrupted, rather than stopping production at the plant, a *surge bin* may be installed and used for temporarily storing the hot mix. This is usually a round, silo-type structure, the lower end of which is cone shaped. Hot mix is dumped into the top of the silo so as to fall vertically along the vertical axis of the structure. The bin is designed so that segregation of the mix is held to a minimum. As it is withdrawn from the bottom, its uniformity is maintained.

Surge bins also speed the loading of trucks with hot mix. They can be filled in a matter of seconds, while a truck at the plant has to wait for the production of several batches before it is loaded.

Surge bins are insulated and can store 50 to 100 tons of mix. They can usually store hot mix up to 12 hours with no significant loss of heat or quality.

Where paving operations can lay the hot mix at a rate faster than the plant can produce it, full surge bins at the beginning of the day will increase the plant's effective daily output.

Sometimes it is necessary or desirable to store hot-asphalt mixes for more than 12 hours. Storage silos, similar to surge bins, are used for this purpose. The capacity of these heated silos may be as much as 350 tons. Hot-mix asphalt ages quite rapidly during exposure to air. The oxidizing process hardens the asphalt. For long-term storage, an atmosphere free of oxygen is used to fill the silo to prevent age-hardening of the hot mix.

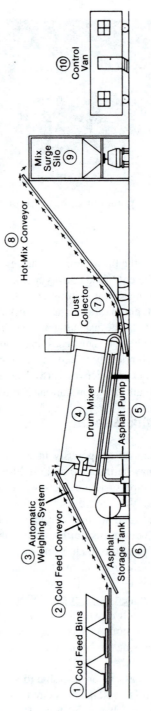

FIGURE 3-24 Basic drum mix facility (*Courtesy The Asphalt Institute*)

FIGURE 3–25 Asphalt concrete drum mix plant with surge/storage silos (*Courtesy Astec Industries, Inc.*)

Storage silos may be remotely located. This makes it possible for the asphalt plant to serve a larger area and provide paving mix at times when the plant would normally not be operating. (See Figure 3–25.)

ESTIMATING ASPHALT CONCRETE

The unit of measure for the purchase of asphalt concrete is the ton (2000 lb). Therefore, the number of tons of asphalt concrete required to complete a paving job must be determined. Some paving contractors utilize quantity charts or slide-rule-type paving calculators to determine required quantities of material while others produce their own tables based upon local materials.

On small paving jobs the quantities are usually determined using a rule of thumb which states that 1 ton of asphalt concrete will cover 80 sq ft, 2 in. thick.

EXAMPLE

$$\text{Area to be paved} = 2600 \text{ sq ft}$$
$$\text{Thickness} = 2 \text{ in.}$$
$$\frac{2600 \text{ sq ft}}{80 \text{ sq ft/ton}} = 32.5 \text{ tons}$$

Larger paving estimates are based upon the unit weight of the asphalt concrete. Asphalt concrete's unit weight will range from 140 to 150 lb per cu ft. The formula used is:

$$T = \frac{A \times t \times uw}{2000 \text{ lb}}$$

where T = tons of asphalt concrete required

A = area to be paved in sq ft

t = thickness of pavement in ft

uw = unit weight of asphalt concrete

EXAMPLE

Area to be paved = 180,000 sq ft

Thickness = 3 in. = 0.25 ft

Unit weight of asphalt concrete = 150 lb/cu ft

$$T = \frac{180,000 \text{ sq ft} \times 0.25 \text{ ft} \times 150 \text{ lb/cu ft}}{2000 \text{ lb/ton}}$$

$$T = 3375 \text{ tons}$$

PREPARATION OF UNPAVED SURFACES

The following roadway surfaces are generally considered unpaved surfaces:

1. Compacted subgrade,

2. Improved subgrade,

3. Untreated base, and

4. Nonsurfaced aggregate roadway.

Certain treated or stabilized granular bases are considered unpaved surfaces when being prepared for asphalt paving. Bases that have been treated or stabilized with either asphalt or portland cement are considered paved surfaces and are excluded from this classification.

Typical asphalt pavement structures are illustrated in Figure 3–26.

Prepared Subgrade

A *prepared subgrade* is one that has been worked and compacted. This may be the foundation soil or a layer of stabilized soil, select soil, or otherwise improved subgrade material.

The riding quality of the pavement surface depends largely on proper construction and preparation of the foundation material. The roadway should be shaped and proof-rolled so that the paving equipment has no difficulty in placing the material at a uniform thickness to a smooth grade.

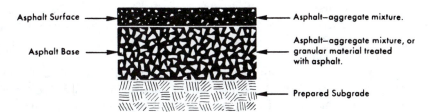

FULL DEPTH ASPHALT PAVEMENT

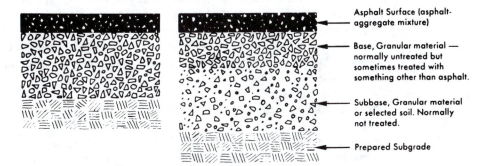

ASPHALT PAVEMENT WITH UNTREATED BASE (AND SUBBASE)

**ASPHALT PAVEMENT WITH PORTLAND CEMENT CONCRETE OR
COMBINED PORTLAND CEMENT CONCRETE AND ASPHALT BASE**

FIGURE 3–26   Asphalt pavement cross sections showing typical asphalt pavement structures (*Courtesy The Asphalt Institute*)

Weather conditions should be suitable and the roadway surface should be firm, dust-free, and dry, or just slightly damp when paving operations are started.

Untreated Base

Untreated aggregate bases and some chemically stabilized bases other than portland cement and asphalt-treated bases should be properly shaped and proof-rolled.

When asphalt pavement courses are to be placed on an untreated aggregate base, loose aggregate particles should be swept from the surface of the roadway using power brooms. Care should be taken, however, not to dislodge or otherwise disturb the bond of the aggregate in the surface of the base. When the loose material has been properly removed, only the tops of the aggregate in the surface will be exposed, and the pieces solidly embedded in the base. When the surface has been cleaned, it is ready to be primed with asphalt.

For priming, an asphalt distributor sprays about 0.2 to 0.5 gal per sq yd liquid asphalt, usually MC-30 or MC-70, over the surface. The asphalt then penetrates or soaks into the surface. If it is not absorbed within 24 hours after application, too much prime has been used. To correct this condition, sand should be spread over the surface to blot the excess asphalt. Care should be taken to prevent overpriming. The prime should be fully set and cured before placing the asphalt mixture on the base.

Asphalt sometimes is mixed into the top 2 or 3 in. of base material in lieu of priming when it is difficult to obtain uniform and thorough penetration. This provides a tough working surface for equipment, a waterproof protective layer, and a bond to the superimposed construction.

Nonsurfaced Aggregate Roadways

Nonsurfaced aggregate roadways are similar to untreated aggregate bases. They differ primarily in that they have been used as a roadway by traffic and, typically, have been in use for a considerable time.

Again, it cannot be stressed too strongly that the riding quality of the surface depends to a great degree on conditioning and preparing the underlying pavement structure. It is advisable, where the aggregate-surfaced roadway is rough and uneven, to bring the surface to grade by scarifying the top few inches of material, blending in more aggregate as may be necessary, compacting, and priming with asphalt. If the aggregate roadway has had a previous asphalt treatment and is rough and uneven, it is advisable to place a *leveling course* of hot-asphalt plant mix ahead of the first layer of the surface course.

Placing a leveling course is an operation employed when the road surface is so irregular that it exceeds the leveling capabilities of the paver. The paver is usually effective on irregularities of lengths not longer than $1\frac{1}{2}$ to 2 times the wheel base of the machine. Beyond these lengths, outside help is needed. Generally, irregularities no longer than 40 or 50 ft can be handled with a traveling stringline device and automatic screed control on the paver.

PAVED SURFACES

Flexible-Type Pavements

Structural distress occurring in old asphalt pavements is usually the result of inadequate design, inadequate execution of the design including compaction, or both. Poor mix design can also cause several types of distress, and excess asphalt may cause corrugation or rutting. Cracking may be caused by excessive pavement deflection under traffic due to an inadequate pavement structure or a spongy foundation. Insufficient or oxidized asphalt may also cause cracking because the mix may be brittle.

Before the old pavement receives an overlaying course of asphalt, it should first be inspected. The remedy for whatever failures exist depends on the type and extent of the distress. If failure is extensive, reconstruction will probably be necessary. In any case, all needed repairs to the old surface should be made before paving.

A slick surface on an old pavement may be caused by aggregate polishing under traffic or by too much asphalt in the mix. If the cause is excess asphalt, it should be either burned off or removed with a *heater-planer* before placing the overlay.

Old pavements having small cracks should be given a fog seal before overlaying. A *fog seal* is a light application of emulsified asphalt diluted with water and sprayed over the surface. Larger cracks warrant having the surface treated with an emulsion slurry seal. The *slurry seal* is a mixture of emulsified asphalt, fine aggregate, and mineral filler, with water added to produce a slurry consistency.

Potholes in an old pavement that is otherwise strong should be filled with asphalt concrete and compacted before the roadway surface is paved (see Figure 3–27). If the base beneath the old pavement has failed, the damaged areas will eventually show in the new paved surface. Patching, of course, must be done before paving, and the patch should be deep enough to strengthen the base.

All bleeding and unsuitable patches, excess asphaltic crack or joint filler, loose scale, and any surplus bituminous material should be removed from the surface of the existing pavement.

All depressions of 1 in. or more should be overlaid with a leveling course and compacted ahead of the surfacing operation. All surfaces, both horizontal and vertical,

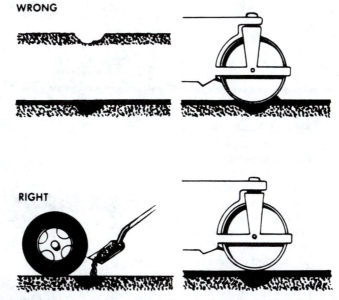

FIGURE 3–27 Potholes should be filled and compacted before spreading the first course (*Courtesy The Asphalt Institute*)

that will be in contact with the new asphalt surface must be thoroughly cleaned. Cleaning flat surfaces is usually done with rotary brooms, but washing or flushing may be necessary to remove clay or dirt. A tack coat should be applied to the existing pavement and to all vertical faces. These include curbs, gutters, drainage gratings, manholes, and other contact surfaces. A uniform coating of liquid asphalt or asphalt emulsion will provide a closely bonded waterproof joint. For repairs to pavements that will not be resurfaced, the procedure illustrated in Figure 3–28 should be used.

Rigid-Type Pavements

Distress in rigid-type pavements also must be corrected before resurfacing. Additional layers of asphalt mixtures must be thick enough not only to provide required additional strength but also to minimize the reflection of cracks from old pavement in the new surface.

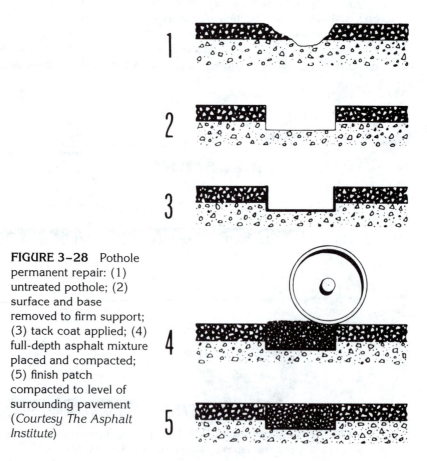

FIGURE 3–28 Pothole permanent repair: (1) untreated pothole; (2) surface and base removed to firm support; (3) tack coat applied; (4) full-depth asphalt mixture placed and compacted; (5) finish patch compacted to level of surrounding pavement (*Courtesy The Asphalt Institute*)

Preparation of damaged or distressed rigid pavements differs from that for asphalt pavements. Preparation may include one or more of the following:

1. Breaking large cracked slabs into smaller pieces and seating them firmly with heavy rollers,
2. Cracking slabs that rock under traffic and seating them with heavy rollers,
3. Undersealing to provide uniform support,
4. Patching disintegrated and spalled areas,
5. Sealing cracks to prevent the intrusion of water from below.

Pumping at the joints is caused by the rocking of slabs under traffic. The wet subgrade is removed from beneath the slab, and this causes cracking and breaking in the joint area. Usually a pavement can be stabilized by undersealing with asphalt specially prepared for this purpose. Otherwise, the rocking slabs should be cracked into smaller pieces and seated.

In some cases portions of the pavement may be disintegrated or so badly broken up that the pavement fragments should be removed. In such cases, these areas should be prepared and patched with asphalt concrete prior to the resurfacing operation.

Filler material is removed from joints and cracks in the slabs to a depth of at least $\frac{1}{4}$ in. The joints are refilled with an asphalt joint-filling material. Any asphalt patches having excess asphalt, as well as any excess crack filler that may have accumulated next to cracks and joints, are removed.

As a final step, before any asphalt paving is placed, the pavement surface should be swept clean and given a tack coat. Where preparation measures have caused settlement or pavement roughness, a leveling course of asphalt concrete should be placed prior to the resurfacing operation.

INSPECTION OF MIX

Close cooperation between the paving crew and the asphalt plant is essential in securing a satisfactory and uniform job. A fast means of communication should be established between the paving operation and the asphalt plant so that any change in the mixture can be made promptly. When possible, the paving inspector and the plant inspector should frequently exchange visits. When the paving inspector is familiar with plant operations, he can easily determine if changes at the plant are necessary to improve the mix. The plant inspector, on the other hand, by being familiar with the paving operation can better understand problems attendant to it.

Every truckload of material should be observed as it arrives. The mix temperature should be checked regularly. If it is not within specified tolerance, the mix should not be used.

Mistakes in batching, mixing, and temperature control can and do occur, and these errors may sometimes go unnoticed by the plant inspector. Consequently, loads arriving at the spreader may be unsatisfactory. When the paving inspector rejects a load, he should record his action, with the reason for rejection, both on the ticket and in his diary so that the proper deduction can be made from the pay quantities. If appropriate, a sample should be obtained for laboratory analysis. A record should also be kept of the loads accepted and placed. These records should be checked daily, or more frequently, with those of the plant inspector so no discrepancies exist when work is completed.

Mix Deficiencies

Some mix deficiencies that may justify discarding the mix are as follows:

1. *Too hot:* Blue smoke rising from the mix usually indicates an overheated batch. The temperature should be checked immediately. If the batch exceeds maximum specification limits, it should be discarded. If it exceeds optimum placing temperature but does not exceed the specification limit, the batch is usually not discarded, but immediate steps should be taken to correct the condition.

2. *Too cold:* A generally stiff appearance, or improper coating of the larger aggregate particles, indicates a cold mixture. Again, the temperature should be checked immediately. If it is below the specification limit, it should be discarded. If it is within the specification limit but below optimum placing temperature, steps should be taken immediately to correct the situation.

3. *Too much asphalt:* When loads have been arriving at the spreader with the material domed up or peaked and suddenly a load appears lying flat, it may contain too much asphalt. Excessive asphalt may be detected under the screed by the way the mix slacks off.

4. *Too little asphalt:* A mix containing too little asphalt generally can be detected immediately if the asphalt deficiency is severe. It has a lean, granular appearance and improper coating, and lacks the typical shiny, black luster. The pavement surface has a dull, brown appearance, and the roller does not compact it satisfactorily. A less severe deficiency is difficult to detect by appearance; suspicions should be checked by testing.

5. *Nonuniform mixing:* Nonuniform mixing shows up as spots of lean, brown, dull-appearing material within areas having a rich, shiny appearance.

6. *Excess coarse aggregate:* A mix with excess coarse aggregate can be detected by the poor workability of the mix and by its coarse appearance when it is on the road. Otherwise, it resembles an overrich mix.

7. *Excess fine aggregate:* A mix with an excess of fine aggregate has a different texture from a properly graded mix after it has been rolled. Otherwise, it resembles a lean mix.

8. *Excess moisture:* Steam rising from the mix as it is dumped into the hopper of the spreader indicates moisture in the mix. It may be bubbling or popping as if it were boiling. The mix may also foam so that it appears to have too much asphalt.

9. *Miscellaneous:* Segregation of the aggregates in the mix may occur because of improper handling and may be serious enough to warrant rejection. Loads that have become contaminated because of spilled gasoline, kerosene, oil, and the like should not be used in the roadway.

THE PAVING OPERATION

Spreading and compacting asphalt mixtures is the operation to which all the other processes are directed. Aggregates have been selected and combined; the mix designed; the plant and its auxiliary equipment set up, calibrated, and inspected; and the materials mixed together and delivered to the paver.

Asphalt mix is brought to the paving site in trucks and deposited directly into the paver or in windrows in front of the paver. The paver then spreads the mix at a set width and thickness as it moves forward. In doing so, the paver partially compacts the material. Immediately or shortly thereafter and while the mix is still hot, steel-wheeled and rubber-tired rollers are driven over the freshly paved strip, further compacting the mix. Rolling is usually continued until the pavement is compacted to the required density, or until the temperature has dropped to a point where further compaction may produce detrimental results.

Figure 3–29 shows a paver and roller placing and compacting asphalt pavement. The flow of materials through the paver is illustrated in Figure 3–30.

After the pavement course has been compacted and allowed to cool, it is ready for additional paving courses or ready to support traffic loads.

The Asphalt Paver

The *asphalt paver* spreads the mixture in a uniform layer of desired thickness and shape, or finishes the layer to the desired elevation and cross section, ready for compaction. Modern pavers are supported on crawler treads or wheels. These machines can place a paved layer of less than 1 in. to about 10 in. in thickness over a width of 6 to 32 ft. Working speeds generally range from 10 to 70 ft per minute.

FIGURE 3–29 Paver and steel-wheeled roller placing and compacting asphalt pavement (*Courtesy Constructioneer*)

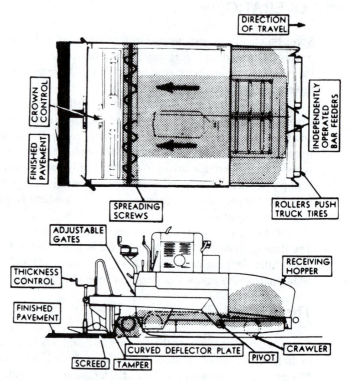

FIGURE 3–30 Flow of materials through a typical asphalt paver (*Courtesy Barber-Greene Co.*)

On small paving jobs it is sometimes more convenient and economical to use a tow-type paver than to use the larger, self-powered pavers. Tow-type pavers (Figure 3–31) are attached to the rear of the dump truck that hauls the asphalt mix from the plant.

Hand-Spreading Operations

The increasing use of asphalt in construction has resulted in an increased number of related projects in which asphalt mixes are used. For example, asphalt paving mixes are used for constructing driveways, parking areas, shoulders, and sidewalks. Such incidental construction is becoming more and more a part of the paving contract.

Normally, mix requirements for these jobs are the same as for roadway mixes. However, where it is anticipated that the major portion of placing will be by hand, mixes should be designed for good workability. This is easily achieved by decreasing the amount of coarse aggregate in the mix. Placing and compaction methods for hand-placed asphalt mixes are the same as for machine-spread paving.

Certain differences in construction methods are required, especially where special equipment such as sidewalk pavers are not available. In addition, there are apt to be places on a regular road-paving job where spreading with a paver is either impractical or impossible. In these cases, hand spreading may be permitted.

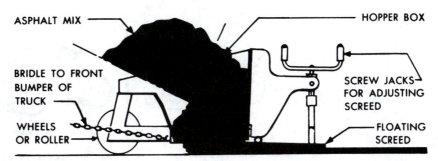

FIGURE 3–31 Flow of material through a tow-type paver (*Courtesy The Asphalt Institute*)

Placing and spreading by hand should be done very carefully and the material distributed uniformly to avoid segregation.

Material should not be broadcast or spread from shovels since this causes segregation. Rather, it should be deposited by shovels or wheelbarrows into small piles and spread with asphalt rakes or wide-blade lutes. Any part of the mix that has formed into lumps and does not break down easily should be discarded.

The Roller Operation

Rolling should start as soon as possible after material has been spread. Rolling consists of three consecutive phases: *breakdown* or *initial rolling, intermediate rolling,* and *finish rolling.*

Breakdown rolling compacts the material beyond that imparted by the paver, to obtain practically all of the density it needs. Intermediate rolling densifies and seals the surface. Finish rolling removes roller marks and other blemishes left from previous rolling. Rollers available for these operations are illustrated in Figure 3–32 and include:

1. steel-wheeled,
2. pneumatic-tired,
3. vibrating, and
4. combination steel-wheeled and pneumatic-tired.

Steel-wheeled rollers have been and may be used for all three rolling phases. A pneumatic-tired roller sometimes is used for breakdown rolling, but is generally preferred for intermediate rolling. Vibrating rollers (see Figure 3–34) are also used primarily for intermediate rolling. During rolling, the roller wheels should be kept moist with only enough water to avoid picking up material. Rollers should move at a slow, uniform speed with the drive roll nearest the paver (see Figure 3–35). Rollers should be in good mechanical condition. The line of rolling should not change suddenly, nor should the roller be reversed quickly, thereby displacing the mix. Any major change in roller direction should be done on stable material. If rolling causes displacement of the material, the area affected should be loosened and restored to original grade with loose new material before being rolled again.

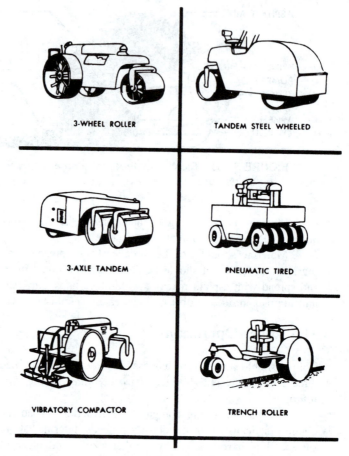

FIGURE 3-32 Types of compactors (*Courtesy The Asphalt Institute*)

Two important areas of rolling are the transverse and longitudinal joints. The transverse joints are perpendicular to the centerline of the pavement, and the longitudinal joints are parallel to the centerline.

The roller should be placed on the previously compacted material with about 6 in. of the roller wheel on the uncompacted mix. The roller should work successive passes, each covering 6 to 8 in., until the entire width of the drive roll is on the new mix.

If the specified density of asphalt pavement mix is not obtained during construction, subsequent traffic will further consolidate the pavement. This consolidation occurs principally in the wheel paths and appears as channels in the pavement surface.

Most mixtures compact quite readily if spread and rolled at temperatures that assure proper asphalt density. Refer to Figure 3-33 for items that influence compaction and suggested corrective measures.

FIGURE 3–33 Summary of influences on compaction

ITEM	EFFECT	CORRECTIONS*
Aggregate		
● Smooth Surfaced	Low interparticle friction	Use light rollers
		Lower mix temperature
● Rough Surfaced	High interparticle friction	Use heavy rollers
● Unsound	Breaks under steel-wheeled rollers	Use sound aggregate
		Use pneumatic rollers
● Absorptive	Dries mix—difficult to compact	Increase asphalt in mix
Asphalt		
● Viscosity		
—High	Particle movement restricted	Use heavy rollers
		Increase temperature
—Low	Particles move easily during compaction	Use light rollers
		Decrease temperature
● Quantity		
—High	Unstable & plastic under roller	Decrease asphalt in mix
—Low	Reduced lubrication—difficult compaction	Increase asphalt in mix
		Use heavy rollers
Mix		
● Excess Coarse Aggregate	Harsh mix—difficult to compact	Use heavy rollers
● Oversanded	Too workable—difficult to compact	Reduce sand in mix
		Use light rollers
● Too Much Filler	Stiffens mix—difficult to compact	Reduce filler in mix
		Use heavy rollers
● Too Little Filler	Low cohesion—mix may come apart	Increase filler in mix
Mix temperature		
● High	Difficult to compact—mix lacks cohesion	Decrease mixing temperature
● Low	Difficult to compact—mix too stiff	Increase mixing temperature
Course Thickness		
● Thick Lifts	Hold heat—more time to compact	Roll normally
● Thin lifts	Lose heat—less time to compact	Roll before mix cools
		Increase mix temperature
Weather Conditions		
● Low Air Temperature	Cools mix rapidly	Roll before mix cools
● Low Surface Temperature	Cools mix rapidly	Increase mix temperature
● Wind	Cools mix—crusts surface	Increase lift thickness

*Corrections may be made on a trial basis at the plant or job site. Additional remedies may be derived from changes in mix design.

Courtesy The Asphalt Institute

FIGURE 3-34   Vibratory roller compacting asphalt overlay (*Courtesy Constructioneer*)

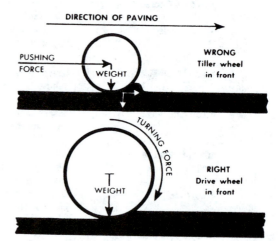

FIGURE 3-35   Rolling direction is important (*Courtesy The Asphalt Institute*)

Pavement Density

The degree or amount of compaction obtained by rolling is determined by *Density tests.* Ordinarily, specifications require that a pavement be compacted to a minimum percentage of either maximum theoretical density or density obtained by laboratory compaction. Density determinations of the finished pavement are necessary to check this requirement. These are made in the laboratory in accordance with the test method, Specific Gravity of Compressed Bituminous Mixtures (AASHTO T166), on samples submitted by the paving inspector.

Care should be exercised in obtaining and transporting these samples to the field laboratory to ensure a minimum of disturbance. Sampling of compacted mixes from the roadway should be done in accordance with AASHTO T168, Sampling Bituminous Paving Mixtures. A pavement power saw or coring machine used for taking samples provides the least disturbance of samples and compacted pavement.

EXAMPLE

The density of an asphalt concrete mix is determined by laboratory tests to be 148.9 pcf. The density of a field core taken from a section of compacted pavement by test is 146.2 pcf.

$$PC = \frac{\gamma_F \, (\text{pcf})}{\gamma_L (\text{pcf})} \times 100$$

where: PC = percent compaction (%)

γ_F = density of field core (pcf)

γ_L = density of laboratory specimen (pcf)

$$PC = \frac{146.2}{148.9} \times 100 = 98.2\%$$

Currently Air Permeability tests and Nuclear Density tests have progressed to the point where compaction may be controlled without having to obtain a sample of compacted pavement. These nondestructive tests also make possible the rapid determination of density so that additional compaction may be given, if required, while the pavement is still hot.

AUXILIARY EQUIPMENT

Asphalt Distributor

The asphalt distributor is used to apply either a prime coat or a tack coat to the surface to be paved. Prime coats are applications of liquid asphalt to an absorbent surface such as granular base. Tack coats are very light applications of liquid asphalt to an existing paved surface.

The *distributor* (Figure 3–36) consists of a truck or trailer on which is mounted an insulated tank with a heating system, usually oil burning. The distributor has a power-driven pump and a system of spray bars and nozzles through which the asphalt is forced, under pressure, onto the construction surface.

It is important that asphalt sprayed from a distributor be spread over the surface uniformly at the desired rate of application. This requires a pump in good working order and free-flowing spray bars and nozzles.

To obtain a desired rate of application, the speed of the distributor must be determined for a given pumping rate and coverage width. Distributors usually have a

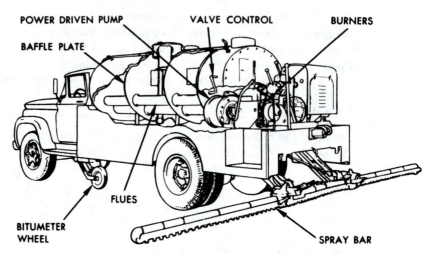

POWER DRIVEN PUMP   VALVE CONTROL   BURNERS

BAFFLE PLATE

FLUES

BITUMETER
WHEEL

SPRAY BAR

FIGURE 3–36 Bituminous distributor truck (*Courtesy The Asphalt Institute*)

bitumeter which indicates the forward speed of the distributor in feet per minute. This speed must be held constant if the asphalt coverage is to be uniform.

Motor Grader

In some situations the *motor grader* may be used to spread asphalt plant mixes, for example, in the placement of leveling courses. A leveling course is a thin layer of asphalt plant mix placed under a pavement's wearing surface. The leveling course helps the paver lay a smooth, uniform-wearing course by removing irregularities in the old pavement.

Windrowing Equipment

Windrows of asphalt plant mixes are sometimes placed in the roadway and in front of the asphalt paver. An elevator attachment fixed to the front end of the paver picks up the asphalt mix and discharges it into the hopper. This eliminates the necessity of having trucks backing up and discharging their loads as the paver moves forward.

Windrowing equipment may also be used for controlling the amount of material for leveling courses spread by a motor grader.

Incidental Tools

Adequate hand tools and proper equipment for cleaning and heating them should be available for the paving operation. Incidental tools include:

1. Rakes;
2. Shovels;

3. Lutes;

4. Tool heating torch;

5. Cleaning equipment;

6. Hand tampers;

7. Small mechanical vibrating compactors;

8. Blocks and shims for supporting the screed of the paver when beginning operations;

9. Rope, canvas, or timbers for construction of joints at ends of runs;

10. Joint cutting and painting tools; and

11. Straightedge.

Not all of these tools are necessarily used on every paving project or every day of a particular job. Rakes, shovels, and lutes are frequently used by personnel around the paver. While the paver is operating, the laborers work or rework a portion of the mix to fit the paving around objects or fill in areas that the paver does not pave adequately or cannot reach during the paving operation. Ramps, intersections, and areas broken up by bridge columns and piers are typical areas where hand paving will be required.

ASPHALT ROOFING PRODUCTS

The preservative and waterproofing characteristics of asphalt make it an ideal material for roofing systems.

Asphalts used in the production of roofing products include *saturant* or oil-rich asphalts, and a harder, more viscous asphalt known as a "*coating asphalt.*" The softening point of saturants varies from 100 to 160°F, and the softening point of coating asphalt may run as high as 260°F.

The sheet material used in the production of roofing products may be either an *organic felt sheet* or an *inorganic glass fiber mat.* Cellulose fibers from rags, paper, and wood are processed into a dry felt which must have certain characteristics of strength, absorptive capacity, and flexibility. The glass fiber mat is composed of continuous or random thin glass fibers bonded with plastic binders. Glass mats are coated and impregnated with asphalt in one operation, while the felt sheets are impregnated with the saturant first and then coated with the coating asphalt. Coating asphalts generally contain a finely ground mineral stabilizer, giving the coating increased weathering resistance and increased resistance to shattering in cold weather. Some mineral stabilizers used are silica, slate dust, talc, micaceous materials, dolomite, and traprock.

Certain asphalt roofing products are coated with mineral aggregate granules. The granules protect the coating asphalt from light and offer a weathering protection. The mineral granules also increase the fire resistance of asphalt roofing. The mineral granules also impart the various colors or color blends that are available in roofing products.

The manufacturer distributes finely ground talc or mica powder on the surfaces of rolled roofing and shingles to prevent their sticking together before they are used. The powder has no other purpose and usually disappears from exposed surfaces soon after the roofing is installed.

The flow diagram in Figure 3–37 illustrates the production of asphalt roofing. During production, the materials are rigidly inspected to ensure conformance with standards. Some important items checked are:

1. Saturation of felt to determine quantity of saturant and efficiency of saturation,
2. Thickness and distribution of coating asphalt,
3. Adhesion and distribution of mineral granules,
4. Weight, count, size, coloration, and other characteristics of finished product before and after it is packaged.

The installation of asphalt roofing usually will require small amounts of accessory asphaltic materials. *Flashing cements* are used as part of a flashing system at points of vertical intersection such as where the roof meets a wall, chimney, or vent pipes. Flashing cements are processed to remain elastic through the normal temperature ranges of summer to winter. They are elastic after setting, and normal expansion and contraction of the roof deck should not cause separation to occur.

Lap cements are thinner than flashing cements and are used to make a watertight bond between laps of roll roofing. *Roof coatings* are thin liquids applied with brush or by spraying to resurface old roofs and may be either emulsified or cutback asphalts.

Manufactured asphalt roofing products are produced to American Society for Testing and Materials standards. Asphalt roofing that is listed by the Underwriters Laboratories, Inc. (UL) as *A, B,* or *C* will not ignite easily, readily spread flames, or create flaming brands to endanger nearby buildings. Underwriters Laboratories also rate shingles for wind resistance. They must withstand a 60-mph wind for 2 hours to carry the UL label.

Prepared roofing products are those products which are manufactured and packaged ready to apply to the roof deck, usually by nailing. Asphalt shingles and certain roll roofings are considered prepared roofing products.

Another asphalt roofing system is the built-up roof. The *built-up roof* is used on flat or almost flat roofs and consists of alternate layers of roofing felt and asphalt covered with an aggregate coating.

Roofing asphalt is heated in an asphalt kettle, and is raised to the roof by pulley or pumped directly from the kettle to the roof. The hot asphalt is mopped or distributed by hot-asphalt applicators and covered with roofing felt in layers until the last coat of asphalt is applied, depending upon the number of plies specified. The last asphalt application is a flood coat which is immediately covered with mineral aggregates before it cools. The aggregate is generally spread mechanically, but can be done by hand.

Asphalts used for built-up roofs are softer asphalts and have greater temperature susceptibility so that they soften and flow slightly during warm weather. This softening enables the asphalt to "heal" small cracks which may develop from contraction, expansion, or minor movements due to settlement of the building.

There is a roofing asphalt available for use in any climate and on any slope on which built-up roofing can be used. Refer to ASTM D312 Section 4 for the types and general applications.

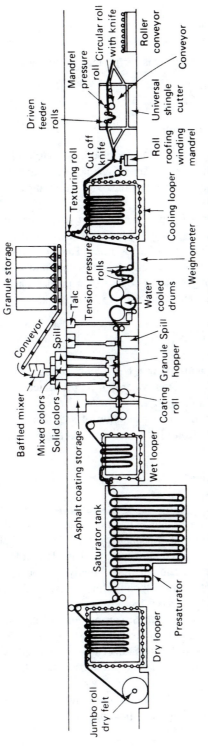

FIGURE 3-37 Flow diagram of a typical roofing plant (*Courtesy Asphalt Roofing Manufacturers' Association*)

ASPHALT PIPE COATINGS

There are three major systems for protecting pipe with asphalt coating:

1. Wrapped systems
2. Mastic systems
3. Interior coating systems

Asphalt-wrapped systems for pipelines consist of a prime coat followed by either one or two applications of asphalt enamel in conjunction with one or more layers of reinforcing and protective wrapping. The wrapping material is asphalt-saturated felt or asphalt-saturated glass wrap.

Mastic systems for pipelines consist of a prime coat followed by a coating of a dense, impervious, essentially voidless mixture of asphalt, mineral aggregate, and mineral filler which may include asbestos fiber. The minimum thickness is usually $\frac{1}{4}$ in. The finished mastic coating is usually coated with whitewash.

Interior coating systems consist of a prime coat followed by a centrifugally cast layer of asphalt enamel about $\frac{1}{32}$ in. to $\frac{3}{32}$ in. thick.

ASPHALT MULCH TREATMENTS

Stabilizing slopes and flat areas on construction projects is a chronic problem. Soil erosion caused by wind and water can be prevented by the establishment of vegetation which anchors the soil in place.

However, during the germination of seed and early plant growth, mulch must be used to prevent erosion. There are two acceptable methods for using asphalt in the mulching process:

1. Asphalt spray mulch
2. Asphalt mulch tie-down

The *asphalt spray mulch* is usually an emulsified asphalt sprayed on the newly seeded area. The thin film of asphalt has three beneficial effects. First, it holds the seed in place against erosion. Second, by virtue of its dark color, it absorbs and conserves solar heat during the germination period. Finally, it holds moisture in the soil, promoting speedy plant growth. The asphalt film shrinks and cracks, permitting plant growth. Eventually, after it has served its purpose, the asphalt film disintegrates.

An *asphalt mulch tie-down* can be done using either of two acceptable methods. The first method is to spread straw or hay on the graded slope. When the mulch is in place, a mixture of seed, fertilizer, and water is sprayed over the mulch. The liquid passes through the mulch to the soil. The liquid asphalt is then sprayed over the mulch to lock it in place.

The second method requires the spreading of the seed and fertilizer upon the prepared soil, followed by the spraying of the asphalt and mulching material simultaneously.

ASPHALT JOINT MATERIALS

Asphalt is used as a *joint* and *crack filler* in pavements and other structures. The joint between two concrete pavement slabs may be filled with hot asphalt. The asphalt's properties of adhesion and flexibility allow the two separate slabs to expand and contract without permitting moisture to penetrate the joint. The asphalt material used may also be premolded in strips. The strips are composed of asphalt mixed with fine mineral substances, fibrous materials, cork, or sawdust, manufactured in dimensions suitable for use in joints. The premolded strips are inserted at joint locations before placement of the portland cement concrete and eliminate the filling of the joint openings after the slabs have cured.

Asphalt is a widely used construction material with many diverse applications. To ensure that asphalt and its products are used properly, organizations such as the Asphalt Institute, Asphalt Roofing Manufacturers' Association, and others produce technical literature concerning asphalt uses. For an in-depth treatment of the material, this technical literature is recommended.

REVIEW QUESTIONS

1. How are natural asphalts formed?
2. What are the differences between asphalt and tar?
3. What are bituminous materials?
4. What are the classifications of petroleum crude oil based upon their asphalt content?
5. How is the percentage of asphalt in a crude oil determined?
6. What distillation processes are used to produce asphalt?
7. What are blown asphalts, and what are they used for?
8. How are asphalt cements liquified other than by heat?
9. What do the basic tests on asphalt materials measure?
10. Why are asphalt cement temperature-viscosity curves important in the production process of asphalt concrete?
11. What are the basic requirements for an asphalt pavement?
12. What factors must be considered when designing an asphalt pavement's thickness?
13. What objectives must the design of an asphalt pavement mix meet?
14. What are tack coats and prime coats?
15. What is the suggested pavement thickness for a full-depth asphalt concrete driveway, if the in situ soils are nonplastic clayey loams?
16. What is surge storage, and how is it used in asphalt concrete production?
17. Calculate the number of tons of asphalt concrete required to pave a 300-sq-ft area 3 in. thick. The asphalt concrete has a density of 150 lb per cu ft.

18. How many tons of asphalt concrete will be required to overlay a 2.5-mile-long, 24-ft-wide road with 3 in. of wearing course asphalt concrete that has a density of 147.9 pcf?

19. Briefly detail the paving operation utilizing mechanized equipment.

20. The core densities listed were obtained from a compacted asphalt concrete pavement, core A = 142.9 pcf, core B = 149.9 pcf, and core C = 143.4 pcf. Determine the percentage of compaction if the laboratory density of the mix was 147.1 pcf. Do any of the cores indicate potential problems with the pavement?

21. What is an asphalt distributor truck, and what functions does it serve on a pavement project?

22. Describe briefly how asphalt roofing materials are produced.

23. How is asphalt used for slope stabilization in highway construction?

24. Calculate the number of tons of asphalt concrete required to pave a 500-sq-ft area 2 in. thick. The asphalt concrete has a density of 148.6 lb per cu ft.

25. How many tons of asphalt concrete will be required to overlay a 3-mile-long, 24-ft-wide road with $2\frac{1}{2}$ in. of wearing course asphalt concrete that has a density of 146.3 pcf?

26. What are the suggested thicknesses for an asphalt concrete surface parking area for heavy trucks on gravelly or sandy well-drained soils?

27. Calculate the metric tons of asphalt concrete required to pave 2 km of roadway 4 m wide and 80 mm thick. The density of the paving material is 2370 kg/m³.

4

Portland Cement Concrete

Concrete has many characteristics that make it a widely used construction material. Among them are raw material availability, the ability of concrete to take the shape of the form it is placed in, and the ease with which its properties can be modified. The ability to modify such properties as its strength, durability, economy, watertightness, and abrasion resistance is most important. As illustrated in Figure 4–1, there are a great many variables that affect the properties of concrete. The ease with which concrete can be modified by its variables can often work to the disadvantage of the user if quality control is not maintained from the first to the last operations in concrete work.

Basically, *concrete* is 60 to 80 percent aggregates (i.e., sand, stone), which are considered "inert" ingredients, and 20 to 40 percent "paste" (i.e., water, portland cement), considered the active ingredients. These materials are combined or mixed, and cured to develop the hardened properties of concrete.

During this production sequence, concrete is very often produced by one firm with products supplied by three or four other firms and sold in an unfinished state to a contractor who will place, finish, and cure it. During this process it will be subject to the weather and other variables. Therefore, in order to ensure that the concrete initially designed for a specific function is the same concrete that ends up in service, careful consideration must be given to all of the variables which may affect it.

HISTORY

The development of cementing materials can be traced back to the Egyptians and Romans, and their use of masonry construction. The Egyptians used a cement produced

145

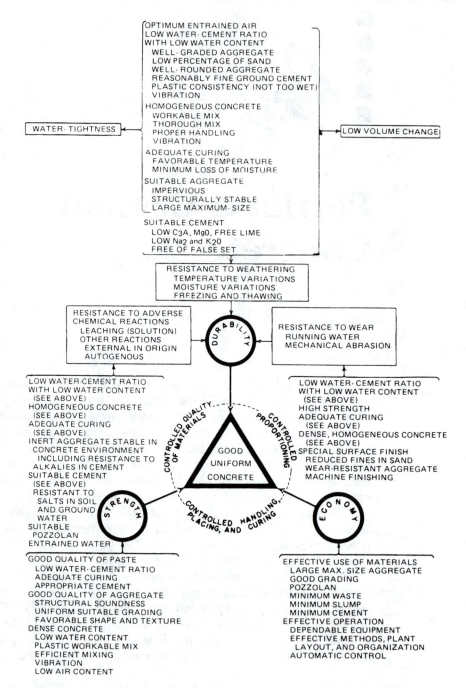

FIGURE 4–1 Chart showing the principal properties of good concrete, their relationships, and the elements which control them. Many factors are involved in the production of good, uniform concrete. 288-D-795 (*Courtesy U.S. Department of the Interior, Water and Power Resources Service*)

by a heating process, and this may have been the start of the technology. Roman engineering upgraded simple lime mortars with the addition of volcanic ash which increased their durability, as evidenced by the sound structures which still stand.

The development of a concrete or cement technology as we know it probably can be traced back to England, where in 1824 Joseph Aspdin produced a portland cement from a heated mixture of limestone and clay. He was awarded a British patent and the name portland cement was used because when the material hardened, it resembled a stone from the quarries of Portland, England. There is evidence that several of Joseph Aspdin's contemporaries were involved in the same research, but evidence shows that he fired his product above the clinkering temperature, thus producing a superior product.

The production of portland cement in the United States dates back to 1872, when the first portland cement plant was opened at Coplay, Pennsylvania.

Today, the industry is considered a basic industry, and the production of portland cement occurs in all regions of the world.

MANUFACTURE OF PORTLAND CEMENT

The manufacture of portland cement requires raw materials which contain lime, silica, alumina, and iron. The sources of these elements vary from one manufacturing location to another, but once these materials are obtained, the process is rather uniform. (See Figure 4–2.)

FIGURE 4–2 Sources of raw materials used in manufacture of portland cement

Lime, CaO	Iron, Fe_2O_3	Silica, SiO_2	Alumina, Al_2O_3	Gypsum, $CaSO_4 \cdot 2H_2O$	Magnesia, MgO
Alkali waste	Blast-furnace flue dust	Calcium silicate	Aluminum-ore refuse*	Anhydrite	Cement rock
Aragonite*	Clay*	Cement rock	Bauxite	Calcium sulfate	Limestone
Calcite*	Iron ore*	Clay*	Cement rock	Gypsum	Slag
Cement-kiln dust	Mill scale*	Fly ash	Clay*		
Cement rock	Ore washings	Fuller's earth	Copper slag		
Chalk	Pyrite cinders	Limestone	Fly ash*		
Clay	Shale	Loess	Fuller's earth		
Fuller's earth		Marl*	Granodiorite		
Limestone*		Ore washings	Limestone		
Marble		Quartzite	Loess		
Marl*		Rice-hull ash	Ore washings		
Seashells		Sand*	Shale*		
Shale*		Sandstone	Slag		
Slag		Shale*	Staurolite		
		Slag			
		Traprock			

Note: As a generalization, probably 50 percent of all industrial byproducts have potential as raw materials for the manufacture of portland cement.
*Most common sources.
Source: Portland Cement Association

As illustrated in Figure 4–3, the process begins with the acquisition of raw materials such as limestone, clay, and sand. The limestone is reduced to an approximately 5-in. size in the primary crusher and further reduced to 3/4-in. in the secondary crusher. All of the raw materials are stored in the bins and proportioned prior to delivery to the grinding mill. The wet process results in a slurry, which is mixed and pumped to storage basins. The dry process produces a fine ground powder which is stored in bins.

Both systems feed rotary kilns where the actual chemical changes will take place. The material is fed into the upper end of the kiln, and as the kiln rotates, the material passes slowly from the upper to the lower end at a rate controlled by the slope and speed of rotation of the kiln. As the material passes through the kiln, its temperature is raised to the point of *incipient fusion* or clinkering temperature where the chemical reactions take place. Depending upon the raw materials, this temperature is usually between 2400°F (1316°C) and 2700°F (1482°C). Chemical recombinations of the raw ingredients take place in this temperature range to produce the basic chemical components of portland cement.

The *clinker* produced is black or greenish black in color and rough textured. Its size makes it relatively inert in the presence of moisture. From clinker storage the material is transported to final grinding where approximately 2 to 3 percent gypsum will be added to control the setting time of the portland cement when it is mixed with water.

The portland cement produced is either distributed in bulk by rail, barge, or truck, or packaged in bags. Bulk cement is sold by the barrel, which is the equivalent of four bags or 376 lb, or by the ton. Bag cement weighs 94 lb ± 3% and is considered to be 1 bulk cubic foot of cement.

The manufacture of portland cement involves the use of many technical skills to ensure a uniform product. Engineers, chemists, and technicians are all employed in the process of determining and controlling the various chemical and physical properties of the cements produced. For practical purposes, Type I portland cement contains the oxides illustrated in Figure 4–4.

CHEMICAL COMPOSITION OF PORTLAND CEMENT

Portland cements are composed of four basic chemical compounds shown with their names, chemical formulas, and abbreviations.

1. Tricalcium silicate $3CaO\ SiO_2 = C_3S$
2. Dicalcium silicate $2CaO\ SiO_2 = C_2S$
3. Tricalcium aluminate $3CaO\ Al_2O_3 = C_3A$
4. Tetracalcium aluminoferrite $4CaO\ Al_2O_3FeO_3 = C_4AFe$

The relative percentages of these compounds can be determined by chemical analysis. Each of the components exhibits a particular behavior, and it can be shown that by modifying the relative percentages of these compounds, the behavior of the cement can be altered.

Tricalcium silicate hardens rapidly and is largely responsible for initial set and early strength. In general, the early strength of portland cement concretes will be higher with increased percentages of C_3S. However, if moist curing is continued, the later strength after about 6 months will be greater for cements with a higher percentage of C_2S.

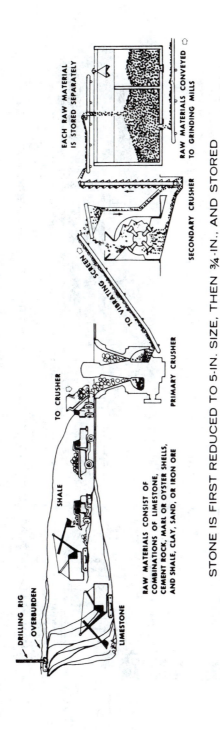

STONE IS FIRST REDUCED TO 5-IN. SIZE, THEN ¾-IN., AND STORED

FIGURE 4-3 Flow chart of manufacture of portland cement (*Courtesy Portland Cement Association*)

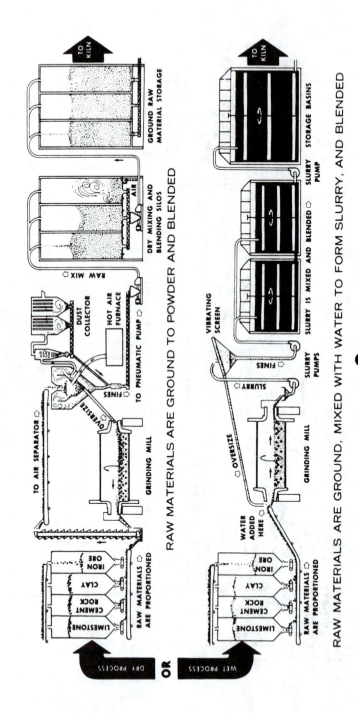

RAW MATERIALS ARE GROUND TO POWDER AND BLENDED

RAW MATERIALS ARE GROUND, MIXED WITH WATER TO FORM SLURRY, AND BLENDED

FIGURE 4-3 (Continued)

150

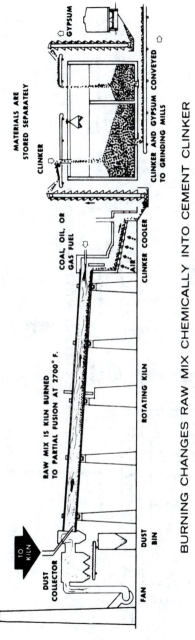

3

BURNING CHANGES RAW MIX CHEMICALLY INTO CEMENT CLINKER

FIGURE 4-3 (Continued)

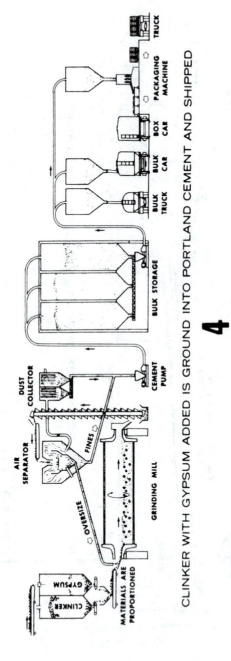

CLINKER WITH GYPSUM ADDED IS GROUND INTO PORTLAND CEMENT AND SHIPPED

FIGURE 4–3 (Continued)

Dicalcium silicate hardens slowly, and its effect on strength increases occurs at ages beyond one week.

Tricalcium aluminate contributes to strength development in the first few days because it is the first compound to hydrate. It is, however, the least desirable component because of its high heat generation and its reactiveness with soils and water containing moderate to high sulfate concentrations. Cements made with low C_3A contents usually generate less heat, develop higher strengths, and show greater resistance to sulfate attacks.

The tetracalcium aluminoferrite compound assists in the manufacture of portland cement by allowing lower clinkering temperature. C_4AFe contributes very little to the strength of concrete even though it hydrates very rapidly.

Most specifications for portland cements place limits on certain physical properties and chemical composition of the cements. Therefore, the study of this material requires an understanding of some of these basic properties.

PHYSICAL PROPERTIES OF PORTLAND CEMENT

One factor which affects the hydration of cement, regardless of its chemical composition, is its *fineness*. The finer a cement is ground, the higher the heat of hydration and resulting accelerated strength gain. The strength gain due to fineness is evident during the first 7 days. For a given weight of cement, the surface area of the grains of a coarse-ground cement is less than for a fine-ground cement. Since the water is in contact with more surface area in a fine-ground cement, the hydration process occurs more rapidly in a fine-ground cement. If the cement is ground too finely, however, there is a possibility of prehydration due to moisture vapor during manufacturing and storage, with the resulting loss in cementing properties of the material. There is evidence to show that in some cases very coarse-ground particles may never completely hydrate.

Figure 4–4 shows the compound composition and fineness of each type of portland cement. Currently the fineness of cement is stated as *specific surface* (i.e., the calculated surface area of the particles in square meters per kilogram m^2/kg of cement). Even

FIGURE 4–4   Chemical and compound composition and fineness of some typical cements

Type of Portland Cement	Chemical Composition (%)						Loss on Ignition (%)	Insoluble Residue (%)	Potential Compound Composition (%)*				Blaine fineness (m^2/kg)
	SiO_2	Al_2O_3	Fe_2O_3	CaO	MgO	SO_3			C_3S	C_2S	C_3A	C_4AF	
Type I	20.9	5.2	2.3	64.4	2.8	2.9	1.0	0.2	55	19	10	7	370
Type II	21.7	4.7	3.6	63.6	2.9	2.4	0.8	0.4	51	24	6	11	370
Type III	21.3	5.1	2.3	64.9	3.0	3.1	0.8	0.2	56	19	10	7	540
Type IV	24.3	4.3	4.1	62.3	1.8	1.9	0.9	0.2	28	49	4	12	380
Type V	25.0	3.4	2.8	64.4	1.9	1.6	0.9	0.2	38	43	4	9	380
White	24.5	5.9	0.6	65.0	1.1	1.8	0.9	0.2	33	46	14	2	490

*Potential Compound Composition refers to the maximum compound composition allowable by ASTM C150 calculations using the chemical composition of the cement. The actual compound composition may be less due to incomplete or altered chemical reactions.
Source: Portland Cement Association

though the specific surface is only an approximation of the true area, good correlations have been obtained between specific surfaces and those properties influenced by particle fineness. Higher specific surfaces indicate finer-ground cements and usually a more active cement.

Soundness is the ability of a cement to maintain a stable volume after setting. An unsound cement will exhibit cracking, disruption, and eventual disintegration of the material mass. This delayed-destruction expansion is caused by excessive amounts of free lime or magnesium.

The free lime is enclosed in cement particles, and eventually the moisture reaches the lime after the cement has set. At that time the lime expands with considerable force, disrupting the set cement.

The current test for soundness in cement is the ASTM Autoclave test. Standard specimens of neat cement paste are subjected to high pressure and temperature for 3 hours. After cooling, the length of bars is compared with the length before testing and cements which exhibit an expansion of no more than 0.50 percent are considered to be sound. Since the introduction of the Autoclave test, there have been almost no cases of delayed expansion due to unsound cements.

WATER-CEMENT REACTION

Hydration is the chemical reaction that takes place when portland cement and water are mixed together. The hydration reaction is considered complete at 28 days. The reaction is dependent upon available moisture. Figure 4–5 indicates strength gains for different curing conditions.

When cement is mixed with water to form a fluid paste, the mixture will eventually become stiff and then hard. This process is called *setting*. A cement used in concrete must not set too fast, for then it would be unworkable, that is, it would stiffen and become hard before it could be placed or finished. When it sets too slowly, valuable construction time would be lost. Most portland cements exhibit initial set in about 3 hours and final set in about 7 hours. If gypsum were not added during final grinding of normal portland cement, the set would be very rapid and the material unworkable.

False set of portland cement is a stiffening of a concrete mixture with little evidence of significant heat generation. To restore plasticity, all that is required is further mixing without additional water. There are cases where a *flash set* is exhibited by a cement, and in this case the cement has *hydrated* and further remixing will do no good. The actual setting time of the concrete will vary from job to job depending upon the temperature of the concrete and wind velocity, humidity, placing conditions, and other variables.

The ability of a cement to develop compressive strength in a concrete is an important property. (See Figure 4–6.) The compressive strengths of cements are usually determined on standard 2-in. (50.8-mm) cubes. The results of these tests are useful in comparing strengths of various cements in neat paste conditions. *Neat paste* is water, cement, and a standard laboratory sand used to standardize tests. The tests will not predict concrete strength values due to the variables in concrete mixtures that also influence strength.

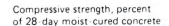

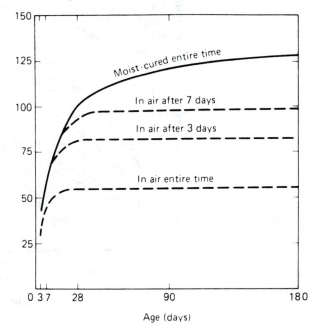

Compressive strength, percent
of 28-day moist-cured concrete

FIGURE 4–5 Strength of concrete continues to increase as long as moisture is present for hydration of cement (*Courtesy Portland Cement Association*)

FIGURE 4–6 Approximate relative strength of concrete as affected by type of cement

Type of Portland Cement		Compressive Strength (Percent of Strength of Type I or Normal Portland Cement Concrete)			
ASTM	CSA	1 day	7 days	28 days	3 mos.
I	Normal	100	100	100	100
II		75	85	90	100
III	High-Early-Strength	190	120	110	100
IV		55	55	75	100
V	Sulfate-Resisting	65	85	100	

Source: Portland Cement Association

    The heat generated when water and cement chemically react is called the *heat of hydration,* and it can be a critical factor in concrete use. The total amount of heat generated is dependent upon the chemical composition of the cement, and the rate is affected by the fineness, chemical composition, and curing temperatures. (See Figure 4–7).

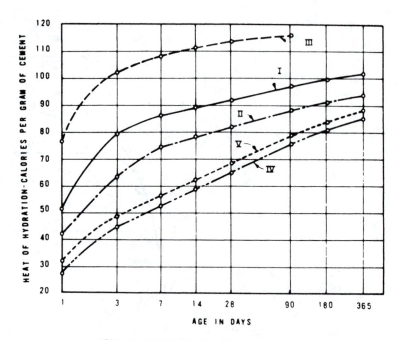

HEAT OF HYDRATION FOR VARIOUS TYPES OF CEMENT

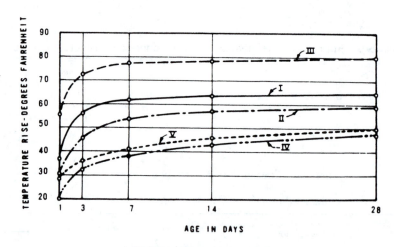

TEMPERATURE RISE OF CONCRETE

Tests of mass concrete with $4\frac{1}{2}$-in. maximum aggregate,
containing 376 pounds of cement per cubic yard in
17-by 17-in. cylinders, sealed and cured in adiabatic
calorimeter rooms

FIGURE 4–7 Heat of hydration and temperature rise for concretes made
with various types of cement. 288-D-118 (*Courtesy U.S. Department of
the Interior, Water and Power Resources Service*)

Approximate amounts of heat generation during the first 7 days of curing using Type I cement as the base are as follows:

Type I	100%
Type II	80–85%
Type III	150%
Type IV	40–60%
Type V	60–75%

Concrete has a low tensile strength; it is approximately 11 percent of concrete's compressive strength. To allow the use of concrete in locations where tensile strength is important or increased compressive strength is required, steel is used to reinforce the concrete. Refer to Figure 4–11 for reinforcing steel sizes. Steel used for reinforcing concrete can be welded wire mesh, deformed reinforcing bars, or cable tendons. Steel has a high strength-to-weight ratio, and its coefficient of thermal expansion is almost the same as concrete's.

Plain reinforced concrete can be used for most construction. The steel is positioned in the form and the concrete placed around it. When the concrete has cured, the materials will be bonded together and act as one.

Prestressed concrete requires the application of a load to the steel before concrete placement. When the concrete has cured, the load is removed from the steel and the concrete is placed in compression. Posttensioned concrete involves the application of a load to the steel after the concrete has cured. Open ducts are left in the concrete through which steel tendons are placed, or plastic-coated steel tendons are draped in the formwork before the concrete is placed. When the concrete has cured, loads are applied to the steel. Posttensioned concrete is versatile because the loads applied to the steel can be changed according to actual conditions of structure loading.

TYPES OF PORTLAND CEMENT

ASTM Type I (Normal)

This type is a general concrete construction cement utilized when the special properties of the other types are not required. It is used where the concrete will not be subjected to sulfate attack from soil or water or be exposed to severe weathering conditions. It is generally not used in large masses because of the heat of hydration generated. Its uses include pavements and sidewalks, reinforced concrete buildings, bridges, railway structures, tanks, reservoirs, culverts, water pipes, and masonry units.

ASTM Type II (Moderate Heat or Modified)

Type II cement is used where resistance to moderate sulfate attack is important, as in areas where sulfate concentration in groundwater is higher than normal but not severe. Type II cements produce less heat of hydration than Type I, hence their use in structures of mass such as piers, abutments, and retaining walls. They are used in warm-weather concreting because of their lower temperature rise than Type I. The use of Type II for highway pavements will give the contractor more time to saw control joints because of the lower heat generation and resulting slower setting and hardening.

ASTM Type III (High-Early-Strength)

Type III cements are used where an early strength gain is important and heat generation is not a critical factor. When forms have to be removed for reuse as soon as possible, Type III supplies the strength required in shorter periods of time than the other types. In cold-weather concreting, Type III allows a reduction in the heated curing time with no loss in strength.

ASTM Type IV (Low Heat)

Type IV cement is used where the rate and amount of heat generated must be minimized. The strength development for Type IV is at a slower rate than Type I. It is primarily used in large mass placements such as gravity dams where the amount of concrete at any given time is so large that the temperature rise resulting from heat generation during hardening becomes a critical factor.

ASTM Type V (Sulfate-Resisting)

Type V is primarily used where the soil or groundwater contains high sulfate concentrations and the structure would be exposed to severe sulfate attack.

Air-Entraining Portland Cements

ASTM C175 governs the air-entraining cements, Types IA, IIA, and IIIA. The three cements correspond to Types I, II, and III, with the addition of small quantities of air-entraining materials integrated with the clinker during the manufacturing process. These cements provide the concrete with improved resistance to freeze-thaw action and to scaling caused by chemicals and salts used for ice and snow removal. Concrete made with these cements contains microscopic air bubbles, separated, uniformly distributed, and so small that there are many billions in a cubic foot.

White Portland Cement

White portland cement is a true portland cement, its color being the principal difference between it and normal portland cement. The cement is manufactured to meet ASTM C150 and C175 specifications. The selected raw materials used in the manufacture of white cement have negligible amounts of iron and manganese oxide, and the process of manufacture is controlled to produce the white color. Its primary use is for architectural concrete products, cement paints, tile grouts, and decorative concrete. Its use is recommended wherever white or colored concrete or mortar is desired. Colored concretes are produced by using a coloring additive, and the white cement allows for more accurate control of colors desired.

Portland Blast-Furnace Slag Cements

In these cements, granulated blast-furnace slag of selected quality is interground with portland cement. The slag is obtained by rapidly chilling or quenching molten slag in water, steam, or air. Portland blast-furnace slag cements include two types, Type IS and Type IS-A, conforming to ASTM C595. These cements can be used in general concrete construction wherever the specific properties of the other types are not required. However, moderate heat of hydration (MH), moderate sulfate resistance (MS), or both are optional provisions. Type IS has about the same rate of strength development as Type I cement, and both have the same compressive strength requirements.

Portland-Pozzolan Cements

IP, IP-A, P, and P-A designate the Portland-Pozzolan cements with the A denoting air-entraining additives as specified in C595. They are used principally for large hydraulic structures such as bridge piers and dams. These cements are manufactured by intergrinding portland cement clinker with a suitable pozzolan such as volcanic ash, fly ash from power plants, or diatomaceous earth, or by blending the portland cement or portland blast-furnace slag cement and a pozzolan.

Masonry Cements

Type I and Type II masonry cements are manufactured to conform to ASTM C91 and contain portland cement, air-entraining additives, and materials selected for their ability to impart workability, plasticity, and water-retention properties to the masonry mortars.

Special Portland Cements

Oil Well Cement   Oil well cement is used for sealing oil wells. It is usually slow setting and resistant to high pressures and temperatures. The American Petroleum Institute Specifications for Oil Well Cements (API standard 10A) cover requirements for six classes of cements. Each class is applicable for use at a certain range of well depths. Conventional portland cements are also used with suitable set-modifying admixtures.

Waterproofed Portland Cements   Waterproofed portland cement is manufactured by the addition of a small amount of calcium, aluminum, or other stearate to the clinker during final grinding. It is manufactured in either white or gray color, and is used to reduce water penetration through the concrete.

MIXING WATER

In the production of concrete, water plays an important role. It is used to wash aggregates, as mixing water, and during the curing process.

The use of an impure water for aggregate washing may result in aggregate particles being coated with silt, salts, or organic materials. Aggregates that have been contaminated by such impure water may produce distressed concrete due to chemical reactions with the cement paste or poor aggregate bonding. In most cases, comparative tests should be run on possible contaminated aggregates.

It is generally accepted that any potable water can be used as mixing water in the manufacture of concrete. Duff Abrams found sea water having a 3.5 percent salt content adequate in producing concrete so that some waters used in concrete making are not potable.

Questionable water may be used for concrete if mortar cubes made with this water have 7- and 28-day strengths equal to at least 90 percent of the strength of cubes made with a known water supply. Impurities in water may also affect setting time and volume stability, and may cause *efflorescence* (the leaching of free lime), discoloration, and excessive reinforcement corrosion. (See Figure 4–8.)

A water source similar in analysis to any of the water in Figure 4–9 is probably satisfactory for use in concrete. The waters represent the approximate compositions of water supplies for most cities with populations over 20,000 in the United States and Canada. The units used to designate foreign matter in water are ppm (parts per million) and designate the weight of foreign matter to the weight of water.

The upper limit of total dissolved solids is usually 2000 ppm. Although higher concentrations are not always harmful, certain cements may react adversely. Therefore, possible higher concentrations should be avoided.

The effects of many common impurities have been well documented in technical literature.

Carbonates and bicarbonates of sodium and potassium affect the setting times of concrete. Sodium carbonate may cause very rapid setting; bicarbonates may either accelerate or retard the set. In large concentrations these salts can materially reduce concrete strength. When the sum of these dissolved salts exceeds 1000 ppm (0.1 percent), tests for setting time and 28-day strength should be made.

Sodium chloride or sodium sulfate can be tolerated in large quantities; waters having concentrations of 20,000 ppm of sodium chloride and 10,000 ppm of sodium sulfate have been used successfully. Carbonates of calcium and magnesium are not very soluble in water and are seldom found in high enough concentrations to affect concrete

FIGURE 4–8   Acceptance criteria for questionable water supplies (ASTM C94)

	Limits	*Test Method*
Compressive strength, minimum percentage of control at 7 days	90	C109*
Time of set, deviation from control (hour:min)	from 1:00 earlier to 1:30 later	C191*

*Comparisons should be based on fixed proportions and the same volume of test water compared to control mix using city water or distilled water.
Source: Portland Cement Association

FIGURE 4–9 Typical analyses of city water supplies and sea water (parts per million)

Chemical	Analysis Number						Sea water*
	1	2	3	4	5	6	
Silica (SiO$_2$)	2.4	0.0	6.5	9.4	22.0	3.0	—
Iron (Fe)	0.1	0.0	0.0	0.2	0.1	0.0	—
Calcium (Ca)	5.8	15.3	29.5	96.0	3.0	1.3	50–480
Magnesium (Mg)	1.4	5.5	7.6	27.0	2.4	0.3	260–1,410
Sodium (Na)	1.7	16.1	2.3	183.0	215.0	1.4	2,190–12,200
Potassium (K)	0.7	0.0	1.6	18.0	9.8	0.2	70–550
Bicarbonate (HCO$_3$)	14.0	35.8	122.0	334.0	549.0	4.1	—
Sulfate (SO$_4$)	9.7	59.9	5.3	121.0	11.0	2.6	580–2,810
Chloride (Cl)	2.0	3.0	1.4	280.0	22.0	1.0	3,960–20,000
Nitrate (NO$_3$)	0.5	0.0	1.6	0.2	0.5	0.0	—
Total dissolved solids	31.0	250.0	125.0	983.0	564.0	19.0	35,000

*Different seas contain different amounts of dissolved salts.
Source: Portland Cement Association

properties. Bicarbonates of calcium and magnesium are present in some municipal water supplies, and concentrations of the bicarbonate of up to 400 ppm are not considered harmful.

Concentrations of magnesium sulfate and magnesium chloride up to 40,000 ppm have been used without harmful effects on concrete strength. Calcium chloride is often used as an accelerator in concrete in quantities up to 2 percent by weight of the cement. It cannot be used in prestressed concrete or in concrete containing aluminum conduit or pipe.

Iron salts in concentrations of up to 40,000 ppm have been used successfully; however, natural groundwater usually contains no more than 20 to 30 ppm.

The salts of manganese, tin, zinc, copper, and lead may cause reductions in strength and variations in setting times. Salts that act as retarders include sodium iodate, sodium phosphate, sodium arsenate, and sodium borate, and when present in amounts as little as a few tenths of 1 percent by weight of cement, they can greatly retard set and strength development. Concentrations of sodium sulfide as low as 100 ppm warrant testing.

Generally, sea water containing 35,000 ppm of salt can be used in nonreinforced concrete, which will exhibit higher early strength with a slight reduction in 28-day strength. The reduction in 28-day strength is usually compensated for in the mix design. Sea water has been used in reinforced concrete; however, if the steel does not have sufficient cover or if the concrete is not watertight, the risk of corrosion is increased greatly. Sea water should never be used in prestressed concrete.

Aggregates from the sea may be used with fresh mixing water since the salt coating would amount to about 1 percent by weight of the mixing water.

Generally, mixing waters having common inorganic acid concentrations as high as 10,000 ppm have no adverse effects on concrete strength. The acceptance of mixing waters containing acid should be based on concentrations of acids in ppm rather than the pH value, since the latter is an intensity index.

Sodium hydroxide concentrations of 0.5 percent by weight of cement do not greatly affect the concrete strength, providing quick set does not occur. Potassium hydroxide in concentrations up to 1.2 percent by weight of cement can reduce strengths of certain cements while not materially affecting strengths of others.

Industrial waste water and sanitary sewage can be used in concretes. After sewage passes through a good disposal system, the concentration of solids is usually too low to have any significant effect on concrete. Waste waters from tanneries, paint factories, coke plants, chemical plants, and galvanizing plants, etc., may contain harmful impurities. As with all questionable water sources, it pays to run the comparative strength tests before using such waters in concrete manufacturing.

Sugar in concentrations of as little as 0.03 to 0.15 percent by weight of cement will usually retard the setting time of cement. There may be a reduction in 7-day strength and an increase in 28-day strength. When the amount of sugar is raised to 0.20 percent by weight of cement, the set is accelerated. When the sugar exceeds 0.25 percent, there may be rapid setting and a reduction in 28-day strength. Water containing an excess of 500 ppm of sugar should be tested.

Clay or fine particles can be tolerated in concentrations of up to 2000 ppm. Though the clay may affect other properties of cement, the strength should not be affected at higher concentrations.

Silty water should settle in basins before use to reduce the suspended silts and clays.

Mineral oils have less effect on strength development than vegetable or animal oils; however, when concentrations are greater than 2 percent by weight of cement, a strength loss of approximately 20 percent or more will occur.

Organic impurities such as algae in mixing water may cause excessive strength reductions by affecting bond or by excessive air entrainment.

As with all of the ingredients used in concrete production, if the water available is questionable, the comparative property tests should be run. Sometimes the concrete mix can be modified to compensate for water which produces low strength or exhibits other adverse characteristics.

The use of water containing acids or organic substances should be questioned because of the possibility of surface reactions or retardation. The other concern with curing water is the possibility of staining or discoloration due to impurities in the water.

AGGREGATES

The aggregate component of a concrete mix occupies 60 to 80 percent of the volume of concrete, and their characteristics influence the properties of the concrete. The selection of aggregates will determine the mix design proportion and the economy of the resulting concrete. It is therefore necessary to understand the importance of aggregate selection, testing, and handling as discussed in Chapter 2.

Aggregates selected for use should be clean, hard, strong, and durable particles, free of chemicals, coatings of clay, or other materials that will affect the bond of the cement paste. Aggregates containing shale or other soft and porous organic particles should be avoided because they have poor resistance to weathering. Coarse aggregates can usually be inspected visually for weaknesses. Any aggregates that do not have adequate service records should be tested for compliance with requirements. Most concrete aggregate sources are periodically checked to ensure that the aggregates being produced meet the concrete specifications.

The commonly used aggregates such as sand, gravel, and crushed stone produce normal-weight concrete weighing 135 to 160 lb per cu ft. Various expanded shales and clays produce structural lightweight concrete having unit weights ranging from 85 to 115 lb per cu ft. Much lighter concretes weighing 15 to 90 lb per cu ft, using vermiculite, pumice, and perlite as aggregates, are called insulating concretes. The use of materials such as barites, limonite, magnetic iron, and iron particles produces heavyweight concretes with weights going as high as 400 lb per cu ft.

Aggregates must possess certain characteristics to produce a workable, strong, durable, and economical concrete. These basic characteristics are shown in Figure 4–10 with their significant ASTM test or practice designation and specification requirement.

The most common test used to measure abrasion resistance of an aggregate is the Los Angeles rattler. A quantity of aggregate is placed in a steel drum with steel balls, the drum is rotated for a preset number of revolutions, and the percentage of material worn away is determined. While the test is a general index of aggregate quality, there is no direct correlation generally with concrete abrasion using the same aggregate. If wear resistance is critical, it is more accurate to run abrasion tests on the concrete itself.

Porosity, absorption, and pore structure determine the freeze-thaw resistance of an aggregate. If an aggregate particle absorbs too much water, when it is exposed to freezing there will be little room for water expansion. At any freezing rate there may be a critical particle size above which the particle will fail if completely saturated.

There are two ways to determine the resistance to freezing-thawing of an aggregate: past performance records, if available, and the freeze-thaw test on concrete specimens containing the aggregates. Specimens are cast and cyclically exposed to freezing and thawing temperatures, with the deterioration measured by the reduction in the dynamic modulus of elasticity of the specimens.

While aggregates are generally considered to be the "inert" component of a concrete mix, alkali-aggregate reactions do occur. Past performance records are usually adequate, but if no records are available or if a new aggregate source is being used, laboratory tests should be performed to determine the aggregate's alkali reactiveness.

Fresh concrete is affected by particle texture and shape more than hardened concrete. Rough-textured or flat aggregates require more water to produce a workable concrete than rounded or cubical, well-shaped aggregates. The National Ready Mix Concrete Association, based upon the use of well-shaped cubical aggregate as the standard, suggests that flat, elongated, or sharply angular aggregates will require 25 lb of water more per cubic yard, thus requiring more cement to maintain the same water-cement ratio. The use of rounded gravel aggregates will usually allow a 15-lb reduction in mixing water, with the resulting reduction in cement, thus producing a savings to the concrete producer. It is recommended that long, flat particles not exceed 15 percent by weight of the total aggregate. This requirement is important when using manufactured sand because it contains more flat, elongated particles than natural sand.

As described in Chapter 2, the method of determining aggregate gradation and maximum aggregate size is by sieve analysis. The grading and maximum size of

FIGURE 4–10 Characteristics and tests of aggregates

Characteristic	Significance	Test Designation*	Requirement or Item Reported
Resistance to abrasion and degradation	Index of aggregate quality; wear resistance of floors, pavements	ASTM C131 ASTM C535 ASTM C779	Maximum percentage of weight loss. Depth of wear and time
Resistance to freezing and thawing	Surface scaling, roughness, loss of section, and unsightliness	ASTM C666 ASTM C682	Maximum number of cycles or period of frost immunity; durability factor
Resistance to disintegration by sulfates	Soundness against weathering action	ASTM C88	Weight loss, particles exhibiting distress
Particle shape and surface texture	Workability of fresh concrete	ASTM C295 ASTM D3398	Maximum percentage of flat and elongated pieces
Grading	Workability of fresh concrete; economy	ASTM C117 ASTM C136	Minimum and maximum percentage passing standard sieves
Bulk unit weight or bulk density	Mix design calculations; classification	ASTM C29	Compact weight and loose weight
Specific gravity	Mix design calculations	ASTM C127, fine aggregate ASTM C128, coarse aggregate	—
Absorption and surface moisture	Control of concrete quality	ASTM C70 ASTM C127 ASTM C128 ASTM C566	—
Compressive and flexural strength	Acceptability of fine aggregate failing other tests	ASTM C39 ASTM C78	Strength to exceed 95% of strength achieved with purified sand
Definitions of constituents	Clear understanding and communication	ASTM C125 ASTM C294	—
Aggregate constituents	Determine amount of deleterious and organic materials	ASTM C40 ASTM C87 ASTM C117 ASTM C123 ASTM C142 ASTM C295	Maximum percentage of individual constituents
Resistance to alkali reactivity and volume change	Soundness against volume change	ASTM C227 ASTM C289 ASTM C295 ASTM C342 ASTM C586	Maximum length change, constituents and amount of silica, and alkalinity

Source: Portland Cement Association

*The majority of the tests and characteristics listed are referenced in ASTM C33. Reference 4-22 presents additional test methods and properties of concrete influenced by aggregate properties.

FIGURE 4-11 Standard rebar sizes and weights

Bar Number	Area (mm²)	Weight (kg/m)	Diameter (in.)	Weight (lb/ft)
3	71	0.559	0.375	0.376
4	127	0.994	0.500	0.668
5	198	1.552	0.625	1.043
6	285	2.235	0.750	1.502
7	388	3.041	0.875	2.044
8	507	3.973	1.000	2.670
9	645	5.059	1.128	3.400
10	817	6.403	1.270	4.303
11	1007	7.906	1.410	5.313
14	1452	11.38	1.693	7.65
18	2581	20.24	2.257	13.60

Source: ASTM A615

aggregates affect relative aggregate proportion as well as cement and water requirements, workability, economy, porosity, and shrinkage of concrete. Variations in grading may seriously affect the uniformity of concrete from one batch to another. Harsh sands often produce unworkable mixes and very fine sands often produce uneconomical concretes. Generally, aggregates that have smooth grading curves, that is, no excesses or deficiencies, produce the most satisfactory results. For workability in leaner mixes, a grading that approaches the maximum recommended percentage passing through each sieve is desirable. Coarse grading is required for economy in richer mixes. Generally, if the water-cement ratio is held constant and if the proper ratio of coarse to fine aggregate is chosen, a wide range in grading may be used with no effect on strength.

Usually more water is required for smaller aggregates than for larger maximum sizes. Conversely, the larger sizes require less water, and therefore less cement, to maintain a constant ratio with its resulting economy. The higher cost of obtaining or handling aggregates in the 2-in.-plus range usually offsets the saving in cement.

Generally, in higher-strength ranges, smaller aggregates will produce higher strengths than larger aggregates.

In certain cases, aggregates that have been gap graded may be used to produce higher strengths in stiff concrete mixes. Close control of gap-graded mixes is required because the variations may produce segregation.

The maximum sizes for coarse aggregates are usually based on the following ACI 211.1 recommendations (refer to Figure 4-11 for rebar diameters):

EXAMPLE

1. One-fifth the minimum dimension of nonreinforced members. Assume a minimum dimension of 15 in.

$$\tfrac{1}{5} \times 15 \text{ in.} = 3\text{-in. maximum aggregate size}$$

2. Three-fourths the clear spacing between reinforcing bars or between reinforcing bars and forms.

Subtract the distance occupied by stirrups, bars, and covers from the total dimension.

$$
\begin{array}{lr}
\text{Width of member} & 14 \text{ in.} \\
\text{Two } \tfrac{1}{4}\text{-in. stirrups} & -\tfrac{1}{2} \text{ in.} \\
\text{Two } 1\tfrac{1}{2}\text{-in. covers} & -3 \text{ in.} \\
\text{Four } \tfrac{3}{4}\text{-in. bars} & -3 \text{ in.} \\
\text{Clear space} & 7\tfrac{1}{2} \text{ in.}
\end{array}
$$

$7\tfrac{1}{2}$ in. divided into 3 spaces $= 3 \; 2\tfrac{1}{2}$-in. spaces

$$\tfrac{3}{4} \times 2\tfrac{1}{2} \text{ in.} = 1.875 \text{ in.} = 1\tfrac{7}{8} \text{ in.}$$

Check cover

$$\tfrac{3}{4} \times 1\tfrac{1}{2} \text{ in.} = 1\tfrac{1}{8} \text{ in.}$$

In this example, cover governs. Select the next lower commercially available aggregate, 1 in.

3. One-third the depth of nonreinforced slabs on grade. Assume a 6-in. slab on grade.

$$6 \text{ in} \times \tfrac{1}{3} = 2\text{-in. maximum aggregate size}$$

If, in the judgment of the engineer, the concrete is workable and can be placed without honeycomb or excessive voids, these requirements may be modified.

The weight of an aggregate per unit volume is called its bulk unit weight because the volume is occupied by aggregates and voids. A known container is filled with aggregate following ASTM C29 and then weighed to find the aggregate's bulk unit weight.

Insulating lightweight aggregates	6–70 lb per cu ft
Structural lightweight aggregates	30–70 lb per cu ft
Normal-weight concrete aggregates	75–110 lb per cu ft
Heavyweight concrete aggregates	110–290 lb per cu ft

The specific gravity is not a measure of aggregate quality, but is used to design and control mixes. The specific gravity is defined as the ratio of the weight of a substance to the weight of an equal volume of water. In the metric system under standard conditions the unit weight of water may be taken as unity; therefore, the weight of a substance in grams per cubic centimeter is equal to its specific gravity. In the English system the unit weight of water, 62.4 lb per cu ft, is divided into the solid unit weight of the substance to find its specific gravity.

For use in concrete design the bulk specific gravity is determined on aggregates in a saturated, surface-dry state. The bulk specific gravity is not the true specific gravity. It is defined as the ratio of the weight of an equal volume of water in air at standard temperatures.

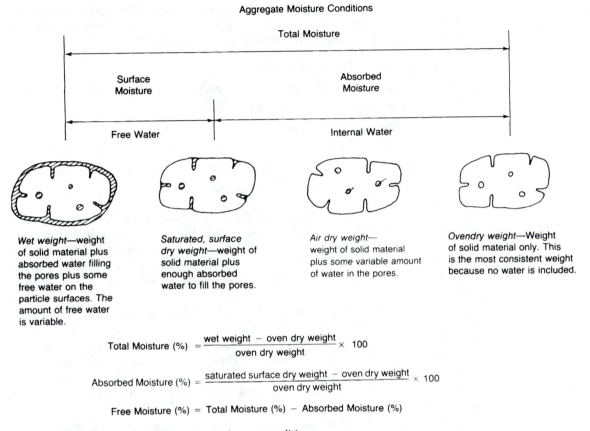

FIGURE 4-12 Aggregate moisture conditions

The moisture content of the aggregate is separated into internal moisture called absorbed moisture and external or surface moisture. Refer to Figure 4-12.

The moisture content of an aggregate must be known so that the batch weights and water content of concrete may be controlled. Some concrete production facilities have automatic equipment to measure moisture conditions of the aggregates and make adjustments in batch weights.

ADMIXTURES

The basic concrete mix design can be modified by the addition of an admixture. *Admixtures* are defined as any material other than portland cement, aggregates, and water added to a concrete or mortar mix before or during mixing. Usually good concrete-mixing practice will impart the qualities that will be required of the concrete when it is placed into service. Very often by using a different type of cement or modifying the mix design desired, property changes can be obtained for special concrete service.

There are times, however, where it is important to modify the design, and the only way of making a change is through the use of an admixture. Admixtures are generally used for one or more of the following reasons (see Figure 4–13):

1. To improve workability of the fresh concrete;
2. To reduce water content, thereby increasing strength for a given water-cement ratio;
3. To increase durability of the hardened cement;
4. To retard setting time or increase it;
5. To impart color to concrete;
6. To maintain volume stability by reducing or offsetting shrinkage during curing;
7. To increase concrete resistance to freezing and thawing.

Most admixtures perform more than one function; for example, when an air-entraining admixture is used, increased resistance to freeze-thaw cycles in the hardened concrete, a reduction in bleedwater, and increased workability in the fresh concrete can be expected. Sometimes the admixture produces an adverse reaction in conjunction with the desired one. For example, some finely powdered workability admixtures tend to increase drying shrinkage.

Since the effectiveness of an admixture varies with the type and amount of cement, aggregate shape, gradation, proportion, mixing time, water content, concrete, and air temperature, it is usually advisable to make trial mixes before using an admixture.

Trial mixes or small sample batches duplicate job conditions as close as possible so that the admixture dosages and results will be close to job expectations. Trial mixes also will allow study of the admixtures' compatibility if more than one admixture is to be used in the concrete.

When deciding whether to use a certain admixture or not, the designer should consider a mix design modification, a comparison of costs between the modification, and the admixture cost including purchase, storage, and batching costs and any adverse reactions that can be expected.

It is advised that any admixture being considered meet or exceed appropriate specifications and that the manufacturer's recommendations be followed.

The most commonly used admixtures today are air-entraining agents, accelerators, retarders, and water reducers. The air-entraining admixtures are covered by ASTM C260; the others are covered by ASTM C494. Although both of the specifications set no limits on chemical composition and are based more upon performance, they require the producer of the admixture to state the chloride content of the product.

The air-entraining admixture is used to increase the durability of concrete by protecting it against freeze-thaw cycle damage. When a concrete has been placed in service and it is subjected to water saturation followed by freezing temperatures, the resulting expansion of the water into ice usually will damage the concrete. By entraining air in concrete to form a microscopic air-void system, the expansion is provided a relief valve system. The air-void system in the hardened concrete paste allows water to freeze, with the empty air voids providing room for the expansion that occurs as water changes to ice.

FIGURE 4–13 Concrete admixtures by classification

Type of Admixture	Desired Effect	Material
Accelerators (ASTM C494, Type C)	Accelerate setting and early-strength development	Calcium chloride (ASTM D98) Triethanolamine, sodium thiocyanate, calcium formate, calcium nitrite, calcium nitrate
Air detrainers	Decrease air content	Tributyl phosphate, dibutyl phthalate, octyl alcohol, water-insoluble esters of carbonic and boric acid, silicones
Air-entraining admixtures (ASTM C260)	Improve durability in environments of freeze-thaw, de-icers, sulfate, and alkali reactivity Improve workability	Salts of wood resins (Vinsol resin) Some synthetic detergents Salts of sulfonated lignin Salts of petroleum acids Salts of proteinaceous material Fatty and resinous acids and their salts Alkylbenzene sulfonates Salts of sulfonated hydrocarbons
Alkali-reactivity reducers	Reduce alkali-reactivity expansion	Pozzolans (fly ash, silica fume), blast-furnace slag, salts of lithium and barium, air-entraining agents
Bonding admixtures	Increase bond strength	Rubber, polyvinyl chloride, polyvinyl acetate, acrylics, butadiene-styrene copolymers.
Coloring agents	Colored concrete	Modified carbon black, iron oxide, phthalocyanine, umber, chromium oxide, titanium oxide, cobalt blue (ASTM C979)
Corrosion inhibitors	Reduce steel corrosion activity in a chloride environment	Calcium nitrite, sodium nitrite, sodium benzoate, certain phosphates or fluosilicates, fluoaluminates
Dampproofing admixtures	Retard moisture penetration into dry concrete	Soaps of calcium or ammonium stearate or oleate Butyl stearate Petroleum products
Finely divided mineral admixtures Cementitious	Hydraulic properties Partial cement replacement	Ground granulated blast-furnace slag (ASTM C989) Natural cement Hydraulic hydrated lime (ASTM C141)
Pozzolans	Pozzolanic activity Improve workability, plasticity, sulfate resistance; reduce alkali reactivity, permeability, heat of hydration Partial cement replacement Filler	Diatomaceous earth, opaline cherts, clays, shales, volcanic tuffs, pumicites (ASTM C618, Class N), fly ash (ASTM C618, Classes F and C), silica fume
Pozzolanic and cementitious	Same as cementitious and pozzolan categories	High calcium fly ash (ASTM C618, Class C) Ground granulated blast-furnace slag (ASTM C989)
Nominally inert	Improve workability Filler	Marble, dolomite, quartz, granite

FIGURE 4–13 (Continued)

Type of Admixture	Desired Effect	Material
Fungicides, germicides, and insecticides	Inhibit or control bacterial and fungal growth	Polyhalogenated phenols Dieldrin emulsions Copper compounds
Gas formers	Cause expansion before setting	Aluminum powder Resin soap and vegetable or animal glue Saponin Hydrolized protein
Grouting agents	Adjust grout properties for specific applications	See Air-entraining admixtures, Accelerators, Retarders, Workability agents
Permeability reducers	Decrease permeability	Silica fume Fly ash (ASTM C618) Ground slag (ASTM C989) Natural pozzolans Water reducers Latex
Pumping aids	Improve pumpability	Organic and synthetic polymers Organic flocculents Organic emulsions of paraffin, coal tar, asphalt, acrylics Bentonite and pyrogenic silicas Natural pozzolans (ASTM C618, Class N) Fly ash (ASTM C618, Classes F and C) Hydrated lime (ASTM C141)
Retarders (ASTM C494, Type B)	Retard setting time	Lignin Borax Sugars Tartaric acid and salts
Superplasticizers* (ASTM C1017, Type 1)	Flowing concrete Reduce water-cement ratio	Sulfonated melamine formaldehyde condensates Sulfonated naphthalene formaldehyde condensates Lignosulfonates
Superplasticizer* and retarder (ASTM C1017, Type 2)	Flowing concrete with retarded set Reduce water	See Superplasticizers and also Water reducers
Water reducer (ASTM C494, Type A)	Reduce water demand at least 5%	Lignosulfonates Hydroxylated carboxylic acids Carbohydrates (Also tend to retard set so accelerator is often added)
Water reducer and accelerator (ASTM C494, Type E)	Reduce water (minimum 5%) and accelerate set	See Water reducer, Type A (Accelerator is added)
Water reducer and retarder (ASTM C494, Type D)	Reduce water (minimum 5%) and retard set	See Water reducer, Type A

FIGURE 4–13 (Continued)

Type of Admixture	Desired Effect	Material
Water reducer—high range (ASTM C494, Type F)	Reduce water demand (minimum 12%)	See Superplasticizers
Water reducer—high range—and retarder (ASTM C494, Type G)	Reduce water demand (minimum 12%) and retard set	See Superplasticizers and also Water reducers
Workability agents	Improve workability	Air-entraining admixtures Finely divided admixtures, except silica fume Water reducers

*Superplasticizers are also referred to as high-range water reducers or plasticizers. These admixtures often meet both ASTM C494 and C1017 specifications simultaneously.
Source: Portland Cement Association

The normal mixing of concrete will entrap a certain percentage of air depending upon aggregate size, temperature, and other variables, but this air is usually in the form of widely spaced large bubbles and under a microscope can be distinguished from entrained air. The ability to handle the expansion of the water is a function of the spacing factor or average distance from any point in the paste to the nearest air void. The recommended spacing factor is 0.008 in. (See Figure 4–14.)

The size of the effective air voids is in the range of 50 to 500 microns, the largest and smallest voids having little effect in protecting the paste.

The actual dosages required to produce a given air content will vary. If excess fines are present, for example, a higher dose of admixture is required to produce the required air content.

Generally, if air-entraining admixtures are used, the water content may be decreased 0.3 to 4 lb per 1 percent of air with the same workability due to the ball bearing action of the air voids. If no reduction in water content is made and cement content is maintained, a decrease in compressive strength of 3 to 4 percent for each 1 percent of air entrained will result.

To accelerate the setting time of concrete, the admixtures used are usually soluble chlorides, carbonates, and silicates, the most widely used being calcium chloride. The general dosage of calcium chloride should not exceed 2 percent by weight of cement, and it should not be used in prestressed concrete because of corrosion. Calcium chloride may be used during the winter to speed up initial setting time to allow earlier finishing. Calcium chloride is not an antifreeze and does not substantially lower freezing temperatures of the concrete. It does, however, get the concrete through its early setting stage faster, and it is during these early stages when freezing will damage the concrete the most. The effects of calcium chloride on the strength of concrete are shown in Figure 4–15.

For concrete placements during warm weather, a retarder is generally used. The retarders are primarily organic compounds such as lignosulfonic acid salts or hydroxylated carboxylic acid salts.

FIGURE 4–14   Effect of production procedures, construction practices, and environment on control of air content in concrete

Variable	Effects	Corrective Action
Admixture metering	Accuracy, reliability of metering system will affect uniformity of air content.	Avoid manual-dispensing gravity-feed system, timers. Positive displacement devices preferred. Establish frequent maintenance and calibration program.
Batching sequence	Simultaneous batching lowers air.	Avoid slurry-mix addition of AEA.*
	Late addition of AEA raises air.	Do not batch AEA onto cement. Maintain uniformity in batching sequence.
Consolidation	Air content decreases under prolonged vibration or at high frequencies.	Do not overvibrate. Avoid high-frequency vibrators. Avoid multiple passes of vibratory screeds.
Finishing	Air content reduced in surface layer by excessive finishing.	Avoid finishing with bleedwater still on surface. Avoid overfinishing. Do not sprinkle water on surface prior to finishing.
Haul time	Long hauls reduce air, especially in hot weather.	Optimize delivery schedules. Maintain concrete temperatures in recommended ranges.
Mixer capacity	Air increases as capacity is approached.	Run mixer close to full capacity, avoid overloading, clean mixer frequently.
Mixing speed	Air increases up to approximately 20 rpm. Decreases at higher speeds.	Avoid high drum speeds.
Mixing time	Central mixers—air increases up to 90 seconds. Truck mixers—air increases up to 10 minutes. Air decreases after optimum time is reached.	Establish optimum mixing time for particular mixer. Avoid overmixing.
Retempering	Air content increases after retempering. Ineffective beyond 4 hours.	Retemper only enough to restore workability. Avoid addition of excess water.
Temperature	Air content decreases with increase in temperature.	Increase AEA dosage as temperature increases.
Transport	Some air (1% to 2%) normally lost during transport. Air lost in pumping and on belt conveyors, especially at higher air contents.	Avoid high air contents in pumped concrete. Do not use aluminum pipelines, dump trucks.

Source: Portland Cement Association
*Air-entraining admixture.
Note: The table information may not apply to all situations.

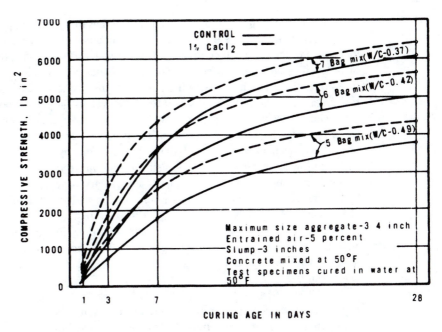

FIGURE 4–15 The effects of calcium chloride on the strength of concrete of different cement contents and at different ages with Type II cement. 288-D-1530 (*Courtesy U.S. Department of the Interior, Water and Power Resources Service*)

For normal conditions the setting time of concrete can be reduced 30 to 50 percent for normal dosages. The use of a retarder during warm weather helps to offset the decreased setting time due to higher placement temperatures. Retarders can also be used to reduce cold joints, allow smaller crews to finish flat work, and permit later control joint sawing. Water reducers are usually retarders that have been modified to suppress or modify the retarding effect.

Superplasticizers or high-range water reducers are chemical dispersants that, when added to a concrete mix with a 3- to $3\frac{1}{2}$-in. slump, can increase the slump to 8 to 10 in. depending on the dosage rate and other mix components. This increase is temporary and with the passage of time the mix will revert to the original slump. The admixtures work by increasing the dispersion of cement particles thereby reducing interparticle friction. The increased dispersion of the cement particles allows for a more complete hydration to take place and as a result higher compressive and flexural strengths are achieved.

Superplasticizers are used to solve difficult placement problems such as tight constricted formwork, dense rebar configurations, and situations where the concrete must be pumped, conveyored, or chuted over long distances.

Microsilica or silica fume is a byproduct of the silicon and ferrosilicon industries. During the production of these materials a silica-based gas is given off. As it rises it cools rapidly into tiny, glassy spherical particles, which are collected in a bag house, a system used to filter the hot gases vented from the submerged electric-arc furnaces.

The chemical makeup of microsilica is similar to fly ash and portland cement in that all three contain the same basic chemical compounds. However, the relative distribution by percent of the chemical compounds is somewhat different. The physical characteristics of microsilica are quite different. Average diameters of particles of microsilica are 100 times finer than cement, the specific gravity of microsilica is 2.2 versus a common 3.15 for cement, and the bulk density is 9 to 25 pcf versus 94 pcf for portland cement.

During the hydration process, two products are formed: (1) calcium silicate hydrate, the glue or binder of the system, and (2) a nonbinder calcium hydroxide, which may occupy as much as a quarter of the volume of the hydration products. The calcium hydroxide, when present in large quantities, may make the concrete more vulnerable to chemical and sulfate attack as well as to adverse alkali-aggregate reactions. The calcium hydroxide can also combine with carbon dioxide to form a soluble salt, which causes efflorescence as the salt is leached out of the concrete.

Microsilica's pozzolanic reaction with calcium hydroxide and water produces more aggregate-binding calcium silicate gel, which improves bonding within the matrix, reduces permeability, and increases compressive and flexural strengths, abrasion resistance, and durability.

ASTM C618 is the standard specification that governs the use of fly ash, a byproduct of the combustion of powdered coal as a mineral admixture. The fly ashes are classified as pozzolanic materials; that is, they possess little or no cementitious value but will, in the presence of moisture, chemically react with calcium hydroxide to form cementitious compounds. The standard describes Class F fly ash as the byproduct of burning anthracite or bituminous coal and having pozzolanic properties. Class C, produced from the burning of lignite or subbituminous coal, has both pozzolanic and some cementitious properties.

The use of fly ash as a mineral admixture or cement substitute is discussed in ACI 211 with examples of the methods used to determine the fly ash content in a properly designed concrete mix.

When concrete is manufactured with the addition of fly ash, its placeability, workability, and pumpability increase because of the ball bearing effect of the microscopic ash particles. Concrete with fly ash will normally take longer to set, thus extending the finishing time, and overall will take longer to reach the desired compressive strength. Since the required strengths are not usually reached at 28 days, it is advisable to prepare enough test specimens to allow for testing at later ages up to 56 days.

PROPORTIONING CONCRETE INGREDIENTS

Since concrete strength is inversely proportional to the water-cement ratio, a reduction in water while maintaining cement content will give an increase in strength. A rule of thumb for good concrete of 0.45 to 0.58 water-cement ratio says that each 0.01 reduction in the water-cement ratio will increase 28-day strength by 100 psi. It also follows that for a given strength, if the water is reduced, then the cement may be reduced with resulting economy.

In higher-strength concretes, the use of a water reducer is required because of the low water-cement ratio being used, 0.30 to 0.35. If concrete of this water-cement ratio is to be workable, a water reducer is required to raise the workability of such a mix.

The determination of the relative amounts of materials required to produce a concrete that will be economical and workable in the plastic state and that will have the required properties in the hardened state is called mix design or proportioning. Proportioning may vary from the simple 1:2:3 formula, which means 1 part cement, 2 parts fine aggregate, 3 parts coarse aggregate, to the ACI 211.1 mix design procedure which is included in the appendix. Some of the proportioning is based on empirical information and some on tests and calculations. What is important is that the concrete to be produced from the initial proportioning satisfies its service requirements. When proportioning concrete, the technician or engineer must look at the entire job. Factors such as mixing apparatus, concrete handling and transportation, finishing, curing, and strength requirements must be considered.

Concrete economy is basically a matter of reducing cement content, since it is usually the most expensive ingredient, without sacrificing the service requirements.

Admixtures such as water reducers have played a part in reducing cement contents while still maintaining required strengths. Cement reductions are also possible by utilizing the stiffest mix placeable, the largest maximum aggregate size, and the proper ratio of fine to coarse aggregates. Generally, labor, handling, and forming costs are the same for varying concretes so that basic savings can only be recognized in the initial design.

The workability of the fresh concrete is an important factor during mix design. Maximum aggregate sizes, water contents, method of transporting, and finishing must be considered here. Concrete that can be placed in slabs on grade with little reinforcing may not be easily placed in heavily reinforced walls or beams. A very stiff concrete that is to be machine finished would be useless to a contractor who must hand trowel a concrete slab.

The service requirements such as strength and exposure must also be considered. All concretes do not have the same strength requirement; mix designs may range from 2000 to 10,000 psi. Exposure conditions may vary from sulfate groundwater conditions to freezing and thawing conditions, but whatever the exposure condition, the mix design must produce concrete to meet the service needs.

Trial batches are usually produced and tested before actual production of concrete begins. A materials testing laboratory usually performs this operation. The laboratory is supplied the mix requirements and samples of materials to be used on the job. Their job is to design the most economical concrete mix that will satisfy the job requirements. One of the problems inherent in this system is the size of the trial mixes, and usually when production begins, adjustments are made in the design.

Concrete proportioning can be performed by trial batching. If the cement ratio is given, the technician can produce a paste (water and cement) for that water-concrete ratio, and vary the fine aggregate and coarse aggregate to produce different aggregate ratios. The batches are usually produced based on past trial batches so that the analysis of all possible combinations is not required. The trial batch that meets the design requirements is then enlarged to job batch sizes, and if it requires further refinement, it can be made when production starts.

Another method used is to base designs on past experience. If the concrete producer has good records, it could possibly supply concrete based on past performance.

A widely used method for mix designs is ACI 211.1, Recommended Practice for Designing Normal and Heavyweight Concrete. The complete procedure will be found in the appendix.

The proportioning of concrete mixes is not an exact science, and human judgment is an important factor to be considered. The technician or engineer will not find all of the mix design solutions in charts and tables, but in a blend of his skill and judgment and the technical information available.

CONCRETE MANUFACTURING

The production of concrete for the job covers a wide range of methods. Concrete can be mixed by hand in small portable mixers, in transit mix trucks, and in large stationary mixers. But no matter how the concrete is mixed, the end result desired is the same—a quality concrete meeting the design requirements. To produce quality concrete, the batching and measuring of ingredients must be done accurately. Therefore, most specifications require that materials be weighed and combined rather than combined by volume. Water is the one ingredient that is usually measured out either way, by weight or by volume. Weighing materials allows for adjustments in moisture conditions, especially in the fine aggregates where bulking can occur due to moisture.

ASTM C94 specifies weight measurements be made to required tolerances. Refer to the appendix for this document.

All weighing equipment should be checked periodically and adjustments made when required. Admixture equipment should be checked daily since overdoses can be very detrimental to quality concrete production. From the discussion on air-entraining admixtures, it can be seen that an overdose here could possibly reduce the concrete strength considerably.

Concrete Mixing

The actual mixing of concrete is performed for the most part by mixing equipment. The mixing equipment is usually rated for two functions: first, the actual mixing of the ingredients to produce concrete, and second, the agitating of already mixed concrete. The agitating capacity is higher than the mixing capacity. The mixing equipment can be stationary, mounted on wheels and towable, mounted on a truck for transit mix, or mounted on crawlers for paving operations.

Stationary mixing equipment can be found on jobs which require large amounts of concrete at steady rates. A good example is a large concrete dam; the amount of concrete required and the steady placement scheduled permit the semipermanent installation. Large highway paving jobs also may utilize stationary mixers. The concrete is produced at one central location and transported to the paving equipment by special agitator trucks or in ordinary dump trucks if conditions permit. The economy of such a system should be evident when comparing the cost of transit mix trucks to dump or agitator trucks. The actual mixing drums may vary from 2 to 12 cu yd and may be placed in tandem so that while one drum is discharging, the other drum is mixing a batch.

The required mixing time of a stationary mixer may vary, but generally 1 minute is required for the first cubic yard and 15 seconds for each additional cubic yard or fraction of a cubic yard. The mixing time is measured from the time all of the solid ingredients are in the drum, provided that all of the water has been added before one-fourth of the mixing time has elapsed. Many of the stationary mixers have timing devices which can be set and locked to prevent the discharge of the concrete before proper mixing time has elapsed.

ASTM C94 specifies mixing time based on drum revolutions. Generally, 70 to 100 revolutions at a rotation rate designated by the manufacturer of the mixer is required to produce uniform concrete. No more than 100 revolutions at mixing speed can be made. All revolutions over 100 must be made at agitating speed. ASTM C94 also specifies that discharge of the concrete shall be completed within $1\frac{1}{2}$ hours or before the drum has revolved 300 revolutions—whichever comes first—after the introduction of the mixing water to the cement and aggregates, or after the introduction of cement to the aggregates.

Concrete Mixing Methods

Stationary mixers are also used by some ready-mix producers. The concrete is mixed at the central yard and delivered to various jobsites in transit mix trucks (Figures 4–16 and 4–17). The trucks are able to deliver more concrete per trip because they are operating at agitating capacity which is higher than mixing capacity.

Many of the stationary mixers in use today are actually portable in that the components are maintained on trailers, and after the job's completion, the plant can be disassembled easily and transported to the next site.

For smaller concrete jobs many contractors will rely on the portable mixer or construction mixer. The capacities of these mixers are generally in cubic feet, and they are used for small concrete placement or when time of placement must be controlled.

The biggest problem with concrete produced with construction mixers is quality control. Most contractors do not bother to weigh batch ingredients, but instead use volumetric batching. While the total cubic yards placed by this method today is rather small, the same care should be exercised by those contractors who still use it as is used in a modern concrete producer's plant.

Paving mixers are concrete mixers mounted on crawler treads. The materials are fed into the mixer from dry-batch trucks, and the machine travels along the finish grade and

FIGURE 4–16 Front-discharge transit mixer (*Courtesy Clemente Latham Concrete Corporation*)

FIGURE 4–17 Mobile concrete dispensers allow the production of custom concrete mixes on site (*Courtesy Cemen Tech, Inc.*)

deposits fresh concrete behind itself to be screeded and finished by the rest of the paving train.

Shotcrete is a nonproprietary term used to describe mortar or concrete that is placed by high-velocity compressed air and adheres to the surface on which it is projected. In the dry-mix process, the dry materials are thoroughly mixed with enough water to prevent dusting. The dry mixture is forced through the delivery hose by compressed air, and the water is added at the mixing nozzle. The wet mix utilizes wet mortar or concrete forced through the delivery hose to the nozzle, where compressed air is introduced to increase the velocity of the material. Because of the velocity at impact, a certain amount of material bounces off the surface of the structure; this material is called *rebound*. With dry-mix shotcrete, rebound may average 30 percent on overhanging surfaces or squaring corners, about 25 percent for vertical surfaces, and on nearly level surfaces about 20 percent. The rebound material must be cleared away from the application area, since it is mostly the sand and coarse particles rather than cement that make up rebound. In fact, the cement content of the shotcrete in place is higher than the cement content of the rebound.

Either sand or coarse aggregate shotcrete can be applied to the surfaces of various materials. The primary uses of shotcrete are in repairing and strengthening existing structures, as protective coatings for structural steel and masonry, in tunnel and canal construction, and in the building of free-form swimming pools.

Shotcrete's strength is usually evaluated by cores removed from sample panels or from the application itself, if the shotcrete is thick enough.

The most familiar concrete production system is ready mix. Ready mix is concrete delivered to the jobsite ready for placement. Ready-mix concrete is produced by one of three methods: central mix, transit mix, and shrink mix. Central-mix concrete is mixed in a stationary mixer at the producer's yard and delivered to the jobsite in a transit mixer operating at agitating speeds, in an agitator truck, or in dump trucks. Transit-mixed concrete is completely mixed in the truck. The ingredients are batched, water is added, and the concrete is mixed in the drum mounted on a truck. Shrink-mixed concrete is a combination of central mix and transit mix, with mixing requirements split between the central plant and the transit truck.

Concrete mixing equipment loads should not exceed rated capacities. When capacities are exceeded to increase production, the quality of the concrete produced is lowered. The interior of the mixing drum should be periodically checked for worn blades and hardened concrete buildup, as both factors decrease mixing efficiency.

The final quality of the concrete produced by a ready-mix supplier is determined by the contractor's operations, which include forming, placing, and curing. This joint involvement in material production can cause problems. If the contractor's placing and curing operations are faulty, concrete which should have met all requirements may not meet job service requirements.

The division of responsibilities generally requires a third party, the materials testing laboratory, to become involved in concrete construction. The materials laboratory will monitor the concrete production, placement, and curing operations by performing ASTM or other specified tests during these operations. Most ready-mix firms have quality control programs to monitor their products' performance. When concrete is produced by any method, jobsite or ready mixed, several basic tests are performed to measure quality. It is advised that the technician read the specifications carefully and note the who, what, when, and where of the tests.

TESTING CONCRETE

It is important that the samples of concrete to be tested be representative samples. If they are not, then the results obtained by testing will not represent the concrete placed. ASTM makes provision for sampling fresh concrete in C172. It spells out procedures for sampling various production systems and specifies a sample size of 1 cu ft except for routine Slump and Air-Content tests. The sample must be tested within 15 minutes and during testing must be protected from the weather.

A major requirement of fresh concrete is *workability*, a composite term used to denote the ease with which concrete can be mixed, transported, placed, and finished without segregation. Workability is a relative term because concrete which satisfies its requirements under one set of conditions may not satisfy its requirements under different conditions. A concrete used in a nonreinforced footing may not be usable in a reinforced wall or column.

A major requirement of fresh concrete is *consistency*, denoted by the fluidity of the concrete as measured by the Slump test. If the slump of a concrete mix is controlled, the consistency and workability necessary for proper placement and indirectly the water-cement ratio can be controlled. Changes in water content have a pronounced effect on slump. A 3 percent change in water content will increase the slump about 1 in. If the surface moisture on the sand changes by about 1 percent, the slump may increase 1 to $1\frac{1}{2}$ in.

In conjunction with slump, the term *workability* is often used to denote the ease with which concrete can be mixed, transported, placed, and finished without segregation. The workability of a concrete mix can be estimated by the Slump test and by observations of the concrete for stickiness and harshness. Wet concretes are usually more workable than dry concretes, but concretes of the same slump may vary in workability depending on the paste and aggregates involved.

The ASTM C143 test for slump of portland cement concrete details the procedure for performing Slump tests on fresh concrete. A slump cone is filled in three layers of equal volume so the first layer is about $2\frac{5}{8}$ in. (76 mm) high, and the second layer is $6\frac{1}{8}$ in. (155 mm) high. Each layer is rodded 25 times with a tamping rod 24 in. (600 mm) long and $\frac{5}{8}$ in. (16 mm) in diameter, with a hemispherical tip with a $\frac{5}{8}$-in. diameter. The rodding is uniformly distributed and is full depth for the first layer and just penetrating previous layers for the second and third layers. If the level of concrete falls below the top of the cone during the last rodding, add additional concrete as required to keep an excess above the top of the mold. Strike off the surface of concrete by a screeding motion and rolling the rod across the top of the cone. In 5 ± 2 seconds, raise the cone straight up. Set the slump cone next to the concrete, and measure the difference in height between the slump cone and the original center of the specimen. With the rod set on the cone, this slump measurement can be read to the nearest $\frac{1}{4}$ in. (6 mm). The test from filling of the slump cone to measuring the slump should take no longer than $2\frac{1}{2}$ minutes. If two consecutive tests on a sample show a falling away of a portion of the sample, the concrete probably lacks the cohesiveness for the Slump test to be applicable.

The *air content* of fresh concrete is a very important value. If a mix design for a certain air content is to meet exposure requirements, that air content must be maintained. As shown in Figure 4–18, if air content decreases, durability decreases; if it increases, strength decreases about 3 percent for each 1 percent of air. There are three field procedures in use today: the ASTM C173 test for air content of freshly mixed concrete by the volumetric system, the ASTM C231 test for air content of freshly mixed concrete by the pressure method, and the ASTM C138 unit weight, yield, and air content (gravimetric) of concrete.

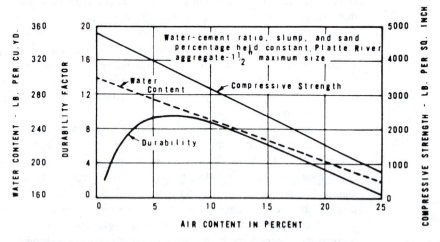

FIGURE 4–18 Effects of air content on durability, compressive strength, and required water content of concrete. Durability increases rapidly to a maximum and then decreases as the air content is increased. Compressive strength and water content decrease as the air content is increased. 288-D-1520 (*Courtesy U.S. Department of the Interior, Water and Power Resources Service*)

The volumetric method can be used with all types of aggregates and is recommended for lightweight or porous aggregates. A sample of concrete is placed in the bowl in three layers, each layer is rodded 25 times, and the side of the bowl is tapped with a mallet 10 to 15 times after each rodding. After filling and rodding, strike off the excess concrete, clean the bowl flange, and clamp the top section onto the bowl. Using the special funnel, fill the top section with water, remove the funnel, and adjust the water level with a syringe until the bottom of the meniscus is at zero. Attach and tighten the screw cap. Invert and agitate until the concrete settles from the base; then rock and roll the apparatus until no further drops in water level occur. Dispel the foam by removing the cap and adding isopropyl alcohol in 1-cup increments. Make a direct reading of the liquid in the neck, reading to the bottom of the meniscus and estimating to the nearest 0.1 percent. The air content is that reading plus the number of cupfuls of alcohol used.

The pressure method cannot be used with lightweight or porous aggregates since the water will be forced into the aggregate's pore structure and erroneous results will be obtained. Correction factors are relatively constant for normal-weight aggregates and, even though small, should be determined and applied when air contents are determined by the pressure method. The pressure method of determining air content is based on Boyle's Law which relates pressure to volume. When the pressure is applied, the air in the concrete sample is compressed. ASTM C231 recognizes two types of apparatus, Meter Type A and Meter Type B.

Operation of the Type A meter involves the introduction of water in a glass tube to a predetermined height above a sample of concrete of known volume and the application of a predetermined air pressure over the water. By observing the reduction in the water level, the percentage of air in the concrete can be read from the glass tube.

The Type B meter involves the equalizing of a known volume of air at a known pressure in a sealed air chamber with the unknown volume of air in the concrete sample, the dial and the pressure gauge being calibrated in terms of percentage of air for the pressure at which equalization takes place.

A nonstandardized test used to measure air content of plastic concrete is the Chace air indicator. The utilization of this simple, inexpensive test is usually restricted to determining the presence of or lack of entrained air in plastic concrete. The testing device consists of a graduated glass tube and a rubber stopper that has a brass cup attached to it. The brass cup is filled with cement paste containing no aggregate particles larger than one-tenth of an inch and inserted into the bottom of the glass tube. The glass tube is filled with isopropyl alcohol up to the zero line and with the thumb held over the open end shaken to remove the air from the mortar. The drop in alcohol level is read and multiplied by a factor based on the mortar content of the concrete mix to determine air content. Because the test is not standardized no concrete should be rejected; however, the load in question should be tested by a standard method to determine its air content.

The unit weight of fresh concrete and yield determinations are covered by ASTM C138. The *unit weight* of fresh concrete is determined in pounds per cubic foot or kilograms per cubic meter, and yield is the number of cubic feet of concrete produced from a mixture of known quantities of materials.

The unit weight determination is made with a standard cylindrical measure which is filled in three equal layers with each layer rodded 25 times. The sides of the container must be rapped 10 to 15 times until no large air bubbles appear and the holes left from rodding have closed. The surface of the concrete must be struck off, the sides of the container cleaned, and the container full of concrete weighed. Subtract the weight of the container from the weight of the container full of concrete and multiply the resulting number by the calibration factor as determined by ASTM C29. The resulting number is the weight of the concrete per cubic foot or cubic meter. The unit weight of concrete is often used as a guide for air contents. If the unit weight falls, it usually indicates that the air content is rising. It is also an indicator of strength for a given class of concrete.

Yield determinations are important in that the volume of concrete being produced for a given batch can be checked. If the total weight of all of the ingredients batched is divided by the unit weight of concrete, the result is the yield in cubic feet.

EXAMPLE

Batch Weights

Water	265 lb
Cement	510
C/A	1917
F/A	1350
	4042 lb total

Unit weight = 149.2 lb/cu ft

$$\text{Yield} = \frac{4042 \text{ lb}}{149.2 \text{ lb/cu ft}} = 27.1 \text{ cu ft}$$

The volume of concrete produced as determined by yield calculations enables a ready-mix producer to check his production, and the contractor can check that he is getting the material he is paying for. The yield calculation can be used to solve disputes concerning the cubic yards of concrete required to fill a set of forms. If the forms move during placement, the yardage required to fill them will increase and the contractor may claim he was shortchanged. If the yield determinations are available, then some problems can be easily solved.

While the tests are being completed on a sample of concrete, the temperature of the concrete should also be taken and recorded, since placement temperature may govern setting times, curing, and strength development. In hot weather, the maximum placement temperature is often limited to 90°F; in cold weather, a minimum temperature of 55 or 60°F is sometimes specified. Refer to ASTM C1064 and C94 in the Appendix.

COMPRESSIVE STRENGTH TESTS

A very important property of hardened concrete is its compressive strength. Compressive strength is the measured maximum resistance to axial loading, expressed as force per unit of cross-sectional area in pounds per square inch (psi).

The designer of a concrete structure selects a desired compressive strength (f'_c) for the concrete. The various parts of the structure are designed so that f'_c, reduced by an appropriate safety factor, is not exceeded. Suitable safety factors for various parts of the structure (beams, columns, floors, etc.) and for various kinds of loads (static, moving traffic, etc.) are determined and published by organizations such as the American Concrete Institute (ACI). The concrete that is placed in the structure is tested at 28 days and evaluated based upon ASTM or ACI criteria to determine that it has the required compressive strength (f'_c).

ASTM C31 is the test procedure for making compressive test cylinders. The standard test cylinder is 6 in. in diameter by 12 in. high for aggregates up to 2 in. For larger aggregates, the diameter should be at least three times the aggregate size and the height at least twice the diameter. The molds used are generally waxed cardboard or plastic, and ASTM C470 is the governing specification.

The test cylinders are filled in three equal layers and each layer rodded 25 times. Concretes of 1- to 3-in. slump may be rodded or vibrated; concretes under 1-in. slump must be vibrated, while concretes over 3-in. slump must be rodded. After the cylinders have been filled, they are struck off level and covered with a glass or steel plate or damp burlap and allowed to set for 24 hours. During the first 24 hours the specimen can be affected by movement, temperature changes, or drying. The cylinders are then moved to proper curing facilities where moist curing will take place for the required time. The strengths of cylinders are generally taken at 7 and 28 days. Figures 4–19, 4–20, and 4–21 indicate strength properties of concrete subjected to different curing conditions. Figure 4–22 represents a typical stress-strain diagram for hardened concrete.

The speed with which construction takes place has cast some doubt on the usefulness of the 7- and 28-day concrete strength tests. If concrete strengths are not adequate in the footings of a building, the engineer may not receive the information until the walls have already been cast on the questionable footing concrete.

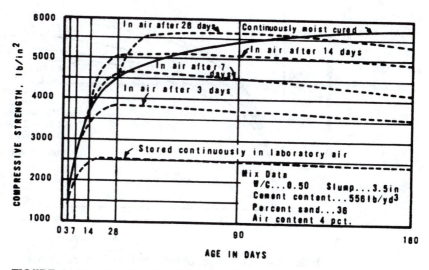

FIGURE 4–19 Compressive strength of concrete dried in laboratory air after preliminary moist curing. 288-D-2644 (*Courtesy U.S. Department of the Interior, Water and Power Resources Service*)

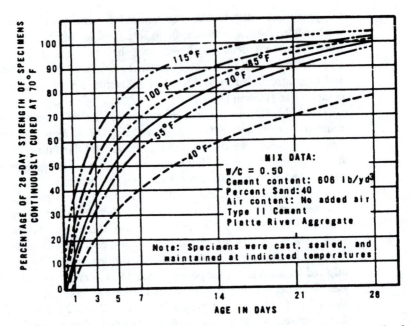

FIGURE 4-20 Effect of curing temperature on compressive strength of concrete. 288-D-2645 (*Courtesy U.S. Department of the Interior, Water and Power Resources Service*)

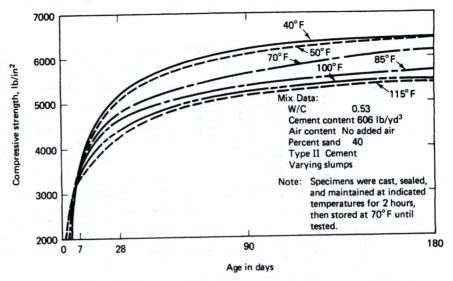

FIGURE 4-21 Effect of initial temperature on compressive strength of concrete. 288-D-2646 (*Courtesy U.S. Department of the Interior, Water and Power Resources Service*)

Accelerated tests are being developed to allow earlier acquisition of strength information. Systems currently being tested or approved include 2-day breaks of cylinders that have been cured in boiling water or in autogenous curing boxes, 5-hour breaks of cylinders cured under heat and pressure, and a system that will chemically analyze plastic concrete before placement for its potential strength. These systems will require extensive correlation testing with 28-day cylinders before they gain wide acceptance. The compressive strength of the concrete is determined by loading the cylinders to failure.

EXAMPLE

Cylinder diameter = 6 in.
Load at failure = 115,000 lb
$$s = P/A$$
s = compressive strength
P = load in lb
A = area in sq in.
$$s = \frac{115,000 \text{ lb}}{28.27 \text{ sq in.}}$$
$$s = 4070 \text{ lb/sq in.}$$

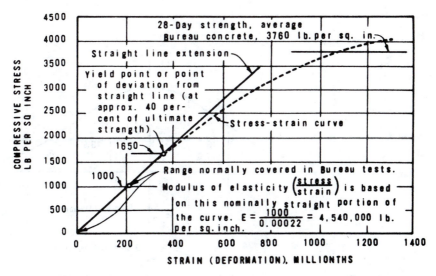

FIGURE 4-22 Typical stress-strain diagram for thoroughly hardened concrete that has been moderately preloaded. The stress-strain curve is very nearly a straight line within the range of usual working stresses. 288-D-799 (*Courtesy U.S. Department of the Interior, Water and Power Resources Service*)

The specimens made under controlled curing conditions are generally the specimens used to judge the quality of the concrete for the job and are called *record cylinders*.

The contractor may have cylinders made and cured under jobsite conditions to determine when forms may be stripped or the structure may be put into service.

The evaluation of compressive strength test results is usually based on ASTM C94 or ACI 214 criteria. The evaluations use statistical methods to determine the adequacy of concrete strengths.

Statistical computations used to control the quality of concrete can be performed manually or by using simple calculators. The results of concrete strength tests will, if plotted, assume the "normal distribution"—that is, the familiar bell-shaped curve (see Figure 4–23). The curve can be described by two characteristics: the mean or average denoted by the letter $\bar{x}$ and the standard deviation denoted by the Greek letter sigma, σ.

$$\text{Mean } \bar{x} = \frac{\Sigma x}{n}$$

$$\text{Standard deviation } \sigma = \sqrt{\frac{\Sigma (x - \bar{x})^2}{n - 1}}$$

where $\bar{x}$ = mean
$\quad x$ = test strength
$\quad n$ = number of tests
$\quad \sigma$ = standard deviation

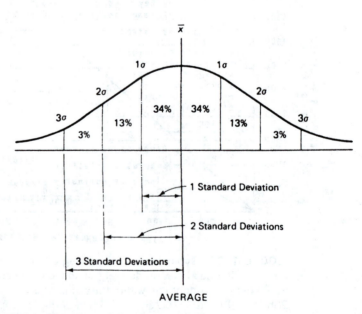

FIGURE 4–23 Normal distribution curve

The smaller the standard deviation, the steeper the curve, indicating results grouped tightly around the mean; the higher the standard deviation, the shallower the normal distribution curve, indicating widespread test results.

Whatever the value of the standard deviation, vertical lines drawn at one, two, and three standard deviations on either side of the mean always include the same proportion of area under the curve. For example, if $\bar{x}$ = 3500 psi and σ = 250 psi, approximately 68 percent of the test results would fall between 3750 and 3250 psi, 94 percent between 4000 and 3000 psi, and almost 100 percent (99.73 percent) between 4250 and 2750 psi.

To measure the degree of uniformity of concrete production at a given concrete plant, the coefficient of variation is usually determined.

$$V = \frac{\sigma}{\bar{x}} \times 100$$

where V = coefficient of variation
σ = standard deviation
$\bar{x}$ = mean

The coefficient of variation is used as a rating for the degree of control the concrete plant has over production variables. If the value of V is low, it indicates a fairly uniform product; conversely, if the value of V is high, the product will not be very uniform.

Direct tests for tensile strength of concrete are seldom made, but a convenient, reliable test to determine indirectly the tensile strength of concrete is in use today. Developed in Brazil and standardized by ASTM, the test gives a splitting tensile strength value which is about 15 percent higher than values obtained through direct tensile tests.

The method utilizes standard 6-by-12-in. cylinders which are loaded along the length of the cylinder. (See Figure 4–24.) The splitting tensile strength is determined by using a formula based on the theory of elasticity.

$$f_t = \frac{2P}{\pi l d}$$

where f_t = splitting tensile strength, psi
P = maximum load, lb
l = length of cylinder, in.
d = diameter of cylinder, in.

When tests are not conducted on concrete specimens, reasonable approximations of tensile and splitting tensile strengths may be obtained using these empirical equations:

$$\text{Tensile strength} = f'_t = 4.5\sqrt{f'_c}$$
$$\text{Splitting tensile strength} = f'_{sp} = 6.5\sqrt{f'_c}$$

Concrete used for pavement slabs is subjected to bending loads, and the flexure strength or modulus of rupture of the concrete is usually determined with 6-by-6 concrete

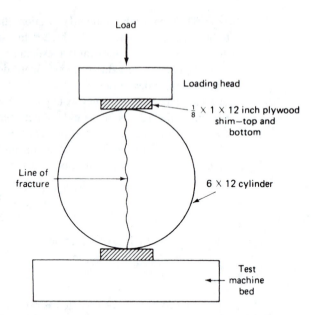

FIGURE 4–24 Splitting tensile test

beam specimens. The test procedure is ASTM C78 and utilizes simple beams with third-point loading. When the full ASTM procedure is not used, an adequate estimate of flexure strength using the compressive strength of the concrete can be determined.

$$R = k\sqrt{f'_c}$$

where R = modulus of rupture, psi
$f'c$ = compressive strength, psi
k = a constant value between 8 and 10

NONDESTRUCTIVE TEST METHODS

The need to determine the in-place strength of concrete occurs frequently in the construction industry. For example, when a building is going to be renovated to serve a new purpose, part of the design procedure may require strength testing of the structure's existing concrete. The other main use of in-place testing is during the construction process where the tests are utilized to monitor and evaluate concrete. In this situation the testing may be used to determine when formwork and/or shoring may be removed safely or to assist in the evaluation of concrete that has not reached design strength requirements. The most widely used in-place test methods are:

1. the rebound hammer,

2. the penetration probe,

3. pullouts, and

4. ultrasound.

Each of the tests used for nondestructive testing has limitations and requires the development of empirical correlations to the standard compressive strength test. Refer to Figure 4–25.

The Rebound Hammer

The impact rebound test ASTM C805 is often referred to as the Schmidt or Swiss Hammer Test. The rebound hammer is held perpendicular to the concrete surface and pushed toward the surface, stretching the internal spring to its limit. At the limit the spring releases and pulls the hammer toward the concrete and the plunger rebounds off the concrete. The plunger is locked in its rebound position, and the rebound number is read and recorded. Ten readings are taken and no two readings should be obtained closer together than 1 in. The ten readings are averaged, and any reading that differs by more than seven from the average is discarded; then average the remaining values. If more than two readings differ from the average by more than seven, discard all ten readings and repeat the test. Most hammers have a graph printed on them that indicates compressive strengths of concrete based on the rebound numbers obtained by test. Even though the test results are not precise, they indicate relative strengths of in-place concrete; that is, for the same class of concrete, higher numbers represent stronger concretes than lower numbers. To obtain more usable information from the rebound test, concrete specimens of the class of concrete are restrained in a compression testing machine while rebound numbers are read from the specimen surface. The specimen is then loaded to failure and a correlation graph is plotted of compressive strength versus rebound numbers.

While the test is simple to perform, the user should be aware of the factors that influence the rebound numbers. One of these factors is that the test is a surface test and may not be representative of the interior concrete conditions. Also, the concrete surface smoothness, surface carbonation, coarse aggregate type, moisture conditions, as well as the age, size, shape, and rigidity of the concrete being tested all have varying degrees of influence on the test results. Despite its limitations, the rebound hammer is still a very useful tool for determining relative strengths and uniformity of in-place concrete materials.

The Penetration Probe

The penetration probe method ASTM C803 is usually referred to by its commercial name, the Windsor Probe. The test uses a powder-activated gun to drive a hardened alloy probe into concrete. ASTM C803 requires that the exit muzzle velocity of the probes have a coefficient of variation no greater than 3 percent based on 10 approved method ballistic tests.

The test procedure can be used on lightweight concretes of less than 125 pcf and normal-weight concretes using different probes. The gold probe has a 56 percent greater cross-sectional area than the silver probe and is used for lightweight concrete. The power setting of low is used for concretes that have an expected compressive strength below 3200 psi and the high power setting for concretes above 3200 psi. The probes are fired into concrete through a triangular template, which allows for the rejection of an anomalous reading, and by shifting the template setting of a new probe. The average penetration of the three probes is measured using a pair of triangular plates attached to the probes. At the completion of the test the probes are removed from the concrete and the

FIGURE 4–25   Comparison among five nondestructive tests

Item to Compare	Test Device				
	Rebound Hammer	Ultrasonic Pulse Velocity	Penetration Probe	Pullout	Pin Penetration
Cost of purchase	Inexpensive	Expensive	Expensive	Expensive	Inexpensive
Cost of operation	Inexpensive	Inexpensive	Expensive	Expensive	Inexpensive
Time required to perform test	About 10 to 20 sec per shot	About 1 to 2 min per reading	About 3 to 4 min per shot	About 2 to 3 min per pull	About 1 min per shot
Appearance of surface of concrete after testing	Leaves an indentation on the surface	Grease used is difficult to remove and leaves stain on concrete	Leaves a small hole, and may cause some minor cracking	Leaves a large hole in the concrete. Damage to the concrete must be repaired	Leaves tiny hole
Surface finish of concrete	Trowelled surface gives higher values than formed surface	Smooth surface is required	Not very important	Not important	Not important
Moisture content of the concrete	Dry concrete gives higher values than wet concrete	Pulse velocity increases with increased moisture content	Dry concrete gives higher value than wet concrete	Dry concrete gives higher value than wet concrete	Dry concrete gives higher value than wet concrete
Temperature	Frozen concrete will give very high values and must be thawed before testing. Temperature of the hammer will also affect the rebound number	Not sensitive to temperature in the range 5 to 30°C. At higher temperatures, the pulse velocity is decreased, and at temperature below freezing it is increased	Not investigated	Not investigated	Not investigated
Effect of carbonation of the surface	Can increase the hardness values by as much as 50 percent	Does not have great effect on the test	Relatively not important	Does not have any effect on the test	Not investigated
Effect of hard aggregate	Different size of aggregate affects the rebound number	Different calibration chart is required with change in source of aggregate	Tends to give higher compressive strength	Sometimes might increase the strength	Minor effect

FIGURE 4–25 (Continued)

Item to Compare	Test Device				
	Rebound Hammer	Ultrasonic Pulse Velocity	Penetration Probe	Pullout	Pin Penetration
Length and size of specimen tested	Small test pieces give consistently lower rebound number and higher scatter of results	Pulse velocity depends on the path length and size of structure is limited by the leads and transducer size	Not suitable for very small structures	Not suitable for very small structures	Minor effect
Existence of steel bars inside the structure	Does not have great effect	Tends to increase pulse velocity	Does not have great effect	Does not have great effect	Does not have great effect
General remarks	Useful in checking the uniformity of concrete and in comparing one concrete against another	Efficient for determining concrete quality	Device must be calibrated for the material tested; also different type of probes are required for different types of aggregate	Gives direct measure of the strength. It is suitable to evaluate existing structures where the concrete quality is suspect	Useful in checking the uniformity of concrete and in determining its quality

Source: The American Concrete Institute

holes patched. Charts designed to adjust compressive strength values based upon Moh's hardness of the coarse aggregate, type of probe, and power setting are used with the average penetration value to determine the compressive strength.

Pullout

The pullout test ASTM C900 is often referred to as the Danish Pullout Test. A steel rod with an enlarged head is cast in the concrete to be tested. When the concrete is ready for testing a tension jack is placed over the protruding steel rod and a tensile force is applied to the rod until failure occurs in the concrete.

The feature of the pullout test is that it produces a well-defined failure and it does measure a static strength property of concrete that can be analyzed. The measured strength value determined by the pullout test can be correlated to the compressive strength of concrete provided that the test configuration and concrete materials are held constant.

Since the standard pullout test requires the inserts to be preplaced in the concrete, their use requires preplanning as to location. This insert requirement also means they cannot be used to test existing concrete; however, at this time various expanding-type anchors are being investigated for use in testing existing concrete.

Ultrasonic

The pulse velocity test ASTM C597 measures the velocity of a sound wave through concrete. The time required for the pulse to travel through the concrete from the transmitter to the receiver is divided into the straight-line distance the signal travels to determine the pulse velocity. The pulse velocity can be correlated to the elastic modulus and mass density of the concrete being tested. The compressive strength can then be empirically inferred from the test results.

The test results are affected by the age of the concrete, moisture content, cracks, voids, and reinforcing steel. The pulse velocity through steel is about 40 percent greater than through concrete. Therefore, if reinforcement bars run parallel to the pulse, the velocity readings will be much higher, indicating a higher compressive strength.

The test method for cores and sawed beam specimens is ASTM C42. The method covers the removal of the concrete specimens from the structure, followed by their preparation and testing to failure. The area of concrete to be tested should be aged at least 14 days to assure adequate bond development between the coarse aggregate and mortar.

The preparation of the specimens before test requires the removal of projections from the ends of the core, checking end diameter values, and correcting any deficiencies by sawing or tooling. The specimens are then submerged in saturated lime water at 73.4 ± 3°F for at least 40 hours prior to test. This requirement may be altered by the specifying authority for the project so that specimens may also be tested at their normal moisture content. The core's length-to-diameter ratio is important. If a capped specimen has an L/D ratio greater than 2.10, it must be trimmed so that the L/D ratio falls between 2.10 and 1.94. When the L/D ratio of a specimen falls below 1.94, a correction factor is applied to the compressive strength. The specification requires that a core having a maximum height of 95 percent of its diameter before capping or a height less than its diameter after capping shall not be tested. Chapter 4 of the Building Code ACI 318 specifies that the average strength of three cores equal at least 85 percent of the design strength $f'c$ and no single core strength fall below 75 percent of the design strength $f'c$. When these criteria are met, the concrete represented by the core tests is considered structurally adequate. Locations represented by erratic core strength tests may be retested to verify testing accuracy. If the conditions of ACI 318 Chapter 4 are not met, then the specifying authority may order load tests as described in ACI 318 Chapter 20 or take other appropriate action. (See Figure 4–26.)

If a load test is required, the test procedures should be performed under the direction of a qualified engineer with experience in structural investigations. The specified total test load shall be 85 percent of the dead and live load design strength required by the code.

The general criterion for acceptance of test load results is that the structure show no visible signs of failure. Visible signs of failure are evidenced by cracking, spalling, or excessive deflections. There are no simple rules developed that apply to all structures and situations, but if sufficient damage is evident no retest is permitted. If no visible signs of damage or failure occur, then the structure's adequacy is governed by deflection recovery.

FIGURE 4-26   Concrete masonry units used here to apply a uniform
load to a roof deck, for deflection testing (*Courtesy American Concrete
Institute*)

Except for obvious failures, the specifying authority may permit the use of a structure at
a lower load rating if based on load test results; the structure is considered safe.

PLACEMENT OF CONCRETE

During the testing of fresh concrete, the contractor's crews will be placing the concrete in
the forms. Depending upon the job conditions, various methods of concrete placement are
utilized. Equipment will vary from simple chutes, wheelbarrows, and buggies to
sophisticated conveyor or pump systems. Figures 4-27 and 4-28 illustrate correct and
incorrect methods of concrete placement utilizing different types of equipment. Regardless of how the concrete is placed, extreme care must be taken to ensure that the concrete
is not changed by transporting it and that it does not become segregated during
placement. *Segregation* or the separation of coarse aggregate from the mortar or the water
from the ingredients can be very detrimental to the quality of the hardened concrete.

One versatile method of handling plastic concrete on many construction sites is the
concrete pump. The concrete pump transports plastic concrete through a pipeline system
from the ready-mix truck to the point of placement without changing the basic
characteristics of the concrete mix.

The normal pumping distances will range from 300 to 1000 ft horizontally or 100
to 300 ft vertically. In some instances, concrete has been successfully pumped over 2000
ft horizontally and 900 ft vertically. Curves, vertical lifts, and harsh mixes tend to reduce
maximum pumping distances. A 90° bend in the pipe is the equivalent of about 40 ft of
straight horizontal line, and each 1 ft of vertical lift is the equivalent of about 8 ft of
horizontal line.

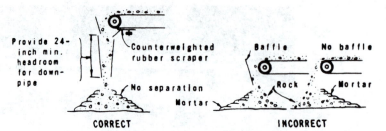

Provide 24-
inch min.
headroom
for down-
pipe

Counterweighted
rubber scraper

No separation

Mortar

CORRECT

The above arrangement prevents
separation of concrete whether
it is being discharged into
hoppers, buckets, cars, trucks,
or forms.

Baffle   No baffle

Rock   Mortar

INCORRECT

Improper or complete lack of control
  at end of belt
Usually a baffle or shallow hopper
  merely changes the direction of
  separation.

CONTROL OF SEPARATION OF CONCRETE AT THE END OF CONVEYOR BELT

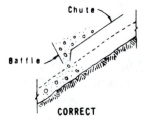   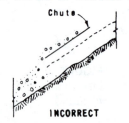

Chute

Baffle

CORRECT

Place baffle and drop at end of
chute so that separation is
avoided and concrete remains
on slope.

Chute

INCORRECT

Concrete discharged from a free
end chute on a slope to be paved.
Rock is separated and goes to bottom
of slope. Velocity tends to carry concrete down slope.

PLACING CONCRETE ON A SLOPING SURFACE

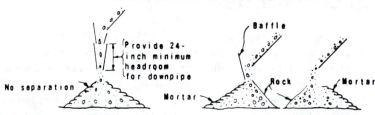

Provide 24-
inch minimum
headroom
for downpipe

No separation

Mortar

CORRECT

The above arrangement prevents
separation, no matter how short
the chute, whether concrete is
being discharged into hoppers,
buckets, cars, trucks, or forms.

Baffle

Rock   Mortar

INCORRECT

Improper or lack of control at end
  of any concrete chute, no matter
  how short.
Usually a baffle merely changes
  direction of separation.

CONTROL OF SEPARATION AT THE END OF CONCRETE CHUTES

This applies to sloping discharges from mixers, truck mixers, etc. as well
as to longer chutes, but not when concrete is discharged into another chute
or onto a conveyor belt.

FIGURE 4–27 Correct and incorrect methods of concrete placement
using conveyor belts and chutes. Proper procedures must be used if
separation at the ends of conveyors and chutes is to be controlled.
288-D-854 (*Courtesy U.S. Department of the Interior, Water and Power
Resources Service*)

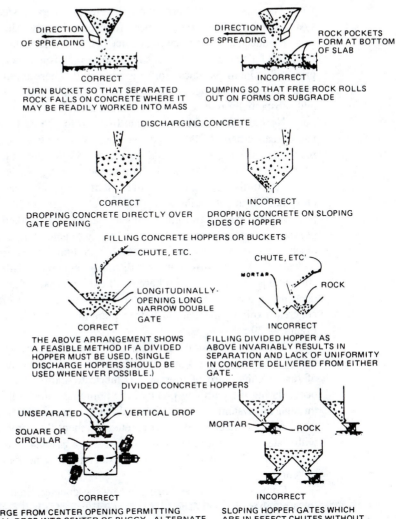

DISCHARGING CONCRETE

FILLING CONCRETE HOPPERS OR BUCKETS

DIVIDED CONCRETE HOPPERS

DISCHARGE OF HOPPERS FOR LOADING CONCRETE BUGGIES

FIGURE 4–28 Correct and incorrect methods for loading and discharging concrete buckets, hoppers, and buggies. Use of proper procedures avoids separation of the coarse aggregate from the mortar. 288-D-3276 (*Courtesy U.S. Department of the Interior, Water and Power Resources Service*)

The pipe used to carry the concrete is generally steel; however, on small pump systems heavy rubber hose has been found satisfactory. Aluminum pipe, which originally was introduced as a labor-saving device because of its light weight, is no longer permitted for most federal and state construction work. (The concrete passing through the pipe grinds aluminum particles from the pipe wall. These aluminum particles, reacting with lime from the concrete, create hydrogen gas, which increases the voids in the concrete and substantially reduces concrete strengths.)

Normal pump capacities range from 10 to 125 cu yd per hour, with special pumps having capacities of 200 cu yd per hour. Aggregate sizes are important; generally, the maximum size aggregate should not exceed 40 percent of the diameter of the pipe if the aggregate has a well-rounded shape. Since ideally shaped aggregates are not always available, further reductions in maximum aggregate size may be require for flat and elongated aggregates. Pumping lightweight aggregate concrete presents no problem, provided that the lightweight aggregate has been presoaked. Without the presoak, pump pressures tend to force water into the aggregate during pumping, and the concrete discharge becomes dry and unworkable. Slump ranges for lightweight concretes run between 2 to 5 in. Most pumps will handle concretes with slumps of 3 to 4 in. In this slump range the concrete discharge will exhibit no segregation. In fact, any concrete that does not segregate before pumping will not tend to segregate during pumping. If a concrete exhibits segregation before pumping, it usually is not a pumpable mix. (See Figure 4–29.)

Before actual pumping begins, the pump lines are lubricated with a concrete mix that contains no coarse aggregate. The amount of mortar used will depend on the length of run. A cubic yard of mortar will lubricate approximately 1000 ft of pipe. If delays occur during the pumping process, the pump operator will have to move some concrete through the system at regular intervals to prevent plugs from forming in the system.

After completion of the concrete placement the pump and lines can be washed out with water. Some lines may require the use of a *go-devil,* a dumbbell-shaped insert placed in the pipe which will push out the concrete, leaving clean interior walls in the pipe system.

Conveyor belts have been used by the concrete industry to move plastic concrete for a number of years. The first successful use of a belt conveyor appears to be a 1929 concrete placement utilizing a 600-ft conveyor to transport concrete on a bridge job. Early belt conveyors had capacities of 30 to 40 cu yd per hour, while today equipment with capacities of up to 300 cu yd per hour is available for massive concrete placements. The volume of concrete transported by a conveyor is determined by the belt width, conveyor speed, angle of incline or decline, and the properties of the concrete mix itself, such as aggregate size and shape, mix proportions, and slump. Conveyors, charging hoppers, transfer devices, and belt wipers generally do not modify any of the important characteristics of the concrete being carried to the placement area. However, if placement is delayed excessively or weather conditions are not optimum, some provision may have to be made to cover the conveyor system.

The conveying system must be properly designed with enough power to start and stop with fully loaded belts during placement delays. The individual sections are designed for high mobility because the delivery of fresh concrete must be continuous over the

FIGURE 4-29 Methods and equipment for transporting and handling concrete

Equipment	Type and Range of Work for Which Equipment is Best Suited	Advantages	Points to Watch For
Belt conveyors	For conveying concrete horizontally or to a higher or lower level. Usually used between main discharge point and secondary discharge point.	Belt conveyors have adjustable reach, traveling diverter, and variable speed both forward and reverse. Can place large volumes of concrete quickly when access is limited.	End-discharge arrangements needed to prevent segregation, leave no mortar on return belt. In adverse weather (hot, windy) long reaches of belt need cover.
Belt conveyors mounted on truck mixers	For conveying concrete to a lower, horizontal, or higher level.	Conveying equipment arrives with the concrete. Adjustable reach and variable speed.	End-discharge arrangements needed to prevent segregation, leave no mortar on return belt.
Buckets	Used with cranes, cableways, and helicopters for construction of buildings and dams. Convey concrete directly from central discharge point to formwork or to secondary discharge point.	Enable full versatility of cranes, cableways, and helicopters to be exploited. Clean discharge. Wide range of capacities.	Select bucket capacity to conform to size of the concrete batch and capacity of placing equipment. Discharge should be controllable.
Chutes	For conveying concrete to lower level, usually below ground level, on all types of concrete construction.	Low cost and easy to maneuver. No power required, gravity does most of the work.	Slopes range between 1 to 2 and 1 to 3 and chutes must be adequately supported in all positions. Arrange for discharge at end (downpipe) to prevent segregation.
Cranes	The right tool for work above ground level.	Can handle concrete, reinforcing steel, formwork, and sundry items in high-rise, concrete-framed buildings.	Has only one hook. Careful scheduling between trades and operations are needed to keep it busy.
Dropchutes	Used for placing concrete in vertical forms of all kinds. Some chutes are one piece, others are assembled from loosely connected segments.	Dropchutes direct concrete into formwork and carry it to bottom of forms without segregation. Their use avoids spillage of grout and concrete on the form sides, which is harmful when off-the-form surfaces are specified. They also will prevent segregation of coarse particles.	Dropchutes should have sufficiently large, splayed-top openings into which concrete can be discharged without spillage. The cross section of dropchute should be chosen to permit inserting into the formwork without interfering with reinforcing steel.

FIGURE 4-29 (Continued)

Equipment	Type and Range of Work for Which Equipment is Best Suited	Advantages	Points to Watch For
Mobile batcher mixers	Used for intermittent production of concrete at jobsite.	A combined materials transporter and mobile batching and mixing system for quick, precise proportioning of specified concrete. One-man operation.	Trouble-free operation requires good preventive maintenance program on equipment. Materials must be identical to those in original mix design.
Nonagitating trucks	Used to transport concrete on short hauls over smooth roadways.	Capital cost of nonagitating equipment is lower than that of truck agitators or mixers.	Concrete slump should be limited. Possibility of segregation. Height is needed for high lift of truck body upon discharge.
Pneumatic guns (shotcrete)	Used where concrete is to be placed in difficult locations and where thin sections and large areas are needed.	Ideal for placing concrete in freeform shapes, for repairing and strengthening buildings, for protective coatings, and thin linings.	Quality of work depends on skill of those using equipment. Only experienced nozzlemen should be employed.
Pumps	Used to convey concrete directly from central discharge point at jobsite to formwork or to secondary discharge point.	Pipelines take up little space and can be readily extended. Delivers concrete in continuous stream. Pumps can move concrete both vertically and horizontally. Mobile pumps can be delivered when necessary to small or large projects. Stationary pump booms provide continuous concrete for tall building construction.	Constant supply of freshly mixed concrete is needed with average consistency and without any tendency to segregate. Care must be taken in operating pipeline to ensure an even flow and to clean out at conclusion of each operation. Pumping vertically, around bends, and through flexible hose will considerably reduce the maximum pumping distance.
Screw spreaders	Used for spreading concrete over flat areas, as in pavements.	With a screw spreader a batch of concrete discharged from bucket or truck can be quickly spread over a wide area to a uniform depth. The spread concrete has good uniformity of compaction before vibration is used for final compaction.	Screw spreaders are usually used as part of a paving train. They should be used for spreading before vibration is applied.

FIGURE 4-29 (Continued)

Equipment	Type and Range of Work for Which Equipment is Best Suited	Advantages	Points to Watch For
Tremies	For placing concrete underwater.	Can be used to funnel concrete down through the water into the foundation or other part of the structure being cast.	Precautions are needed to ensure that the tremie discharge end is always buried in fresh concrete, so that a seal is preserved between water and concrete mass. Diameter should be 10 to 12 in. unless pressure is available. Concrete mixture needs more cement, 7 to 8 bags per cubic yard, and greater slump, 6 to 9 in., because concrete must flow and consolidate without any vibration.
Truck agitators	Used to transport concrete for all uses in pavements, structures, and buildings. Haul distances must allow discharge of concrete within 1 1/2 hours, but limit may be waived under certain circumstances.	Truck agitators usually operate from central mixing plants where quality concrete is produced under controlled conditions. Discharge from agitators is well controlled. There is uniformity and homogeneity of concrete on discharge.	Timing of deliveries to suit job organization. Concrete crew and equipment must be ready on site to handle concrete.
Truck mixers	Used to transport concrete for all uses in pavements, structures, and buildings. Haul distances must allow discharge of concrete within 1 1/2 hours, but limit may be waived under certain circumstances.	No central mixing plant needed, only a batching plant, since concrete is completely mixed in truck mixer. Discharge is same as for truck agitator.	Timing of deliveries to suit job organization. Concrete crew and equipment must be ready on site to handle concrete. Control of concrete quality is not as good as with central mixing.
Wheelbarrows and buggies	For short flat hauls on all types of on site concrete construction, especially where accessibility to work area is restricted.	Very versatile and therefore ideal inside and on jobsites where placing conditions are constantly changing.	Slow and labor intensive.

Source: Portland Cement Association

FIGURE 4-30 Concrete placement using a conveyor system (*Courtesy Morgen Manufacturing Co.*)

placement area without excessive construction joints. Figure 4–30 illustrates a feeder-type belt system which operates in series with end discharge transfer points and a radial discharge conveyor at the point of placement. The radial discharge allows placement through a 360° arc. This type of system has an appreciable setup time and cost; therefore, it is only used on large-volume placements.

On construction projects utilizing pumps or conveyors there tends to be some discussion as to the proper location for concrete testing. Should the tests be performed on the concrete as discharged from the truck into the transporting system, or after the concrete has traveled through the system to the placement area? The general recommendation is to make tests at both locations; if satisfactory correlation can be made, tests may be performed at the most accessible location as long as placement conditions do not change.

Like all materials used in construction, concrete expands and contracts under different conditions of moisture and temperature. To control random cracking, joints must be placed in the concrete to allow cracking to occur at the proper location. Figure 4–31 illustrates the types of joints.

A *control joint* is a cut made into the surface of the concrete. The slab is weakened at that point and cracks should develop in the joint rather than randomly. The joint may be sawed, made with a groover, or formed with divider strips.

The *isolation joint* is designed to physically separate areas of concrete from one another or from columns, poles, and walls; this separation allows for differential settlement. The joint is usually formed with a premolded filler which is left in place just slightly below the concrete surface's tooled edges.

Construction joints are used when concrete cannot be placed continuously. They separate one concrete placement from the next concrete placement. Construction joints should be located in the concrete so that they may act as control joints. Some load-transfer device must be used to carry loads across the joint. Dowels or keyways can be used.

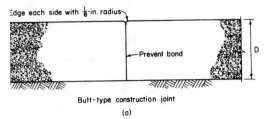

Edge each side with $\frac{1}{8}$-in. radius

Prevent bond

D

Butt-type construction joint

(a)

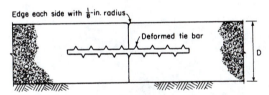

Edge each side with $\frac{1}{8}$-in. radius

Prevent bond

0.1 D

1:4 slope

0.2 D

D/2

D

Tongue-and-groove construction joint

(b)

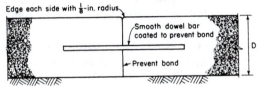

Edge each side with $\frac{1}{8}$-in. radius

Smooth dowel bar coated to prevent bond

Prevent bond

D

Butt-type construction joint with dowels

(c)

Edge each side with $\frac{1}{8}$-in. radius

Deformed tie bar

D

Butt-type construction joint with tie bars
(not a contraction joint)

(d)

Construction joints are stopping places in the process of construction. Construction-joint types a, b, and c are also used as contraction joints.

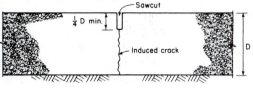

Sawcut

$\frac{1}{4}$ D min.

Induced crack

D

Sawed contraction joint

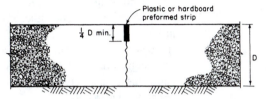

Plastic or hardboard preformed strip

$\frac{1}{4}$ D min.

D

Premolded insert contraction joint

Contraction joints provide for horizontal movement in the plane of a slab or wall and induce controlled cracking caused by drying shrinkage.

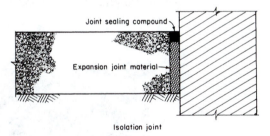

Joint sealing compound

Expansion joint material

Isolation joint

Isolation joints permit horizontal and vertical movements between abutting faces of the slab and fixed parts of a structure.

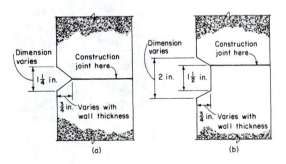

Dimension varies

Construction joint here

$1\frac{1}{4}$ in.

$\frac{3}{4}$ in. Varies with wall thickness

(a)

Dimension varies

Construction joint here

2 in.

$1\frac{1}{2}$ in.

$\frac{3}{4}$ in. Varies with wall thickness

(b)

Horizontal construction joints in walls with V-shaped (a) and beveled (b) rustication strips.

FIGURE 4-31 Joints used in concrete placement (*Courtesy Portland Cement Association*)

After the concrete has been properly placed and consolidated by rodding or vibration and the final screeding operations have been completed, the contractor must apply the proper surface finish and curing system. (See Figure 4–32.)

During concrete placement the contractor must consolidate the plastic concrete. The consolidation must eliminate as far as practical the voids in the concrete. Well-consolidated concrete is free of rock pockets or honeycomb or bubbles of entrapped air and is in close contact with forms, reinforcement, and other embedded items such as anchor bolts and pipe sleeves.

Vibrators may be either immersion or external form-mounted systems powered by air or electricity. The contractor must determine a vibrator pattern and the amplitude and frequency of vibration, as well as the depth of the vibrator into the concrete, to ensure good consolidation. Care must be taken so as not to overvibrate fresh concrete, which will cause the coarse aggregate to settle and leave a wet mortar film at the surface of the concrete placement.

There is considerable evidence to indicate that revibration is beneficial to concrete, provided that the concrete is brought back to a plastic condition. The revibrated concrete exhibits a higher strength and less settlement cracking, and the effects of internal bleeding are reduced.

The finish of a concrete surface may vary from a wood float, broomed finish up to a hard troweled finish. Wood float and broom finishes are usually used on exterior

FIGURE 4–32 Laser screed maintains accurate elevation control while screeding concrete (*Courtesy Somero Enterprises, Inc.*)

FIGURE 4–33 Concrete slip form paver (*Courtesy CMI Corporation*)

flatwork while the trowel finish is an interior finish. Contractors may choose to finish small areas by hand trowels and larger areas by power trowels. The power trowels are usually gasoline powered and have three or four steel blades which rotate on the surface of the concrete (see Figure 4–33).

CURING CONCRETE

Proper curing must begin after surfaces have been worked to proper finish for concrete to adequately gain its design strength, increase its resistance to freeze-thaw, and improve its watertightness and wear resistance. This requires that hydration of the cement be continued. During the curing period, drying shrinkage may occur if the concrete was placed at an excess water content. Figure 4–34 shows the relationship of water content per cubic yard of concrete to drying shrinkage. The continued hydration of the cement requires moisture and favorable temperatures to be maintained for an adequate time. The time required will depend upon type of cement, mix proportions, design strength, size and shape of the concrete structure, and future exposure conditions.

The optimum concrete temperature at placement will vary with conditions, but generally 90°F (32.2°C) is set as the upper limit. To obtain the specified placement temperature in hot weather often requires the use of prechilled aggregates and possibly the substitution of shaved ice for mix water. During cold weather the aggregates and mixing water may be heated to raise the concrete temperature.

During hot-weather concreting, the loss of moisture after placement is critical, and various methods can be used to prevent the moisture loss or to add additional curing water to the concrete. (See Figure 4–35.)

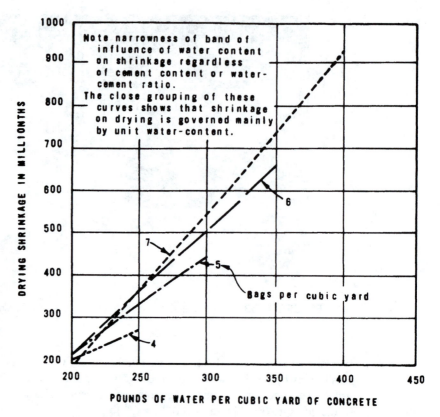

FIGURE 4-34 The interrelation of shrinkage, cement content, and water content. The chart indicates that shrinkage is a direct function of the unit water content of fresh concrete. 288-D-2647 (*Courtesy U.S. Department of the Interior, Water and Power Resources Service*)

Methods used to prevent moisture loss may include the use of waterproof papers, plastic film, and liquid curing compounds which form a membrane and the leaving of forms in place. During hot weather, dark coverings should not be used, as they will absorb the sun's rays.

The additional water methods are by ponding, sprinkling, and using wet coverings such as burlap, sand, and straw. The methods utilized will vary, but care should be taken so that the entire concrete surface is protected, especially corners and edges, and that the material used as a curing system will not stain the concrete.

Cold-weather concreting requires the maintenance of internal heat or the use of additional heat to provide the proper curing temperatures. To maintain internal heat, insulating blankets and straw may be used. The external heat may be supplied by salamanders, space heaters, or live steam. If fuel-burning heaters are used, care must be taken to see that they are properly vented to prevent *carbonation*. The carbon dioxide produced by the combustion of fossil fuels reacts with the calcium hydroxide in the fresh concrete to form a calcium carbonate layer on the surface of the concrete. This surface

FIGURE 4-35 Effect of concrete and air temperatures, relative humidity, and wind velocity on rate of evaporation of surface moisture from concrete. There is no way to predict with certainty when plastic shrinkage cracking will occur. However, when the rate of evaporation exceeds 0.2 lb per square foot per hour, precautionary measures are almost mandatory. Cracking is possible if the rate of evaporation exceeds 0.1 lb per square foot per hour. (*Courtesy of Portland Cement Association*)

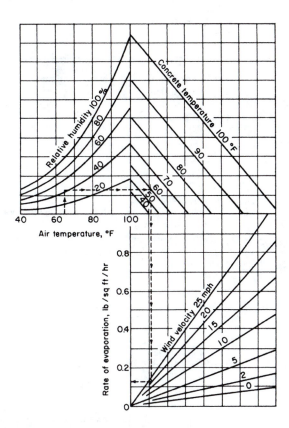

weakness will cause the floor to dust when put into service. Some common materials that come in contact with concrete and their effect on hardened concrete are shown in Figure 4-36.

No two concrete jobs are alike, and the specifications must be checked carefully to determine what will be required for hot- or cold-weather concrete placement and what methods of curing will be allowed.

PRECAST CONCRETE PRODUCTS

Precast concrete products are construction items usually manufactured off site and delivered to the construction site ready for installation into the structure. During the manufacturing process the same quality control measures applied to site-cast concrete are used to ensure the use of quality materials in the production of precast items. Precast concrete pipe, catch basins, septic systems, and structural elements such as beams, columns, and floor units are concrete items that can be precast in standard sizes and shapes and marketed as products ready for installation at the construction site. (See Figure 4-37.)

FIGURE 4-36 Effects of various substances on hardened concrete

Substance	Effect on Unprotected Concrete
Petroleum oils, heavy, light, and volatile	None
Coal tar distillates	None, or very slight
Inorganic acids	Disintegration
Organic materials	
Acetic acid	Slow disintegration
Oxalic and dry carbonic acids	None
Carbonic acid in water	Slow attack
Lactic and tannic acids	Do
Vegetable oils	Slight or very slight attack
Inorganic salts	
Sulfates of calcium, sodium, magnesium, potassium, aluminum, iron	Active attack
Chlorides of sodium, potassium	None*
Chlorides of magnesium, calcium	Slight attack*
Miscellaneous	
Milk	Slow attack
Silage juices	Do
Molasses, corn syrup, and glucose	Slight attack*
Hot distilled water	Rapid disintegration

*Absence of moisture.
Courtesy of U.S. Department of the Interior, Water and Power Resources Services

Precast concrete pipe is classified by the production method utilized to manufacture the pipe. Cast concrete pipe is usually 48 in. in diameter or larger, with varying lengths. The split steel forms stand upright, and the concrete is placed between the inner and outer steel form. The pipe is reinforced with steel rebar and wire mesh. The concrete usually has a 3-in. or less slump and is consolidated by external form-mounted vibrators. Special care must be taken to ensure tight form connections; otherwise, as the concrete is vibrated, objectionable mortar leaks will occur at the joints. The concrete pipe will be removed from the mold and cured, steam or moist curing being used.

The centrifugally spun system is used to produce reinforced pipe 42 in. in diameter or less. The system utilizes a single outside form which can be rotated at high speeds. The concrete is deposited inside the spinning mold by a conveyor belt and compacted by centrifugal force. Variations used to aid compaction are vibration and steel rollers in direct contact with the concrete being placed. The concrete used has a slump of 0 to 2 in. and is deposited in the form to ensure a specified wall thickness with minimum variations. The duration and speed of spinning must be sufficient to prevent the concrete from sagging when the rotation stops. The pipe is cured with the same methods as cast pipe.

Tamped and packerhead pipe are usually nonreinforced concrete pipe made by compacting very dry concrete into steel molds. The mold is split and can be removed as soon as the pipe section is completed without damaging the pipe. The packerhead system utilizes a stationary mold, with the packerhead placing and shaping the interior surface. The tamped system uses a fixed interior cylinder with the outside mold rotating while the

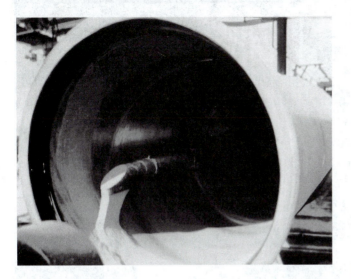

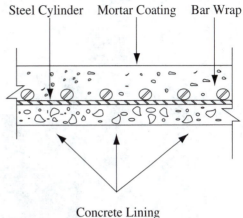

Steel Cylinder   Mortar Coating   Bar Wrap

Concrete Lining

Centrifugal Lining: A measured amount of concrete or cement mortar is fed into the rotating cylinder. After placement, the rotation of the cylinder is increased to the packing velocity and maintained at that velocity until the excess water is removed, resulting in a densely compacted lining with exceptional long-term flow characteristics.

FIGURE 4–37 (*Courtesy of Ameron International® Concrete and Steel Pipe Group, Rancho Cucamonga, California*)

concrete is compacted by vertical tampers. When the pipe unit is completed, the form is removed and moist or steam curing is used to produce required concrete strengths.

Lined cylinder prestressed concrete pipe is used for high-pressure water distribution systems. This pipe is made in stages. The core of the pipe is produced by means of the centrifugal system. When the core has cured, it is wrapped with high-tensile-strength reinforcing steel under tension. Some systems utilize longitudinal steel in tension also. The wrapped core is then coated with mortar and cured to complete the pipe assembly.

Precast structural elements such as beams, columns, and highway median barriers are produced in casting beds of varying shapes and lengths. (See Figures 4–38, 4–39, and 4–40.) The forms or casting beds are usually set with the top of the form at grade; external vibrators are mounted on them. The forms are adjusted to the required dimensions of the finished beam; all required reinforcement is set, and the concrete is deposited in the form. Generally, precast operations attempt a 24-hour turnover or cycle for form use. To aid the initial set of the concrete, external heat is applied to the mold with electric heaters or a pipe system containing heated oil.

Using high-early-strength cements, water reducers, and heated curing, precast plants attain concrete strengths of 3000 psi or more within a 24-hour cycle. The concrete beams cast are removed from the molds and stored on the plant site for delivery when needed, and the casting cycle is repeated.

FIGURE 4–38 Pretied rebar cage being lowered into a highway median barrier form (*Courtesy Fort Miller Co., Inc.*)

FIGURE 4–39 Concrete placement using a bucket and front-discharge ready-mix truck while a materials technician tests the plastic concrete (*Courtesy Fort Miller Co., Inc.*)

FIGURE 4–40 The completed highway median barrier is removed from the form after 24 hours (*Courtesy Fort Miller Co., Inc.*)

Whether site cast or precast, the concrete structure or product must be constructed with careful attention and quality control to ensure a long service life with a minimum of maintenance and repairs.

Concrete as a construction material is a complex subject. In order to deal with it, many organizations have been formed which share technical information with the users of concrete. The serious student of concrete should study the literature of organizations such as the American Concrete Institute, the Portland Cement Institute, the National Ready Mix Concrete Association, and others to keep abreast of new developments and to help understand the behavior of concrete as a construction material.

REVIEW QUESTIONS

1. List the basic types of portland cement, and describe their characteristics and uses.

2. What is the heat of hydration? What factors affect the rate of heat generation?

3. What factors influence the air content of concrete in the plastic state?

4. What are the four basic chemical compounds which make up portland cement, and what effect do they have on portland cement concrete?

5. If water from an untested source is to be used for concrete manufacturing, what test must be made for strength?

6. What are admixtures and what are they used for?

7. What modification is made to concrete to increase its resistance to freeze-thaw damage?

8. Why is concrete such a widely used construction material?

9. What factors are important during hot- and cold-weather concrete placement?

10. What is the maximum aggregate size which can be used in concrete for the following conditions:

a. Nonreinforced walls

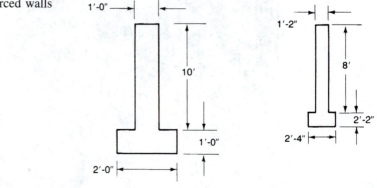

b. Slabs on grade

Portland Cement Concrete

c. Reinforced beams

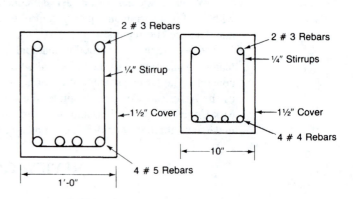

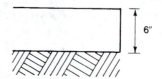

11. What is the difference between the types of air meters used to measure air content of fresh concrete, and why is the difference important?

12. Do the results of the listed strength tests satisfy ASTM C94 requirements? The concrete strength specified was 3000 psi.

3100 psi	3210 psi
2850 psi	2985 psi
3200 psi	3170 psi
2950 psi	2890 psi
3050 psi	2920 psi

13. Calculate the percentage of free moisture on a fine aggregate based on the given data.

Percent absorption = 1.7
Wet weight = 503.7 g
Oven-dry weight = 480.2 g

14. Calculate the mean, standard deviation, and coefficient of variation for the following test data:

3700 psi	2920 psi
4310 psi	3680 psi
3890 psi	4010 psi
4100 psi	3980 psi

15. Determine the yield of the following concrete batches:
    a. γ_{conc} = 147.6 pcf

Water	265 lb
Cement	530 lb
Coarse aggregate	1900 lb
Fine aggregate	1290 lb

b. γ_{conc} = 149.2 pcf

Water	325 lb
Cement	500 lb
Coarse aggregate	1875 lb
Fine aggregate	1330 lb

16. Determine the compressive strengths of:
    a. a 6-in.-diameter concrete cylinder that failed at a test load of 135,000 lb.
    b. a 3-in.-diameter specimen that failed at a test load of 30,000 lb.

17. Design a concrete mix to satisfy the following requirements:
    $f'c$ = 2000 psi

Nonair-entrained   Interior slab on grade
Nonreinforced   Maximum aggregate size = 1 in.

			Aggregate Data		
			Bulk Unit Weight	Percent Moisture	
	Sp. Gr.	F. M.	(pcf)	ABS	Free
CA	2.68	6.00	95	0.5	1
FA	2.59	2.70	105	1	3

18. Design a concrete mix to satisfy the following requirements:

$f'_c = 4000$ psi

Air-entrained	Exterior slab on grade
Nonreinforced	Moderate exposure
	Maximum aggregate size $= 1\frac{1}{2}$ in.

| | | | Aggregate Data | | |
| | | | Bulk Unit Weight | Percent Moisture | |
	Sp. Gr.	F. M.	(pcf)	ABS	Free
CA	2.71	6.10	98	0.4	0.7
FA	2.65	2.80	112	0.9	2.1

19. Design a concrete mix to satisfy the following requirements:

$f'_c = 5000$ psi

Air-entrained	Exterior column
Reinforced	Severe exposure
Slump 5 in.	Maximum aggregate size $= \frac{3}{4}$ in.

| | | | Aggregate Data | | |
| | | | Bulk Unit Weight | Percent Moisture | |
	Sp. Gr.	F. M.	(pcf)	ABS	Free
CA	2.62	6.70	96.5	0.3	0.9
FA	2.58	2.90	111.6	1.2	6.2

20. Design a concrete mix to satisfy the following requirements:

$f'_c = 3000$ psi

| Nonair-entrained | Interior slab on grade |
| Nonreinforced | Maximum aggregate size $= 1$ in. |

| | | | Aggregate Data | | |
| | | | Bulk Unit Weight | Percent Moisture | |
	Sp. Gr.	F. M.	(pcf)	ABS	Free
CA	2.69	6.10	95	0.4	0.7
FA	2.59	2.70	110	0.9	3.0

21. Design a concrete mix to satisfy the following requirements:

$f'c$ = 30 Mpa

Nonair-entrained   Maximum aggregate size = 25 mm
Slump 75 mm

			Aggregate Data		
			Dry-rodded Unit Weight	Percent Moisture	
	Sp. Gr.	F. M.	(Kg/m³)	ABS	Free
CA	2.67	6.70	1545	0.3	0.9
FA	2.63	2.90	1762	1.2	3.1

22. Calculate the modulus of rupture for a 6-by-6-in. square concrete flexure beam with a span length of 18 in. if failure occurs:
   a. within the middle third at a load of 5150 lb.
   b. 0.5 in. outside of the middle third.
   c. 1.2 in. outside of the middle third.
   Refer to ASTM C78 in the appendix.

23. Determine the approximate modulus of rupture of a concrete with a compressive strength of 4100 psi. Assume $K = 9$.

24. A splitting tensile test was performed on a standard 6-by-12-in. cylinder; the cylinder fractured at 49,800 lb. Calculate the splitting tensile strength and the approximate direct tensile strength of the concrete.

25. Three concrete cores were tested in accordance with ASTM C42. Determine the structural adequacy of the concrete if the required $f'c$ = 3500 psi.

Core	Strength (psi)
1	3150
2	2975
3	3220

26. Calculate the compressive strength of a standard concrete test cylinder that has an L/D ratio of 1.25 if failure occurs at 112,900 lb. Refer to ASTM C39 in the appendix.

27. Calculate the quantity of concrete required to place a 40-by-40-ft 6-in.-thick slab in cubic yards and cubic meters.

5

Iron and Steel

Iron in its various forms, including steel, is by far the most important of the metals used in the construction industry. All forms of iron and steel are included in the term *ferrous metals*. They are manufactured to meet a wide variety of specifications for various uses. Chemical composition and internal structure are accurately controlled during manufacturing. Therefore, strength and other mechanical properties can be determined with a high degree of reliability.

Ferrous products are fabricated in shops to desired size and shape. The finished products are ordinarily delivered to a construction site ready to be installed, with inspection and testing completed. Ferrous metals are seldom damaged during transportation because of their strength and hardness. Therefore, people in the construction field have little opportunity to control the quality of iron or steel. Compared to aggregates, asphalt concrete, or portland cement concrete, all of which are partially "manufactured" during installation at the construction site, there is little that can be done to improve or harm a ferrous metal product once it leaves the fabrication shop.

STRUCTURE AND COMPOSITION

Iron and steel appear to be smooth and uniform, yet they consist of particles called *grains* or *crystals* that can be distinguished under a microscope. The grains are formed as the metal passes from the liquid to the solid state. This internal crystalline structure called the *constitution* determines to a great extent what mechanical properties the metal has. Each grain consists of a symmetrical pattern of atoms which is the same in all iron and steel. The grains are not all similar because they press on each other as they form, causing variations in size, shape, and arrangement. The size, shape, and arrangement of grains account for many of the differences in the behavior of various irons and steels.

Some types of iron and steel also contain a different kind of grain interspersed among the typical grains. These have an influence on the material's behavior. The internal structure is determined by the way the metal is cooled and by the way the metal is given its final shape. Grain size, shape, and arrangement are generally the same throughout a finished piece of metal, but special procedures can be used to make them different in different areas of the same piece.

The strength of the metal depends on the cohesion of the atoms in each crystal and the cohesion between adjacent crystals. In this respect, the structure is somewhat like that of aggregate surrounded by adhesive to make concrete. Instead of adhesion holding the crystals or grains together, an atomic bond which is much stronger holds them. Iron and steel therefore have a higher tensile strength than any aggregate-adhesive combination.

Strain of any kind consists of movement of the atoms, closer together in compression or farther apart in tension. Atoms arranged close together allow more stretching or, in other words, more ductility than less-concentrated atomic arrangements. As long as the atoms retain their spatial relationships, even in a distorted way, they return to their original positions when stress is removed. The extent to which the atoms can move and still return to their original positions is the limit of elastic deformation. Beyond this extent, the pattern cannot be distorted without slippage along a plane or parallel planes through the grains. Any distortion in this range is plastic or permanent.

The final temperature and rate of heating do not affect the internal structure at the time materials are melted to make pig iron or when pig iron is melted to make iron or steel. However, the rate of cooling is important. Rapid cooling causes large crystals. Metal with large crystals is more brittle and does not have the strength, ductility, or shock resistance of metal with the smaller crystals caused by slower cooling. However, large

FIGURE 5–1 Ferrous metal properties

Element	Common Content	Effects
Carbon	Up to 0.90%	Increases hardness, tensile strength, and responsiveness to heat treatment with corresponding increases in strength and hardness.
	Over 0.90%	Increases hardness and brittleness; over 1.2%, causes loss of malleability.
Manganese	0.50% to 2.0%	Imparts strength and responsiveness to heat treatment; promotes hardness, uniformity of internal grain structure.
Silicon	Up to 2.50%	Same general effects as manganese.
Sulfur	Up to 0.050%	Maintained below this content to retain malleability at high temperatures, which is reduced with increased content.
	0.05% to 3.0%	Improves machinability.
Phosphorus	Up to 0.05%	Increases strength and corrosion resistance, but is maintained below this content to retain malleability and weldability at room temperature.

Source: "Construction Lending Guide," courtesy U.S. League of Savings Associations

crystals produce better machinability. Any elongation and alignment of grains in one direction increase the strength of the metal to resist stresses in that direction. The means of producing ferrous metals, both the refining with heat and the working into final shape, affect the mechanical properties of the material.

No ferrous metal is pure iron. All include the elements shown in Figure 5–1 which have great effect on the properties of the metal, even if present in very small amounts. Phosphorus occasionally may not be included. Chemical content is determined by the composition of the iron ore, the way in which the metal is heated, and the elements added. Iron ore contains varying percentages of manganese, silicon, and sulfur, and may or may not contain some phosphorus. Carbon comes from the burning coke, and additional carbon may be added to the molten metal. Excess sulfur may be removed by the addition of manganese.

Generally speaking, longer or hotter treatment in a furnace decreases the percentages of carbon, manganese, phosphorus, silicon, and sulfur. Increases are made by adding the desired element to the liquid metal. Other elements also may be added to the liquid metal. These are shown in Figure 5–7.

PRODUCTION OF FERROUS METALS

The first step in the manufacture of iron or steel is to produce a low grade of iron in a continuously operating furnace called a *blast furnace*. These furnaces are about 200 ft high and about 50 ft in diameter. (See Figure 5–2.) Iron ore, coke, and limestone are loaded continuously at the top. Iron ore is an oxide of iron found in nature mixed with rock or soil called *gangue*. Coke is produced by heating coal to drive the impurities out. It then burns with greater heat than coal. Limestone is a type of rock that occurs in nature. Burning the coke and supporting the combustion with a strong blast of hot air melt the iron ore and limestone at a temperature of about 1500°F (815°C). The heat melts the iron, frees it of oxygen, and forms carbon monoxide gas which imparts carbon to the liquid iron.

Melting permits separation of iron from the gangue which combines with the molten limestone to form slag. Iron is much heavier than slag, so there is a natural separation of the two as they melt. Iron flows to the bottom of the furnace and molten slag floats on the iron. Iron is removed from a tap near the bottom and slag from a tap slightly higher. These are removed a half dozen times per 24 hours of operation. Use of the slag as an aggregate is discussed in Chapter 2. The iron flows into molds and is allowed to solidify into shapes called *pigs,* or it is taken in a ladle while still liquid to be refined into steel or a better grade of iron. In either case, the product of the blast furnace is called *pig iron.*

The makeup of the iron resulting from this process is not accurately controlled. It contains about 4 percent carbon, about 2 percent silicon, about 1 percent manganese, and about 0.05 percent sulfur. It may contain up to 2 percent phosphorus depending on the type of ore used.

Pig iron is not useful for construction because it is weak and brittle, although it is very hard. The general term *iron* refers to a ferrous metal that is of a higher quality than pig iron. To produce useful iron or steel, a second melting is needed for further purification. In the future, iron and steel will be produced in one operation, but it is not yet economically feasible.

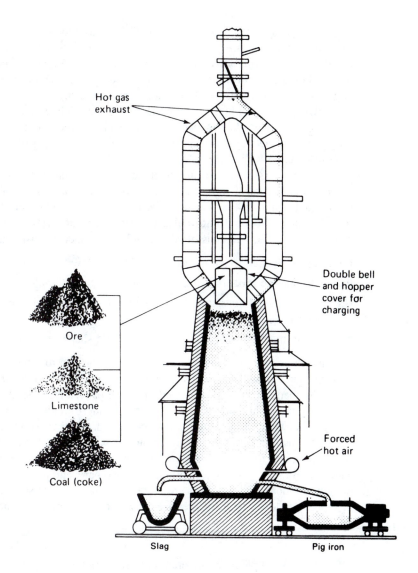

Hot gas exhaust

Double bell and hopper cover for charging

Ore

Limestone

Coal (coke)

Forced hot air

Slag

Pig iron

FIGURE 5-2 Typical blast furnace

Iron

It is possible to refine pig iron until it is nearly pure iron containing little more than traces of impurities. In this form, iron is suitable for construction. It is highly resistant to corrosion, highly ductile, and readily machined. It is drawn into wires and rolled into sheets for roofing, siding, and corrugated pipe. Vitreous enamel coatings adhere well to this type of iron. Despite these qualities, the high cost of refining prevents this type of iron from being one of the major construction materials.

The types of iron more common to the construction industry are gray and white cast iron, malleable cast iron, and wrought iron. *Cast iron* is a general term denoting ferrous metals composed primarily of iron, carbon, and silicon, and shaped by being cast in a mold. They are too brittle to be shaped any other way. The brittleness is caused by the large amount of carbon, which also increases strength.

Wrought iron is highly refined iron with slag deliberately incorporated but not in chemical union with the iron. The slag forms one-directional fibers uniformly distributed throughout the metal. Chemical compositions of various types of iron are shown with cast steel in Figure 5–3.

Pig iron is remelted in small furnaces to make the cast metals. Chemical composition is controlled by the addition of scrap iron or steel of various kinds and of silicon and manganese as needed. The molten metal flows from the furnace to a ladle from which it is poured into molds to be formed into useful shapes. This operation is called *casting*. The materials of which molds are made are listed here:

molding sand: a cohesive mixture of sand and clay.

loam: a cohesive mixture of sand, silt, and clay.

shell mold: a mold consisting of a mixture of sand and resin that hardens when heated prior to the casting.

metal dies: molds machined to the proper mold shape.

The first three types of mold are used once and broken to remove the casting. The dies may be used thousands of times. The first two types are formed around a *pattern* which is usually made of wood. For a shell mold the pattern is made of metal which is heated to solidify the mold material. The size of the pattern in all cases must allow for cooling shrinkage of the casting. Patterns may be reused, whether wood or metal.

The mold material is packed around the pattern, which has been heated in the case of a shell mold. Removal of the pattern leaves a mold of the desired shape. The molds, except a few very simple ones, are made in two parts and placed together for the casting. Sometimes more than two parts are needed and intermediate sections are placed between the upper and lower molds. Cores are inserted to supplement the mold when necessary. A

FIGURE 5–3 Typical composition of ferrous metals

Metal	Typical Composition (Percent)				
	C	Si	Mn	P	S
Cast steel	0.5–0.9	0.2–0.7	0.5–1.0	0.05	0.05
Gray cast iron	2.5–3.8	1.1–2.8	0.4–1.0	0.15	0.10
White cast iron	1.8–3.6	0.5–2.0	0.2–0.8	0.18	0.10
Malleable cast iron	2.0–3.0	0.6–1.3	0.2–0.6	0.15	0.10
Wrought iron	<0.035	0.075–0.15	<0.06	0.10–0.15	0.006–0.015
Pure iron	0.015	Trace	0.025	0.005	0.025
Pig iron	3–5	1–4	0.2–1.5	0.1–2.0	0.04–0.10

typical mold is shown in Figure 5–4. Manhole frames and covers, storm water inlet grates, pump casing, fire hydrants, sinks, and bathtubs are made of iron castings.

Iron is also cast in centrifugal molds which are of cylindrical shape with metal or sand linings. They are spun rapidly as the molten iron is poured, forcing the metal to the outside by centrifugal force and causing it to solidify as a hollow cylinder. Iron pipe for water, sewage, and gas is made this way.

The projections shown in Figure 5–4 must be broken off and machined smooth. After casting, the metal surface has the roughness of the mold material. Even if die cast, the surface is not smooth because of cooling shrinkage. Certain areas of a casting may be required to fit tightly against another surface. These areas must be machined to a smooth finish. Often castings are made in two parts and bolted together. The contact surfaces are machined for a tight fit, and bolt holes are drilled through the flanges of the two castings. (See Figure 5–5.)

Gray cast iron, the most widely used type of iron, has a high carbon content and contains large numbers of graphite flakes. The flakes give a gray appearance to a fractured surface. Properties of gray iron include low viscosity when molten (so that fairly intricate castings can be made), excellent machinability, high resistance to abrasion, and rather poor ductility and toughness. ASTM A48, Gray Iron Castings, contains specifications for gray cast iron.

White cast iron contains its carbon completely combined with the iron. A fractured surface appears bright white. The advantages of white iron over gray iron are that it is

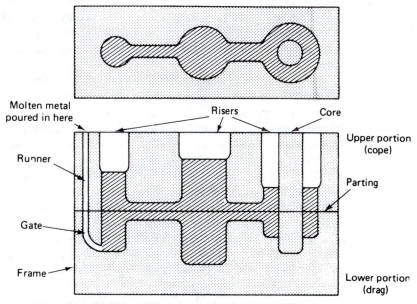

Molten metal in the risers fills the mold as cooling contraction takes place.

FIGURE 5–4 Mold and casting

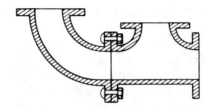

FIGURE 5-5 Cast iron
pipe fittings bolted
together

harder and more resistant to wear from abrasion. However, it is more difficult to machine, less resistant to corrosion, more brittle, and more difficult to cast. By controlling chemical composition and cooling rate, castings with cores of gray iron and surfaces of white iron can be made. These are called *chilled iron* castings. White iron is used in machinery such as crushers, grinders, chutes, and mixers where resistance to abrasion is critical.

Cast iron with the carbon reformed from flakes into tiny spheroids by the addition of magnesium to the molten iron is known as *ductile iron.* The basic nature of the iron is not changed, except that tensile strength, ductility, and the ability to withstand shock loads are greatly increased. Ductile iron pipe is used for water, sewage, and gas.

Malleable cast iron consists of white iron made tough and ductile by *annealing,* which consists of heating to about 1600°F (870°C), holding that temperature for a time, and cooling very slowly to about 1275°F (710°C). This process requires several days. During the entire process, carbon is precipitated from the solution as small lumps in the metal until there is no combined carbon. Some carbon may be allowed to remain combined to increase hardness, strength, and resistance to abrasion. There is then a loss of ductility and toughness. Brittleness is eliminated by removal of carbon from solution, and machinability is improved by the carbon lumps. Malleable iron is used for pipe fittings, guardrail fittings, and other items which require machining and which are subject to shock loads.

Wrought iron is made by refining pig iron in a furnace in a way similar to the refining of steel. The iron silicate slag is melted, and the relatively pure molten iron is poured into the slag. A pasty mixture of the two is formed, with the slag evenly distributed as individual particles. The mixture forms a semisolid ball, which is dumped out and pressed into a rectangular block, squeezing the excess slag out in the process. The block is rolled to the desired shape, aligning the slag as strings or ribbons in the direction of rolling. It is then readily shaped further by drawing, bending, or forging, and can be made into thin, intricate shapes. It is easily welded and machined.

The fibrous structure of wrought iron results in a material with different mechanical properties parallel and perpendicular to the fibers or the axis of the grains. Tensile strength is 10 to 15 percent lower across the fibers than parallel to them, and ductility is only about 20 percent as much. Shearing strength across the fibers is much greater than shearing strength along the fibers. A rod, twisted until it fails in torsion, comes apart along the axis, separating between fibers.

Wrought iron has excellent corrosion resistance which is greater on faces that have been rolled than on sheared or machined faces. Wrought iron pipe is used extensively where corrosion resistance is needed. This type of pipe has threaded joints because wrought iron is easily machined. Cast and ductile iron pipe joints must be of another kind.

FIGURE 5-6
Ornamental wrought iron
grille

Wrought iron is also used extensively for ornamental ironwork, as well as for miscellaneous ironwork where corrosion resistance, machinability, or ductility and malleability are needed. (See Figure 5-6.)

Steel

Pig iron is further oxidized in another furnace at about 3000°F (1650°C) to produce steel. Most steel is made by the basic oxygen process, electric-arc process, open-hearth process, or vacuum process. Each has unique features, but in all cases, pig iron, scrap steel, and sometimes iron ore are melted together with a flux of limestone or lime. The process is a repetition of the blast-furnace operation with variations. The purpose is the same—to remove impurities. Impurities are removed as gases and in the slag.

Phosphorus and sulfur are reduced to less than 0.05 percent of the steel. Manganese content is reduced to an amount from 0.2 to 2.0 percent; silicon from 0.01 to 0.35 percent. The final amounts depend on the specifications for the steel. Carbon is the key element in controlling the properties of ordinary steel called *carbon steel.* Strength and hardness increase with an increase in carbon up to about 1.2 percent. Brittleness increases and ductility decreases as carbon increases. Usually an amount less than 1.2 percent is specified in order to obtain a product satisfactory in all respects.

Carbon in an amount up to 2 percent is completely soluble in molten iron, and when cooled, the mixture forms a solid chemical solution. Carbon in greater amounts forms separate grains of graphite or iron carbide throughout the metal.

Steel is defined as a chemical union of iron and carbon (carbon is, therefore, less than 2 percent by weight) plus other elements. This definition does not exclude every kind of iron. However, almost all iron contains carbon in excess of 2 percent and steel usually contains less than 1.2 percent carbon. Therefore, it is usually obvious whether a ferrous metal is iron or steel. Customary terminology should be used for borderline cases. The term *iron* is used to refer to cast iron, malleable cast iron, ductile iron, wrought iron, or pure iron. As can be seen in Figure 5–3, some of these metals may have less than 2 percent carbon.

Carbon, manganese, silicon, phosphorus, and sulfur are considered impurities because generally they must all be reduced below the amount found in iron ore. However, each one improves the final product when present in the correct amount. In some cases, due to the characteristics of the iron ore, there is a deficiency of one or more of these elements, and they must be added to the molten steel.

Any added element is considered an *alloying element,* but when only these five elements are involved, the steel is not considered an alloy steel. Other elements may be added to impart certain properties to steel. These are also called alloying elements, and the steel that results is called *alloy steel.* See Figure 5–7 for the effects of alloying elements.

Steels are identified according to a classification system of the Society of Automotive Engineers (SAE). Each type of steel is designated by a group of numbers.

FIGURE 5–7   Effects of alloying elements

Element	Amount	Effect
Aluminum	Variable	Promotes small grain size and uniformity of internal grain structure in the as-cast metal or during heat treatment.
Copper	Up to 0.25%	Increases strength and corrosion resistance.
Lead	0.15% to 0.35%	Improves machinability without detrimental effect on mechanical properties.
Chromium	0.50% to 1.50%	In alloy steels, increases responsiveness to heat treatment and hardenability.
	4.0% to 12%	In heat-resisting steels, causes retention of mechanical properties at high temperatures.
	Over 12%	Increases corrosion resistance and hardness.
Nickel	1.0% to 4.0%	In alloy steels, increases strength, toughness, and impact resistance.
	Up to 27.0%	In stainless steels, improves performance at elevated temperatures and prevents work hardening.
Molybdenum	0.10% to 0.40%	In alloy steels, increases toughness and hardenability.
	Up to 4.0%	In stainless steels, increases corrosion resistance and strength retention at high temperatures.
Tungsten	17% to 20%	In tool steels, promotes hardness at high cutting temperatures; in stainless steels, smaller amounts assure strength retention at high temperatures.
Vanadium	0.15% to 0.20%	Promotes small grain size and uniformity of internal grain structure in the as-cast metal or during heat treatment; improves resistance to thermal fatigue and shock.
Tellurium	Up to 0.05%	Improves machinability when added to leaded steels.
Titanium	Variable	Prevents loss of effective chromium through carbide precipitation in "18-8" stainless steels.
Cobalt	17.0% to 36.0%	Increases magnetic properties of alloy steels. In smaller amounts, promotes strength at high temperatures in heat resisting steels.

Source: "Construction Lending Guide" courtesy U.S. League of Savings Associations

The first digit indicates the class of steel. For example, carbon steel is designated by No. 1 and nickel steel by No. 2. The next one or two digits indicate the approximate percentage of the major alloying element for alloy steels. The last two or three digits indicate the carbon content in hundredths of a percent. The classification system is outlined in Figure 5–8.

Besides the key information shown directly by the classification number, percentage ranges for all impurities and alloying elements are also designated indirectly when the system is used. The system provides a simplified way to specify steel. For example, a 1018 steel is a carbon steel containing 0.15 to 0.20 percent carbon, 0.60 to 0.90 percent manganese, 0.040 maximum percent phosphorus, and 0.050 maximum percent sulfur; and 4320 steel is a molybdenum steel containing 0.17 to 0.22 percent carbon, 0.45 to 0.65 percent manganese, 0.040 percent phosphorus, 0.040 percent sulfur, 0.20 to 0.35 percent silicon, 1.65 to 2.00 percent nickel, 0.40 to 0.60 percent chromium, and 0.20 to 0.30 percent molybdenum.

The American Iron and Steel Institute has adopted the SAE system with some variations and has added letter prefixes to designate the steel-making process used and other letters to designate special conditions. These designations are also shown in Figure 5–8.

Figure 5–14 shows the American Institute of Steel Construction, Inc. (AISC) system of designating structural steel. Each steel is known by the number of the ASTM standard that describes it. However, manufacturers may call them by trade names. The figure shows which rolled plates, bars, and shapes are made of each type of steel. As an example, it can be seen that A529 steel is carbon steel with a yield stress of 42 Ksi or more and ultimate tensile stress of 60 to 85 Ksi, and that only shapes listed in group 1, table A of ASTM A6 and plates and bars up to $\frac{1}{2}$ in. thickness are manufactured. ASTM A529 specifies manufacturing methods, chemical content, and mechanical properties required of steel to be supplied when A529 steel is specified.

The chemical composition of steel is determined by the composition of the materials used, the temperature, the length of time in the furnace, the medium surrounding the steel (whether air, oxygen, or vacuum), and whether open flame or heat. The surrounding medium depends on the process used, and the other variables can be controlled for each process. The steel is tested at intervals during the process, and adjustments are made. Alloying elements are added just before the melt is tapped to flow from the furnace to a ladle. The steel may be poured directly from the ladle into molds to make castings. Steel castings are made the same way and used for the same purposes as iron castings. Steel is stronger and tougher, but more expensive.

Most of the steel is poured into ingot molds prior to further shaping. The ingots are of various sizes and shapes, depending on future plans for them. Their weight ranges from hundreds of pounds to many tons. They are tall compared to their cross sections, which are square or rectangular. A common size is about 6 ft tall with a cross section 2 ft by 2 ft and a weight over 4 tons. An ingot is cooled to a uniform temperature throughout in a *soaking pit,* which is a furnace where the steel temperature is allowed to decrease to about 2300°F (1260°C). It is then taken to a mill to be given its final shape.

Steel properties are influenced to a great extent by the mechanical operations that change an ingot of steel into a useful shape. The operations are rolling, extruding, drawing, forging, and casting. All except casting may be performed while the steel is in

FIGURE 5–8 Classification of steels (SAE and AISI)

SAE Classification System

Carbon steels	1xxx
Plain carbon	10xx
Free-cutting (screw stock)	11xx
Free-cutting, manganese	X13xx*
High-manganese	T13xx**
Nickel steels	2xxx
0.50% nickel	20xx
1.50% nickel	21xx
3.50% nickel	23xx
5.00% nickel	25xx
Nickel-chromium steels	3xxx
1.25% nickel, 0.60% chromium	31xx
1.75% nickel, 1.00% chromium	32xx
3.50% nickel, 1.50% chromium	33xx
3.00% nickel, 0.80% chromium	34xx
Corrosion- and heat-resisting steels	30xxx
Molybdenum steels	4xxx
Chromium	41xx
Chromium-nickel	43xx
Nickel	46xx and 48xx
Chromium steels	5xxx
Low-chromium	51xx
Medium-chromium	52xxx
Chromium-vanadium steels	6xxx
Tungsten steels	7xxx and 7xxxx
Triple-alloy steels	8xxx
Silicon-manganese steels	9xxx

---

*X indicates manganese or sulfur content has been varied from the standard for that number.
**T indicates manganese content has been varied in 1300 range steels.

Additional Symbols Used in AISI System

10xx	Basic open-hearth and acid Bessemer carbon steel grades, nonsulfurized and nonphosphorized.
11xx	Basic open-hearth and acid Bessemer carbon steel grades, sulfurized but not phosphorized.
12xx	Basic open-hearth carbon steel grades, phosphorized.

Prefix	
B	Acid Bessemer carbon steel.
C	Basic open-hearth carbon steel.
CB	Either acid Bessemer or basic open-hearth carbon steel at the option of the manufacturer.
D	Acid open-hearth carbon steel.
E	Electric furnace alloy steel.

---

a plastic condition at a temperature of about 2000°F (1090°C), or as low as room temperature. The operations are called *hot working* or *cold working.*

Hot working breaks up coarse grains and increases density by closing tiny air holes and forcing the grains closer together. Cold working elongates grains in the direction of the steel elongation, increases strength and hardness, and decreases ductility. Cold working results in more accurately finished products, because there is no cooling shrinkage to be estimated. The surfaces are smoother, because oxide scale does not form as it does during hot working. Overworking, whether hot or cold, causes brittleness.

For all but very large objects, working to final shape is done in two stages. The first stage consists of squeezing the ingot into a smaller cross section between two rollers, called *blooming rolls,* which exert a very high pressure. This operation is always performed while the steel is hot. The ingot is rolled into a much longer piece with a square or rectangular cross section closer to its final size. The desired cross section is obtained by turning the ingot 90° to be rolled on the sides as it is passed back and forth through the rolls. If it is approximately square in cross section, it is called a *bloom* if large (over 36 sq in.) and a *billet* if smaller. It is called a *slab* if the width is twice the thickness or more. The appropriate shape is used to manufacture beams, rails, plate, sheets, wire, pipe, bolts, or other items by one of the following methods.

Rolling consists of compressing and shaping an ingot into a useful shape by squeezing it through a succession of rollers, each succeeding set of rollers squeezing the material smaller in cross section and closer to the final shape. The piece being rolled becomes longer and wider as it is compressed. It may be made narrower by cutting or by rolling after turning 90° so that the rolling reduces the width. A wide variety of cross sections useful for construction of buildings and bridges can be rolled in long pieces by means of specially shaped rollers. (See Figure 5–9.) Flat sheets can be rolled by rollers of a constant diameter. Corrugated sheets can be rolled from flat sheets by using corrugated rollers. Corrugated steel roof deck can be seen in Figure 5–21. Hot rolling usually precedes cold rolling until the steel is close to its final shape. Hot rolling is usually the first step in reducing the size of an ingot prior to extruding, drawing, or forging.

Extrusion consists of forcing a billet of hot, plastic steel through a die of the desired shape to produce a continuous length of material of reduced cross section in the shape of the die. The resulting product has the shape of a rolled product. That is, it is long with a constant cross section. However, more intricate shapes can be formed by extrusion than by rolling, and the surface is of higher quality. An extrusion is made in one operation rather than repetitive operations as in the case of rolling. An extruded section can sometimes be used in place of a section that requires several operations if formed any other way. (See Figure 5–10.) Extrusions can be made with cross sections having a maximum dimension of nearly 2 ft.

Drawing consists of pulling steel through a small die to form wire or a small rod of round, square, oval, or other cross section. Steel is hot rolled to form a rod of a size not much larger than the shape to be drawn. It is then finished by cold drawing. Seamless steel pipe may also be finished by cold drawing over a round, bullet-shaped mandrel to form a hollow center and through a die to form the outside. The advantages of cold drawing are a smoother finish, more accurate size, more strength, and better machinability.

To vary the area and weight within a given nominal size, the flange width, the flange thickness, and the web thickness are changed.

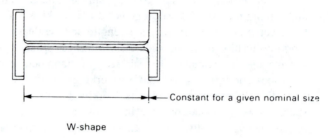

Constant for a given nominal size

W-shape

To vary the area and weight within a given nominal size, the web thickness and the flange width are changed by an equal amount.

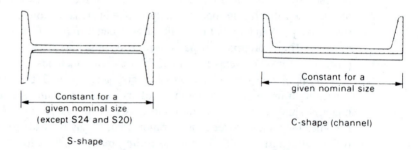

Constant for a given nominal size (except S24 and S20)

S-shape

Constant for a given nominal size

C-shape (channel)

To vary area and weight for a given leg length, the thickness of each leg is changed. Note that leg length is changed slightly by this method.

L-shape (angle)

FIGURE 5-9 Typical rolled sections (AISC)

Forging consists of deforming steel by pressure or blows into a desired shape. The forging may be made from an ingot or from a rolled shape. The steel is usually heated to a semisolid state at a temperature over 2000°F (1090°C). In some cases it is forged cold. It is forced to fill the shape between dies by pressure or blows of the upper die upon the lower one. The shape may be formed more accurately by successive forgings, each succeeding operation performed with smaller dies closer to the desired final shape. Instead, the final shape may be achieved by machining. Many shapes can be either cast or forged. Economics often determine which method is used. However, forging is preferred if strength of the part is important. Forging improves the mechanical properties of the

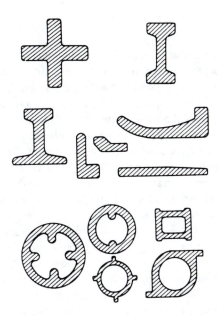

FIGURE 5–10 Typical extruded sections

metal, as does other hot working or cold working, and produces a stronger, more ductile, more uniform product with smaller grain size than is produced by casting.

After steel cools and is given its final shape, further heating and cooling processes can change the internal structure and thereby impart certain properties. Heat treatment consists of heating, holding the metal at the high temperature, and cooling. Even here the rate of heating is not important, except for high-carbon alloyed steels. The metal is held at the upper temperature so that it can be heated to a uniform temperature throughout. The rate of cooling is very important.

Normalizing consists of heating the steel to a temperature of about 1500°F (815°C) or higher, depending on the type of metal, and cooling several hundred degrees slowly in air. This process increases uniformity of structure.

Annealing consists of heating the steel to a temperature slightly lower than for normalizing and cooling it several hundred degrees very slowly, usually in a furnace. Methods vary somewhat depending on the purpose, which may be to soften the metal, produce a special structure, facilitate machining, facilitate cold shaping, or reduce stresses.

Quenching consists of cooling steel very rapidly in oil, water, or brine from a temperature of about 1500°F (815°C). Quenching increases hardness and strength, but reduces ductility and toughness. Residual stresses are introduced by quenching and should be relieved by tempering.

Tempering consists of reheating the quenched steel to a temperature of 300 to 1200°F (150 to 650°C) and cooling in air to reduce the residual stresses and increase ductility. Heating to the lower temperature range produces greater hardness, strength, and wear resistance, while higher heat produces greater toughness.

STEEL TENSILE TEST

Mechanical tests for steel include tension, bending, hardness, and impact. For structural steel the tension, or tensile, test is the most important. (See Figure 5–11.) The purchaser may specify that the test be performed on steel from the furnace, after rolling, or after fabrication. Specimens for testing are poured separately as an ingot is being made or are cut from the waste material of a rolled member. Specimens may be of various sizes.

The typical tensile test specimen is a 0.500-in.-diameter cylinder machined to a smooth, accurate circular cross section. The specimen is clamped at each end or threaded into a testing machine that applies an axial pull at a uniformly increasing rate until the specimen breaks. As the pulling proceeds, the force is constantly indicated in digits or by a dial on the machine. Tensile stress is calculated by dividing the force by the original cross-sectional area.

Before the force is applied, two marks are made on the specimen two inches apart in the direction of the applied force. The two marks are drawn farther apart as the specimen deforms under the tension. Strain is calculated by dividing the increase in distance between the marks by the original 2-in. distance.

Stress and strain are determined at regular intervals from readings of force and the measured increase in distance between the marks. A curve of stress versus strain is plotted to determine whatever information is desired. The yield stress and rupture stress are often specified as lower limits for acceptance of steel. (See Figure 1–4a for a typical stress-strain diagram for steel.) In many cases, a complete stress-strain curve is plotted by an automatic recorder as the test proceeds.

FIGURE 5–11   The application of tensile loads to a steel specimen; note the stress-strain recorder (*Courtesy Al Gaudreau*)

Automatic devices are available to determine yield strength by noting the strength at the correct plastic (permanent) deformation as the sample is being tested without plotting a stress-strain curve.

STEEL PROTECTION

Rusting is oxidation or combining of the iron with oxygen, which occurs in the presence of moisture. It proceeds more rapidly where there is noticeable dampness, but it occurs in any air with a relative humidity higher than 70 percent. It progresses more rapidly in salt air and in an industrial atmosphere. The thickness of metal lost by rusting is $\frac{1}{2}$ mil (a mil is 0.001 in.) or less per year in average conditions. It may be much higher in the presence of industrial air pollution. The rust is formed from the solid metal, reducing its size so that the member becomes weaker and loses any decorative finish it might have. The rust penetrates deeper as time goes on. Painting the steel prevents rust. However, painting is expensive and paint must be replaced periodically at additional cost. Carbon steel may be made more rust resistant by the addition of copper as an alloying element.

Ordinary steel cannot be used where it is exposed to high temperatures. At a very high temperature it melts to the liquid state, and it begins the process of liquifying at moderately high temperatures. Steel weakens at 800 to 900°F (430 to 480°C) and cannot support any load at 1200°F (650°C). Steel may be used economically for structural support of industrial furnaces, incinerators, and other heat-producing devices, but it must be insulated from the heat.

Structural steel that is ordinarily subjected to normal temperatures may be subjected to great heat during an accidental fire. The steel will then melt or at least become soft from the heat unless protected by insulation. Usually the steel is encased in concrete to insulate it.

A fire must always be considered a possibility. However, if the possibility is remote and the cost of insulating is high compared to the cost of failure from heat, it may be decided to leave the steel unprotected. A steel highway bridge, for example, is protected from the burning of an automobile by the concrete pavement; and the possibility of a damaging fire under the bridge is usually very slight. Adding the weight of a heat-protective covering over all the steel would greatly increase the required bridge size and cost. Therefore, the steel is not insulated for fire protection.

The protection of ordinary steel in a moderately corrosive atmosphere requires thorough cleansing of the steel followed by the application of three coats of various types of oil-based paint with a total thickness of 4 mils (0.004 in.). The prevention of rust can be made easier by careful design to avoid pockets or crevices that hold water, spots that are inaccessible for repainting, and sharp edges that are difficult to coat with the required thickness of paint.

Another type of protection commonly used is galvanizing, or coating with zinc or with zinc-pigmented paints. Zinc adheres readily to iron or steel to form a tight seal against the atmosphere. It prolongs the life of iron and steel because it corrodes much more slowly than they do. Zinc continues to protect the iron or steel even after it has been eaten through in spots, because corrosion will take place in the zinc in preference to the ferrous metal. The zinc coating has a shiny, silvery appearance which is not suitable for all uses.

Bituminous coatings are used to protect iron and steel from the effects of atmosphere, water, or soil. The usefulness of bitumens as protective coatings is discussed in Chapter 3. The appearance and odor of bitumens make them unsuitable for many applications.

Stainless steels, which are known as high-alloy steels, have chromium and nickel as their chief alloying elements. They contain 16 to 28 percent chromium and may contain up to 22 percent nickel. Chromium may be used alone or in combination with nickel. Adding manganese increases ductility and acid resistance. Stainless steels have high resistance to corrosion, and their wide variety of finishes, from dull to mirrorlike, last indefinitely. They are used where appearance or sanitation is important, as in kitchens, laboratories, and exterior building trim. They are also used for mechanisms in wet or corrosive atmospheres, such as rockers and rocker plates for bridges, water valves and gates, and smokestack controls. Corrosion resistance is due to the forming of a thin, transparent coating of chromium oxide over the surface. Stainless steel may be made harder at a sacrifice of some of the corrosion resistance.

Stainless steels are available with various characteristics, such as good corrosion resistance at high temperatures, no magnetic property, good weldability, and a low coefficient of thermal expansion. For some kinds of stainless steel, the tendency toward galvanic corrosion when in contact with other metals and a higher than normal coefficient of thermal expansion can lead to trouble unless precautions are taken in design.

Heat-resisting steel contains chromium as the primary alloying element. This steel does not lose a significant amount of strength at temperatures up to 1100°F (590°C). It can be hardened by heat treatment.

STRUCTURAL STEEL

Structural steel includes rolled shapes and plates used in structural frames, connectors, plates, or bracing needed to hold the frame in place, and most other steel attached directly to the frame. Exceptions are grating and metal deck, open-web steel joists, ornamental metal, stacks, tanks, and steel required for assembly or erection of materials supplied by trades other than structural steel fabricators or erectors.

Figure 5–12 shows a typical structural steel frame building under construction. Steel erection consists of connecting precut pieces of rolled sections (see Figure 5–9) together as shown on construction drawings to form a structure.

Yield stress (see Figure 1–4 for explanation) is used as a basis for the design of all steel structures. It is the yield point for all structural steels that produce a yield point on their stress-strain curves. This includes most structural steels. It is the yield strength determined at a plastic (permanent) strain of 0.002 (0.2 percent) for steel having no yield point. Of the steels listed in Figure 5–13, only A514 is of this type. Yield stresses range from 24 to 100 Ksi for structural steels.

Maximum allowable stresses (described in Chapter 1) in compression, tension, and shear for various types of structural members and connections and for various types of loads are published by the American Institute of Steel Construction, Inc. (AISC), American Association of State Highway and Transportation Officials (AASHTO), and other organizations. These published stresses are all computed by reducing the yield

FIGURE 5-12 Steel frame building under construction

stress for each type of steel by a safety factor. (Safety factors are discussed in Chapter 1.) The designer selects the type of steel and the size and arrangement for each member and connection so that the expected loads are carried economically, without exceeding the published allowable stresses.

Structural steels designated as carbon steel in Figure 5–13 are mild carbon steels containing 0.29 maximum percent carbon, 1.20 maximum percent manganese, 0.04 maximum percent phosphorus, and 0.05 maximum percent sulfur. Silicon is required only for plates at 0.15 to 0.40 percent. These steels have yield stresses from 32 to 42 Ksi. Strength of these steels is closely related to carbon content. Corrosion resistance may be doubled by adding copper. A36 is all-purpose steel, widely used for buildings and bridges.

Alloying elements added to steel can impart properties impossible to impart by heating and cooling or by working. (See Figure 5–7.) An important reason for adding alloys is to improve mechanical properties. High-strength, low-alloy steels contain alloying elements that improve mechanical properties and resistance to rust. The total amount of alloying elements added is 2 or 3 percent. Specifications for these steels require that they meet certain performance standards rather than certain chemical formulas. Each manufacturer has his own method of producing a product that meets the standards.

Those designated as high-strength, low-alloy steel in Figure 5–13 have the carbon content of mild carbon steel with columbium, vanadium, nitrogen, or copper, or

Steel Type	ASTM Designation	F_y Minimum Yield Stress (ksi)	F_u Tensile Stress[a] (ksi)	Shapes — Group per ASTM A6 [b]1	2	3	4	5	Plates and Bars To ½" Incl.	Over ½" to ¾" Incl.	Over ¾" to 1¼" Incl.	Over 1¼" to 1½" Incl.	Over 1½" to 2" Incl.	Over 2" to 2½" Incl.	Over 2½" to 4" Incl.	Over 4" to 5" Incl.	Over 5" to 6" Incl.	Over 6" to 8" Incl.	Over 8"
Carbon	A36	32	58–80																
		36	58–80[c]																
	A529	42	60–85																
High-Strength Low Alloy	A441	40	60																
		42	63																
		46	67																
		50	70																
	A572—Grade 42	42	60																
	A572—Grade 50	50	65																
	A572—Grade 60	60	75																
	A572—Grade 65	65	80																
Corrosion-Resistant High-Strength Low-Alloy	A242	42	63																
		46	67																
		50	70																
	A588	42	63																
		46	67																
		50	70																
Quenched & Tempered Alloy	A514[d]	90	100–130																
		100	110–130																

[a] Minimum unless a range is shown.
[b] Includes bar-size shapes.
[c] For shapes over 426 lbs./ft. minimum of 58 ksi only applies.
[d] Plates only.

■ Available.
☐ Not available.

FIGURE 5-13 Classification of steels (AISC)

combinations of them added as alloys in small amounts. Maximum percentages are: carbon, 0.26; manganese, 1.65; phosphorus, 0.04; sulfur, 0.05; and silicon, 0.40. These steels have yield stresses from 40 to 65 Ksi. Strength is increased beyond that of ordinary carbon steel by means of a finer structure that occurs during cooling with no additional heat treatment.

Those designated as corrosion-resistant, high-strength, low-alloy steels in Figure 5–13 have four times the corrosion resistance of carbon structural steel or two times that of carbon structural steel with copper and are also known as *weathering steels*.

Exposure to the atmosphere forms a thin, rust-colored, protective coating of iron oxide, which eventually becomes blue-gray and which prevents any further corrosion. Two or three years are required for the coating to form completely. The coating does not protect against corrosion from concentrated, corrosive industrial fumes, from wetting with salt water, or from being submerged in water or buried in the ground. During the early stages of weathering, rainwater dripping from the steel carries corroded materials which stain concrete, brick, and other light-colored, porous materials.

Weathering steels have the carbon content of mild-carbon steel or low-carbon steel with various small percentages of chromium, nickel, silicon, vanadium, titanium, zirconium, molybdenum, copper, and columbium added as alloys. Yield stresses range from 42 to 50 Ksi. These steels also attain high strength through finer structure occurring during cooling.

Those designated as quenched and tempered alloy steel in Figure 5–13 are available only as plates. They also have the carbon content of mild-carbon steel or low-carbon steel and alloys of silicon, nickel, chromium, molybdenum, vanadium, titanium, zirconium, copper, and boron. These steels have yield stresses of 90 or 100 Ksi. These steels are intended for use in welded structures, and special precautions must be taken to weld them. The steel is fully killed, fine grain. It must be heated to at least 1650°F then quenched and tempered by reheating to not less than 1150°F and allowed to cool slowly. Quenching produces martensite causing great strength and hardness along with brittleness. Tempering greatly improves ductility and toughness, but at the cost of some reduction in strength and hardness.

Judging by the high strengths of the alloy steels in Figure 5–13, one might wonder why carbon steel is still used. Carbon steel is so much cheaper by the pound that a member made of it may be cheaper than a smaller member of the same strength made of stronger, more expensive steel. In addition to this, the size of many members is dictated by considerations other than strength, and they cannot be smaller, no matter how strong the material is. In these cases, the least expensive material is used unless corrosion resistance or heat resistance is of great importance.

Steel is produced in mills to standard shapes; plates and bars of standard thicknesses; pipe, tubing, plain rods, deformed rods, and wire of standard diameters; and various rolled shapes of standard dimensions. Figure 5–14 lists these products. Designers ordinarily select standard shapes that best suit their purposes and adapt their designs to conform to the shapes that are available. In some cases they modify standard shapes to conform to their design requirements. Some examples of modified standard shapes are T shapes cut from W or S shapes, L's cut from C shapes, and tapered members fabricated from various shapes.

Steel produced in a mill is not sent directly to a construction project. It goes next to a fabricating shop. Detail drawings that show exactly how separate parts fit together to form a structure are used to determine the finished lengths and any fabrication needed to facilitate the assembly of the parts at the jobsite. Fabrication takes place in the shop as much as possible to make field work simpler.

The operations performed in the fabricating shop include cutting or shearing to the correct length. Steel is cut with an oxygen torch machine or sheared with a mechanical cutting device with a large blade that drops onto the steel to shear it to the correct length. When smoother ends are needed, the cut or sheared surfaces are finished by planing or grinding to a smooth surface. Holes for rivets or bolts are drilled through thick sections and punched through thinner ones. Holes may also be punched and reamed smooth. If connections are to be made by welding, the work is partially done in the fabricating shop. As a general rule, the less riveting, bolting, or welding left for the field, the more efficient the entire operation is. Examples of fabrication are shown in Figure 5–15.

FIGURE 5-14   Designations of rolled steel shapes

Designation	Type of Shape
W 24 × 76	W shape
W 14 × 26	
S 24 × 100	S shape
M 8 × 18.5	M shape
M 10 × 9	
M 8 × 34.3	
C 12 × 20.7	American standard channel
MC 12 × 45	Miscellaneous channel
MC 12 × 10.6	
HP 14 × 73	HP shape
L 6 × 6 × $\frac{3}{4}$	Equal leg angle
L 6 × 4 × $\frac{5}{8}$	Unequal leg angle
WT 12 × 38	Structural Tee cut from W shape
WT 7 × 13	
ST 12 × 50	Structural Tee cut from S shape
MT 4 × 9.25	Structural Tee cut from M shape
MT 5 × 4.5	
MT 4 × 17.15	
PL $\frac{1}{2}$ × 18	Plate
Bar 1 □	Square bar
Bar $1\frac{1}{4}$ φ	Round bar
Bar $2\frac{1}{2}$ × $\frac{1}{2}$	Flat bar
Pipe 4 Std.	Pipe
Pipe 4 X—Strong	
Pipe 4 XX—Strong	
TS 4 × 4 × 0.375	Structural tubing: square
TS 5 × 3 × 0.375	Structural tubing: rectangular
TS 3 OD × 0.250	Structural tubing: circular

Open-web steel joists are fabricated of angles and rods and are stocked in standard lengths, grouped according to the roof load or floor load they are able to support. They are Warren trusses with a top chord fabricated to support a roof deck or floor. They are designed to be spaced close together and are available in lengths from 4 to 96 ft. Open-web steel joists can be seen in Figure 5–21.

Steel, especially the more complicated shapes, may cool unevenly while being rolled. The final cooling then causes a variation in the amount of shrinkage of various areas, which results in curved or twisted members. These are straightened in the mill after rolling. Shapes that are to be used as beams are then deliberately curved upward so that when they deflect downward in use they will be approximately straight. The curve or *camber* is a smooth curve, roughly part of a circle, and may be applied over almost the entire length of the beam or between any two points specified, depending on how the beam is expected to deflect in use. The designer specifies the curvature by designating the ordinate (also called camber) at the middle of the curve.

Usually sufficient camber is induced to balance the expected dead load deflection so that in use the beam will be straight except when deflected by live load. Camber is

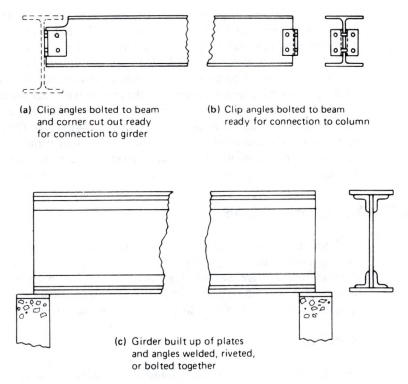

(a) Clip angles bolted to beam
and corner cut out ready
for connection to girder

(b) Clip angles bolted to beam
ready for connection to column

(c) Girder built up of plates
and angles welded, riveted,
or bolted together

FIGURE 5-15   Examples of fabricated steel

induced by bending the beam while the steel is cold. Approximately a quarter of the mill-induced camber is lost before the beam reaches the construction site. The remainder is permanent.

Camber for complicated loading arrangements may be built into beams and also trusses at the fabricating shop. It is done by rapid heating with a blowtorch of a short section of the bottom of the beam, which attempts to expand but is restrained by the cold steel on each side, resulting in sufficient compression to cause permanent plastic shortening in the heated area when it cools. As a result of the bottom flange shortening, the beam or truss bows upward. This method is also used in the shop and field to straighten members that are accidentally bent.

Steel is painted in the fabricating shop with a "shop coat" of paint having the required dry film thickness in mils (one thousandth of an inch). The shop coat is the prime coat of the protective paint system and will not protect against corrosive atmospheres nor against prolonged exposure to normal atmosphere. It is meant to protect the steel until it is erected and painting can be completed.

The steel must be cleaned by wire brushing or comparable means before painting. The paint may be applied with a brush or roller or by spraying, dipping, or flow coating. Required dry thickness of the paint film may be 1 mil or more. Touch-up painting required to replace paint removed by handling after the shop coat is applied is the responsibility of the builder.

Paint thickness may be measured with a dial comparator, dial indicator, or micrometer by measuring the thickness of painted metal, removing a small portion of paint, and measuring the thickness of bare metal. The difference is the paint thickness.

Another method depends on the reduction in magnetic force caused by a nonmagnetic coat of paint between a permanent magnet and the magnetic metal covered by the paint. The thicker the coating, the greater the reduction in magnetic force. A small magnet is placed in contact with the paint, and its force field, which passes through the paint in order to reach the steel, is measured. The value obtained is converted to paint thickness by referring to a calibration curve for that apparatus. A variation of this method is to measure the impedance to electric eddy currents set up by magnetism. Impedance to the flow of electricity through the paint is proportional to its thickness.

STRUCTURAL CONNECTIONS

Steel members must be connected to form a structure. They may be connected by riveting, welding, or bolting. A connection is not designed on a purely rational basis as the structural members are. Stresses at connections are so complex that the connections are designed according to empirical methods based on successful experience. A connection includes a group of rivets or bolts or a predetermined length of weld.

Riveting

Riveting was once the most common method of making connections. It is now used only for shop connections and seldom used even there. Holes are punched or drilled through the members to be connected, and a steel rivet (shown in Figure 5–16) slightly smaller than the holes is heated to a cherry red color (1000° to 1950°F) and inserted through the

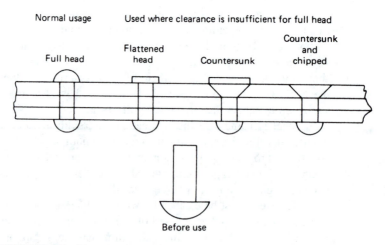

FIGURE 5–16   Rivets

holes. The head is braced and the shank end is hammered until it flattens to a head, compressing the members between the two rivet heads, as shown in the figure. Cooling of the rivet causes the rivet to shorten, compressing the members still further.

Welding

A welded connection is neat in appearance and the metal of a weld is stronger than the metal being connected. Weld metal is manufactured to more demanding specifications than structural steel and is protected from the atmosphere while cooling. The weld metal also benefits somewhat by combining with constituents of the welding rod coating. The result is a steel with better crystalline structure and higher mechanical properties.

Chemical and mechanical properties of weld metal must be matched to the metal being welded. Therefore, a wide variety of welding electrodes is available. The American Welding Society and ASTM have established a numbering system for electrodes. All designations begin with the letter E, which is followed by a four- or five-digit number. The first two or three digits indicate the minimum tensile strength in kips per square inch. The next digit indicates the recommended welding positions. Digit 3 is for flat only; 2 is for flat and horizontal, and 1 is for all positions including vertical and overhead. The next digit indicates current supply and recommended welding techniques. The four welding positions are shown in Figure 5–18.

Welding consists of heating the two pieces to be joined until they melt enough to fuse. The heat comes from an electric arc that is formed between a welding rod and the two pieces to be welded. A portable electric generator is connected to the structural steel

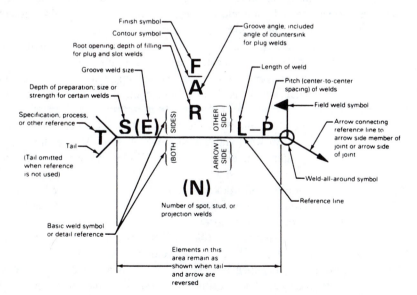

FIGURE 5–17 Welding arrow symbol (*Courtesy American Welding Society*)

FIGURE 5–18 The four welding positions (*Courtesy U.S. Department of the Interior, Bureau of Reclamation*)

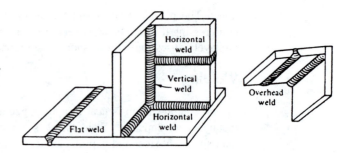

and to the welding rod, and either an alternating or a direct current is passed through the rod and the structural members when the rod touches or nearly touches the members. The tip of the rod and some depth of the base metal, called *penetration,* are melted. The two metals combine and harden upon cooling. The liquid metal rapidly absorbs oxygen and nitrogen, which causes it to be brittle and lose its resistance to corrosion unless it is protected from the atmosphere.

Four welding methods are allowed by the American Institute of Steel Construction for structural work. In the *shielded metal-arc method,* the metal welding rod is coated with a *flux,* which melts as the weld metal melts and covers the molten metal, shielding it from the atmosphere. The flux is partially converted to gas, which surrounds the working area, helping to protect the weld from oxygen and nitrogen. Shielded metal-arc welding is a manual method suited for field use. The three other methods discussed here are suitable for semiautomatic or automatic use.

In the *submerged-arc method,* powdered flux is automatically spread ahead of the electrode and completely covers the welding arc and also protects the new weld metal.

In *gas metal-arc welding,* a coil of electrode wire is constantly fed to a holder as the electrode melts. The new weld metal is protected from the air by CO_2 or other gas constantly fed to the location as the welding proceeds.

In *flux-cored arc welding,* the welding rod consists of a core of flux surrounded by weld metal. This is used to facilitate continuous feeding of the electrode as welding takes place.

The fillet weld is the most frequently used type. Other types commonly used are the butt or groove weld and the plug or slot weld. All are shown in Figure 5–19. The *fillet weld* is triangular in cross section and is placed at a right-angle joint formed by the pieces to be connected.

For a *butt* or *groove weld,* the ends to be connected are butted together and welded. The abutting edges may be smooth, flat surfaces, or they may be shaped to form a groove. Grooves of several shapes are used. Flat edges and the two most common grooves are shown in the figure. Most butt welding is done to join plates edge to edge. Butt welding requires that the pieces to be welded be cut precisely to size or they will not meet properly. This expensive, precise cutting is avoided if the pieces are lapped and welded with fillet welds. This economy accounts for the greater popularity of fillet welds, even though butt welds are stronger.

A *plug* or *slot weld* consists of filling with weld metal a circular or oblong hole in one piece, which is positioned on top of the piece to which it is to be connected. This type

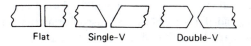

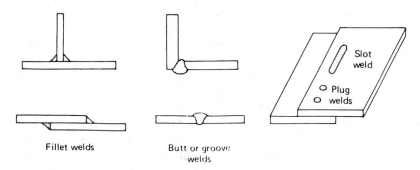

FIGURE 5-19 Weld types

of weld is useful for joining pieces that must act together over an area too large to be satisfactorily connected at the edges, such as elements of the flange of a plate girder. They are also used on plate joints that are overlapped to avoid overhead welding in the field. Fillet welds may be used inside the plugged or slotted holes.

Welds, and also any other ferrous materials, are tested for cracks or any other discontinuity by magnetic particle examination. Methods are described in ASTM E709. This type of test is useful for testing welds or steel members for acceptance. It is useful for checking ferrous products from pig iron to finished castings or forgings. It is also useful for preventive maintenance examinations of structures already in use. The method is accurate enough to test whether or not a specimen meets measurable standards.

The test method depends on the principle that magnetic lines of force are distorted by a discontinuity in the material through which the lines of force pass. Magnetic particles spread loosely on a ferrous metal surface will collect at points of discontinuity at or near the surface when magnetic lines of force are present in the ferrous material. An entire object or any part of it may be tested with proper size equipment and proper placing.

Three steps are required: the part to be tested must be magnetized, the proper type of magnetic particles must be applied, and particle accumulations must be observed and evaluated.

The part may be magnetized by passing an electric current through it or by placing it within a magnetic field from a separate source. A narrow crack parallel to the lines of force may not be detectable. The test must often be performed twice or more in different directions to catch all the cracks.

Finely divided ferromagnetic particles, colored and even fluorescent for visibility, are used dry or suspended in a liquid. To give a clear picture, they must have high attraction to a discontinuity in the material and low attraction to each other. For field inspection, dry powder sprayed or dusted onto the object is commonly used. Particles suspended in water or oil are used normally indoors with a reservoir and recirculation of the particle-bearing liquid. The liquid may also be sprayed for use only once. Wet particles are more sensitive to very small discontinuities because of their smaller size, but dry particles are less affected by heat or cold and more easily carried and applied on the jobsite. Fluorescent particles require a black light for viewing so are not often used on a construction site. Fluorescent particles are the easiest to see against any background, so they are often used in liquid indoors.

Heavy oil containing flake-like particles may be brushed into overhead or steeply inclined surfaces before magnetizing. Because of its high viscosity, the suspension remains in place long enough to be tested. It may even be used under water.

Particle-bearing liquid polymers that solidify in place forming a thin permanent record are useful for investigating hard-to-see areas. The thin coating containing the particles gathered at discontinuities is removed for examination.

When dry particles are used, the part is magnetized before the particles are applied because they do not move readily once in contact with the metal to be tested. With wet particles it is more convenient to flood the part with the suspended particles and then magnetize the part briefly.

The magnetic field must be strong enough to cause all discontinuities larger than allowable to be discovered and must be reasonably consistent for the same reason. Strength depends on the source of magnetism (electric current or magnetic field) and on the size, shape, and type of steel being tested.

Determining and holding the proper strength can be difficult. It may be necessary to experiment with identical pieces of material having discontinuities of known size in order to set the proper strength.

Bolts

A *bolt* is manufactured with a head at one end and threads at the other end to which a nut can be threaded. Washers may be used. They fit loosely on the shank of the bolt at either or both ends and increase the area that bears on the member when the nut is tightened. When the bolt is in position to hold two members together, a tightening of the nut pulls the bolt with a tensile force and presses inward on the two members, causing friction between them to resist movement. (See Figure 5–20.)

A bolted joint is subject to two types of loading from the structure. Tension tends to pull the plates apart in a line parallel with the bolt axis, and shear tends to make the plates slip against the friction between their surfaces in a direction perpendicular to the bolt axis. The friction available to resist shear is proportional to the bolt tension. Movement perpendicular to the bolt axis cannot occur until the friction between the members is overcome. If the friction is overcome, there is slight movement, and both members bear on the bolt. A bearing connection is satisfactory, provided slight movement is permissible and the load is static. If the joint is subject to load changes, stress reversal, impact, or vibration, a bearing connection is unsatisfactory, because it may loosen. The joint must then be designed so that sufficient friction is developed between the members to resist any load perpendicular to the bolt axis and so that the load parallel with the bolt is not sufficient to stretch it and thereby reduce that friction.

The load (T) is resisted by the bolt in tension. The
load (S) is resisted by friction between the two
members. The friction is caused by compression of
the members between the bolt head and the nut.

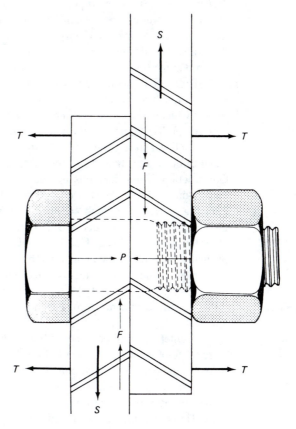

FIGURE 5–20 Principle
of high-strength bolting

Like rivets, common bolts have an uncertain tension, and therefore the friction
caused between members cannot be accurately determined. Nevertheless, common bolts
and rivets have been and still are used successfully. In many connections where little
strength is required and there are no vibrations, impact loads, or stress cycles, common
bolts should be used because they are less expensive and easier to install than
high-strength bolts. However, common bolts are much weaker than high-strength bolts;
they loosen under vibration, impact loads, or cyclic loads, especially if there is stress
reversal.

High-Strength Bolts

High-strength steel bolts can be installed to produce a predetermined tension greater than
that of a common bolt. Because of the great friction developed between members, there
is very little movement between them when loads are applied to the members.
High-strength bolts are several times as strong in tension as common bolts. They are the

most recently developed fastening devices, but have become the most popular by far, especially for field connections.

Tables of minimum tension loads for various size high-strength bolts have been prepared by AISC. In a properly constructed joint, nuts are tightened until each bolt has at least the minimum tension. Greater tension is permitted because the tabulated minimum tension loads are only 70 percent of the specified minimum tensile strength of the bolts. The designer must select the number and size of bolts so that the friction required at that joint is provided when all bolts are under the minimum allowable tension.

Bolts are tightened with wrenches powered by electricity or compressed air. These power wrenches operate by impacting against the object to be turned and are called *impact wrenches*. The nut is usually turned, but the bolt may be turned by its head if more convenient. The opposite end is held with a hand wrench while tightening takes place.

Each nut in a group of high-strength bolts must be tightened until bolt tension is equal to or greater than that specified for the bolt size by the American Institute of Steel Construction. Three methods of obtaining the required bolt tension are approved. The turn-of-nut method depends on the fact that tightening of the nut elongates the bolt, inducing tension in the bolt and therefore friction between the members in proportion to the bolt elongation. All nuts are first tightened as tight as they can be by one person using an ordinary spud wrench. This *snug-tight* position is the starting position for all methods of final tightening and may also be obtained by a few impacts of an impact wrench. Any turning of the nut beyond this original tightening draws the end of the bolt into the nut, thereby stretching the bolt. All nuts are then rotated the additional amount prescribed by AISC ($\frac{1}{3}$ turn to one full turn, depending on bolt size) to obtain correct elongation and tension.

Tightening may be done with a calibrated wrench. To calibrate a wrench, at least three bolts of each size to be used on that job are tightened in a calibrating device that indicates the tension in each bolt. Torque delivered by the wrench becomes greater as the nut is turned. The wrench is set to stall at the average torque load that produces the correct tension. Each bolt on the job is then turned until the wrench stalls.

Tightening may also be controlled by the use of a direct tension indicator on each bolt as it is tightened. One type of indicator is a load indicator washer manufactured by Bethlehem Steel Corporation. The washer has small projections on one of its flat faces that bear against the bolt head (or nut if the bolt head is to be turned).

As the nut is turned, the washer projections are compressed, causing the washer to move closer to the bolt head. The width of the gap can be related to bolt tension. The gap will be a predetermined width at proper bolt tension. The gap is measured with a feeler gauge to determine when proper tension is reached.

Inspection of high-strength bolt installation starts with witnessing the calibration of the wrench and proper tightening of each bolt. After completion of the bolting, the inspector also checks to see that no bolt is skipped. Nut surfaces are examined to determine that none was missed. The impact wrench almost always leaves its mark on the nut or bolt head.

A *torque wrench* is used to inspect a percentage of bolts chosen at random. A torque wrench is a long, hand-operated wrench that includes an indicator dial to indicate torque while the wrench is used. The wrench is calibrated to determine the torque needed to produce the required bolt tension. This wrench is applied to each bolt to be tested until the

FIGURE 5–21 Steel framing with bolted column-to-beam connection

bolt moves slightly in the tightening direction. The torque required to do this must be as large as the torque determined by calibration.

Bolts installed using load-indicating washers are tested by the insertion of a metal feeler gauge. If the gauge fits into the opening, the washer projections have not been compressed enough and nuts must be tightened until the gap is too narrow for the gauge.

High-strength bolts are of two types: A325, described in ASTM A325, and A490, described in ASTM A490. The A325 bolts are of carbon steel and the A490 bolts are of alloy steel. There are four types of A325 bolts: medium-carbon steel, low-carbon martensite, weathering steel, and hot-dip galvanized. There are two types of A490 bolts: alloy steel and weathering steel. An A325 bolt has the strength of one and one-half rivets of the same size, and an A490 bolt has the strength of one and one-half A325 bolts of the same size. Figure 5–21 shows a typical connection made with high-strength bolts. Clip angles were shop welded to the beams, and the angles were bolted to the column in the field. Also shown are open-web steel joists and corrugated sheet steel roof decking.

REINFORCING STEEL

Steel is used as the reinforcing in combination with portland cement concrete for reinforced concrete structural members. Members are constructed so that steel resists all tension and compression is resisted by concrete or by concrete and steel together. Reinforcing steel is shown tied in place for a concrete column in Figure 5–22. Rods are bent outward to join those of the beams that will be supported by the column.

Reinforcing bars are made either plain or deformed. Figure 5–23 shows standard bar markings. Deformed bars create a better bond between concrete and steel. They are

FIGURE 5–22
Reinforcing steel for a
reinforced concrete
column

designated by the number of eighths of an inch in their diameter and are available in sizes from #2, or $\frac{1}{4}$ in. diameter, to #18, or $2\frac{1}{4}$ in. diameter. A table of rebar sizes and weights is given in Chapter 4.

Rebars are made from Bessemer or open-hearth carbon steel with 0.40 to 0.70 percent carbon; from scrap carbon steel axles of railroad cars; and from standard section T rails. The bars are hot rolled and furnished in the grades shown in Figure 5–24. Figure 5–25 shows steel reinforcing bars being bent.

FERROUS METAL PIPE

Both gray cast iron and ductile iron have been used extensively for pipe installed underground. Ductile iron has all but replaced cast iron for this purpose because of its greater ability to withstand the stresses of handling and underground installation. It is used to carry liquids or gases under pressure and also to carry nonpressurized flows of liquid. Water, sewage, and natural gas are frequently transported through iron pipe.

Pipe is cast in a cylindrical, water-cooled steel mold, with or without resin lining, and with no core. The mold is nearly horizontal but is inclined slightly so that liquid metal flows toward one end. At the other end, molten metal is poured into a trough that is suspended inside the mold and extends to the opposite, lower end. As the molten iron flows out the lower end of the trough into the mold, the mold spins rapidly, forming a uniform layer on the inside surface of the mold. The mold is withdrawn horizontally from the trough at a rate matched to the rate of flow so that the desired pipe wall thickness is obtained.

Unequal settling and shifting of the earth may subject buried pipes to tensile stresses under beam or arch loading conditions. Handling pipe between the manufacturing

IDENTIFICATION MARKS*—ASTM STANDARD REBARS

The ASTM specifications for billet-steel, rail-steel, axle-steel and low-alloy reinforcing bars (A 615, A 616, A 617 and A 706, respectively) require identification marks to be rolled into the surface of one side of the bar to denote the producer's mill designation, bar size, type of steel, and minimum yield designation. Grade 60 bars show these marks in the following order.

1st – Producing Mill (usually a letter)

2nd – Bar Size Number (#3 through #18)

3rd – Type of Steel: **S** for Billet (A 615)

⊥ for Rail (A 616)

⊥R for Rail meeting Supplementary Requirements S1 (A 616)

A for Axle (A 617)

W for Low-Alloy (A 706)

4th – Minimum Yield Designation

Minimum yield designation is used for Grade 60 and Grade 75 bars only. Grade 60 bars can either have one (1) single longitudinal line (grade line) or the number 60 (grade mark). Grade 75 bars can either have two (2) grade lines or the grade mark 75.

A grade line is smaller and is located between the two main ribs which are on opposite sides of all bars made in the United States. A grade line must be continued through at least 5 deformation spaces, and it may be placed on the side of the bar opposite the bar marks. A grade mark is the 4th mark on the bar.

Grade 40 and 50 bars are required to have only the first three identification marks (no minimum yield designation).

VARIATIONS: Bar identification marks may also be oriented to read horizontally (at 90° to those illustrated).

Grade mark numbers may be placed within separate consecutive deformation spaces to read vertically or horizontally.

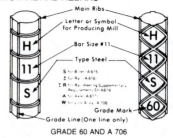

GRADE 60 AND A 706

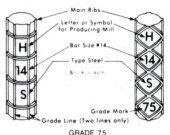

GRADE 75

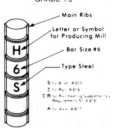

GRADE 40 AND 50

ACI BUILDING CODE – REQUIREMENTS FOR REINFORCING BARS

The current ACI Building Code requires billet-steel reinforcing to conform to the ASTM A 615 specification.

Rail-steel reinforcing bars must meet A 616 including supplementary requirement (S1). As shown in the mechanical requirements table on page 1-2, the supplementary requirement (S1) prescribes more-restrictive bend tests. S1 also requires that A 616 reinforcing bars fur-nished to these supplementary requirements must be designated for type of steel by the symbol "R", in addition to the rail symbol.

The ACI Code does not have special requirements for axle-steel (A 617) and low-alloy (A 706) reinforcing bars, nor take any exceptions to the ASTM specifications for these bars.

FIGURE 5-23 Identification marks*—ASTM standard bars (*Courtesy Concrete Reinforcing Steel Institute*)

plant and the jobsite often causes impact or shock loads due to bumping and jarring the pipe. The ability of ductile iron to withstand these stresses is very high compared to its cost.

Corrosion resistance is important for any material to be buried underground. Ductile iron and gray cast iron are much more resistant to corrosion than steel, though not as resistant as clay and plastics that are also used for pipes. The two are about equal in corrosion resistance, with ductile iron possibly a little more resistant. It is, nevertheless, standard manufacturing procedure to coat the outside of both types of pipe with a 1-mil (one thousandth of an inch)-thick coat of bituminous material.

FIGURE 5-24 Mechanical requirements for standard ASTM deformed reinforcing bars

Type of Steel and ASTM Designation	Bar Nos. Range	Grade[1]	Minimum[2] Yield, psi	Minimum Tensile strength, psi	Minimum Percentage Elongation in 8 in.	Cold Bend test[3] Pin Diameter (d = nominal diameter of specimen)
Billet-Steel A615	3-6	40	40,000	70,000	#3 . . . 11 #4, #5, #6 . . . 12	#3, #4, #5 . . . 3½d #6 . . . 5d
	3-11, 14, 18	60	60,000	90,000	#3, #4, #5, #6 . . . 9 #7, #8 . . . 8 #9, #10, #11, #14, #18 . . . 7	#3, #4, #5 . . . 3½d #6, #7, #8 . . . 5d #9, #10, #11 . . . 7d #14, #18 (90 deg) . . . 9d
	11, 14 18	75	75,000	100,000	#11, #14, #18 . . . 6	#11 . . . 7d #14, #18 (90 deg) . . . 9d
Rail-Steel A616	3-11	50	50,000	80,000	#3, #7 . . . 6 #4, #5, #6 . . . 7 #8, #9, #10, #11 . . . 5	For Grades 50 and 60: #3, #4, #5 . . . 6d per S1[4] . . . 3½d #6, #7, and #8 . . . 6d per S1[4] . . . 5d #9, #10 . . . 8d per S1[4] . . . 7d #11 (90 deg) . . . 8d per S1[4] . . . 7d
	3-11	60	60,000	90,000	#3, #4, #5, #6 . . . 6 #7 . . . 5 #8, #9, #10, #11 . . . 4½	
Axle-Steel A617	3-11	40	40,000	70,000	#3, #7 . . . 11 #4, #5, #6 . . . 12 #8 . . . 10 #9 . . . 9 #10 . . . 8 #11 . . . 7	#3, #4, #5 . . . 3½d #6 through #11 . . . 5d
	3-11	60	60,000	90,000	#3, #4, #5, #6, #7 . . . 8 #8, #9, #10, #11 . . . 7	#3, #4, #5 . . . 3½d #6, #7, #8 . . . 5d #9, #10, #11 . . . 7d
Low-Alloy Steel A706	3-11, 14, 18	60	60,000[5]	80,000[6]	#3, #4, #5, #6 . . . 14 #7, #8, #9, #10, #11 . . . 12 #14, #18 . . . 10	#3, #4, #5 . . . 3d #6, #7, #8 . . . 4d #9, #10, #11 . . . 6d #14, #18 . . . 8d

[1] Minimum yield designation.
[2] Yield point or yield strength. See ASTM specifications.
[3] Test bends 180° unless noted otherwise.
[4] Under supplementary requirements S1 of ASTM A 616 only. ACI 318 requires rail-steel bars (ASTM A 616) to meet Supplementary Requirement S1.
[5] Maximum yield strength 78,000 psi (ASTM A 706 only).
[6] Tensile strength shall not be less than 1.25 times the actual yield strength (ASTM A 706 only).

Source: Concrete Reinforcing Steel Institute.

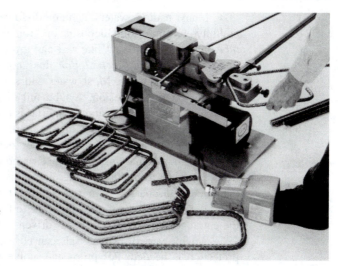

FIGURE 5–25 Steel reinforcing bars can be cut and bent on portable machines or shop fabricated (*Courtesy Fascut Industries, Inc.*)

A loose tube of polyethylene has proven to be an effective deterrent to all types of corrosion in gray cast iron or ductile iron pipe. The tube is inserted over the pipe at the time of installation. The covering need not be watertight, although contact between soil and pipe must be prevented. Groundwater that seeps between the polyethylene sheet and the pipe surface does not cause a measurable amount of corrosion. Sheets of polyethylene may be wrapped around the pipe and secured with tape. However, use of the tubes is usually more economical. Standards for protection with loose polyethylene encasement are contained in American Water Works Association Standard C105.

Steel pipe is also used as an underground conduit for liquids and gases under pressure. Narrow, rolled sheets of steel are wound spirally and are butt welded at the spiral joint to form a tube. Steel pipe is also fabricated with one straight, longitudinal joint butt welded. Steel has a greater tensile strength, toughness, and ductility than ductile iron, but is not as resistant to corrosion as gray cast iron or ductile iron. However, all these characteristics in a pipeline depend on wall thickness, bedding and backfill conditions, and corrosion protection. All must be properly designed to suit the installation conditions. That is, the pipe wall must be thick enough not to be overstressed by the external load or the internal pressure of the liquid or gas; the soil must be arranged under, around, and over the pipe so that it does not concentrate forces on the pipe; and the material must be protected from external and internal corrosion.

Steel pipe is protected from external corrosion by a coating of coal tar enamel. The coal tar enamel is protected from scratches or abrasion by tough paper or fabric wrapped tightly around the enamel.

Coal tar is also used as a lining for iron and steel pipe. However, cement mortar made of portland cement and sand is much more popular for coating pipe interiors. A lining is necessary to protect the ferrous metal from being corroded by some of the many substances that are transported through pipes.

Many natural waters contain dissolved iron on which iron bacteria feed and multiply, forming solid deposits on iron or steel pipe walls. These deposits, called *tubercles,* look somewhat like rust and grow nearly large enough to fill the pipe so that flow is inadequate. *Tuberculation* does not take place if the metal is protected from contact with the water. Most water and sewer pipe is cement-mortar lined to prevent tuberculation and corrosion. A tube full of mortar is inserted into a rapidly spinning horizontal length of pipe, and the mortar is dumped uniformly along the pipe length. The pipe continues to spin, compacting the mortar to a uniform thickness by centrifugal force. The finished thickness is $\frac{3}{16}$ in. or thinner, depending on the pipe size.

The mortar may instead be discharged from the end of the tube and spread with a trowel attached to the tube as the pipe spins; the tube is withdrawn at a rate matched to the rate of discharge of mortar so that the desired thickness of mortar is applied. Centrifugal force and vibration combine to form a dense lining of uniform thickness with the entrapped air and excess water driven out.

A wide variety of materials can be used to line iron and steel pipe when special protection is needed. Polypropylene, polyethylene, and glass linings are among those available.

Steel, usually a copper or other rust-resisting alloy, is also used for corrugated pipe up to 10 ft in diameter for storm drains, sanitary sewers, and other nonpressurized flows. The pipe is made of thin metal sheets (from 0.05 to 0.17 in. thick) which have been corrugated between rollers. They are made of rectangles curved to circular shape and riveted together or of long, narrow strips wound spirally and joined with one long, spiral lock seam.

The strength of corrugated steel pipe comes partly from the deep section given to it by the corrugations. The corrugations cause the pipe to be much stronger than a noncorrugated pipe of the same wall thickness. However, most of its strength is due to the fact that it is flexible. The thin metal deflects extensively under load before it breaks. To achieve its potential strength, it must be confined all around by soil. A heavy weight on flexible, corrugated pipe flattens the top and bottom and bulges the sides outward unless they are restrained. A properly constructed pipeline is surrounded by solidly tamped soil so that the sides cannot bulge and, therefore, the top cannot deflect. Nonflexible pipe cracks before it deflects noticeably, and therefore soil pressure from the sides causes very little increase in its resistance to loading.

Corrugated steel pipe is protected from corrosion by galvanizing as a standard procedure for ordinary usage. It is coated inside and out by dipping in hot asphalt in addition to the galvanizing for protection from corrosive soil or corrosive water. Asbestos fibers may be used to join the zinc and asphalt, thereby improving the bond between them.

The interior may be paved with asphalt thick enough to cover the corrugations with a smooth surface to decrease resistance to flow and to protect the inside of the pipe from corrosion or erosion by solid particles carried in the liquid. The paving may cover the entire circumference or just the lower part, depending on where flow improvement and protection are needed.

Elliptical cross sections and cross sections approximating a circle with the bottom flattened are popular for special uses and are easily fabricated of corrugated steel. Very large sizes of all the cross sections are shipped as curved plates completely fabricated for erection by bolting the plates together at the jobsite.

REVIEW QUESTIONS

1. What two treatments determine the internal structure of ferrous metals?

2. Describe the raw materials and the product of a blast furnace.

3. What conditions of use would require a chilled iron casting?

4. What is the difference between steel and iron, chemically and in physical properties?

5. How is steel improved by cold working?

6. What are the advantages of extrusion compared to rolling?

7. How does forging improve steel compared to casting?

8. What improvements can be made in steel by heat treatment?

9. How does steel fail in a fire?

10. In what environments does weathering steel need protection from corrosion?

11. What is the chief characteristic of stainless steel?

12. Sketch the three most common types of weld.

13. Describe the two methods of tightening high-strength bolts.

14. Determine the number of pounds and kilograms of rebar required for a construction project with the following bar list:
    700 #6—20 ft long
    300 #5—8 ft long
    400 #4—4 ft long

15. What methods can be used to inhibit corrosion in buried steel pipe?

16. Calculate the stress in a #7 rebar subjected to a tensile load of 10,600 lb.

17. Calculate the stress in a #7 rebar subjected to a tensile load of 9700 lb in psi and MPa.

▪6

Wood

Wood has universal appeal. It is generally pleasant in appearance, no matter how it is cut or finished. Certain types can be extremely beautiful if properly cut and finished.

Most wood has a pleasant odor for a long time after it is removed from the forest. Because of its poor heat-conducting properties, wood does not remove heat from the hand and so feels warm to the touch. Metals, plastics, stone, and concrete conduct heat rapidly from the hand whenever they are lower in temperature than the human body. Because normal room temperature is lower than body temperature, these materials feel unpleasantly cold to the touch when compared to wood.

Wood is an excellent material for doors, door and window frames, flooring, trim, and other items where appearance is of primary importance. Wood is used extensively in dwellings where feelings of comfort and well-being are especially desired. Some uses of wood are shown in Figure 6–1.

GROWTH OF TREES

Trees are either *deciduous,* having broad leaves and usually shedding them in the fall, or *coniferous,* having needles and cones containing seeds. In the wood industry the deciduous trees are called *hardwoods* and the conifers are called *softwoods.* Hardwoods are generally harder than softwoods, but there are many exceptions. As examples, Douglas fir and southern pine are harder than some hardwoods, and basswood and poplar are softer than many softwoods.

The way a tree grows explains much about the characteristics of lumber. (See Figure 6–2.) Wood consists of long, narrow, hollow cells called *fibers.* New fibers grow at the outside of the tree, increasing the diameter layer by layer. The thin, growing layer is called the *cambium layer.* The *sapwood* is within the cambium layer, and its fibers are

FIGURE 6-1 Uses of wood: (a) flooring (*Courtesy Memphis Hardwood Flooring Co.*); (b) chapel ceiling (*Courtesy American Institute of Timber Construction*); (c) railroad bridge (*Courtesy American Institute of Timber Construction*)

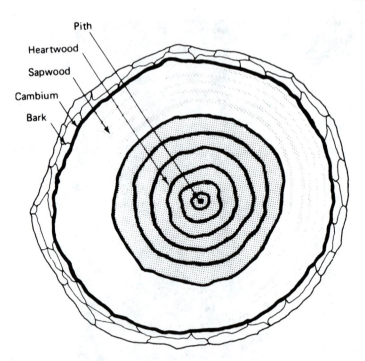

FIGURE 6-2   Cross section of tree

active in the life processes of the tree, but they do not grow. The *heartwood* at the center of the tree consists of dead fibers. Heartwood and sapwood do not differ in mechanical properties. However, heartwood is a darker shade because of the resins, gums, and minerals it contains. At the center is a thin vein of soft tissue called *pith* extending the length of the tree and having no strength. Outside the cambium layer is the *bark,* which protects the growing cells from insects but is useless as a structural material.

The fibers of all wood species consist of a structurally sound material called *cellulose* (approximately 70 percent of the volume) cemented with *lignin* (approximately 25 percent), plus miscellaneous substances that are of less importance. Paper is made of the cellulose from wood.

Forming of new fibers and growth of fibers proceed rapidly in the spring and early summer, forming large, thin-walled fibers with a small percentage of wall material in their cross section. In the summer and autumn, growth is slower with a greater percentage of fiber wall material. In cold weather, there is no growth. Springwood and summerwood form alternating concentric bands around the tree. This circular pattern is easily seen when the tree is sawed transversely. Summerwood is heavier, darker, harder, and stronger than springwood.

The age of the tree can be determined by the number of rings. Something about the weather during the tree's lifetime can be told by the width of the individual rings of springwood and summerwood. They indicate whether or not conditions were favorable for growth. The strength of a piece of wood can be judged by the percentage of summerwood compared to springwood showing in cross section. The strength can also be judged by the unit weight or specific gravity. A higher percentage of summerwood results in greater strength and greater weight.

Some fibers grow transversely, forming radial lines from the center. These lines are called *rays* and are useful in the life processes of the tree. They do not affect strength, but they do have an influence on the appearance of finished lumber.

The hollow fiber structure of wood makes it an excellent insulator against the passage of heat and sound. Generally, wood is not used primarily as an insulator, but the insulation is an added benefit when wood is selected for the siding or roofing of a building. However, fiber boards intended primarily as insulation are manufactured of pressed wood chips and sawdust.

The solid matter in wood is heavier than water. Wood floats because it consists of hollow fibers containing air that cause its overall unit weight to be less than that of water. Wood with the fibers saturated with water is heavier than water and will sink in it. A pack of drinking straws held together with rubber bands approximates the fibrous structure of wood.

The hollow fibers are easily crushed or pulled apart in a transverse direction. They have a great deal more strength longitudinally because fiber walls make up a greater percentage of the cross section in this direction than in a transverse direction. Figure 6–3 shows how there is more cell wall material to resist stresses along the axis of a tree or the axis of a piece of wood sawed from a tree. Notice how lateral forces can collapse the long, narrow fibers without crushing any fiber walls. This is not true in the longitudinal direction where the resisting walls are too long and close together. Refer to Figure 6–16 for the allowable stresses parallel and perpendicular to the grain of various species of wood.

If stress is applied in any direction between longitudinal and transverse, the resisting strength varies from maximum in the longitudinal direction to minimum in the transverse direction.

The coefficient of thermal expansion of wood varies from 0.000001 to 0.000003 per °F (0.0000005 to 0.000002 per °C) parallel to the grain, and from 0.000015 to 0.000035 per °F (0.000008 to 0.000019 per °C) perpendicular to the grain. It varies with the species and is seldom important because expansion and contraction due to moisture changes are greater unless the humidity is nearly constant and the temperature varies greatly.

The hollow cells of a tree contain water both within the hollow space and within the cell walls. The total weight of water often exceeds the weight of solid material. Moisture evaporates from the wood after the tree is dead until an equilibrium moisture is reached that depends on air temperature and humidity. The *free water* in the hollow space evaporates first with no change in the volume of the wood. When the free water is gone, *absorbed water* evaporates from the cell walls causing shrinkage of the wood. This shrinkage is the cause of cracks in the wood called *checks*. (See Figure 6–13.)

When wood is sawed parallel to the length of the tree, the light and dark annual rings appear as stripes called *grain*. The width of the grain is determined by the angle between the rings and the sawed surface. The stripes are the same width as the annual rings if the cut is perpendicular to the rings and become wider as the cut varies more from the perpendicular. (See Figure 6–4.)

The grain (and therefore the fibers) may be inclined to the axis of the piece of wood because of a branch nearby or because of a bend in the tree. This deviation in direction of

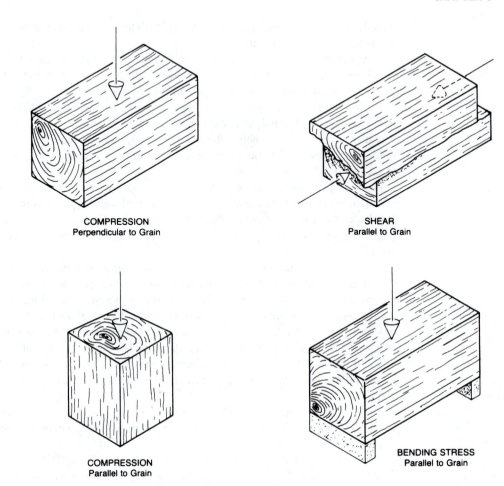

FIGURE 6–3 Wood Stress (*Courtesy Timothy Dennis*)

grain is called *slope of grain.* Figure 6–5 shows how a branch causes slope of grain. A bend in a tree trunk or a fork in a tree obviously causes the grain to slope in a piece of wood sawed straight. Because nearly all major stresses on a piece of wood are parallel to the long axis, a slope in grain away from the axis weakens the wood for normal usage. The greater the angle between axis and grain, the weaker the wood. (See the discussion of the Hankinson formula and the Scholten nomographs later in the chapter.)

The outward growth of new cells partially encloses branches that have started to grow and forms a discontinuity in the annual ring pattern. The discontinuity appears as a knot in a piece of lumber. (See Figure 6–6.) The branch may die and the branch stub become completely enclosed within the trunk, forming a loose knot. The branch may continue to grow by adding cells the same way the trunk does and form a solid knot.

Whether loose or tight, the knot causes weakness. The center of a loose knot has no more strength than a hole. If the knot is solid, the center is still weak, because its cells are approximately perpendicular to the long axis of the wood. The nearby cells are at various

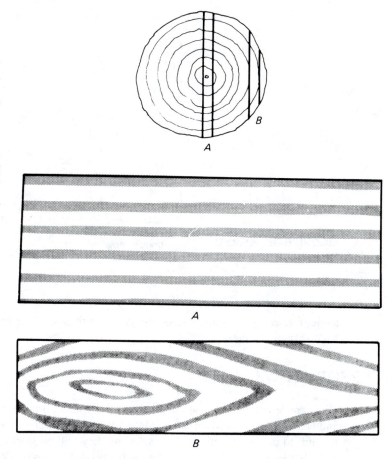

FIGURE 6-4 Pattern of grain depends on how wood is cut from log

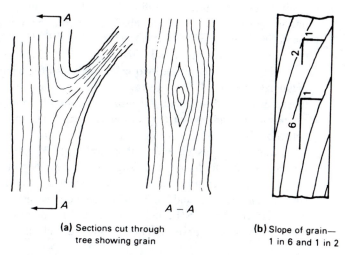

(a) Sections cut through
tree showing grain

(b) Slope of grain—
1 in 6 and 1 in 2

FIGURE 6-5 Slope of grain caused by a branch

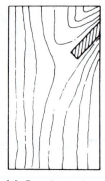

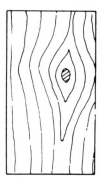

FIGURE 6-6 Knots in lumber

(a) Board sawed on axis of branch showing spike knot

(b) Board sawed perpendicular to axis of branch

angles caused by the spreading of the new growth around the branch, and they therefore have varying strengths.

LUMBER PRODUCTION

Trees are felled and cut and trimmed into logs with portable, power-driven chain saws and hauled to a sawmill for sawing into lumber. The logs are kept moist while stored at the mill to prevent shrinkage cracks, unless they will be stored only a short time.

Blades remove bark before the log is sawed. The sawyer decides how to saw the log for maximum production on the basis of its size, shape, and irregularities. The log is then sawed lengthwise into large rectangular and semiround shapes for further sawing into lumber sizes, or it may be cut directly into lumber thickness by gang saws cutting the log into many slices at once. Saws called *edgers* trim the rough-edged slabs longitudinally to the desired lumber width and cut off the rounded edges. Saws called *trimmers* then saw the lumber transversely into desired lengths and trim away defective portions.

Figure 6-7 shows the two basic methods of sawing a log into lumber and also a combination method. The slash-cut lumber is called *plain sawed* in the terminology of the hardwood industry and *flat grain* in softwood terminology. The rift-cut lumber is called *quarter sawed* when referring to hardwoods and *edge grain* when referring to softwoods.

Lumber is finished in one of several ways. *Rough lumber* remains as sawed on all four sides with no further finishing. *Dressed lumber* or *surfaced lumber* is planed or surfaced on at least one face. It is designated as S1S if surfaced on one side, S1E if surfaced on one edge, and S1S1E if surfaced on one side and one edge. The abbreviations S2S, S2E, S1S2E, S2S1E, and S4S are used for other combinations of sides and edges that are surfaced. *Worked lumber* is dressed and also worked to provide tongue-and-

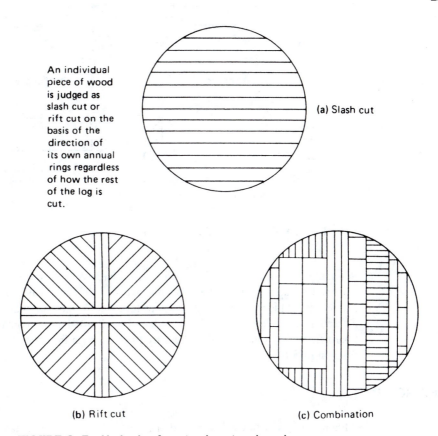

An individual piece of wood is judged as slash cut or rift cut on the basis of the direction of its own annual rings regardless of how the rest of the log is cut.

(a) Slash cut

(b) Rift cut

(c) Combination

FIGURE 6–7 Methods of sawing logs into boards

groove or shiplap joints and/or to change the cross section in some other way. See Figure 6–8 for typical cross sections of worked lumber.

Lumber to be finished may be planed while green, or it may be seasoned first and planed later. *Seasoning* is the process of reducing the moisture until a suitable moisture level is reached. The cross section of the wood becomes smaller during seasoning. If lumber is planed to the proper size after seasoning, it will remain the proper size. If it is planed first, it must be left larger than the proper size to allow for shrinkage to the proper size.

Lumber is sawed to nominal sizes (usually to the whole inch), but the width of the saw blade reduces the size somewhat. Planing reduces the size further to the correct net or finished size at which the lumber is sold. Nominal sizes and net sizes before and after seasoning are shown in Figure 6–9.

Quantities of lumber are measured and sold by the *foot board measure (fbm)*. One *board foot* is a quantity 1 sq ft by 1 in. thick. When fbm of finished lumber is calculated,

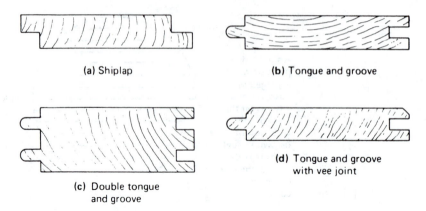

(a) Shiplap   (b) Tongue and groove

(c) Double tongue and groove   (d) Tongue and groove with vee joint

FIGURE 6–8 Typical cross sections of worked lumber

nominal dimensions are used so width and thickness are always in full inches. Finished lumber less than an inch thick is considered 1 in. thick when computing board feet. Lumber length is taken to the next lower foot if its length is a number of whole feet plus a fraction. For example, a 12 ft 3 in. length of 2 × 4 lumber contains $12 \times 2 \times \frac{4}{12} = 8$ board ft. Multiply the length in feet by the thickness in inches by the width in feet or fraction of a foot.

SEASONING

Although the moisture of green wood is very high, it will eventually reach equilibrium with the surrounding atmosphere by losing moisture to the atmosphere. (See Figures 6–10, 6–11, and 6–12.)

Moisture in wood is expressed as *moisture content* (*m.c.*), which is the weight of water in the wood expressed as a percentage of the weight of the oven-dry wood. Moisture content can be determined by weighing a piece of wood including the water, and then driving all water out by drying in an oven and weighing the same piece of wood in the oven-dry condition. The difference between weight with water and weight without water is the weight of the water. Dividing this weight by the oven-dry weight gives a ratio of weight of water to oven-dry weight of wood. This ratio expressed as a percentage is the moisture content.

Reaching equilibrium takes months or years for green wood. Wood may be seasoned in the air, or much time may be saved by seasoning it in a kiln. Wood being dried in a kiln is subjected to warm, moist air or steam and loses sufficient moisture in a period of several days to several months. This is far less than the 4 years sometimes needed for air drying some hardwoods.

Seasoning can take place through the use of hygroscopic chemicals applied to the wood. This method reduces shrinkage cracks (checks) because the chemical keeps the surface of the wood moist and partially replaces moisture lost from the cell walls with the chemical. After the chemical is applied, the wood is dried in a solution of the chemical, in a kiln, or in the air.

FIGURE 6-9 Standard sizes of yard lumber and timbers

NOMINAL AND MINIMUM-DRESSED SIZES OF BOARDS, DIMENSION, AND TIMBERS

Item		Thickness			Face Widths	
		Minimum Dressed			Minimum Dressed	
	Nominal	Dry** (in.)	Green** (in.)	Nominal	Dry* (in.)	Green* (in.)
Boards	1	$\frac{3}{4}$	$\frac{25}{32}$	2	$1\frac{1}{2}$	$1\frac{9}{16}$
	$1\frac{1}{4}$	1	$1\frac{1}{32}$	3	$2\frac{1}{2}$	$2\frac{9}{16}$
	$1\frac{1}{2}$	$1\frac{1}{4}$	$1\frac{9}{32}$	4	$3\frac{1}{2}$	$3\frac{9}{16}$
				5	$4\frac{1}{2}$	$4\frac{5}{8}$
				6	$5\frac{1}{2}$	$5\frac{5}{8}$
				7	$6\frac{1}{2}$	$6\frac{5}{8}$
				8	$7\frac{1}{4}$	$7\frac{1}{2}$
				9	$8\frac{1}{4}$	$8\frac{1}{2}$
				10	$9\frac{1}{4}$	$9\frac{1}{2}$
				11	$10\frac{1}{4}$	$10\frac{1}{2}$
				12	$11\frac{1}{4}$	$11\frac{1}{2}$
				14	$13\frac{1}{4}$	$13\frac{1}{2}$
				16	$15\frac{1}{4}$	$15\frac{1}{2}$
Dimension	2	$1\frac{1}{2}$	$1\frac{9}{16}$	2	$1\frac{1}{2}$	$1\frac{9}{16}$
	$2\frac{1}{2}$	2	$2\frac{1}{16}$	3	$2\frac{1}{2}$	$2\frac{9}{16}$
	3	$2\frac{1}{2}$	$2\frac{9}{16}$	4	$3\frac{1}{2}$	$3\frac{9}{16}$
	$3\frac{1}{2}$	3	$3\frac{1}{16}$	5	$4\frac{1}{2}$	$4\frac{5}{8}$
				6	$5\frac{1}{2}$	$5\frac{5}{8}$
				8	$7\frac{1}{4}$	$7\frac{1}{2}$
				10	$9\frac{1}{4}$	$9\frac{1}{2}$
				12	$11\frac{1}{4}$	$11\frac{1}{2}$
				14	$13\frac{1}{4}$	$13\frac{1}{2}$
				16	$15\frac{1}{4}$	$15\frac{1}{2}$
Dimension	4	$3\frac{1}{2}$	$3\frac{9}{16}$	2	$1\frac{1}{2}$	$1\frac{9}{16}$
	$4\frac{1}{2}$	4	$4\frac{1}{16}$	3	$2\frac{1}{2}$	$2\frac{9}{16}$
				4	$3\frac{1}{2}$	$3\frac{9}{16}$
				5	$4\frac{1}{2}$	$4\frac{5}{8}$
				6	$5\frac{1}{2}$	$5\frac{5}{8}$
				8	$7\frac{1}{4}$	$7\frac{1}{2}$
				10	$9\frac{1}{4}$	$9\frac{1}{2}$
				12	$11\frac{1}{4}$	$11\frac{1}{2}$
				14	—	$13\frac{1}{2}$
				16	—	$15\frac{1}{2}$
Timbers	5 and thicker	—	$\frac{1}{2}$off	5 and wider	—	$\frac{1}{2}$off

*The thicknesses apply to all widths and all widths to all thicknesses.
**Dry lumber is defined as lumber which has been seasoned to a moisture content of 19 percent or less.
Green lumber is defined as lumber having a moisture content in excess of 19 percent.
Source: National Forest Products Association

FIGURE 6–10 Average moisture content of green heartwood and sapwood of 20 species of American trees

Species	Average Moisture Content (Percent of Dry Weight)	
	Heartwood	*Sapwood*
Hardwoods		
Ash, white	38	40
Beech	53	78
Birch, yellow	68	71
Elm, American	95	92
Gum, black	50	61
Maple, silver	60	88
Maple, sugar	58	67
Softwoods		
Douglas fir	36	117
Fir, lowland white	91	136
Hemlock, eastern	58	119
Hemlock, western	42	170
Pine, loblolly	34	94
Pine, lodgepole	36	113
Pine, longleaf	34	99
Pine, Norway	31	135
Pine, ponderosa	40	148
Pine, shortleaf	34	108
Redwood	100	210
Spruce, Engelmann	54	167
Spruce, Sitka	33	146

Source: U.S. Forest Products Laboratory

   Seasoning is continued until a moisture content is reached that approximates the average equilibrium m.c. for the conditions in which the lumber will be used. This varies, depending on the geographical area in which the lumber will be used and on whether it is to be used indoors or outdoors. (See Figure 6–11.) The m.c. of wood does not exceed 19 percent in normal outdoor usage.

   In use, wood never ceases to change its moisture content with the seasons or other influencing factors. It takes moisture from the atmosphere or releases its moisture to the atmosphere continuously in response to changing atmospheric conditions. However, it never again approaches the high moisture content it had while living. Figure 6–12 shows how wood m.c. varies with temperature and humidity of the surrounding air.

   The strength of a given piece of wood increases as the moisture content decreases. This fact is acknowledged by allowing higher stresses in seasoned wood. (See Figure 6–18.) This is sufficient reason for drying wood before using it, and also sufficient reason for specifying maximum allowable moisture contents when ordering wood to be used where strength is important.

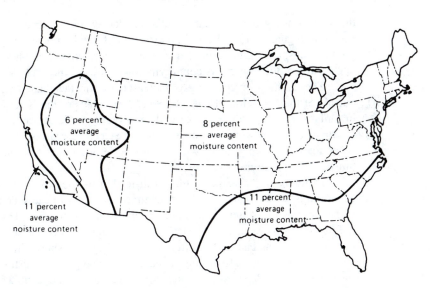

FIGURE 6-11   Recommended moisture content averages for interior finish woodwork in various parts of the United States (*Courtesy U.S. Forest Products Laboratory*)

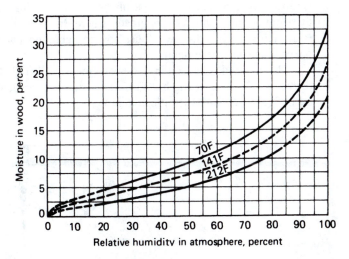

FIGURE 6-12   Relation of the equilibrium moisture content of wood to the relative humidity of the surrounding atmosphere at three temperatures (*Courtesy U.S. Forest Products Laboratory*)

Another reason for drying wood before use is that it shrinks in size when dried, but it does not shrink uniformly. Longitudinal size change is negligible. Transverse shrinkage is greatest in the curved direction of the annual rings and varies to a minimum of one-half to one-third this amount radially or in a direction perpendicular to the annual rings. For this reason, a log develops large radial cracks (*checks*) if dried too rapidly. Checks are shown in Figure 6–13. Because the direction of maximum shrinkage is along the annual growth rings, shrinkage is greater as the circumference is greater. Thus, the cracks are open wider at the outside, becoming narrower toward the center.

The splitting or checking is increased by the fact that drying takes place at the outside of the log before the inside dries. The outer portion is restrained from shrinking inward by the unyielding center and the cracks are larger as a result. It is therefore advantageous to saw wood into smaller sizes before seasoning to minimize checking. After seasoning, when there will be very little additional change in size, the wood is finished to its final cross section size.

Differential shrinkage results in distortion as the wood dries. In many cases the distortion is insignificant, but it is sometimes sufficient to cause construction difficulties. If the wood is too distorted, it cannot be used for construction. However, if green wood is fastened in place, it pulls fastenings loose and distorts the structure as it dries. The various distortions caused by differential shrinkage are shown in Figure 6–14.

Seasoned wood also changes shape with changes in moisture content. Doors that swell and stick in damp weather and shrink, leaving open cracks, when the weather is dry are common evidence of volume change with change in moisture content. The shrinkage is most noticeable indoors when wintertime heating causes the air to be very dry.

Joints in wooden door and window frames open during a period when the air is dry and close again when moisture is normal. Figure 6–15 shows how a joint opens. The shrinkage is a certain percentage of the original width for a given moisture loss, and therefore the total shrinkage is greater where the wood is wider. Longitudinal shrinkage is negligible, so length of wood has no noticeable influence. This explains why the joint opens as shown in the figure.

If the wood is cut so that the wide dimension is radial to the annual rings (rift cut), there is less change in width than if the wood is cut tangential to the annual rings (slash cut). (See Figure 6–14 for illustration.)

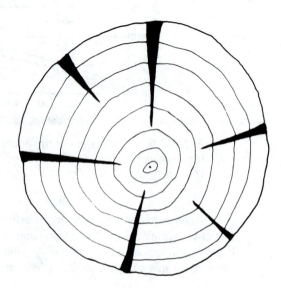

FIGURE 6–13 Checks in a log

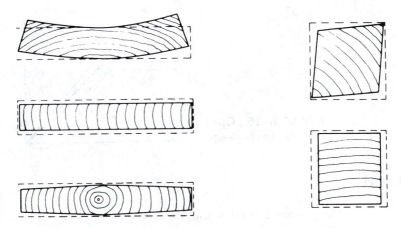

(a) Typical unequal shrinkage determined by direction of annual rings

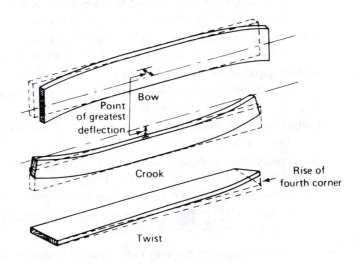

Point of greatest deflection

Bow

Crook

Rise of fourth corner

Twist

(b) Warping caused by various combinations of shrinkage

FIGURE 6–14 Shrinkage and distortion

If the wood gains moisture greatly in excess of the amount it contained when it was installed, the resulting expansion can cause damage. For example, if the wood at the joint in Figure 6–15 expanded instead of contracting, the corner of the frame would be pushed apart, cracking the wood or loosening the nails. Shrinkage may be unsightly, but damage from it is less likely. For this reason, the m.c. at the time of construction should approximate the upper level the wood is expected to have during ordinary usage.

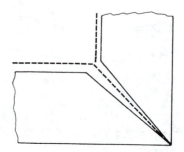

FIGURE 6-15 Open
joint due to shrinkage

STRENGTH

The important stresses and corresponding strengths of wood are divided into the following six types:

modulus of elasticity (E): This is a measure of the stiffness or resistance to deflection. It is not usually considered a measure of strength, but is a measure of the ability to resist failure due to excessive deformation. It is used to predict movement under load and avoid failure due to excessive movement.

extreme fiber stress in bending (F_b): This is the stress (compression at the top, tension at the bottom) that must be resisted in a beam undergoing bending.

tension parallel to grain (F_t): This is the stress induced by pulling apart in a longitudinal direction. Resistance to tension perpendicular to grain is so weak that it is usually considered negligible.

compression parallel to grain (F_c): This is the stress induced by pressing together longitudinally.

compression perpendicular to grain ($F_{c\perp}$): This is the stress induced by pressing together in a transverse direction. There is no appreciable difference in strength to resist this compression perpendicular to the annual rings or parallel to them.

horizontal shear (F_v): This is the stress induced by the tendency for upper fibers to slide over lower fibers as a beam bends.

The first step in obtaining useful allowable stresses and an accurate modulus of elasticity is to test small, perfect samples of wood to determine the stresses at failure and the modulus of elasticity for each species. This testing is done in accordance with ASTM D2555, Methods for Establishing Clear Wood Strength Values. The samples tested have no defects to reduce their strength or stiffness.

Allowable stresses for lumber are determined by reducing the stresses in the samples at failure to provide a safety factor of approximately 2.5. By this means, basic allowable stresses are established for each species of tree. These, along with moduli of elasticity, are published in ASTM D245, Methods for Establishing Structural Grades for Visually Graded Lumber, as Basic Stresses for Clear Lumber Under Long-Time Service at Full Design Load.

Because individual pieces of lumber contain defects that reduce strength and stiffness, studies and tests are conducted to determine the reduction in strength and stiffness caused by the various kinds of defects. The allowable stresses and correct modulus of elasticity are determined for wood with defects by reducing the values for clear wood using the procedures of ASTM D245.

These procedures require determination of the location, magnitude, and condition of defects that reduce strength and stiffness in order to determine the total amount of that reduction. Each defect reduces the strength somewhat, and the total effect of these reductions is expressed as a ratio that represents the strength of the piece of lumber being graded compared to the strength of clear wood. This ratio is used to establish usable allowable stresses by multiplying the allowable stresses for clear wood and the modulus of elasticity for clear wood by the ratio.

National Design Specification for Stress-Grade Lumber and Its Fastenings includes grades established for each species of wood with usable allowable stresses for each grade. These stresses are derived by multiplying the basic allowable clear wood stresses by adjustments (see Figure 6–17). A sample of allowable stresses from the National Design Specification is shown in Figure 6–16.

Each manufacturers' association then establishes grading rules to categorize its lumber products according to the various grades. The grading rules take into account the strength and modulus of elasticity reductions due to defects and describe the location, magnitude, and condition of defects permitted for each grade. Each piece of lumber is assigned to the correct grade according to the association's rules and may be used with the specified allowable stresses for that grade.

Lumber may also be stress-graded by machine with a supplementary visual inspection (see Figure 6–18). Lumber so graded is called *machine stress-rated* (MSR). Each piece is subjected to beam loading, and the modulus of elasticity is determined from the resulting deflection without damaging the piece. The piece is then examined for characteristics and manufacturing imperfections that fall below standards. If it is acceptable, it is stamped with the value of modulus of elasticity and allowable fiber stress in bending.

The fiber stress and the tension and compression parallel to grain are inferred from the modulus of elasticity and verified by visual inspection. The E values recognized by the Western Wood Products Association are shown in Figure 6–16. Note that the allowable compression perpendicular to grain and horizontal shear are constant for each species, regardless of the modulus of elasticity.

Allowable compression is much greater parallel to grain than perpendicular to grain (see Figure 6–16) and is intermediate in value for any other direction. The Hankinson formula is used to compute the allowable compression or bearing at other angles. The formula follows:

$$F_n = \frac{F_c \times F_c'}{F_c \sin^2 \theta + F_c' \cos^2 \theta}$$

where: F_c = allowable stress in compression parallel to grain
F_c' = allowable stress in compression perpendicular to grain
θ = angle between direction of grain and direction of load
F_n = allowable compressive stress at angle θ with the direction of grain

FIGURE 6–16   Allowable unit stresses—visual grading

Species or Group	Grade	Extreme Fiber Stress in Bending "F_b" — Single	Tension Parallel to Grain "F_t"	Horizontal Sheer "F_v"	Compression Perpendicular "F_c⊥"	Compression Parallel to Grain "F_c∥"	Modulus of Elasticity "E"
Douglas Fir-Larch	Select Structural	1450	1000	95	625	1700	1,900,000
	No. 1 & Btr.	1150	775	95	625	1500	1,800,000
	No. 1	1000	675	95	625	1450	1,700,000
Douglas Fir	No. 2	875	575	95	625	1300	1,600,000
Western Larch	No. 3	500	325	95	625	750	1,400,000
	Construction	1000	650	95	625	1600	1,500,000
	Standard	550	375	95	625	1350	1,400,000
	Utility	275	175	95	625	875	1,300,000
	Stud	675	450	95	625	825	1,400,000
Douglas Fir-South	Select Structural	1300	875	90	520	1550	1,400,000
	No. 1	900	600	90	520	1400	1,300,000
	No. 2	825	525	90	520	1300	1,200,000
Douglas Fir South	No. 3	475	300	90	520	750	1,100,000
	Construction	925	600	90	520	1550	1,200,000
	Standard	525	350	90	520	1300	1,100,000
	Utility	250	150	90	520	875	1,000,000
	Stud	650	425	90	520	825	1,100,000
Hem-Fir	Select Structural	1400	900	75	405	1500	1,600,000
	No. 1 & Btr.	1050	700	75	405	1350	1,500,000
Western Hemlock	No. 1	950	600	75	405	1300	1,500,000
Noble Fir	No. 2	850	500	75	405	1250	1,300,000
California Red Fir	No. 3	500	300	75	405	725	1,200,000
Grand Fir	Construction	975	575	75	405	1500	1,300,000
Pacific Silver Fir	Standard	550	325	75	405	1300	1,200,000
White Fir	Utility	250	150	75	405	850	1,100,000
	Stud	675	400	75	405	800	1,200,000
Spruce-Pine-Fir (South)	Select Structural	1300	575	70	335	1200	1,300,000
	No. 1	850	400	70	335	1050	1,200,000
Western Species	No. 2	750	325	70	335	975	1,100,000
Engelmann Spruce	No. 3	425	200	70	335	550	1,000,000
Sitka Spruce	Construction	850	375	70	335	1200	1,000,000
Lodgepole Pine	Standard	475	225	70	335	1000	900,000
	Utility	225	100	70	335	650	900,000
	Stud	575	250	70	335	600	1,000,000

FIGURE 6-16 (Continued)

Species or Group	Grade	Extreme Fiber Stress in Bending "F_b" Single	Tension Parallel to Grain "F_t"	Horizontal Sheer "F_v"	Compression Perpendicular "$F_{c\perp}$"	Compression Parallel to Grain "$F_{c\parallel}$"	Modulus of Elasticity "E"
Western Cedars	Select Structural	1000	600	75	425	1000	1,100,000
	No. 1	725	425	75	425	825	1,000,000
Western Red Cedar	No. 2	700	425	75	425	650	1,000,000
Incense Cedar	No. 3	400	250	75	425	375	900,000
Port Orford Cedar	Construction	800	475	75	425	850	900,000
Alaska Cedar	Standard	450	275	75	425	650	800,000
	Utility	225	125	75	425	425	800,000
	Stud	550	325	75	425	400	900,000
Western Woods	Select Structural	875	400	70	335	1050	1,200,000
	No. 1	650	300	70	335	925	1,100,000
Any of the species in the	No. 2	650	275	70	335	875	1,000,000
first four species groups	No. 3	375	175	70	335	500	900,000
above plus any or all	Construction	725	325	70	335	1050	1,000,000
of the following:	Standard	400	175	70	335	900	900,000
Idaho White Pine	Utility	200	75	70	335	600	800,000
Ponderosa Pine	Stud	500	225	70	335	550	900,000
Sugar Pine							
Alpine Fir							
Mountain Hemlock							

Note: These represent base values for western dimension lumber (2 to 4 in. thick by 2 in. and wider). They should be used in conjunction with appropriate adjustments given in Figure 6–17. The design values are given in pounds per square inch.
Source: National Forest Products Association

FIGURE 6–17 Adjustment factors for base values

BASE VALUE EQUATIONS

The basic difference between using BASE VALUES and the design values that were published for dimension lumber prior to the results of the In-Grade Testing Program, is that BASE VALUES must be adjusted for SIZE before conditions of use. The table below shows how the adjustments are applied to BASE VALUES.

BASE VALUE EQUATIONS

Apply to Dimension Lumber Values in Table 1

Base Value	x	Size Adjustment Factor	x	Routine Adjustment Factors	x	Special Use Factors	=	Design Value
F_b	x	C_F	x	C_D x C_r	x	C_M x C_R x C_t x C_{fu}	=	F'_b
F_t	x	C_F	x	C_D	x	C_M x C_R x C_t	=	F'_t
F_v			x	C_D x C_H	x	C_M x C_R x C_t	=	F'_v
$F_{c\perp}$*					x	C_M x C_R x C_t	=	$F'_{c\perp}$
$F_{c/}$	x	C_F	x	C_D x		C_M x C_R x C_t	=	$F'_{c/}$
E					x	C_M x C_R x C_t	=	E'

* For $F_{c\perp}$ value of 0.02˝ deformation basis, see Table F.

Note: C_F = Size Factor C_M = Wet Use Factor
       C_r = Repetitive Member Factor C_R = Fire Retardant Factor, refer to the
       C_H = Horizontal Shear   National Design Specification
       C_D = Duration of Load C_t = Temperature Factor, refer to the
       C_{fu} = Flat Use Factor   National Design Specification

SIZE FACTORS (C_F)   Table A

Apply to Dimension Lumber Base Values

Grades	Nominal Width (depth)	F_b 2˝ & 3˝ thick nominal	F_b 4˝ thick nominal	F_t	$F_{c/}$	Other Properties
Select Structural, No. 1 & Btr., No. 1, No. 2 & No. 3	2˝, 3˝ & 4˝	1.5	1.5	1.5	1.15	1.0
	5˝	1.4	1.4	1.4	1.1	1.0
	6˝	1.3	1.3	1.3	1.1	1.0
	8˝	1.2	1.3	1.2	1.05	1.0
	10˝	1.1	1.2	1.1	1.0	1.0
	12˝	1.0	1.1	1.0	1.0	1.0
	14˝ & wider	0.9	1.0	0.9	0.9	1.0
Construction & Standard	2˝, 3˝ & 4˝	1.0	1.0	1.0	1.0	1.0
Utility	2˝ & 3˝	0.4	—	0.4	0.6	1.0
	4˝	1.0	1.0	1.0	1.0	1.0
Stud	2˝, 3˝ & 4˝	1.1	1.1	1.1	1.05	1.0
	5˝ & 6˝	1.0	1.0	1.0	1.0	1.0

Source: Western Wood Products Association

FIGURE 6–17 (Continued)

REPETITIVE MEMEBER FACTOR (C_r)   Table B

Apply to Size-adjusted F_b

Where 2″ to 4″ thick lumber is used repetitively, such as for joists, studs, rafters and decking, the pieces side by side share the load and the strength of the entire assembly is enhanced. Therefore, where three or more members are adjacent or are not more than 24″ apart and are joined by floor, roof or other load distributing elements, the F_b value can be increased 1.15 for repetitive member use.	**REPETITIVE MEMBER USE** **F_b x 1.15**

DURATION OF LOAD ADJUSTMENT (C_D)   Table C

Apply to Size-adjusted Values

Wood has the property of carrying substantially greater maximum loads for short durations than for long durations of loading. Tabulated design values apply to normal load duration. (Factors do not apply to MOE or $F_{c\perp}$)

LOAD DURATION	FACTOR
Permanent	0.9
Ten Years (Normal Load)	1.0
Two Months (Snow Load)	1.15
Seven Day	1.25
One Day	1.33
Ten Minutes (Wind and Earthquake Loads)	1.6
Impact	2.0

Confirm load requirements with local codes. Refer to Model Building Codes or the National Design Specification for high-temperature or fire-retardant treated adjustment factors.

HORIZONTAL SHEAR ADJUSTMENT (C_H)   Table D

Apply to F_v Values

Horizontal shear values published in Tables 1-6 are based upon the maximum degree of shake, check or split that might develop in a piece. When the actual size of these characteristics is known, the following adjustments may be taken.

2″ THICK LUMBER		3″ and THICKER LUMBER	
For convenience, the table below may be used to determine horizontal shear values for any grade of 2″ thick lumber in any species when the length of split or check is known and any increase in them is not anticipated.		Horizontal shear values for 3″ and thicker lumber also are established as if a piece were split full length. When specific lengths of splits are known and any increase in them is not anticipated, the following adjustments may be applied.	
When length of split on wide face is:	**Multiply Tabulated Fv value by:**	**When length of split on wide face is:**	**Multiply Tabulated Fv value by:**
No split	2.00	No split	2.00
1/2 of wide face	1.67	1/2 of narrow face	1.67
3/4 of wide face	1.50	1 of narrow face	1.33
1 of wide face	1.33	1½ of narrow or more	1.00
1½ of wide face or more	1.00		

FIGURE 6–17 (Continued)

FLAT USE FACTORS (C_{fu})　　Table E

Apply to Size-adjusted F_b

NOMINAL WIDTH	NOMINAL THICKNESS	
	2" & 3"	4"
2" & 3"	1.00	—
4"	1.10	1.00
5"	1.10	1.05
6"	1.15	1.05
8"	1.15	1.05
10" & wider	1.20	1.10

ADJUSTMENTS FOR COMPRESSION PERPENDICULAR TO GRAIN ($C_{c\perp}$)　　Table F

For Deformation Basis of 0.02"
Appply to $F_{c\perp}$ Values

Design values for compression perpendicular to grain ($F_{c\perp}$) are established in accordance with the procedures set forth in ASTM Standards D 2555 and D 245. ASTM procedures consider deformation under bearing loads as a serviceability limit state comparable to bending deflection because bearing loads rarely cause structural failures. Therefore, ASTM procedures for determining compression perpendicular to grain values are based on a deformation of 0.04" and are considered adequate for most classes of structures. Where more stringent measures need to be taken in design, the following formula permits the designer to adjust design values to a more conservative deformation basis of 0.02":

$$Y_{02} = 0.73\,Y_{04} + 5.60$$

EXAMPLE:　Douglas Fir-Larch: Y_{04} = 625 psi
Y_{02} = 0.73 (625) + 5.60 = 462 psi

WET USE FACTORS (C_M)　　Table G

Apply to Size-adjusted values

The design values shown in the accompanying tables are for routine construction applications where the moisture content of the wood does not exceed 19%. When use conditions are such that the moisture content of dimension lumber will exceed 19%, the Wet Use Adjustment Factors below are recommended:

	PROPERTY	ADJUSTMENT FACTOR
F_b	Extreme Fiber Stress in Bending	0.85*
F_t	Tension Parallel to Grain	1.0
F_c	Compression Parallel to Grain	0.8**
F_v	Horizontal Shear	0.97
$F_{c\perp}$	Compression Perpendicular to Grain	0.67
E	Modulus of Elasticity	0.9

*Fiber Stress in Bending Wet Use Factor 1.0 for size-adjusted F_b not exceeding 1150 psi
**Compression Parallel to Grain in Wet Use Factor 1.0 for size-adjusted F_c not exceeding 750 psi

FIGURE 6–18   Allowable unit stresses—machine stress-rated lumber

MSR LUMBER DESIGN VALUES*   Table 3

2" and less in thickness, 2" and wider

Grades described in Section 52.00 of *Western Lumber Grading Rules*

Grade Designation [1]	Extreme Fiber Stress in Bending "F_b" [2] Single	Modulus of Elasticity "E"	Tension Parallel to Grain "F_t"	Compression Parallel to Grain "$F_{c\parallel}$"
2850 Fb-2.3E	2850	2,300,000	2300	2150
2700 Fb-2.2E	2700	2,200,000	2150	2100
2550 Fb-2.1E	2550	2,100,000	2050	2025
2400 Fb-2.0E	2400	2,000,000	1925	1975
2250 Fb-1.9E	2250	1,900,000	1750	1925
2100 Fb-1.8E	2100	1,800,000	1575	1875
1950 Fb-1.7E	1950	1,700,000	1375	1800
1800 Fb-1.6E	1800	1,600,000	1175	1750
1650 Fb-1.5E	1650	1,500,000	1020	1700
1500 Fb-1.4E	1500	1,400,000	900	1650
1450 Fb-1.3E	1450	1,300,000	800	1625
1350 Fb-1.3E	1350	1,300,000	750	1600
1200 Fb-1.2E	1200	1,200,000	600	1400
900 Fb-1.0E	900	1,000,000	350	1050

*Design values in pounds per square inch. Design values for compression perpendicular to grain, $F_{c\perp}$, and horizontal shear, F_v, are the same as assigned visually graded lumber of the appropriate species.

[1] For any given value of F_b, the average modulus of elasticity, E, may vary depending upon the species, timber source and other variables. The E value included in the F_b-E grade designations in the table are those usually associated with each F_b level. Grade stamps may show higher or lower E values (in increments of 100,000 psi), if machine rating indicates the assignment is appropriate. When an E value varies from the designated F_b level in the table, the tabulated F_b, F_t, and F_c values associated with the designated F_b value are applicable.

[2] The tabulated F_b values are applicable to lumber loaded on edge. When loaded flatwise, refer to Table E.

ADJUSTMENTS FOR   Checklist 3
MSR LUMBER

☐	Repetitive Member Use Factor (C_r)	Table B,
☐	Duration of Load (C_D)	Table C,
☐	Horizontal Shear (C_H)	Table D,
☐	Flat Use Factor (C_{fu})	Table E,
☐	Compression Perpendicular ($C_{c\perp}$)	Table F,
☐	Wet Use Factor (C_M) (only when appropriate)	Table G

Source: Western Wood Products Association

FIGURE 6-19 Example allowable floor joist and ceiling joist spans

FLOOR JOIST SPANS

40# Live Load
10# Dead Load
L/360

Design Criteria: *Strength* - 10 lbs per sq. ft. dead load plus 40 lbs. per sq. ft. live load.
Deflection - Limited in span in inches divided by 360 for live load only.

Species or Group	Grade*	2 x 6			2 x 8			2 x 10			2 x 12		
		12" oc	16" oc	24" oc	12" oc	16" oc	24" oc	12" oc	16" oc	24" oc	12" oc	16" oc	24" oc
Douglas Fir-Larch	1 & Btr	11-2	10-2	8-10	14-8	13-4	11-8	18-9	17-0	14-5	22-10	20-5	16-8
	1	10-11	9-11	8-8	14-5	13-1	11-0	18-5	16-5	13-5	22-0	19-1	15-7
	2	10-9	9-9	8-1	14-2	12-7	10-3	17-9	15-5	12-7	20-7	17-10	14-7
	3	8-8	7-6	6-2	11-0	9-6	7-9	13-5	11-8	9-6	15-7	13-6	11-0
Douglas Fir-South	1	10-0	9-1	7-11	13-2	12-0	10-5	16-10	15-3	12-9	20-6	18-1	14-9
	2	9-9	8-10	7-9	12-10	11-8	10-0	16-5	14-11	12-2	19-11	17-4	14-2
	3	8-6	7-4	6-0	10-9	9-3	7-7	13-1	11-4	9-3	15-2	13-2	10-9
Hem-Fir	1 & Btr	10-6	9-6	8-3	13-10	12-7	11-0	17-8	16-0	13-9	21-6	19-6	16-0
	1	10-6	9-6	8-3	13-10	12-7	10-9	17-8	16-0	13-1	21-6	18-7	15-2
	2	10-0	9-1	7-11	13-2	12-0	10-2	16-10	15-2	12-5	20-4	17-7	14-4
	3	8-8	7-6	6-2	11-0	9-6	7-9	13-5	11-8	9-6	15-7	13-6	11-0
Spruce-Pine-Fir (South)	1	9-9	8-10	7-8	12-10	11-8	10-2	16-5	14-11	12-5	19-11	17-7	14-4
	2	9-6	8-7	7-6	12-6	11-4	9-6	15-11	14-3	11-8	19-1	16-6	13-6
	3	8-0	6-11	5-8	10-2	8-9	7-2	12-5	10-9	8-9	14-4	12-5	10-2
Western Woods	1	9-6	8-7	7-0	12-6	10-10	8-10	15-4	13-3	10-10	17-9	15-5	12-7
	2	9-2	8-4	7-0	12-1	10-10	8-10	15-4	13-3	10-10	17-9	15-5	12-7
	3	7-6	6-6	5-4	9-6	8-3	6-9	11-8	10-1	8-3	13-6	11-8	9-6

Span (feet and inches)

*Spans were computed for commonly marketed grades and species. Spans for other grades and species and Western Cedars can be computed using the WWPA *Span Computer*

FIGURE 6-19 (Continued)

CEILING JOIST SPANS

20# Live Load (limited attic storage)
10# Dead Load

Design Criteria: *Strength* - 10 lbs per sq. ft. dead load plus 20 lbs. per sq. ft. limited storage.
Deflection - Limited in span in inches divided by 240 for live load only.

L/240

Species or Group	Grade*	2 x 6			2 x 8			2 x 10			2 x 12		
		12" oc	16" oc	24" oc	12" oc	16" oc	24" oc	12" oc	16" oc	24" oc	12" oc	16" oc	24" oc
Douglas Fir-Larch	1 & Btr	16-1	14-7	12-0	21-2	18-8	15-3	26-4	22-9	18-7	30-6	26-5	21-7
	1	15-9	13-9	11-2	20-1	17-5	14-2	24-6	21-3	17-4	28-5	24-8	20-1
	2	14-10	12-10	10-6	18-9	16-3	13-3	22-11	19-10	16-3	26-7	23-0	18-10
	3	11-2	9-8	7-11	14-2	12-4	10-0	17-4	15-0	12-3	20-1	17-5	14-3
Douglas Fir-South	1	14-5	13-0	10-8	19-0	16-6	13-6	23-3	20-2	16-5	27-0	23-4	19-1
	2	14-1	12-6	10-2	18-3	15-9	12-11	22-3	19-3	15-9	25-10	22-4	18-3
	3	10-11	9-6	7-9	13-10	12-0	9-9	16-11	14-8	11-11	19-7	17-0	13-10
Hem-Fir	1 & Btr	15-2	13-9	11-6	19-11	17-10	14-7	25-2	21-9	17-9	29-2	25-3	20-7
	1	15-2	13-5	10-11	19-7	16-11	13-10	23-11	20-8	16-11	27-9	24-0	19-7
	2	14-5	12-8	10-4	18-6	16-0	13-1	22-7	19-7	16-0	26-3	22-8	18-6
	3	11-2	9-8	7-11	14-2	12-4	10-0	17-4	15-0	12-3	20-1	17-5	14-3
Spruce-Pine-Fir (South)	1	14-1	12-8	10-4	18-6	16-0	13-1	22-7	19-7	16-0	26-3	22-8	18-6
	2	13-8	11-11	9-8	17-5	15-1	12-4	21-3	18-5	15-0	24-8	21-4	17-5
	3	10-4	8-11	7-4	13-1	11-4	9-3	16-0	13-10	11-4	18-6	16-1	13-1
Western Woods	1	12-9	11-1	9-0	16-2	14-0	11-5	19-9	17-1	14-0	22-11	19-10	16-3
	2	12-9	11-1	9-0	16-2	14-0	11-5	19-9	17-1	14-0	22-11	19-10	16-3
	3	9-8	8-5	6-10	12-4	10-8	8-8	15-0	13-0	10-7	17-5	15-1	12-4

Span (feet and inches)

*Spans were computed for commonly marketed grades and species. Spans for other grades and Western Cedars can be computed using the WWPA *Span Computer*

The Scholten nomographs in Figure 6–20 are used to solve the equation. The equation or nomograph is used with allowable stresses F_c and F_c' to find the allowable stress at any angle desired.

LUMBER CLASSIFICATION

Standards have been established for the classification of lumber according to appearance, strength, shape, and use. Each piece of lumber is assigned to a grade according to certain rules. Softwoods come mainly from the southeastern area of the United States, the western part of the United States, or Canada, where they are graded to meet widely recognized standards and are used throughout the world. Hardwoods are produced throughout a greater area, although total production is much less and distribution from any one mill is usually not so extensive.

Organizations

Grading standards for softwoods are published by the U.S. Department of Commerce in Product Standard PS 20 (American Softwood Lumber Standard), which is recognized by the associations that issue grading rules throughout the United States and Canada. Grading rules for each region are established by organizations whose rules conform to PS 20 with additions for special conditions of each region.

The Western Wood Products Association, consisting of lumber producers within the states of Arizona, California, Colorado, Idaho, Montana, Nevada, New Mexico, Oregon, South Dakota, Utah, Washington, and Wyoming, provides grading rules for the following: Douglas fir, Engelmann spruce, mountain hemlock, western hemlock, Idaho white pine, incense cedar, larch, lodgepole pine, ponderosa pine, sugar pine, the true firs, and western red cedar.

The California Redwood Association is similar, but covers only 12 northern California counties and provides rules for redwood and some other softwood species.

The Southern Forest Products Association, consisting of lumber producers within the states of Alabama, Arkansas, Florida, Georgia, Louisiana, Maryland, Mississippi, Missouri, North Carolina, Oklahoma, South Carolina, Texas, and Virginia, provides grading rules for shortleaf, longleaf, loblolly, slash, Virginia, and ponderosa pine.

The National Lumber Grades Authority, a Canadian government agency, provides grading rules effective throughout Canada for Sitka spruce, Douglas fir, western larch, eastern hemlock, tamarack, eastern white pine, western hemlock, amabilis fir, ponderosa pine, red pine, white spruce, red spruce, black spruce, Engelmann spruce, lodgepole pine, jack pine, alpine fir, balsam fir, western red cedar, Pacific coast yellow cedar, western white pine, and several hardwoods.

The Northeastern Lumber Manufacturers' Association, consisting of lumber producers within the states of Connecticut, Maine, Massachusetts, New Hampshire, New York, Pennsylvania, Rhode Island, and Vermont, provides grading rules for red spruce, white spruce, black spruce, balsam fir, white pine, jack pine, Norway pine, pitch pine, hemlock, tamarack, white cedar, and several hardwoods.

Bearing strength of wood at angles to the grain (Hankinson formula)
The compressive strength of wood depends on the direction of the
grain with respect to the direction of the applied load. It is highest
parallel to the grain, and lowest perpendicular to the grain. The variation
in strength, at angles between parallel and perpendicular, is determined
by the Hankinson formula. The Scholten nomographs, shown here, are
a graphical solution of this formula which is –

$$F_n = \frac{F_c F_{c\perp}}{F_c \sin^2 \theta + F_{c\perp} \cos^2 \theta}$$

F_c Unit stress in compression parallel to the grain.

$F_{c\perp}$ Unit stress in compression perpendicular to the grain.

θ Angle between the direction of grain and direction of
load normal to the face considered.

F_n Unit compressive stress at inclination θ with the direction
of grain.

The difference between the two charts is in scale, the one on the
right to units of 1000 pounds, and the one on the left to units
of 100 pounds. These units may be applied to allowable lumber
stresses in pounds per square inch, or to total loads in the case of
bolts, timber connectors, or lag screws.

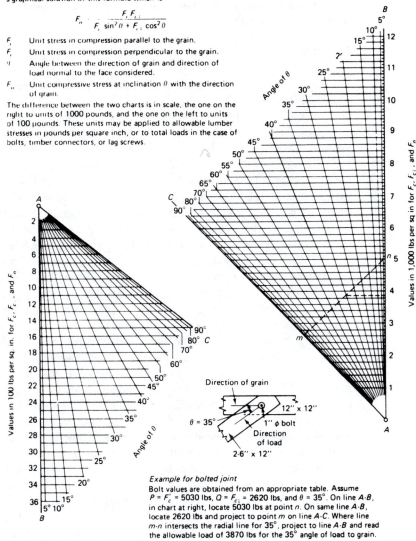

Example for bolted joint
Bolt values are obtained from an appropriate table. Assume
$P = F_c' = 5030$ lbs, $Q = F_{c\perp} = 2620$ lbs, and $\theta = 35°$. On line A-B,
in chart at right, locate 5030 lbs at point n. On same line A-B,
locate 2620 lbs and project to point m on line A-C. Where line
m-n intersects the radial line for 35°, project to line A-B and read
the allowable load of 3870 lbs for the 35° angle of load to grain.

FIGURE 6–20 Scholten nomographs (*Courtesy National Forest Products
Association*)

The National Hardwood Lumber Association, consisting of lumber producers throughout the United States, provides grading rules for hardwoods. The lumber produced to meet these rules is used to manufacture products such as furniture, paneling, tool handles, flooring, and a wide variety of other products. Hardwood used directly in construction is usually purchased from local mills according to specifications agreed on between producer and user.

Grading

Lumber is a term including all finished or semifinished wood shaped with parallel longitudinal surfaces. Those pieces $1\frac{1}{2}$ in. or less in thickness and 2 in. or more in width are *boards*. Pieces at least 2 in. thick and less than 5 in. thick and 2 in. or more wide are *dimension* lumber. Pieces 5 in. or more in thickness and width are *timbers*. These are nominal dimensions and finished sizes are smaller.

Each piece of lumber is assigned on the basis of expected use to the category of *factory and shop lumber* or *yard lumber.* Factory and shop lumber includes pieces to be used in making sash, doors, jambs, sills, and other millwork items. This lumber is graded on the basis of how much is usable and how much must be wasted because of defects. Yard lumber is that which is used structurally and includes most of that used in construction. Figure 6–21 illustrates the categories into which it is divided.

Yard lumber is divided according to size and shape into boards, dimension lumber, and timbers as shown in the figure. Boards are used for roofs, floors, siding, paneling, and trim. Dimension lumber is used for joists, studs, and rafters. Timbers are used infrequently as part of a structure. They are used more often for shoring earthwork or mine tunnels, or as bracing for concrete forms.

Dimensions and timbers are almost always *stress-graded,* which means each piece is assigned to a grade depending on its strength. Allowable stresses are specified for each grade and the design stresses cannot exceed these. A structure is designed by selecting members of cross section sizes and stress grades in the most appropriate combinations to perform the required functions. Each piece may have design stresses up to the allowable stresses for its grade. (See Figure 6–16 for an example of commercial grades with their allowable stresses.) The lumber for the structure must be of the correct grade. A lower grade is too weak and a higher grade is unnecessarily expensive.

Wood frame construction consists of studs, joists, and rafters which act in unison to support loads on the structure. (See Figure 6–22 for illustration.) If one member is weaker and sags or moves out of line more than adjacent members, those adjacent members receive a greater load and the sagging one is relieved of part of its load. If the added load on the adjacent members causes them to move excessively, they are helped out by the next members. Therefore, these members, called *repetitive members,* are not required to support the design load independently. If most of them can bear a slightly greater load, the occasional weaker one is assisted by them. Therefore, a smaller safety factor is justified.

Figure 6–16 shows that the National Design Specification's allowable stresses provide a lower safety factor for repetitive members by specifying a higher allowable stress for the extreme fiber in bending. This means that lumber of any particular

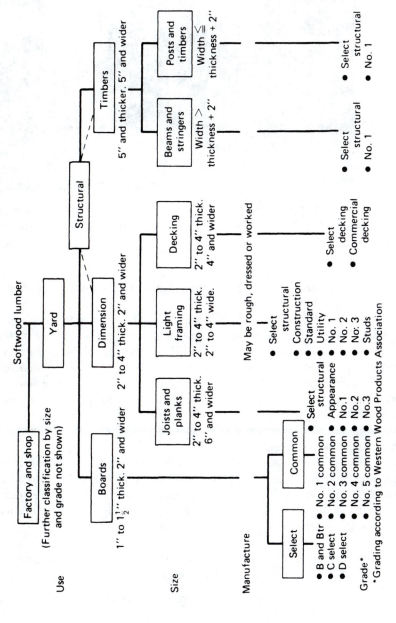

FIGURE 6–21 Softwood lumber classification (*Courtesy Western Wood Products Association*)

277

FIGURE 6-22 Wood frame building under construction. Note glu-lam garage door header (*Courtesy APA—The Engineered Wood Association*)

commercial grade can be designed with a higher stress when used for repetitive members subjected only to beam loading.

The grade for each piece of lumber depends on its appearance and strength. The two are related. Often a flaw that is considered to mar the appearance is also a weakness. Standards are established for each grade. The standards consist of the maximum size or degree of each characteristic and manufacturing imperfection allowed for each grade. *Characteristics* are natural marks resulting from the tree's growth or from seasoning, and manufacturing imperfections are imperfections resulting from sawing, planing, or other manufacturing operations. Some of the characteristics affect appearance, others affect strength, and still others affect both appearance and strength. Manufacturing imperfections affect only appearance.

Each piece of lumber is visually inspected to compare its natural characteristics and manufacturing imperfections with the standards. It is then assigned to the correct grade, which is stamped onto the piece. Some grade stamps are shown in Figure 6–23.

If a graded piece is cut into parts, each part must be regraded, since the parts do not necessarily rate the same grade as the original.

Boards Boards are ordinarily graded strictly on the basis of appearance. Factors considered in grading boards are listed here:

stains: Discolorations that affect appearance but not strength. They are allowed to some extent in all grades.

checks: Lengthwise separations of the wood normally occurring across the annual growth rings and caused by seasoning or by the flattening of a piece of cupped

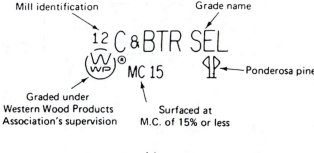

(a)

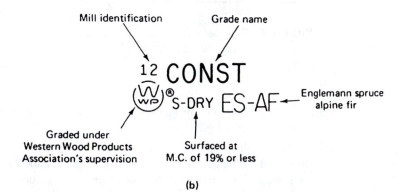

(b)

FIGURE 6–23 Typical grade stamps (*Courtesy Western Wood Products Association*)

lumber between rollers. They affect appearance and strength. Some are allowed in all grades. (See Figure 6–24.)

shakes: Lengthwise separations caused by slippage occurring between the annual growth rings and sometimes outward from the pith through the rings. Shakes are caused while the tree is growing. They affect appearance and strength, and are permitted only in the lower grades. (See Figure 6–24.)

cup and crook: Distortions caused by unequal shrinkage during seasoning. They affect appearance and are permitted to some extent in all grades. (See Figures 6–14 and 6–24.)

wane: Bark or missing wood on an edge or corner of a piece of lumber. It affects appearance and strength, and is permitted to some extent in all grades. (See Figure 6–24.)

splits: Separation of the wood due to the tearing apart of wood cells. They affect appearance and strength, and are permitted to some extent in all but the highest grades.

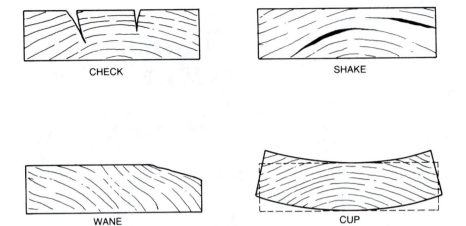

FIGURE 6–24 Defects in wood due to uneven shrinkage and other factors (*Courtesy Timothy Dennis*)

pitch: An accumulation of resinous material. It affects appearance and is permitted to some extent in all grades.

pockets: Well-defined openings between the annual growth rings which develop during the growth of the tree and usually contain pitch or bark. They affect appearance and strength, and are permitted to some extent in all grades.

pith: The small, soft core in the structural center of a log. It affects appearance and strength, and is permitted to some extent in most grades.

holes: These may occur and extend partly or completely through the wood. They affect appearance and strength, and are permitted to some extent in most grades.

knots: Portions of branches over which the tree has grown. They affect appearance and strength, and are permitted to some extent in all grades. They may be desirable for appearance. The sizes and conditions of knots are important. A knot may be decayed or sound, have a hole in it, be loose or tight, and be intergrown with the growth rings of the surrounding wood or "encased" with no intergrowth.

unsound wood: The result of disintegration of the wood substance due to action of wood-destroying fungi. It is also known as rotten or decayed wood. There are several kinds of unsound wood caused by fungi that cease activity when the tree is felled. Additional decay is no more likely to take place in this kind of lumber than in lumber with no decay. Unsound wood affects appearance and strength, and is permitted only in lower grades.

torn grain: An irregularity in the surface of a piece where wood has been torn or broken out by surfacing. It affects appearance and is permitted to some extent in all grades. It could affect strength only if very severe, in which case it would not be acceptable from an appearance standpoint either.

raised grain: An unevenness between springwood and summerwood on the surface of dressed lumber. It affects appearance and is permitted to some extent in nearly all grades.

skips: Areas that did not surface cleanly. They affect appearance and are permitted to some extent in all grades.

These characteristics and manufacturing imperfections do not detract from a good appearance if they are on the side of the lumber that does not show. Most pieces have one side with a better appearance than the other, and because only one side shows in normal usage, the grading rules allow the grade to be determined by judging the better side for many of the grading factors.

Rules for each of the grades shown in Figure 6–21 describe the maximum extent to which each characteristic or imperfection is permitted. Some are not permitted at all in the higher grades. Requirements become more lenient for each succeeding grade from Select B and better to No. 5 common. Stress-rated boards are available for trusses, box beams, structural bracing, and other engineered construction.

Dimension Lumber   Dimension lumber is graded for use as joists and planks, light framing, or decking according to the same characteristics and manufacturing imperfections as boards. Some additional characteristics are also considered. Because of the greater thickness of dimension lumber, bow and twist (see Figure 6–14) are subject to limits. They are not considered for boards because a board is flexible enough to be forced into a flat, untwisted position and nailed into place.

Two other characteristics are considered because strength is a major consideration. The direction of grain is not permitted to vary by too great an angle from the axis of the piece of lumber, and a minimum density of wood is required. *Slope* of grain is the deviation between the general grain direction and the axis of the lumber. It is determined by measuring a unit length of offset between grain and axis, and measuring the length along the axis in which the deviation takes place. It is the tangent of the angle between grain and axis expressed as a fraction with 1 as the numerator. As an example, the slope of grain may be expressed as 1 in 8.

Determining the density is a way of determining the proportion of summerwood compared to the total amount of wood. It is determined by measuring the thickness of summerwood and springwood annual rings or by determining the specific gravity.

For dimension joists and planks and light framing, checks, shakes, and splits are limited only at the ends of the lumber pieces, and larger knots are allowed along the longitudinal centerline than near the edges. See the discussion on timber stress grading below for an explanation.

Timbers   Timbers are graded as beams and stringers or as posts and timbers. Beams and stringers are pieces with a width more than 2 in. greater than the thickness, and posts and timbers have a width not more than 2 in. greater than the thickness. The grading rules for each take into account the proposed usage. A piece graded under beams and stringers rules can be used most efficiently by being stressed to its allowable stress under beam loading. If graded under posts and timbers rules, it can be used most efficiently by being stressed to its allowable stress under column loading. However, any member can sustain any of the allowable stresses listed for its grade, and therefore it may be used in any way as long as it is not stressed beyond the allowable stresses.

The chief difference in grading requirements between the two categories is in the allowed locations for characteristics that lower the strength of the member. The greatest tension and compression fiber stresses (due to bending) under beam loading are at the center of the beam's length at the top and bottom edges of the beam. The greatest tendency for the fibers of a beam to move relative to each other (fail in shear) under beam loading is at both ends along the center line between top and bottom. A column is stressed more uniformly throughout its entire length and cross section.

This difference is reflected in the grading requirements. Larger knots are allowed near the longitudinal centerline than near the top and bottom edges of beams and stringers where they have more effect in lessening the resistance to fiber stress. Checks, shakes, and splits are limited only near the ends of beams and stringers and, even there, not in the vicinity of the top and bottom edges where unit shearing stress is negligible.

For posts and timbers, the knot location is not considered. Checks, shakes, and splits are measured at the ends for posts and timbers. The shorter of the two projections of a shake onto the faces of the member is considered in grading posts and timbers; and for beams and stringers, the horizontal projection of the shake while the member is in use is considered.

Special-Use Wood

Wood meets the requirements for several special construction items so perfectly that entire industries are in operation, producing these items.

Wood *shingles* and *shakes* are used for roofing and siding. Most are made of western red cedar, a species with high resistance to decay and weathering and highly impermeable to water. This wood has a high strength-to-weight ratio. This is advantageous for any roofing material because it means that the structural frame has only a lightweight roof to support. The close, straight grain of the cedar allows the wood to be sawed into thin shingles parallel to the grain with very little cutting across the grain. This is an advantage over most other woods because each shingle has its flexure loading parallel to grain or nearly so.

The grain permits thin shakes to be split from a block of wood either by hand or with a machine. Shakes are thicker than shingles and have a hand-hewn look. Shingles and shakes can be treated with fire-resistant chemicals so that they do not support combustion.

Wood is frequently used for *flooring*. Both hardwoods and softwoods of many kinds are used, and both rift-cut and slash-cut lumber are used. Abrasion resistance is important for any floor, and close-grained species are preferred. The wood is installed in strips or blocks with side grain showing where appearance is important, or in blocks with end grain showing where appearance is not important. Wear resistance is greater on end grain.

The pieces of wood are usually of tongue-and-groove construction or interlocked in some way to prevent uneven warping. Wood is highly valued as flooring where appearance (in homes) or proper resilience (for basketball courts) is important. Wood is difficult to maintain under heavy usage if appearance is important, but easy to maintain even under heavy industrial usage if appearance is not important. It is valued for industrial floors in certain cases because of its resistance to acids, petroleum products, and salts. It is also nonsparking and is less tiring to the feet and legs of workers than harder floors.

DETERIORATION OF WOOD

Wood has four major enemies: insects, marine borers, fungi, and fire. Any of the four can destroy the usefulness of wood. However, wood can be protected to a great extent from any of them by the use of chemicals. Certain woods, such as cedar, cypress, locust, and redwood, are more resistant to fungi (decay) than other wood, and have long been used for fence posts and foundations of small buildings. The heartwood of all trees is more resistant to decay and insect attack than the sapwood because some of the substances that give the heartwood its color are poisonous to fungi and insects. However, sapwood absorbs preservative chemicals better because its cells are not occupied by these poisonous substances. The sapwood can be made more resistant with chemicals than the untreated heartwood.

Insects of various types damage wood by chewing it. Termites are the best known. They are antlike creatures that consume cellulose as food, digesting the cellulose content of cardboard, paper, and cloth, as well as wood. They do not fly ordinarily, but do fly in swarms to form new colonies in the spring and lose their wings thereafter. They are most easily seen before a new colony is established and therefore are often seen with wings. Once they establish a colony, they do not venture out into daylight, and in fact cannot survive long in the sun's rays. Once they enter a piece of lumber, they are capable of consuming most of it without ever eating their way to the outside. A structural member that appears sound may be eaten hollow and may fail before the termites are discovered.

Subterranean termites, which are found throughout the United States, eat wood but live in the earth. They cannot live without the moisture they find there. Since they die quickly by drying out in sunlight, they construct passageways from their dwelling place in the moist soil to the food supply. These passageways may be tunnels underground directly to wood in contact with the ground. If the wood is not in contact with the ground, they construct a mud tube attached to a wall, pier, or whatever provides a route to the wood. The tube may even be built from ground to wood across a vertical gap. The termites are protected from the sun as long as they use the passageway for their travels. The tube passageway, which can easily be seen, gives away the presence of these termites.

Nonsubterranean termites are found in the southern part of the United States and are far fewer in number than the subterranean kind. They can live in wood, whether damp or dry, without returning to the ground for moisture. They therefore do not give themselves away by building passageways and are not as easily discovered as the subterranean variety. The termites' excrement of very tiny pellets resembling sawdust and their discarded wings are signs that indicate their presence inside wood structural members. Wings are found when the termites have just moved in, usually in late spring or early summer. These termites may be within lumber that is delivered to the construction site, and lumber should be inspected for evidence of infestation before it is used.

Two methods of protecting wood structures from termites are to provide either a physical barrier or a chemical barrier to keep them from reaching the wood. The physical barrier consists of concrete or steel supports that provide a space between the ground and all wood. A projecting metal shield may be installed around the supports. A physical barrier is not guaranteed to keep termites out, but makes it possible to discover their passageways through regular inspections.

A chemical barrier consists of saturating the soil adjacent to the structure with poison. This method is used against subterranean termites when their passageways are found. The termites cannot pass the poison barrier. Therefore, those that are in the wood will dry out and die, and those in the soil will have to leave or starve to death.

The wood adjacent to the soil may be saturated with poison to get rid of either type of termite. It is better to treat the wood before construction and prevent the entrance of termites. A coat of paint prevents nonsubterranean termites from entering wood; but repainting is required and may be difficult to do in the areas under a building where termites are likely to enter.

Carpenter ants are a problem in some parts of the United States. They excavate hollows for shelter within wood, although they do not eat wood. They can be as destructive as termites, but do not attack the harder woods.

Marine borers, which include several kinds of mollusks and crustaceans, attack wood from its outer surface, eating it much more rapidly than termites would. They are found occasionally in fresh water, but are much more numerous in salt water and are particularly active in warm climates. Docks and other structures are often supported over water on wood piles, and their protection is a major problem. Heavy impregnation of the wood fibers with creosote oil or creosote–coal tar solution slows the attack of borers, but does not prevent it completely. The only complete protection available is complete encasement of the wood within concrete.

Fungi, which are microscopic, plantlike organisms, feed on wood fibers, leaving a greatly weakened residue of rotten wood. All forms of rot or decay are caused by some type of this microorganism, which is carried on air currents and deposited on the wood. Fungi require air, moisture, and a temperature above 40°F (4°C) to be active. They are most active at temperatures around 80°F (27°C). Wood with a moisture content of 19 percent or below, which is normal outdoors, is not subject to decay. Wood which is indoors is normally drier.

Wood kept below water does not decay because there is no air for the fungi. Logs that have been at the bottom of lakes or rivers since the earliest logging days have been recovered and found to be completely sound. Wood continuously below the groundwater table does not decay because it lacks air. Wood marine piles in water and foundation piles in soil remain sound below water. They do not decay above water either because of the lack of moisture.

The length of pile between high and low water elevations is alternately above water and below water. If in tidal water, it never dries completely when out of water, and when submerged, it is seldom, if ever, so saturated that there is no air. Even underground, with a fluctuating water table, moisture and air are both available much of the time. Fungi thrive in this zone, and the wood may be completely rotten there while the dry wood above and the saturated wood below are still sound. Wood is often used for the lower part of a pile and concrete or steel for the part above low water level. Various chemicals are used to protect wood from fungi when the wood must survive conditions favorable to the fungi.

FIRE

Fire is the obvious enemy of wood, yet buildings of wood construction can be as fire-safe as buildings of any other type of construction. Large timbers do not support combustion except where there are corners or narrow openings next to them, and when they do burn, the square edges burn first. This is demonstrated by the way logs burn in a fireplace. One log alone does not burn unless the fire is constantly fed by other fuel, but two or three logs close together support combustion in the spaces between them with no additional fuel. The sharp edges of a split log burn better than a rounded natural log.

The charred exterior caused by fire is a partially protective coating for the inner wood, cutting the rate of consumption by fire to less than half the rate for unburned wood. A large timber may have enough sound wood remaining to be effective after a protective covering is built up.

A construction method called *heavy timber construction* has been devised to take advantage of these observations. It consists of using large structural members with their exposed edges trimmed to remove the square shape and with corners blocked in to remove "pockets" of heat concentration. Siding, decking, and flooring are thick, with tight joints that permit no cracks to support combustion and allow no heat or flames to burst through. A building of this type does not burn unless the contents maintain a very hot fire for an extended period of time. In that case, no other kind of building can resist the fire either. Even though other building materials do not burn, they fail by melting, expanding excessively, or simply losing strength.

Protected construction consists of ordinary wood frame construction with a protective coating of plaster, gypsum board, or acoustical tile protecting the joists and with plywood used for walls, floors, and roof. With joists having some protection, structural failure is delayed so that there is time for people within the building to escape. The plywood is a barrier to the passage of flames and heat from the source of the fire to other parts of the building.

Wood can be impregnated with fire-retardant chemicals which decrease flame spread and smoke generation. Burning occurs when wood becomes heated sufficiently (300°F, 149°C) and escaping gases burst into flame. The absorbed chemicals prevent this from happening by changing these combustible gases to water plus noncombustible gases.

Fire-retardant paints which have an appearance satisfactory for a finish coat can also provide reduction in flame spread and smoke generation through their insulating properties. Impregnation is more effective than painting and is not detrimental to appearance or strength. However, if wood is to be impregnated with a chemical, it must be done before the wood is part of a structure.

Therefore, paint is usually used to increase the fire resistance of existing buildings, and impregnation is used for new construction. It is done by saturating the wood cells with a fire-retardant chemical dissolved in water. Wood swells when it absorbs the water and shrinks when it dries again. These size changes can cause problems if no allowance is made for them.

Because of the way a fire is fueled, the rapidity with which it causes damage, and the ways in which it causes damage, there is much more involved in fire protection than the selection of materials. Building contents in many cases include trash, cleaning supplies which often burn readily, flammable waxes and polishes applied to floors and furniture, drapes, spilled liquids which may be flammable, and many kinds of flammable stored materials.

People cannot survive in a room with a fire for more than a few minutes, even if the space is large. They are killed by heat, smoke, or lack of oxygen in less than 10 minutes and sometimes in a minute or two. The contents of a room are very quickly damaged by smoke and heat, even if not actually burned. Water damage may also be extensive. The material that burns and the damage done by the burning are largely beyond the control of the designer of the building.

Therefore, the strategy employed by designers and by firefighters is to delay collapse of any part of a building so that all occupants can get out, to provide safe passageways for them to get out, and to prevent the spread of the fire to other spaces. It is not feasible to accomplish more than this unless the contents of the building do not burn. The fire safety of a building depends on the contents and how they are stored, good housekeeping, sprinkler and fire alarm systems, firefighting methods, and the type of construction more than on building materials.

PRESERVATION OF WOOD

Preserving wood involves treating it with a poison so that fungi and insects do not consume it. Strength is not affected by the poisonous preservative. The preservative may be brushed onto the surface of the wood. This provides a small amount of protection. More protection is obtained by dipping the wood into a solution containing the preservative. These two methods are used only for small projects or for wood requiring little protection.

The best protection is obtained by forcing the preservative into the fibers of the wood. A certain retention of preservative in pounds per cubic foot of wood is required, depending on the type of preservative, species of wood, and conditions under which the wood is to be used. Some woods must be punctured with sharp points (*incised*) before the operation to retain the specified amount of preservative. All wood must have the bark removed before being treated because the preservatives do not penetrate bark well. If at all possible, wood is cut to final size before treatment to avoid wasting preservative on excess wood and to avoid later cutting into parts of the wood not penetrated by the preservative. If later cutting exposes any untreated wood, it should be painted with a heavy coat of the preservative.

Preservatives commonly used are of three kinds. Water-soluble salts with such chemicals as sodium fluoride, copper sulfate, or zinc chloride as their primary ingredient are injected into wood in weak solutions (less than 5 percent). The water evaporates, leaving the salts within the wood in the required amounts which vary but are about 1 lb per cu ft for protection against fungi and insects. Salts containing zinc chloride are retained in quantities up to 5 lb per cu ft for protection against fire in addition to fungi and insects.

These preservatives, which are suitable for indoor use, are inoffensive in appearance and odor, and the wood can be painted after it is treated. There are some disadvantages, however. The wood expands and increases in weight when water is injected, and some time is required to dry the wood to an acceptable m.c. for use. Because these preservatives are soluble in water, the wood treated with them cannot be used in water or exposed to rain without the loss of some of the salts by leaching. Therefore, they are not suitable for outdoor use.

Poisonous organic materials such as pentachlorophenol or copper naphthenate dissolved in petroleum oil are used to protect wood from fungi and insects. Since these poisonous materials are not soluble in water, they are effective on wood used in wet places. The oil evaporates rapidly after treatment so that the wood is ready for use sooner than that treated with waterborne salts. The wood cannot be painted after treatment, but does not have an unpleasant appearance. Required retention is in the range of $\frac{1}{2}$ lb per cu ft.

Creosote, a liquid byproduct of the refining of tar, is the most effective preservative against fungi and insects and the only one effective at all against marine borers. It is used alone, mixed with coal tar, or mixed with petroleum. Railroad ties and utility poles are treated with one of the three. Mixing with petroleum is an economy measure to increase the quantity of preservative for uses where less effective preservation is satisfactory. Creosote and creosote–coal tar mixtures are used for more demanding conditions and are the only types used in salt water.

Creosote is a black or dark brown, foul smelling, sticky substance and is therefore not satisfactory for all uses. Wood treated with creosote is very difficult to paint. Creosote after application burns very readily until it cures by drying. Generally, it is not a fire hazard by the time the wood is put to use. Creosote must be used in larger quantities than the other preservatives. However, it is so much cheaper that it is more economical to use it wherever its unpleasant appearance and odor are not objectionable.

Typical retention requirements are 8 lb per cu ft for installation above ground, 10 lb per cu ft for wood in contact with the ground, and 25 lb per cu ft for piling in salt water.

Pressure treatment of wood includes placing seasoned wood into a pressure vessel, flooding it with the preservative, and forcing the preservative into the cells of the wood with air pressure. The full-cell method results in the cell walls being completely coated and hollow cells being nearly filled with preservative. The empty-cell method results in the cells being nearly empty but with the cell walls completely coated. The weight of preservative retained is greater after the full-cell operation. It is more costly, but it is necessary to achieve the high retention needed for the most severe conditions.

Wood exposed to the weather becomes eroded, often turns gray, and develops checks. It may be protected from the weather by a surface coating of paint, enamel, varnish, or sealer. All should be applied with the wood at the moisture content it will have in use so that there will be a minimum of shrinkage or swelling to loosen the coating. Satisfactory performance requires the finish to be hard enough for protection, to be flexible enough not to crack when the wood shrinks and swells, and to adhere strongly to the wood.

These same finishes may be used primarily for appearance rather than protection. They may be designed for interior use solely to improve appearance by providing a desired color, enhancing the natural wood appearance, hiding blemishes, making the surface smooth, or improving lighting with a more reflective surface.

paint: Finely divided solids suspended in a liquid vehicle to allow it to spread over a surface, where it dries to a solid, protective film covering the wood from view. It is normally applied in two coats: the first (prime coat) to bond to the wood, and the second (cover coat) to provide protection.

enamel: Similar to paint and provides a smoother, harder, and more brittle surface. Because of the brittleness, it is not suitable for exterior use in wet or cold climates because swelling and shrinking or expansion and contraction cause it to crack and chip.

varnish: Resins dissolved in a liquid vehicle. It provides a clear coat through which the wood grain shows.

sealer: A water-repellant substance dissolved in a solvent and used to seal and moistureproof the wood by penetration into the pores while allowing the grain to show.

GLUED LAMINATED WOOD

Construction with sawn wood is limited by the size, shape, and characteristics of readily available trees. Lumber longer than 24 ft (7.2 m) or with a cross section dimension greater than 12 in. × 12 in. is difficult to obtain in large quantities. When lumber of these sizes is sawed, each piece is more likely to have some characteristic that seriously reduces strength or lowers the quality of its appearance than is likely with smaller pieces. Even if there are no serious weaknesses at the time of sawing, it is difficult and time consuming to season large timbers without producing serious checks, and difficult to season long pieces without serious warping. Heavy timber construction and long spans are not feasible with sawn lumber. Sawn lumber cannot be bent into curves except in small cross sections and is ordinarily used straight.

However, structural members of any length and cross section and with just about any desired curve can be made by gluing smaller pieces together. The smaller pieces, which are of standard lumber cross section, are glued one over the other, wide face to wide face, as laminations. No one lamination need be as long as the member. They are glued end to end to reach the full length. A structural member made this way is called a *glu-lam member* (short for glued and laminated), and construction with members of this kind is called *glu-lam construction*. The supporting members for heavy timber construction are glu-lam timbers. Almost all glu-lam members are made of Douglas fir or southern pine. (See Figure 6–25.)

Lumber of 2 in. nominal thickness is ordinarily used for laminations. These laminations can be used straight in columns or beams and can be bent to form arches or for desired architectural effects. For sharper curves, thinner laminations are used. Bending lumber introduces deformation, as shown in Figure 6–26. Deformation causes stresses just as stresses cause deformation, both in accordance with the modulus of

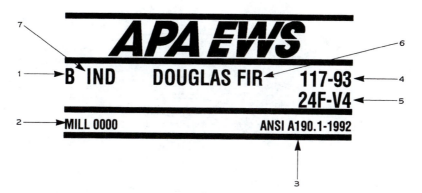

(1) Indicates structural use: B-Simple span bending member. C-Compression member. T-Tension member. CB-Continuous or cantilevered span bending member.

(2) Mill number.

(3) Identification of ANSI Standard A190.1, Structural Glued Laminated Timber. ANSI A190.1 is the American National Standard for glulam beams.

(4) Applicable laminating specification.

(5) Applicable combination number. In the example shown: 24F means the allowable bending stress in fiber is 2400 psi; V4 indicates that the laminations were visually graded and designates the grade of laminations used in the beam layup.

(6) Species of lumber used. Some common species used in APA EWS glulams include Douglas-fir, hem-fir, Alaska cedar, spruce-pine-fir (SPF) and southern pine.

(7) Designation of appearance grade. INDUSTRIAL, ARCHITECTURAL or PREMIUM.

FIGURE 6-25 Typical APA *EWS* trademark (*Courtesy APA—The Engineered Wood Association*)

elasticity of the material. The figure demonstrates how the same curvature introduces greater stress in a thicker lamination. Sharper curves can be made using thinner lams as long as the allowable F_b is not exceeded. Horizontal shear is also induced by bending, and the allowable F_v must not be exceeded in the wood.

Preparation of wood to fabricate a glu-lam structural member is shown in Figure 6-27, and a finished product is shown in Figure 6-28. The individual laminations are placed so that:

1. Weak spots are separated from each other to avoid a concentration of weaknesses.

2. Disfiguring characteristics are hidden within the member.

3. End joints between lams are separated from each other to avoid a plane of weakness.

4. The strongest wood is placed where stresses are the highest.

5. The wood with the best appearance is placed where appearance is important.

Usually the lamination width is the full width of the member. If laminations must be placed side by side to equal the proper width, their side joints must be glued and not be located one over another. End joints and side joints are shown in Figure 6-29.

The use of glu-lam construction allows wood to be used in large projects for which only concrete or steel would have been considered previously. Glu-lam members can be made stronger than the strongest sawn lumber of the same size. Large members can be made entirely from small trees or from the small pieces left after the weak parts are cut

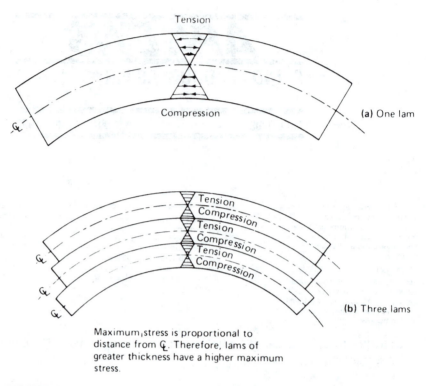

Tension

Compression

(a) One lam

Tension
Compression
Tension
Compression
Tension
Compression

(b) Three lams

Maximum stress is proportional to distance from $\mathcal{C}$. Therefore, lams of greater thickness have a higher maximum stress.

FIGURE 6-26   Stress due to bending laminations

FIGURE 6-27   Manufacturing of glu-lam arches (*Courtesy Weyerhaeuser*)

FIGURE 6-28 Finished curved roof beam (*Courtesy Weyerhaeuser*)

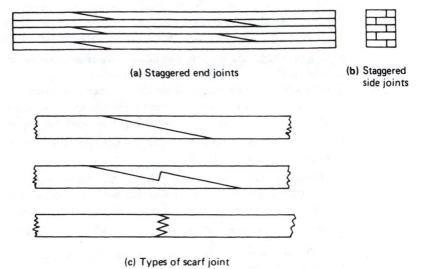

(a) Staggered end joints

(b) Staggered side joints

(c) Types of scarf joint

FIGURE 6-29 Joints in glu-lam members

out of large trees. Glu-lam has proven particularly popular for roof arches such as those for churches, auditoriums, and supermarkets.

PLYWOOD

Plywood is another type of glued laminated wood. The laminations are thin and are arranged with the grain of each one running perpendicular to the grain of the laminations adjacent to it. The laminations are called *veneers.* The center veneer is called the *core,* the outside veneers are the *face* and *back,* and the inner veneers with grain perpendicular to the face and back are called *cross bands.* There is always an odd number of veneers, usually three or five.

Alternating the grain direction tends to equalize the strength in all directions, although the strength is less parallel to grain than it would be if the grain of all veneers were in the same direction. The advantages far outweigh this disadvantage, however.

The advantages of plywood over sawn lumber of comparable thickness are listed here:

1. Plywood's greater transverse strength stiffens or braces the entire structure to a greater degree than lumber sheathing when plywood is used over studs, joists, and rafters for wood frame construction.

2. Plywood's greater stiffness allows it to bridge wider spaces between beams without excessive deflection, thus reducing the number of beams required.

3. Plywood resists concentrated loads better because its mutually perpendicular grain structure spreads the loads over a larger area.

4. Plywood can be worked closer to the edges without splitting, allowing it to be bolted, screwed, or nailed with less excess material.

5. Desired appearance can be obtained by using thin veneers of high-quality wood only where they show. A matching repetitive pattern can be obtained by using one log for all the face veneer and wood with less desirable appearance for the other veneers.

6. Length change and warping due to moisture change are much less in plywood than in sawn lumber because shrinkage parallel to grain is negligible, and wood grain running both ways prevents excessive shrinkage either way. Using an odd number of veneers results in the grain on top and bottom running in the same direction so that shrinkage and expansion are equalized on the two faces and warping is prevented.

7. Plywood can be more easily bent to form curves for concrete forms or for curved wood construction.

8. Plywood is fabricated in large sheets that can be handled more efficiently at the construction site than sawn lumber. Because one sheet covers the same area as half a dozen boards, plywood requires less handling and fitting into place.

9. Plywood has demonstrated greater fire resistance than boards of the same thickness.

Plywood does not have equal strength in both directions. If there is an equal thickness of veneers in each direction, the tensile and compressive strengths are equal.

However, bending strength is greater parallel to the grain of the face and back, unless there is a much greater thickness of cross bands with their grain in the other direction. If cross bands are thick enough to provide equal bending strength perpendicular to face grain, tensile and compressive strengths are much greater perpendicular to the face grain.

Plywood is usually made in 4-by-8-ft sheets with the face grain in the long direction. If the panel is subjected to bending across a 4-by-8-ft opening, the bending unit stress (F_b) is less in the 4-ft dimension than in the 8-ft dimension. The unit stresses resulting from a uniform load are therefore balanced. This means they reach roughly the same percentage of allowable unit stress in each direction, since the direction of greater allowable unit stress is also the direction of greater actual unit stress.

Veneers of plywood are manufactured by being cut from logs slightly longer than the 8-ft length of a finished plywood veneer. The cutting is done with a knife blade held in place while the log rotates against it. A thin, continuous layer is peeled from the ever-decreasing circumference and cut into sheet-size veneers.

The veneers cannot always be made 4 ft wide and must sometimes be made from more than one piece and neatly joined side by side. The desired combination of these veneers is dried in an oven, glued together, and pressed into plywood sheets. Sometimes veneers are cut in slices across the log parallel to the axis of the log in the same direction as slash-cut lumber to obtain a special appearance. The veneers are usually $\frac{1}{16}$ to $\frac{3}{16}$ in. thick.

Softwood Plywood

The types and grades of softwood plywood are described in the U.S. Department of Commerce's Product Standard PSI for Softwood Plywood—Construction and Industrial. Softwood plywood sheet thicknesses in common use are $\frac{1}{4}$, $\frac{5}{16}$, $\frac{3}{8}$, $\frac{1}{2}$, $\frac{5}{8}$, $\frac{3}{4}$, $\frac{7}{8}$, $1\frac{1}{8}$, and $1\frac{1}{4}$ in. Veneers are classified into five *grades* based on finished appearance as judged by knots, pitch pockets, discoloration, and other characteristics similar to those used in grading lumber. The grades, starting with the best, are A, B, C, C plugged, and D. Only the face and back veneers are judged. These may be repaired by cutting out defects and replacing them with patches that will match so well in grain and color and fit so tightly in the hole that they are difficult to see.

Plywood is classified into five *species groups* according to strength and stiffness, with Group 1 the strongest and stiffest. The species of wood included in each group are shown in Figure 6–30. The sheet is considered to be in a group if the face and back are of a species from that group, although the inner veneers may be of another group. This is logical because the stiffness and bending strength depend mostly on the outer veneers. Although more than 50 species are listed, most plywood is made from Douglas fir.

Two general *types* of plywood are manufactured: interior and exterior. *Interior type plywood* is made with glue that is adequate for service indoors, and *exterior type plywood* is made with hot, phenolic resin glue that is unaffected by water and resists weathering as well as wood does. Exterior type plywood does not include any veneers, outer or inner, below C grade. It is intended for permanent outdoor installation. Interior plywood may be made in any grade.

The interior type is available in three categories. Interior glue is used for plywood intended for use where it may be exposed briefly to weather. Intermediate glue is used for

FIGURE 6–30 Classification of species

Group 1	Group 2		Group 3	Group 4	Group 5
Apitong* **	Cedar, Port Orford	Maple, black	Alder, red	Aspen	Basswood
Beech, American	Cypress	Mengkulang*	Birch, paper	Bigtooth	Poplar, balsam
Birch	Douglas fir 2†	Meranti, red* ‡	Cedar, Alaska	Quaking	
Sweet	Fir	Mersawa*	Fir, subalpine	Cativo	
Yellow	Balsam	Pine	Hemlock, eastern	Cedar	
Douglas fir 1†	California red	Pond	Maple, bigleaf	Incense	
Kapur*	Grand	Red	Pine	Western red	
Keruing* **	Noble	Virginia	Jack	Cottonwood	
Larch, western	Pacific silver	Western white	Lodgepole	Eastern	
Maple, sugar	White	Spruce	Ponderosa	Black (western	
Pine	Hemlock, western	Black	Spruce	poplar)	
Caribbean	Lauan	Red	Redwood	Pine	
Ocote	Almon	Sitka	Spruce	Eastern white	
Pine, southern	Bagtikan	Sweetgum	Engelmann	Sugar	
Loblolly	Mayapis	Tamarack	White		
Longleaf	Red lauan	Yellow poplar			
Shortleaf	Tangile				
Slash	White lauan				
Tanoak					

*Each of these names represents a trade group of woods consisting of a number of closely related species.
**Species from the genus *Dipterocarpus* marketed collectively: Apitong if orginating in the Philippines, Keruing if originating in Malaysia or Indonesia.
†Douglas fir from trees grown in the states of Washington, Oregon, California, Idaho, Montana, Wyoming, and the Canadian provinces of Alberta and British Columbia shall be classed as Douglas fir No. 1. Douglas fir from trees grown in the states of Nevada, Utah, Colorado, Arizona, and New Mexico shall be classed as Douglas fir No. 2.
‡Red Meranti shall be limited to species having a specific gravity of 0.41 or more based on green volume and oven-dry weight.
Source: APA—The Engineered Wood Association

plywood intended for use in high humidity or for exposure to the weather for a short time. Exterior glue is used for plywood expected to be exposed to weather for an extended period during construction.

Plywood is graded for strength, although not in the same way as lumber. Based on the thickness and classification of species, strength is indicated by stamping two *identification index* numbers on the plywood sheet. The first number gives the maximum span if the sheet is used for a roof, and the second gives the maximum span if the sheet is used for a subfloor.

Plywood is specified and graded primarily either for appearance or for strength, depending on how it is to be used. Descriptions of the appearance veneer grades are listed in Figure 6–31. If an appearance grade is desired, the grade, number of veneers, species group, type, and thickness are specified. If an engineered grade is desired for strength, the grade, identification index, number of veneers, and thickness are specified. These specified requirements are verified by a certification of quality stamped on the back or edge of each piece of plywood. Examples of such grade stamps are shown in Figure 6–32.

FIGURE 6–31   Veneer grades used in plywood

A	Smooth, paintable. Not more than 18 neatly made repairs, boat, sled, or router type, and parallel to grain, permitted. Wood or synthetic repairs permitted. May be used for natural finish in less demanding applications.
B	Solid surface. Shims, sled or router repairs, and tight knots to 1 in. across grain permitted. Wood or synthetic repairs permitted. Some minor splits permitted.
$C_{plugged}$	Improved C veneer with splits limited to $\frac{1}{8}$-in. width and knotholes or other open defects limited to $\frac{1}{4} \times \frac{1}{2}$ in. Admits some broken grain. Wood or synthetic repairs permitted.
C	Tight knots to $1\frac{1}{2}$ in. Knotholes to 1 in. across grain and some to $1\frac{1}{2}$ in. if total width of knots and knotholes is within specified limits. Synthetic or wood repairs. Discoloration and sanding defects that do not impair strength permitted. Limited splits allowed. Stitching permitted.
D	Knots and knotholes to $2\frac{1}{2}$ in. width across grain and $\frac{1}{2}$ in. larger within specified limits. Limited splits allowed. Stitching permitted. Limited to Interior, Exposure 1, and Exposure 2 panels.

Source: APA—The Engineered Wood Association

Structural members can be fabricated of plywood, or of plywood in combination with sawn lumber or glu-lam lumber. The plywood is fastened to the lumber by nailing or gluing. Glue may be held under pressure by specialized equipment while drying, or the pressure may be applied by nailing tightly immediately after gluing in a procedure called *nail gluing.*

Plywood is used for the gusset plates and splices of sawn wood trusses. It is also used for *box beams,* where it serves as the web with sawn or glu-lam lumber as the flanges. *Stressed-skin panels* are made with the materials reversed. The upper and lower flanges (panel covers) are made of plywood with webs of sawn lumber. The assembly is very wide compared to its depth, but is stressed like a beam while having the shape of a panel.

Sandwich panels consist of plywood panel covers separated by a comparatively weak material with no need for sawn lumber except at the edges of the panels in some cases. The material between panel faces may be plastic foam or resin-impregnated paper in a honeycomb pattern. The material need only be strong enough to unite the load-bearing upper and lower panel faces, which act structurally like the upper and lower chords of a truss. Truss chords are held apart by a thin network of web members, and the panel faces are also held apart by a thin network of material. See Figure 6–33 for illustrations of the various types of structural components.

Plywood siding is manufactured with face materials of various kinds to provide a particular effect while retaining the desirable properties of plywood. *Overlaid plywood* has a resin-treated surface, hot-bonded to the plywood sheet. The surface is smooth and intended for paint finish of the best quality. It is also used for concrete forms because its smooth surface makes a better concrete surface and allows forms to be removed easily. *Coated plywood* is surfaced with metal or plastic designed to produce a special effect. Coatings that simulate stucco or exposed aggregate are available as well as metal coatings of various textures and colors and clear plastic coating for protection only.

HOW TO READ THE BASIC TRADEMARKS OF *APA – THE ENGINEERED WOOD ASSOCIATION*

Product Standard PS 1-95 is intended to provide for clear understanding between buyer and seller. To identify plywood manufactured by association member mills under the requirements of Product Standard PS 1-95, four types of trademarks and one typical edge mark are illustrated. They include the plywood's exposure durability classification, grade and group, and class or Span Rating. Here's how they look, together with notations on what each element means.

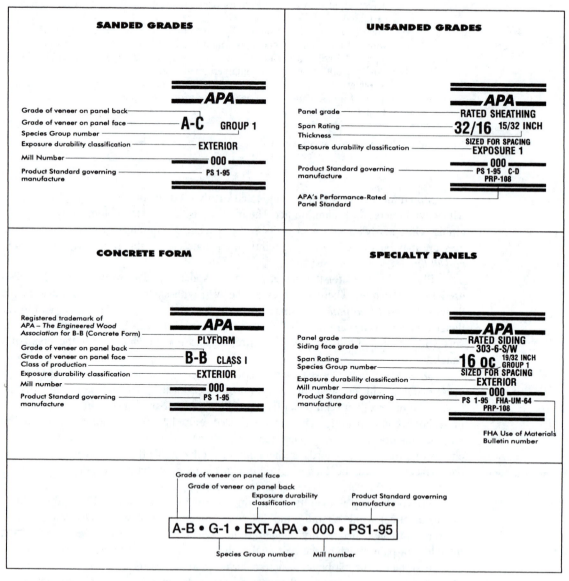

FIGURE 6–32 Plywood grades (*Courtesy APA—The Engineered Wood Association*)

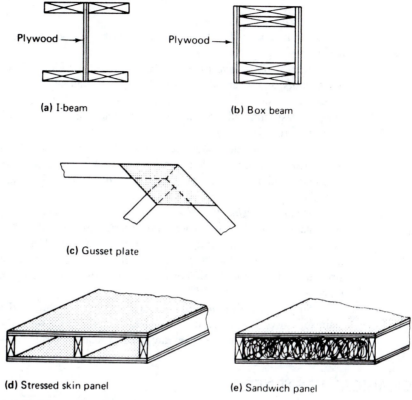

(a) I-beam   (b) Box beam

(c) Gusset plate

(d) Stressed skin panel   (e) Sandwich panel

FIGURE 6-33   Structural uses of plywood

Hardwood Plywood

The types and grades of hardwood plywood are described in the U.S. Department of Commerce's Product Standard PS51 for Hardwood and Decorative Plywood. Hardwood plywood is usually selected for its appearance to be used as the face of cabinets, furniture, doors, flooring, and wall paneling. Many special effects can be obtained in wood pattern by the way the veneer is cut from the log. Knots, crooked grain, and other characteristics that indicate weakness are valued for their appearance.

Wall paneling is made with a face veneer selected for its appearance and then stained or treated for special effects. It may be sand blasted, antiqued, striated, or grooved to give the appearance of individual boards. It is made in sheets as thin as $\frac{1}{8}$ in. with little strength and little care for the appearance of the back.

The core material behind hardwood veneers may be sawn lumber with a thin veneer on one or both faces for cabinets or furniture. It may be made from sawdust, shavings, and other scraps of wood mixed with glue and pressed into flat sheets called particle boards. It may also be made of noncombustible material for fire-resistant construction.

GLUE

Glues commonly used in the manufacturing of plywood and in other wood fabrication are listed here.

Animal glues have traditionally been used for gluing wood. They are made from hides, hoofs, and other animal parts. They are heated before application and pressed cold, set quickly, show little stain, develop high strength, do not dull tools excessively, are not moisture resistant, and are low priced. They are used mostly for furniture, millwork, and cabinet work.

Casein glues are made from milk. They are used cold, set quickly, stain some woods excessively, develop high strength, cause tools to become dull, and perform well in damp conditions. They are used for structural joining and glu-lam and plywood manufacturing.

Melamine resin, phenol resin, resorcinol resin, and *resorcinol resin–phenol resin* combinations are used when waterproof glues are needed. All except resorcinol require high temperatures for curing, although some resorcinol-phenol combinations may use temperatures as low as 100°F (38°C). All of them show little stain, develop very high strength, and are expensive. They are used for structural joining and glu-lam and plywood manufacturing.

Some *vegetable glues* are made from starch. They are used cold, set at various rates, stain some woods slightly, develop high strength, cause some dulling of tools, and have low resistance to moisture. They are used in manufacturing plywood.

MECHANICAL FASTENERS

Wood members are fastened together and to other materials with metal fasteners of various kinds. The traditional nails made of steel and sometimes aluminum, copper, zinc, or brass are widely used. The standard lengths of nails are made in three diameters called box nails, common nails, and spikes, with box nails being the thinnest and spikes the thickest. Spikes are also made in longer sizes than the others. The tendency of wood to split when nailed is proportional to its specific gravity, and it is necessary to use several thinner nails rather than one thick one in heavy wood. The three diameters allow flexibility in the design of nailed joints.

Unseasoned wood that is nailed causes the nails to loosen as it shrinks during seasoning. Wood must be nailed dry if it is to be dry in use. However, wet wood may be nailed if it is going to stay wet.

A nail may be subjected to an axial force tending to pull it out of the wood. The nail is said to be subjected to *withdrawal loading*. The resistance to withdrawal depends on the nail diameter and the length driven into the wood and on the specific gravity of the wood, being much greater for heavier wood. Wood is much better able to resist withdrawal from side grain than from end grain. Nails subjected to withdrawal from end grain have half the resistance of those in side grain and are not permitted by the National Design Specification. Nails are sometimes coated with cement or rosin to make them more resistant to withdrawal.

The most common load on the wood of a nailed joint is a lateral load in side grain. The load that can be resisted depends on the specific gravity of the wood and on the length and diameter of the nail embedded in the wood. It does not depend on the direction of load. The nails connecting flanges and webs of box beams and the nails connecting truss joints are loaded laterally. Resistance to lateral loads in end grain is two-thirds of the side grain resistance. Wood offers more resistance to lateral loads than to withdrawal, and nails should be loaded laterally in preference to withdrawal whenever possible. See Figure 6–34 for illustrations of nailed joints.

Wood screws are used for the same purpose as nails and transmit withdrawal or lateral loads to the wood in much the same way. Strength depends on the length and width of the screw and on the specific gravity of the wood. It is independent of direction for lateral loads. Screws can resist stronger forces than nails of comparable size because of the grip of the threads in the wood. Resistance to lateral loads is greater, and the design should require them rather than withdrawal loads if at all possible. Resistance to withdrawal from end grain is low, and screws are not permitted by the National Design Specification to be loaded this way. Lateral resistance in end grain is two-thirds of the resistance in side grain.

Bolts are used to transmit lateral forces from one wood member to another and are not loaded in withdrawal. A bolt is inserted into a predrilled hole and held in place between the bolt head and a nut. The load transmitted by a laterally loaded bolt is different from the load transmitted by a laterally loaded nail or screw. The resistance is a function of the compressive strength of the wood and the area (length × width of bolt) bearing against the wood. Just as wood is strongest in compression parallel to grain and weakest in compression perpendicular to grain, so the bolted joint is strongest when the load is parallel to grain and weakest when the load is perpendicular to grain, and has an intermediate strength at any other angle. The allowable load at other angles is determined by using the Hankinson formula or Scholten nomographs and the allowable loads parallel and perpendicular to grain.

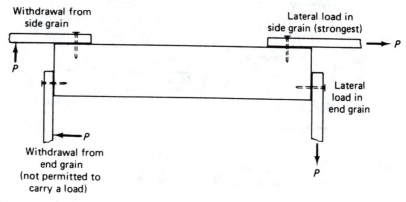

FIGURE 6–34 Loads on nails

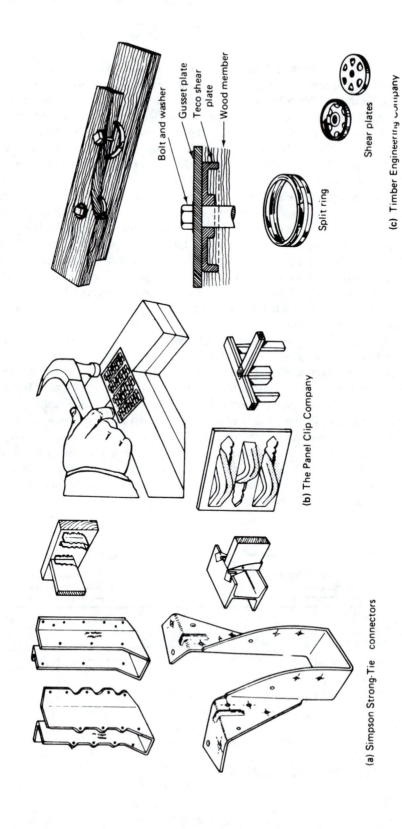

FIGURE 6-35 Typical connectors used with wood: (a) Simpson Strong-Tie® connectors (*Courtesy Simpson Co.*); (b) top plate tie with truss clip (*Courtesy Panel Clip Co.*); (c) split rings and shear plates (*Courtesy Timber Engineering Co.*)

(a) Simpson Strong-Tie connectors

(b) The Panel Clip Company

(c) Timber Engineering Company

Split ring

Shear plates

Bolt and washer

Gusset plate

Teco shear plate

Wood member

Lag screws, which are threaded at the pointed end for one-half to three-quarters of the length and unthreaded toward the head, provide good withdrawal resistance like a screw and strong lateral resistance like a bolt.

Two types of connectors are used in combination with bolts to increase the area of wood in compression. One split ring or a pair of shear plates is used for wood-to-wood connections and one shear plate for metal-to-wood connections. Several may be used in one joint. Both types are inserted into tight-fitting prefabricated holes. They may be used in side grain or end grain at any angle. Their strength depends on the area of wood in contact with the connector and the compressive strength of the wood at the angle as determined by the Hankinson formula or Scholten nomographs. Split rings transfer the load from wood to wood through the ring, and the bolt takes no load, but only holds the joint together. Shear connectors fit tightly over the bolt, and the load is transferred from one member to another through the bolt. Many other specialized fasteners are designed for connecting wood rapidly and securely. See Figure 6–35 for illustrations of some of the types in use.

REVIEW QUESTIONS

1. At what time of year was the tree in Figure 6–2 cut down? Explain your answer.

2. Indicate in a sketch the pattern of grain in a straight board sawed from a tree with a bend in it. Show boards sawed parallel to the plane of the bend and those sawed perpendicular to it.

3. Give the fbm of the following quantities of wood:
   a. 800 lineal ft of $\frac{3}{4}$ in. × 8 in.
   b. 15 pieces of 2 × 4 from 12 ft 0 in. to 12 ft 11 in. in length
   c. one post 10 ft long, 14 × 14 in. in cross section

4. Should a window frame, as shown in Figure 6–15, be slash-cut or rift-cut to keep the joint opening to a minimum? Explain your answer.

5. In what ways do springwood and summerwood differ?

6. What are the moisture content values used to define greenwood and dry wood? Why is this an important distinction?

7. A sample of Douglas fir sapwood had a wet weight of 1315.8 g and an oven-dry weight of 612 g. Calculate the moisture content of the sapwood and determine if it is a reasonable value.

8. Define equilibrium moisture content.

9. Describe three methods of seasoning wood.

10. If the stress at failure in bending is 7200 psi for small, perfect samples of a certain species of wood, what is the allowable bending stress for a piece of lumber with defects that are judged to reduce the strength by 40 percent?

11. **a.** Determine the allowable fiber stress in bending for a Douglas fir south select structural grade 2 × 4 for single and repetitive member use.
    b. What are the allowable spans for a Hem fir number 2, 2 × 8 set at 12 in. o.c., 16 in. o.c., and 24 in. o.c.?

12. What methods are used to grade lumber? What agencies provide the grading rules used to perform lumber grading?

13. Explain the difference between single member and repetitive member allowable stresses in bending. Cite an example.

14. What are the differences among boards, dimension lumber, and timber?

15. What is the difference between a characteristic and a manufacturing imperfection?

16. If other factors are equal, which piece of lumber is weaker: one with a slope of grain of 1 in 5 or one with a slope of grain of 1 in 6?

17. How do preservatives protect wood from rotting, insects, and marine borers?

18. Discuss the advantages and disadvantages of creosote as a preservative.

19. Why can glu-lam timbers be stronger than sawn timbers?

20. Briefly describe the manufacturing process used to manufacture plywood.

21. What characteristic of plywood is indicated by the veneer grade? by the species group?

22. What does the designation 24/16 mean on a plywood grade trademark?

7

Masonry

Masonry is an important aspect of the construction industry that utilizes manufactured products, field-produced materials, and skilled workmanship to produce walls and floor surfaces. Masonry construction must have adequate strength to carry loads, be highly durable, and, when used in exterior applications, be watertight.

Masonry construction is also a very aesthetic material, providing the designer with a number of variables to work with such as size of units, color, texture, and type of bond. Masonry construction may also be used as an acoustical material and for the construction of fire-rated wall systems. The materials associated with masonry construction include concrete block, clay brick, clay tile, stone, mortar, and metal reinforcing systems.

CLAY MASONRY

One of the oldest manufactured building materials still in use today is the clay brick. The remains of structures found in the Tigris-Euphrates basin indicate the use of sunbaked brick as early as 6000 B.C. By 500–600 B.C., bricks were being hard-burned in kilns to produce a more durable construction material.

The brickworks were usually owned by royal families, and they would have the family's name or insignia molded into the brick, much the same as some brick manufacturers still do today. While the process of brick making has been improved through technological advances, the basic theory of hard-burned brick manufacturing has remained virtually unchanged.

Brick

The term *brick* is used to denote solid clay masonry units. Cored units are considered solid as long as the cores do not exceed 25 percent of the total cross-sectional area of the unit. The cores, which vary in size and number, reduce the weight of the brick, increase bond strength, and allow a more even drying of the units during the burning phase of brick manufacturing. Most brick produced today is of standard nominal modular sizes and shapes, as illustrated by Figures 7–1 and 7–2. The nominal dimensions of a masonry unit include the thickness of the mortar joint.

Tile

Hollow clay masonry units are called *clay tile* and are produced with core areas in excess of 25 percent of the gross cross-sectional area of the unit. The main classifications of hollow masonry are structural clay tile (Figure 7–3) and structural facing tile, the latter having a surface that has been treated with a ceramic glaze, color, or surface texture treatment. When the tile units are designed to be used with the cores horizontal, they are called side construction tile; when cores are set vertical, the units are called end construction tile.

Raw Materials for Clay Masonry

Chemically, the clays used to manufacture brick and tile are compounds of alumina and silica with differing amounts of metallic oxides and other impurities. The metallic oxides act as fluxes during burning and also influence the color of clay masonry units.

Manufacturers of brick will blend clays from different locations as well as vary the manufacturing processes to reduce variations in the finished product. However, slight differences in the properties of clay masonry units are normal.

The clays used to produce brick and tile must have enough plasticity to be shaped and molded when wet and adequate tensile strength to retain the molded shape until the units are fired in the kilns. The clay particles must also fuse together when subjected to the elevated kiln temperatures.

The raw materials used to manufacture brick and tile are:

1. *Surface clays* are clays found at or close to the surface of the earth.
2. *Shales* are clays that have been subjected to high pressures and have hardened into a rock formation.
3. *Fire clays* are deep-mined clays having more uniform chemical and physical properties and fewer impurities, and are used to produce brick with refractory qualities.

Manufacturing Clay Masonry

The manufacturer of brick and tile will use individual clays or blends of clays, depending upon the specific end product required.

The steps in the manufacturing process of clay masonry units are illustrated in Figure 7–4.

Winning or mining is the process of obtaining the raw clays from surface pits or underground mines. The clays are blended for color, to increase uniformity, and to allow more control of the raw material's suitability for a given product run.

Unit Name		Actual Size (inches)	Actual Size (mm)	Modular Metric Size (mm)	Vertical Coursing
Modular	width	3-1/2	89	90	3:200 mm
	height	2-1/4	57	57	
	length	7-1/2	190	190	
Engineer Modular	width	3-1/2	89	90	5:400 mm
	height	2-3/4	70	70	
	length	7-1/2	190	190	
Closure Modular	width	3-1/2	89	90	2:200 mm
	height	3-1/2	89	90	
	length	7-1/2	190	190	
Roman	width	3-1/2	89	90	4:200 mm
	height	1-5/8	41	40	
	length	11-1/2	292	290	
Norman	width	3-1/2	89	90	3:200 mm
	height	2-1/4	57	57	
	length	11-1/2	292	290	
Engineer Norman	width	3-1/2	89	90	5:400 mm
	height	2-3/4	70	70	
	length	11-1/2	292	290	
Utility	width	3-1/2	89	90	2:200 mm
	height	3-1/2	89	90	
	length	11-1/2	292	290	
Standard *	width	3-5/8	92		3:200 mm
	height	2-1/4	57	57	
	length	8	203		
Engineer Standard *	width	3-5/8	92		5:400 mm
	height	2-13/16	71	70	
	length	8	203		
King *	width	3	76		5:400 mm
	height	2-3/4	70	70	
	length	9-5/8	245		

* Not a modular unit in either the inch-pound or the metric system.

FIGURE 7–1   Common brick sizes (*Courtesy Construction Metrication Council of the National Institute of Building Sciences, Washington, D.C.*)

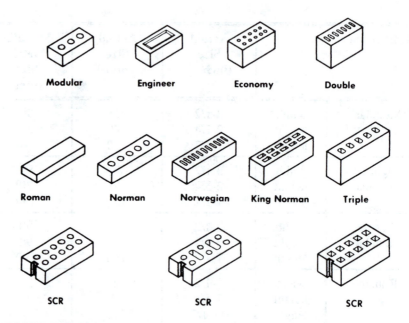

FIGURE 7-2 Typical clay brick (Construction—Principles, Materials, and Methods, *Institute of Financial Education, 5th ed., 1983*)

The clays are crushed to break up large chunks, screened to remove stones, and then pulverized with 4- to 8-ton grinding wheels. The clays are then screened to control particle sizes going to the pugmills. Pugmills are large mixing chambers where the clays are blended with water. The operation is called *tempering* and produces a plastic, relatively homogeneous mass ready for molding.

Three types of forming methods are used to produce clay masonry units: stiff-mud, soft-mud, and dry-press. The most common method in use is the stiff-mud method. It accounts for all structural tile production and most brick production.

The stiff-mud method utilizes a clay blended with approximately 10 to 15 percent water by weight to produce a plastic mass which is then de-aired in a vacuum to reduce the air content of the wet clay. The clay is then extruded through a die. As it leaves the die, any required surface texture may be applied to the clay ribbon. Cutter wires, spaced to compensate for normal drying and burning shrinkage, cut the brick to size. The bricks are then sorted off of a continuous-belt conveyor, with acceptable bricks being placed on dryer carts and the rejects being returned to the pugmill.

The soft-mud process is used for clays which contain 20 to 30 percent water in their natural state. The clays are mixed and then molded in forms. Either sand or water can be used as a release agent to prevent the clay from sticking to the mold. Brick produced this way is called water-struck or sand-struck, depending upon the material used as a release agent.

The dry-press process is utilized for low-plasticity clays. These clays are blended with less than 10 percent water and formed in molds under pressures ranging from 500 to 1500 psi.

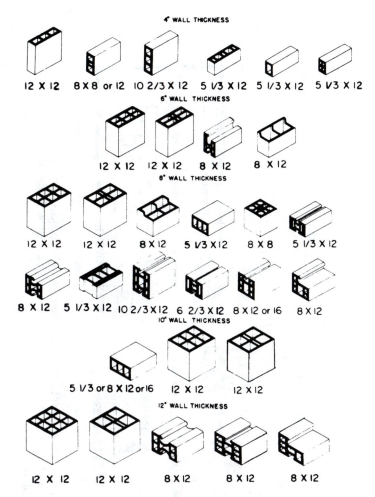

FIGURE 7–3 Structural clay tile (Construction—Principles, Materials, and Methods, *Institute of Financial Education, 5th ed., 1983*)

The wet units coming from the cutting or molding machines will normally have moisture contents ranging from 7 to 30 percent. This water is removed in dryers at temperatures ranging from 100 to 300°F over a period of one to two days.

When brick or tile units require a glazed finish, two methods are utilized. High-fired glazes are applied to the units before or after drying and the units are then kiln-burned at normal temperatures. Low-fired glazes are applied after the clay unit has been kiln-burned and allowed to cool. The clay units are then sprayed with the glazing compound and refired at low temperatures to set the glaze.

Brick and tile are fired in continuous tunnel kilns or periodic kilns, with the process requiring two to five days. The tunnel kiln allows the brick to move through various temperature zones on special carts. The periodic kiln requires the brick to be stacked

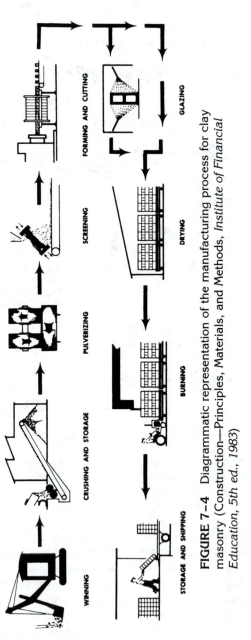

FIGURE 7-4 Diagrammatic representation of the manufacturing process for clay masonry (Construction—Principles, Materials, and Methods, *Institute of Financial Education, 5th ed., 1983*)

WINNING

CRUSHING AND STORAGE

PULVERIZING

SCREENING

FORMING AND CUTTING

STORAGE AND SHIPPING

BURNING

DRYING

GLAZING

inside, with the temperature of the interior space fluctuating as required by the burning and cooling operations.

The burning of the brick is a very critical stage in the production process, and kiln temperatures are monitored constantly because variations during the burn will affect finish color, strength, absorption, and size of the units.

The first stage in the burning process is called water smoking and occurs at temperatures up to 400°F. The second stage is dehydration and occurs in the range of 300 to 1800°F. The third stage is oxidation and occurs between 1000 and 1800°F, with the final stage, vitrification, occurring between 1600 and 2400°F. Near the end of the burning, the units may be flashed to produce different colors and color shading. Flashing is the creation in the kiln of a reducing atmosphere (oxygen reduction to reduce combustion).

The cooling down of the clay units will normally require two to three days in a periodic kiln and no more than two days in a continuous kiln. The rate of cooling will affect color, cracking, and checking of the clay unit and is therefore carefully controlled.

After cooling, the units are removed from the kilns, sorted, graded, and prepared for direct shipping or storage.

Strength of Clay Masonry

The compressive strength of brick and clay tile will vary based upon the clay source, method of manufacture, and the degree of burning. Plastic clays used in the stiff-mud process generally yield higher compressive strengths than soft-mud or dry-press methods. When the same clay and methods of manufacturing are utilized, higher degrees of burning will yield higher compressive strengths. Compressive strengths of brick usually range from 1500 to 20,000 psi.

Absorption of Clay Masonry

The absorption of water by brick is dependent upon the clay, the process of manufacturing, and the amount of burn to which the brick has been subjected. Plastic clays and higher degrees of burning generally produce brick units having low absorptions.

Brick which will be exposed to weathering, especially alternate freezing and thawing, should have low absorption capacities. High compressive strengths or low absorption values usually indicate brick or tile that will exhibit adequate durability when exposed to alternate freezing and thawing conditions.

Suction is the initial rate of absorption of clay masonry units and has a great influence upon bond strength. When a brick is laid in a bed of mortar, water is drawn up into the brick's surface. If the brick is highly absorptive, this process will leave a dry bed of mortar which will not develop adequate bond between the brick units. If the unit has very low absorption, the water will allow the brick to float and when the mortar dries, inadequate bond strengths will result.

Maximum bond strength will generally occur when the brick suction rate does not exceed 0.7 oz (20 g) per minute. Brick having suction rates in excess of this limit should be sprayed with water prior to use; however, the surfaces should be allowed to dry before the brick is used.

To determine in the field whether brick should be prewet or not is relatively easy. Simply sprinkle a few drops of water on the flat side of a brick. If the drops are absorbed in less than a minute, prewetting is required. A more accurate field test requires a quarter, a wax marker, and an eyedropper. Draw a circle on the brick using the quarter and wax marker and place 20 drops of water within the circle. If the water is absorbed in less than 1½ minutes the brick should be presoaked.

Clay Masonry Colors

Colors of brick cover a wide range and include tones of pearl gray, cream, red, purple, and black. The chemical composition of the clay, method of burning, and the degree of burn all affect the color of brick. The most important oxide present in clay with respect to color is iron. Iron oxides in clays will produce red brick when exposed to an oxidizing fire, and purple when burned in a reducing atmosphere. Generally, lighter colors are the result of underburning. Overburning produces clinker brick, which is dark red, black, or dark brown, depending upon the original clays. Underburned brick is softer and more absorptive and has lower compressive strengths than brick produced at higher temperatures.

Clay Masonry Standards

Standard specifications for the numerous types and grades of brick and tile have been developed by the American Society for Testing and Materials (ASTM) and are widely accepted. It is recommended that the appropriate ASTM specification be included by reference for all clay masonry construction.

CONCRETE MASONRY

The first concrete masonry units used in construction were large, cumbersome blocks of solid concrete that had been cast in wood forms. Late in the nineteenth century builders began experimenting with the production of hollow concrete masonry units. These blocks were much lighter than the solid type, yet still retained adequate load-carrying capacity.

The first patent for a hollow concrete masonry unit mold and manufacturing process was issued to Harold S. Palmer in 1900. The molds were filled with a relatively dry concrete and hand-tamped. Production rates varied, but 80 units per day was average. By the 1920s, automatic machines were producing about 3000 concrete masonry units per day.

It is not unusual today to see manufacturing equipment in a block plant producing over 20,000 block units per day, depending upon size, shape, and materials being used to produce the block.

Typical shapes of concrete block are illustrated in Figure 7–5. The sizes of concrete blocks are stated as nominal dimensions. For example, an 8-in., 8 × 18 concrete block is actually 7⅝ in. wide and 7⅝ in. high by 17⅝ in. long. The ⅜-in. difference from nominal to actual represents the head and bed mortar joint when the block is installed. Therefore, when an 8 × 18-in. block is placed in a wall, the occupied wall surface area is 1 sq ft; when an 8 × 16 block is installed in a wall, it occupies 0.89 sq ft of wall surface.

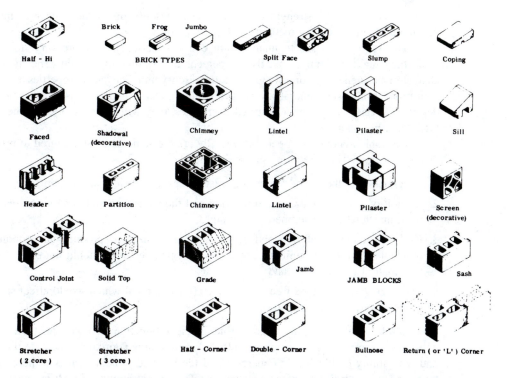

FIGURE 7-5 Typical shapes of concrete block (Construction—Principles, Materials, and Methods, *Institute of Financial Education, 5th ed., 1983*)

The term *concrete masonry unit (CMU)* refers to molded concrete units used in construction to build load-bearing and nonload-bearing walls. The units are cored or solid and manufactured off site. However, like most masonry construction, the units are integrated into the structure on site, utilizing field materials (mortars) and skilled workmanship.

Raw Materials for Concrete Masonry Units

Concrete masonry units are manufactured from portland cement, water, aggregates, and in some cases admixtures, which may include coloring agents, air-entraining materials, water repellents, and other additives.

Most of the cementitious material used to manufacture block is Type I portland cement; however, Type III high-early-strength cements are also used to increase early strengths and reduce breakage during handling and delivery. Most block plants utilize liquid and powder admixture systems to alter the concrete properties rather than special cements. These systems allow greater control of the concrete mix properties going into the block molds.

Portland blast-furnace slag cements, fly ash, silica flour, and other pozzolanic materials may also be substituted for some of the Type I cement. When the pozzolanic materials are used, the strength of the concrete masonry unit takes longer to mature, depending upon the curing method used and type of aggregate.

The aggregates used to manufacture concrete masonry units are very important, since they make up approximately 90 percent of the unit by weight. The aggregate characteristics generally control the concrete masonry units' physical properties as well as their production costs. Generally, local availability governs aggregate use; however, when designers specify certain manufactured aggregates, they will be transported to the block manufacturing plant.

Desirable aggregate properties generally are the same as those required to produce quality concrete. These required properties include:

1. Toughness, hardness, and strength to resist impact, abrasion, and loading;

2. Durability to resist freezing and thawing and the expansion and contraction resulting from moisture and/or temperature changes;

3. Uniform gradation of fine and coarse aggregate sizes to produce an economical, moldable mixture and uniform appearance (aggregates used should not exceed ⅓ of the smallest block shell); and

4. The aggregate should be free of any deleterious material which would affect strength or cause surface imperfections.

While admixtures play a great role in the production of concrete, their use in concrete masonry unit production is limited. Air-entraining admixtures increase plasticity and workability of block mix concretes and the air-void system increases the concrete masonry units' ability to resist weathering. The air-entraining admixtures also allow greater compaction, producing denser units with more uniform surfaces and less breakage of freshly molded units. Metallic stearates are somewhat effective in reducing absorption rates and capillary action in concrete masonry units; however, their use is limited.

Calcium chloride and other accelerating admixtures are used by some manufacturers to allow faster production rates during cold weather.

Manufacturing Concrete Masonry Units

The production of concrete masonry units will vary to some degree from plant to plant. However, the basic sequencing is fairly common to all facilities. (See Figure 7–6.)

Raw materials are delivered to the production site by truck, railroad, or barge, where they are usually stored in open stockpiles. The cement is delivered by bulk tankers and blown into storage silos. The aggregates are fed by conveyor from stockpiles to bins located above the weigh hoppers. Aggregate gradations generally run toward the fine side, with maximum sizes rarely exceeding ⅜ in.

The concrete block mix is proportioned by weight into a weigh batcher, with the ingredients carefully controlled to maintain a uniform mix from batch to batch. Electronic sensors determine the moisture content of the aggregates and vary accordingly the amount of mixing water required. The materials are dropped into the mixer, the required water is added, and the materials are mixed for six to eight minutes. Admixtures are normally added with the mixing water. Since the block mix is relatively dry when

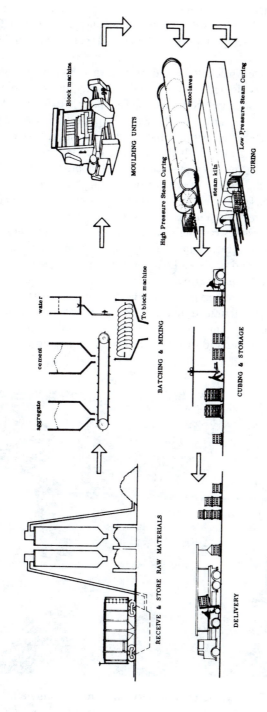

FIGURE 7-6 Manufacturing flow chart for concrete masonry units (CMU) (Construction—Principles, Materials, and Methods, *Institute of Financial Education, 5th ed., 1983*)

compared to concrete, longer mixing or blending times are required. Concrete masonry units are produced with lower water-cement ratios and cement factors than structural concretes. Cement factors run from 250 to 375 lb per cu yd, and the mix is considered to be zero slump.

The completed batch is then deposited in a holding bin located over the block machine. The mix is fed into the block molds in measured quantities and then consolidated with pressure and vibration. The mold is then lifted from the molded block units (see Figure 7–7) and repositioned for a repeat cycle. The green block (uncured block) sits on a steel tray pallet, which is then transferred to a curing rack (see Figure 7–8). When a curing rack is filled, it is moved to the curing area (see Figure 7–9).

Low-pressure steam curing accounts for approximately 80 percent of all block production, with the balance of production utilizing high-pressure steam curing and, when climatic conditions are favorable, moist curing at normal temperatures of 70 to 100°F.

Low-pressure steam curing is performed in tunnel kilns at atmospheric pressures, with steam temperatures ranging from 150 to 185°F. The curing sequence starts once the kiln is loaded with green units. The green units are allowed to obtain some initial hardening for a period of 1 to 3 hours prior to steam exposure. This time is customarily referred to as the *holding period.*

Following the holding period, the heating-up period or steaming-up period begins. According to a predetermined time-temperature program, saturated steam or moist air is fed into the kiln. The temperature of the units is raised at a rate not exceeding 60°F per hour, to a maximum of 150 to 165°F for normal aggregates.

FIGURE 7–7 Concrete masonry units immediately after molding. Note shape retention (*Courtesy Dagostino Building Blocks, Inc.*)

FIGURE 7–8 Curing racks being loaded with "green" block prior to curing (*Courtesy Dagostino Building Blocks, Inc.*)

FIGURE 7–9 Curing area (*Courtesy Dagostino Building Blocks, Inc.*)

When the units have reached the desired temperature in the kiln, the steam is turned off and the block undergoes a soaking period of from 12 to 18 hours. The kiln is operating during this timeframe on residual steam and heat, and the units are said to be *soaking*. After soaking and if required, an artificial drying condition may be induced by elevating the kiln temperature for approximately 4 hours. Steam curing's principal benefit is economy, accelerating the strength gain of the units so they may be placed into inventory quicker, with 2- to 4-day strengths of 90 percent or more of their ultimate strength. The strength of steam-cured block is more than double that of moist-cured block, which at the 2- to 4-day age would normally exhibit 40 percent of its ultimate strength.

High-pressure steam curing accelerates the block setting time, using saturated steam at pressures ranging from 125 to 150 psi. The curing is performed in a pressure vessel called an *autoclave*. The green masonry units are allowed to gain initial hardening for a 2- to 3-hour holding period before being placed in the autoclave. Once the units are placed in the autoclave, the temperature is raised slowly over a period of 3 hours so that the green units are not subjected to full steam pressure too soon. When a 350°F temperature is reached, the block is allowed to soak for 5 to 10 hours, depending on unit sizes at a constant temperature and pressure.

The pressure release is called the *blowdown* and usually takes ½ hour or less to perform. The rapid blowdown allows the masonry units to lose moisture quickly without building up shrinkage stresses in the individual units. Enough moisture is removed during the blowdown phase that the concrete masonry units are very close to a relatively stable air-dry condition.

The strengths of high-pressure-cured concrete masonry units at one-day age are equal to the 28-day strengths of moist-cured block. The high-pressure steam process produces dimensionally stable units that exhibit less volume change than moist-cured block when subjected to environmental changes related to moisture conditions. The shrinkage of high-pressure steam-cured units, moving from a saturated condition to a relatively dry condition in a heated space, is about 50 percent less than for moist-cured concrete masonry units.

When the curing procedures have been completed, the concrete masonry units are moved to cubing stations. Concrete masonry units are handled in cubes which consist of six layers of block, each layer containing 15 to 18 blocks, depending upon the individual unit's size. Normally a cube of 8 × 8 × 16 concrete block will contain both stretcher and corner blocks; however, larger units are usually cubed separately.

Concrete masonry units are normally stored outside two to three cubes high and require no special protection from the weather (see Figure 7–10). However, architectural concrete masonry units are covered with protection. The inventory time usually runs from a few days to several weeks. If concrete masonry units are shipped to a construction project too soon, the breakage from handling may be quite high; therefore, most producers allow their inventories to age, thereby reducing contractor complaints about "green" block.

In general, much of the technical knowledge relating to concrete is applicable to the production of concrete masonry units. Like concrete, the physical properties of the concrete masonry units are determined by the physical properties of the hardened cement

FIGURE 7-10 Architectural concrete masonry units are protected with a poly film prior to storage and shipping (*Courtesy Dagostino Building Blocks, Inc.*)

paste and the aggregate (see Figure 7-11). Mix composition and consistency, consolidation methods, textural requirements, and curing also affect the concrete masonry units' physical properties.

Strength of Concrete Masonry Units

Compressive strengths of concrete masonry units are difficult to predict because the useful water-cement ratio concept is not valid for harsh block mixes. The production of concrete masonry units requires careful control of water quantities in the block mix. Wetter mixes are easier to mold and generally yield higher compressive strengths; however, breakage of green units increases during handling operations. The use of very dry mixes produces consolidation problems during molding operations and ultimately lowers compressive strengths. Therefore, each block-manufacturing facility, through experimentation, will develop mix designs that will produce concrete masonry units of adequate strength without sacrificing other required properties.

The factors which affect compressive strength values for concrete block include: the type and gradation of aggregate, the type and amount of cementitious material, the degree of consolidation attained during molding, the curing method, the size and shape of the concrete masonry unit, and the conditions of the block with regard to moisture and temperature at the time of test.

FIGURE 7-11 Typical properties of concrete block made with different aggregates

	Aggregate (Graded: 3/8" to 0.)		Weight lbs/cu. ft. of Concrete	Weight 8" × 8" × 16" Unit	Compressive Strength (gross area) psi*	Water Absorption lbs/cu. ft. of Concrete	Thermal Expansion Coefficient (per °F) × 10^{-6}
	TYPE	Density (air-dry) lbs/cu. ft.					
NORMAL	Sand and Gravel	130–145	135	40	1200–1800	7–10	5.0
	Limestone	120–140	135	40	1100–1800	8–12	5.0
	Air-cooled Slag	100–125	120	35	1100–1500	9–13	4.6
LIGHT	Expanded Shale	75– 90	85	25	1000–1500	12–15	4.5
	Expanded Slag	80–105	95	28	700–1200	12–16	4.0
	Cinders	80–105	95	28	700–1000	12–18	2.5
	Pumice	60– 85	75	22	700– 900	13–19	4.0
	Scoria	75–100	95	28	700–1200	12–26	4.0

*Multiply these values by 1.80 to obtain approximate corresponding values of strength of the concrete (strength of unit on net area).

Source: Construction—Principles, Materials, and Methods, Institute of Financial Education, 5th ed., 1983

Tensile strength, flexural strength, and modulus of elasticity values vary with the compressive strength values of a concrete masonry unit. Tensile strength will normally range from 7 to 10 percent of the compressive strength, flexural strength from 15 to 20 percent of compressive strength, and the modulus of elasticity from 300 to 1200 times the compressive strength. Strength and absorption requirements for concrete masonry units are given in ASTM C90 in the appendix.

Absorption of Concrete Masonry Units

Absorption tests provide a measure of the density of the concrete in concrete masonry units. The absorption value is calculated in pounds of water per cubic foot of concrete and varies over a wide range, depending upon the aggregates used in the unit. Values for water absorption may vary from 4 lb per cu ft for dense sands and stones to as much as 20 lb per cu ft for lightweight aggregates.

The porosity of the concrete will also influence other properties, such as permeability, thermal conductivity, weight reduction, and acoustical properties. When these properties are required, the absorption values will rise. However, since these properties are usually required of interior or protected masonry, the higher absorption values are not detrimental to the concrete masonry units' durability. A high initial rate of absorption or suction indicates concrete masonry units of high permeability and low durability, because the concrete contains a large number of interconnected pores and voids. However, unconnected air-filled voids present in lightweight aggregates and air-entrained cement paste impart some of the desired porosity properties to the concrete masonry unit while limiting the permeability of the unit to water.

Even though concrete masonry units may have reasonably high suction rates, unlike clay masonry, concrete masonry units are never presoaked and in some cases may require a covering system to prevent moisture content changes in the units because of weather conditions.

Dimensional Changes in Concrete Masonry Units

Concrete masonry units normally undergo dimensional changes due to changes in temperature, moisture content, and a chemical reaction called *carbonation.*

Temperature changes cause units to expand and contract when heated and cooled. These volume changes are reversible through the same temperature ranges. The thermal expansion and contraction of concrete masonry units is governed primarily by the type of aggregate in the unit, since aggregates normally comprise 80 percent of the concrete volume. These volume changes, while relatively small in a single unit, can cause serious problems in the construction of long walls. Therefore, the designers of masonry structures will place control joints in long walls as relief areas for the compounded volume changes occurring in individual masonry units.

Moisture content changes cause concrete masonry units to expand when wet and shrink when dried. During the first few cycles of wetting and drying, the concrete masonry units may not return to their original sizes, because the concrete has a tendency toward a permanent contraction state. However, during subsequent wetting and drying cycles, the volume changes are reversible.

Original drying shrinkage is an important factor in crack development in concrete masonry walls. If concrete masonry units are placed in a wall before they have been allowed to shrink to a dimensionally stable volume, wherever the wall is restrained tensile stresses will develop and cracks will occur. Drying shrinkage is greatly reduced by properly curing and drying units so that when they are placed in the structure the moisture content of the unit is in equilibrium with the surrounding air.

Carbonation causes irreversible shrinkage in concrete masonry units when carbon dioxide is absorbed into the hardened concrete paste of masonry units. The changes in volume are approximately the same as those caused by moisture condition fluctuations. One method of reducing carbonation on the jobsite during cold weather masonry construction is to require all heat sources to be properly vented to the exterior of the work area.

Mortar

Mortar is a combination of one or more cementitious materials, a clean, well graded sand, and enough water to produce a plastic mix. Mortar serves as the binding medium in masonry construction and its functions are to bond individual units together while sealing the spaces between units, compensate for size variation in units, cause metal ties and reinforcing and masonry units to act together in a structural system, and provide aesthetic qualities to the structure through the use of color and type of joint.

Mortar is used while plastic and then hardens; thus, both plastic and hardened properties will determine a mortar's suitability for a specific construction project. The workability of a mortar is determined by its uniformity, cohesiveness, and consistency. A mortar is considered workable when the mix does not segregate easily, is easily spread, supports the weight of units, makes alignment easy, clings to vertical faces of masonry units, and is easily forced from mortar joints without excessive smearing of the wall. There are no tests in use that will measure a mortar mix's workability; however, the mason in the field will be able to tell very quickly if a particular mix is workable or not.

Water retention in a mortar prevents rapid loss of water from mortar in contact with a highly absorptive masonry unit. If the mortar has a low water retention value, the plasticity of the mortar would be greatly reduced. When low-absorption units are placed on mortar, a high water retentivity is required to prevent bleeding, which is the formation of a thin layer of water between the unit and the mortar. The water will cause the unit to float, drastically reducing bond strength.

Mortar flow is determined by laboratory test using a truncated cone and flow table. A cone of mortar is formed on the table with an original base diameter of 4 in., then the table is raised and dropped 25 times in 15 seconds and the diameter of the mortar mass is measured. If the original 4-in. diameter measures 8 in. after the test, the mortar would have a flow of 100 percent. Flow values that range from 130 to 150 percent are required for construction projects.

Flow after suction is a test used to measure water retentivity and is stated as the ratio of flow after suction to initial flow, expressed as a percentage value. The initial flow test is repeated after the mortar sample being tested has been subjected to a vacuum for one minute, thereby removing some water from the mortar mix.

Bond strength is the most important property of hardened mortar and is affected by mortar properties, type and condition of masonry unit, workmanship, and curing.

When the air content of a mortar mix is increased, there usually will be a decrease in bond strength; however, water retention properties improve and the durability of the hardened paste increases.

The relationship of flow to tensile bond strength is direct for all mortars, with an increase in flow causing an increase in bond strength.

The compressive strength of mortar depends largely upon the quantity of portland cement in the mix. Compressive strength increases with an increase in cement content and decreases with an increase in water content. However, since there have been very few reports of structural failure or distress associated with mortar, most masonry construction work is performed utilizing moderate-strength mortars. Tests have shown that concrete masonry wall compressive strengths increase only about 10 percent when mortar cube compressive strengths are increased 130 percent. Composite wall strengths increase 25 percent when mortar cube compressive strengths increase 160 percent. Generally, bond strength, workability, and water retentivity are considered more important than compressive strength and are usually given more consideration in specifications.

The strong concern placed upon bond strength is evident when specifications allow retempering of mortar mixes. *Retempering* is the addition of water to mortar mixes that have lost water while sitting in mortar pans. The practice of retempering will reduce compressive strengths, but the loss is more than compensated for by the increase of bond strength of the retempered mortar mix. The usual time limit for mortar use is around 2½ hours from time of initial mixing, after which time the mortar should be discarded. Many specifications limit the number of retemperings permitted as well as set a specified time limit for the use of a mortar mix.

Straight lime mortars—lime, sand, and water hardened at a slow variable rate—have low compressive strengths and poor durability, but do have good workability and high water retentivity. The lime hardens when exposed to air and the hardening process occurs over long periods of time. Lime mortars have the ability to heal or recement small cracks and reduce water infiltration.

Portland cement, sand, and water combine to form portland cement mortars which harden quickly and attain high compressive strengths with good durability; however, workability is poor and water retention is low.

Portland cement, lime, sand, and water are combined to produce mortars which have good durability, high compressive strengths, and consistent hardening rates. The lime component increases workability, elasticity, and water retentivity. Both cementitious materials contribute to good bond strength.

Masonry cement, sand, and water mortars are used for convenience. The proprietary masonry cement is preblended by the manufacturer and will normally include lime, an air-entraining agent, and other ingredients which produce desired properties in mortars utilizing masonry cements.

Individual mortar materials are required to conform to ASTM specifications, which are the result of extensive laboratory testing and field-use experiences over a long period of time.

Portland cement used in mortar mixes is governed by ASTM C150 and Types I, II, and III are permitted. Air-entraining portland cements may also be used in mortar mixes, with ASTM C175 as the governing standard. Types IA, IIA, and IIIA are available for use; however, since experience has shown that wide variations in actual measured air contents may occur with those cements, their use requires extreme caution.

ASTM C91 controls masonry cement properties and while Type I and Type II masonry cements are manufactured, Type II is the recommended masonry cement for use in mortars.

The lime component of mortar mixes may be either quicklime or hydrated lime, with the latter being the preferred material. Quicklime is calcium oxide, which must be carefully mixed with water (slaked) and stored for as long as two weeks before use. When used on a jobsite, quicklime is prepared in barrels and added to the mortar at a soft, putty consistency. ASTM C5 covers the properties of quicklime. Hydrated lime is quicklime that has been slaked into a calcium hydroxide before packaging. Hydrated lime can be used without the delay of the slaking process and therefore is more convenient to use on construction projects. ASTM C207 covers Type S and Type N hydrated limes; however, only Type S hydrated lime is specified for use in mortars.

The sand used in mortars may be manufactured or natural sand and should meet ASTM C144 requirements. The sand used should be clean, sound, and well graded, with a top size of ¼ in. Both workability and durability of mortars are affected by the quality of sand used. Sands containing less than 5 to 15 percent fines produce unworkable, harsh mortars that will require additional cement or lime to make the mix usable, while sands deficient in top sizes or large particles tend to produce weak mortars.

While there is no standard specification for the water used in mortar mixes, the general guidelines for water in concrete mixes are also applicable to mortars. Water suitable to produce mortars should be clean and free of deleterious acids, alkalis, or organic materials.

The selection of type of mortar depends upon a number of variables. However, none of the recognized mortar types will produce a mortar that will rate highest in all properties required for a specific job requirement. Therefore, the properties of the various types of mortars are usually evaluated and a mortar type chosen which will reasonably satisfy end-use requirements. (See Figure 7–12.)

ASTM C270 currently recognizes four types of mortars for plain masonry, M, S, N, and O. The recommended construction applications are shown in Figure 7–13.

FIGURE 7–12
Multiwythe wall construction with wire joint reinforcement set in mortar (*Courtesy DUR-O-WALL, Inc.*)

FIGURE 7–13 Recommended mortar types for various construction applications

Construction Application	Recommended Minimum ASTM Mortar Types	Order of Relative Importance of Principal Properties		
		Plasticity*	Compressive Strength	Weather Resistance
Foundations, basements, walls, isolated piers**	M, S	3	2	1
Exterior walls	S, N	2	3	1
Solid masonry unit veneer over wood frame	N	2	3	1
Interior walls—load-bearing	S, N	1	2	3
Interior partitions—nonload-bearing	N, O	1	—	—
Reinforced masonry (columns, pilasters, walls, beams)	M, S†	3	1	2

Source: Construction—Principles, Materials, and Methods, Institute of Financial Education, 5th ed., 1983
*Adequate workability and a minimum water retention (flow after suction of 70 percent) assumed for all mortars.
**Also any masonry wall subject to unusual lateral loads for earthquakes, hurricanes, etc.
†Only portland cement-lime Type S and M mortars.

Type M mortar is a high-strength mortar that has a greater durability than other mortar types. It is generally recommended for use below grade in foundation walls, retaining walls, walks, sewers, and manholes. It is also specified where high compressive strengths are required.

Type S mortar is a medium-high-strength mortar which is used where Type M is recommended, but where bond and lateral strength are more important than compressive strength. Tensile bond strength between brick and Type S mortars approaches the maximum obtainable with cement-lime mortars. Type S mortar is used in reinforced and nonreinforced masonry where maximum flexural strengths are required.

Type N mortar is a medium-strength mortar recommended for use above grade in severe exposure conditions. Typical areas of use include chimneys, parapet walls, and exterior building walls.

Type O mortars are medium-low-strength mortars for general interior use in nonload-bearing walls. However, if compressive stresses are expected to stay below 100 lb per sq in., exposures are not severe, there are no high winds or other significant lateral loads, and the walls are solid masonry, they may be used in load-bearing wall systems. Type O mortars should never be used where they will be exposed to freeze-thaw cycling.

Two types of mortars, PM and PL, are specified for structural reinforced masonry, and are governed by ASTM C476, Standard Specification for Mortar and Grout for Reinforced Masonry. This type of construction utilizes standard deformed reinforcing rods, vertically and horizontally spaced in the wall system to produce high-strength masonry systems.

Grout

ASTM C476 also governs construction grouts, which are an essential element of reinforced concrete masonry. Mortar is not grout and the two are not interchangeable, since they have different characteristics and are used differently.

Grouts are essential elements of reinforced concrete masonry. In reinforced load-bearing walls, grout is usually placed in the wall spaces or cores that contain steel reinforcement. The grout bonds the deformed steel reinforcement to the masonry units so that the two act together to resist imposed loads. Grout may also be used in cores that do not contain steel to further increase the load-carrying capabilities of a wall system. The strength of nonreinforced load-bearing walls may also be increased with the use of a grout mix by filling a portion or all of the cores in the wall assembly.

The size of the space to be grouted as well as the height of the lift to be grouted will generally determine the specific grout mix selected. However, since building codes and standards differ on specific values of maximum aggregate size versus clear opening, the governing documents for the work should be consulted. The maximum size of the aggregate and mix consistency should be determined with regard to specific job conditions to ensure satisfactory grout placement and adequate embedment of the steel reinforcement.

The compressive strengths of grouts will vary from 600 to 2500 psi. Grout strengths are typically affected by water content, sampling methods, and testing methods.

Grouts in place will generally have strength values in excess of 2500 psi, because the surrounding masonry units will absorb water from the grout rapidly, thereby reducing the in-place water-cement ratio of the grout and causing an increase in compressive strength. Grout strengths are also aided by the moisture trapped in the surrounding masonry unit, which produces a moist condition essential to cement hydration and strength gain.

Grouts should be produced with a fluid consistency adequate for pouring or pumping without segregation. The grout should flow around the steel and into all masonry voids without bridging or honeycombing. ASTM C143 slump measurements can be used as guides for grout consistency for high- and low-absorption units, with 8-in. slumps recommended for low-absorption units and 10-in. slumps for high-absorption units.

Batching, mixing, and delivery of grout mixes should, whenever possible, follow ASTM C94 standard specifications for ready-mixed concrete.

Grout specimens for compressive strength testing are cast in molds with concrete masonry units having the same absorption characteristics and moisture content as the units being used in the construction. This molding system simulates the conditions existing in the wall system where the masonry units will absorb water from the grout, thereby reducing the grout's water-cement ratio and increasing its strength.

To prepare a test specimen, a firm, flat location should be selected where the mold can remain undisturbed for 48 hours. A $\frac{5}{8}$-in.-thick piece of wood $3\frac{1}{2}$ in. square is placed on the level surface with four masonry units typical of the project. Paper toweling or a similar permeable paper is taped to the face of each concrete masonry unit and the units are set around the $3\frac{1}{2}$-in. piece of wood. The mold is twice as high as it is wide. The grout is then poured into the mold in two layers and each layer is rodded 25 times with a thin metal or wood puddling stick.

The bottom layer is puddled throughout its depth and uniformly across its surface area. The second layer puddling should penetrate about ½ in. into the first layer. Vibrating tools may also be used to consolidate the grout if the structure is being vibrated.

The tops of the specimens are leveled and covered and the specimens are protected from extreme temperature variations for 48 hours. When the specimens are two days old, the blocks are removed and the specimens are carefully transported to a testing area where compression tests are run on them according to applicable ASTM standards C617 and C39.

Fire Ratings of Concrete Masonry

Two concerns of fire safety codes deal with structural integrity during a fire and containment of the fire. Therefore, the materials used in construction must have measurable values for resistance to heat transmission and flame spread, depending upon occupancy classifications, fire zone classifications, and the nature of combustible materials which may be in a structure. The structural integrity requirement includes resistance to thermal shock, impact, and overturning forces during the most severe fire possible for the building area's occupancy.

Fire resistance or fire rating values are expressed in terms of time that a material or type of construction will withstand the standard fire test and still perform its design purpose. A fire rating of four or more hours can be readily achieved utilizing concrete masonry walls.

The standard test for determining the fire ratings of construction materials is ASTM E119, Methods of Fire Tests of Building Construction and Materials. The extent and severity of the fire in the test apparatus must conform to ASTM E119 criteria.

Three criteria are used to develop a fire rating for a wall or partition assembly. Any one of the criteria will be decisive should it occur first.

1. Structural failure of the system while carrying design loads when subjected to the standard fire test.
2. Heat transmission through the wall that will cause an average rise in temperature of the side not exposed to direct flame (9 locations are averaged) or a rise of 325°F at one location. This criterion governs the spread of a fire by ignition of combustible materials placed against or near the wall surface away from the fire.
3. Passage of flame or heated gases which will ignite cotton waste, or passage of water from a fire hose through the wall assembly. After cooling but within 72 hours, the wall must carry twice the safe superimposed design load.

The generally accepted practice in building codes is to state the fire rating of concrete masonry walls in terms of equivalent solid thickness. Equivalent solid thickness is the solid thickness that would be obtained if the same amount of concrete contained in a hollow concrete masonry unit were recast without core holes. The percentage of solids used in the calculations can be determined from net area or net volume values obtained by using ASTM C140, Methods of Testing Concrete Masonry Units. When walls are plastered or otherwise faced with fire-resistant materials, the thickness of the materials is included in the calculations of the equivalent thickness effective for fire resistance.

Calculation of equivalent thickness is illustrated in Figure 7–14. Estimated fire resistance ratings are shown in Figure 7–15 and are for fully protected construction in which all structural members are of noncombustible materials. Where combustible members are formed into walls, equivalent solid thickness protecting such members should be not less than 93 percent of the thicknesses shown.

The fire resistance of masonry-constructed walls can be increased by filling core spaces with various fire-resistant materials. Standard fire tests have shown that by filling

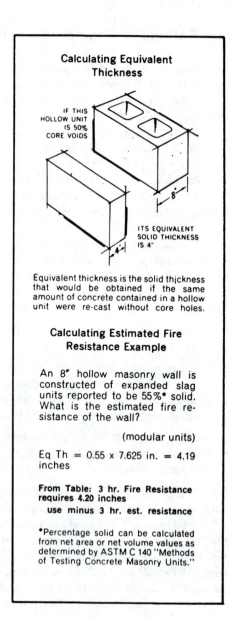

Calculating Equivalent Thickness

IF THIS HOLLOW UNIT IS 50% CORE VOIDS

8″

ITS EQUIVALENT SOLID THICKNESS IS 4″

4″

Equivalent thickness is the solid thickness that would be obtained if the same amount of concrete contained in a hollow unit were re-cast without core holes.

Calculating Estimated Fire Resistance Example

An 8″ hollow masonry wall is constructed of expanded slag units reported to be 55%* solid. What is the estimated fire resistance of the wall?

(modular units)

Eq Th = 0.55 x 7.625 in. = 4.19 inches

From Table: 3 hr. Fire Resistance requires 4.20 inches
   use minus 3 hr. est. resistance

*Percentage solid can be calculated from net area or net volume values as determined by ASTM C 140 "Methods of Testing Concrete Masonry Units."

FIGURE 7–14
Calculating equivalent thickness (*Courtesy National Concrete Masonry Association*)

CONCRETE MASONRY
ESTIMATED FIRE-RESISTANCE RATINGS

AGGREGATE TYPE	MINIMUM EQUIVALENT THICKNESS, INCHES, FOR RATING OF:			
	1 hr.	2 hr.	3 hr.	4 hr.
PUMICE	1.8	3.0	4.0	4.7
EXPANDED SLAG	2.2	3.3	4.2	5.0
EXPANDED SHALE OR CLAY	2.5	3.7	4.7	5.5
LIMESTONE, SCORIA, CINDERS, OR UNEXPANDED SLAG	2.7	4.0	5.0	5.9
CALCAREOUS GRAVEL	2.8	4.2	5.3	6.2
SILICEOUS GRAVEL	3.0	4.5	5.7	6.7

FIGURE 7–15   Estimated fire resistance ratings of concrete masonry
(*Courtesy National Concrete Masonry Association*)

the cores in hollow masonry units or the air space in cavity walls with dry granular material, substantial reductions in heat transfer and increases in fire endurance are obtained.

Thermal Properties of Concrete Masonry

Concrete masonry walls offer insulation qualities combined with architectural appeal. While the design of walls and insulation are important, the heat flow through wall systems is a small percentage of the total heat loss in building construction. One square foot of single-pane glass has a heat flow six or seven times as great as a square foot of lightweight concrete block wall with filled cores.

Resistance values of single-wythe concrete masonry walls with hollow cells empty and filled with bulk insulation are given in Figure 7–16.

FIGURE 7–16 Resistance values ($R = 1/C$) of single-wythe concrete masonry walls with hollow cells empty and filled with bulk insulation

CM Units (in.)	Insulation in Cells	Unit Weight (lb/cu ft)				
		60	*80*	*100*	*120*	*140*
4	Filled	3.36	2.79	2.33	1.92	1.14
	Empty	2.07	1.68	1.40	1.17	0.77
6	Filled	5.59	4.59	3.72	2.95	1.59
	Empty	2.25	1.83	1.53	1.29	0.86
8	Filled	7.46	6.06	4.85	3.79	1.98
	Empty	2.30	2.12	1.75	1.46	0.98
10	Filled	9.35	7.46	5.92	4.59	. 2.35
	Empty	3.00	2.40	1.97	1.63	1.08
12	Filled	10.98	8.70	6.80	5.18	2.59
	Empty	3.29	2.62	2.14	1.81	1.16

Source: National Concrete Masonry Association

Heat-transfer values increase as moisture content increases. When concrete masonry walls become saturated, heat transfer increases based upon the masonry unit's density. Therefore, exterior masonry walls are usually protected from moisture.

Masonry construction is considered heavy-wall construction as opposed to light-wall construction of wood and metal stud. Heavy construction does not respond to temperature changes as rapidly as light construction, even though the two walls' systems may have the same U values. (See Figure 7–17.) U values are the coefficients of total heat flow rate. They express the total amount of heat in British thermal units (Btu) that 1 sq ft of wall, ceiling, or floor will transmit per hour for each degree Fahrenheit of temperature difference between the warm and cool sides of the material or assembly.

Acoustical Properties of Concrete Masonry

Concrete masonry is an excellent sound barrier because of its density and in some situations its absorption qualities. Sound is composed of two elements, tone (frequency) and loudness (decibels). Tone is measured in vibrations per second, or frequency, and the unit of measure is the hertz (Hz). Loudness is measured in decibels (db). A 20-db increase in loudness indicates a tenfold increase in pressure. The human ear can adjust its sensitivity to noise somewhat, thereby reducing the pressure. The decibel as a unit of measure rates thunder at 120 db, average office noise 60 db, and normal breathing 10 db.

Building codes generally regulate the amount of noise stopped by floors, walls, and ceilings at 40 to 55 db of sound loss for airborne and impact sounds.

Concrete masonry units' ability to reduce sound transmission will vary depending upon wall construction, type of block, painted or unpainted surfaces, and other characteristics. Therefore, the reader is encouraged to consult the National Concrete Masonry Association's TEK literature relative to sound-loss characteristics.

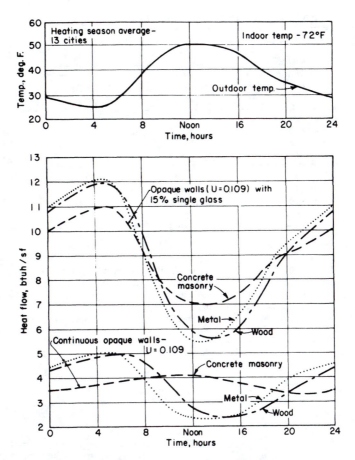

FIGURE 7-17 Heat loss through masonry and nonmasonry walls, U values being equal (*Courtesy Portland Cement Association*)

Estimating Masonry Materials

The quantities of masonry materials, such as concrete block and mortar, required to construct a wall are relatively easy to determine. The number of units required may be determined based on the face surface area of the concrete masonry unit or an estimating guide such as the one illustrated in Figure 7–18. Usually corners are only counted once, any openings over 10 sq ft are deducted from the wall area, and variable waste factors are added to complete the determination of material quantities. Quantity determinations are part of a process that must take into account the costs of labor, material handling, equipment, and site conditions, all of which are covered in detail in estimating texts. (See Figure 7–19.)

FIGURE 7–18 Wall weights and material quantities for single-wythe concrete masonry construction*

Nominal Wall Thickness (in.)	Nominal Size (width × height × length) of Concrete Masonry Units (in.)	Average Weight of 100-sq-ft Wall Area (lb)**		Material Quantities for 100-sq-ft. Wall Area		
		Units Made with Sand-Gravel Aggregate†	Units Made with Lightweight Aggregate†	Number of Units	Mortar (cu ft)	Mortar for 100 Units (cu ft)‡
4	4×4×16	4550	3550	225	13.5	6.0
6	6×4×16	5100	3900	225	13.5	6.0
8	8×4×16	6000	4450	225	13.5	6.0
4	4×8×16	4050	3000	112.5	8.5	7.5
6	6×8×16	4600	3350	112.5	8.5	7.5
8	8×8×16	5550	3950	112.5	8.5	7.5
12	12×8×16	7550	5200	112.5	8.5	7.5

Source: Portland Cement Association
*Based on ⅜-in. mortar joints.
**Actual weight of 100 sq ft of wall can be computed by the formula $WN + 145M$ where W is the actual weight of a single unit; N, the number of units for 100 sq ft of wall; and M, the mortar (cu ft) for 100 sq ft of wall.
†Using a concrete density of 138 pcf for units made with sand-gravel aggregate and 87 pcf for lightweight-aggregate units, and the average weight of unit for two- and three-core block.
‡With face-shell mortar bedding. Mortar quantities include 10 percent allowance for waste.

FIGURE 7–19 Masonry construction projects depend on high lift equipment to move materials on site (*Courtesy JCB, Inc.*)

EXAMPLE

Determine the number of 8 × 16-in. concrete masonry units required to build a wall 8 ft high and 44 ft long with four 3 × 4-ft openings.

Total wall area	8 × 44 ft =	352 sq ft
Subtract the openings	4(3 × 4 ft) =	−48 sq ft
Net wall area		304 sq ft

$$\text{Number of CMUs} = \frac{304 \text{ sq ft}}{0.89 \text{ sq ft}} = 341.6 = 342$$

Using Figure 7–18:

$$\text{Net wall area in squares (100 sq ft)} = \frac{304 \text{ sq ft}}{100 \text{ sq ft}} = 3.04 \text{ square}$$

$$3.04 \text{ square} \times 112.5 \text{ units/square} = 342 \text{ units}$$

The mortar required to place 342 concrete blocks from Figure 7–18 is 7.5 cu ft per 100 units:

$$3.42 \times 7.5 \text{ cu ft} = 25.65 \text{ cu ft}$$

QUALITY OF MASONRY CONSTRUCTION

The material presented in Chapter 1 relative to the inspection and testing of construction materials and processes is a very important aspect of masonry construction.

The question of construction quality may arise during the design phase, construction phase, or after construction has been completed. Construction quality is governed by several factors, including but not limited to the knowledge and attitudes relative to required quality levels, the assignment of responsibility for quality construction, and familiar criteria to measure and evaluate levels of quality obtained.

Construction and protection requirements to ensure quality of masonry construction are given in Figures 7–20 and 7–21, respectively.

Quality control is the term used to describe a contractor or manufacturer's effort to achieve a specified end result. It involves measuring, testing, and evaluating a product or process at regular intervals to maintain acceptable levels of quality. Quality assurance is the measuring, testing, and evaluation done by the purchaser to measure quality obtained in a product or structure.

In the construction industry, the roles of quality control and quality assurance inspectors entail much more than performing or witnessing materials tests and inspecting finished work. Inspectors must have a very good working knowledge of the job drawings and specifications as well as a familiarity with reference specifications. On construction projects where quality is important, the architect and/or engineer or their authorized project representatives should be available on site during all phases of construction. ACI

FIGURE 7–20   Construction requirements (*Courtesy National Concrete Masonry Association*)

Air Temperature (°F)	Construction Requirements
40–32	Heat mixing water *or* sand to minimum of 70°F and maximum of 160°F.
32–25	Heat mixing water *and* sand to minimum of 70°F and maximum of 160°F.
25–20	Heat mixing water and sand to minimum of 70°F and maximum of 160°F. Utilize sources of heat on both sides of walls under construction. Employ windbreaks when wind is in excess of 15 mph.
20 and below	Heat mixing water and sand to minimum of 79°F and maximum of 160°F. Provide enclosure and auxiliary heat to maintain air temperature above 32°F. Temperature of units when laid shall not be less than 20°F.

FIGURE 7–21   Protection requirements (*Courtesy National Concrete Masonry Association*)

Mean Daily Air Temperature (°F)	Protection Requirements (*completed masonry or sections not being worked on*)
40–32	Protect masonry from rain or snow for 24 hours.
32–25	Completely cover masonry for 24 hours.
25–20	Completely cover masonry with insulating blankets for 24 hours.
20 and below	Maintain masonry temperature above 32°F for 24 hours by enclosure and supplementary heat, by electric heating blankets, infrared heat lamps, or other approved method.

Committee 531, Concrete Masonry Structures—Design and Construction, provides for reductions in allowable stresses when on-site inspection does not exist for structural masonry construction.

Occasionally in masonry construction work the designer will require the building of one or more sample wall panels. These panels are usually 4 × 8 and should include all of the materials specified or selected for actual wall construction. Typically, the panels include the masonry units and reinforcement accessories, and show workmanship, coursing, bonding, wall thickness, color and texture range of units, and mortar joint color and tooling. After the designer or his representative approves the panel as fabricated, it is then used as a standard to measure actual construction work quality.

The appendix to this text includes selected ASTM specifications that are relevant to various aspects of masonry construction. The readers of this text are encouraged to familiarize themselves with these specifications.

REVIEW QUESTIONS

1. What is the difference between solid- and hollow-core masonry units?

2. What three clays are used to manufacture clay masonry?

3. Describe the manufacturing system most commonly used to manufacture clay masonry.

4. What factors influence the compressive strength of clay masonry?

5. Describe the procedures for field testing clay brick suction rates.

6. What materials are used in the manufacture of concrete masonry units?

7. Describe the manufacturing process used to produce concrete masonry units.

8. What is the main advantage of autoclaved concrete masonry units?

9. What factors influence the compressive strength of concrete masonry units?

10. What functions does mortar serve in masonry construction?

11. Describe grout and how it is used in concrete masonry construction.

12. A 12-in. hollow masonry wall is constructed of expanded shale reported to be 55 percent solid. What is the estimated fire resistance of the wall?

13. What criteria are used to develop a fire rating for a wall or partition assembly?

14. What is the difference between heavy-wall and light-wall construction and why is this difference important in building construction?

15. What is the difference between quality control and quality assurance?

16. Explain why an architect might specify a sample wall panel for a masonry construction project.

17. Based on the data given, complete the required ASTM C140 calculations and compare them to the ASTM C90 requirements.

    Concrete masonry unit 8×8×16 in.
    Sampled weight   29.41 lb
    Submerged weight   14.23 lb
    Saturated surface-dry weight   31.74 lb
    Oven-dry weight   28.21 lb

18. Three concrete masonry units of the type tested in the previous problem were loaded to failure with the listed results. Do these units meet ASTM C90 strength requirements?

CMU	Load (lb)
1	221,490
2	212,610
3	219,000

19. Determine the cubic feet of mortar and number of 12×8×16-in. concrete blocks required to construct a 35-ft-wide, 55-ft-long, 8-ft-high foundation. Assume a 5 percent waste factor for the block and a 50 percent waste factor for the mortar.

20. What procedure can be used to determine if a cored brick is considered solid or hollow?

21. How many grades and types of brick are covered by ASTM C216? Summarize the major differences between the grades and types of brick.

22. What are the normally specified finish and appearance requirements for concrete block?

■ Appendixes

METRIC CONVERSION FACTORS

The following list provides the conversion relationship between U.S. customary units and SI (International System) units. The proper conversion procedure is to multiply the specified value on the left (primarily U.S. customary values) by the conversion factor exactly as given below and then round to the appropriate number of significant digits desired. For example, to convert 11.4 ft to meters: 11.4 × 0.3048 = 3.47472, which rounds to 3.47 meters. Do not round either value before performing the multiplication, as accuracy would be reduced. A complete guide to the SI system and its use can be found in ASTM E 380, Metric Practice.

To convert from	to	multiply by
Length		
inch (in.)	micron (μ)	25,400 E*
inch (in.)	centimeter (cm)	2.54 E
inch (in.)	meter (m)	0.0254 E
foot (ft)	meter (m)	0.3048 E
yard (yd)	meter (m)	0.9144
Area		
square foot (sq ft)	square meter (sq m)	0.09290304 E
square inch (sq in.)	square centimeter (sq cm)	6.452 E
square inch (sq in.)	square meter (sq m)	0.00064516 E
square yard (sq yd)	square meter (sq m)	0.8361274
Volume		
cubic inch (cu in.)	cubic centimeter (cu cm)	16.387064
cubic inch (cu in.)	cubic meter (cu m)	0.00001639
cubic foot (cu ft)	cubic meter (cu m)	0.02831685
cubic yard (cu yd)	cubic meter (cu m)	0.7645549
gallon (gal) Can. liquid	liter	4.546
gallon (gal) Can. liquid	cubic meter (cu m)	0.004546
gallon (gal) U.S. liquid**	liter	3.7854118
gallon (gal) U.S. liquid	cubic meter (cu m)	0.00378541
fluid ounce (fl oz)	milliliters (ml)	29.57353
fluid ounce (fl oz)	cubic meter (cu m)	0.00002957
Force		
kip (1000 lb)	kilogram (kg)	453.6
kip (1000 lb)	newton (N)	4,448.222
pound (lb) avoirdupois	kilogram (kg)	0.4535924
pound (lb)	newton (N)	4.448222
Pressure or stress		
kip per square inch (ksi)	megapascal (MPa)	6.894757
kip per square inch (ksi)	kilogram per square centimeter (kg/sq cm)	70.31
pound per square foot (psf)	kilogram per square meter (kg/sq m)	4.8824
pound per square foot (psf)	pascal (Pa)†	47.88
pound per square inch (psi)	kilogram per square centimeter (kg/sq cm)	0.07031
pound per square inch (psi)	pascal (Pa)†	6,894.757
pound per square inch (psi)	megapascal (MPa)	0.00689476
Mass (weight)		
pound (lb) avoirdupois	kilogram (kg)	0.4535924
ton, 2000 lb	kilogram (kg)	907.1848
grain	kilogram (kg)	0.0000648

To convert from	to	multiply by
Mass (weight) per length		
kip per linear foot (klf)	kilogram per meter (kg/m)	0.001488
pound per linear foot (plf)	kilogram per meter (kg/m)	1.488
Mass per volume (density)		
pound per cubic foot (pcf)	kilogram per cubic meter (kg/cu m)	16.01846
pound per cubic yard (lb/cu yd)	kilogram per cubic meter (kg/cu m)	0.5933
Temperature		
degree Fahrenheit (°F)	degree Celsius (°C)	$t_C = (t_F - 32)/1.8$
degree Fahrenheit (°F)	degree Kelvin (°K)	$t_K = (t_F + 459.7)/1.8$
degree Kelvin (°K)	degree Celsius (C°)	$t_C = t_K - 273.15$
Energy and heat		
British thermal unit (Btu)	joule (J)	1055.056
calorie (cal)	joule (J)	4.1868 E
Btu/°F · hr · ft²	W/m² · °K	5.678263
kilowatt-hour (kwh)	joule (J)	3,600,000. E
British thermal unit per pound (Btu/lb)	calories per gram (cal/g)	0.55556
British thermal unit per hour (Btu/hr)	watt (W)	0.2930711
Power		
horsepower (hp) (550 ft-lb/sec)	watt (W)	745.6999 E
Velocity		
mile per hour (mph)	kilometer per hour (km/hr)	1.60934
mile per hour (mph)	meter per second (m/s)	0.44704
Permeability		
darcy	centimeter per second (cm/sec)	0.000968
feet per day (ft/day)	centimeter per second (cm/sec)	0.000352

*E indicates that the factor given is exact.
**One U.S. gallon equals 0.8327 Canadian gallon.
†A pascal equals 1.000 newton per square meter.

Note:
One U.S. gallon of water weighs 8.34 pounds (U.S.) at 60°F.
One cubic foot of water weighs 62.4 pounds (U.S.).
One milliliter of water has a mass of 1 gram and has a volume of one cubic centimeter.
One U.S. bag of cement weighs 94 lb.

The prefixes and symbols listed below are commonly used to form names and symbols of the decimal multiples and submultiples of the SI units.

Multiplication Factor	Prefix	Symbol
$1,000,000,000 = 10^9$	giga	G
$1,000,000 = 10^6$	mega	M
$1,000 = 10^3$	kilo	k
$1 = 1$	—	—
$0.01 = 10^{-2}$	centi	c
$0.001 = 10^{-3}$	milli	m
$0.000001 = 10^{-6}$	micro	μ
$0.000000001 = 10^{-9}$	nano	n

THE CONSTRUCTION TRADES

Here are the metric units that will be used by the construction trades. The term "length" includes all linear measurements--length, width, height, thickness, diameter, and circumference.

	Quantity	Unit	Symbol
Surveying	length	kilometer, meter	km, m
	area	square kilometer hectare (10 000 m^2) square meter	km^2 ha m^2
	plane angle	degree (non-metric) minute (non-metric) second (non-metric)	° ' "
Excavating	length	meter, millimeter	m, mm
	volume	cubic meter	m^3
Trucking	distance	kilometer	km
	volume	cubic meter	m^3
	mass	metric ton (1000 kg)	t
Paving	length	meter, millimeter	m, mm
	area	square meter	m^2
Concrete	length	meter, millimeter	m, mm
	area	square meter	m^2
	volume	cubic meter	m^3
	temperature	degree Celsius	°C
	water capacity	liter (1000 cm^3)	L
	mass (weight)	kilogram, gram	kg, g
	cross-sectional area	square millimeter	mm^2

Source: The Construction Metrication Council of the National Institute of Building Sciences, Washington, D.C.

	Quantity	Unit	Symbol
Masonry	length	meter, millimeter	m, mm
	area	square meter	m^2
	mortar volume	cubic meter	m^3
Steel	length	meter, millimeter	m, mm
	mass	metric ton (1000 kg) kilogram, gram	t kg, g
Carpentry	length	meter, millimeter	m, mm
Plastering	length	meter, millimeter	m, mm
	area	square meter	m^2
	water capacity	liter (1000 cm^3)	L
Glazing	length	meter, millimeter	m, mm
	area	square meter	m^2
Painting	length	meter, millimeter	m, mm
	area	square meter	m^2
	capacity	liter (1000 cm^3) milliliter (cm^3)	L mL
Roofing	length	meter, millimeter	m, mm
	area	square meter	m^2
	slope	millimeter/meter	mm/m
Plumbing	length	meter, millimeter	m, mm
	mass	kilogram, gram	kg, g
	capacity	liter (1000 cm^3)	L
	pressure	kilopascal	kPa
Drainage	length	meter, millimeter	m, mm
	area	hectare (10 000 m^2) square meter	ha m^2
	volume	cubic meter	m^3
	slope	millimeter/meter	mm/m

	Quantity	Unit	Symbol
HVAC	length	meter, millimeter	m, mm
	volume	cubic meter	m^3
	capacity	liter (1000 cm^3)	L
	airflow	meter/second	m/s
	volume flow	cubic meter/second liter/second	m^3/s L/s
	temperature	degree Celsius	°C
	force	newton, kilonewton	N, kN
	pressure	kilopascal	kPa
	energy, work	kilojoule, megajoule	kJ, MJ
	rate of heat flow	watt, kilowatt	W, kW
Electrical	length	meter, millimeter	m, mm
	frequency	hertz	Hz
	power	watt, kilowatt	W, kW
	energy	megajoule kilowatt hour	MJ kWh
	electric current	ampere	A
	electric potential	volt, kilovolt	V, kV
	resistance	ohm	Ω

ROUNDING TABLE, 1/32 INCH TO 4 INCHES

Underline denotes exact conversion
Shaded figures are too exact for most uses

Inches	Nearest 0.1 mm (1/254")	Nearest 1 mm (1/25")	Nearest 5 mm (1/5")
1/32"	0.8	1	
1/16"	1.6	2	
3/32"	2.4	2	
1/8"	3.2	3	
3/16"	4.8	5	
1/4"	6.4	6	
5/16"	7.9	8	
3/8"	9.5	10	
7/16"	11.1	11	
1/2"	<u>12.7</u>	13	
9/16"	14.3	14	
5/8"	15.9	16	
3/4"	19.0	19	
7/8"	22.2	22	
1"	<u>25.4</u>	25	25
1-1/4"	31.8	32	30
1-1/2"	<u>38.1</u>	38	40
1-3/4"	44.4	44	45
2"	<u>50.8</u>	51	50
2-1/4"	57.2	57	55
2-1/2"	<u>63.5</u>	64	65
2-3/4"	69.8	70	70
3"	<u>76.2</u>	76	75
3-1/4"	82.6	83	85
3-1/2"	<u>88.9</u>	89	90
3-3/4"	95.2	95	95
4"	<u>101.6</u>	102	100

ROUNDING TABLE, 4 INCHES TO 100 FEET

Underline denotes exact conversion
Shaded figures are too exact for most uses

Inches and Feet	Nearest 0.1 mm (1/254")	Nearest 1 mm (1/25")	Nearest 5 mm (1/5")	Nearest 10 mm (2/5")	Nearest 50 mm (2")	Nearest 100 mm (4")	1" = 25 mm exactly
4"	101.6	102	100	100			100
5"	127	127	125	130			125
6"	152.4	152	150	150			150
7"	177.8	178	180	180			175
8"	203.2	203	205	200			200
9"	228.6	229	230	230			225
10"	254	254	255	250			250
11"	279.4	279	280	280			275
1-0"	304.8	305	305	300	300		300
2-0"	609.6	610	610	610	600		600
3'-0"	914.4	914	915	910	900		900
4'-0"	1219.2	1219	1220	1220	1200		1200
5'-0"		1524	1525	1520	1500		1500
6'-0"		1829	1830	1830	1850		1800
7'-0"		2134	2135	2130	2150		2100
8'-0"		2438	2440	2440	2450		2400
9'-0"		2743	2745	2740	2750		2700
10'-0"		3048	3050	3050	3050	3000	3000
15'-0"		4572	4570	4570	4550	4600	4500
20'-0"		6096	6095	6100	6100	6100	6000
25'-0'		7620	7620	7620	7600	7600	7500
30'-0"		9144	9145	9140	9150	9100	9000
40'-0"		12 192	12 190	12 190	12 200	12 200	12 000
50'-0"		15 240	15 240	15 240	15 250	15 200	15 000
75'-0"		22 860	22 860	22 860	22 850	22 900	22 500
100'-0"		30 480	30 480	30 480	30 500	30 500	30 000

Designation: C 29/C 29M – 91a   AMERICAN SOCIETY FOR TESTING AND MATERIALS
1916 Race St. Philadelphia, Pa 19103
Reprinted from the Annual Book of ASTM Standards. Copyright ASTM
If not listed in the current combined index, will appear in the next edition.

American Association of State
Highway and Transportation Officials Standard
AASHTO No.: T 19/T19M

Standard Test Method for
Unit Weight and Voids in Aggregate[1]

This standard is issued under the fixed designation C 29/C 29M; the number immediately following the designation indicates the year of original adoption or, in the case of revision, the year of last revision. A number in parentheses indicates the year of last reapproval. A superscript epsilon (ε) indicates an editorial change since the last revision or reapproval.

This test method has been approved for use by agencies of the Department of Defense. Consult the DoD Index of Specifications and Standards for the specific year of issue which has been adopted by the Department of Defense.

1. Scope

1.1 This test method covers the determination of unit weight in a compacted or loose condition and calculated voids in fine, coarse, or mixed aggregates based on the same determination. This test method is applicable to aggregates not exceeding 6 in. (150 mm) in nominal maximum size.

NOTE 1—Unit weight is the traditional terminology used to describe the property determined by this test method. Some believe the proper term is unit mass, or density, or bulk density, but consensus on this alternate terminology has not been obtained.

1.2 The values stated in either inch-pound units or acceptable metric units are to be regarded separately as standard, as appropriate for a specification with which this test method is used. An exception is with regard to sieve sizes and nominal size of aggregate, in which the metric values are the standard as stated in Specification E 11. Within the text, metric units are shown in parentheses. The values stated in each system may not be exact equivalents; therefore each system must be used independently of the other, without combining values in any way.

1.3 *This standard does not purport to address all of the safety problems, if any, associated with its use. It is the responsibility of the user of this standard to establish appropriate safety and health practices and determine the applicability of regulatory limitations prior to use.*

2. Referenced Documents

2.1 *ASTM Standards:*
C 125 Terminology Relating to Concrete and Concrete Aggregates[2]
C 127 Test Method for Specific Gravity and Absorption of Coarse Aggregate[2]
C 128 Test Method for Specific Gravity and Absorption of Fine Aggregate[2]
C 138 Test Method for Unit Weight, Yield, and Air Content (Gravimetric) of Concrete[2]
C 670 Practice for Preparing Precision and Bias Statements for Test Methods for Construction Materials[2]
C 702 Practice for Reducing Field Samples of Aggregate to Testing Size[2]

D 75 Practice for Sampling Aggregates[3]
D 123 Terminology Relating to Textile Materials[4]
E 11 Specification for Wire-Cloth Sieves for Testing Purposes[5]
2.2 *AASHTO Standard:*
T19 Method of Test for Unit Weight and Voids in Aggregate[6]

3. Terminology

3.1 *Definitions*—Definitions are in accordance with Terminology C 125 unless otherwise indicated.

3.1.1 *mass, n*—the quantity of matter in a body. (See **weight.**)

3.1.1.1 *Discussion*—Units of mass are the kilogram (kg), the pound (lb), or units derived from these. Mass may also be visualized as equivalent to inertia, or the resistance offered by a body to change of motion (acceleration). Masses are compared by weighing the bodies, which amounts to comparing the forces of gravitation acting on them.   **D 123.**

3.1.2 *unit weight, n*—weight per unit volume.

3.1.2.1 *Discussion*—The term weight means the force of gravity acting on the mass.

3.1.3 *weight, n*—the force exerted on a body by gravity. (See **mass.**)

3.1.3.1 *Discussion*—Weight is equal to the mass of the body multiplied by the acceleration due to gravity. Weight may be expressed in absolute units (newtons, poundals) or in gravitational units (kgf, lbf), for example: on the surface of the earth, a body with a mass of 1 kg has a weight of 1 kgf (approximately 9.81 N), or a body with a mass of 1 lb has a weight of 1 lbf (approximately 4.45 N or 32.2 poundals). Since weight is equal to mass times the acceleration due to gravity, the weight of a body will vary with the location where the weight is determined, while the mass of the body remains constant. On the surface of the earth, the force of gravity imparts to a body that is free to fall an acceleration of approximately 9.81 m/s² (32.2 ft/s²).   **D 123.**

3.2 *Description of Term Specific to this Standard:*

3.2.1 *voids, n—in unit volume of aggregate*—the space between particles in an aggregate mass not occupied by solid

---

[1] This test method is under the jurisdiction of ASTM Committee C-9 on Concrete and Concrete Aggregates and is the direct responsibility of Subcommittee C09.03.05 on Methods of Testing and Specifications for Physical Characteristics of Concrete Aggregates.
Current edition approved Dec. 15, 1991. Published February 1992. Originally published as C 29 – 20 T. Last previous edition C 29/C 29M – 91.
[2] *Annual Book of ASTM Standards*, Vol 04.02.

[3] *Annual Book of ASTM Standards*, Vol 04.03.
[4] *Annual Book of ASTM Standards*, Vol 07.01.
[5] *Annual Book of ASTM Standards*, Vols 04.02 and 14.02.
[6] Available from American Association of State Highway and Transportation Officials, 444 N. Capitol St. NW, Suite 225, Washington, DC 20001.

⑤ C 29/C 29M

mineral matter.

3.2.1.1. *Discussion*—Voids within particles, either permeable or impermeable, are not included in voids as determined by this test method.

4. Significance and Use

4.1 This test method is often used to determine unit weight values that are necessary for use for many methods of selecting proportions for concrete mixtures.

4.2 The unit weight may also be used for determining mass/volume relationships for conversions in purchase agreements. However, the relationship between degree of compaction of aggregates in a hauling unit or stockpile and that achieved in this test method is unknown. Further, aggregates in hauling units and stockpiles usually contain absorbed and surface moisture (the latter affecting bulking), while this test method determines the unit weight on a dry basis.

4.3 A procedure is included for computing the percentage of voids between the aggregate particles based on the unit weight determined by this test method.

5. Apparatus

5.1 *Balance*—A balance or scale accurate within 0.1 % of the test load at any point within the range of use, graduated to at least 0.1 lb (0.05 kg). The range of use shall be considered to extend from the mass of the measure empty to the mass of the measure plus its contents at 120 lb/ft³ (1920 kg/m³).

5.2 *Tamping Rod*—A round, straight steel rod, ⅝ in. (16 mm) in diameter and approximately 24 in. (600 mm) in length, having one end rounded to a hemispherical tip of the same diameter as the rod.

5.3 *Measure*—A cylindrical metal measure, preferably provided with handles. It shall be watertight, with the top and bottom true and even, and sufficiently rigid to retain its form under rough usage. The measure shall have a height approximately equal to the diameter, but in no case shall the height be less than 80 % nor more than 150 % of the diameter. The capacity of the measure shall conform to the limits in Table 1 for the aggregate size to be tested. The thickness of metal in the measure shall be as described in Table 2. The top rim shall be smooth and plane within 0.01 in. (0.25 mm) and shall be parallel to the bottom within 0.5° (Note 2). The interior wall of the measure shall be a smooth and continuous surface.

NOTE 2—The top rim is satisfactorily plane if a 0.01-in. (0.25-mm) feeler gage cannot be inserted between the rim and a piece of ¼-in. (6-mm) or thicker plate glass laid over the measure. The top and bottom are satisfactorily parallel if the slope between pieces of plate glass in contact with the top and bottom does not exceed 0.87 % in any direction.

5.3.1 If the measure may also be used for testing for unit weight of concrete according to Test Method C 138, the measure should be made of steel or other suitable metal not readily subject to attack by cement paste.

NOTE 3—Reactive materials such as aluminum alloys may be used where, as a consequence of an initial reaction, a surface film is formed which protects the metal against further corrosion. Measures larger than nominal 1 ft³ (28 L) capacity should be made of steel for rigidity, or the minimum thicknesses of metal listed in Table 2 should be suitably increased.

TABLE 1   Capacity of Measures

Nominal Maximum Size of Aggregate		Capacity of Measure[A]	
in.	mm	ft³	L (m³)
½	12.5	⅒	2.8 (0.0028)
1	25.0	⅓	9.3 (0.0093)
1½	37.5	½	14 (0.014)
3	75	1	28 (0.028)
4½	112	2½	70 (0.070)
6	150	3½	100 (0.100)

[A] The indicated size of measure shall be used to test aggregates of a nominal maximum size equal to or smaller than that listed. The actual volume of the measure shall be at least 95 % of the nominal volume listed.

TABLE 2   Requirements for Measures

Capacity of Measure	Thickness of Metal, min		
	Bottom	Upper 1½ in. or 38 mm of wall[A]	Remainder of wall
Less than 0.4 ft³	0.20 in.	0.10 in.	0.10 in.
0.4 ft³ to 1.5 ft³, incl	0.20 in.	0.20 in.	0.12 in.
over 1.5 to 2.8 ft³, incl	0.40 in.	0.25 in.	0.15 in.
over 2.8 to 4.0 ft³, incl	0.50 in.	0.30 in.	0.20 in.
Less than 11 L	5.0 mm	2.5 mm	2.5 mm
11 to 42 L, incl	5.0 mm	5.0 mm	3.0 mm
over 42 to 80 L, incl	10.0 mm	6.4 mm	3.8 mm
over 80 to 133 L, incl	13.0 mm	7.6 mm	5.0 mm

[A] The added thickness in the upper portion of the wall may be obtained by placing a reinforcing band around the top of the measure.

5.4 *Shovel or Scoop*—A shovel or scoop of convenient size for filling the measure with aggregate.

5.5 *Calibration Equipment*—A piece of plate glass, preferably at least ¼ in. (6 mm) thick and at least 1 in. (25 mm) larger than the diameter of the measure to be calibrated. A supply of water-pump or chassis grease that can be placed on the rim of the container to prevent leakage.

6. Sampling

6.1 Sampling should generally be accomplished in accordance with Practice D 75 and sample reduction in accordance with Practice C 702.

7. Test Sample

7.1 The size of the sample shall be approximately 125 to 200 % of the quantity required to fill the measure, and shall be handled in a manner to avoid segregation. Dry the aggregate sample to essentially constant mass, preferably in an oven at 230 ± 9°F (110 ± 5°C).

8. Calibration of Measure

8.1 Fill the measure with water at room temperature and cover with a piece of plate glass in such a way as to eliminate bubbles and excess water.

8.2 Determine the mass of the water in the measure using the balance described in 5.1.

8.3 Measure the temperature of the water and determine its density from Table 3, interpolating if necessary.

8.4 Calculate the volume, V, of the measure by dividing the mass of the water required to fill the measure by its density. Alternatively, calculate the factor for the measure $(1/V)$ by dividing the density of the water by the mass required to fill the measure.

C 29/C 29M

TABLE 3 Density of Water

Temperature		lb/ft³	kg/m³
°F	°C		
60	15.6	62.366	999.01
65	18.3	62.336	998.54
70	21.1	62.301	997.97
(73.4)	(23.0)	(62.274)	(997.54)
75	23.9	62.261	997.32
80	26.7	62.216	996.59
85	29.4	62.166	995.83

NOTE 4—For the calculation of unit weight, the volume of the measure in acceptable metric units should be expressed in cubic metres, or the factor as 1/m³. However, for convenience the size of the measure may be expressed in litres.

8.5 Measures shall be recalibrated at least once a year or whenever there is reason to question the accuracy of the calibration.

9. Selection of Procedure

9.1 The shoveling procedure for loose unit weight shall be used only when specifically stipulated. Otherwise, the compact unit weight shall be determined by the rodding procedure for aggregates having a nominal maximum size of 1½ in. (37.5 mm) or less, or by the jigging procedure for aggregates having a nominal maximum size greater than 1½ in. (37.5 mm) and not exceeding 6 in. (150 mm).

10. Rodding Procedure

10.1 Fill the measure one-third full and level the surface with the fingers. Rod the layer of aggregate with 25 strokes of the tamping rod evenly distributed over the surface. Fill the measure two-thirds full and again level and rod as above. Finally, fill the measure to overflowing and rod again in the manner previously mentioned. Level the surface of the aggregate with the fingers or a straightedge in such a way that any slight projections of the larger pieces of the coarse aggregate approximately balance the larger voids in the surface below the top of the measure.

10.2 In rodding the first layer, do not allow the rod to strike the bottom of the measure forcibly. In rodding the second and third layers, use vigorous effort, but not more force than to cause the tamping rod to penetrate to the previous layer of aggregate.

NOTE 5—In rodding the larger sizes of coarse aggregate, it may not be possible to penetrate the layer being consolidated, especially with angular aggregates. The intent of the procedure will be accomplished if vigorous effort is used.

10.3 Determine the mass of the measure plus its contents, and the mass of the measure alone, and record the values to the nearest 0.1 lb (0.05 kg).

11. Jigging Procedure

11.1 Fill the measure in three approximately equal layers as described in 10.1, compacting each layer by placing the measure on a firm base, such as a cement-concrete floor, raising the opposite sides alternately about 2 in. (50 mm), and allowing the measure to drop in such a manner as to hit with a sharp, slapping blow. The aggregate particles, by this procedure, will arrange themselves in a densely compacted condition. Compact each layer by dropping the measure 50 times in the manner described, 25 times on each side. Level the surface of the aggregate with the fingers or a straightedge in such a way that any slight projections of the larger pieces of the coarse aggregate approximately balance the larger voids in the surface below the top of the measure.

11.2 Determine the mass of the measure plus its contents, and the mass of the measure alone, and record the values to the nearest 0.1 lb (0.05 kg).

12. Shoveling Procedure

12.1 Fill the measure to overflowing by means of a shovel or scoop, discharging the aggregate from a height not to exceed 2 in. (50 mm) above the top of the measure. Exercise care to prevent, so far as possible, segregation of the particle sizes of which the sample is composed. Level the surface of the aggregate with the fingers or a straightedge in such a way that any slight projections of the larger pieces of the coarse aggregate approximately balance the larger voids in the surface below the top of the measure.

12.2 Determine the mass of the measure plus its contents, and the mass of the measure alone, and record the values to the nearest 0.1 lb (0.05 kg).

13. Calculation

13.1 *Unit Weight*—Calculate the unit weight for the rodding, jigging, or shoveling procedure as follows:

$$M = (G - T)/V \qquad (1)$$

or

$$M = (G - T) \times F \qquad (2)$$

where:
M = unit weight of the aggregate, lb/ft³ (kg/m³),
G = mass of the aggregate plus the measure, lb (kg),
T = mass of the measure, lb (kg),
V = volume of the measure, ft³ (m³), and
F = factor for measure, ft⁻³ (m⁻³).

13.1.1 The unit weight determined by this test method is for aggregate in an oven-dry condition. If the unit weight in terms of saturated-surface-dry (SSD) condition is desired, use the exact procedure in this test method, and then calculate the SSD unit weight using the following formula:

$$M_{SSD} = M[1 + (A/100)] \qquad (3)$$

where:
M_{SSD} = unit weight in SSD condition, lb/ft³ (kg/m³), and
A = % absorption, determined in accordance with Test Method C 127 or Test Method C 128.

13.2 *Void Content*—Calculate the void content in the aggregate using the unit weight determined by either the rodding, jigging, or shoveling procedure, as follows:

$$\% \text{ Voids} = 100[(S \times W) - M]/(S \times W) \qquad (4)$$

where:
M = unit weight of the aggregate, lb/ft³ (kg/m³),
S = bulk specific gravity (dry basis) as determined in accordance with Test Method C 127 or Test Method C 128, and
W = density of water, 62.3 lb/ft³ (998 kg/m³).

14. Report

14.1 Report the results for the unit weight to the nearest 1 lb/ft³ (10 kg/m³) as follows:

14.1.1 Unit weight by rodding, or

14.1.2 Unit weight by jigging, or

14.1.3 Loose unit weight.

14.2 Report the results for the void content to the nearest 1 % as follows:

14.2.1 Voids in aggregate compacted by rodding, %, or

14.2.2 Voids in aggregate compacted by jigging, %, or

14.2.3 Voids in loose aggregate, %.

15. Precision and Bias

15.1 The following estimates of precision for this test method are based on results from the AASHTO Materials Reference Laboratory (AMRL) Reference Sample Program, with testing conducted using this test method and AASHTO Method T19. There are no significant differences between the two test methods. The data are based on the analyses of more than 100 paired test results from 40 to 100 laboratories.

15.2 *Coarse Aggregate* (*unit weight*):

15.2.1 *Single-Operator Precision*—The single-operator standard deviation has been found to be 0.88 lb/ft³ (14 kg/m³) (1S). Therefore, results of two properly conducted tests by the same operator on similar material should not differ by more than 2.5 lb/ft³ (40 kg/m³) (D2S).

15.2.2 *Multilaboratory Precision*—The multilaboratory standard deviation has been found to be 1.87 lb/ft³ (30 kg/m³) (1S). Therefore, results of two properly conducted tests from two different laboratories on similar material should not differ by more than 5.3 lb/ft³ (85 kg/m³) (D2S).

15.2.3 These numbers represent, respectively, the (1S) and (D2S) limits as described in Practice C 670. The precision estimates were obtained from the analysis of AMRL reference sample data for unit weight by rodding of normal weight aggregates having a nominal maximum aggregate size of 1 in. (25.0 mm), and using a ½-ft³ (14-L) measure.

15.3 *Fine Aggregate* (*unit weight*):

15.3.1 *Single-Operator Precision*—The single-operator standard deviation has been found to be 0.88 lb/ft³ (14 kg/m³) (1S). Therefore, results of two properly conducted tests by the same operator on similar material should not differ by more than 2.5 lb/ft³ (40 kg/m³) (D2S).

15.3.2 *Multilaboratory Precision*—The multilaboratory standard deviation has been found to be 2.76 lb/ft³ (44 kg/m³) (1S). Therefore, results of two properly conducted tests from two different laboratories on similar material should not differ by more than 7.8 lb/ft³ (125 kg/m³) (D2S).

15.3.3 These numbers represent, respectively, the (1S) and (D2S) limits as described in Practice C 670. The precision estimates were obtained from the analysis of AMRL reference sample data for loose unit weight from laboratories using a ¹⁄₁₀-ft³ (2.8-L) measure.

15.4 No precision data on void content are available. However, as the void content in aggregate is calculated from unit weight and bulk specific gravity, the precision of the voids content reflects the precision of these measured parameters given in 15.2 and 15.3 of this test method and in Test Methods C 127 and C 128.

15.5 *Bias*—The procedure in this test method for measuring unit weight and void content has no bias because the values for unit weight and void content can be defined only in terms of a test method.

16. Keywords

16.1 aggregates; coarse aggregate; density; fine aggregate; unit weight; voids in aggregates

AMERICAN SOCIETY FOR TESTING AND MATERIALS
100 Barr Harbor Dr., West Conshohocken, PA 19428
Reprinted from the Annual Book of ASTM Standards. Copyright ASTM
If not listed in the current combined index, will appear in the next edition.

Designation: C 33 – 93

Standard Specification for
Concrete Aggregates[1]

This standard is issued under the fixed designation C 33; the number immediately following the designation indicates the year of original adoption or, in the case of revision, the year of last revision. A number in parentheses indicates the year of last reapproval. A superscript epsilon (ε) indicates an editorial change since the last revision or reapproval.

This specification has been approved for use by agencies of the Department of Defense. Consult the DoD Index of Specifications and Standards for the specific year of issue which has been adopted by the Department of Defense.

1. Scope

1.1 This specification defines the requirements for grading and quality of fine and coarse aggregate (other than lightweight or heavyweight aggregate) for use in concrete.[2]

1.2 This specification may be used by a contractor, concrete supplier, or other purchaser as part of the purchase document describing the material to be furnished.

NOTE 1—This specification is regarded as adequate to ensure satisfactory materials for most concrete. It is recognized that, for certain work or in certain regions, it may be either more or less restrictive than needed. For example, where aesthetics are important, more restrictive limits may be considered regarding impurities that would stain the concrete surface. The specifier should ascertain that aggregates specified are or can be made available in the area of the work, with regard to grading, physical, or chemical properties, or combination thereof.

1.3 This specification may also be referenced in project specifications to define the quality of aggregate, the nominal maximum size of the aggregate, and other specific grading requirements. Those responsible for selecting the proportions for the concrete mixture shall have the responsibility of determining the proportions of fine and coarse aggregate and the addition of blending aggregate sizes if required or approved.

1.4 *Units of Measurement:*

1.4.1 With regard to sieve sizes and the size of aggregate as determined by the use of testing sieves, the values in inch-pound units are shown for the convenience of the user; however, the standard sieve designation shown in parentheses is the standard value as stated in Specification E 11.

1.4.2 With regard to other units of measure, the values stated in inch-pound units are to be regarded as standard.

2. Referenced Documents

2.1 *ASTM Standards:*

C 29/C 29M Test Method for Unit Weight and Voids in Aggregate[3]

C 40 Test Method for Organic Impurities in Fine Aggregates for Concrete[3]

C 87 Test Method for Effect of Organic Impurities in Fine Aggregate on Strength of Mortar[3]

C 88 Test Method for Soundness of Aggregates by Use of Sodium Sulfate or Magnesium Sulfate[3]

C 117 Test Method for Materials Finer than 75-μm (No. 200) Sieve in Mineral Aggregates by Washing[3]

C 123 Test Method for Lightweight Pieces in Aggregate[3]

C 125 Terminology Relating to Concrete and Concrete Aggregates[3]

C 131 Test Method for Resistance to Degradation of Small-Size Coarse Aggregate by Abrasion and Impact in the Los Angeles Machine[3]

C 136 Test Method for Sieve Analysis of Fine and Coarse Aggregates[3]

C 142 Test Method for Clay Lumps and Friable Particles in Aggregates[3]

C 227 Test Method for Potential Alkali Reactivity of Cement-Aggregate Combinations (Mortar-Bar Method)[3]

C 289 Test Method for Potential Reactivity of Aggregates (Chemical Method)[3]

C 295 Guide for Petrographic Examination of Aggregates for Concrete[3]

C 330 Specification for Lightweight Aggregates for Structural Concrete[3]

C 331 Specification for Lightweight Aggregates for Concrete Masonry Units[3]

C 332 Specification for Lightweight Aggregates for Insulating Concrete[3]

C 342 Test Method for Potential Volume Change of Cement-Aggregate Combinations[3]

C 535 Test Method for Resistance to Degradation of Large-Size Coarse Aggregate by Abrasion and Impact in the Los Angeles Machine[3]

C 586 Test Method for Potential Alkali Reactivity of Carbonate Rocks for Concrete Aggregates (Rock Cylinder Method)[3]

C 637 Specification for Aggregates for Radiation-Shielding Concrete[3]

C 638 Descriptive Nomenclature of Constituents of Aggregates for Radiation-Shielding Concrete[3]

C 666 Test Method for Resistance of Concrete to Rapid Freezing and Thawing[3]

D 75 Practice for Sampling Aggregates[4]

D 3665 Practice for Random Sampling of Construction Materials[4]

E 11 Specification for Wire-Cloth Sieves for Testing Purposes[5]

---

[1] This specification is under the jurisdiction of ASTM Committee C-9 on Concrete and Concrete Aggregates and is the direct responsibility of Subcommittee C09.20 on Normal Weight Aggregates.

Current edition approved Oct. 15, 1993. Published December 1993. Originally published as C 33 – 21 T. Last previous edition C 33 – 92a.

[2] For lightweight aggregates, see Specifications C 331, C 332, and C 330; for heavyweight aggregates see Specification C 637 and Descriptive Nomenclature C 638.

[3] *Annual Book of ASTM Standards,* Vol 04.02.

[4] *Annual Book of ASTM Standards,* Vol 04.03.

[5] *Annual Book of ASTM Standards,* Vol 14.02.

C 33

3. Terminology

3.1 For definitions of terms used in this standard, refer to Terminology C 125.

4. Ordering and Specifying Information

4.1 The direct purchaser of aggregates shall include the information in 4.2 in the purchase order as applicable. A project specifier shall include in the project documents information to describe the aggregate to be used in the project from the applicable items in 4.3.

4.2 Include in the purchase order for aggregates the following information, as applicable:

4.2.1 Reference to this specification, as C 33-_____,

4.2.2 Whether the order is for fine aggregate or for coarse aggregate,

4.2.3 Quantity, in tons or metric tons (Note 2),

4.2.4 When the order is for fine aggregate:

4.2.4.1 Whether the optional grading in 6.2 applies,

4.2.4.2 Whether the restriction on reactive materials in 7.3 applies,

4.2.4.3 In the case of the sulfate soundness test (8.1) which salt is to be used. If none is stated, either salt may be used,

4.2.4.4 The appropriate limit for material finer than No. 200 sieve (Table 1). If not stated, the 3.0 % limit shall apply,

4.2.4.5 The appropriate limit for coal and lignite (Table 1). If not stated, the 1.0 % limit shall apply,

4.2.5 When the order is for coarse aggregate:

4.2.5.1 The grading (size number) (11.1 and Table 2), or alternate grading as agreed between the purchaser and aggregate supplier.

4.2.5.2 The class designation (11.1 and Table 3),

4.2.5.3 Whether the restriction on reactive materials in 11.2 applies,

4.2.5.4 In the case of the sulfate soundness test (Table 3), which salt is to be used. If none is stated, either salt may be used, and

4.2.6 Any exceptions or additions to this specification (see Note 1).

NOTE 2—The weight should be determined as loaded in the hauling unit, including any natural moisture present. No water should be added at the time of loading.

4.3 Include in project specifications for aggregates the following information, as applicable:

4.3.1 Reference to this specification, as C 33_____.

4.3.2 When the aggregate being described is fine aggregate:

4.3.2.1 Whether the restriction on reactive materials in 7.3 applies,

4.3.2.2 In the case of the sulfate soundness test (8.1) which salt is to be used. If none is stated, either salt may be used.

4.3.2.3 The appropriate limit for material finer than the No. 200 sieve (Table 1). If not stated, the 3.0 % limit shall apply, and

4.3.2.4 The limit that applies with regard to coal and lignite (Table 1). If not stated, the 1.0 % limit shall apply.

4.3.3 When the aggregate being described is coarse aggregate:

4.3.3.1 The nominal maximum size or sizes permitted, based on thickness of section or spacing of reinforcing bars or other criteria. In lieu of stating the nominal maximum size, the specifier may designate an appropriate size number or numbers (10.1 and Table 2). Designation of a size number to indicate a nominal size shall not restrict the person responsible for selecting proportions from combining two or more gradings of aggregate to obtain a desired grading, provided that the gradings are not otherwise restricted by the project specifier and the nominal maximum size indicated by the size number is not exceeded,

4.3.3.2 The class designation (11.1 and Table 3),

4.3.3.3 Whether the restriction on reactive materials in 10.2 applies,

4.3.3.4 In the case of the sulfate soundness test (Table 3), which salt is to be used. If none is stated, either salt may be used,

4.3.3.5 The person responsible for selecting the concrete proportions if other than the concrete producer, and

4.3.3.6 Any exceptions or additions to this specification (See Note 1).

FINE AGGREGATE

5. General Characteristics

5.1 Fine aggregate shall consist of natural sand, manufactured sand, or a combination thereof.

6. Grading

6.1 *Sieve Analysis*—Fine aggregate, except as provided in 6.2, 6.3, and 6.4, shall be graded within the following limits:

Sieve (Specification E 11)	Percent Passing
⅜-in. (9.5 mm)	100
No. 4 (4.75-mm)	95 to 100
No. 8 (2.36-mm)	80 to 100
No. 16 (1.18-mm)	50 to 85
No. 30 (600-μm)	25 to 60
No. 50 (300-μm)	10 to 30
No. 100 (150-μm)	2 to 10

6.2 The minimum percent shown above for material passing the No. 50 (300-μm) and No. 100 (150-μm) sieves may be reduced to 5 and 0, respectively, if the aggregate is to be used in air-entrained concrete containing more than 400 lb of cement per cubic yard (237 kg/m³) or in nonair-entrained concrete containing more than 500 lb of cement per cubic yard (297 kg/m³) or if an approved mineral admixture is used to supply the deficiency in percent passing these sieves. Air-entrained concrete is here considered to be concrete containing air-entraining cement or an air-entraining agent and having an air content of more than 3 %.

TABLE 1   Limits for Deleterious Substances in Fine Aggregate for Concrete

Item	Weight Percent of Total Sample, max
Clay lumps and friable particles	3.0
Material finer than No. 200 (75-μm) sieve:	
Concrete subject to abrasion	3.0[A]
All other concrete	5.0[A]
Coal and lignite:	
Where surface appearance of concrete is of importance	0.5
All other concrete	1.0

[A] In the case of manufactured sand, if the material finer than the No. 200 (75-μm) sieve consists of the dust of fracture, essentially free of clay or shale, these limits may be increased to 5 and 7 %, respectively.

⏣ C 33

TABLE 2 Grading Requirements for Coarse Aggregates

Size Number	Nominal Size (Sieves with Square Openings)	Amounts Finer than Each Laboratory Sieve (Square-Openings), Weight Percent												
		4 in. (100 mm)	3½ in. (90 mm)	3 in. (75 mm)	2½ in. (63 mm)	2 in. (50 mm)	1½ in. (37.5 mm)	1 in. (25.0 mm)	¾ in. (19.0 mm)	½ in. (12.5 mm)	⅜ in. (9.5 mm)	No. 4 (4.75 mm)	No. 8 (2.36 mm)	No. 16 (1.18 mm)
1	3½ to 1½ in. (90 to 37.5 mm)	100	90 to 100	...	25 to 60	...	0 to 15	...	0 to 5	...	...	...	...	...
2	2½ to 1½ in. (63 to 37.5 mm)	...	...	100	90 to 100	35 to 70	0 to 15	...	0 to 5	...	...	...	...	...
3	2 to 1 in. (50 to 25.0 mm)	...	...	...	100	90 to 100	35 to 70	0 to 15	...	0 to 5	...	...	...	...
357	2 in. to No. 4 (50 to 4.75 mm)	...	...	...	100	95 to 100	...	35 to 70	...	10 to 30	...	0 to 5	...	...
4	1½ to ¾ in. (37.5 to 19.0 mm)	...	...	...	...	100	90 to 100	20 to 55	0 to 15	...	0 to 5	...	...	...
467	1½ in. to No. 4 (37.5 to 4.75 mm)	...	...	...	...	100	95 to 100	...	35 to 70	...	10 to 30	0 to 5	...	...
5	1 to ½ in. (25.0 to 12.5 mm)	...	...	...	...	...	100	90 to 100	20 to 55	0 to 10	0 to 5	...	...	...
56	1 to ⅜ in. (25.0 to 9.5 mm)	...	...	...	...	...	100	90 to 100	40 to 85	10 to 40	0 to 15	0 to 5	...	...
57	1 in. to No. 4 (25.0 to 4.75 mm)	...	...	...	...	...	100	95 to 100	...	25 to 60	...	0 to 10	0 to 5	...
6	¾ to ⅜ in. (19.0 to 9.5 mm)	...	...	...	...	...	...	100	90 to 100	20 to 55	0 to 15	0 to 5	...	...
67	¾ in. to No. 4 (19.0 to 4.75 mm)	...	...	...	...	...	...	100	90 to 100	...	20 to 55	0 to 10	0 to 5	...
7	½ in. to No. 4 (12.5 to 4.75 mm)	...	...	...	...	...	...	...	100	90 to 100	40 to 70	0 to 15	0 to 5	...
8	⅜ in. to No. 8 (9.5 to 2.36 mm)	...	...	...	...	...	...	...	...	100	85 to 100	10 to 30	0 to 10	0 to 5

6.3 The fine aggregate shall have not more than 45 % passing any sieve and retained on the next consecutive sieve of those shown in 6.1, and its fineness modulus shall be not less than 2.3 nor more than 3.1.

6.4 Fine aggregate failing to meet the sieve analysis and fineness modulus requirements of 6.1, 6.2, or 6.3, may be accepted provided that concrete made with similar fine aggregate from the same source has an acceptable performance record in similar concrete construction; or, in the absence of a demonstrable service record, provided that it is demonstrated that concrete of the class specified, made with the fine aggregate under consideration, will have relevant properties at least equal to those of concrete made with the same ingredients, with the exception that a reference fine aggregate be used which is selected from a source having an acceptable performance record in similar concrete construction.

NOTE 3—Fine aggregate that conforms to the grading requirements of a specification, prepared by another organization such as a state transportation agency, which is in general use in the area, should be considered as having a satisfactory service record with regard to those concrete properties affected by grading.

NOTE 4—Relevant properties are those properties of the concrete which are important to the particular application being considered. STP 169B[6] provides a discussion of important concrete properties.

6.5 For continuing shipments of fine aggregate from a given source, the fineness modulus shall not vary more than 0.20 from the base fineness modulus. The base fineness modulus shall be that value that is typical of the source. If necessary, the base fineness modulus may be changed when approved by the purchaser.

---

[6] *Significance of Tests and Properties of Concrete and Concrete Making Materials, STP 169B, ASTM, 1978.*

NOTE 5—The base fineness modulus should be determined from previous tests, or if no previous tests exist, from the average of the fineness modulus values for the first ten samples (or all preceding samples if less than ten) on the order. The proportioning of a concrete mixture may be dependent on the base fineness modulus of the fine aggregate to be used. Therefore, when it appears that the base fineness modulus is considerably different from the value used in the concrete mixture, a suitable adjustment in the mixture may be necessary.

7. Deleterious Substances

7.1 The amount of deleterious substances in fine aggregate shall not exceed the limits prescribed in Table 1.

7.2 *Organic Impurities:*

7.2.1 Fine aggregate shall be free of injurious amounts of organic impurities. Except as herein provided, aggregates subjected to the test for organic impurities and producing a color darker than the standard shall be rejected.

7.2.2 A fine aggregate failing in the test may be used, provided that the discoloration is due principally to the presence of small quantities of coal, lignite, or similar discrete particles.

7.2.3 A fine aggregate failing in the test may be used, provided that, when tested for the effect of organic impurities on strength of mortar, the relative strength at 7 days, calculated in accordance with Test Method C 87, is not less than 95 %.

7.3 Fine aggregate for use in concrete that will be subject to wetting, extended exposure to humid atmosphere, or contact with moist ground shall not contain any materials that are deleteriously reactive with the alkalies in the cement in an amount sufficient to cause excessive expansion of mortar or concrete, except that if such materials are present in injurious amounts, the fine aggregate may be used with a cement containing less than 0.60 % alkalies calculated as sodium oxide equivalent ($Na_2O + 0.658K_2O$) or with the

ⓈⓉⓂ C 33

TABLE 3 Limits for Deleterious Substances and Physical Property Requirements of Coarse Aggregate for Concrete

NOTE—See Fig. 1 for the location of the weathering regions and Note 10 for guidance in using the map. The weathering regions are defined as follows:
(S) Severe Weathering Region—A cold climate where concrete is exposed to deicing chemicals or other aggressive agents, or where concrete may become saturated by continued contact with moisture or free water prior to repeated freezing and thawing.
(M) Moderate Weathering Region—A climate where occasional freezing is expected, but where concrete in outdoor service will not be continually exposed to freezing and thawing in the presence of moisture or to deicing chemicals.
(N) Negligible Weathering Region—A climate where concrete is rarely exposed to freezing in the presence of moisture.

Class Designation	Type or Location of Concrete Construction	Maximum Allowable, %						
		Clay Lumps and Friable Particles	Chert[C] (Less Than 2.40 sp gr SSD)	Sum of Clay Lumps, Friable Particles, and Chert (Less Than 2.40 sp gr SSD)[C]	Material Finer Than No. 200 (75-μm) Sieve	Coal and Lignite	Abrasion[A]	Magnesium Sulfate Soundness (5 cycles)[B]
	Severe Weathering Regions							
1S	Footings, foundations, columns and beams not exposed to the weather, interior floor slabs to be given coverings	10.0	...	...	1.0[D]	1.0	50	...
2S	Interior floors without coverings	5.0	...	...	1.0[D]	0.5	50	...
3S	Foundation walls above grade, retaining walls, abutments, piers, girders, and beams exposed to the weather	5.0	5.0	7.0	1.0[D]	0.5	50	18
4S	Pavements, bridge decks, driveways and curbs, walks, patios, garage floors, exposed floors and porches, or waterfront structures, subject to frequent wetting	3.0	5.0	5.0	1.0[D]	0.5	50	18
5S	Exposed architectural concrete	2.0	3.0	3.0	1.0[D]	0.5	50	18
	Moderate Weathering Regions							
1M	Footings, foundations, columns, and beams not exposed to the weather, interior floor slabs to be given coverings	10.0	...	...	1.0[D]	1.0	50	...
2M	Interior floors without coverings	5.0	...	...	1.0[D]	0.5	50	...
3M	Foundation walls above grade, retaining walls, abutments, piers, girders, and beams exposed to the weather	5.0	8.0	10.0	1.0[D]	0.5	50	18
4M	Pavements, bridge decks, driveways and curbs, walks, patios, garage floors, exposed floors and porches, or waterfront structures subject to frequent wetting	5.0	5.0	7.0	1.0[D]	0.5	50	18
5M	Exposed architectural concrete	3.0	3.0	5.0	1.0[D]	0.5	50	18
	Negligible Weathering Regions							
1N	Slabs subject to traffic abrasion, bridge decks, floors, sidewalks, pavements	5.0	...	...	1.0[D]	0.5	50	...
2N	All other classes of concrete	10.0	...	...	1.0[D]	1.0	50	...

[A] Crushed air-cooled blast-furnace slag is excluded from the abrasion requirements. The rodded or jigged unit weight of crushed air-cooled blast-furnace slag shall be not less than 70 lb/ft³ (1120 kg/m³). The grading of slag used in the unit weight test shall conform to the grading to be used in the concrete. Abrasion loss of gravel, crushed gravel, or crushed stone shall be determined on the test size or sizes most nearly corresponding to the grading or gradings to be used in the concrete. When more than one grading is to be used, the limit on abrasion loss shall apply to each.

[B] The allowable limits for soundness shall be 12 % if sodium sulfate is used.

[C] These limitations apply only to aggregates in which chert appears as an impurity. They are not applicable to gravels that are predominantly chert. Limitations on soundness of such aggregates must be based on service records in the environment in which they are used.

[D] This percentage may be increased under either of the following conditions: (1) if the material finer than the No. 200 (75-μm) sieve is essentially free of clay or shale the percentage may be increased to 1.5; or (2) if the source of the fine aggregate to be used in the concrete is known to contain less than the specified maximum amount passing the No. 200 (75-μm) sieve (Table 1) the percentage limit (L) on the amount in the coarse aggregate may be increased to $L = 1 + [(P)/(100 - P)] (T - A)$, where P = percentage of sand in the concrete as a percent of total aggregate, T = the Table 1 limit for the amount permitted in the fine aggregate, and A = the actual amount in the fine aggregate. (This provides a weighted calculation designed to limit the maximum mass of material passing the No. 200 (75-μm) sieve in the concrete to that which would be obtained if both the fine and coarse aggregate were supplied at the maximum tabulated percentage for each of these ingredients.)

addition of a material that has been shown to prevent harmful expansion due to the alkali-aggregate reaction. (See Appendix X1.)

8. Soundness

8.1 Except as provided in 8.2 and 8.3, fine aggregate subjected to five cycles of the soundness test shall have a weighted average loss not greater than 10 % when sodium sulfate is used or 15 % when magnesium sulfate is used.

8.2 Fine aggregate failing to meet the requirements of 8.1 may be accepted, provided that concrete of comparable properties, made from similar aggregate from the same source, has given satisfactory service when exposed to weathering similar to that to be encountered.

8.3 Fine aggregate not having a demonstrable service record and failing to meet the requirements of 8.1 may be accepted, provided it gives satisfactory results in concrete subjected to freezing and thawing tests (see Test Method C 666).

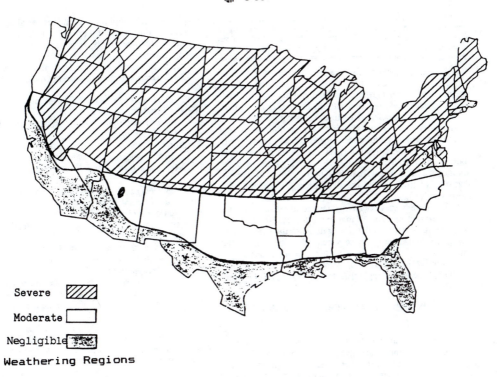

FIG. 1 Location of Weathering Regions

COARSE AGGREGATE

9. General Characteristics

9.1 Coarse aggregate shall consist of gravel, crushed gravel, crushed stone, air-cooled blast furnace slag, or crushed hydraulic-cement concrete, or a combination thereof, conforming to the requirements of this specification.

NOTE 6—Although crushed hydraulic-cement concrete has been used as an aggregate with reported satisfactory results, its use may require some additional precautions. Mixing water requirements may be increased because of the harshness of the aggregate. Partially deteriorated concrete, used as aggregate, may reduce freeze-thaw resistance, affect air void properties or degrade during handling, mixing, or placing. Crushed concrete may have constituents that would be susceptible to alkali-aggregate reactivity or sulfate attack in the new concrete or may bring sulfates, chlorides, or organic material to the new concrete in its pore structure.

10. Grading

10.1 Coarse aggregates shall conform to the requirements prescribed in Table 2 for the size number specified.

NOTE 7—The ranges shown in Table 2 are by necessity very wide in order to accommodate nationwide conditions. For quality control of any specific operation, a producer should develop an average gradation for the particular source and production facilities, and control the gradation within reasonable tolerances from this average. Where coarse aggregate sizes numbers 357 or 467 are used, the aggregate should be furnished in at least two separate sizes.

11. Deleterious Substances

11.1 Except for the provisions of 11.3, the limits given in Table 3 shall apply for the class of coarse aggregate designated in the purchase order or other document (Notes 8 and 9). If the class is not specified, the requirements for Class 3S, 3M, or 1N shall apply in the severe, moderate, and negligible weathering regions, respectively (see Table 3 and Fig. 1).

NOTE 8—The specifier of the aggregate should designate the class of coarse aggregate to be used in the work, based on weathering severity, abrasion, and other factors of exposure. (See Table 3 and Fig. 1.) The limits for coarse aggregate corresponding to each class designation are expected to ensure satisfactory performance in concrete for the respective type and location of construction. Selecting a class with unduly restrictive limits may result in unnecessary cost if materials meeting those requirements are not locally available. Selecting a class with lenient limits may result in unsatisfactory performance and premature deterioration of the concrete. While concrete in different parts of a single structure may be adequately made with different classes of coarse aggregate, the specifier may wish to require the coarse aggregate for all concrete to conform to the same more restrictive class to reduce the chance of furnishing concrete with the wrong class of aggregate, especially on smaller projects.

NOTE 9—For coarse aggregate in concrete exposed to weathering, the map with the weathering regions shown in Fig. 1 is intended to serve only as a guide to probable weathering severity. Those undertaking construction, especially near the boundaries of weathering regions, should consult local weather bureau records for amount of winter precipitation and number of freeze-thaw cycles to be expected, for determining the weathering severity for establishing test requirements of the coarse aggregate. For construction at altitudes exceeding 5000 ft

🏛 C 33

(1520 m) above sea level, the likelihood of more severe weathering than indicated by the map should be considered. In arid areas, severity of weathering may be less than that indicated. In either case, the definitions of weathering severity in Table 3 would govern. If there is doubt in choosing between two regions, select the more severe weathering region.

11.2 Coarse aggregate for use in concrete that will be subject to wetting, extended exposure to humid atmosphere, or contact with moist ground shall not contain any materials that are deleteriously reactive with the alkalies in the cement in an amount sufficient to cause excessive expansion of mortar or concrete except that if such materials are present in injurious amounts, the coarse aggregate may be used with a cement containing less than 0.60 % alkalies calculated as sodium oxide equivalent ($Na_2O + 0.658K_2O$) or with the addition of a material that has been shown to prevent harmful expansion due to the alkali-aggregate reaction. (See Appendix X1.).

11.3 Coarse aggregate having test results exceeding the limits specified in Table 3 may be accepted provided that concrete made with similar aggregate from the same source has given satisfactory service when exposed in a similar manner to that to be encountered; or, in the absence of a demonstrable service record, provided that the aggregate produces concrete having satisfactory relevant properties (see Note 4).

METHODS OF SAMPLING AND TESTING

12. Methods of Sampling and Testing

12.1 Sample and test the aggregates in accordance with the following methods, except as otherwise provided in this specification. Make the required tests on test specimens that comply with requirements of the designated test methods. The same test specimen may be used for sieve analysis and for determination of material finer than the No. 200 (75-µm) sieve. Separated sizes from the sieve analysis may be used in preparation of samples for soundness or abrasion tests. For determination of all other tests and for evaluation of potential alkali reactivity where required, use independent test specimens.

12.1.1 *Sampling*—Practice D 75 and Practice D 3665.

12.1.2 *Grading and Fineness Modulus*—Test Method C 136.

12.1.3 *Amount of Material Finer than No. 200 (75-µm) Sieve*—Test Method C 117.

12.1.4 *Organic Impurities*—Test Method C 40.

12.1.5 *Effect of Organic Impurities on Strength*—Test Method C 87.

12.1.6 *Soundness*—Test Method C 88.

12.1.7 *Clay Lumps and Friable Particles*—Test Method C 142.

12.1.8 *Coal and Lignite*—Test Method C 123, using a liquid of 2.0 specific gravity to remove the particles of coal and lignite. Only material that is brownish-black, or black, shall be considered coal or lignite. Coke shall not be classed as coal or lignite.

12.1.9 *Weight of Slag*—Test Method C 29.

12.1.10 *Abrasion of Coarse Aggregate*—Test Method C 131 or Test Method C 535.

12.1.11 *Reactive Aggregates*—See Appendix X1.

12.1.12 *Freezing and Thawing*—Procedures for making freezing and thawing tests of concrete are described in Test Method C 666.

12.1.13 *Chert*—Test Method C 123 is used to identify particles in a sample of coarse aggregate lighter than 2.40 specific gravity, and Practice C 295 to identify which of the particles in the light fraction are chert.

13. Keywords

13.1 aggregates; coarse aggregate; concrete aggregates; fine aggregate

APPENDIX

(Nonmandatory Information)

XI. METHODS FOR EVALUATING POTENTIAL REACTIVITY OF AN AGGREGATE

X1.1 A number of methods for detecting potential reactivity have been proposed. However, they do not provide quantitative information on the degree of reactivity to be expected or tolerated in service. Therefore, evaluation of potential reactivity of an aggregate should be based upon judgment and on the interpretation of test data and examination of concrete structures containing a combination of fine and coarse aggregates and cements for use in the new work. Results of the following tests may assist in making the evaluation:

X1.1.1 *Practice C 295*—Certain materials are known to be reactive with the alkalies in cements. These include the following forms of silica: opal, chalcedony, tridymite, and cristobalite; intermediate to acid (silica-rich) volcanic glass such as is likely to occur in rhyolite, andesite, or dacite; certain zeolites such as heulandite; and certain constituents of some phyllites. Determination of the presence and quantities of these materials by petrographic examination is helpful in evaluating potential alkali reactivity. Some of these materials render an aggregate deleteriously reactive when present in quantities as little as 1.0 % or even less.

X1.1.2 *Test Method C 289*—In this test method, aggregates represented by points lying to the right of the solid line of Fig. 2 of Test Method C 289 usually should be considered potentially reactive.

X1.1.2.1 If R_c exceeds 70, the aggregate is considered potentially reactive if S_c is greater than R_c.

X1.1.2.2 If R_c is less than 70, the aggregate is considered potentially reactive if S_c is greater than $35 + (R_c/2)$.

X1.1.2.3 These criteria conform to the solid line curve given in Fig. 2 of Test Method C 289. The test can be made quickly and, while not completely reliable in all cases, provides helpful information, especially where results of the more time-consuming tests are not available.

∰ C 33

X1.1.3 *Test Method C 227*—The results of this test method when made with a high-alkali cement, furnish information on the likelihood of harmful reactions occurring. The alkali content of the cement should be substantially above 0.6 %, and preferably above 0.8 %, expressed as sodium oxide. Combinations of aggregate and cement that have produced excessive expansions in this test usually should be considered potentially reactive. While the line of demarcation between nonreactive and reactive combinations is not clearly defined, expansion is generally considered to be excessive if it exceeds 0.05 % at 3 months or 0.10 % at 6 months. Expansions greater than 0.05 % at 3 months should not be considered excessive where the 6-month expansion remains below 0.10 %. Data for the 3-month tests should be considered only when 6-month results are not available.

X1.1.4 *Test Method C 342*—This test method is intended primarily for research concerning the potential expansion of cement-aggregate combinations subjected to variations of temperature and water saturation during storage under prescribed conditions of test. Its use is mainly by those interested in research on aggregates that are found in parts of Kansas, Nebraska, Iowa and possibly other adjoining areas.

X1.1.4.1 In addition to its usefulness in research, this test method has been found useful in the selection of aggregates of the so-called "sand-gravel" type found mainly in some parts of Kansas, Nebraska and Iowa, which contain very little coarse material; generally 5 to 15 % retained on the No. 4 (4.75-mm) sieve. Much work has been done on the problems of using these aggregates successfully in concrete and is reported in summary in the "Final Report of Cooperative Tests of Proposed Tentative Method of Test for Potential Volume Change of Cement-Aggregate Combinations," Appendix to Committee C-9 Report, Proceedings, ASTM, Volume 54, 1954, p. 356. It indicates that cement-aggregate combinations tested by this procedure in which expansion equals or exceeds 0.200 % at an age of 1 year may be considered unsatisfactory for use in concrete exposed to wide variations of temperature and degree of saturation with water. In that geographical region, the problem has been reduced through the use of partial replacement of the "sand-gravel" with limestone coarse aggregate.

X1.1.5 *Potential Reactivity of Carbonate Aggregates*— The reaction of the dolomite in certain carbonate rocks with alkalies in portland cement paste has been found to be associated with deleterious expansion of concrete containing such rocks as coarse aggregate. Carbonate rocks capable of such reaction possess a characteristic texture and composition. The characteristic texture is that in which relatively large crystals of dolomite are scattered in a finer-grained matrix of calcite and clay. The characteristic composition is that in which the carbonate portion consists of substantial amounts of both dolomite and calcite, and the acid-insoluble residue contains a significant amount of clay. Except in certain areas, such rocks are of relatively infrequent occurrence and seldom make up a significant proportion of the material present in a deposit of rock being considered for use in making aggregate for concrete. Test Method C 586 has been successfully used in (*1*) research and (*2*) preliminary screening of aggregate sources to indicate the presence of material with a potential for deleterious expansions when used in concrete.

ASTM Designation: C 40 – 92

AMERICAN SOCIETY FOR TESTING AND MATERIALS
1916 Race St. Philadelphia, Pa 19103
Reprinted from the Annual Book of ASTM Standards. Copyright ASTM
If not listed in the current combined index, will appear in the next edition.

American Association State
Highway and Transportation Officials Standard
AASHTO No.: T 21

Standard Test Method for
Organic Impurities in Fine Aggregates for Concrete[1]

This standard is issued under the fixed designation C 40; the number immediately following the designation indicates the year of original adoption or, in the case of revision, the year of last revision. A number in parentheses indicates the year of last reapproval. A superscript epsilon (ϵ) indicates an editorial change since the last revision or reapproval.

This standard has been approved for use by agencies of the Department of Defense. Consult the DoD Index of Specifications and Standards for the specific year of issue which has been adopted by the Department of Defense.

1. Scope

1.1 This test method covers procedures for an approximate determination of the presence of injurious organic impurities in fine aggregates that are to be used in hydraulic cement mortar or concrete.

1.2 Inch-pound units are to be regarded as standard.

1.3 *This standard does not purport to address all of the safety problems, if any, associated with its use. It is the responsibility of the user of this standard to establish appropriate safety and health practices and determine the applicability of regulatory limitations prior to use.*

2. Referenced Documents

2.1 *ASTM Standards:*
C 33 Specification for Concrete Aggregates[2]
C 87 Test Method for Effect of Organic Impurities in Fine Aggregate on Strength of Mortar[2]
C 702 Practice for Reducing Field Samples of Aggregate to Testing Size[2]
D 75 Practice for Sampling Aggregates[3]
D 1544 Test Method for Color of Transparent Liquids (Gardner Color Scale)[4]

3. Significance and Use

3.1 This test method is used in making a preliminary determination of the acceptability of fine aggregates with respect to the requirements of Specification C 33 that relate to organic impurities.

3.2 The principal value of this test method is to furnish a warning that injurious amounts of organic impurities may be present. When a sample subjected to this test produces a color darker than the reference color solution it is advisable to perform the test for the effect of organic impurities on the strength of mortar in accordance with Test Method C 87.

4. Apparatus

4.1 *Glass Bottles*—Approximately twelve or 16-oz (U.S. fluid) (350 or 470-mL) nominal capacity colorless glass graduated bottles of approximately oval cross section, equipped with watertight stoppers or caps, not soluble in the specified reagents. In no case shall the maximum outside thickness of the bottles, measured along the line of sight used for the color comparison, be greater than 2½ in. (60 mm) or less than 1.5 in. (40 mm). The graduations on the bottles shall be in ounces (U.S. fluid), or millilitres, except that unmarked bottles may be calibrated and scribed with graduations by the user. In such case, graduation marks are required at only three points as follows:

4.1.1 *Reference Color Solution Level*—2½ oz (U.S. fluid) (75 mL),

4.1.2 *Fine Aggregate Level*—4½ oz (U.S. fluid) (130 mL), and

4.1.3 *NaOH Solution Level*—7 oz (U.S. fluid) (200 mL).

5. Reagent and Reference Standard Color Solution

5.1 *Reagent Sodium Hydroxide Solution (3 %)*—Dissolve 3 parts by mass of reagent grade sodium hydroxide (NaOH) in 97 parts of water.

5.2 *Reference Standard Color Solution*—Dissolve reagent grade potassium dichromate ($K_2Cr_2O_7$) in concentrated sulfuric acid (sp gr 1.84) at the rate of 0.250 g/100 mL of acid. The solution must be freshly made for the color comparison using gentle heat if necessary to effect solution.

6. Sampling

6.1 The sample shall be selected in general accordance with Practice D 75.

7. Test Sample

7.1 The test sample shall have a mass of about 1 lb (approximately 450 g) and be taken from the larger sample in accordance with Practice C 702.

8. Procedure

8.1 Fill a glass bottle to the 4½-fluid oz (approximately 130-mL) level with the sample of the fine aggregate to be tested.

8.2 Add the sodium hydroxide solution until the volume of the fine aggregate and liquid, indicated after shaking, is 7 fluid oz (approximately 200 mL).

8.3 Stopper the bottle, shake vigorously, and then allow to stand for 24 h.

9. Determination of Color Value

9.1 *Standard Procedure*—At the end of the 24-h standing period, fill a glass bottle to the 2½-fluid oz (approximately 75-mL) level with the fresh reference color solution, prepared not longer than 2 h previously, as prescribed in 5.2.

---

[1] This test method is under the jurisdiction of ASTM Committee C-9 on Concrete and Concrete Aggregates and is the direct responsibility of Subcommittee C09.20 on Normal Weight Aggregates.
Current edition approved Nov. 15, 1992. Published January 1993. Originally published as C 40 – 21 T. Last previous edition C 40 – 84 (1991)$^{\epsilon 1}$.
[2] *Annual Book of ASTM Standards,* Vol 04.02.
[3] *Annual Book of ASTM Standards,* Vols 04.02 and 04.03.
[4] *Annual Book of ASTM Standards,* Vol 06.01.

C 40

Then compare the color of the supernatant liquid above the test sample with that of the reference standard color solution and record whether it is lighter, darker, or of equal color to that of the reference standard. Make the color comparison by holding the two bottles close together and looking through them.

9.2 *Alternative Procedure*—To define more precisely the color of the liquid of the test sample, five glass standard colors may be used as described in Table 1 of Test Method D 1544, using the following colors:

Gardner Color Standard No.	Organic Plate No.
5	1
8	2
11	3 (standard)
14	4
16	5

The comparison procedure described in 9.1 shall be used, except that the organic plate number which is nearest the color of the supernatant liquid above the test specimen shall be reported. When using this alternative procedure it is not necessary to prepare the reference standard color solution.

NOTE—A suitable instrument consists of the glass color standards mounted in a plastic holder. The instrument is provided with all five organic plate number colors.

10. Interpretation of Results

10.1 If the color of the supernatant liquid is darker than that of the reference standard color solution, the fine aggregate under test shall be considered to possibly contain injurious organic impurities, and further tests should be made before approving the fine aggregate for use in concrete.

11. Precision and Bias

11.1 Since this test produces no numerical values, determination of the precision and bias is not possible.

12. Keywords

12.1 colorimetric test; fine aggregate; organic impurities

AMERICAN SOCIETY FOR TESTING AND MATERIALS
1916 Race St. Philadelphia, Pa 19103
Reprinted from the Annual Book of ASTM Standards. Copyright ASTM
If not listed in the current combined index, will appear in the next edition.

Standard Test Method for
Materials Finer than 75-μm (No. 200) Sieve in Mineral Aggregates by Washing[1]

This standard is issued under the fixed designation C 117; the number immediately following the designation indicates the year of original adoption or, in the case of revision, the year of last revision. A number in parentheses indicates the year of last reapproval. A superscript epsilon (ε) indicates an editorial change since the last revision or reapproval.

This test method has been approved for use by agencies of the Department of Defense. Consult the DoD Index of Specifications and Standards for the specific year of issue which has been adopted by the Department of Defense.

1. Scope

1.1 This test method covers determination of the amount of material finer than a 75-μm (No. 200) sieve in aggregate by washing. Clay particles and other aggregate particles that are dispersed by the wash water, as well as water-soluble materials, will be removed from the aggregate during the test.

1.2 Two procedures are included, one using only water for the washing operation, and the other including a wetting agent to assist the loosening of the material finer than the 75-μm (No. 200) sieve from the coarser material. Unless otherwise specified, Procedure A (water only) shall be used.

1.3 The values stated in SI units are to be regarded as the standard.

1.4 *This standard does not purport to address all of the safety concerns, if any, associated with its use. It is the responsibility of the user of this standard to establish appropriate safety and health practices and determine the applicability of regulatory limitations prior to use.*

2. Referenced Documents

2.1 *ASTM Standards:*
C 136 Test Method for Sieve Analysis of Fine and Coarse Aggregates[2]
C 670 Practice for Preparing Precision and Bias Statements for Test Methods for Construction Materials[2]
C 702 Practice for Reducing Field Samples of Aggregate to Testing Size[2]
D 75 Practice for Sampling Aggregates[3]
E 11 Specification for Wire-Cloth Sieves for Testing Purposes[4]
2.2 *AASHTO Standard:*
T 11 Method of Test for Amount of Material Finer than 0.075-mm Sieve in Aggregate[5]

3. Summary of Test Method

3.1 A sample of the aggregate is washed in a prescribed manner, using either plain water or water containing a

wetting agent, as specified. The decanted wash water, containing suspended and dissolved material, is passed through a 75-μm (No. 200) sieve. The loss in mass resulting from the wash treatment is calculated as mass percent of the original sample and is reported as the percentage of material finer than a 75-μm (No. 200) sieve by washing.

4. Significance and Use

4.1 Material finer than the 75-μm (No. 200) sieve can be separated from larger particles much more efficiently and completely by wet sieving than through the use of dry sieving. Therefore, when accurate determinations of material finer than 75 μm in fine or coarse aggregate are desired, this test method is used on the sample prior to dry sieving in accordance with Test Method C 136. The results of this test method are included in the calculation in Test Method C 136, and the total amount of material finer than 75 μm by washing, plus that obtained by dry sieving the same sample, is reported with the results of Test Method C 136. Usually, the additional amount of material finer than 75 μm obtained in the dry sieving process is a small amount. If it is large, the efficiency of the washing operation should be checked. It could also be an indication of degradation of the aggregate.

4.2 Plain water is adequate to separate the material finer than 75 μm from the coarser material with most aggregates. In some cases, the finer material is adhering to the larger particles, such as some clay coatings and coatings on aggregates that have been extracted from bituminous mixtures. In these cases, the fine material will be separated more readily with a wetting agent in the water.

5. Apparatus and Materials

5.1 *Balance*—A balance or scale readable and accurate to 0.1 g or 0.1 % of the test load, whichever is greater, at any point within the range of use.

5.2 *Sieves*—A nest of two sieves, the lower being a 75-μm (No. 200) sieve and the upper a 1.18-mm (No. 16) sieve, both conforming to the requirements of Specification E 11.

5.3 *Container*—A pan or vessel of a size sufficient to contain the sample covered with water and to permit vigorous agitation without loss of any part of the sample or water.

5.4 *Oven*—An oven of sufficient size, capable of maintaining a uniform temperature of 110 ± 5°C (230 ± 9°F).

---

[1] This test method is under the jurisdiction of ASTM Committee C-9 on Concrete and Concrete Aggregates and is the direct responsibility of Subcommittee C09.20 on Normal Weight Aggregates.
Current edition approved March 15, 1995. Published May 1995. Originally published as C 117 – 35 T. Last previous edition C 117 – 90.
[2] *Annual Book of ASTM Standards*, Vol 04.02.
[3] *Annual Book of ASTM Standards*, Vol 04.03.
[4] *Annual Book of ASTM Standards*, Vol 14.02.
[5] Available from the American Association of State Highway and Transportation Officials, 444 N. Capitol St., NW, Suite 225, Washington, DC 20001.

C 117

5.5 *Wetting Agent*—Any dispersing agent, such as liquid dishwashing detergents, that will promote separation of the fine materials.

NOTE 1—The use of a mechanical apparatus to perform the washing operation is not precluded, provided the results are consistent with those obtained using manual operations. The use of some mechanical washing equipment with some samples may cause degradation of the sample.

6. Sampling

6.1 Sample the aggregate in accordance with Practice D 75. If the same test sample is to be tested for sieve analysis according to Test Method C 136, comply with the applicable requirements of that test method.

6.2 Thoroughly mix the sample of aggregate to be tested and reduce the quantity to an amount suitable for testing using the applicable methods described in Practice C 702. If the same test sample is to be tested according to Test Method C 136, the minimum mass shall be as described in the applicable sections of that method. Otherwise, the mass of the test sample, after drying, shall conform with the following:

Nominal Maximum Size	Minimum Mass, g
4.75 mm (No. 4) or smaller	300
9.5 mm (⅜ in.)	1000
19.0 mm (¾ in.)	2500
37.5 mm (1½ in.) or larger	5000

The test sample shall be the end result of the reduction. Reduction to an exact predetermined mass shall not be permitted.

7. Selection of Procedure

7.1 Procedure A shall be used, unless otherwise specified by the Specification with which the test results are to be compared, or when directed by the agency for which the work is performed.

8. Procedure A—Washing with Plain Water

8.1 Dry the test sample to constant mass at a temperature of 110 ± 5°C (230 ± 9°F). Determine the mass to the nearest 0.1 % of the mass of the test sample.

8.2 If the applicable specification requires that the amount passing the 75-µm (No. 200) sieve shall be determined on a portion of the sample passing a sieve smaller than the nominal maximum size of the aggregate, separate the sample on the designated sieve and determine the mass of the material passing the designated sieve to 0.1 % of the mass of this portion of the test sample. Use this mass as the original dry mass of the test sample in 10.1.

NOTE 2—Some specifications for aggregates with a nominal maximum size of 50 mm or greater, for example, provide a limit for material passing the 75-µm (No. 200) sieve determined on that portion of the sample passing the 25.0-mm sieve. Such procedures are necessary since it is impractical to wash samples of the size required when the same test sample is to be used for sieve analysis by Test Method C 136.

8.3 After drying and determining the mass, place the test sample in the container and add sufficient water to cover it. No detergent, dispersing agent, or other substance shall be added to the water. Agitate the sample with sufficient vigor to result in complete separation of all particles finer than the 75-µm (No. 200) sieve from the coarser particles, and to bring the fine material into suspension. Immediately pour

the wash water containing the suspended and dissolved solids over the nested sieves, arranged with the coarser sieve on top. Take care to avoid, as much as feasible, the decantation of coarser particles of the sample.

8.4 Add a second charge of water to the sample in the container, agitate, and decant as before. Repeat this operation until the wash water is clear.

NOTE 3—If mechanical washing equipment is used, the charging of water, agitating, and decanting may be a continuous operation.

8.5 Return all material retained on the nested sieves by flushing to the washed sample. Dry the washed aggregate to constant mass at a temperature of 110 ± 5°C (230 ± 9°F) and determine the mass to the nearest 0.1 % of the original mass of the sample.

NOTE 4—Following the washing of the sample and flushing any material retained on the 75-µm (No. 200) sieve back into the container, no water should be decanted from the container except through the 75-µm sieve, to avoid loss of material. Excess water from flushing should be evaporated from the sample in the drying process.

9. Procedure B—Washing Using a Wetting Agent

9.1 Prepare the sample in the same manner as for Procedure A.

9.2 After drying and determining the mass, place the test sample in the container. Add sufficient water to cover the sample, and add wetting agent to the water (Note 5). Agitate the sample with sufficient vigor to result in complete separation of all particles finer than the 75-µm (No. 200) sieve from the coarser particles, and to bring the fine material into suspension. Immediately pour the wash water containing the suspended and dissolved solids over the nested sieves, arranged with the coarser sieve on top. Take care to avoid, as much as feasible, the decantation of coarser particles of the sample.

NOTE 5—These should be enough wetting agent to produce a small amount of suds when the sample is agitated. The quantity will depend on the hardness of the water and the quality of the detergent. Excessive suds may overflow the sieves and carry some material with them.

9.3 Add a second charge of water (without wetting agent) to the sample in the container, agitate, and decant as before. Repeat this operation until the wash water is clear.

9.4 Complete the test as for Procedure A.

10. Calculation

10.1 Calculate the amount of material passing a 75-µm (No. 200) sieve by washing as follows:

$$A = [(B - C)/B] \times 100$$

where:
A = percentage of material finer than a 75-µm (No. 200) sieve by washing,
B = original dry mass of sample, g, and
C = dry mass of sample after washing, g.

11. Report

11.1 Report the following information:

11.1.1 Report the percentage of material finer than the 75-µm (No. 200) sieve by washing to the nearest 0.1 %, except if the result is 10 % or more, report the percentage to the nearest whole number.

⑭ C 117

TABLE 1 Precision

	Standard Deviation (1s)[A], %	Acceptable Range of two Results (d2s)[A], %
Coarse Aggregate[B]		
Single-Operator Precision	0.10	0.28
Multilaboratory Precision	0.22	0.62
Fine Aggregate[C]		
Single-Operator Precision	0.15	0.43
Multilaboratory Precision	0.29	0.82

[A] These numbers represent the (1s) and (d2s) limits as described in Practice C 670.

[B] Precision estimates are based on aggregates having a nominal maximum size of 19.0 mm (¼ in.) with less than 1.5% finer than the 75-μm (No. 200) sieve.

[C] Precision estimates are based on fine aggregates having 1.0 to 3.0% finer than the 75-μm (No. 200) sieve.

11.1.2 Include a statement as to which procedure was used.

12. Precision and Bias

12.1 *Precision*—The estimates of precision of this test method listed in Table 1 are based on results from the AASHTO Materials Reference Laboratory Proficiency Sample Program, with testing conducted by this test method and AASHTO Method T 11. The significant differences between the methods at the time the data were acquired is that Method T 11 required, and Test Method C 117 prohibited, the use of a wetting agent. The data are based on the analyses of more than 100 paired test results from 40 to 100 laboratories.

12.1.1 The precision values for fine aggregate in Table 1 are based on nominal 500-g test samples. Revision of this test method in 1994 permits the fine aggregate test sample size to be 300 g minimum. Analysis of results of testing of 300-g and 500-g test samples from Aggregate Proficiency Test Samples 99 and 100 (Samples 99 and 100 were essentially identical) produced the precision values in Table 2, which indicates only minor differences due to test sample size.

Note 6—The values for fine aggregate in Table 1 will be revised to reflect the 300-g test sample size when a sufficient number of Aggregate Proficiency Tests have been conducted using that sample size to provide reliable data.

12.2 *Bias*—Since there is no accepted reference material suitable for determining the bias for the procedure in this test method, no statement on bias is made.

13. Keywords

13.1 aggregate; coarse aggregate; fine aggregate; grading; loss by washing; 75 μm (No. 200) sieve; size analysis

TABLE 2 Precision Data for 300-g and 500-g Test Samples

Fine Aggregate Proficiency Sample				Within Laboratory		Between Laboratory	
Test Result	Sample Size	No. of Labs	Average	1s	d2s	1s	d2s
AASHTO T 11/ASTM C 117 Total material passing the No. 200 sieve by washing (%)	500 g	270	1.23	0.08	0.24	0.23	0.66
	300 g	264	1.20	0.10	0.29	0.24	0.68

ASTM Designation: C 127 – 88 (Reapproved 1993)$^{\epsilon 1}$

AMERICAN SOCIETY FOR TESTING AND MATERIALS
1916 Race St. Philadelphia, Pa 19103
Reprinted from the Annual Book of ASTM Standards. Copyright ASTM
If not listed in the current combined index, will appear in the next edition.

Standard Test Method for
Specific Gravity and Absorption of Coarse Aggregate[1]

This standard is issued under the fixed designation C 127; the number immediately following the designation indicates the year of original adoption or, in the case of revision, the year of last revision. A number in parentheses indicates the year of last reapproval. A superscript epsilon (ϵ) indicates an editorial change since the last revision or reapproval.

This test method has been approved for use by agencies of the Department of Defense. Consult the DoD Index of Specifications and Standards for the specific year of issue which has been adopted by the Department of Defense.

[1] NOTE—Keywords were added in December 1993.

1. Scope

1.1 This test method covers the determination of specific gravity and absorption of coarse aggregate. The specific gravity may be expressed as bulk specific gravity, bulk specific gravity (SSD) (saturated-surface-dry), or apparent specific gravity. The bulk specific gravity (SSD) and absorption are based on aggregate after 24 h soaking in water. This test method is not intended to be used with lightweight aggregates.

1.2 The values stated in SI units are to be regarded as the standard.

1.3 *This standard does not purport to address all of the safety problems, if any, associated with its use. It is the responsibility of the user of this standard to establish appropriate safety and health practices and determine the applicability of regulatory limitations prior to use.*

2. Referenced Documents

2.1 *ASTM Standards:*

C 29/C 29M Test Method for Unit Weight and Voids in Aggregate[2]

C 125 Terminology Relating to Concrete and Concrete Aggregates[2]

C 128 Test Method for Specific Gravity and Absorption of Fine Aggregate[2]

C 136 Test Method for Sieve Analysis of Fine and Coarse Aggregates[2]

C 566 Test Method for Total Moisture Content of Aggregate by Drying[2]

C 670 Practice for Preparing Precision and Bias Statements for Test Methods for Construction Materials[2]

C 702 Practice for Reducing Field Samples of Aggregate to Testing Size[2]

D 75 Practice for Sampling Aggregates[3]

D 448 Classification for Sizes of Aggregate for Road and Bridge Construction[3]

E 11 Specification for Wire-Cloth Sieves for Testing Purposes[4]

E 12 Terminology Relating to Density and Specific Gravity of Solids, Liquids, and Gases[5]

2.2 *AASHTO Standard:*

AASHTO No. T 85 Specific Gravity and Absorption of Coarse Aggregate[6]

3. Terminology

3.1 *Definitions:*

3.1.1 *absorption*—the increase in the weight of aggregate due to water in the pores of the material, but not including water adhering to the outside surface of the particles, expressed as a percentage of the dry weight. The aggregate is considered "dry" when it has been maintained at a temperature of 110 ± 5°C for sufficient time to remove all uncombined water.

3.1.2 *specific gravity*—the ratio of the mass (or weight in air) of a unit volume of a material to the mass of the same volume of water at stated temperatures. Values are dimensionless.

3.1.2.1 *apparent specific gravity*—the ratio of the weight in air of a unit volume of the impermeable portion of aggregate at a stated temperature to the weight in air of an equal volume of gas-free distilled water at a stated temperature.

3.1.2.2 *bulk specific gravity*—the ratio of the weight in air of a unit volume of aggregate (including the permeable and impermeable voids in the particles, but not including the voids between particles) at a stated temperature to the weight in air of an equal volume of gas-free distilled water at a stated temperature.

3.1.2.3 *bulk specific gravity (SSD)*—the ratio of the weight in air of a unit volume of aggregate, including the weight of water within the voids filled to the extent achieved by submerging in water for approximately 24 h (but not including the voids between particles) at a stated temperature, compared to the weight in air of an equal volume of gas-free distilled water at a stated temperature.

[1] This test method is under the jurisdiction of ASTM Committee C-9 on Concrete and Concrete Aggregates and is the direct responsibility of Subcommittee C09.20 on Normal Weight Aggregates.

Current edition approved Oct. 31, 1988. Published December 1988. Originally published as C 127 – 36 T. Last previous edition C 127 – 84.

[2] *Annual Book of ASTM Standards*, Vol 04.02.

[3] *Annual Book of ASTM Standards*, Vol 04.03.

[4] *Annual Book of ASTM Standards*, Vol 14.02.

[5] *Annual Book of ASTM Standards*, Vol 15.05.

[6] Available from American Association of State Highway and Transportation Officials, 444 North Capitol St. N.W., Suite 225, Washington, DC 20001.

⬧ C 127

NOTE 1—The terminology for specific gravity is based on terms in Terminology E 12, and that for absorption is based on that term in Terminology C 125.

4. Summary of Test Method

4.1 A sample of aggregate is immersed in water for approximately 24 h to essentially fill the pores. It is then removed from the water, the water dried from the surface of the particles, and weighed. Subsequently the sample is weighed while submerged in water. Finally the sample is oven-dried and weighed a third time. Using the weights thus obtained and formulas in this test method, it is possible to calculate three types of specific gravity and absorption.

5. Significance and Use

5.1 Bulk specific gravity is the characteristic generally used for calculation of the volume occupied by the aggregate in various mixtures containing aggregate, including portland cement concrete, bituminous concrete, and other mixtures that are proportioned or analyzed on an absolute volume basis. Bulk specific gravity is also used in the computation of voids in aggregate in Test Method C 29. Bulk specific gravity (SSD) is used if the aggregate is wet, that is, if its absorption has been satisfied. Conversely, the bulk specific gravity (oven-dry) is used for computations when the aggregate is dry or assumed to be dry.

5.2 Apparent specific gravity pertains to the relative density of the solid material making up the constituent particles not including the pore space within the particles which is accessible to water.

5.3 Absorption values are used to calculate the change in the weight of an aggregate due to water absorbed in the pore spaces within the constituent particles, compared to the dry condition, when it is deemed that the aggregate has been in contact with water long enough to satisfy most of the absorption potential. The laboratory standard for absorption is that obtained after submerging dry aggregate for approximately 24 h in water. Aggregates mined from below the water table may have a higher absorption, when used, if not allowed to dry. Conversely, some aggregates when used may contain an amount of absorbed moisture less than the 24-h soaked condition. For an aggregate that has been in contact with water and that has free moisture on the particle surfaces, the percentage of free moisture can be determined by deducting the absorption from the total moisture content determined by Test Method C 566.

5.4 The general procedures described in this test method are suitable for determining the absorption of aggregates that have had conditioning other than the 24-h soak, such as boiling water or vacuum saturation. The values obtained for absorption by other test methods will be different than the values obtained by the prescribed 24-h soak, as will the bulk specific gravity (SSD).

5.5 The pores in lightweight aggregates may or may not become essentially filled with water after immersion for 24 h. In fact, many such aggregates can remain immersed in water for several days without satisfying most of the aggregates' absorption potential. Therefore, this test method is not intended for use with lightweight aggregate.

6. Apparatus

6.1 *Balance*—A weighing device that is sensitive, read-

able, and accurate to 0.05 % of the sample weight at any point within the range used for this test, or 0.5 g, whichever is greater. The balance shall be equipped with suitable apparatus for suspending the sample container in water from the center of the weighing platform or pan of the weighing device.

6.2 *Sample Container*—A wire basket of 3.35 mm (No. 6) or finer mesh, or a bucket of approximately equal breadth and height, with a capacity of 4 to 7 L for 37.5-mm (1½-in.) nominal maximum size aggregate or smaller, and a larger container as needed for testing larger maximum size aggregate. The container shall be constructed so as to prevent trapping air when the container is submerged.

6.3 *Water Tank*—A watertight tank into which the sample container may be placed while suspended below the balance.

6.4 *Sieves*—A 4.75-mm (No. 4) sieve or other sizes as needed (see 7.2, 7.3, and 7.4), conforming to Specification E 11.

7. Sampling

7.1 Sample the aggregate in accordance with Practice D 75.

7.2 Thoroughly mix the sample of aggregate and reduce it to the approximate quantity needed using the applicable procedures in Methods C 702. Reject all material passing a 4.75-mm (No. 4) sieve by dry sieving and thoroughly washing to remove dust or other coatings from the surface. If the coarse aggregate contains a substantial quantity of material finer than the 4.75-mm sieve (such as for Size No. 8 and 9 aggregates in Classification D 448), use the 2.36-mm (No. 8) sieve in place of the 4.75-mm sieve. Alternatively, separate the material finer than the 4.75-mm sieve and test the finer material according to Test Method C 128.

7.3 The minimum weight of test sample to be used is given below. In many instances it may be desirable to test a coarse aggregate in several separate size fractions; and if the sample contains more than 15 % retained on the 37.5-mm (1½-in.) sieve, test the material larger than 37.5 mm in one or more size fractions separately from the smaller size fractions. When an aggregate is tested in separate size fractions, the minimum weight of test sample for each fraction shall be the difference between the weights prescribed for the maximum and minimum sizes of the fraction.

Nominal Maximum Size, mm (in.)	Minimum Weight of Test Sample, kg (lb)
12.5 (½) or less	2 (4.4)
19.0 (¾)	3 (6.6)
25.0 (1)	4 (8.8)
37.5 (1½)	5 (11)
50 (2)	8 (18)
63 (2½)	12 (26)
75 (3)	18 (40)
90 (3½)	25 (55)
100 (4)	40 (88)
112 (4½)	50 (110)
125 (5)	75 (165)
150 (6)	125 (276)

7.4 If the sample is tested in two or more size fractions, determine the grading of the sample in accordance with Test Method C 136, including the sieves used for separating the size fractions for the determinations in this method. In calculating the percentage of material in each size fraction, ignore the quantity of material finer than the 4.75-mm (No. 4) sieve (or 2.36-mm (No. 8) sieve when that sieve is used in accordance with 7.2).

8. Procedure

8.1 Dry the test sample to constant weight at a temperature of 110 ± 5°C (230 ± 9°F), cool in air at room temperature for 1 to 3 h for test samples of 37.5-mm (1½-in.) nominal maximum size, or longer for larger sizes until the aggregate has cooled to a temperature that is comfortable to handle (approximately 50°C). Subsequently immerse the aggregate in water at room temperature for a period of 24 ± 4 h.

NOTE 2—When testing coarse aggregate of large nominal maximum size requiring large test samples, it may be more convenient to perform the test on two or more subsamples, and the values obtained combined for the computations described in Section 9.

8.2 Where the absorption and specific gravity values are to be used in proportioning concrete mixtures in which the aggregates will be in their naturally moist condition, the requirement for initial drying to constant weight may be eliminated, and, if the surfaces of the particles in the sample have been kept continuously wet until test, the 24-h soaking may also be eliminated.

NOTE 3—Values for absorption and bulk specific gravity (SSD) may be significantly higher for aggregate not oven dried before soaking than for the same aggregate treated in accordance with 8.1. This is especially true of particles larger than 75 mm (3 in.) since the water may not be able to penetrate the pores to the center of the particle in the prescribed soaking period.

8.3 Remove the test sample from the water and roll it in a large absorbent cloth until all visible films of water are removed. Wipe the larger particles individually. A moving stream of air may be used to assist in the drying operation. Take care to avoid evaporation of water from aggregate pores during the operation of surface-drying. Weigh the test sample in the saturated surface-dry condition. Record this and all subsequent weights to the nearest 0.5 g or 0.05 % of the sample weight, whichever is greater.

8.4 After weighing, immediately place the saturated-surface-dry test sample in the sample container and determine its weight in water at 23 ± 1.7°C (73.4 ± 3°F), having a density of 997 ± 2 kg/m³. Take care to remove all entrapped air before weighing by shaking the container while immersed.

NOTE 4—The container should be immersed to a depth sufficient to cover it and the test sample during weighing. Wire suspending the container should be of the smallest practical size to minimize any possible effects of a variable immersed length.

8.5 Dry the test sample to constant weight at a temperature of 110 ± 5°C (230 ± 9°F), cool in air at room temperature 1 to 3 h, or until the aggregate has cooled to a temperature that is comfortable to handle (approximately 50°C), and weigh.

9. Calculations

9.1 *Specific Gravity:*

9.1.1 *Bulk Specific Gravity*—Calculate the bulk specific gravity, 23/23°C (73.4/73.4°F), as follows:

$$\text{Bulk sp gr} = A/(B - C)$$

where:
A = weight of oven-dry test sample in air, g,
B = weight of saturated-surface-dry test sample in air, g, and
C = weight of saturated test sample in water, g.

9.1.2 *Bulk Specific Gravity (Saturated-Surface-Dry)*—Calculate the bulk specific gravity, 23/23°C (73.4/73.4°F), on the basis of weight of saturated-surface-dry aggregate as follows:

$$\text{Bulk sp gr (saturated-surface-dry)} = B/(B - C)$$

9.1.3 *Apparent Specific Gravity*—Calculate the apparent specific gravity, 23/23°C (73.4/73.4°F), as follows:

$$\text{Apparent sp gr} = A/(A - C)$$

9.2 *Average Specific Gravity Values*—When the sample is tested in separate size fractions the average value for bulk specific gravity, bulk specific gravity (SSD), or apparent specific gravity can be computed as the weighted average of the values as computed in accordance with 9.1 using the following equation:

$$G = \frac{1}{\dfrac{P_1}{100\, G_1} + \dfrac{P_2}{100\, G_2} + \ldots \dfrac{P_n}{100\, G_n}} \quad \text{(see Appendix X1)}$$

where:
G = average specific gravity. All forms of expression of specific gravity can be averaged in this manner.
$G_1, G_2 \ldots G_n$ = appropriate specific gravity values for each size fraction depending on the type of specific gravity being averaged.
$P_1, P_2, \ldots P_n$ = weight percentages of each size fraction present in the original sample.

NOTE 5—Some users of this test method may wish to express the results in terms of density. Density may be determined by multiplying the bulk specific gravity, bulk specific gravity (SSD), or apparent specific gravity by the weight of water (997.5 kg/m³ or 0.9975 Mg/m³ or 62.27 lb/ft³ at 23°C). Some authorities recommend using the density of water at 4°C (1000 kg/m³ or 1.000 Mg/m³ or 62.43 lb/ft³) as being sufficiently accurate. Results should be expressed to three significant figures. The density terminology corresponding to bulk specific gravity, bulk specific gravity (SSD), and apparent specific gravity has not been standardized.

9.3 *Absorption*—Calculate the percentage of absorption, as follows:

$$\text{Absorption, \%} = [(B - A)/A] \times 100$$

9.4 *Average Absorption Value*—When the sample is tested in separate size fractions, the average absorption value is the average of the values as computed in 9.3, weighted in proportion to the weight percentages of the size fractions in the original sample as follows:

$$A = (P_1 A_1/100) + (P_2 A_2/100) + \ldots (P_n A_n/100)$$

where:
A = average absorption, %,
$A_1, A_2 \ldots A_n$ = absorption percentages for each size fraction, and
$P_1, P_2, \ldots P_n$ = weight percentages of each size fraction present in the original sample.

10. Report

10.1 Report specific gravity results to the nearest 0.01, and indicate the type of specific gravity, whether bulk, bulk (saturated-surface-dry), or apparent.

10.2 Report the absorption result to the nearest 0.1 %.

10.3 If the specific gravity and absorption values were determined without first drying the aggregate, as permitted in 8.2, it shall be noted in the report.

11. Precision and Bias

11.1 The estimates of precision of this test method listed in Table 1 are based on results from the AASHTO Materials Reference Laboratory Reference Sample Program, with testing conducted by this test method and AASHTO Method T 85. The significant difference between the methods is that Test Method C 127 requires a saturation period of 24 ± 4 h, while Method T 85 requires a saturation period of 15 h minimum. This difference has been found to have an insignificant effect on the precision indices. The data are based on the analyses of more than 100 paired test results from 40 to 100 laboratories.

11.1 *Bias*—Since there is no accepted reference material for determining the bias for the procedure in this test

TABLE 1 Precision

	Standard Deviation (1S)[A]	Acceptable Range of Two Results (D2S)[A]
Single-Operator Precision:		
Bulk specific gravity (dry)	0.009	0.025
Bulk specific gravity (SSD)	0.007	0.020
Apparent specific gravity	0.007	0.020
Absorption[B], %	0.088	0.25
Multilaboratory Precision:		
Bulk specific gravity (dry)	0.013	0.038
Bulk specific gravity (SSD)	0.011	0.032
Apparent specific gravity	0.011	0.032
Absorption[B], %	0.145	0.41

[A] These numbers represent, respectively, the (1S) and (D2S) limits as described in Practice C 670. The precision estimates were obtained from the analysis of combined AASHTO Materials Reference Laboratory reference sample data from laboratories using 15 h minimum saturation times and other laboratories using 24 ± 4 h saturation times. Testing was performed on normal-weight aggregates, and started with aggregates in the oven-dry condition.

[B] Precision estimates are based on aggregates with absorptions of less than 2 %.

method, no statement on bias is being made.

12. Keywords

12.1 absorption; aggregate; coarse aggregate; specific gravity

---

APPENDIXES

(Nonmandatory Information)

X1. DEVELOPMENT OF EQUATIONS

X1.1 The derivation of the equation is apparent from the following simplified cases using two solids. Solid 1 has a weight W_1 in grams and a volume V_1 in millilitres; its specific gravity (G_1) is therefore W_1/V_1. Solid 2 has a weight W_2 and volume V_2, and $G_2 = W_2/V_2$. If the two solids are considered together, the specific gravity of the combination is the total weight in grams divided by the total volume in millilitres:

$$G = (W_1 + W_2) / (V_1 + V_2)$$

Manipulation of this equation yields the following:

$$G = \cfrac{1}{\cfrac{V_1 + V_2}{W_1 + W_2}} = \cfrac{1}{\cfrac{V_1}{V_1 + V_2} \cdot \cfrac{1}{W_1} + \cfrac{V_2}{W_1}}$$

$$G = \cfrac{1}{\cfrac{W_1}{W_1 + W_2}\left(\cfrac{V_1}{W_1}\right) + \cfrac{W_2}{W_1 + W_2}\left(\cfrac{V_2}{W_2}\right)}$$

However, the weight fractions of the two solids are:

$$W_1/(W_1 + W_2) = P_1/100 \text{ and } W_2/(W_1 + W_2) = P_2/100$$

and,

$$1/G_1 = V_1/W_1 \text{ and } 1/G_2 = V_2/W_2$$

TABLE X1.1 Example of Calculation of Average Values of Specific Gravity and Absorption for a Coarse Aggregate Tested in Separate Sizes

Size Fraction, mm (in.)	% in Original Sample	Sample Weight Used in Test, g	Bulk Specific Gravity (SSD)	Absorption, %
4.75 to 12.5 (No. 4 to ½)	44	2213.0	2.72	0.4
12.5 to 37.5 (½ to 1½)	35	5462.5	2.56	2.5
37.5 to 63 (1½ to 2½)	21	12593.0	2.54	3.0

Average Specific Gravity (SSD)

$$G_{SSD} = \cfrac{1}{\cfrac{0.44}{2.72} + \cfrac{0.35}{2.56} + \cfrac{0.21}{2.54}} = 2.62$$

Average Absorption

$$A = (0.44)(0.4) + (0.35)(2.5) + (0.21)(3.0) = 1.7\%$$

Therefore,

$$G = 1/[(P_1/100)(1/G_1) + (P_2/100)(1/G_2)]$$

An example of the computation is given in Table X1.1.

X2. INTERRELATIONSHIPS BETWEEN SPECIFIC GRAVITIES AND ABSORPTION AS DEFINED IN TEST METHODS C 127 AND C 128

X2.1 Let:

S_d = bulk specific gravity (dry basis),
S_s = bulk specific gravity (SSD basis),
S_a = apparent specific gravity, and
A = absorption in %.

X2.2 Then,

$$S_s = (1 + A/100)S_d \tag{1}$$

$$S_a = \cfrac{1}{\cfrac{1}{S_d} - \cfrac{A}{100}} = \cfrac{S_d}{1 - \cfrac{AS_d}{100}} \tag{2}$$

$$S_a = \cfrac{1}{\cfrac{1 + A/100}{S_s} - \cfrac{A}{100}} = \cfrac{S_s}{1 - \left[\cfrac{A}{100}(S_s - 1)\right]} \tag{2a}$$

$$A = \left(\frac{S_s}{S_d} - 1\right)100 \tag{3}$$

$$A = \left(\frac{S_a - S_s}{S_a(S_s - 1)}\right)100 \tag{4}$$

Standard Test Method for
Specific Gravity and Absorption of Fine Aggregate[1]

This standard is issued under the fixed designation C 128; the number immediately following the designation indicates the year of original adoption or, in the case of revision, the year of last revision. A number in parentheses indicates the year of last reapproval. A superscript epsilon (ε) indicates an editorial change since the last revision or reapproval.

This standard has been approved for use by agencies of the Department of Defense. Consult the DoD Index of Specifications and Standards for the specific year of issue which has been adopted by the Department of Defense.

1. Scope

1.1 This test method covers the determination of bulk and apparent specific gravity, 23/23°C (73.4/73.4°F), and absorption of fine aggregate.

1.2 This test method determines (after 24 h in water) the bulk specific gravity and the apparent specific gravity as defined in Terminology E 12, the bulk specific gravity on the basis of weight of saturated surface-dry aggregate, and the absorption as defined in Definitions C 125.

NOTE 1—The subcommittee is considering revising Test Methods C 127 and C 128 to use the term "density" instead of "specific gravity" for coarse and fine aggregate, respectively.

1.3 The values stated in SI units are to be regarded as the standard.

1.4 *This standard does not purport to address all of the safety problems, if any, associated with its use. It is the responsibility of the user of this standard to establish appropriate safety and health practices and determine the applicability of regulatory limitations prior to use.*

2. Referenced Documents

2.1 *ASTM Standards:*

C 29/C 29M Test Method for Unit Weight and Voids in Aggregate[2,3]

C 70 Test Method for Surface Moisture in Fine Aggregate[2]

C 125 Terminology Relating to Concrete and Concrete Aggregates[2,3]

C 127 Test Method for Specific Gravity and Absorption of Coarse Aggregate[2,3]

C 188 Test Method for Density of Hydraulic Cement[4]

C 566 Test Method for Total Moisture Content of Aggregate by Drying[2]

C 670 Practice for Preparing Precision and Bias Statements for Test Methods for Construction Materials[2,3,4]

C 702 Practice for Reducing Field Samples of Aggregate to Testing Size[2]

D 75 Practices for Sampling Aggregates[2,3]

E 12 Terminology Relating to Density and Specific Gravity of Solids, Liquids, and Gases[2,5]

E 380 Practice for Use of the International System of Units (SI) (the Modernized Metric System)[6]

2.2 *AASHTO Standard:*

AASHTO No. T 84 Specific Gravity and Absorption of Fine Aggregates[7]

3. Significance and Use

3.1 Bulk specific gravity is the characteristic generally used for calculation of the volume occupied by the aggregate in various mixtures containing aggregate including portland cement concrete, bituminous concrete, and other mixtures that are proportioned or analyzed on an absolute volume basis. Bulk specific gravity is also used in the computation of voids in aggregate in Test Method C 29 and the determination of moisture in aggregate by displacement in water in Test Method C 70. Bulk specific gravity determined on the saturated surface-dry basis is used if the aggregate is wet, that is, if its absorption has been satisfied. Conversely, the bulk specific gravity determined on the oven-dry basis is used for computations when the aggregate is dry or assumed to be dry.

3.2 Apparent specific gravity pertains to the relative density of the solid material making up the constituent particles not including the pore space within the particles that is accessible to water. This value is not widely used in construction aggregate technology.

3.3 Absorption values are used to calculate the change in the weight of an aggregate due to water absorbed in the pore spaces within the constituent particles, compared to the dry condition, when it is deemed that the aggregate has been in contact with water long enough to satisfy most of the absorption potential. The laboratory standard for absorption is that obtained after submerging dry aggregate for approximately 24 h in water. Aggregates mined from below the water table may have a higher absorption when used, if not allowed to dry. Conversely, some aggregates when used may contain an amount of absorbed moisture less than the 24 h-soaked condition. For an aggregate that has been in contact with water and that has free moisture on the particle surfaces, the percentage of free moisture can be determined by deducting the absorption from the total moisture content determined by Test Method C 566 by drying.

[1] This test method is under the jurisdiction of ASTM Committee C-9 on Concrete and Concrete Aggregates and is the direct responsibility of Subcommittee C09.20 on Normal Weight Aggregates.

Current edition approved April 15, 1993. Published June 1993. Originally published as C 128 – 36. Last previous edition C 128 – 88.

[2] *Annual Book of ASTM Standards,* Vol 04.02.

[3] *Annual Book of ASTM Standards,* Vol 04.03.

[4] *Annual Book of ASTM Standards,* Vol 04.01.

[5] *Annual Book of ASTM Standards,* Vol 15.05.

[6] *Annual Book of ASTM Standards,* Vol 14.02. Excerpts in all volumes.

[7] Available from American Association of State Highway and Transportation Officials, 444 North Capitol St. N.W., Suite 225, Washington, DC 20001.

C 128

4. Apparatus

4.1 *Balance*—A balance or scale having a capacity of 1 kg or more, sensitive to 0.1 g or less, and accurate within 0.1 % of the test load at any point within the range of use for this test. Within any 100-g range of test load, a difference between readings shall be accurate within 0.1 g.

4.2 *Pycnometer*—A flask or other suitable container into which the fine aggregate test sample can be readily introduced and in which the volume content can be reproduced within ±0.1 cm³. The volume of the container filled to mark shall be at least 50 % greater than the space required to accommodate the test sample. A volumetric flask of 500 cm³ capacity or a fruit jar fitted with a pycnometer top is satisfactory for a 500-g test sample of most fine aggregates. A Le Chatelier flask as described in Test Method C 188 is satisfactory for an approximately 55-g test sample.

4.3 *Mold*—A metal mold in the form of a frustum of a cone with dimensions as follows: 40 ± 3 mm inside diameter at the top, 90 ± 3 mm inside diameter at the bottom, and 75 ± 3 mm in height, with the metal having a minimum thickness of 0.8 mm.

4.4 *Tamper*—A metal tamper weighing 340 ± 15 g and having a flat circular tamping face 25 ± 3 mm in diameter.

5. Sampling

5.1 Sampling shall be accomplished in general accordance with Practice D 75.

6. Preparation of Test Specimen

6.1 Obtain approximately 1 kg of the fine aggregate from the sample using the applicable procedures described in Practice C 702.

6.1.1 Dry it in a suitable pan or vessel to constant weight at a temperature of 110 ± 5°C (230 ± 9°F). Allow it to cool to comfortable handling temperature, cover with water, either by immersion or by the addition of at least 6 % moisture to the fine aggregate, and permit to stand for 24 ± 4 h.

6.1.2 As an alternative to 6.1.1, where the absorption and specific gravity values are to be used in proportioning concrete mixtures with aggregates used in their naturally moist condition, the requirement for initial drying to constant weight may be eliminated and, if the surfaces of the particles have been kept wet, the 24-h soaking may also be eliminated.

NOTE 2—Values for absorption and for specific gravity in the saturated surface-dry condition may be significantly higher for aggregate not oven dried before soaking than for the same aggregate treated in accordance with 6.1.1.

6.2 Decant excess water with care to avoid loss of fines, spread the sample on a flat nonabsorbent surface exposed to a gently moving current of warm air, and stir frequently to secure homogeneous drying. If desired, mechanical aids such as tumbling or stirring may be employed to assist in achieving the saturated surface-dry condition. Continue this operation until the test specimen approaches a free-flowing condition. Follow the procedure in 6.2.1 to determine whether or not surface moisture is present on the constituent fine aggregate particles. It is intended that the first trial of the cone test will be made with some surface water in the specimen. Continue drying with constant stirring and test at frequent intervals until the test indicates that the specimen

has reached a surface-dry condition. If the first trial of the surface moisture test indicates that moisture is not present on the surface, it has been dried past the saturated surface-dry condition. In this case thoroughly mix a few millilitres of water with the fine aggregate and permit the specimen to stand in a covered container for 30 min. Then resume the process of drying and testing at frequent intervals for the onset of the surface-dry condition.

6.2.1 *Cone Test for Surface Moisture*—Hold the mold firmly on a smooth nonabsorbent surface with the large diameter down. Place a portion of the partially dried fine aggregate loosely in the mold by filling it to overflowing and heaping additional material above the top of the mold by holding it with the cupped fingers of the hand holding the mold. Lightly tamp the fine aggregate into the mold with 25 light drops of the tamper. Each drop should start about 5 mm (0.2 in.) above the top surface of the fine aggregate. Permit the tamper to fall freely under gravitational attraction on each drop. Adjust the starting height to the new surface elevation after each drop and distribute the drops over the surface. Remove loose sand from the base and lift the mold vertically. If surface moisture is still present, the fine aggregate will retain the molded shape. When the fine aggregate slumps slightly it indicates that it has reached a surface-dry condition. Some angular fine aggregate or material with a high proportion of fines may not slump in the cone test upon reaching a surface-dry condition. This may be the case if fines become airborne upon dropping a handful of the sand from the cone test 100 to 150 mm onto a surface. For these materials the saturated surface-dry condition should be considered as the point that one side of the fine aggregate slumps slightly upon removing the mold.

NOTE 3—The following criteria have also been used on materials that do not readily slump:

(1) *Provisional Cone Test*—Fill the cone mold as described in 6.2.1 except only use 10 drops of the tamper. Add more fine aggregate and use 10 drops of the tamper again. Then add material two more times using 3 and 2 drops of the tamper, respectively. Level off the material even with the top of the mold, remove loose material from the base; and lift the mold vertically.

(2) *Provisional Surface Test*—If airborne fines are noted when the fine aggregate is such that it will not slump when it is at a moisture condition, add more moisture to the sand, and at the onset of the surface-dry condition, with the hand lightly pat approximately 100 g of the material on a flat, dry, clean, dark or dull nonabsorbent surface such as a sheet of rubber, a worn oxidized, galvanized, or steel surface, or a black-painted metal surface. After 1 to 3 s remove the fine aggregate. If noticeable moisture shows on the test surface for more than 1 to 2 s then surface moisture is considered to be present on the fine aggregate.

(3) Colorimetric procedures described by Kandhal and Lee, Highway Research Record No. 307, p. 44.

(4) For reaching the saturated surface-dry condition on a single size material that slumps when wet, hard-finish paper towels can be used to surface dry the material until the point is just reached where the paper towel does not appear to be picking up moisture from the surfaces of the fine aggregate particles.

7. Procedure

7.1 Make and record all weight determinations to 0.1 g.

7.2 Partially fill the pycnometer with water. Immediately introduce into the pycnometer 500 ± 10 g of saturated surface-dry fine aggregate prepared as described in Section 6, and fill with additional water to approximately 90 % of capacity. Roll, invert, and agitate the pycnometer to elimi-

C 128

nate all air bubbles (Note 4). Adjust its temperature to 23 ± 1.7°C (73.4 ± 3°F), if necessary by immersion in circulating water, and bring the water level in the pycnometer to its calibrated capacity. Determine the total weight of the pycnometer, specimen, and water.

NOTE 4—It normally takes about 15 to 20 min to eliminate air bubbles. Dipping the tip of a paper towel into the pycnometer has been found to be useful in dispersing the foam that sometimes builds up when eliminating the air bubbles. Optionally, a small amount of isopropyl alcohol may be used to disperse the foam. Do *not* use either of these procedures when using the alternate method described in 7.2.1.

7.2.1 *Alternative to Weighing in 7.2*—The quantity of added water necessary to fill the pycnometer at the required temperature may be determined volumetrically using a buret accurate to 0.15 mL. Compute the total weight of the pycnometer, specimen, and water as follows:

$$C = 0.9975 \, V_a + S + W \qquad (1)$$

where:

C = weight of pycnometer with specimen and water to calibration mark, g,
V_a = volume of water added to pycnometer, mL,
S = weight of the saturated surface-dry specimen, and
W = weight of the empty pycnometer, g.

7.2.2 *Alternative to the Procedure in 7.2*—Use a Le Chatelier flask initially filled with water to a point on the stem between the 0 and the 1-mL mark. Record this initial reading with the flask and contents within the temperature range of 23 ± 1.7°C (73.4 ± 3°F). Add 55 ± 5 g of fine aggregate in the saturated surface-dry condition (or other weight as necessary to result in raising the water level to some point on the upper series of gradation). After all fine aggregate has been introduced, place the stopper in the flask and roll the flask in an inclined position, or gently whirl it in a horizontal circle so as to dislodge all entrapped air, continuing until no further bubbles rise to the surface (Note 5). Take a final reading with the flask and contents within 1°C (1.8°F) of the original temperature.

NOTE 5—When using the Le Chatelier flask method, the operator may use a small measured amount (not to exceed 1 mL) of isopropyl alcohol to eliminate foam appearing on the water surface. The volume of alcohol used must be subtracted from the final reading (R_2).

7.3 Remove the fine aggregate from the pycnometer, dry to constant weight at a temperature of 110 ± 5°C (230 ± 9°F), cool in air at room temperature for 1 ± ½ h, and weigh.

7.3.1 If the Le Chatelier flask method is used, a separate sample portion is needed for the determination of absorption. Weigh a separate 500 ± 10-g portion of the saturated surface-dry fine aggregate, dry to constant weight, and reweigh.

7.4 Determine the weight of the pycnometer filled to its calibration capacity with water at 23 ± 1.7°C (73.4 ± 3°F).

7.4.1 *Alternative to Weighing in 7.4*—The quantity of water necessary to fill the empty pycnometer at the required temperature may be determined volumetrically using a buret accurate to 0.15 mL. Calculate the weight of the pycnometer filled with water as follows:

$$B = 0.9975 \, V + W \qquad (2)$$

where:

B = weight of flask filled with water, g,

V = volume of flask, mL, and
W = weight of the flask empty, g.

8. Bulk Specific Gravity

8.1 Calculate the bulk specific gravity, 23/23°C (73.4/73.4°F), as defined in Terminology E 12, as follows:

$$\text{Bulk sp gr} = A/(B + S - C) \qquad (3)$$

where:

A = weight of oven-dry specimen in air, g,
B = weight of pycnometer filled with water, g,
S = weight of the saturated surface-dry specimen, and
C = weight of pycnometer with specimen and water to calibration mark, g.

8.1.1 If the Le Chatelier flask method was used, calculate the bulk specific gravity, 23/23°C, as follows:

$$\text{Bulk sp gr} = \frac{S_1(A/S)}{0.9975 \, (R_2 - R_1)} \qquad (4)$$

where:

S_1 = weight of saturated surface-dry specimen used in Le Chatelier flask, g,
R_1 = initial reading of water level in Le Chatelier flask, and
R_2 = final reading of water level in Le Chatelier flask.

9. Bulk Specific Gravity (Saturated Surface-Dry Basis)

9.1 Calculate the bulk specific gravity, 23/23°C (73.4/73.4°F), on the basis of weight of saturated surface-dry aggregate as follows:

$$\text{Bulk sp gr (saturated surface-dry basis)} = S/(B + S - C) \qquad (5)$$

9.1.1 If the Le Chatelier flask method was used, calculate the bulk specific gravity, 23/23°C, on the basis of saturated surface-dry aggregate as follows:

$$\text{Bulk sp gr (saturated surface-dry basis)} = \frac{S_1}{0.9975 \, (R_2 - R_1)} \qquad (6)$$

10. Apparent Specific Gravity

10.1 Calculate the apparent specific gravity, 23/23°C (73.4/73.4°F), as defined in Terminology E 12, as follows:

$$\text{Apparent sp gr} = A/(B + A - C) \qquad (7)$$

11. Absorption

11.1 Calculate the percentage of absorption, as defined in Terminology C 125, as follows:

$$\text{Absorption, \%} = [(S - A)/A] \times 100 \qquad (8)$$

12. Report

12.1 Report specific gravity results to the nearest 0.01 and absorption to the nearest 0.1 %. The Appendix gives mathematical interrelationships among the three types of specific gravities and absorption. These may be useful in checking the consistency of reported data or calculating a value that was not reported by using other reported data.

12.2 If the fine aggregate was tested in a naturally moist condition other than the oven dried and 24 h-soaked condition, report the source of the sample and the procedures used to prevent drying prior to testing.

◈⟡ C 128

TABLE 1 Precision

	Standard Deviation (1S)[A]	Acceptable Range of Two Results (D2S)[A]
Single-Operator Precision:		
Bulk specific gravity (dry)	0.011	0.032
Bulk specific gravity (SSD)	0.0095	0.027
Apparent specific gravity	0.0095	0.027
Absorption[B], %	0.11	0.31
Multilaboratory Precision:		
Bulk specific gravity (dry)	0.023	0.066
Bulk specific gravity (SSD)	0.020	0.056
Apparent specific gravity	0.020	0.056
Absorption[B], %	0.23	0.66

[A] These numbers represent, respectively, the (1S) and (D2S) limits as described in Practice C 670. The precision estimates were obtained from the analysis of combined AASHTO Materials Research Laboratory reference sample data from laboratories using 15 to 19 h saturation times and other laboratories using 24 ± 4 h saturation time. Testing was performed on normal weight aggregates, and started with aggregates in the oven-dry condition.
[B] Precision estimates are based on aggregates with absorptions of less than 1 % and may differ for manufactured fine aggregates and fine aggregates having absorption values greater than 1 %.

13. Precision and Bias

13.1 *Precision*—The estimates of precision of this test method (listed in Table 1) are based on results from the AASHTO Materials Reference Laboratory Reference Sample Program, with testing conducted by this test method and AASHTO Method T 84. The significant difference between the methods is that Test Method C 128 requires a saturation period of 24 ± 4 h, and Method T 84 requires a saturation period of 15 to 19 h. This difference has been found to have an insignificant effect on the precision indices. The data are based on the analyses of more than 100 paired test results from 40 to 100 laboratories.

13.2 *Bias*—Since there is no accepted reference material suitable for determining the bias for this test method, no statement on bias is being made.

14. Keywords

14.1 absorption; aggregate; fine aggregate; specific gravity

APPENDIX

(Nonmandatory Information)

X1. INTERRELATIONSHIPS BETWEEN SPECIFIC GRAVITIES AND ABSORPTION AS DEFINED IN TEST METHODS C 127 AND C 128

X1.1 Let:
S_d = bulk specific gravity (dry-basis),
S_s = bulk specific gravity (SSD-basis),
S_a = apparent specific gravity, and
A = absorption in %.

Then:

$$(1) \quad S_s = (1 + A/100)S_d$$

$$(2) \quad S_a = \frac{1}{\dfrac{1}{S_d} - \dfrac{A}{100}} = \frac{S_d}{1 - \dfrac{AS_d}{100}}$$

$$(2a) \quad \text{or } S_a = \frac{1}{\dfrac{1 + A/100}{S_s} - \dfrac{A}{100}}$$

$$= \frac{S_s}{1 - \dfrac{A}{100}(S_s - 1)}$$

$$(3) \quad A = \left(\frac{S_s}{S_d} - 1\right)100$$

$$(4) \quad A = \left(\frac{S_a - S_s}{S_a(S_s - 1)}\right)100$$

ASTM C 128

AMERICAN SOCIETY FOR TESTING AND MATERIALS
100 Barr Harbor Dr., West Conshohocken, PA 19428
Reprinted from the Annual Book of ASTM Standards. Copyright ASTM
If not listed in the current combined index, will appear in the next edition.

Designation: C 131 – 89

Standard Test Method for
Resistance to Degradation of Small-Size Coarse Aggregate by Abrasion and Impact in the Los Angeles Machine[1]

This standard is issued under the fixed designation C 131; the number immediately following the designation indicates the year of original adoption or, in the case of revision, the year of last revision. A number in parentheses indicates the year of last reapproval. A superscript epsilon (ε) indicates an editorial change since the last revision or reapproval.

1. Scope

1.1 This test method covers a procedure for testing sizes of coarse aggregate smaller than 1½ in. (37.5 mm) for resistance to degradation using the Los Angeles testing machine.

NOTE 1—A procedure for testing coarse aggregate larger than ¾ in. (19 mm) is covered in Test Method C 535.

2. Referenced Documents

2.1 *ASTM Standards:*

C 136 Method for Sieve Analysis of Fine and Coarse Aggregates[2]
C 535 Test Method for Resistance to Degradation of Large-Size Coarse Aggregate by Abrasion and Impact in the Los Angeles Machine[2]
C 670 Practice for Preparing Precision and Bias Statements for Test Methods for Construction Materials[2]
C 702 Practice for Reducing Field Samples of Aggregate to Testing Size[2]
D 75 Practice for Sampling Aggregates[2]
E 11 Specification for Wire-Cloth Sieves for Testing Purposes[3]

3. Summary of Test Method

3.1 The Los Angeles test is a measure of degradation of mineral aggregates of standard gradings resulting from a combination of actions including abrasion or attrition, impact, and grinding in a rotating steel drum containing a specified number of steel spheres, the number depending upon the grading of the test sample. As the drum rotates, a shelf plate picks up the sample and the steel spheres, carrying them around until they are dropped to the opposite side of the drum, creating an impact-crushing effect. The contents then roll within the drum with an abrading and grinding action until the shelf plate impacts and the cycle is repeated. After the prescribed number of revolutions, the contents are removed from the drum and the aggregate portion is sieved to measure the degradation as percent loss.

4. Significance and Use

4.1 The Los Angeles test has been widely used as an indicator of the relative quality or competence of various sources of aggregate having similar mineral compositions. The results do not automatically permit valid comparisons to be made between sources distinctly different in origin, composition, or structure. Specification limits based on this test should be assigned with extreme care in consideration of available aggregate types and their performance history in specific end uses.

5. Apparatus

5.1 *Los Angeles Machine*—The Los Angeles testing machine, conforming in all its essential characteristics to the design shown in Fig. 1, shall be used. The machine shall consist of a hollow steel cylinder, closed at both ends, having an inside diameter of 28 ± 0.2 in. (711 ± 5 mm), and an inside length of 20 ± 0.2 in. (508 ± 5 mm). The cylinder shall be mounted on stub shafts attached to the ends of the cylinder but not entering it, and shall be mounted in such a manner that it may be rotated with the axis in a horizontal position within a tolerance in slope of 1 in 100. An opening in the cylinder shall be provided for the introduction of the test sample. A suitable, dust-tight cover shall be provided for the opening with means for bolting the cover in place. The cover shall be so designed as to maintain the cylindrical contour of the interior surface unless the shelf is so located that the charge will not fall on the cover, or come in contact with it during the test. A removable steel shelf extending the full length of the cylinder and projecting inward 3.5 ± 0.1 in. (89 ± 2 mm) shall be mounted on the interior cylindrical surface of the cylinder, in such a way that a plane centered between the large faces coincides with an axial plane. The shelf shall be of such thickness and so mounted, by bolts or other suitable means, as to be firm and rigid. The position of the shelf shall be such that the distance from the shelf to the opening, measured along the outside circumference of the cylinder in the direction of rotation, shall be not less than 50 in. (1.27 m).

NOTE 2—The use of a shelf of wear-resistant steel, rectangular in cross section and mounted independently of the cover, is preferred. However, a shelf consisting of a section of rolled angle, properly mounted on the inside of the cover plate, may be used provided the direction of rotation is such that the charge will be caught on the outside face of the angle. If the shelf becomes distorted from its original shape to such an extent that the requirements given in X1.2 of the Appendix to this method are not met, the shelf shall either be repaired or replaced before additional tests are made.

---

[1] This test method is under the jurisdiction of ASTM Committee C-9 on Concrete and Concrete Aggregates and is the direct responsibility of Subcommittee C09.03.05 on Methods of Testing and Specifications for Physical Characteristics of Concrete Aggregates.
Current edition approved June 15, 1989. Published June 1989. Originally published as C 131 – 37 T. Last previous edition C 131 – 81(1987).
[2] *Annual Book of ASTM Standards*, Vols 04.02 and 04.03.
[3] *Annual Book of ASTM Standards*, Vol 14.02.

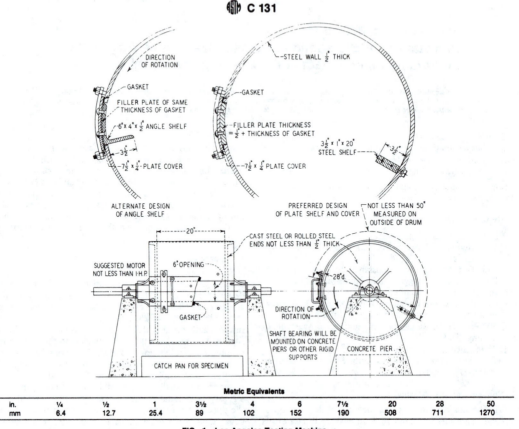

Metric Equivalents									
in.	¼	½	1	3½	4	6	7½	20	28	50
mm	6.4	12.7	25.4	89	102	152	190	508	711	1270

FIG. 1 Los Angeles Testing Machine

5.1.1 The machine shall be so driven and so counterbalanced as to maintain a substantially uniform peripheral speed (Note 3). If an angle is used as the shelf, the direction of rotation shall be such that the charge is caught on the outside surface of the angle.

NOTE 3—Back-lash or slip in the driving mechanism is very likely to furnish test results which are not duplicated by other Los Angeles machines producing constant peripheral speed.

5.2 *Sieves*, conforming to Specification E 11.

5.3 *Balance*—A balance or scale accurate within 0.1 % of test load over the range required for this test.

5.4 *Charge*—The charge shall consist of steel spheres averaging approximately 1²⁷/₃₂ in. (46.8 mm) in diameter and each weighing between 390 and 445 g.

5.4.1 The charge, depending upon the grading of the test sample as described in Section 7, shall be as follows:

Grading	Number of Spheres	Weight of Charge, g
A	12	5000 ± 25
B	11	4584 ± 25
C	8	3330 ± 20
D	6	2500 ± 15

NOTE 4—Steel ball bearings 1¹³/₁₆ in. (46.0 mm) and 1⅞ in. (47.6 mm) in diameter, weighing approximately 400 and 440 g each,

respectively, are readily available. Steel spheres 1²⁷/₃₂ in. (46.8 mm) in diameter weighing approximately 420 g may also be obtainable. The charge may consist of a mixture of these sizes conforming to the weight tolerances of 5.4 and 5.4.1.

6. Sampling

6.1 The field sample shall be obtained in accordance with Practice D 75 and reduced to test portion size in accordance with Methods C 702.

7. Test Sample

7.1 The test sample shall be washed and oven-dried at 221 to 230°F (105 to 110°C) to substantially constant weight (Note 5), separated into individual size fractions, and recombined to the grading of Table 1 most nearly corresponding to the range of sizes in the aggregate as furnished for the work. The weight of the sample prior to test shall be recorded to the nearest 1 g.

8. Procedure

8.1 Place the test sample and the charge in the Los Angeles testing machine and rotate the machine at a speed of 30 to 33 rpm for 500 revolutions. After the prescribed number of revolutions, discharge the material from the

$(\$T\!M)$ **C 131**

TABLE 1 Gradings of Test Samples

Sieve Size (Square Openings)		Weight of Indicated Sizes, g			
Passing	Retained on	Grading			
		A	B	C	D
37.5 mm (1½ in.)	25.0 mm (1 in.)	1 250 ± 25	...	...	...
25.0 mm (1 in.)	19.0 mm (¾ in.)	1 250 ± 25	...	...	...
19.0 mm (¾ in.)	12.5 mm (½ in.)	1 250 ± 10	2 500 ± 10	...	...
12.5 mm (½ in.)	9.5 mm (⅜ in.)	1 250 ± 10	2 500 ± 10	...	...
9.5 mm (⅜ in.)	6.3 mm (¼ in.)	...	...	2 500 ± 10	...
6.3 mm (¼ in.)	4.75-mm (No. 4)	...	...	2 500 ± 10	...
4.75-mm (No. 4)	2.36-mm (No. 8)	...	...	...	5 000 ± 10
Total		5 000 ± 10	5 000 ± 10	5 000 ± 10	5 000 ± 10

machine and make a preliminary separation of the sample on a sieve coarser than the 1.70-mm (No. 12). Sieve the finer portion on a 1.70-mm sieve in a manner conforming to Method C 136. Wash the material coarser than the 1.70-mm sieve (Note 5), oven-dry at 221 to 230°F (105 to 110°C) to substantially constant weight, and weigh to the nearest 1 g (Note 6).

NOTE 5—If the aggregate is essentially free of adherent coatings and dust, the requirement for washing before and after test may be waived. Elimination of washing after test will seldom reduce the measured loss by more than about 0.2 % of the original sample weight.

NOTE 6—Valuable information concerning the uniformity of the sample under test may be obtained by determining the loss after 100 revolutions. This loss should be determined without washing the material coarser than the 1.70-mm sieve. The ratio of the loss after 100 revolutions to the loss after 500 revolutions should not greatly exceed 0.20 for material of uniform hardness. When this determination is made, take care to avoid losing any part of the sample; return the entire sample, including the dust of fracture, to the testing machine for the final 400 revolutions required to complete the test.

9. Calculation

9.1 Express the loss (difference between the original weight and the final weight of the test sample) as a percentage of the original weight of the test sample. Report this value as the percent loss.

NOTE 7—The percent loss determined by this method has no known consistent relationship to the percent loss for the same material when tested by Test Method C 535.

10. Precision

10.1 For nominal 19.0-mm (¾-in.) maximum size coarse aggregate with percent losses in the range of 10 to 45 %, the multilaboratory coefficient of variation has been found to be 4.5 %.[4] Therefore, results of two properly conducted tests from two different laboratories on samples of the same coarse aggregates should not differ from each other by more than 12.7 %[4] of their average. The single-operator coefficient of variation has been found to be 2.0 %.[4] Therefore, results of two properly conducted tests by the same operator on the same coarse aggregate should not differ from each other by more than 5.7 % of their average.[4]

10.2 *Bias*—Since there is no accepted reference material suitable for determining the bias for this procedure, no statement on bias is being made.

---

[4] These numbers represent, respectively, the (1S%) and (D2S%) limits as described in Practice C 670.

AMERICAN SOCIETY FOR TESTING AND MATERIALS
1916 Race St. Philadelphia, Pa 19103
Reprinted from the Annual Book of ASTM Standards. Copyright ASTM
If not listed in the current combined index, will appear in the next edition.

Standard Test Method for
Sieve Analysis of Fine and Coarse Aggregates[1]

This standard is issued under the fixed designation C 136; the number immediately following the designation indicates the year of original adoption or, in the case of revision, the year of last revision. A number in parentheses indicates the year of last reapproval. A superscript epsilon (ϵ) indicates an editorial change since the last revision or reapproval.

This standard has been approved for use by agencies of the Department of Defense. Consult the DoD Index of Specifications and Standards for the specific year of issue which has been adopted by the Department of Defense.

1. Scope

1.1 This test method covers the determination of the particle size distribution of fine and coarse aggregates by sieving.

1.2 Some specifications for aggregates which reference this method contain grading requirements including both coarse and fine fractions. Instructions are included for sieve analysis of such aggregates.

1.3 The values stated in SI units (SI units and units specifically approved in Practice E 380 for use with SI units) are to be regarded as the standard. The values in parentheses are provided for information purposes only.

1.4 *This standard does not purport to address all of the safety concerns, if any, associated with its use. It is the responsibility of the user of this standard to establish appropriate safety and health practices and determine the applicability of regulatory limitations prior to use.*

2. Referenced Documents

2.1 *ASTM Standards:*

C 117 Test Method for Materials Finer Than 75-μm (No. 200) Sieve in Mineral Aggregates by Washing[2]

C 125 Terminology Relating to Concrete and Concrete Aggregates[2]

C 670 Practice for Preparing Precision and Bias Statements for Test Methods for Construction Materials[2]

C 702 Practice for Reducing Field Samples of Aggregate to Testing Size[2]

D 75 Practice for Sampling Aggregates[3]

E 11 Specification for Wire-Cloth Sieves for Testing Purposes[4]

E 380 Practice For Use of the International System of Units (SI) (the Modernized Metric System)[5]

2.2 *AASHTO Standard:*

AASHTO No. T 27 Sieve Analysis of Fine and Coarse Aggregates[6]

3. Terminology

3.1 *Definitions*—For definitions of terms used in this standard, refer to Terminology C 125.

4. Summary of Test Method

4.1 A weighed sample of dry aggregate is separated through a series of sieves of progressively smaller openings for determination of particle size distribution.

5. Significance and Use

5.1 This test method is used primarily to determine the grading of materials proposed for use as aggregates or being used as aggregates. The results are used to determine compliance of the particle size distribution with applicable specification requirements and to provide necessary data for control of the production of various aggregate products and mixtures containing aggregates. The data may also be useful in developing relationships concerning porosity and packing.

5.2 Accurate determination of material finer than the 75-μm (No. 200) sieve cannot be achieved by use of this method alone. Test Method C 117 for material finer than 75-μm sieve by washing should be employed.

6. Apparatus

6.1 *Balances*—Balances or scales used in testing fine and coarse aggregate shall have readability and accuracy as follows:

6.1.1 For fine aggregate, readable to 0.1 g and accurate to 0.1 g or 0.1 % of the test load, whichever is greater, at any point within the range of use.

6.1.2 For coarse aggregate, or mixtures of fine and coarse aggregate, readable and accurate to 0.5 g or 0.1 % of the test load, whichever is greater, at any point within the range of use.

6.2 *Sieves*—The sieves shall be mounted on substantial frames constructed in a manner that will prevent loss of material during sieving. The sieves shall conform to Specification E 11. Sieves with openings larger than 125 mm (5 in.) shall have a permissible variation in average opening of ±2 % and shall have a nominal wire diameter of 8.0 mm (5/16 in.) or larger.

NOTE 1—It is recommended that sieves mounted in frames larger than standard 203-mm (8 in.) diameter frames be used for testing coarse aggregate.

6.3 *Mechanical Sieve Shaker*—A mechanical sieve shaker, if used, shall impart a vertical, or lateral and vertical, motion to the sieve, causing the particles thereon to bounce and turn so as to present different orientations to the sieving

[1] This test method is under the jurisdiction of ASTM Committee C-9 on Concrete and Concrete Aggregates and is the direct responsibility of Subcommittee C09.20 on Normal Weight Aggregates.

Current edition approved April and May 15, 1995. Published July 1995. Originally published as C 136 – 38 T. Last previous edition C 136 – 93.

[2] *Annual Book of ASTM Standards*, Vol 04.02.

[3] *Annual Book of ASTM Standards*, Vol 04.03.

[4] *Annual Book of ASTM Standards*, Vol 14.02.

[5] *Annual Book of ASTM Standards*, Vol 14.02. Excerpts in all volumes.

[6] Available from American Association of State Highway and Transportation Officials, 444 North Capitol St. N.W., Suite 225, Washington, DC 20001.

C 136

surface. The sieving action shall be such that the criterion for adequacy of sieving described in 8.4 is met in a reasonable time period.

NOTE 2—Use of a mechanical sieve shaker is recommended when the size of the sample is 20 kg or greater, and may be used for smaller samples, including fine aggregate. Excessive time (more than approximately 10 min) to achieve adequate sieving may result in degradation of the sample. The same mechanical sieve shaker may not be practical for all sizes of samples, since the large sieving area needed for practical sieving of a large nominal size coarse aggregate very likely could result in loss of a portion of the sample if used for a small sample of coarse aggregate or fine aggregate.

6.4 *Oven*—An oven of appropriate size capable of maintaining a uniform temperature of 110 ± 5°C (230 ± 9°F).

7. Sampling

7.1 Sample the aggregate in accordance with Practice D 75. The size of the field sample shall be the quantity shown in Practice D 75 or four times the quantity required in 7.4 and 7.5 (except as modified in 7.6), whichever is greater.

7.2 Thoroughly mix the sample and reduce it to an amount suitable for testing using the applicable procedures described in Practice C 702. The sample for test shall be approximately the quantity desired when dry and shall be the end result of the reduction. Reduction to an exact predetermined quantity shall not be permitted.

NOTE 3—Where sieve analysis, including determination of material finer than the 75-µm sieve, is the only testing proposed, the size of the sample may be reduced in the field to avoid shipping excessive quantities of extra material to the laboratory.

7.3 *Fine Aggregate*—The size of the test sample, after drying, shall be 300 g minimum.

7.4 *Coarse Aggregate*—The size of the test sample of coarse aggregate shall conform with the following:

Nominal Maximum Size, Square Openings, mm (in.)	Test Sample Size, min, kg (lb)
9.5 (3/8)	1 (2)
12.5 (1/2)	2 (4)
19.0 (3/4)	5 (11)
25.0 (1)	10 (22)
37.5 (1 1/2)	15 (33)
50 (2)	20 (44)
63 (2 1/2)	35 (77)
75 (3)	60 (130)
90 (3 1/2)	100 (220)
100 (4)	150 (330)
112 (4 1/2)	200 (440)
125 (5)	300 (660)
150 (6)	500 (1100)

7.5 *Coarse and Fine Aggregate Mixtures*—The size of the test sample of coarse and fine aggregate mixtures shall be the same as for coarse aggregate in 7.4.

7.6 The size of sample required for aggregates with large nominal maximum size is such as to preclude testing except with large mechanical sieve shakers. However, the intent of this method will be satisfied for samples of aggregate larger than 50-mm nominal maximum size if a smaller test sample size is used, provided that the criterion for acceptance or rejection of the material is based on the average of results of several samples, such that the sample size used times the number of samples averaged equals the minimum size of sample shown in 7.4.

7.7 In the event that the amount of material finer than the

75-µm (No. 200) sieve is to be determined by Test Method C 117, proceed as follows:

7.7.1 For aggregates with a nominal maximum size of 12.5 mm (1/2 in.) or less, use the same test sample for testing by Test Method C 117 and this method. First test the sample in accordance with Test Method C 117 through the final drying operation, then dry sieve the sample as stipulated in 8.2 through 8.7 of this method.

7.7.2 For aggregates with a nominal maximum size greater than 12.5 mm (1/2 in.), a single test sample may be used as described in 7.7.1, or separate test samples may be used for Test Method C 117 and this method.

7.7.3 Where the specifications require determination of the total amount of material finer than the 75-µm sieve by washing and dry sieving, use the procedure described in 7.7.1.

8. Procedure

8.1 Dry the sample to constant mass at a temperature of 110 ± 5°C (230 ± 9°F).

NOTE 4—For control purposes, particularly where rapid results are desired, it is generally not necessary to dry coarse aggregate for the sieve analysis test. The results are little affected by the moisture content unless: (*1*) the nominal maximum size is smaller than about 12.5 mm (1/2 in.); (*2*) the coarse aggregate contains appreciable material finer than 4.75 mm (No. 4); or (*3*) the coarse aggregate is highly absorptive (a lightweight aggregate, for example). Also, samples may be dried at the higher temperatures associated with the use of hot plates without affecting results, provided steam escapes without generating pressures sufficient to fracture the particles, and temperatures are not so great as to cause chemical breakdown of the aggregate.

8.2 Suitable sieve sizes shall be selected to furnish the information required by the specifications covering the material to be tested. The use of additional sieves may be desirable to provide other information, such as fineness modulus, or to regulate the amount of material on a sieve. Nest the sieves in order of decreasing size of opening from top to bottom and place the sample on the top sieve. Agitate the sieves by hand or by mechanical apparatus for a sufficient period, established by trial or checked by measurement on the actual test sample, to meet the criterion for adequacy or sieving described in 8.4.

8.3 Limit the quantity of material on a given sieve so that all particles have opportunity to reach sieve openings a number of times during the sieving operation. For sieves with openings smaller than 4.75-mm (No. 4), the quantity retained on any sieve at the completion of the sieving operation shall not exceed 7 kg/m² of sieving surface. For sieves with openings 4.75 mm (No. 4) and larger, the quantity retained in kg/m² of sieving surface shall not exceed the product of 2.5 × (sieve opening in mm). In no case shall the quantity retained be so great as to cause permanent deformation of the sieve cloth.

NOTE 5—The 7 kg/m² amounts to 200 g for the usual 203.2-mm (8-in.) diameter sieve (with effective sieving diameter of 190.5 mm (7.5 in.)) with openings smaller than 4.75 mm. See Appendix X1 for the maximum amount that may be retained on sieves of various sizes with openings of 4.75 mm and larger. The amount of material retained on a sieve may be regulated by (*1*) the introduction of a sieve with larger openings immediately above the given sieve or (*2*) testing the sample in a number of increments.

8.4 Continue sieving for a sufficient period and in such

C 136

manner that, after completion, not more than 1 mass % of the residue on any individual sieve will pass that sieve during 1 min of continuous hand sieving performed as follows: Hold the individual sieve, provided with a snug-fitting pan and cover, in a slightly inclined position in one hand. Strike the side of the sieve sharply and with an upward motion against the heel of the other hand at the rate of about 150 times per minute, turn the sieve about one sixth of a revolution at intervals of about 25 strokes. In determining sufficiency of sieving for sizes larger than the 4.75-mm (No. 4) sieve, limit the material on the sieve to a single layer of particles. If the size of the mounted testing sieves makes the described sieving motion impractical, use 203-mm (8 in.) diameter sieves to verify the sufficiency of sieving.

8.5 In the case of coarse and fine aggregate mixtures, the portion of the sample finer than the 4.75-mm (No. 4) sieve may be distributed among two or more sets of sieves to prevent overloading of individual sieves.

8.5.1 Alternatively, the portion finer than the 4.75-mm (No. 4) sieve may be reduced in size using a mechanical splitter according to Practice C 702. If this procedure is followed, compute the mass of each size increment of the original sample as follows:

$$A = \frac{W_1}{W_2} \times B$$

where:

A = mass of size increment on total sample basis,
W_1 = mass of fraction finer than 4.75-mm (No. 4) sieve in total sample,
W_2 = mass of reduced portion of material finer than 4.75-mm (No. 4) sieve actually sieved, and
B = mass of size increment in reduced portion sieved.

8.6 Unless a mechanical sieve shaker is used, hand sieve particles larger than 75 mm (3 in.) by determining the smallest sieve opening through which each particle will pass. Start the test on the smallest sieve to be used. Rotate the particles, if necessary, in order to determine whether they will pass through a particular opening; however, do not force particles to pass through an opening.

8.7 Determine the mass of each size increment on a scale or balance conforming to the requirements specified in 5.1 to the nearest 0.1 % of the total original dry sample mass. The total mass of the material after sieving should check closely with original mass of sample placed on the sieves. If the amounts differ by more than 0.3 %, based on the original dry sample mass, the results should not be used for acceptance purposes.

8.8 If the sample has previously been tested by Test Method C 117, add the mass finer than the 75-μm (No. 200) sieve determined by that method to the mass passing the 75-μm (No. 200) sieve by dry sieving of the same sample in this method.

9. Calculation

9.1 Calculate percentages passing, total percentages retained, or percentages in various size fractions to the nearest 0.1 % on the basis of the total mass of the initial dry sample. If the same test sample was first tested by Test Method C 117, include the mass of material finer than the 75-μm (No. 200) size by washing in the sieve analysis calculation;

and use the total dry sample mass prior to washing in Test Method C 117 as the basis for calculating all the percentages.

9.2 Calculate the fineness modulus, when required, by adding the total percentages of material in the sample that is coarser than each of the following sieves (cumulative percentages retained), and dividing the sum by 100: 150-μm (No. 100), 300-μm (No. 50), 600-μm (No. 30), 1.18-mm (No. 16), 2.36-mm (No. 8), 4.75-mm (No. 4), 9.5-mm (3/8-in.), 19.0-mm (3/4-in.), 37.5-mm (1½-in.), and larger, increasing in the ratio of 2 to 1.

10. Report

10.1 Depending upon the form of the specifications for use of the material under test, the report shall include the following:

10.1.1 Total percentage of material passing each sieve, or

10.1.2 Total percentage of material retained on each sieve, or

10.1.3 Percentage of material retained between consecutive sieves.

10.2 Report percentages to the nearest whole number, except if the percentage passing the 75-μm (No. 200) sieve is less than 10 %, it shall be reported to the nearest 0.1 %.

TABLE 1 Precision

	Total Percentage of Material Passing		Standard Deviation (1s), %[A]	Acceptable Range of Two Results (d2s), %[A]
Coarse Aggregate:[B]				
Single-operator precision	<100	≥95	0.32	0.9
	<95	≥85	0.81	2.3
	<85	≥80	1.34	3.8
	<80	≥60	2.25	6.4
	<60	≥20	1.32	3.7
	<20	≥15	0.96	2.7
	<15	≥10	1.00	2.8
	<10	≥5	0.75	2.1
	<5	≥2	0.53	1.5
	<2	>0	0.27	0.8
Multilaboratory precision	<100	≥95	0.35	1.0
	<95	≥85	1.37	3.9
	<85	≥80	1.92	5.4
	<80	≥60	2.82	8.0
	<60	≥20	1.97	5.6
	<20	≥15	1.60	4.5
	<15	≥10	1.48	4.2
	<10	≥5	1.22	3.4
	<5	≥2	1.04	3.0
	<2	>0	0.45	1.3
Fine Aggregate:				
Single-operator precision	<100	≥95	0.26	0.7
	<95	≥60	0.55	1.6
	<60	≥20	0.83	2.4
	<20	≥15	0.54	1.5
	<15	≥10	0.36	1.0
	<10	≥2	0.37	1.1
	<2	>0	0.14	0.4
Multilaboratory precision	<100	≥95	0.23	0.6
	<95	≥60	0.77	2.2
	<60	≥20	1.41	4.0
	<20	≥15	1.10	3.1
	<15	≥10	0.73	2.1
	<10	≥2	0.65	1.8
	<2	>0	0.31	0.9

[A] These numbers represent, respectively, the (1s) and (d2s) limits described in Practice C 670.

[B] The precision estimates are based on aggregates with nominal maximum size of 19.0 mm (¾ in.).

C 136

TABLE 2 Precision Data for 300-g and 500-g Test Samples

Test Result	Fine Aggregate Proficiency Sample			Within Laboratory		Between Laboratory	
	Sample Size	Number Labs	Average	1s	d2s	1s	d2s
AASIITO T27/ASTM C136							
Total material passing the No. 4 sieve (%)	500 g	285	99.992	0.027	0.066	0.037	0.104
	300 g	276	99.990	0.021	0.060	0.042	0.117
Total material passing the No. 8 sieve (%)	500 g	281	84.10	0.43	1.21	0.63	1.76
	300 g	274	84.32	0.39	1.09	0.69	1.92
Total material passing the No. 16 sieve (%)	500 g	286	70.11	0.53	1.49	0.75	2.10
	300 g	272	70.00	0.62	1.74	0.76	2.12
Total material passing the No. 30 sieve (%)	500 g	287	48.54	0.75	2.10	1.33	3.73
	300 g	276	48.44	0.87	2.44	1.36	3.79
Total material passing the No. 50 sieve (%)	500 g	286	13.52	0.42	1.17	0.98	2.73
	300 g	275	13.51	0.45	1.25	0.99	2.76
Total material passing the No. 100 sieve (%)	500 g	287	2.55	0.15	0.42	0.37	1.03
	300 g	270	2.52	0.18	0.52	0.32	0.89
Total Material passing the No. 200 sieve (%)	500 g	278	1.32	0.11	0.32	0.31	0.85
	300 g	266	1.30	0.14	0.39	0.31	0.85

10.3 Report the fineness modulus, when required, to the nearest 0.01.

11. Precision and Bias

11.1 *Precision*—The estimates of precision for this test method are listed in Table 1. The estimates are based on the results from the AASHTO Materials Reference Laboratory Proficiency Sample Program, with testing conducted by Test Method C 136 and AASHTO Test Method T 27. The data are based on the analyses of the test results from 65 to 233 laboratories that tested 18 pairs of coarse aggregate proficiency test samples and test results from 74 to 222 laboratories that tested 17 pairs of fine aggregate proficiency test samples (Samples No. 21 through 90). The values in the table are given for different ranges of total percentage of aggregate passing a sieve.

11.1.1 The precision values for fine aggregate in Table 1 are based on nominal 500-g test samples. Revision of this test method in 1994 permits the fine aggregate test sample size to be 300 g minimum. Analysis of results of testing of 300-g and 500-g test samples from Aggregate Proficiency Test Samples 99 and 100 (Samples 99 and 100 were essentially identical) produced the precision values in Table 2, which indicate only minor differences due to test sample size.

NOTE 6—The values for fine aggregate in Table 1 will be revised to reflect the 300-g test sample size when a sufficient number of Aggregate Proficiency Tests have been conducted using that sample size to provide reliable data.

11.2 *Bias*—Since there is no accepted reference material suitable for determining the bias in this test method, no statement on bias is made.

12. Keywords

12.1 aggregate; coarse aggregate; fine aggregate; gradation; grading; sieve analysis; size analysis

C 136

APPENDIX

(Nonmandatory Information)

X1. MAXIMUM QUANTITIES OF AGGREGATE PERMITTED TO BE RETAINED ON INDIVIDUAL SIEVES

X1.1 This Test Method contains a restriction in the section on Procedure limiting the quantity of aggregate material retained on an individual sieve at the completion of sieving. This restriction is to prevent overloading of the sieve, and to permit all particles to have a reasonable chance to reach a sieve opening and to be able to pass through the sieve if the particle is smaller than the sieve opening. The limit is expressed in the procedure as a formula. Table X1.1 expresses the maximum quantity that may be retained on an individual sieve based on the nominal sieve size (for several sizes in common use) and nominal sieve opening.

X1.1.1 The sieve area for round sieve frames is based on an effective diameter 12.7 mm (0.5 in.) less than the nominal frame diameter, because Specification E 11 permits the sealer between the sieve cloth and the frame to extend 6.4 mm (¼ in.) over the sieve cloth. Thus the effective sieving diameter for a 203.2-mm (8-in.) diameter sieve frame is 190.5 mm (7.5 in.). Some sieve manufacturers may not infringe on the sieve cloth by the full 6.4 mm (0.25 in.).

TABLE X1.1 Maximum Allowable Quantity of Material Retained on a Sieve, kg

Sieve Designation, mm	Nominal Dimensions of Sieve[A]				
	8-in. Diameter	10-in. Diameter	12-in. Diameter	12 by 12 in.	18 by 24 in.
	Sieving Area, m²				
	0.028502	0.045730	0.067012	0.092903	0.301935
150	[B]	[B]	[B]	34.84	113.23
125	[B]	[B]	[B]	29.03	94.35
112	[B]	[B]	[B]	26.01	84.54
100	[B]	[B]	[B]	23.23	75.48
90	[B]	[B]	15.08	20.90	67.94
75	[B]	8.57	12.56	17.42	56.61
63	[B]	7.20	10.55	14.63	47.55
50	3.56	5.72	8.38	11.61	37.74
37.5	2.67	4.29	6.28	8.71	28.31
25.0	1.78	2.86	4.19	5.81	18.87
19.0	1.35	2.17	3.18	4.41	14.34
12.5	0.89	1.43	2.09	2.90	9.44
9.5	0.67	1.09	1.59	2.21	7.17
4.75	0.33	0.54	0.80	1.10	3.59

[A] Sieve dimensions in SI units: 203.2-mm diameter; 254-mm diameter; 304.8-mm diameter; 304.8 by 304.8 mm; 457.2 by 609.6 mm.
[B] Sieves indicated have less than five full openings and should not be used for sieve testing except as provided in 8.6.

ASTM Designation: C 330 – 89

AMERICAN SOCIETY FOR TESTING AND MATERIALS
1916 Race St. Philadelphia, Pa 19103
Reprinted from the Annual Book of ASTM Standards. Copyright ASTM
If not listed in the current combined index, will appear in the next edition.

Standard Specification for
Lightweight Aggregates for Structural Concrete[1]

This standard is issued under the fixed designation C 330; the number immediately following the designation indicates the year of original adoption or, in the case of revision, the year of last revision. A number in parentheses indicates the year of last reapproval. A superscript epsilon (ε) indicates an editorial change since the last revision or reapproval.

This specification has been approved for use by agencies of the Department of Defense. Consult the DoD Index of Specifications and Standards for the specific year of issue which has been adopted by the Department of Defense.

1. Scope

1.1 This specification covers lightweight aggregates intended for use in structural concrete in which prime considerations are lightness in weight and compressive strength of the concrete. Procedures covered in this specification are not intended for job control of concrete.

1.2 With regard to sieve sizes and the size of aggregate as determined by the use of testing sieves, the values in inch-pound units are shown for the convenience of the user; however, the standard sieve designation shown in parentheses is the standard value as stated in Specification E 11.

1.2.1 With regard to other units of measure, the values stated in inch-pound units are to be regarded as standard.

NOTE 1—This specification is regarded as adequate to ensure satisfactory lightweight aggregates for most concrete. It is recognized that it may be either more or less restrictive than needed for some conditions and for special purposes, such as fire resistance, fill, and concrete constructions, the use of which is based on load tests rather than conventional design procedures.

2. Referenced Documents

2.1 *ASTM Standards:*
C 29/C 29M Test Method for Unit Weight and Voids in Aggregate[2]
C 33 Specification for Concrete Aggregates[2]
C 39 Test Method for Compressive Strength of Cylindrical Concrete Specimens[2]
C 40 Test Method for Organic Impurities in Fine Aggregates for Concrete[2]
C 114 Test Methods for Chemical Analysis of Hydraulic Cement[3]
C 136 Method for Sieve Analysis of Fine and Coarse Aggregates[2]
C 142 Test Method for Clay Lumps and Friable Particles in Aggregates[2]
C 151 Test Method for Autoclave Expansion of Portland Cement[3]
C 157 Test Method for Length Change of Hardened Hydraulic-Cement Mortar and Concrete[2,3]
C 192 Practice for Making and Curing Concrete Test Specimens in the Laboratory[2]

C 496 Test Method for Splitting Tensile Strength of Cylindrical Concrete Specimens[2]
C 567 Test Method for Unit Weight of Structural Lightweight Concrete[2]
C 641 Test Method for Staining Materials in Lightweight Concrete Aggregates[2]
C 666 Test Method for Resistance of Concrete to Rapid Freezing and Thawing[2]
D 75 Practice for Sampling Aggregates[2]
E 11 Specification for Wire-Cloth Sieves for Testing Purposes[4]

3. General Characteristics

3.1 Two general types of lightweight aggregates are covered by this specification, as follows:

3.1.1 Aggregates prepared by expanding, pelletizing, or sintering products such as blast-furnace slag, clay, diatomite, fly ash, shale, or slate, and

3.1.2 Aggregates prepared by processing natural materials, such as pumice, scoria, or tuff.

3.2 The aggregates shall be composed predominately of lightweight-cellular and granular inorganic material.

4. Chemical Composition

4.1 Lightweight aggregates shall not contain excessive amounts of deleterious substances, as determined by the following limits:

4.1.1 *Organic Impurities (Test Method C 40)*—Lightweight aggregates that, upon being subjected to test for organic impurities, produce a color darker than the standard shall be rejected, unless it can be demonstrated that the discoloration is due to small quantities of materials not harmful to the concrete.

4.1.2 *Staining (Test Method C 641)*—An aggregate producing a heavy or very heavy stain shall be rejected when the material making up the stain is found upon chemical analysis to contain an iron content, expressed as Fe_2O_3, equal to or greater than 1.5 mg/200 g of sample.

4.1.3 *Loss on Ignition (Methods C 114)*—The loss on ignition of lightweight aggregates shall not exceed 5 %.

NOTE 2—Certain processed aggregates may be hydraulic in character, and may be partially hydrated during production; if so, the quality of the product is not usually reduced thereby. Therefore, consideration should be given to the type of material when evaluating the product in terms of ignition loss.

---

[1] This specification is under the jurisdiction of ASTM Committee C-9 on Concrete and Concrete Aggregates and is the direct responsibility of Subcommittee C 09.21 on Lightweight Aggregates.
Current edition approved Oct. 27 1989. Published December 1989. Originally published as C 330 – 53 T. Last previous edition C 330 – 87.
[2] *Annual Book of ASTM Standards,* Vol 04.02.
[3] *Annual Book of ASTM Standards,* Vol 04.01.

[4] *Annual Book of ASTM Standards,* Vols 04.01, 04.02, and 14.02.

⬤ C 330

5. Physical Properties

5.1 Lightweight aggregate under test shall meet the following requirements:

5.1.1 *Clay Lumps*—The amount of clay lumps shall not exceed 2 % by dry weight.

5.1.2 *Grading*—The grading shall conform to the requirements shown in Table 1.

5.1.3 *Uniformity of Grading*—To ensure reasonable uniformity in the grading of successive shipments of lightweight aggregate, fineness modulus shall be determined on samples taken from shipments at intervals stipulated by the purchaser. If the fineness modulus of the aggregate in any shipment differs by more than 7 % from that of the sample submitted for acceptance tests, the aggregate in the shipment shall be rejected, unless it can be demonstrated that it will produce concrete of the required characteristics.

5.1.4 *Unit Weight*—The unit weight of the lightweight aggregates shall conform to the requirements shown in Table 2.

5.1.5 *Uniformity of Unit Weight*—The reported unit weight of lightweight aggregate shipments, sampled and tested, shall not differ by more than 10 % from that of the sample submitted for acceptance tests.

5.2 Concrete specimens containing lightweight aggregate under test shall meet the following requirements:

5.2.1 *Compressive Strength (Test Method C 39), Unit Weight (Test Method C 567), and Splitting Tensile Strength (Test Method C 496)*—Compressive strength and unit weight shall be an average of three specimens and the splitting tensile strength shall be the average of eight specimens. It shall be possible to produce structural concrete using the lightweight aggregates under test, so that from the same batch of concrete one or more of the compressive strength requirements and splitting tensile strength requirements in the following table will be satisfied without exceeding the corresponding maximum unit weight values. Intermediate values for strength and corresponding unit weight values may be established by interpolation (see Note 3).

Average Air Dry 28-day Unit Weight max, lb/ft³ (kg/m³)	Average 28-day Splitting Tensile Strength, min, psi (MPa)	Average 28-day Compressive Strength, min, psi (MPa)
All Lightweight Aggregate		
110 (1760)	320 (2.2)	4000 (28)
105 (1680)	300 (2.1)	3000 (21)
100 (1600)	290 (2.0)	2500 (17)
Sand/Lightweight Aggregate		
115 (1840)	330 (2.3)	4000 (28)
110 (1760)	310 (2.1)	3000 (21)
105 (1680)	300 (2.1)	2500 (17)

NOTE 3—Materials that do not meet the minimum average splitting tensile strength requirement may be used provided the design is modified to compensate for the lower value.

5.2.2 *Natural Sand*—Natural sand replacement for part, or all, of the lightweight-aggregate fines may be used to determine compliance with these minimum requirements, provided that the proposed structural concrete usage contemplates similar combination of materials. The test report shall record the proportion of all ingredients and the characteristics of the natural sand as specified in Specification C 33.

5.2.3 *Drying Shrinkage*—The drying shrinkage of con-

crete specimens prepared and tested as described in the method for preparation of samples for shrinkage of concrete shall not exceed 0.07 %.

5.2.4 *Popouts*—Concrete specimens prepared as described in the method for preparation of sample for shrinkage of concrete and tested in accordance with Test Method C 151 shall show no surface popouts.

5.2.5 *Durability*—In the absence of a proven record of satisfactory durability in structural concrete, lightweight aggregates may be required to pass a concrete freezing and thawing test satisfactory to the purchaser.

6. Sampling

6.1 Sample lightweight aggregates in accordance with Practice D 75.

7. Number of Tests

7.1 *Tests on Aggregate*—One representative sample is required for each test for organic impurities, staining, loss on ignition, grading, unit weight, and clay lumps.

7.2 *Tests on Concrete*—At least three specimens are required for each of the following tests of concrete: compressive strength, shrinkage, unit weight, resistance to freezing and thawing, and presence of popout materials. At least eight concrete specimens are required for splitting tensile strength tests.

8. Test Methods

8.1 *Compressive Strength (Test Method C 39)*—Make test specimens in accordance with Practice C 192. Cure specimens in accordance with Practice C 192 until the time of test, or follow the curing procedures for the air dry unit weight (Test Method C 567). When the latter procedure is used, remove the specimens from the moist curing at the age of 7 days and store at 73.4 ± 3°F (23 ± 1.7°C) with a relative humidity of 50 ± 5 % until the time of test.

8.2 *Splitting Tensile Strength*—Make 6 by 12-in. (152 by 305-mm) cylindrical test specimens in accordance with Practice C 192, cure, and test in accordance with Test Method C 496.

8.3 *Unit Weight of Concrete (Test Method C 567)*—Follow the procedures in Test Method C 567.

8.4 *Shrinkage of Concrete (Test Method C 157)*—Follow the procedures of Test Method C 157 with the following exceptions:

8.4.1 Prepare the concrete mixture using 564 lb of cement/yd³ (335 kg/m³), admixture (if any), and with an air content of 6 ± 1 %. Adjust the water content so as to produce a slump of 2 to 4 in. (50 to 100 mm). Thoroughly consolidate the concrete in steel molds not smaller than 2 by 2 in. (50 by 50 mm) nor larger than 4 by 4 in. (100 by 100 mm) in cross section, and long enough to provide a 10 in. (250 mm) gage length. The surface of the concrete shall be steel troweled.

8.4.2 *Curing*—To prevent evaporation of water from the unhardened concrete, cover the specimen with a nonabsorptive, nonreactive plate or sheet of tough, durable, impervious plastic. Wet burlap may be used for covering, but care must be exercised to keep the burlap wet until the specimens are removed from the molds. Placing a sheet of

⟨ASTM⟩ C 330

TABLE 1 Grading Requirements for Lightweight Aggregates for Structural Concrete

Size Designation	Percentages (by Weight) Passing Sieves Having Square Openings								
	1 in. (25.0 mm)	¾ in. (19.0 mm)	½ in. (12.5 mm)	⅜ in. (9.5 mm)	No. 4 (4.75- mm)	No. 8 (2.36- mm)	No. 16 (1.18- mm)	No. 50 (300- μm)	No. 100 (150- μm)
Fine aggregate:									
No. 4 to 0	...	...	...	100	85–100	...	40–80	10–35	5–25
Coarse aggregate:									
1 in. to No. 4	95–100	...	25–60	...	0–10	...	...	...	...
¾ in. to No. 4	100	90–100	...	10–50	0–15	...	...	...	...
½ in. to No. 4	...	100	90–100	40–80	0–20	0–10	...	...	...
⅜ in. to No. 8	...	...	100	80–100	5–40	0–20	0–10	...	...
Combined fine and coarse aggregate:									
½ in. to 0	...	100	95–100	...	50–80	...	...	5–20	2–15
⅜ in. to 0	...	...	100	90–100	65–90	35–65	...	10–25	5–15

TABLE 2 Unit Weight Requirements of Lightweight Aggregates for Structural Concrete

Size Designation	Dry Loose Weight, max, lb/ft³ (kg/m³)
Fine aggregate	70 (1120)
Coarse aggregate	55 (880)
Combined fine and coarse aggregate	65 (1040)

TABLE 3 Weight of Sieve Test Sample for Fine Lightweight Aggregates

Range of Nominal Weight of Aggregate		Weight of Test Sample, g
lb/ft³	kg/m³	
5–15	80–240	50
15–25	240–400	100
25–35	400–560	150
35–45	560–720	200
45–55	720–880	250
55–65	880–1040	300
65–70	1040–1120	350

plastic over the burlap will facilitate keeping it wet. Remove specimens from the molds not less than 20 nor more than 48 h after casting and store in a moist room maintained at 73.4 ± 3°F (23 ± 1.7°C) with a relative humidity of not less than 95 %. At the age of 7 days, remove the specimens from the moist room, measure for length, and store in a curing cabinet maintained at 100 ± 2°F (37.8 ± 1.1°C) with a relative humidity of 32 ± 2 %.

NOTE 4—The air immediately above a saturated solution of magnesium chloride ($MgCl_2$) at 100°F (37.8°C) is approximately 32 % relative humidity.

8.4.3 *Report*—After storage in the cabinet for 28 days, determine the change in length of each specimen to the nearest 0.01 % of the effective gage length. Report the change in length as the drying shrinkage of the specimen; report the average drying shrinkage of the specimens as the drying shrinkage of the concrete.

8.5 *Test for Popout Materials*—Prepare concrete specimens for the test for popout materials as described in method for preparation of samples for shrinkage of concrete. Cure and autoclave the specimens in accordance with Test Method C 151. Visually inspect the autoclaved specimens for the number of popouts that have developed on the surface. Report the average number of popouts per specimen.

8.6 *Test for Freezing and Thawing*—Make freezing and thawing tests of concrete, when required, in accordance with Test Method C 666.

8.7 *Grading (Method C 136)*—Follow the procedures of Method C 136, except that the weight of the test sample for fine aggregate shall be in accordance with Table 3. The test sample for coarse aggregate shall consist of 0.1 ft³ (2830 cm³) or more of the material used for the determination of unit weight. The aggregate, when mechanically sieved, shall be sieved for only 5 min.

8.8 *Unit Weight (Loose) (Test Method C 29)*—The aggregate shall be tested in an oven dry condition utilizing the shoveling procedure.

8.9 *Clay Lumps and Friable Particles in Aggregates*— Test Method C 142.

9. Rejection

9.1 Material that fails to conform to the requirements of this specification may be rejected. Rejection shall be reported to the producer or supplier promptly and in writing.

10. Certification

10.1 When specified in the purchase order or contract, a producer's or supplier's certification shall be furnished to the purchaser that the material was manufactured, sampled, and tested in accordance with this specification and has been found to meet the requirements. When specified in the purchase order or contract, a report of the test results shall be furnished.

ASTM Designation: C 566 – 96

AMERICAN SOCIETY FOR TESTING AND MATERIALS
100 Barr Harbor Dr., West Conshohocken, PA 19428
Reprinted from the Annual Book of ASTM Standards. Copyright ASTM
If not listed in the current combined index, will appear in the next edition.

Standard Test Method for
Total Moisture Content of Aggregate by Drying[1]

This standard is issued under the fixed designation C 566; the number immediately following the designation indicates the year of original adoption or, in the case of revision, the year of last revision. A number in parentheses indicates the year of last reapproval. A superscript epsilon (ε) indicates an editorial change since the last revision or reapproval.

This test method has been approved for use by agencies of the Department of Defense. Consult the DoD Index of Specifications and Standards for the specific year of issue which has been adopted by the Department of Defense.

1. Scope

1.1 This test method covers the determination of the percentage of evaporable moisture in a sample of aggregate by drying, both surface moisture and moisture in the pores of the aggregate. Some aggregate may contain water that is chemically combined with the minerals in the aggregate. Such water is not evaporable and is not included in the percentage determined by this test method.

1.2 The values stated in SI units are to be regarded as the standard. The values stated in parentheses are provided for information only.

1.3 *This standard does not purport to address all of the safety concerns, if any, associated with its use. It is the responsibility of the user of this standard to establish appropriate safety and health practices and determine the applicability of regulatory limitations prior to use. For specific precautionary statements, see 5.3.1, 7.2.1, and 7.3.1.*

2. Referenced Documents

2.1 *ASTM Standards:*
C 29/C 29M Test Method for Unit Weight and Voids in Aggregate[2]
C 125 Terminology Relating to Concrete and Concrete Aggregates[2]
C 127 Test Method for Specific Gravity and Absorption of Coarse Aggregate[2]
C 128 Test Method for Specific Gravity and Absorption of Fine Aggregate[2]
C 670 Practice for Preparing Precision Statements for Test Methods for Construction Materials[2]
D 75 Practice for Sampling Aggregates[3]
E 11 Specification for Wire Cloth and Sieves for Testing Purposes[2]

3. Terminology

3.1 *Definitions:*
3.1.1 For definitions of terms used in this test method, refer to Terminology C 125.

4. Significance and Use

4.1 This test method is sufficiently accurate for usual purposes, such as adjusting batch quantities of ingredients for concrete. It will generally measure the moisture in the test sample more reliably than the sample can be made to represent the aggregate supply. In cases where the aggregate itself is altered by heat, or where more refined measurement is required, the test should be conducted using a ventilated, controlled temperature oven.

4.2 Large particles of coarse aggregate, especially those larger than 50 mm (2 in.), will require greater time for the moisture to travel from the interior of the particle to the surface. The user of this test method should determine by trial if rapid drying methods provide sufficient accuracy for the intended use when drying large size particles.

5. Apparatus

5.1 *Balance*—A balance or scale accurate, readable, and sensitive to within 0.1 % of the test load at any point within the range of use. Within any interval equal to 10 % of the capacity of the balance or scale, the load indication shall be accurate within 0.1 % of the difference in masses.

5.2 *Source of Heat*—A ventilated oven capable of maintaining the temperature surrounding the sample at 110 ± 5°C (230 ± 9°F). Where close control of the temperature is not required (see 4.1), other suitable sources of heat may be used, such as an electric or gas hot plate, electric heat lamps, or a ventilated microwave oven.

5.3 *Sample Container*—A container not affected by the heat, and of sufficient volume to contain the sample without danger of spilling, and of such shape that the depth of sample will not exceed one fifth of the least lateral dimension.

5.3.1 **Precaution**—When a microwave oven is used, the container shall be nonmetallic.

NOTE 1—Except for testing large samples, an ordinary frying pan is suitable for use with a hot plate, or any shallow flat-bottomed metal pan is suitable with heat lamps or oven. Note precaution in 5.3.1.

5.4 *Stirrer*—A metal spoon or spatula of convenient size.

6. Sampling

6.1 Sample in accordance with Practice D 75, except for the sample size.

6.2 Secure a sample of the aggregate representative of the moisture content in the supply being tested and having a mass not less than the amount listed in Table 1. Protect the sample against loss of moisture prior to determining the mass.

7. Procedure

7.1 Determine the mass of the sample to the nearest 0.1 %.

---

[1] This test method is under the jurisdiction of ASTM Committee C-9 on Concrete and Concrete Aggregates and is the direct responsibility of Subcommittee C09.20 on Normal Weight Aggregates.
Current edition approved Jan. 10, 1996. Published March 1996. Originally issued as C 566 – 65 T. Last previous edition C 566 – 95.
[2] Annual Book of ASTM Standards, Vol 04.02.
[3] Annual Book of ASTM Standards, Vol 04.03.

ASTM C 566

TABLE 1 Sample Size for Aggregate

Nominal Maximum Size of Aggregate, mm (in.)[A]	Mass of Normal Weight Aggregate Sample, min, kg[B]
4.75 (0.187) (No. 4)	0.5
9.5 (3/8)	1.5
12.5 (1/2)	2
19.0 (3/4)	3
25.0 (1)	4
37.5 (1 1/2)	6
50 (2)	8
63 (2 1/2)	10
75 (3)	13
90 (3 1/2)	16
100 (4)	25
150 (6)	50

[A] Based on sieves meeting Specification E 11.
[B] Determine the minimum sample mass for lightweight aggregate by multiplying the value listed by the dry-loose unit mass of the aggregate in kg/m³ (determined using Test Method C 29/C 29M) and dividing by 1600.

7.2 Dry the sample thoroughly in the sample container by means of the selected source of heat, exercising care to avoid loss of any particles. Very rapid heating may cause some particles to explode, resulting in loss of particles. Use a controlled temperature oven when excessive heat may alter the character of the aggregate, or where more precise measurement is required. If a source of heat other than the controlled temperature oven is used, stir the sample during drying to accelerate the operation and avoid localized overheating. When using a microwave oven, stirring of the sample is optional.

7.2.1 **Caution:** When using a microwave oven, occasionally minerals are present in aggregates that may cause the material to overheat and explode. If this occurs it can damage the microwave oven.

7.3 When a hot plate is used, drying can be expedited by the following procedure. Add sufficient anhydrous denatured alcohol to cover the moist sample. Stir and allow suspended material to settle. Decant as much of the alcohol as possible without losing any of the sample. Ignite the remaining alcohol and allow it to burn off during drying over the hot plate.

7.3.1 **Warning**—Exercise care to control the ignition operation to prevent injury or damage from the burning alcohol.

7.4 The sample is thoroughly dry when further heating causes, or would cause, less than 0.1 % additional loss in mass.

7.5 Determine the mass of the dried sample to the nearest 0.1 % after it has cooled sufficiently not to damage the balance.

8. Calculation

8.1 Calculate total evaporable moisture content as follows:

$$p = 100 \, (W - D)/D$$

where:
p = total evaporable moisture content of sample, percent,
W = mass of original sample, g, and
D = mass of dried sample, g.

8.2 Surface moisture content is equal to the difference between the total evaporable moisture content and the absorption, with all values based on the mass of a dry sample. Absorption may be determined in accordance with Test Method C 127 or Test Method C 128.

9. Precision and Bias

9.1 *Precision:*

9.1.1 The within-laboratory single operator standard deviation for moisture content of aggregates has been found to be 0.2790 % (Note 2). Results of two properly conducted tests by the same operator in the same laboratory on the same type of aggregate sample, therefore, should not differ by more than 0.7891 % (Note 2) from each other in 95 % of the cases.

9.1.2 The between-laboratory single operator standard deviation for moisture content of aggregates has been found to be 0.28012 % (Note 2). Results of properly conducted tests from two laboratories on the same aggregate sample, therefore, should not differ by more than 0.7923 % (Note 2) from each other in 95 % of the cases.

NOTE 2—These numbers represent, respectively, the 1s and d2s limits as described in Practice C 670.

9.2 *Bias:*

9.2.1 When experimental results are compared with known values from accurately compounded specimens, the following has been derived.

9.2.1.1 The bias of moisture tests on one aggregate material has been found to have a mean of +0.0615 %. The bias of individual test values from the same aggregate material has been found with 95 % confidence to lie between −0.074 % and +0.197 %.

9.2.1.2 The bias of moisture tests on a second aggregate material has been found to have a mean of +0.0007 %. The bias of individual test values from the same aggregate material has been found with 95 % confidence to lie between −0.135 % and +0.136 %.

9.2.1.3 The bias of moisture tests overall on both aggregate materials has been found to have a mean of +0.0311 %. The bias of individual test values overall from both aggregate materials has been found with 95 % confidence to lie between −0.116 % and +0.179 %.

NOTE 3—These precision and bias statements were derived from aggregate moisture data provided by 17 laboratories participating in the Strategic Highway Research Program (SHRP) Soil Moisture Proficiency Sample Program that is fully described in the National Research Council Report SHRP-P-619.[4] Details of the statistical derivation are contained in appendix V of the report. A complete description of the program, including raw data, source of the aggregate samples, participating laboratories, etc., is also contained in the report. All samples in this program were dried to a constant mass in a drying oven maintained at 110 ± 5°C. When other drying procedures are used, the precision and bias of the results may be significantly different than that indicated above.

10. Keywords

10.1 aggregate; drying; moisture content

---

[4] Available from the National Research Council, 2101 Constitution Ave., N.W., Washington, DC 20418.

C 566

AMERICAN SOCIETY FOR TESTING AND MATERIALS
1916 Race St. Philadelphia, Pa 19103
Reprinted from the Annual Book of ASTM Standards. Copyright ASTM
If not listed in the current combined index, will appear in the next edition.

Standard Practice for
Bituminous Mixing Plant Inspection[1]

This standard is issued under the fixed designation D 290; the number immediately following the designation indicates the year of original adoption or, in the case of revision, the year of last revision. A number in parentheses indicates the year of last reapproval. A superscript epsilon (ε) indicates an editorial change since the last revision or reapproval.

1. Scope

1.1 This practice defines the authority and duties of the inspector at the bituminous mixing plant. These duties are performed in order to ensure the contractor's compliance with the contract and applicable specifications and do not in any way relieve the contractor of the responsibility to produce uniform mixtures in compliance with the contract.

1.2 The values stated in inch-pound units are to be regarded as the standard.

1.3 *This standard does not purport to address all of the safety problems, if any, associated with its use. It is the responsibility of the user of this standard to establish appropriate safety and health practices and determine the applicability of regulatory limitations prior to use.*

2. Referenced Documents

2.1 *ASTM Standards:*

C 136 Method for Sieve Analysis of Fine and Coarse Aggregates[2,3]

D 75 Practice for Sampling Aggregates[3]

D 140 Practice for Sampling Bituminous Materials[3]

D 242 Specification for Mineral Filler for Bituminous Paving Mixtures[3]

D 546 Test Method for Sieve Analysis of Mineral Filler for Road and Paving Materials[3]

D 979 Practice for Sampling Bituminous Paving Mixtures[3]

D 995 Specification for Mixing Plants for Hot-Mixed, Hot-Laid Bituminous Paving Mixtures[3]

D 3666 Practice for Evaluating and Qualifying Agencies Testing and Inspecting Bituminous Paving Materials[3]

3. Terminology

3.1 *Descriptions of Terms Specific to This Standard:*

3.1.1 *engineer, n*—the party in responsible charge of the work or the engineer's duly recognized or authorized representative.

3.1.2 *inspector, n*—the engineer's (or in the absence of the engineer, the purchaser's) authorized representative delegated to perform inspections, tests, and duties hereinafter indicated.

3.1.2.1 *Discussion*—The inspector shall be qualified as a technician in accordance with the applicable requirements of Practice D 3666.

3.1.3 *contractor, n*—the party to the contract who has agreed to supply materials and perform work in accordance with the specifications, or the contractor's duly authorized representative at the plant.

3.1.4 *laboratory, n*—any supervising laboratory duly authorized by the engineer to direct and advise the inspector in the discharge of assigned duties.

3.1.4.1 *Discussion*—The laboratory shall satisfy the applicable requirements of Practice D 3666.

3.1.5 *plant laboratory, n*—the laboratory operated by or under the direction of the plant inspector at the plant, or the contractor's laboratory for use by the contractor's representative for the control of plant production.

4. Significance and Use

4.1 This practice defines the authority and duties of the inspection personnel assigned to bituminous mixing plants.

4.2 The intent of the practice is to assure by inspection, that the contractor's facilities, production operations, materials handling, required testing, and finally, the finished mix product comply with applicable specifications.

5. Responsibilities and General Duties of Inspector

5.1 *Authority*—In the absence of authority conferred by the specifications or contract provisions, the inspector shall be provided with written authority from the engineer to ensure fulfillment of specifications covering materials, plant procedure, and products, and reject such materials, procedures, and products failing to conform to specifications. The inspector shall have available a copy of the specifications and any contract special provisions applying to the particular project, and shall be furnished immediately in writing with copies of all modifications, amendments, and instructions affecting the product of the plant. The inspector shall recognize the right of the contractor to use such apparatus, methods, and personnel as deemed proper, provided that no specification requirements are thereby violated. Any appeal on the part of the contractor from rejections shall be made in writing to the engineer, with a copy to the inspector, unless otherwise provided in the contract.

5.2 *Cooperation*—The plant inspector shall cooperate with the contractor in every reasonable way to obtain efficient and economical plant operation consistent with production of a mixture of satisfactory quality, and with the paving inspector on matters of mutual concern relating to obtaining a mixture of satisfactory placement characteristics, all within the limits of the specifications.

5.3 *Duties*—In addition to the responsibilities specified in 5.1 and 5.2, the duties of the plant inspector shall be:

5.3.1 To ensure that the plant is equipped and operated at all times in conformity with the specifications (Section 6),

---

[1] This practice is under the jurisdiction of ASTM Committee D-4 on Road and Paving Materials and is the direct responsibility of Subcommittee D04.23 on Plant-Mixed Bituminous Surfaces and Bases.

Current edition approved Sept. 15, 1991. Published November 1991. Originally published as D 290 – 28 T. Last previous edition D 290 – 91.

[2] *Annual Book of ASTM Standards*, Vol 04.02.

[3] *Annual Book of ASTM Standards*, Vol 04.03.

⑩ D 290

TABLE 1   Index of Sampling

Material	Method	Quantity	When Collected	By Whom Tested
Fine aggregate (cold feed)	Practice D 75	Case I[A]—25 lb (11.3 kg) Case II[B]—5 lb (2.3 kg)	preliminary or first shipments from given source and when source of supply changes, when material characteristics change, or by special instructions from engineer	laboratory or plant laboratory
Coarse aggregate (cold feed)	Same as for Fine Aggregate	Case I[A]—50 lb (22.7 kg) Case II[B]—50 lb (22.7 kg)	same as for fine aggregate	laboratory or plant laboratory
Filler	Specification D 242	5 lb (2.3 kg)	each shipment	laboratory or plant laboratory
Aggregates (plant bins)	By use of approved sampling device capable of obtaining a representative bin sample	5 (2.3 kg) to 35 lb (15.9 kg) or more depending on maximum particle size as required under Method C 136	at least daily	plant laboratory
Bituminous material	Practice D 140	1 qt (1 L)	each car, tank truck, or boat	plant laboratory
Finished mixtures: A. To determine average daily analysis of mixture. B. For determination of uniformity of individual or different batches	Practice D 979	Practice D 979	A. Daily B. As directed	laboratory
Pavement sample	Practice D 979	1 square piece of size specified by Practice D 979	as directed	laboratory

[A] When job-mix is formulated by Laboratory.
[B] When job-mix is formulated by Contractor.

5.3.2 To obtain samples as required for testing at the plant laboratory or submission to the laboratory (Section 7),

5.3.3 To inform the contractor when mixture or conditions violate specifications and disapprove subsequent production if corrections are not made (Section 8),

5.3.4 To conduct tests to check the adequacy of (1) materials to be used in mixture production and (2) plant control in maintaining a mixture which is in conformance with the job-mix formula and tolerance limits for uniformity (Section 9),

5.3.5 To maintain required inventory and production records (see 10.1), and

5.3.6 To submit daily reports (see 10.2 and 10.3).

6. Plant Equipment and Operation

6.1 General requirements for plant equipment shall be determined in accordance with Specification D 995 and supplementing contract requirements.

6.2 The inspector shall ascertain as early as possible, by a thorough inspection of the plant site, plant, and appurtenances, that all elements are in compliance with the contract. Specific attention shall be given to materials storage and handling, cold aggregate feeds, drier, mixture production plant, batching and mixing components, truck scales (when required), and hauling units. The inspector shall witness checks on the accuracy of the scales, using standard weights, and of volumetric meters if used in the proportioning of mixtures. During the operation of the plant, a periodic check shall be made on the accuracy of scales or meters used in determining the mass or volume of each component material.

7. Sampling

7.1 *Materials (General):*

7.1.1 A recommended schedule of sampling is indicated in Table 1, Index of Sampling.

7.1.2 As far as possible in advance, but within the time limitation imposed by contract requirements, representative samples of each material proposed for use in the bituminous mixture shall be obtained by, or under approval and observation of, the inspector and submitted to the laboratory or tested by the inspector as directed.

NOTE 1—Requirements for lead time, size of samples, and specific sampling procedures will vary with contracting agencies, for example, different conditions will prevail as between job-mix formulation by the contractor or the engineer.

7.1.3 Should the source of supply of any material, or the characteristics of any material affecting specification requirements change from that represented by the initially submitted samples, new samples shall be submitted to the laboratory by the inspector.

7.1.4 Daily control samples of bituminous material and mixtures shall be collected and, at the end of the day's work, forwarded to the laboratory without delay.

NOTE 2—When forwarding samples of crude asphalt, refined asphalt, hard natural asphalt, oxidized asphalt or any other bituminous materials in inspections covering the production of bituminous pavements incorporating such materials, information shall also be furnished relative to the proportions by mass being used so that proper combinations can be made for analysis and check determinations.

7.2 *Bituminous Mixtures:*

7.2.1 Samples of bituminous mixtures shall be taken by the contractor daily, or as directed, and witnessed by the inspector for the purpose of checking average aggregate grading, and if desired, bituminous material content of the produced mixture by means of extraction procedures. Samples may also be taken, if directed, to determine uniformity within a batch, or batch-to-batch (time-to-time for continuous mixing plants).

7.2.1.1 In the case of plants automatically recording batch

◈ D 290

mass of aggregate and the bituminous material, the engineer may elect to check bituminous material content of the mixture on the basis of batch mass, or comparison of actual versus theoretical consumptions, instead of extraction tests on samples of produced mixture.

7.2.2 Sampling of bituminous paving mixtures shall be done in accordance with Practice D 979, except as modified below, for determination of within batch variation.

7.2.3 *Composite Sample*—Samples obtained for the purpose of checking aggregate grading and bituminous material content shall be composited by accumulating fractions from occasional batches produced during the day, or shorter check interval, and stored on a metal plate or in another suitable container. The sample, of a size required for testing, shall be obtained from the accumulated fractional samplings by quartering after thorough remixing. To facilitate remixing, the entire mass should be warmed, avoiding overheating to the degree necessary to permit satisfactory mixing.

7.2.4 *Uniformity Samples*—Samples used to determine uniformity within a single batch or from batch to batch shall be obtained as follows:

7.2.4.1 *With Batch Variation*—Individual samples shall be taken by means of a sampling thief from three uniformly separated locations in a single batch and individually analysed.

7.2.4.2 *Batch to Batch Variation*—Samples shall be taken from three or more separate batches throughout a day's production by Practice D 979, and remixed, quartered, and analysed separately.

7.2.5 All sampling of mixtures shall be done with extreme care to assure representativeness and to preclude contamination with foreign material. Samples submitted to the laboratory should be completely identified and accompanied with required data.

7.3 *Rejected Materials*—Samples of all materials rejected by the inspector may be forwarded to the laboratory.

7.4 *Marking Samples*—Beginning at the start of operations on a given contract, the inspector shall assign class designations to each class of material being sampled, and each sample selected shall be numbered serially in that class, continuing numerically until the completion of the work. Care shall be taken that the series of numbers is not broken or numbers duplicated. All samples sent to the laboratory shall be marked in such a manner as to ensure complete identification. Letters and numbers may be scratched or punched clearly on tin cans, and marked with ink or paint on other sample containers or on sections of pavement.

8. Preparation of Mixtures

8.1 *Job-Mix Formula*—The inspector shall receive instructions from the engineer with regard to the job-mix formula establishing the percentage of bituminous material (in relation to either the total mixture or aggregate fraction) and aggregate gradation, and the specification tolerance limits for deviation in either bituminous material content or gradation of the produced mixture from the job-mix values.

8.2 *Combining Cold-Feed Aggregates*—The inspector shall check to assure that proper attention is given to the combining of aggregates before they enter the dryer. Settings of feeders should be noted as established by the contractor, any changes in settings which will change the relative feed

rates between aggregates, and make certain that feeding is continuous and uniform, especially with fine aggregates of high moisture content.

8.3 *Drying Aggregates*—The inspector shall make certain that the aggregate is properly dried and heated to the desired temperature, and that the feed of aggregates to the dryer is consistent with the capacity of the dryer at the given moisture content.

8.4 *Proportioning by Mass:*

8.4.1 The inspector shall witness a check on calibration and accuracy of batching scales, initially and periodically thereafter (at least weekly or when suspect). The batching operation should be observed frequently (continuously when feasible or required) to determine that proper care is being exercised in weighing batches, that aggregate hoppers and bitumen bucket swing freely during weighings, and that the mass indicators read zero after discharge of the batch. The inspector should observe that the bitumen bucket is drained completely for each batch and check the tare mass of the empty bucket at frequent intervals to determine if any compensation should be made for the amount of bituminous material clinging to it. (This latter element requires more attention in cool weather or at times when there is a long interval between loads.)

8.4.2 The inspector shall make certain that the aggregates are deposited in the mixer in a proper sequence for satisfactory mixing, that the specified dry-mixing and wet-mixing periods are accomplished, and that the mixing time is sufficient to produce a homogeneous mixture of uniform color and texture.

8.5 *Proportioning by Volume:*

8.5.1 *Aggregate Feed*—The inspector shall witness the "calibration" of the hot-bin and mineral filler feeders at various gate openings or control-arm settings, and check the contractor's computations for and plot of the calibration graphs relating to volume flow of aggregate from the respective bins to pounds delivered per revolution of the feeder mechanism.

8.5.2 *Bituminous Material Feed*—The inspector shall witness a check on the bituminous material pump delivery per revolution of the aggregate feeder mechanism (continuous mixing plant) or accuracy of the batch meter (volumetric metering batch plant).

8.5.3 *Batch Proportions*—The contractor's batch proportions per revolution shall be subject to the approval of the inspector to assure compliance of the bituminous mixture with the job-mix formula.

8.6 *Mixtures (General):*

8.6.1 The inspector shall ascertain that the aggregates in the hot bins are of known and uniform gradation so they may be batched in the prescribed proportions and consistently produce a mixture within specification limits of tolerance.

8.6.2 The inspector shall make periodic visual observations of the produced mixture to ensure homogeneous batches of continuously uniform color and texture.

8.6.3 When bituminous material is batched by volume, its mass per gallon, at operating temperature, shall be determined and the batching meter adjusted to deliver the required volume at this temperature.

8.6.4 It is recommended that, whenever possible, entire

✿ D 290

loads of the mixture proportioned either by mass or volume, be weighed as a check against individual batches.

8.7 *Temperature of Materials and Mixtures:*

8.7.1 The inspector shall check the temperature of all ingredients of the mixture, especially mineral aggregates, and of the mixtures as frequently as possible. The inspector shall assist in keeping temperatures uniform by notifying the plant foreman of any marked changes observed. In the event of improper temperature, mixing operations shall be discontinued until aggregates of the proper temperature are obtained.

8.7.2 The desired temperatures at the plant will depend upon the kind of mixture being prepared, the type of bituminous material being used, weather conditions, and the length of haul. The inspector should, therefore, receive instructions from the engineer as to the temperatures applicable under the various conditions.

9. Plant Testing of Materials

9.1 *Filler*—A minimum of one thoroughly dry sample of filler, representing each shipment received at the plant, shall be tested in accordance with Test Method D 546.

9.2 *Cold Aggregates*—Fine and coarse aggregate shall be tested in accordance with Method C 136. Samples shall be tested daily, or more often if necessary, in order to provide data for making adjustments to the combination of aggregates at the cold-feed to the dryer. When two or more aggregates are being received for use in combination, separate sieve analysis shall be made on each aggregate and the required combination to meet the job-mix gradation calculated and shown on the daily report. The proportions in which all aggregates, including added filler, are combined in the batch shall also be shown on the report.

9.3 *Heated Aggregates:*

9.3.1 Samples of aggregates as discharged from the hot storage bins into the mixer shall be taken and tested at least twice during a full day's operation, or more frequently if necessary, in order to determine the uniformity and gradation suitability of bin materials to maintain the mixture within tolerance limits. Samples shall be secured from the stream of aggregate as it flows from the storage bin by any means which provides a truly representative sample of the material in the bin.

9.3.2 All tests of these materials shall be recorded on the daily plant report. The results will show: (*1*) when blended materials are being used, whether cold-feed blending is being carried on satisfactorily and (*2*) whether separation of aggregates by sizes has been uniform. If the screened fine aggregate bin is contaminated with coarse aggregate or the screened coarse aggregate bins contain an excessive change in the amount of fine material carried over from the next finer bin, steps shall be taken to determine the cause and to make correction.

10. Report

10.1 *Production of Plant*—The inspector shall maintain a daily record of (*1*) time and hours of plant production, (*2*) number of batches (or tons) of the various mixtures produced, (*3*) the batch mass proportions of hot-bin aggregates and bituminous material, and (*4*) when possible, a balance sheet comparison of bituminous materials actually used (based on receipts, disbursements, and tank inventories) and theoretically used (based on number of batches produced multiplied by quantity per batch). Other miscellaneous information shall be recorded as required to complete specific report forms.

10.2 *Daily Reports*—At the close of each working day, whether the plant is in operation or not, the inspector shall forward to the engineer and laboratory a consecutively numbered daily report, using a form which gives all the required information. All data pertinent to the work not covered by the form should be given on the reverse side of the report sheet, and communications of exceptional importance only should be sent separately from the report. When work is suspended for several days, the inspector may not be required to submit reports daily, but the last report should state why and for what periods work has been discontinued. The inspector shall retain copies of these reports and communications and, in addition, keep a daily record of all matters pertaining to the work inspected, particularly as to any action in the acceptance or rejection of materials with reasons therefore, instruction or suggestions to the contractor, and the receipt of instructions from the engineer or laboratory.

10.3 *Report Form*—A standard form of report is not practicable for all conditions and types of pavement, but the report form shown in Table 2 is a typical form showing the kind of information which should be included; additional data may be called for as required.

◀⑨▶ D 290

TABLE 2 Bituminous Mixing Plant Inspector's Daily Report

NOTE: This report is intended as a guide. When more materials are being used, or more than one mix type is being produced, additional spaces may be necessary.

Project _____ County _____ State _____ Date _____

Report No _____

Bituminous Mixture:
Produced by _____ At _____
Consigned to _____ At _____
Type of Plant _____ Continous-Batch _____ Mix Time Per Batch _____ Seconds

Component Materials

Bituminous Material	Type/Grade	Source	Car or Truck Number						Date Received							Amount	

Aggregate	Type	Source	2½ in.	1½ in.	1 in.	¾ in.	½ in.	⅜ in.	No. 4	No. 8	No. 16	No. 30	No. 50	No. 100	No. 200
Coarse															
Intermediate															
Fine															
Filler															
Combined Gradation	Coarse ___% Intermediate ___%	Fine ___% Filler ___%													
Job Mix Formula															

Analysis of Hot Bin Aggregates

Bin No.	2½ in.	1½ in.	1 in.	¾ in.	½ in.	⅜ in.	No.4	No. 8	No.16	No. 30	No. 50	No. 100	No. 200
1													
2													
3													
4													
Mineral Filler													

Sand Equivalent Value _____ Correction Factor From Washed Analysis (No. 200) _____

Batch Weights, lbs, or lbs per revolution

Mix Type	Bin 1	Bin 2	Bin 3	Bin 4	Filler	Bituminous Material	Total
Total Mix, %							

Analysis of Mix

Sample	Hour	Temperature °F	2½ in.	1½ in.	1 in.	¾ in.	½ in.	⅜ in.	No. 4	No. 8	No. 16	No. 30	No.50	No. 100	No. 200	ASPH
Averages for Day																
Job Mix Formula																

Temperature of Mix, °F

Time								
°Farenheit								

Characteristics of Mix

Sample Location	Time or Load No.	Theoretical Density	Specimen Density	Theoretical Density, %	Stability	Flow .01 inch	Cohesionmeter Value
From Truck							
From Truck							

Weather: a.m. _____ p.m. _____ Temperature: a.m. _____ p.m. _____

Plant Operated: Production: Type of Mix:

From: _____ Tons Previous _____ _____

To _____ Tons Today _____ _____

Tons Total _____

Sample No. _____ Represents _____ Tons of _____ Surface _____ For Dates _____

Sample No. _____ Represents _____ Tons of _____ Surface _____ For Dates _____

Remarks _____

Signed _____

Plant Inspector, Resident Engineer, etc.

D 290

Standard Specification for
Mixing Plants for Hot-Mixed, Hot-Laid Bituminous Paving Mixtures[1]

This standard is issued under the fixed designation D 995; the number immediately following the designation indicates the year of original adoption or, in the case of revision, the year of last revision. A number in parentheses indicates the year of last reapproval. A superscript epsilon (ε) indicates an editorial change since the last revision or reapproval.

This specification has been approved for use by agencies of the Department of Defense. Consult the DoD Index of Specifications and Standards for the specific year of issue which has been adopted by the Department of Defense.

1. Scope

1.1 This specification covers requirements for plants suitable for producing hot-mixed, hot-laid bituminous paving mixtures.

1.2 The values stated in inch-pound units are to be regarded as the standard.

2. Referenced Documents

2.1 *ASTM Standards:*
C 136 Test Method for Sieve Analysis of Fine and Coarse Aggregates[2]
D 8 Terminology Relating to Materials for Roads and Pavements[3]
D 140 Practice for Sampling Bituminous Materials[3]

3. Terminology

3.1 For definitions of terms see Terminology D 8.

3.2 *Descriptions of Terms Specific to This Standard:*

3.2.1 *batch plant, n*—a manufacturing facility for producing bituminous paving mixtures that proportions the aggregate and bituminous constituents into the mix by weighed batches, adds bituminous material by either weight or volume, and mixes the blend.

3.2.2 *continuous mix plant, n*—a manufacturing facility for producing bituminous paving mixtures that continuously proportions the aggregate and bituminous constituents into the mix by a continuous volumetric proportioning system without definite batch intervals.

3.2.3 *drum mix plant, n*—a manufacturing facility for producing bituminous paving mixtures that continuously proportions aggregates, heats and dries them in a rotating drum, and simultaneously mixes them with a controlled amount of bituminous material. The same plant may produce cold-mixed bituminous paving mixtures without heating and drying the aggregates.

4. Requirements for All Plants

4.1 *Uniformity*—The plant shall be capable of uniformly combining and mixing various sizes of aggregate from stockpiles, reclaimed asphalt pavement, if required, and bituminous material.

4.2 *Equipment for Preparation of Bituminous Material:*

4.2.1 Tanks for storage of bituminous material shall be equipped for heating the material, under effective and positive control at all times, to the temperature required in the paving mixture specifications. Heating shall be by steam or oil coils, electricity, or other means such that no flame shall contact the heating tank.

4.2.2 The circulating system for the bituminous material shall be of adequate capacity to provide proper and continuous circulation between storage tank and proportioning units during the entire operating period.

4.2.2.1 The discharge end of the bituminous material circulating pipe shall be kept below the surface of the bituminous material in the storage tank to prevent discharging the hot bituminous material into the open air.

4.2.2.2 All pipe lines and fittings shall be steam or oil-jacketed or otherwise properly insulated to prevent heat loss. When the bituminous material is emulsified asphalt, provisions should be made in the bitumen transfer system that will enable the operator to turn off or reduce the heat media from all lines, pumps, and jacketed bituminous material buckets as soon as the system is open and circulating properly.

4.2.3 Storage tank capacity shall be such as to ensure continuous operation of the plant and uniform temperature of the bituminous material when it is introduced into the aggregate. Tanks shall be calibrated accurately to 100-gal (378.5-L) intervals and shall be accessible for measuring the volume of bituminous material at any time.

4.2.4 A sampling tap, complying with the requirements of Practice D 140, shall be provided in the bituminous material feed lines connecting the storage tanks to the bituminous control unit.

4.2.5 When filled or native bituminous materials are used, means shall be provided for agitation to maintain a uniform product.

4.3 *Mineral Filler*—Adequate dry storage shall be provided for mineral filler, when required, and provision shall be made for accurate proportioning.

4.4 *Cold Aggregate Feeder*—The plant shall be provided with mechanical means for uniformly feeding the aggregates into the dryer so that uniform production and temperature may be assured. When aggregates must be blended from two or more bins at the cold feed to meet the requirements of the

---

[1] This specification is under the jurisdiction of ASTM Committee D-4 on Road and Paving Materials and is the direct responsibility of Subcommittee D04.23 on Plant-Mix Bituminous Surfaces and Bases.
Current edition approved Sept. 10, 1995. Published November 1995. Originally published as D 995 – 48 T. Last previous edition D 995 – 95a.
[2] *Annual Book of ASTM Standards,* Vol 04.02.
[3] *Annual Book of ASTM Standards,* Vol 04.03.

paving mixture specifications, a synchronized proportioning method shall be provided.

4.4.1 If recycling capability is required, the plant shall be equipped with mechanical means for feeding the desired weight of reclaimed asphalt pavement into the mix. Facilities shall be provided for obtaining samples of the reclaimed asphalt pavement.

4.5 *Dryer*—A dryer of satisfactory design capable of drying and heating the aggregate to the moisture and temperature requirements of the paving mixture specifications shall be provided.

4.6 *Bituminous Control Unit:*

4.6.1 Satisfactory means, either by weighing or metering, shall be provided to obtain the proper amount of bituminous material. Accuracy of the metering devices shall be within 1.0 % of the actual weight being measured when that weight has been determined using another measuring device and shall be within 0.5 % when that weight has been determined using test weights. Bituminous material scales shall conform to 8.5.

4.6.2 Suitable means shall be provided, either by steam or oil jacketing, or other insulation, for maintaining the specified temperature of the bituminous material in the pipe lines, meters, weigh buckets, spray bars, and other containers or flow lines.

4.7 *Thermometric Equipment:*

4.7.1 An armored recording thermometer of suitable range shall be fixed in the bituminous material feed line at a suitable location near the discharge at the mixer unit.

4.7.2 Approved recording thermometers, pyrometers, or other recording thermometric instruments shall be fixed at the discharge chute of the dryer and, when applicable, in the hot fines bin to register and record automatically the temperature of the heated aggregate or heated mixture.

4.8 *Emission Controls:*

4.8.1 A dust collecting system shall be provided. The system shall be made to waste the material so collected, or to return all or any part uniformly to the mixture.

4.8.2 Other emissions, such as smoke but excepting water vapor, shall be controlled to be in compliance with applicable limits.

4.9 *Surge and Storage Bins*—If bins are used for surge or storage, they shall be such that mixture drawn from the bin meets the requirements of the paving mixture specification.

4.10 *Safety Requirements:*

4.10.1 Adequate and safe stairways to the mixer platform shall be provided if applicable. Guarded ladders to other plant units shall be located where required.

4.10.2 All gears, pulleys, chains, sprockets, and other dangerous moving parts shall be thoroughly protected.

4.10.3 Ample unobstructed space shall be provided on the mixing platform if applicable.

4.10.4 An unobstructed passage shall be maintained at all times in and around the truck-loading space. This space shall be kept free of drippings from the mixing platform. A ladder or platform shall be located at the truck-loading space to permit easy and safe inspection of the mixture as it is delivered into the trucks. Overhead protection shall be provided where necessary.

5. Significance and Use

5.1 This specification describes the various components of batch, continuous mix, and drum mix plants. This standard is useful to help evaluate existing plants and for specifying new plants to ensure the plant is capable of producing a quality product. This standard does not address plant operation and control or mixture production.

6. Requirements for Plants Controlling Gradation of Hot, Dry Aggregates

6.1 *Plant Screens:*

6.1.1 Plants shall be equipped with plant screens located between the dryer and hot aggregate bins and shall have adequate capacity and size range to separate the heated aggregate into the sizes required for proportioning so that they may be recombined consistently within the specification limits.

6.1.2 The nominal maximum size aggregate in the fines bin shall be specified. The screen type and size shall be determined by the operator. No aggregate shall be larger than the maximum specified.

6.1.3 Control shall be based on frequent bin samples tested in accordance with Test Method C 136. Aggregate in each bin, including mineral filler, shall be combined in proper proportions, and the composite shall be checked for compliance with the paving mixture specifications.

6.2 *Hot Aggregate Bins:*

6.2.1 Hot-bin storage of sufficient capacity to ensure uniform and continuous operation shall be provided. Bins shall be divided into the specified number of compartments arranged to ensure separate and adequate storage of appropriate fractions of the aggregate.

6.2.2 Each compartment shall be provided with an overflow chute of such size and at such a location to prevent any backing up of material into other compartments or into contact with the screen.

6.2.3 Bins shall be equipped with "tell-tale" devices to indicate the position of the aggregate in the bins at the lower quarter points. An automatic plant shut-off shall be provided to operate when any aggregate bin becomes empty.

6.2.4 Adequate and convenient facilities shall be provided for obtaining aggregate samples from each bin.

7. Requirements for Plants Controlling Gradation of Cold, Damp Aggregates

7.1 *Maximum Aggregate Size*—Oversize aggregate shall be rejected by suitable methods or devices before the aggregate enters the cold feed, or by plant screens complying with 6.1.

7.2 *Cold Feed Bins:*

7.2.1 Cold feed bins for storing aggregates prior to proportioning shall be equipped with "tell-tale" devices to indicate the position of the aggregate in the bins at the lower quarter points. An automatic plant shut-off shall be provided to operate when any aggregate bin becomes empty or the flow from any bin gate becomes restricted.

7.2.2 Adequate and convenient facilities shall be provided for obtaining samples of the full flow of aggregate from each cold feed bin and from the total cold feed.

7.2.3 Adequate and convenient facilities shall be provided for diverting aggregate flow into trucks or other suitable

⬡ D 995

containers to check the accuracy of the aggregate delivery system.

7.2.4 Control shall be based on frequent samples from each cold-feed bin and the total cold feed tested by Test Method C 136. Results of total cold-feed samples shall be checked for compliance with the paving mixture specifications.

8. Requirements for Batch Plants

8.1 *Control of Aggregate Gradation*—The plant shall be equipped to control aggregate gradation in accordance with the requirements of either Section 6 or Section 7.

8.2 *Weigh Box or Hopper:*

8.2.1 Means shall be provided for weighing aggregate from each bin into a weigh box or hopper, suspended on scales, and ample in size to hold a full batch.

8.2.2 The weigh box or hopper shall be supported on fulcrums and knife edges that will not easily be thrown out of alignment or adjustment.

8.2.3 Gates, both on the bins and the hopper, shall not leak.

8.3 *Aggregate scales:*

8.3.1 Scales for any weigh box or hopper may be either beam or springless-dial type and shall be of standard make and design. The accuracy of the weighing device shall be within 1.0 % of the actual weight being measured when that weight has been determined using another measuring device and shall be within 0.5 % when that weight has been determined using test weights.

8.3.2 The change in load required to alter noticeably the position of rest of the indicating element (or elements) of a nonautomatic indicating scale shall not be greater than 0.1 % of the nominal scale capacity.

8.3.3 Beam type scales shall be equipped with a device to indicate that the required load is being approached. This device shall indicate at least the last 200 lb (91 kg) of the load.

8.3.4 Graduation intervals for either beam or dial scales shall not be greater than 0.1 % of the nominal scale capacity. Scale graduations and markings shall be plainly visible.

8.3.5 On dial scales, parallax effects shall be reduced to the practical minimum with clearance between the indicator index and scale graduations not exceeding 0.06 in. (1.5 mm).

8.3.6 Scales shall be equipped with adjustable pointers for marking the weight of each material to be weighed into the batch.

8.3.7 Not less than ten test weights, each of 50-lb (22.7-kg) nominal weight and each stamped with its actual weight to within ±0.05 %, shall be provided for the purpose of testing and calibrating the scales. For each scale a suitable cradle or platform shall be provided for applying the test loads. The test weights shall be kept clean and conveniently located for calibration of the scale.

8.4 *Bituminous Material Bucket:*

8.4.1 If a bucket is used, it shall be large enough to handle a batch in a single weighing.

8.4.2 The filling system and bucket shall be of such design, size, and shape that the bituminous material will not overflow, splash, or spill outside the bucket during filling and weighing.

8.4.3 The time required to add the bituminous material shall not exceed 20 s. Where the quantity of bituminous material is metered, provision shall be made to check the delivery of the meter by actual weight.

8.4.4 The bucket shall be steam or oil-jacketed or equipped with properly insulated electric heating units. It shall be arranged to deliver the bituminous material in a thin uniform sheet or in multiple sprays over the full length of the mixer.

8.5 *Bituminous Material Scales*—Scales for the weighing of bituminous material shall meet the requirements for aggregate scales, as specified in 8.3 except a device to indicate at least the last 20 lb (9.1 kg) of the approaching total load shall be provided. Beam-type scales shall be equipped with a tare beam or adequate counterbalance for balancing the bucket and compensating periodically for the accumulation of bituminous material on the bucket.

8.6 *Mixer Unit for Batch Method:*

8.6.1 The plant shall include a batch mixer of an approved twin-shaft pugmill type capable of producing a uniform mixture.

8.6.1.1 The mixer shall be designed to provide means of adjusting the clearance between the mixer blades and liner plates to ensure proper and efficient mixing.

8.6.1.2 If not enclosed, the mixer box shall be equipped with a dust hood to prevent loss of dust by dispersion.

8.6.1.3 The mixer shall be constructed to prevent leakage of the contents.

8.6.1.4 Mixer discharge shall not cause appreciable segregation.

8.6.2 The mixer shall be equipped with a positive means for governing mixing time and an accurate time lock to control the operation of a complete mixing cycle by locking the weigh-box gate after the charging of the mixer until the closing of the mixer gates at the completion of the cycle; it shall lock the bituminous material bucket throughout the dry-mixing period and shall lock the mixer gate throughout the dry- and wet-mixing periods.

8.6.2.1 The dry-mixing period is defined as the interval of time between the opening of the weigh-box gate and the application of bituminous material. The wet-mixing period is the interval of time between the start of the application of bituminous material and the opening of the mixer gate.

8.6.2.2 The timing control shall be flexible and capable of being set at intervals of not more than 5 s throughout cycles up to 3 min.

8.6.2.3 If required by the specifications, a mechanical batch counter shall be installed as part of the timing device and shall be designed to register only completely mixed batches.

8.7 *Automation of Batching:*

8.7.1 If required by the specifications, an automatic weighing, cycling, and monitoring system shall be installed as part of the batching equipment.

8.7.2 The system shall include equipment for accurately proportioning the various components of the mixture by weight or by volume in the proper order, and equipment for controlling the cycle sequence and timing of mixture operations. There shall be auxiliary interlock cut-off circuits to interrupt and stop the automatic batching operations whenever an error exceeding the acceptable tolerance occurs in proportioning.

8.7.3 *Accuracy*—The automatic proportioning system shall be capable of consistently delivering materials within the full range of batch sizes within the following tolerances:

	Total Batch Weight of Paving Mix, %
Batch aggregate component	±1.5
Mineral filler	±0.5
Bituminous material	±0.1
Zero return (aggregate)	±0.5
Zero return (bituminous material)	±0.1

The electrical circuits for the above delivery tolerances of each cut-off interlock shall be capable of providing the total span for the full allowable tolerance for maximum batch size. Tolerance controls shall be automatically or manually adjustable to provide spans suitable for less than full-size batches (Note 1). The automatic controls and interlock cut-off circuits shall be capable of being consistently coordinated with the batching scale or meter within an accuracy of 0.2 % of the nominal capacity (Note 2) of said scale or meter throughout the full range of the batch sizes.

NOTE 1—If separate tolerance controls are not provided for the batching of mineral filler, it will be necessary to reduce the aggregate tolerances to ±0.5 % for those batches requiring mineral filler.

NOTE 2—The term "nominal capacity" of a scale or meter where referred to herein is defined as the maximum quantity which the scale or meter is capable of measuring.

8.8 *Recording of Batching:*

8.8.1 If required by the specifications, an automatic graphic or digital record shall be produced for each batch of bituminous concrete indicating the proportions of each aggregate component, mineral filler, and bituminous material. Such records of the batches shall be further identified through a print of day and date. Bituminous material proportions shall be recorded either as weight or volume. If recorded as volume, the record shall be either in gallons at 60°F (16°C), gallons converted to weight in pounds, or actual gallons with an additional recording of bituminous material temperature.

8.8.2 If a digital tape or ticket recorder is used, it shall record the proportions as indicated on the batching scale or meter within an accuracy of 0.5 % of maximum batch size.

8.8.3 If graphical recording is used, it shall be designed so that the stylus will traverse at least 9 in. (229 mm) of the recorder width for the total aggregate weight and maximum bituminous material weight or volume; the preceding based on maximum batch size.

8.8.3.1 The charts shall be designed so that all quantities, including zero can be read directly and shall have a resolution of at least ten lines per inch. The chart speed shall be such that individual aggregate weights, when batched cumulatively, can be clearly identified.

8.8.3.2 The recorder shall record the proportions as indicated on the batching scale or meter within an accuracy of 0.5 % of the maximum batch size.

9. Requirements for Continuous Mix Plants

9.1 *Control of Aggregate Gradation*—The plant shall be equipped to control aggregate gradation in accordance with the requirements of either Section 6 or Section 7. Accurate means of checking the proportioning of each hot bin size by weight shall be provided.

9.1.1 Hot-aggregate bins shall include interlocked feeders

mounted under the bin compartments. The interlocked feeders shall be equipped with a dust-proof revolution counter with minimum graduations of one tenth of a revolution. The mix proportions shall be set up on the basis of pounds (or kilograms) of each aggregate bin size per revolution.

9.1.2 Each bin shall have a feeder mechanism, subject to control by positive mechanical means, to control the rate of flow of aggregate drawn from each respective bin compartment. Where the gate orifice-type feeder is used, it shall have at least one dimension adjustable by positive mechanical means. Locks shall be provided on each gate. Calibrated gages with minimum graduations of not more than 1/10 in. (2.5 mm) shall be provided for each gate to establish gate openings.

9.1.3 When added mineral filler is specified, a separate bin and feeder shall be furnished with its drive interlocked with the aggregate feeders.

9.1.4 Means shall be provided to establish the rate of flow in pounds (or kilograms) per revolution by scale weight.

9.2 *Weight Calibration of Bituminous Material and Aggregate Feed*—The plant shall include a means of calibrating gate openings and bituminous material flow by means of weight test samples in pounds (or kilograms) per revolution.

9.2.1 The aggregate fed out of the bins through individual orifices shall be bypassed into suitable test boxes, and each compartment material shall be confined in individual test receptacles or compartments.

9.2.2 Accessories shall be supplied so that the aggregate in each compartment may be weighed separately.

9.2.3 Test containers shall be of convenient size to obtain a composite weight at least 600 lb (273 kg).

9.3 *Synchronization of Aggregate and Bituminous Material Feed*—Satisfactory means shall be provided to afford positive interlocking or mechanical control between the flow of aggregate through the gates and the flow of bituminous material through the meter or other proportioning device. Means shall be provided to check the rate of flow of the bituminous material by scale weight per revolution.

9.4 *Mixer Unit for Continuous Method*—The plant shall include a continuous mixer of an approved twin-shaft pugmill-type and shall be capable of producing a uniform mixture within the permissible job mix tolerances.

9.4.1 The paddles shall be adjustable for angular position on the shafts and reversible to retard the flow of the mix.

9.4.2 Mixers shall be equipped with discharge hoppers or other facilities to prevent segregation during discharge.

9.4.3 The mixer shall carry a manufacturer's plate giving the net volumetric contents of the mixer at the several heights, inscribed on a permanent gage.

9.4.4 Charts shall be prepared giving the rate of aggregate feed per revolution and per interval of time at the plant operating speed.

9.4.5 Continous mixers not complying in all respects with the above requirements, but capable of producing a uniform mixture within the job mix tolerances, will be considered for approval and may be approved.

9.4.6 The weight per unit volume relationship of the coated loose mix shall be determined and the pugmill capacity at operating height shall be determined by means of the volume gage on the side of the mixer.

D 995

9.4.7 Positive means for governing mixing time shall be provided. Mixing time shall be determined from the following equation:

$$\text{Mixing time, s} = \frac{\text{pugmill dead capacity, lb(kg)}}{\text{pugmill output, lb(kg)/s}}$$

9.5 *Automation of Continuous Mixing Plants:*

9.5.1 If required by the specifications, devices capable of automatically sampling and weighing the quantity of each hot-bin aggregate size and sampling, weighing, or metering the bituminous material fed to the pugmill during either a known number of revolutions of the plant or a known interval of time shall be installed as part of the plant equipment. In addition, each aggregate hot bin, mineral-filler bin, and the bituminous material feed line shall have interlock circuits such that the plant operations will be stopped if either aggregate or bituminous material flow is discontinued or reduced.

9.5.2 The plant shall proportion each size of aggregate to the pugmill with such accuracy that the weight of material from each hot bin shall not deviate from the design value by an amount more than 1.5 % of the total weight of bituminous paving mixture delivered per revolution or interval of time. Where the separate addition of mineral filler is required, it shall be added so as not to deviate more than 0.5 % of the total weight of bituminous paving mixture per revolution or interval of time. The bituminous material shall be added so as not to deviate more than 0.1 % of the total weight of bituminous paving mixture per revolution or interval of time.

9.5.3 The scales or meters, or both, used to determine the quantities of aggregates and bitumen per revolution or interval of time shall be accurate to within 0.20 % of their nominal capacities. The aggregate sampling device shall have a capacity of at least 1 lb for each ton per hour of plant output capacity or 100 lb (45.3 kg) which ever is greater.

9.6 *Recording of Continuous Plants:*

9.6.1 When required by the specifications, each plant shall have an automatic graphic or digital recorder for recording the weights of samples of each hot-bin aggregate size and bituminous material, either individually or cumulatively. In addition to the recording of sample quantities, the time of sampling identified by a time and date accurate to the nearest minute shall also be recorded.

9.6.2 If a digital tape or ticket recorder is used, it shall be capable of accurately recording weights to 0.1 % of the nominal capacity of the weighing system.

9.6.3 If graphical recording is used, it shall be designed so that the stylus will traverse at least 9 in. (229 mm) of the recorder width for the maximum aggregate sample weight and maximum bituminous material weight. The charts shall be designed so that all quantities, including zero, can be read directly and shall have a resolution of at least 10 lines per inch (25.4 mm). The chart speed shall be such that individual aggregate weights, when batched cumulatively, can be clearly identified.

9.6.4 A digital recorder shall be installed as part of the platform truck scales. The recorder shall produce a printed digital record on a ticket of the gross and tare weights of the delivery trucks along with a time and date print for each ticket. Provisions shall be made so that scales may not be manually manipulated during the printing process. In addition, the system shall be so interlocked as to allow printing only when the scale has come to rest. The scales and recorder shall be of sufficient capacity and size to weigh accurately the heaviest loaded trucks or tractor trailers that are used for the delivery of bituminous paving mixtures from the plant.

10. Requirements for Drum-Mix Plants

10.1 *Control of Aggregate Gradation*—The plant shall be equipped to control aggregate gradation in accordance with the requirements of Section 7.

10.2 *Aggregate Delivery System:*

10.2.1 The total cold aggregate feed shall be weighed continuously by an approved belt scale. The accuracy of the weighing device shall be within 1.0 % of the actual weight being measured when that weight has been determined using another measuring device and shall be within 0.5 % when that weight has been determined using test weights.

10.2.2 Provisions shall be made for introducing the moisture content of the total cold feed into the belt weighing signal and correcting wet aggregate weight to dry aggregate weight.

10.2.3 An automatic digital record of the dry weight of aggregate flow shall be displayed, recorded, and totaled in appropriate units of weight and time at least once every 5 min of plant operation, and on demand, at least once every minute of plant operation for a period of at least 5 min.

10.2.4 When mineral filler is specified, a separate bin and feeder shall be provided with its drive interlocked with the aggregate feeders.

10.3 *Bituminous Material System:*

10.3.1 Satisfactory means shall be provided to assure positive interlock between dry weight of aggregate flow and the flow of bituminous material through an approved meter. The interlock shall be capable of adjusting the flow of bituminous material to compensate for any variation in the dry weight of aggregate flow.

10.3.2 An automatic digital record of the flow of bituminous material shall be displayed, recorded, and totaled in appropriate units of volume or weight and time at least once every 5 min of plant operation, and on demand, at least once every minute of plant operation for a period of at least 5 min. The digital record of bitumen flow shall be coordinated with the digital record of dry aggregate flow at the point at which the bitumen is discharged into the aggregate.

10.4 *Drum-Mix Plant*—The drum-mix plant shall be of satisfactory design, capable of drying and heating the aggregate to the moisture and temperature requirements set forth in the paving mixture specifications, and capable of producing a uniform mixture of aggregates and bituminous material. A surge or storage system complying with 4.9 shall be provided.

11. Keywords

11.1 asphalt plants; batch plants; bituminous mixing plants; bituminous paving mixtures; continuous mix plants; drum mix plants

D 995

ASTM Designation: C 31/C 31M – 95

AMERICAN SOCIETY FOR TESTING AND MATERIALS
100 Barr Harbor Dr., West Conshohocken, PA 19428
Reprinted from the Annual Book of ASTM Standards. Copyright ASTM
If not listed in the current combined index, will appear in the next edition.

Standard Practice for
Making and Curing Concrete Test Specimens in the Field[1]

This standard is issued under the fixed designation C 31/C 31M; the number immediately following the designation indicates the year of original adoption or, in the case of revision, the year of last revision. A number in parentheses indicates the year of last reapproval. A superscript epsilon (ε) indicates an editorial change since the last revision or reapproval.

This practice has been approved for use by agencies of the Department of Defense. Consult the DoD Index of Specifications and Standards for the specific year of issue which has been adopted by the Department of Defense.

1. Scope

1.1 This practice covers procedures for making and curing cylindrical and prismatic beam specimens from representative samples of fresh concrete for a construction project.

1.2 The concrete used to make the molded specimens shall have the same levels of slump, air content, and percentage of coarse aggregate as the concrete it represents. This practice is not satisfactory for making specimens from concretes not having a measurable slump or requiring other sizes and shapes of specimens to represent a product or structure.

1.3 The values stated in either inch-pound units or SI units shall be regarded separately as standard. The SI units are shown in brackets. The values stated may not be exact equivalents; therefore each system must be used independently of the other. Combining values from the two units may result in nonconformance.

1.4 *This standard does not purport to address all of the safety concerns, if any, associated with its use. It is the responsibility of the user of this standard to establish appropriate safety and health practices and determine the applicability of regulatory limitations prior to use.*

2. Referenced Documents

2.1 *ASTM Standards:*
C 138 Test Method for Unit Weight, Yield, and Air Content (Gravimetric) of Concrete[2]
C 143 Test Method for Slump of Hydraulic Cement Concrete[2]
C 172 Practice for Sampling Freshly Mixed Concrete[2]
C 173 Test Method for Air Content of Freshly Mixed Concrete by the Volumetric Method[2]
C 192 Practice for Making and Curing Concrete Test Specimens in the Laboratory[2]
C 231 Test Method for Air Content of Freshly Mixed Concrete by the Pressure Method[2]
C 470 Specification for Molds for Forming Concrete Test Cylinders Vertically[2]

C 511 Specification for Moist Cabinets, Moist Rooms, and Water Storage Tanks Used in the Testing of Hydraulic Cements and Concretes[3]
C 617 Practice for Capping Cylindrical Concrete Specimens[2]
C 1064 Test Method for Temperature of Freshly Mixed Portland-Cement Concrete[2]

2.2 *American Concrete Institute Publication:*[4]
CP-1 Concrete Field Testing Technician, Grade I

3. Significance and Use

3.1 This practice provides standardized requirements for making, curing, protecting, and transporting concrete test specimens under field conditions.

3.2 If the specimens are made and standard cured, as stipulated herein, information may be developed for the following purposes:
3.2.1 Acceptance testing for specified strength,
3.2.2 Checking adequacy of mixture proportions for strength, and
3.2.3 Quality control.

3.3 If the specimens are made and field cured, as stipulated herein, information may be developed to serve as a basis for the following purposes:
3.3.1 Determination of the time the structure may be put in service,
3.3.2 Comparison with standard cured specimens test results or with results from various in-place test methods,
3.3.3 Safety and instructure performance evaluation, or
3.3.4 Form or shoring removal time requirements.

4. Apparatus

4.1 *Molds, General*—Molds for specimens or fastenings thereto in contact with the concrete shall be made of steel, cast iron, or other nonabsorbent material, nonreactive with concrete containing portland or other hydraulic cements. Molds shall hold their dimensions and shape under all conditions of use. Molds shall be watertight during use as judged by their ability to hold water poured into them. Provisions for tests of water leakage are given in the Test Methods for Elongation, Absorption, and Water Leakage section of Specification C 470. A suitable sealant, such as heavy grease, modeling clay, or microcrystalline wax shall be

---

[1] This practice is under the jurisdiction of ASTM Committee C-9 on Concrete and Concrete Aggregates and is the direct responsibility of Subcommittee C09.61 on Testing Concrete for Strength.
Current edition approved Nov. 10, 1995. Published January 1996. Originally published as C 31 – 20. Last previous edition C 31 – 91.
[2] *Annual Book of ASTM Standards*, Vol 04.02.

[3] *Annual Book of ASTM Standards*, Vol 04.01.
[4] Available from American Concrete Institute, P.O. Box 19150, Detroit, MI 48219-0150.

◑ C 31/C 31M

used where necessary to prevent leakage through the joints. Positive means shall be provided to hold base plates firmly to the molds. Reusable molds shall be lightly coated with mineral oil or a suitable nonreactive form release material before use.

4.2 *Cylinder Molds:*

4.2.1 *Molds for Casting Specimens Vertically*—Molds for casting concrete test specimens shall conform to the requirements of Specification C 470.

4.3 *Beam Molds*—Beam molds shall be rectangular in shape and of the dimensions required to produce the specimens stipulated in 5.2. The inside surfaces of the molds shall be smooth. The sides, bottom, and ends shall be at right angles to each other and shall be straight and true and free of warpage. Maximum variation from the nominal cross section shall not exceed 1/8 in. [3 mm] for molds with depth or breadth of 6 in. [150 mm] or more. Molds shall produce specimens not more than 1/16 in. [2 mm] shorter than the required length in accordance with 5.2, but may exceed it by more than that amount.

4.4 *Tamping Rod*—The rod shall be a round, straight steel rod with the tamping end rounded to a hemispherical tip of the same diameter. Both ends may be rounded, if preferred. The dimensions shall conform to those in Table 1.

4.5 *Vibrators*—Internal vibrators may have rigid or flexible shafts, preferably powered by electric motors. The frequency or vibration shall be 7000 vibrations per minute or greater while in use. The outside diameter or side dimension of the vibrating element shall be at least 0.75 in. [20 mm] and not greater than 1.5 in. [40 mm]. The combined length of the shaft and vibrating element shall exceed the maximum depth of the section being vibrated by at least 3 in. [75 mm]. For cylinders, the diameter of the vibrating element must be no more than one fourth the diameter of the cylinder. For beams, the diameter of the vibrating element must be no more than one third the width of the mold. A vibrating-reed tachometer should be used to check the frequency of vibration.

4.6 *Mallet*—A mallet with a rubber or rawhide head weighing 1.25 ± 0.50 lb [0.6 ± 0.2 kg] shall be used.

4.7 *Small Tools*—Tools and items which may be required are shovels, pails, trowels, wood float, metal float, blunted trowels, straightedge, feeler gage, scoops, and rules.

4.8 *Slump Apparatus*—The apparatus for measurement of slump shall conform to the requirements of Test Method C 143.

4.9 *Sampling Receptacle*—The receptacle shall be a suitable heavy gage metal pan, wheelbarrow, or flat, clean nonabsorbent board of sufficient capacity to allow easy remixing of the entire sample with a shovel or trowel.

4.10 *Air Content Apparatus*—The apparatus for measuring air content shall conform to the requirements of Test Methods C 173 or C 231.

5. Testing Requirements

5.1 *Cylindrical Specimens*—Compressive or splitting tensile strength specimens shall be cylinders cast and hardened in an upright position, with a length equal to twice the diameter. The standard specimen shall be the 6 by 12-in. [150 by 300-mm] cylinder when the nominal maximum size of the coarse aggregate does not exceed 2 in. [50 mm] (Notes 1 and 2). When the nominal maximum size of the coarse aggregate does exceed 2 in. [50 mm], either the concrete sample shall be treated by wet sieving as described in Practice C 172 or the diameter of the cylinder shall be at least three times the nominal maximum size of coarse aggregate in the concrete. For acceptance testing for specified strength, cylinders smaller than 6 by 12 in. [150 by 300 mm] shall not be used, unless another size is specified (Note 3).

Note 1—The nominal maximum size is the smallest sieve opening through which the entire amount of aggregate is required to pass.

Note 2—When molds in SI units are required and not available, equivalent inch-pound unit size mold should be permitted.

Note 3—For uses other than acceptance testing for specified strength, a 4 by 8 in. [100 by 200 mm] or 5 by 10 in. [125 by 250 mm] cylinder may be suitable. However, the diameter of any cylinder shall be at least three times the nominal maximum size of the coarse aggregate in the concrete (Note 1). When cylinders smaller than the standard size are used, within-test variability has been shown to be higher but not to a statistically significant degree. The compressive strength results are affected by a number of factors including cylinder size.

5.2 *Rectangular Beam Specimens*—Flexural strength specimens shall be rectangular beams of concrete cast and hardened in the horizontal position. The length shall be at least 2 in. [50 mm] greater than three times the depth as tested. The ratio of width to depth as molded shall not exceed 1.5. The standard beam shall be 6 by 6 in. [150 by 150 mm] in cross section, and shall be used for concrete with nominal maximum size coarse aggregate up to 2 in. [50 mm] (Note 2). When the nominal maximum size of the coarse aggregate exceeds 2 in. [50 mm], the smaller cross sectional dimension of the beam shall be at least three times the nominal maximum size of the coarse aggregate. Unless required by project specifications, beams made in the field shall not have a width or depth of less than 6 in. [150 mm].

5.3 *Field Technicians*—The field technicians making and curing specimens for acceptance testing shall be certified ACI Field Testing Technicians, Grade I or equivalent. Equivalent personnel certification programs shall include both written and performance examinations, as outlined in ACI CP-1.

6. Sampling Concrete

6.1 The samples used to fabricate test specimens under this standard shall be obtained in accordance with Practice C 172 unless an alternative procedure has been approved.

6.2 Record the identity of the sample with respect to the location of the concrete represented and the time of casting.

7. Slump, Air Content, and Temperature

7.1 *Slump*—Measure and record the slump of each batch of concrete from which specimens are made immediately after remixing in the receptacle, as required in Test Method C 143.

TABLE 1   Tamping Rod and Rodding Requirements

Diameter of Cylinder, in. (mm)	Rod Dimensions		Number of Roddings/Layer
	Diameter of Rod, in. (mm)	Length of Rod, in. (mm)	
< 6 (150)	3/8 (10)	12 (300)	25
6 (150)	5/8 (16)	24 (600)	25
8 (200)	5/8 (16)	24 (600)	50
10 (250) (or greater)	5/8 (16)	24 (600)	75

🛈 **C 31/C 31M**

TABLE 2 Specimen Size, Type, and Molding Requirements

Specimen Type and Size, as Depth, in. (mm)	Mode of Consolidation	Number of Layers	Approximate Depth of Layer, in. (mm)
Cylinders:			
12 (300) or less	rodding	3 equal	4 (100) or less
Over 12 (300)	rodding	as required	4 (100) or less
12 (300) or less	vibration	2 equal	6 (150) or less
12 (300) to 18 (450)	vibration	2 equal	half depth of specimen
Over 18 (450)	vibration	3 or more	8 (200) or as near as practicable
Beams:			
6 (150) to 8 (200)	rodding	2 equal	half depth of specimen
Over 8 (200)	rodding	3 or more	4 (100)
6 (150) to 8 (200)	vibration	1	depth of specimen
Over 8 (200)	vibration	2 or more	8 (200) as near as practicable

7.2 *Air Content*—Determine and record the air content in accordance with either Test Method C 173 or Test Method C 231. The concrete used in performing the air content test shall not be used in fabricating test specimens.

7.3 *Temperature*—Determine and record the temperature in accordance with Test Method C 1064.

NOTE 4—Some specifications may require the measurement of the unit weight of concrete. The volume of concrete produced per batch may be desired on some projects. Also, additional information on the air content measurements may be desired. Test Method C 138 is used to measure the unit weight, yield, and gravimetric air content of freshly mixed concrete.

8. Molding Specimens

8.1 *Place of Molding*—Mold specimens promptly on a level, rigid surface, free of vibration and other disturbances, at a place as near as practicable to the location where they are to be stored.

8.2 *Casting Cylinders*—From Tables 1, 2, and 3, determine method of consolidation, the number and approximate depth of the layers and number of roddings per layer. If consolidation is by rodding, select the size of the tamping rod from Table 2. If consolidation is by internal vibration, select the proper vibrator to meet the requirements in 4.5. Select a small tool, such as a scoop, blunted trowel, or shovel, of a size and shape large enough so each amount of concrete obtained from the sampling receptacle will be representative and small enough so concrete is not lost when being placed in the mold. While placing the concrete in the mold, move the small tool around the perimeter of the mold opening to ensure an even distribution of the concrete and minimize segregation. Each layer of concrete shall be consolidated as required. In placing the final layer, add an amount of concrete that will fill the mold after consolidation. Underfilled or overfilled molds shall be adjusted with representative concrete during consolidation of the top layer.

8.3 *Casting Beams*—From Tables 2 and 3 determine the method of consolidation, the approximate depth, and number of layers. If consolidation is by rodding use the ⅝-in. [16-mm] tamping rod. Determine the number of roddings

TABLE 3 Method of Consolidation Requirements

NOTE—Use method of consolidation in Table 3 unless another is specified.

Slump in. (mm)	Method of Consolidation
>3 (75)	rodding
1 to 3 (25 to 75)	rodding or vibration
<1 (25)	vibration

per layer, one for each 2 in.² [14 cm²] of the top surface area of the beam. If consolidation is by internal vibration, select the proper vibrator to meet the requirements in 4.5. Select a small tool, such as a scoop, blunted trowel, or shovel, of the size and shape large enough so each amount of concrete obtained from the sampling receptacle is representative and small enough so concrete is not lost when placed in the mold. While placing the concrete in the mold, move the small tool around the opening to ensure even distribution of the concrete and minimize segregation. Each layer shall be consolidated as required. In placing the final layer, add an amount of concrete that will fill the mold after consolidation. Underfilled or overfilled molds shall be adjusted with representative concrete during consolidation of the top layer.

8.4 *Consolidation*—The methods of consolidation for this practice are rodding or internal vibration.

8.4.1 *Rodding*—Place the concrete in the mold, in the required number of layers of approximately equal volume. Rod each layer with the rounded end of the rod using the required number of roddings. Rod the bottom layer throughout its depth. Distribute the roddings uniformly over the cross section of the mold. For each upper layer allow the rod to penetrate about ½ in. [12 mm] into the underlying layer when the depth of the layer is less than 4 in. [100 mm], and about 1 in. [25 mm] when the depth is 4 in. [100 mm] or more. After each layer is rodded, tap the outsides of the mold lightly 10 to 15 times with the mallet, to close any holes left by rodding and to release any large air bubbles that may have been trapped. Use an open hand to tap light-gage single-use cylinder molds which are susceptible to damage if tapped with a mallet. After tapping, spade the concrete along the sides and ends of beam molds with a trowel or other suitable tool.

8.4.2 *Vibration*—Maintain a uniform time period for duration of vibration for the particular kind of concrete, vibrator, and specimen mold involved. The duration of vibration required will depend upon the workability of the concrete and the effectiveness of the vibrator. Usually sufficient vibration has been applied as soon as the surface of the concrete has become relatively smooth. Continue vibration only long enough to achieve proper consolidation of the concrete. Overvibration may cause segregation. Fill the molds and vibrate in the required number of approximately equal layers. Place all the concrete for each layer in the mold before starting vibration of that layer. In compacting the specimen, the vibrator shall not be allowed to rest on the bottom or sides of the mold. Carefully withdraw the vibrator in such a manner that no air pockets are left in the specimen. When placing the final layer, avoid overfilling by more than ¼ in. [6 mm].

8.4.2.1 *Cylinders*—Use three insertions of the vibrator at different points for each layer. Allow the vibrator to penetrate through the layer being vibrated, and into the layer below, approximately 1 in. [25 mm]. After each layer is vibrated, tap the outsides of the mold lightly 10 to 15 times with the mallet, to close any holes that remain and to release any large air bubbles that may have been trapped. Use an open hand to tap light-gage single-use molds which are susceptible to damage if tapped with a mallet.

8.4.2.2 *Beams*—Insert the vibrator at intervals not exceeding 6 in. [150 mm] along the center line of the long dimension of the specimen. For specimens wider than 6 in., use alternating insertions along two lines. Allow the shaft of the vibrator to penetrate into the bottom layer approximately 1 in. (25 mm). After each layer is vibrated, tap the outsides of the mold lightly 10 to 15 times with the mallet to close any holes left by vibrating and to release any large air bubbles that may have been trapped.

8.5 *Finishing*—After consolidation, strike off excess concrete from the surface and float or trowel as required. Perform all finishing with the minimum manipulation necessary to produce a flat even surface that is level with the rim or edge of the mold and that has no depressions or projections larger than ⅛ in. [3.3 mm].

8.5.1 *Cylinders*—After consolidation, finish the top surfaces by striking them off with the tamping rod where the consistency of the concrete permits or with a wood float or trowel. If desired, cap the top surface of freshly made cylinders with a thin layer of stiff portland cement paste which is permitted to harden and cure with the specimen. See section on Capping Materials of Practice C 617.

8.5.2 *Beams*—After consolidation of the concrete, strike off the top surface to the required tolerance to produce a flat, even surface. A wood float may be used.

8.6 *Identification*—Mark the specimens to positively identify them and the concrete they represent. Use a method that will not alter the top surface of the concrete. Do not mark the removable caps. Upon removal of the molds, mark the test specimens to retain their identities.

9. Curing

9.1 *Protection*—Immediately after finishing, precautions shall be taken to prevent evaporation and loss of water from the specimens. Protect the outside surfaces of cardboard molds from contact with wet burlap or other sources of water. Cardboard molds may expand and damage specimens at an early age if the outside of the mold absorbs water. Cover specimens with a nonabsorbent, nonreactive plate or sheet of impervious plastic. Wet burlap may be used over the plate or plastic sheet to help retard evaporation, but the burlap must not be in contact with the surface of the concrete.

9.2 *Standard Curing*—Standard curing is the curing method used when the specimens are made and cured for the purposes stated in 3.2.

9.2.1 *Storage*—Immediately after finishing move the specimens to an initial curing place for storage (Note 5). If cylinders in the single use molds are moved, lift and support

the cylinders from the bottom of the molds with a large trowel or similar device. If the top surface is marred during movement to place of initial storage, immediately refinish.

9.2.2 *Initial Curing*—After molding, the specimens shall be stored in a temperature range between 60 to 80°F [16 to 27°C] and in a moist environment preventing any loss of moisture up to 48 h (Note 5). At all times the temperature in and between specimens shall be controlled by shielding from direct rays of the sun and radiant heating devices. Specimens that are to be transported to the laboratory for final curing of Section 9.2.3 before 48 h shall remain in the molds in a moist environment, until they are received in the laboratory, demolded and placed in final curing. If specimens are not transported within 48 h, the molds shall be removed within 24 ± 8 h and final curing used until transported (see 10.1).

NOTE 5—It may be necessary to create an environment during initial curing to provide satisfactory moisture and to control the temperature. The specimens may be immersed immediately in saturated limewater, and/or stored in tightly constructed wooden boxes, damp sand pits, temporary buildings at construction sites, under wet burlap, or in heavyweight closed plastic bags. Immersing in saturated limewater is not acceptable for specimens in cardboard or other molds that expand when immersed in water. Other suitable methods may be used provided the foregoing requirements limiting specimen temperature and moisture loss are met. The temperature may be controlled by ventilation, or thermostatically controlled cooling devices, or by heating devices such as stoves, light bulbs, or thermostatically controlled heating elements. Temperature record of the specimens may be established by means of maximum-minimum thermometers. Early age results may be lower when stored near 60°F [16°C] and higher when stored near 80°F [27°C].

9.2.3 *Final Curing:*

9.2.3.1 *Cylinders*—Upon completion of initial curing and within 30 min after removing the molds, store specimens in a moist condition with free water maintained on their surfaces at all times at a temperature of 73 ± 3°F [23 ± 2°C]. Temperatures between 68 and 86°F [20 and 30°C] are permitted for a period not to exceed 3 h immediately prior to test if free moisture is maintained on the surfaces of the specimen at all times, except when capping with sulfur mortar capping compound. When capping with this material, the ends of the cylinder will be dried as described in Practice C 617. Specimens shall not be exposed to dripping or running water. The required moist storage can be obtained by immersion in saturated limewater and may be obtained by storage in a moist room or cabinet meeting the requirements of Specification C 511.

9.2.3.2 *Beams*—Beams are to be cured the same as cylinders (see 9.2.3.1) except for a minimum of 20 h prior to testing, they shall be stored in water saturated with calcium hydroxide at 73 ± 3°F [23 ± 2°C]. Drying of the surfaces of the beam shall be prevented between removal from limewater and completion of testing.

NOTE 6—Relatively small amounts of surface drying of flexural specimens can induce tensile stresses in the extreme fibers that will markedly reduce the indicated flexural strength.

9.3 *Field Curing*—Field curing is the curing method used for the specimens made and cured as stated in 3.3.

9.3.1 *Cylinders*—Store cylinders in or on the structure as near to the point of deposit of the concrete represented as possible. Protect all surfaces of the cylinders from the elements in as near as possible the same way as the formed work. Provide the cylinders with the same temperature and

C 31/C 31M

moisture environment as the structural work. Test the specimens in the moisture condition resulting from the specified curing treatment. To meet these conditions, specimens made for the purpose of determining when a structure may be put in service shall be removed from the molds at the time of removal of form work.

9.3.2 *Beams*—As nearly as practicable, cure beams in the same manner as the concrete in the structure. At the end of 48 ± 4 h after molding, take the molded specimens to the storage location and remove from the molds. Store specimens representing pavements of slabs on grade by placing them on the ground as molded, with their top surfaces up. Bank the sides and ends of the specimens with earth or sand that shall be kept damp, leaving the top surfaces exposed to the specified curing treatment. Store specimens representing structure concrete as near the point in the structure they represent as possible, and afford them the same temperature protection and moisture environment as the structure. At the end of the curing period leave the specimens in place exposed to the weather in the same manner as the structure. Remove all beam specimens from field storage and store in limewater at 73 ± 3°F [23 ± 2°C] for 24 ± 4 h immediately before time of testing to ensure uniform moisture condition from specimen to specimen. Observe the precautions given in 9.2.3.2 to guard against drying between time of removal from curing to testing.

10. Transportation of Specimens to Laboratory

10.1 Prior to transporting, specimens shall be cured and protected as required in Section 9. During transportation, the specimens must be protected with suitable cushioning material to prevent damage from jarring and from freezing temperatures, or moisture loss. Moisture loss may be prevented by wrapping the specimens in plastic or surrounding them with wet sand or wet saw dust. The time for transportation shall not exceed 4 h.

11. Report

11.1 Report the following information to the laboratory that will test the specimens:

11.1.1 Identification number,

11.1.2 Location of concrete represented by the samples,

11.1.3 Date, time and name of individual molding specimens,

11.1.4 Slump, air content, and concrete temperature, test results and results of any other tests on the fresh concrete and any deviations from referenced standard test methods, and

11.1.5 Curing method.

12. Keywords

12.1 beams; casting samples; concrete; curing; cylinders; testing

AMERICAN SOCIETY FOR TESTING AND MATERIALS
1916 Race St. Philadelphia, Pa 19103
Reprinted from the Annual Book of ASTM Standards. Copyright ASTM
If not listed in the current combined index, will appear in the next edition.

Standard Test Method for
Compressive Strength of Cylindrical Concrete Specimens[1]

This standard is issued under the fixed designation C 39; the number immediately following the designation indicates the year of original adoption or, in the case of revision, the year of last revision. A number in parentheses indicates the year of last reapproval. A superscript epsilon (ε) indicates an editorial change since the last revision or reapproval.

This test method has been approved for use by agencies of the Department of Defense. Consult the DoD Index of Specifications and Standards for the specific year of issue which has been adopted by the Department of Defense.

1. Scope

1.1 This test method covers determination of compressive strength of cylindrical concrete specimens such as molded cylinders and drilled cores. It is limited to concrete having a unit weight in excess of 50 lb/ft^3 (800 kg/m^3).

1.2 The values stated in inch-pound units are to be regarded as the standard.

1.3 *This standard does not purport to address all of the safety concerns, if any, associated with its use. It is the responsibility of the user of this standard to establish appropriate safety and health practices and determine the applicability of regulatory limitations prior to use.*

2. Referenced Documents

2.1 *ASTM Standards:*
C 31 Practice for Making and Curing Concrete Test Specimens in the Field[2]
C 42 Test Method for Obtaining and Testing Drilled Cores and Sawed Beams of Concrete[2]
C 192 Practice for Making and Curing Concrete Test Specimens in the Laboratory[2]
C 617 Practice for Capping Cylindrical Concrete Specimens[2]
C 670 Practice for Preparing Precision and Bias Statements for Test Methods for Construction Materials[2]
C 873 Test Method for Compressive Strength of Concrete Cylinders Cast in Place in Cylindrical Molds[2]
C 1077 Practice for Laboratories Testing Concrete and Concrete Aggregates for Use in Construction and Criteria for Laboratory Evaluation[2]
C 1231 Practice for Use of Unbonded Caps in Determination of Compressive Strength of Hardened Concrete Cylinders[2]
E 4 Practices for Force Verification of Testing Machines[3]
E 74 Practice for Calibration of Force-Measuring Instruments for Verifying the Load Indication of Testing Machines[3]
Manual of Aggregate and Concrete Testing[2]
2.2 *American Concrete Institute:*

CP-16 Concrete Laboratory Testing Technician, Grade I.[4]

3. Summary of Test Method

3.1 This test method consists of applying a compressive axial load to molded cylinders or cores at a rate which is within a prescribed range until failure occurs. The compressive strength of the specimen is calculated by dividing the maximum load attained during the test by the cross-sectional area of the specimen.

4. Significance and Use

4.1 Care must be exercised in the interpretation of the significance of compressive strength determinations by this test method since strength is not a fundamental or intrinsic property of concrete made from given materials. Values obtained will depend on the size and shape of the specimen, batching, mixing procedures, the methods of sampling, molding, and fabrication and the age, temperature, and moisture conditions during curing.

4.2 This test method may be used to determine compressive strength of cylindrical specimens prepared and cured in accordance with Practices C 31, C 192, C 617 and C 1231 and Test Methods C 42 and C 873.

4.3 The results of this test method may be used as a basis for quality control of concrete proportioning, mixing, and placing operations; determination of compliance with specifications; control for evaluating effectiveness of admixtures and similar uses.

4.4 The individual who tests concrete cylinders for acceptance testing shall have demonstrated a knowledge and ability to perform the test procedure equivalent to the minimum guidelines for certification of Concrete Laboratory Technician, Level I, in accordance with ACI CP-16.

NOTE 1—The testing laboratory performing this test method should be evaluated in accordance with Practice C 1077.

5. Apparatus

5.1 *Testing Machine*—The testing machine shall be of a type having sufficient capacity and capable of providing the rates of loading prescribed in 7.5.

5.1.1 Verification of calibration of the testing machines in accordance with Practices E 4 is required under the following conditions:

5.1.1.1 After an elapsed interval since the previous verifi-

---

[1] This test method is under the jurisdiction of ASTM Committee C-9 on Concrete and Concrete Aggregates and is the direct responsibility of Subcommittee C09.61 on Testing Concrete for Strength.
Current edition approved Nov. 15, 1994. Published January 1995. Originally published as C 39 – 21 T. Last previous edition C 39 – 93a.
[2] *Annual Book of ASTM Standards*, Vol 04.02.
[3] *Annual Book of ASTM Standards*, Vol 03.01.

[4] Available from American Concrete Institute, P.O. Box 19150, Detroit, MI, 48219-0150.

C 39

cation of 18 months maximum, but preferably after an interval of 12 months,

5.1.1.2 On original installation or relocation of the machine,

5.1.1.3 Immediately after making repairs or adjustments which may in any way affect the operation of the force applying system of the machine or the values displayed on the load indicating system, except for zero adjustments that compensate for the weight of tooling, or specimen, or both, or

5.1.1.4 Whenever there is reason to doubt the accuracy of the results, without regard to the time interval since the last verification.

5.1.2 *Design*—The design of the machine must include the following features:

5.1.2.1 The machine must be power operated and must apply the load continuously rather than intermittently, and without shock. If it has only one loading rate (meeting the requirements of 7.5), it must be provided with a supplemental means for loading at a rate suitable for verification. This supplemental means of loading may be power or hand operated.

NOTE 2—High-strength concrete cylinders rupture more intensely than normal strength cylinders. As a safety precaution, it is recommended that the testing machines should be equipped with protective fragment guards.

5.1.2.2 The space provided for test specimens shall be large enough to accommodate, in a readable position, an elastic calibration device which is of sufficient capacity to cover the potential loading range of the testing machine and which complies with the requirements of Practice E 74.

NOTE 3—The types of elastic calibration devices most generally available and most commonly used for this purpose are the circular proving ring or load cell.

5.1.3 *Accuracy*—The accuracy of the testing machine shall be in accordance with the following provisions:

5.1.3.1 The percentage of error for the loads within the proposed range of use of the testing machine shall not exceed ±1.0 % of the indicated load.

5.1.3.2 The accuracy of the testing machine shall be verified by applying five test loads in four approximately equal increments in ascending order. The difference between any two successive test loads shall not exceed one third of the difference between the maximum and minimum test loads.

5.1.3.3 The test load as indicated by the testing machine and the applied load computed from the readings of the verification device shall be recorded at each test point. Calculate the error, E, and the percentage of error, E_p, for each point from these data as follows:

$$E = A - B$$
$$E_p = 100(A - B)/B$$

where:

A = load, lbf (or N) indicated by the machine being verified, and

B = applied load, lbf (or N) as determined by the calibrating device.

5.1.3.4 The report on the verification of a testing machine shall state within what loading range it was found to conform to specification requirements rather than reporting a blanket acceptance or rejection. In no case shall the loading range be stated as including loads below the value which is 100 times the smallest change of load that can be estimated on the load-indicating mechanism of the testing machine or loads within that portion of the range below 10 % of the maximum range capacity.

5.1.3.5 In no case shall the loading range be stated as including loads outside the range of loads applied during the verification test.

5.1.3.6 The indicated load of a testing machine shall not be corrected either by calculation or by the use of a calibration diagram to obtain values within the required permissible variation.

5.2 The testing machine shall be equipped with two steel bearing blocks with hardened faces (Note 4), one of which is a spherically seated block that will bear on the upper surface of the specimen, and the other a solid block on which the specimen shall rest. Bearing faces of the blocks shall have a minimum dimension at least 3 % greater than the diameter of the specimen to be tested. Except for the concentric circles described below, the bearing faces shall not depart from a plane by more than 0.001 in. (0.025 mm) in any 6 in. (152 mm) of blocks 6 in. in diameter or larger, or by more than 0.001 in. in the diameter of any smaller block; and new blocks shall be manufactured within one half of this tolerance. When the diameter of the bearing face of the spherically seated block exceeds the diameter of the specimen by more than ½ in. (13 mm), concentric circles not more than ¹⁄₃₂ in. (0.8 mm) deep and not more than ³⁄₆₄ in. (1.2 mm) wide shall be inscribed to facilitate proper centering.

NOTE 4—It is desirable that the bearing faces of blocks used for compression testing of concrete have a Rockwell hardness of not less than 55 HRC.

5.2.1 Bottom bearing blocks shall conform to the following requirements:

5.2.1.1 The bottom bearing block is specified for the purpose of providing a readily machinable surface for maintenance of the specified surface conditions (Note 5). The top and bottom surfaces shall be parallel to each other. The block may be fastened to the platen of the testing machine. Its least horizontal dimension shall be at least 3 % greater than the diameter of the specimen to be tested. Concentric circles as described in 5.2 are optional on the bottom block.

5.2.1.2 Final centering must be made with reference to the upper spherical block. When the lower bearing block is used to assist in centering the specimen, the center of the concentric rings, when provided, or the center of the block itself must be directly below the center of the spherical head. Provision shall be made on the platen of the machine to assure such a position.

5.2.1.3 The bottom bearing block shall be at least 1 in. (25 mm) thick when new, and at least 0.9 in. (22.5 mm) thick after any resurfacing operations.

NOTE 5—If the testing machine is so designed that the platen itself can be readily maintained in the specified surface condition, a bottom block is not required.

5.2.2 The spherically seated bearing block shall conform to the following requirements:

5.2.2.1 The maximum diameter of the bearing face of the

suspended spherically seated block shall not exceed the values given below:

Diameter of Test Specimens, in. (mm)	Maximum Diameter of Bearing Face, in. (mm)
2 (51)	4 (102)
3 (76)	5 (127)
4 (102)	6½ (165)
6 (152)	10 (254)
8 (203)	11 (279)

NOTE 6—Square bearing faces are permissible, provided the diameter of the largest possible inscribed circle does not exceed the above diameter.

5.2.2.2 The center of the sphere shall coincide with the surface of the bearing face within a tolerance of ±5 % of the radius of the sphere. The diameter of the sphere shall be at least 75 % of the diameter of the specimen to be tested.

5.2.2.3 The ball and the socket must be so designed by the manufacturer that the steel in the contact area does not permanently deform under repeated use, with loads up to 12 000 psi (82.7 MPa) on the test specimen.

NOTE 7—The preferred contact area is in the form of a ring (described as preferred "bearing" area) as shown on Fig. 1.

5.2.2.4 The curved surfaces of the socket and of the spherical portion shall be kept clean and shall be lubricated with a petroleum-type oil such as conventional motor oil, not with a pressure type grease. After contacting the specimen and application of small initial load, further tilting of the spherically seated block is not intended and is undesirable.

5.2.2.5 If the radius of the sphere is smaller than the radius of the largest specimen to be tested, the portion of the bearing face extending beyond the sphere shall have a thickness not less than the difference between the radius of the sphere and radius of the specimen. The least dimension of the bearing face shall be at least as great as the diameter of the sphere (see Fig. 1).

5.2.2.6 The movable portion of the bearing block shall be held closely in the spherical seat, but the design shall be such

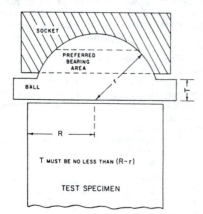

NOTE—Provision shall be made for holding the ball in the socket and for holding the entire unit in the testing machine.

FIG. 1   Schematic Sketch of a Typical Spherical Bearing Block

that the bearing face can be rotated freely and tilted at least 4° in any direction.

5.3 *Load Indication*:

5.3.1 If the load of a compression machine used in concrete testing is registered on a dial, the dial shall be provided with a graduated scale that can be read to at least the nearest 0.1 % of the full scale load (Note 8). The dial shall be readable within 1 % of the indicated load at any given load level within the loading range. In no case shall the loading range of a dial be considered to include loads below the value that is 100 times the smallest change of load that can be read on the scale. The scale shall be provided with a graduation line equal to zero and so numbered. The dial pointer shall be of sufficient length to reach the graduation marks; the width of the end of the pointer shall not exceed the clear distance between the smallest graduations. Each dial shall be equipped with a zero adjustment that is easily accessible from the outside of the dial case, and with a suitable device that at all times until reset, will indicate to within 1 % accuracy the maximum load applied to the specimen.

NOTE 8—As close as can reasonably be read is considered to be ⅟50 in. (0.5 mm) along the arc described by the end of the pointer. Also, one half of a scale interval is about as close as can reasonably be read when the spacing on the load indicating mechanism is between ⅟25 in. (1 mm) and ⅟16 in. (1.6 mm). When the spacing is between ⅟16 in. and ⅛ in. (3.2 mm), one third of a scale interval can be read with reasonable certainty. When the spacing is ⅛ in. or more, one fourth of a scale interval can be read with reasonable certainty.

5.3.2 If the testing machine load is indicated in digital form, the numerical display must be large enough to be easily read. The numerical increment must be equal to or less than 0.10 % of the full scale load of a given loading range. In no case shall the verified loading range include loads less than the minimum numerical increment multiplied by 100. The accuracy of the indicated load must be within 1.0 % for any value displayed within the verified loading range. Provision must be made for adjusting to indicate true zero at zero load. There shall be provided a maximum load indicator that at all times until reset will indicate within 1 % system accuracy the maximum load applied to the specimen.

6. Specimens

6.1 Specimens shall not be tested if any individual diameter of a cylinder differs from any other diameter of the same cylinder by more than 2 %.

NOTE 9—This may occur when single use molds are damaged or deformed during shipment, when flexible single use molds are deformed during molding or when a core drill deflects or shifts during drilling.

6.2 Neither end of compressive test specimens when tested shall depart from perpendicularity to the axis by more than 0.5° (approximately equivalent to ⅛ in. in 12 in. (3 mm in 300 mm)). The ends of compression test specimens that are not planed within 0.002 in. (0.050 mm) shall be capped in accordance with Practice C 617 or they may be sawed or ground to meet that tolerance. The diameter used for calculating the cross-sectional area of the test specimen shall be determined to the nearest 0.01 in. (0.25 mm) by averaging two diameters measured at right angles to each other at about midheight of the specimen.

C 39

6.3 The number of individual cylinders measured for determination of average diameter may be reduced to one for each ten specimens or three specimens per day, whichever is greater, if all cylinders are known to have been made from a single lot of reusable or single-use molds which consistently produce specimens with average diameters within a range of 0.02 in. (0.51 mm). When the average diameters do not fall within the range of 0.02 in. or when the cylinders are not made from a single lot of molds, each cylinder tested must be measured and the value used in calculation of the unit compressive strength of that specimen. When the diameters are measured at the reduced frequency, the cross-sectional areas of all cylinders tested on that day shall be computed from the average of the diameters of the three or more cylinders representing the group tested that day.

6.4 The length shall be measured to the nearest 0.05 D when the length to diameter ratio is less than 1.8, or more than 2.2, or when the volume of the cylinder is determined from measured dimensions.

7. Procedure

7.1 Compression tests of moist-cured specimens shall be made as soon as practicable after removal from moist storage.

7.2 Test specimens shall be kept moist by any convenient method during the period between removal from moist storage and testing. They shall be tested in the moist condition.

7.3 All test specimens for a given test age shall be broken within the permissible time tolerances prescribed as follows:

Test Age	Permissible Tolerance
24 h	± 0.5 h or 2.1 %
3 days	2 h or 2.8 %
7 days	6 h or 3.6 %
28 days	20 h or 3.0 %
90 days	2 days 2.2 %

7.4 *Placing the Specimen*—Place the plain (lower) bearing block, with its hardened face up, on the table or platen of the testing machine directly under the spherically seated (upper) bearing block. Wipe clean the bearing faces of the upper and lower bearing blocks and of the test specimen and place the test specimen on the lower bearing block. Carefully align the axis of the specimen with the center of thrust of the spherically seated block. As the spherically seated block is brought to bear on the specimen, rotate its movable portion gently by hand so that uniform seating is obtained.

7.5 *Rate of Loading*—Apply the load continuously and without shock.

7.5.1 For testing machines of the screw type, the moving head shall travel at a rate of approximately 0.05 in. (1.3 mm)/min when the machine is running idle. For hydraulically operated machines, the load shall be applied at a rate of movement (platen to crosshead measurement) corresponding to a loading rate on the specimen within the range of 20 to 50 psi/s (0.14 to 0.34 MPa/s). The designated rate of movement shall be maintained at least during the latter half of the anticipated loading phase of the testing cycle.

7.5.2 During the application of the first half of the anticipated loading phase a higher rate of loading shall be permitted.

7.5.3 Make no adjustment in the rate of movement of the platen at any time while a specimen is yielding rapidly immediately before failure.

7.6 Apply the load until the specimen fails, and record the maximum load carried by the specimen during the test. Note the type of failure and the appearance of the concrete.

8. Calculation

8.1 Calculate the compressive strength of the specimen by dividing the maximum load carried by the specimen during the test by the average cross-sectional area determined as described in Section 6 and express the result to the nearest 10 psi (69 kPa).

8.2 If the specimen length to diameter ratio is less than 1.8, correct the result obtained in 8.1 by multiplying by the appropriate correction factor shown in the following table:

L/D:	1.75	1.50	1.25	1.00
Factor:	0.98	0.96	0.93	0.87 (Note 10)

NOTE 10—These correction factors apply to lightweight concrete weighing between 100 and 120 lb/ft³ (1600 and 1920 kg/m³) and to normal weight concrete. They are applicable to concrete dry or soaked at the time of loading. Values not given in the table shall be determined by interpolation. The correction factors are applicable for nominal concrete strengths from 2000 to 6000 psi (13.8 to 41.4 MPa).

9. Report

9.1 Report the following information:

9.1.1 Identification number,

9.1.2 Diameter (and length, if outside the range of 1.8D to 2.2D), in inches or millimetres,

9.1.3 Cross-sectional area, in square inches or square centimetres,

9.1.4 Maximum load, in pounds-force or newtons,

9.1.5 Compressive strength calculated to the nearest 10 psi or 69 kPa,

9.1.6 Type of fracture, if other than the usual cone (see Fig. 2),

9.1.7 Defects in either specimen or caps, and,

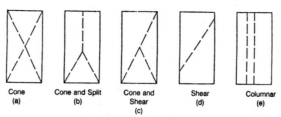

| Cone (a) | Cone and Split (b) | Cone and Shear (c) | Shear (d) | Columnar (e) |

FIG. 2   Sketches of Types of Fracture

C 39

9.1.8 Age of specimen.

10. Precision and Bias

10.1 *Precision*—The single operator precision of tests of individual 6 by 12 in. (150 by 300 mm) cylinders made from a well mixed sample of concrete is given for cylinders made in a laboratory environment and under normal field conditions (see 10.1.1).

	Coefficient of Variation [A]	Acceptable Range of [A]	
		2 results	3 results
Single operator			
Laboratory conditions	2.37 %	6.6 %	7.8 %
Field conditions	2.87 %	8.0 %	9.5 %

[A] These numbers represent respectively the (1s) and (d2s) limits as described in Practice C 670.

10.1.1 The values given are applicable to 6 by 12 in. (150 by 300 mm) cylinders with compressive strength between 2000 and 8000 psi (12 to 55 MPa). They are derived from CCRL concrete reference sample data for laboratory conditions and a collection of 1265 test reports from 225 commercial testing laboratories in 1978.[5]

NOTE 11—Subcommittee C09.03.01 will re-examine recent CCRL Concrete Reference Sample Program data and field test data to see if these values are representative of current practice and if they can be extended to cover a wider range of strengths and specimen sizes.

10.2 *Bias*—Since there is no accepted reference material, no statement on bias is being made.

[5] Research report RR:C09-1006 is on file at ASTM Headquarters.

ASTM Designation: C 78 – 94

AMERICAN SOCIETY FOR TESTING AND MATERIALS
1916 Race St. Philadelphia, Pa 19103
Reprinted from the Annual Book of ASTM Standards. Copyright ASTM
If not listed in the current combined index, will appear in the next edition.

Standard Test Method for
Flexural Strength of Concrete (Using Simple Beam with Third-Point Loading)[1]

This standard is issued under the fixed designation C 78; the number immediately following the designation indicates the year of original adoption or, in the case of revision, the year of last revision. A number in parentheses indicates the year of last reapproval. A superscript epsilon (ϵ) indicates an editorial change since the last revision or reapproval.

This test method has been approved for use by agencies of the Department of Defense. Consult the DoD Index of Specifications and Standards for the specific year of issue which has been adopted by the Department of Defense.

1. Scope

1.1 This test method covers the determination of the flexural strength of concrete by the use of a simple beam with third-point loading.

1.2 The values stated in inch-pound units are to be regarded as the standard. The SI equivalent of inch-pound units has been rounded where necessary for practical application.

1.3 *This standard does not purport to address all of the safety concerns, if any, associated with its use. It is the responsibility of the user of this standard to establish appropriate safety and health practices and determine the applicability of regulatory limitations prior to use.*

2. Referenced Documents

2.1 *ASTM Standards:*

C 31 Practice for Making and Curing Concrete Test Specimens in the Field[2]

C 42 Test Method for Obtaining and Testing Drilled Cores and Sawed Beams of Concrete[2]

C 192 Practice for Making and Curing Concrete Test Specimens in the Laboratory[2]

C 617 Practice for Capping Cylindrical Concrete Specimens[2]

C 1077 Practice for Laboratories Testing Concrete and Concrete Aggregates for Use in Construction and Criteria for Laboratory Evaluation[2]

E 4 Practices for Force Verification of Testing Machines[3]

3. Significance and Use

3.1 This test method is used to determine the flexural strength of specimens prepared and cured in accordance with Test Methods C 42 or Practices C 31 or C 192. Results are calculated and reported as the modulus of rupture. The strength determined will vary where there are differences in specimen size, preparation, moisture condition, curing, or where the beam has been molded or sawed to size.

3.2 The results of this test method may be used to determine compliance with specifications or as a basis for proportioning, mixing and placement operations. It is used in testing concrete for the construction of slabs and pavements (Note 1).

4. Apparatus

4.1 The testing machine shall conform to the requirements of the sections on Basis of Verification, Corrections, and Time Interval Between Verifications of Practices E 4. Hand operated testing machines having pumps that do not provide a continuous loading in one stroke are not permitted. Motorized pumps or hand operated positive displacement pumps having sufficient volume in one continuous stroke to complete a test without requiring replenishment are permitted and shall be capable of applying loads at a uniform rate without shock or interruption.

4.2 *Loading Apparatus*—The third point loading method shall be used in making flexure tests of concrete employing bearing blocks which will ensure that forces applied to the beam will be perpendicular to the face of the specimen and applied without eccentricity. A diagram of an apparatus that accomplishes this purpose is shown in Fig. 1.

4.2.1 All apparatus for making flexure tests of concrete shall be capable of maintaining the specified span length and distances between load-applying blocks and support blocks constant within ±0.05 in. (±1.3 mm).

4.2.2 Reactions shall be parallel to the direction of the applied forces at all times during the test and the ratio of distance between the point of load application and nearest reaction to the depth of the beam shall not be less than one.

4.2.3 If an apparatus similar to that illustrated in Fig. 1 is used: the load-applying and support blocks should not be more than 2½ in. (64 mm) high, measured from the center or the axis of pivot, and should extend entirely across or beyond the full width of the specimen. Each case-hardened bearing surface in contact with the specimen shall not depart from a plane by more than 0.002 in. (0.05 mm) and shall be a portion of a cylinder, the axis of which is coincidental with either the axis of the rod or center of the ball, whichever the block is pivoted upon. The angle subtended by the curved surface of each block should be at least 45° (0.79 rad). The load-applying and support blocks shall be maintained in a vertical position and in contact with the rod or ball by means of spring-loaded screws that hold them in contact with the pivot rod or ball. The uppermost bearing plate and center point ball in Fig. 1 may be omitted when a spherically seated bearing block is used, provided one rod and one ball are used as pivots for the upper load-applying blocks.

---

[1] This test method is under the jurisdiction of ASTM Committee C-9 on Concrete and Concrete Aggregates and is the direct responsibility of Subcommittee C09.61 on Testing Concrete for Strength.

Current edition approved April 15, 1994. Published June 1994. Originally published as C 78 – 30T. Last previous edition C 78 – 84.

[2] *Annual Book of ASTM Standards*, Vol 04.02.

[3] *Annual Book of ASTM Standards*, Vol 03.01.

ⓐ C 78

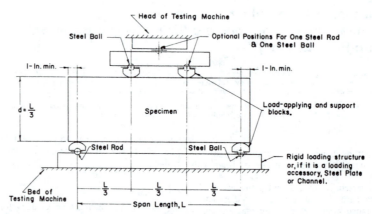

NOTE 1—This apparatus may be used inverted. If the testing machine applies force through a spherically seated head, the center pivot may be omitted, provided one load-applying block pivots on a rod and the other on a ball.
NOTE 2—1 in. = 25.4 mm.

FIG. 1 Diagrammatic View of a Suitable Apparatus for Flexure Test of Concrete by Third-Point Loading Method

5. Testing

5.1 The test specimen shall conform to all requirements of Test Method C 42 or Practices C 31 or C 192 applicable to beam and prism specimens and shall have a test span within 2 % of being three times its depth as tested. The sides of the specimen shall be at right angles with the top and bottom. All surfaces shall be smooth and free of scars, indentations, holes, or inscribed identification marks.

5.2 The technician performing the flexural strength test should be certified as an ACI Technician—Grade II, or by an equivalent written and performance test program.

NOTE 1—The testing laboratory performing this test method may be evaluated in accordance with Practice C 1077.

6. Procedure

6.1 Flexural tests of moist-cured specimens shall be made as soon as practical after removal from moist storage. Surface drying of the specimen results in a reduction in the measured flexural strength.

6.2 When using molded specimens, turn the test specimen on its side with respect to its position as molded and center it on the support blocks. When using sawed specimens, position the specimen so that the tension face corresponds to the top or bottom of the specimen as cut from the parent material. Center the loading system in relation to the applied force. Bring the load-applying blocks in contact with the surface of the specimen at the third points and apply a load of between 3 and 6 % of the estimated ultimate load. Using 0.004 in. (0.10 mm) and 0.015 in. (0.38 mm) leaf-type feeler gages, determine whether any gap between the specimen and the load-applying or support blocks is greater or less than each of the gages over a length of 1 in. (25 mm) or more. Grind, cap, or use leather shims on the specimen contact surface to eliminate any gap in excess of 0.004 in. (0.10 mm) in width. Leather shims shall be of uniform ¼ in. (6.4 mm) thickness, 1 to 2 in. (25 to 50 mm) width, and shall extend across the full width of the specimen. Gaps in excess of 0.015 in. (0.38 mm) shall be eliminated only by capping or

grinding. Grinding of lateral surfaces should be minimized inasmuch as grinding may change the physical characteristics of the specimens. Capping shall be in accordance with the applicable sections of Practice C 617.

6.3 Load the specimen continuously and without shock. The load shall be applied at a constant rate to the breaking point. Apply the load at a rate that constantly increases the extreme fiber stress between 125 and 175 psi/min (0.86 and 1.21 MPa/min), when calculated in accordance with 8.1, until rupture occurs.

7. Measurement of Specimens After Test

7.1 Take three measurements across each dimension (one at each edge and at the center) to the nearest 0.05 in. (1 mm) to determine the average width, average depth, and line of fracture location of the specimen at the section of failure. If fracture occurs at a capped section, include the cap thickness in measurement.

8. Calculation

8.1 If the fracture initiates in the tension surface within the middle third of the span length, calculate the modulus of rupture as follows:

$$R = Pl/bd^2$$

where:
R = modulus of rupture, psi, or MPa,
P = maximum applied load indicated by the testing machine, lbf, or N,
l = span length, in., or mm,
b = average width of specimen, in., or mm, at the fracture, and
d = average depth of specimen, in., or mm, at the fracture.

NOTE 2—The weight of the beam is not included in the above calculation.

8.2 If the fracture occurs in the tension surface outside of the middle third of the span length by not more than 5 % of the span length, calculate the modulus of rupture as follows:

C 78

$$R = 3Pa/bd^2$$

where:

a = average distance between line of fracture and the nearest support measured on the tension surface of the beam, in., (or mm).

NOTE 3—The weight of the beam is not included in the above calculation.

8.3 If the fracture occurs in the tension surface outside of the middle third of the span length by more than 5 % of the span length, discard the results of the test.

9. Report

9.1 Report the following information:

9.1.1 Identification number,

9.1.2 Average width to the nearest 0.05 in. (1 mm),

9.1.3 Average depth to the nearest 0.05 in. (1 mm),

9.1.4 Span length in inches (or millimeters),

9.1.5 Maximum applied load in pound-force (or newtons),

9.1.6 Modulus of rupture calculated to the nearest 5 psi (0.05 MPa),

9.1.7 Curing history and apparent moisture condition of the specimens at the time of test,

9.1.8 If specimens were capped, ground, or if leather shims were used,

9.1.9 Whether sawed or molded and defects in specimens, and

9.1.10 Age of specimens.

10. Precision and Bias

10.1 *Precision*—The coefficient of variation of test results has been observed to be dependent on the strength level of the beams.[4] The single operator coefficient of variation has been found to be 5.7 %. Therefore, results of two properly conducted tests by the same operator on beams made from the same batch sample should not differ from each other by more than 16 %. The multilaboratory coefficient of variation has been found to be 7.0 %. Therefore, results of two different laboratories on beams made from the same batch sample should not differ from each other by more than 19 %.

10.2 *Bias*—Since there is no accepted standard for determining bias in this test method, no statement on bias is made.

11. Keywords

11.1 beams; concrete; flexural strength testing; modulus of rupture

---

[4] See "Improved Concrete Quality Control Procedures Using Third Point Loading" by P. M. Carrasquillo and R. L. Carrasquillo, Research Report 119-1F, Project 3-9-87-1119, Center For Transportation Research, The University of Texas at Austin, November 1987, for possible guidance as to the relationship of strength and variability.

ASTM Designation: C 94 – 96

AMERICAN SOCIETY FOR TESTING AND MATERIALS
100 Barr Harbor Dr., West Conshohocken, PA 19428
Reprinted from the Annual Book of ASTM Standards. Copyright ASTM
If not listed in the current combined index, will appear in the next edition.

Standard Specification for Ready-Mixed Concrete[1]

This standard is issued under the fixed designation C 94; the number immediately following the designation indicates the year of original adoption or, in the case of revision, the year of last revision. A number in parentheses indicates the year of last reapproval. A superscript epsilon (ϵ) indicates an editorial change since the last revision or reapproval.

This specification has been approved for use by agencies of the Department of Defense. Consult the DoD Index of Specifications and Standards for the specific year of issue which has been adopted by the Department of Defense.

1. Scope

1.1 This specification covers ready-mixed concrete manufactured and delivered to a purchaser in a freshly mixed and unhardened state as hereinafter specified. Requirements for quality of concrete shall be either as hereinafter specified or as specified by the purchaser. In any case where the requirements of the purchaser differ from these in this specification, the purchaser's specification shall govern. This specification does not cover the placement, consolidation, curing, or protection of the concrete after delivery to the purchaser.

1.2 The values stated in inch-pound units are to be regarded as the standard. The values in parentheses are for information only.

1.3 As used throughout this specification the manufacturer shall be the contractor, subcontractor, supplier, or producer who furnishes the ready-mixed concrete. The purchaser shall be the owner or representative thereof.

2. Referenced Documents

2.1 *ASTM Standards:*

C 31 Practice for Making and Curing Concrete Test Specimens in the Field[2]

C 33 Specification for Concrete Aggregates[2]

C 39 Test Method for Compressive Strength of Cylindrical Concrete Specimens[2]

C 109 Test Method for Compressive Strength of Hydraulic Cement Mortars (Using 2-in. or 50-mm Cube Specimens)[3]

C 138 Test Method for Unit Weight, Yield, and Air Content (Gravimetric) of Concrete[2]

C 143 Test Method for Slump of Hydraulic Cement Concrete[2]

C 150 Specification for Portland Cement[3]

C 172 Practice for Sampling Freshly Mixed Concrete[2]

C 173 Test Method for Air Content of Freshly Mixed Concrete by the Volumetric Method[2]

C 191 Test Method for Time of Setting of Hydraulic Cement by Vicat Needle[3]

C 231 Test Method for Air Content of Freshly Mixed Concrete by the Pressure Method[2]

C 260 Specification for Air-Entraining Admixtures for Concrete[2]

C 330 Specification for Lightweight Aggregates for Structural Concrete[2]

C 494 Specification for Chemical Admixtures for Concrete[2]

C 567 Test Method for Unit Weight of Structural Lightweight Concrete[2]

C 595 Specification for Blended Hydraulic Cements[3]

C 618 Specification for Fly Ash and Raw or Calcined Natural Pozzolan for Use as a Mineral Admixture in Portland Cement Concrete[2]

C 989 Specification for Ground Granulated Blast-Furnace Slag for Use in Concrete and Mortars[2]

C 1017 Specification for Chemical Admixtures for Use in Producing Flowing Concrete[2]

C 1064 Test Method for Temperature of Freshly Mixed Portland-Cement Concrete[2]

C 1077 Practice for Laboratories Testing Concrete and Concrete Aggregates for Use in Construction and Criteria for Laboratory Evaluation[2]

D 512 Test Methods for Chloride Ion in Water[4]

D 516 Test Method for Sulfate Ion in Water[4]

2.2 *American Concrete Institute Standards:*[6]

CP-1 Technician Workbook for ACI Certification of Concrete Field Testing Technician–Grade I

211.1 Recommended Practice for Selecting Proportions for Normal and Heavyweight Concrete

211.2 Recommended Practice for Selecting Proportions for Structural Lightweight Concrete

301 Specifications for Structural Concrete for Buildings

305R Hot Weather Concreting

306R Cold Weather Concreting

318 Commentary on Building Code Requirements for Reinforced Concrete

2.3 *National Institute of Standards and Technology Document:*[7]

Handbook 44 Specifications, Tolerances, and other Technical Requirements for Commercial Weighing and Measuring Devices

2.4 *Other Documents:*

Bureau of Reclamation Concrete Manual[7]

---

[1] This specification is under the jurisdiction of ASTM Committee C-9 on Concrete and Concrete Aggregates and is the direct responsibility of Subcommittee C09.40 on Ready-Mixed Concrete.

Current edition approved March 10, 1996. Published April 1996. Originally published as C 94 – 33 T. Last previous edition C 94 – 95.

[2] *Annual Book of ASTM Standards*, Vol 04.02.

[3] *Annual Book of ASTM Standards*, Vol 04.01.

[4] *Annual Book of ASTM Standards*, Vol 11.01.

[5] *Annual Book of ASTM Standards*, Vol 14.02.

[6] Available from American Concrete Institute, P.O. Box 19150, Detroit, MI 48219.

[7] Available from Superintendent of Documents, U. S. Government Printing Office, Washington, DC 20402.

C 94

AASHTO T 26 Method of Test for Quality of Water to be Used in Concrete[8]

3. Basis of Purchase

3.1 The basis of purchase shall be the cubic yard or cubic metre of freshly mixed and unhardened concrete as discharged from the mixer.

3.2 The volume of freshly mixed and unhardened concrete in a given batch shall be determined from the total weight of the batch divided by the unit weight of the concrete. The total weight of the batch shall be calculated either as the sum of the weights of all materials, including water, entering the batch or as the net weight of the concrete in the batch as delivered. The unit weight shall be determined in accordance with Test Method C 138 from the average of at least three measurements, each on a different sample using a ½-ft^3 (14 dm^3) container. Each sample shall be taken from the midpoint of each of three different truck loads by the procedure outlined in Practice C 172.

NOTE 1—It should be understood that the volume of hardened concrete may be, or appear to be, less than expected due to waste and spillage, over-excavation, spreading forms, some loss of entrained air, or settlement of wet mixtures, none of which are the responsibility of the producer.

4. Materials

4.1 In the absence of designated applicable specifications covering requirements for quality of materials, the following specifications shall govern:

4.1.1 *Cement*—Cement shall conform to Specification C 150 or Specification C 595. The purchaser should specify the type or types required, but if no type is specified, the requirements of Type I as prescribed in Specification C 150 shall apply.

NOTE 2—These different cements will produce concretes of different properties and should not be used interchangeably.

4.1.2 *Aggregates*—Aggregates shall conform to Specification C 33 or Specification C 330 if lightweight concrete is specified by the purchaser.

4.1.3 *Water:*

4.1.3.1 The mixing water shall be clear and apparently clean. If it contains quantities of substances which discolor it or make it smell or taste unusual or objectionable or cause suspicion, it shall not be used unless service records of concrete made with it or other information indicates that it is not injurious to the quality of the concrete. Water of questionable quality shall be subject to the acceptance criteria of Table 1.

4.1.3.2 Wash water from mixer washout operations may be used for mixing concrete provided tests of wash water comply with the physical test limits of Table 1. Wash water shall be tested at a weekly interval for approximately 4 weeks, and thereafter at a monthly interval provided no single test exceeds the applicable limit (Note 3). Optional chemical limits in Table 2 may be specified by the purchaser when appropriate for the construction. The testing frequency

for chemical limits should be as given above or as specified by the purchaser.

NOTE 3—When recycled wash water is used, attention should be given to effects on the dosage rate and batching sequence of air-entraining and other chemical admixtures, and a uniform amount should be used in consecutive batches.

4.1.4 *Mineral Admixtures*—Fly ash and raw or calcined natural pozzolan shall conform to Specification C 618 as applicable.

4.1.5 *Ground Granulated Blast-Furnace Slag*—Ground granulated blast furnace slag shall conform to Specification C 989.

4.1.6 *Air-Entraining Admixtures*—Air-entraining admixtures shall conform to Specification C 260. (Note 4)

4.1.7 *Chemical Admixtures*—Chemical admixtures shall conform to either Specification C 494 or C 1017 as applicable. (Note 4)

NOTE 4—In any given instance, the required dosage of air-entraining, accelerating, and retarding admixtures may vary. Therefore, a range of dosages should be allowed which will permit obtaining the desired effect.

5. Ordering Information

5.1 In the absence of designated applicable general specifications, the purchaser shall specify the following:

5.1.1 Designated size, or sizes, of coarse aggregate,

5.1.2 Slump, or slumps, desired at the point of delivery (see Section 6 for acceptable tolerances),

5.1.3 When air-entrained concrete is specified, the air content of the samples taken at the point of discharge from the transportation unit (see Section 7 and Table 3 for the total air content and tolerances) (Note 5),

5.1.4 Which of Options A, B, or C shall be used as a basis for determining the proportions of the concrete to produce the required quality, and

5.1.5 When structural lightweight concrete is specified, the unit weight as wet weight, air-dry weight, or oven-dry weight (Note 6).

NOTE 5—In selecting the specified air content, the purchaser should consider the exposure conditions to which the concrete will be subjected. Air contents less than shown in Table 3 may not give the required resistance to freezing and thawing, which is the primary purpose of air-entrained concrete. Air contents higher than the levels shown may reduce strength without contributing any further improvement of durability.

NOTE 6—The unit weight of fresh concrete, which is the only unit weight determinable at the time of delivery, is always higher than the air-dry or oven-dry weight. Definitions of, and methods for determining or calculating air-dry and oven-dry weights, are covered by Test Method C 567.

5.1.6 The purchaser shall ensure that the manufacturer is provided copies of all reports of tests performed on concrete samples taken to determine compliance with specification requirements. Reports shall be provided on a timely basis.

5.2 *Option A:*

5.2.1 When the purchaser requires the manufacturer to assume full responsibility for the selection of the proportions for the concrete mixture (Note 7), the purchaser shall also specify the following:

5.2.1.1 Requirements for compressive strength as determined on samples taken from the transportation unit at the point of discharge evaluated in accordance with Section 17.

---

[8] Available from the American Association of State Highway and Transportation Officials, 444 N. Capitol St., NW, Suite 225, Washington, DC 20001.

(ASTM) **C 94**

TABLE 1   Acceptance Criteria for Questionable Water Supplies

	Limits	Test Method
Compressive strength, min % control at 7 days	90	C 109 [A]
Time of set, deviation from control, h: min	from 1:00 early to 1:30 later	C 191 [A]

[A] Comparisons shall be based on fixed proportions and the same volume of test water compared to control mix using city water or distilled water.

TABLE 2   Optional Chemical Limits for Wash Water

	Limits	Test Method [A]
Chemical requirements, maximum concentration in mixing water, ppm [B]		
Chloride as Cl, ppm:		D 512
Prestressed concrete or in bridge decks	500 [C]	
Other reinforced concrete in moist environments or containing aluminum embedments or dissimilar metals or with stay-in-place galvanized metal forms	1000 [C]	
Sulfate as SO₄, ppm	3000	D 516
Alkalies as (Na₂O + 0.658 K₂O), ppm	600	
Total solids, ppm	50 000	AASHTO T26

[A] Other test methods that have been demonstrated to yield comparable results may be used.

[B] Wash water reused as mixing water in concrete may exceed the listed concentrations if it can be shown that the concentration calculated in the total mixing water, including mixing water on the aggregates and other sources does not exceed the stated limits.

[C] For conditions allowing use of CaCl₂ accelerator as an admixture, the chloride limitation may be waived by the purchaser.

The purchaser shall specify the requirements in terms of the compressive strength of standard specimens cured under standard laboratory conditions for moist curing (see Section 19). Unless otherwise specified the age at test shall be 28 days.

NOTE 7—The purchaser, in selecting requirements for which he assumes responsibility should give consideration to requirements for workability, placeability, durability, surface texture, and density, in addition to those for structural design. The purchaser is referred to American Concrete Institute Standard 211.1 and American Concrete Institute Standard 211.2 for the selection of proportions that will result in concrete suitable for various types of structures and conditions of exposure. The water-cement ratio of most structural lightweight concretes cannot be determined with sufficient accuracy for use as a specification basis.

5.2.2 At the request of the purchaser, the manufacturer shall, prior to the actual delivery of the concrete, furnish a statement to the purchaser, giving the dry weights of cement and saturated surface-dry-weights of fine and coarse aggregate and quantities, type, and name of admixtures (if any) and of water per cubic yard or cubic metre of concrete that will be used in the manufacture of each class of concrete ordered by the purchaser. He shall also furnish evidence satisfactory to the purchaser that the materials to be used and proportions selected will produce concrete of the quality specified.

5.3 *Option B:*

5.3.1 When the purchaser assumes responsibility for the proportioning of the concrete mixture, he shall also specify the following:

5.3.1.1 Cement content in bags or pounds per cubic yard of concrete, or equivalent units,

5.3.1.2 Maximum allowable water content in gallons per cubic yard of concrete, or equivalent units, including surface moisture on the aggregates, but excluding water of absorption (Note 7), and

5.3.1.3 If admixtures are required, the type, name, and dosage to be used. The cement content shall not be reduced

when admixtures are used under this option without the written approval of the purchaser.

5.3.2 At the request of the purchaser, the manufacturer shall, prior to the actual delivery of the concrete, furnish a statement to the purchaser giving the sources, specific gravities, and sieve analyses of the aggregates and the dry weights of cement and saturated-surface-dry weights of fine and coarse aggregate and quantities, type and name of admixture (if any) and of water per cubic yard or cubic metre of concrete that will be used in the manufacture of each class of concrete ordered by the purchaser.

5.4 *Option C:*

5.4.1 When the purchaser requires the manufacturer to assume responsibility for the selection of the proportions for the concrete mixture with the minimum allowable cement content specified (Note 8), the purchaser shall also specify the following:

5.4.1.1 Required compressive strength as determined on samples taken from the transportation unit at the point of discharge evaluated in accordance with Section 17. The purchaser shall specify the requirements for strength in terms of tests of standard specimens cured under standard laboratory conditions for moist curing (see Section 19). Unless otherwise specified the age at test shall be 28 days.

5.4.1.2 Minimum cement content in bags or pounds per cubic yard or kilograms per cubic metre of concrete.

5.4.1.3 If admixtures are required, the type, name, and dosage to be used. The cement content shall not be reduced when admixtures are used.

NOTE 8—Option C can be distinctive and useful only if the designated minimum cement content is at about the same level that would ordinarily be required for the strength, aggregate size, and slump specified. At the same time, it must be an amount that will be sufficient to ensure durability under expected service conditions, as well as satisfactory surface texture and density, in the event specified strength is attained with it. For additional information refer to ACI Standards 211.1 and 211.2 referred to in Note 7.

5.4.2 At the request of the purchaser, the manufacturer

C 94

TABLE 3   Recommended Total Air Content for Air-Entrained Concrete[A,C]

Exposure Condition[B]	Total Air Content, %						
	Nominal Maximum Sizes of Aggregate, in. (mm)						
	3/8 (9.5)	1/2 (12.5)	3/4 (19.0)	1 (25.0)	1 1/2 (37.5)	2 (50.0)	3 (75.0)
Mild	4.5	4.0	3.5	3.0	2.5	2.0	1.5
Moderate	6.0	5.5	5.0	4.5	4.5	4.0	3.5
Severe	7.5	7.0	6.0	6.0	5.5	5.0	4.5

[A] For air-entrained concrete, when specified.
[B] For description of exposure conditions, refer to ACI 211.1, Section 6.3.3, with attention to accompanying footnotes.
[C] Unless exposure conditions dictate otherwise, air contents recommended above may be reduced by up to 1 % for concretes with specified compressive strength, f'_c, of 5000 psi (34.5 MPa) or above.

shall, prior to the actual delivery of the concrete, furnish a statement to the purchaser, giving the dry weights of cement and saturated surface-dry weights of fine and coarse aggregate and quantities, type, and name of admixture (if any) and of water per cubic yard or cubic metre of concrete that will be used in the manufacture of each class of concrete ordered by the purchaser. He shall also furnish evidence satisfactory to the purchaser that the materials to be used and proportions selected will produce concrete of the quality specified. Whatever strengths are attained the quantity of cement used shall not be less than the minimum specified.

5.5 The proportions arrived at by Options A, B, C for each class of concrete and approved for use in a project shall be assigned a designation to facilitate identification of each concrete mixture delivered to the project. This is the designation required in 16.1.7 and supplies information on concrete proportions when they are not given separately on each delivery ticket as outlined in 16.2. A certified copy of all proportions as established in Options A, B, or C shall be on file at the batch plant.

6. Tolerances in Slump

6.1 Unless other tolerances are included in the project specifications, the following shall apply.

6.1.1 When the project specifications for slump are written as a "maximum" or "not to exceed" requirement:

Specified slump:		
	If 3 in. (76 mm) or less	If more than 3 in. (76 mm)
Plus tolerance:	0	0
Minus tolerance:	1 1/2 in. (38 mm)	2 1/2 in. (63 mm)

This option is to be used only if one addition of water is permitted on the job provided such addition does not increase the water-cement ratio above the maximum permitted by the specifications.

6.1.2 When the project specifications for slump are *not* written as a "maximum" or "not to exceed" requirement:

Tolerances for Nominal Slumps

For Specified Slump of:	Tolerance
2 in. (51 mm) and less	±1/2 in. (13 mm)
More than 2 in. through 4 in. (51 to 102 mm)	±1 in. (25 mm)
More than 4 in. (102 mm)	±1 1/2 in. (38 mm)

6.2 Concrete shall be available within the permissible range of slump for a period of 30 min starting either on arrival at the job site or after the initial slump adjustment permitted in 11.7, whichever is later. The first and last 1/4 yd³ or 1/4 m³ discharged are exempt from this requirement. If the

user is unprepared for discharge of the concretes from the vehicle, the producer shall not be responsible for the limitation of minimum slump after 30 min have elapsed starting either on arrival of the vehicle at the prescribed destination or at the requested delivery time, whichever is later.

7. Air-Entrained Concrete

7.1 When air-entrained concrete is desired the purchaser shall specify the total air content of the concrete. See Table 3 for recommended total air contents (Note 4).

7.2 The air content of air-entrained concrete when sampled from the transportation unit at the point of discharge shall be within a tolerance of ± 1.5 of the specified value.

8. Measuring Materials

8.1 Except as otherwise specifically permitted, cement shall be measured by weight. When mineral admixtures (including ground granulated blast furnace slag, fly ash, silica fume, or other pozzolans) are specified in the concrete proportions, they may be weighed cumulatively with cement, but in a weigh hopper and on a scale which is separate and distinct from those used for other materials. Cement shall be weighed before mineral admixtures. When the quantity of cement exceeds 30 % of the full capacity of the scale, the quantity of the cement shall be within ±1 % of the required weight, and the cumulative quantity of cement plus mineral admixtures shall also be within ±1 % of the required weight. For smaller batches to a minimum of 1 yd³ (1 m³), the quantity of the cement and the cumulative quantity of cement plus mineral admixture used shall be not less than the required amount nor more than 4 % in excess. Under special circumstances approved by the purchaser, cement may be measured in bags of standard weight (Note 9). No fraction of a bag of cement shall be used unless weighed.

NOTE 9—In the United States the standard weight of a bag of portland cement is 94 lb (42.6 kg) ±3 %.

8.2 Aggregate shall be measured by weight. Batch weights shall be based on dry materials and shall be the required weights of dry materials plus the total weight of moisture (both absorbed and surface) contained in the aggregate. The quantity of aggregate used in any batch of concrete as indicated by the scale shall be within ±2 % of the required weight when weighed in individual aggregate weigh batchers. In a cumulative aggregate weigh batcher, the cumulative weight after each successive weighing shall be within ±1 % of the required cumulative amount up to that point when the scale is used in excess of 30 % of its capacity. For cumulative weights for less than 30 % of scale capacity, the tolerance shall be ±0.3 % of scale capacity or ±3 % of the required cumulative weight, whichever is less.

8.3 Mixing water shall consist of water added to the batch, ice added to the batch, water occurring as surface moisture on the aggregates, and water introduced in the form of admixtures. The added water shall be measured by weight or volume to an accuracy of 1 % of the required total mixing water. Added ice shall be measured by weight. In the case of truck mixers, any wash water retained in the drum for use in the next batch of concrete shall be accurately measured; if this proves impractical or impossible the wash water shall be discharged prior to loading the next batch of concrete. Total water (including any wash water) shall be measured or weighed to an accuracy of ±3 % of the specified total amount.

8.4 Powdered admixtures shall be measured by weight, and paste or liquid admixtures by weight or volume. Accuracy of weighing admixtures shall be within ±3 % of the required weight. Volumetric measurement shall be within an accuracy of ±3 % of the total amount required or plus and minus the volume of dose required for one sack of cement, whichever is greater.

NOTE 10—Admixture dispensers of the mechanical type capable of adjustment for variation of dosage, and of simple calibration, are recommended.

9. Batching Plant

9.1 Bins with adequate separate compartments shall be provided in the batching plant for fine and for each required size of coarse aggregate. Each bin compartment shall be designed and operated so as to discharge efficiently and freely, with minimum segregation, into the weighing hopper. Means of control shall be provided so that, as the quantity desired in the weighing hopper is approached, the material may be shut off with precision. Weighing hoppers shall be constructed so as to eliminate accumulations of tare materials and to discharge fully.

9.2 Indicating devices shall be in full view and near enough to be read accurately by the operator while charging the hopper. The operator shall have convenient access to all controls.

9.3 Scales shall be considered accurate when at least one static load test within each quarter of the scale capacity can be shown to be within ±0.4 % of the total capacity of the scale.

9.4 Scales for batching concrete ingredients shall meet the accuracy criterion of 9.3 and conform to the applicable sections of the current edition of the National Institute of Standards and Technology Handbook 44.

9.5 Adequate standard test weights shall be available for checking accuracy. All exposed fulcrums, clevises, and similar working parts of scales shall be kept clean. Beam scales shall be equipped with a balance indicator sensitive enough to show movement when a weight equal to 0.1 % of the nominal capacity of the scale is placed in the batch hopper. Pointer travel shall be a minimum of 5 % of the net-rated capacity of the largest weigh beam for underweight and 4 % for overweight.

9.6 The device for the measurement of the added water shall be capable of delivering to the batch the quantity required within the accuracy required in 8.3. The device

shall be so arranged that the measurements will not be affected by variable pressures in the water supply line. Measuring tanks shall be equipped with outside taps and valves to provide for checking their calibration unless other means are provided for readily and accurately determining the amount of water in the tank.

NOTE 11—The scale accuracy limitations of the National Ready Mixed Concrete Association Plant Certification meet the requirements of this specification.

10. Mixers and Agitators

10.1 Mixers may be stationary mixers or truck mixers. Agitators may be truck mixers or truck agitators.

10.1.1 Stationary mixers shall be equipped with a metal plate or plates on which are plainly marked the mixing speed of the drum or paddles, and the maximum capacity in terms of the volume of mixed concrete. When used for the complete mixing of concrete, stationary mixers shall be equipped with an acceptable timing device that will not permit the batch to be discharged until the specified mixing time has elapsed.

10.1.2 Each truck mixer or agitator shall have attached thereto in a prominent place a metal plate or plates on which are plainly marked the gross volume of the drum, the capacity of the drum or container in terms of the volume of mixed concrete, and the minimum and maximum mixing speeds of rotation of the drum, blades, or paddles. When the concrete is truck mixed as described in 11.5, or shrink mixed as described in 11.4, the volume of mixed concrete shall not exceed 63 % of the total volume of the drum or container. When the concrete is central mixed as described in 11.3, the volume of concrete in the truck mixer or agitator shall not exceed 80 % of the total volume of the drum or container. Truck mixers and agitators shall be equipped with means by which the number of revolutions of the drum, blades, or paddles may be readily verified.

10.2 All stationary and truck mixers shall be capable of combining the ingredients of the concrete within the specified time or the number of revolutions specified in 10.5, into a thoroughly mixed and uniform mass and of discharging the concrete so that not less than five of the six requirements shown in Table A1.1 shall have been met.

NOTE 12—The sequence or method of charging the mixer will have an important effect on the uniformity of the concrete.

10.3 The agitator shall be capable of maintaining the mixed concrete in a thoroughly mixed and uniform mass and of discharging the concrete with a satisfactory degree of uniformity as defined by Annex A1.

10.4 Slump tests of individual samples taken after discharge of approximately 15 % and 85 % of the load may be made for a quick check of the probable degree of uniformity (Note 13). These two samples shall be obtained within an elapsed time of not more than 15 min. If these slumps differ more than that specified in Annex A1, the mixer or agitator shall not be used unless the condition is corrected, except as provided in 10.5.

NOTE 13—No samples should be taken before 10 % or after 90 % of the batch has been discharged. Due to the difficulty of determining the actual quantity of concrete discharged, the intent is to provide samples that are representative of widely separated portions, but not the beginning and end of the load.

C 94

10.5 Use of the equipment may be permitted when operation with a longer mixing time, a smaller load, or a more efficient charging sequence will permit the requirements of Annex A1 to be met.

10.6 Mixers and agitators shall be examined or weighed routinely as frequently as necessary to detect changes in condition due to accumulations of hardened concrete or mortar and examined to detect wear of blades. When such changes are extensive enough to affect the mixer performance, the proof-tests described in Annex A1 shall be performed to show whether the correction of deficiencies is required.

11. Mixing and Delivery

11.1 Ready-mixed concrete shall be mixed and delivered to the point designated by the purchaser by means of one of the following combinations of operations:

11.1.1 *Central-Mixed Concrete.*

11.1.2 *Shrink-Mixed Concrete.*

11.1.3 *Truck-Mixed Concrete.*

11.2 Mixers and agitators shall be operated within the limits of capacity and speed of rotation designated by the manufacturer of the equipment.

11.3 *Central-Mixed Concrete*—Concrete that is mixed completely in a stationary mixer and transported to the point of delivery either in a truck agitator, or a truck mixer operating at agitating speed, or in nonagitating equipment approved by the purchaser and meeting the requirements of Section 12, shall conform to the following: The mixing time shall be counted from the time all the solid materials are in the drum. The batch shall be so charged into the mixer that some water will enter in advance of the cement and aggregate, and all water shall be in the drum by the end of the first one fourth of the specified mixing time.

11.3.1 Where no mixer performance tests are made, the acceptable mixing time for mixers having capacities of 1 yd^3 (0.76 m^3) or less shall be not less than 1 min. For mixers of greater capacity, this minimum shall be increased 15 s for each cubic yard or fraction thereof of additional capacity.

11.3.2 Where mixer performance tests have been made on given concrete mixtures in accordance with the testing program set forth in the following paragraphs, and the mixers have been charged to their rated capacity, the acceptable mixing time may be reduced for those particular circumstances to a point at which satisfactory mixing defined in 11.3.3 shall have been accomplished. When the mixing time is so reduced the maximum time of mixing shall not exceed this reduced time by more than 60 s for air-entrained concrete.

11.3.3 *Sampling for Uniformity Tests of Stationary Mixers*—Samples of concrete for comparative purposes shall be obtained immediately after arbitrarily designated mixing times, in accordance with one of the following procedures:

11.3.3.1 *Alternative Procedure 1*—The mixer shall be stopped, and the required samples removed by any suitable means from the concrete at approximately equal distances from the front and back of the drum, or

11.3.3.2 *Alternative Procedure 2*—As the mixer is being emptied, individual samples shall be taken after discharge of approximately 15 % and 85 % of the load. Any appropriate method of sampling may be used, provided the samples are representative of widely separated portions, but not the very ends of the batch (Note 13).

11.3.3.3 The samples of concrete shall be tested in accordance with Section 19, and differences in test results for the two samples shall not exceed those given in Annex A1. Mixer performance tests shall be repeated whenever the appearance of the concrete or the coarse aggregate content of samples selected as outlined in this section indicates that adequate mixing has not been accomplished.

11.4 *Shrink-Mixed Concrete*—Concrete that is first partially mixed in a stationary mixer, and then mixed completely in a truck mixer, shall conform to the following: The time of partial mixing shall be minimum required to intermingle the ingredients. After transfer to a truck mixer the amount of mixing at the designated mixing speed will be that necessary to meet the requirements for uniformity of concrete as indicated in Annex A1. Tests to confirm such performance may be made in accordance with 11.3.3 and 11.3.3.3. Additional turning of the mixer, if any, shall be at a designated agitating speed.

11.5 *Truck-Mixed Concrete*—Concrete that is completely mixed in a truck mixer, 70 to 100 revolutions at the mixing speed designated by the manufacturer to produce the uniformity of concrete indicated in Annex A1. Concrete uniformity tests may be made in accordance with 11.5.1 and if requirements for uniformity of concrete indicated in Annex A1 are not met with 100 revolutions of mixing, after all ingredients including water, are in the drum, that mixer shall not be used until the condition is corrected, except as provided in 10.5. When satisfactory performance is found in one truck mixer, the performance of mixers of substantially the same design and condition of blades may be regarded as satisfactory. Additional revolutions of the mixer beyond the number found to produce the required uniformity of concrete shall be at a designated agitating speed.

11.5.1 *Sampling for Uniformity of Concrete Produced in Truck Mixers*—The concrete shall be discharged at the normal operating rate for the mixer being tested, with care being exercised not to obstruct or retard the discharge by an incompletely opened gate or seal. Separate samples, each consisting of approximately 2 ft^3 (0.1 m^3 approximately) shall be taken after discharge of approximately 15 % and 85 % of the load (Note 13). These samples shall be obtained within an elapsed time of not more than 15 min. The samples shall be secured in accordance with Practice C 172, but shall be kept separate to represent specific points in the batch rather than combined to form a composite sample. Between samples, where necessary to maintain slump, the mixer may be turned in mixing direction at agitating speed. During sampling the receptacle shall receive the full discharge of the chute. Sufficient personnel must be available to perform the required tests promptly. Segregation during sampling and handling must be avoided. Each sample shall be remixed the minimum amount to ensure uniformity before specimens are molded for a particular test.

11.6 When a truck mixer or truck agitator is used for transporting concrete that has been completely mixed in a stationary mixer, any turning during transportation shall be at the speed designated by the manufacturer of the equipment as agitating speed.

11.7 When a truck mixer or agitator is approved for

C 94

mixing or delivery of concrete, no water from the truck water system or elsewhere shall be added after the initial introduction of mixing water for the batch except when on arrival at the job site the slump of the concrete is less than that specified. Such additional water to bring the slump within required limits shall be injected into the mixer under such pressure and direction of flow that the requirements for uniformity specified in Annex A1 are met. The drum or blades shall be turned an additional 30 revolutions or more if necessary, at mixing speed, until the uniformity of the concrete is within these limits. Water shall not be added to the batch at any later time. Discharge of the concrete shall be completed within 1½ h, or before the drum has revolved 300 revolutions, whichever comes first, after the introduction of the mixing water to the cement and aggregates or the introduction of the cement to the aggregates. These limitations may be waived by the purchaser if the concrete is of such slump after the 1½-h time or 300-revolution limit has been reached that it can be placed, without the addition of water, to the batch. In hot weather, or under conditions contributing to quick stiffening of the concrete, a time less than 1½ h may be specified by the purchaser.

11.8 Concrete delivered in cold weather shall have the applicable minimum temperature indicated in the following table. (The purchaser shall inform the producer as to the type of construction for which the concrete is intended.)

Minimum Concrete Temperature as Placed

Section Size, in. (mm)	Temperature, min °F (C)
<12 (<300)	55 (13)
12–36 (300–900)	50 (10)
36–72 (900–1800)	45 (7)
>72 (>1800)	40 (5)

The maximum temperature of concrete produced with heated aggregates, heated water, or both, shall at no time during its production or transportation exceed 90°F (32°C).

NOTE 14—When hot water is used rapid stiffening may occur if hot water is brought in direct contact with the cement. Additional information on cold weather concreting is contained in ACI 306R.

11.9 The producer shall deliver the ready mixed concrete during hot weather at concrete temperatures as low as practicable, subject to the approval of the purchaser.

NOTE 15—In some situations difficulty may be encountered when concrete temperatures approach 90°F (32°C). Additional information may be found in the Bureau of Reclamation Concrete Manual and in ACI 305R.

12. Use of Nonagitating Equipment

12.1 Central-mixed concrete may be transported in suitable nonagitating equipment approved by the purchaser. The proportions of the concrete shall be approved by the purchaser and the following limitations shall apply:

12.2 Bodies of nonagitating equipment shall be smooth, watertight, metal containers equipped with gates that will permit control of the discharge of the concrete. Covers shall be provided for protection against the weather when required by the purchaser.

12.3 The concrete shall be delivered to the site of the work in a thoroughly mixed and uniform mass and discharged with a satisfactory degree of uniformity as prescribed in Annex A1.

12.4 Slump tests of individual samples taken after discharge of approximately 15 % and 85 % of the load may be made for a quick check of the probable degree of uniformity (Note 13). These two samples shall be obtained within an elapsed time of not more than 15 min. If these slumps differ more than that specified in Table A1.1, the nonagitating equipment shall not be used unless the conditions are corrected as provided in 12.5.

12.5 If the requirements of Annex A1 are not met when the nonagitating equipment is operated for the maximum time of haul, and with the concrete mixed the minimum time, the equipment may still be used when operated using shorter hauls, or longer mixing times, or combinations thereof that will result in the requirements of Annex A1 being met.

13. Batch Ticket Information

13.1 The manufacturer of the concrete shall furnish to the purchaser with each batch of concrete before unloading at the site, a delivery ticket on which is printed, stamped, or written, information concerning said concrete as follows:

13.1.1 Name of ready-mix batch plant,

13.1.2 Serial number of ticket,

13.1.3 Date,

13.1.4 Truck number,

13.1.5 Name of purchaser,

13.1.6 Specific designation of job (name and location),

13.1.7 Specific class or designation of the concrete in conformance with that employed in job specifications,

13.1.8 Amount of concrete in cubic yards (or cubic metres),

13.1.9 Time loaded or of first mixing of cement and aggregates, and

13.1.10 Water added by receiver of concrete and his initials.

13.2 Additional information for certification purposes as designated by the purchaser and required by the job specifications shall be furnished when requested; such information may include:

13.2.1 Reading of revolution counter at the first addition of water,

13.2.2 Type and brand, and amount of cement,

13.2.3 Type and brand, and amount of admixtures,

13.2.4 Information necessary to calculate the total mixing water added by the producer. Total mixing water includes free water on the aggregates, water, and ice batched at the plant, and water added by the truck operator from the mixer tank,

13.2.5 Maximum size of aggregate,

13.2.6 Weights of fine and coarse aggregate,

13.2.7 Ingredients certified as being previously approved, and

13.2.8 Signature or initials of ready-mix representative.

14. Plant Inspection

14.1 The manufacturer shall afford the inspector all reasonable access, without charge, for making necessary checks of the production facilities and for securing necessary samples to determine if the concrete is being produced in accordance with this specification. All tests and inspection shall be so conducted as not to interfere unnecessarily with the manufacture and delivery of the concrete.

ASTM C 94

15. Practices, Test Methods, and Reporting

15.1 Test ready-mixed concrete in accordance with the following methods:

15.1.1 *Compression Test Specimens*—Practice C 31, using standard moist curing in accordance with the applicable provisions of Practice C 31.

15.1.2 *Compression Tests*—Test Method C 39.

15.1.3 *Yield, Weight per Cubic Foot*—Test Method C 138.

15.1.4 *Air Content*—Test Method C 138; Test Method C 173 or Test Method C 231.

15.1.5 *Slump*—Test Method C 143.

15.1.6 *Sampling Fresh Concrete*—Practice C 172.

15.1.7 *Temperature*—Test Method C 1064.

15.2 The testing laboratory performing acceptance tests of concrete shall meet the requirements of Practice C 1077.

15.3 Laboratory reports of concrete test results used to determine compliance with this specification shall include a statement that all tests performed by the laboratory or its agents were in accordance with the applicable test methods or shall note all known deviations from the prescribed procedures (Note 16). The reports shall also list any part of the test methods not performed by the laboratory.

NOTE 16—Deviation from standard test methods may adversely affect test results.

NOTE 17—Deviation from standard moisture and temperature curing conditions is often a reason for low strength test results. Such deviations may invalidate the use of such test results as a basis for rejection of the concrete.

16. Sampling and Testing Fresh Concrete

16.1 The contractor shall afford the inspector all reasonable access and assistance, without charge, for the procurement of samples of fresh concrete at time of placement to determine conformance of it to this specification.

16.2 Tests of concrete required to determine compliance with this specification shall be made by a certified ACI Concrete Field Testing Technician, Grade I or equivalent. Equivalent personnel certification programs shall include

TABLE 4 Overdesign Necessary to Meet Strength Requirements[A]

Number of Tests[B]	Standard Deviation, psi					Unknown
	300	400	500	600	700	
15	466	622	851	1122	1392	c
20	434	579	758	1010	1261	c
30 or more	402	526	665	898	1131	c

	Standard Deviation, MPa				Unknown
	2.0	3.0	4.0	5.0	
15	3.1	4.7	7.3	10.0	c
20	2.9	4.3	6.6	9.1	c
30 or more	2.7	4.0	5.8	8.2	c

[A] Add the tabulated amounts to the specified strength to obtain the required average strengths.

[B] Number of tests of a concrete mixture used to estimate the standard deviation of a concrete production facility. The mixture used must have a strength within 1000 psi (7.0 MPa) of that specified and be made with similar materials. See ACI 318.

[C] If less than 15 prior tests are available, the overdesign should be 1000 psi (7.0 MPa) for specified strength less than 3000 psi (20 MPa), 1200 psi (8.5 MPa) for specified strengths from 3000 to 5000 psi (20 to 35 MPa) and 1400 psi (10.0 MPa) for specified strengths greater than 5000 psi (35 MPa).

both written and performance examinations as outlined in ACI CP-1.

16.3 Samples of concrete shall be obtained in accordance with Practice C 172, except when taken to determine uniformity of slump within any one batch or load of concrete (10.4, 11.3.3, 11.5.1, and 12.4).

16.4 Slump, air-content, and temperature tests shall be made at the time of placement at the option of the inspector as often as is necessary for control checks. In addition, these tests shall be made when specified and always when strength specimens are made.

16.5 Strength tests as well as slump, temperature, and air content tests shall generally be made with a frequency of not less than one test for each 150 yd³ (115 m³). Each test be made from a separate batch. On each day concrete is delivered, at least one strength test shall be made for each class of concrete.

16.6 If the measured slump or air content falls outside the specified limits, a check test shall be made immediately on another portion of the same sample. In the event of a second failure, the concrete shall be considered to have failed the requirements of the specification.

17. Strength

17.1 When strength is used as a basis for acceptance of concrete, standard specimens shall be made in accordance to Practice C 31. The specimens shall be cured under standard moisture and temperature conditions in accordance with the applicable provisions of Practice C 31. The technician performing the strength test shall be certified as an ACI Concrete Laboratory Testing Technician—Grade I or II or by an equivalent written and performance test program.

17.2 For a strength test, at least two standard test specimens shall be made from a composite sample secured as required in Section 16. A test shall be the average of the strengths of the specimens tested at the age specified in 5.2.1.1 or 5.4.1.1 (Note 18). If a specimen shows definite evidence other than low strength, of improper sampling, molding, handling, curing, or testing, it shall be discarded and the strength of the remaining cylinder shall then be considered the test result.

NOTE 18—Additional tests may be made at other ages to obtain information for determining form removal time or when a structure may be put in service. Specimens for such tests are cured according to the section on Field Curing in Practice C 31.

17.3 The representative of the purchaser shall ascertain and record the delivery-ticket number for the concrete and the exact location in the work at which each load represented by a strength test is deposited.

17.4 To conform to the requirements of this specification, strength tests representing each class of concrete must meet the following two requirements (Note 19):

17.4.1 The average of any three consecutive strength tests shall be equal to, or greater than, the specified strength, f'_c, and

17.4.2 No individual strength test shall be more than 500 psi (3.4 MPa) below the specified strength, f'_c.

NOTE 19—Due to variations in materials, operations and testing, the average strength necessary to meet these requirements will be substantially higher than the specified strength. The amount higher depends upon the standard deviation of the test results and the accuracy with

C 94

which that value can be estimated from prior data as explained in ACI 318 and ACI 301. Pertinent data is given in Table 4.

18. Failure to Meet Strength Requirements

18.1 In the event that concrete tested in accordance with the requirements of Section 17 fails to meet the strength requirements of this specification, the manufacturer of the ready-mixed concrete and the purchaser shall confer to determine whether agreement can be reached as to what adjustment, if any, shall be made. If an agreement on a mutually satisfactory adjustment cannot be reached by the

manufacturer and the purchaser, a decision shall be made by a panel of three qualified engineers, one of whom shall be designated by the purchaser, one by the manufacturer, and the third chosen by these two members of the panel. The question of responsibility for the cost of such arbitration shall be determined by the panel. Its decision shall be binding, except as modified by a court decision.

19. Keywords

19.1 accuracy; certification; ready-mixed concrete; scales; testing

---

ANNEX

(Mandatory Information)

A1. CONCRETE UNIFORMITY REQUIREMENTS

A1.1 The variation within a batch as provided in Table A1.1 shall be determined for each property listed as the difference between the highest value and the lowest value obtained from the different portions of the same batch. For this specification the comparison will be between two samples, representing the first and last portions of the batch being tested. Test results conforming to the limits of five of the six tests listed in Table A1.1 shall indicate uniform concrete within the limits of this specification.

A1.2 *Coarse Aggregate Content*, using the washout test, shall be computed from the following relations:

$$P = (c/b) \times 100$$

where:

P = weight % of coarse aggregate in concrete,

c = saturated surface-dry-weight in lb (kg) of aggregate retained on the No. 4 (4.75-mm) sieve, resulting from washing all material finer than this sieve from the fresh concrete, and

b = weight of sample of fresh concrete in unit weight container, lb (kg).

A1.3 *Unit Weight of Air Free Mortar* shall be calculated as follows:

Inch-pound units:

$$M = \frac{b - c}{V - \left(\frac{V \times A}{100} + \frac{c}{G \times 62.4}\right)}$$

Metric units:

$$M = \frac{b - c}{V - \left(\frac{V \times A}{100} + \frac{c}{1000G}\right)}$$

where:

M = unit weight of air-free mortar, lb/ft^3 (kg/m^3),

b = weight of concrete sample in unit weight container, lb (kg),

c = saturated surface-dry-weight of aggregate retained on No. 4 (4.75-mm) sieve, lb (kg),

V = volume of unit weight container, ft^3 (m^3),

A = air content of concrete, %, measured in accordance with 19.1.4 on the sample being tested, and

G = specific gravity of coarse aggregate (SSD).

C 94

TABLE A1.1   Requirements for Uniformity of Concrete

Test	Requirement, Expressed as Maximum Permissible Difference in Results of Tests of Samples Taken from Two Locations in the Concrete Batch
Weight per cubic foot (weight per cubic metre) calculated to an air-free basis, lb/ft³ (kg/m³)	1.0 (16)
Air content, volume % of concrete	1.0
Slump:	
If average slump is 4 in. (102 mm) or less, in. (mm)	1.0 (25)
If average slump is 4 to 6 in. (102 to 152 mm), in. (mm)	1.5 (38)
Coarse aggregate content, portion by weight of each sample retained on No. 4 (4.75-mm) sieve, %	6.0
Unit weight of air-free mortar[A] based on average for all comparative samples tested, %.	1.6
Average compressive strength at 7 days for each sample,[B] based on average strength of all comparative test specimens, %	7.5[C]

[A] "Test for Variability of Constituents in Concrete," Designation 26, *Bureau of Reclamation Concrete Manual*, 7th Edition. Available from Superintendent of Documents, U. S. Government Printing Office, Washington, DC 20402.

[B] Not less than 3 cylinders will be molded and tested from each of the samples.

[C] Tentative approval of the mixer may be granted pending results of the 7-day compressive strength tests.

ASTM Designation: C 138 – 92

AMERICAN SOCIETY FOR TESTING AND MATERIALS
1916 Race St. Philadelphia, Pa 19103
Reprinted from the Annual Book of ASTM Standards. Copyright ASTM
If not listed in the current combined index, will appear in the next edition.

American Association State
Highway and Transportation Officials Standard
AASHTO No.: T 121

Standard Test Method for
Unit Weight, Yield, and Air Content (Gravimetric) of Concrete[1]

This standard is issued under the fixed designation C 138; the number immediately following the designation indicates the year of original adoption or, in the case of revision, the year of last revision. A number in parentheses indicates the year of last reapproval. A superscript epsilon (ε) indicates an editorial change since the last revision or reapproval.

This standard has been approved for use by the Department of Defense. Consult the DoD Index of Specifications and Standards for the specific year of issue which has been adopted by the Department of Defense.

1. Scope

1.1 This test method covers determination of the weight per cubic foot or cubic metre of freshly mixed concrete and gives formulas for calculating the yield, cement content, and the air content of the concrete. Yield is defined as the volume of concrete produced from a mixture of known quantities of the component materials.

1.2 The values stated in inch-pound units are to be regarded as the standard.

2. Referenced Documents

2.1 *ASTM Standards:*
C 29/C 29M Test Method for Unit Weight and Voids in Aggregate[2]
C 150 Specification for Portland Cement[2,3]
C 172 Practice for Sampling Freshly Mixed Concrete[2]
C 188 Test Method for Density of Hydraulic Cement[3]
C 231 Test Method for Air Content of Freshly Mixed Concrete by the Pressure Method[2]

3. Symbols

A = air content (percentage of voids) in the concrete
N = actual cement content, lb/yd³ or kg/m³
N_t = weight of cement in the batch, lb or kg
R_y = relative yield
T = theoretical weight of the concrete computed on an airfree basis, lb/ft³ or kg/m³ (Note 1)
V = total absolute volume of the component ingredients in the batch, ft³ or m³
W = unit weight of concrete, lb/ft³ or kg/m³
W_1 = total weight of all materials batched, lb or kg (Note 2)
Y = volume of concrete produced per batch, yd³ or m³
Y_d = volume of concrete which the batch was designed to produce, yd³ (m³)
Y_f = volume of concrete produced per batch, ft³

NOTE 1—The theoretical weight per cubic foot or cubic metre is, customarily, a laboratory determination, the value for which is assumed to remain constant for all batches made using identical component ingredients and proportions. It is calculated from the equation.

$$T = W_1/V$$

The absolute volume of each ingredient in cubic feet is equal to the quotient of the weight of that ingredient divided by the product of its specific gravity times 62.4. The absolute volume of each ingredient in cubic metres is equal to the weight of the ingredient in kilograms divided by 1000 times its specific gravity. For the aggregate components, the bulk specific gravity and weight should be based on the saturated, surface-dry condition. For cement, the actual specific gravity should be determined by Test Method C 188. A value of 3.15 may be used for cements manufactured to meet the requirements of Specification C 150.

NOTE 2—The total weight of all materials batched is the sum of the weights of the cement, the fine aggregate in the condition used, the coarse aggregate in the condition used, the mixing water added to the batch, and any other solid or liquid materials used.

4. Apparatus

4.1 *Balance*—A balance or scale accurate to within 0.3 % of the test load at any point within the range of use. The range of use shall be considered to extend from the weight of the measure empty to the weight of the measure plus its contents at 160 lb/ft³ (2600 kg/m³).

4.2 *Tamping Rod*—A round, straight steel rod, ⅝ in. (16 mm) in diameter and approximately 24 in. (600 mm) in length, having the tamping end rounded to a hemispherical tip the diameter of which is ⅝ in.

4.3 *Internal Vibrator*—Internal vibrators may have rigid or flexible shafts, preferably powered by electric motors. The frequency of vibration shall be 7000 vibrations per minute or greater while in use. The outside diameter or the side dimension of the vibrating element shall be at least 0.75 in. (19 mm) and not greater than 1.50 in. (38 mm). The length of the shaft shall be at least 24 in. (600 mm).

4.4 *Measure*—A cylindrical container made of steel or other suitable metal (Note 3). The minimum capacity of the measure shall conform to the requirements of Table 1 based on the nominal size of aggregate in the concrete to be tested. All measures, except for measuring bowls of air meters which are also used for Test Method C 138 tests, shall conform to

TABLE 1 Capacity of Measures

Nominal Maximum Size of Coarse Aggregate		Capacity of Measure [A]	
in.	mm	ft³	L
1	25.0	0.2	6
1½	37.5	0.4	11
2	50	0.5	14
3	75	1.0	28
4½	112	2.5	70
6	150	3.5	100

[A] The indicated size of measure shall be used to test concrete containing aggregates of a nominal maximum size equal to or smaller than that listed. The actual volume of the measure shall be at least 95 % of the nominal volume listed.

[1] This test method is under the jurisdiction of ASTM Committee C-9 on Concrete and Concrete Aggregates and is the direct responsibility of Subcommittee C09.60 on Fresh Concrete Testing.
Current edition approved Dec. 15, 1992. Published April 1992. Originally published as C 138 – 38 T. Last previous edition C 138 – 81ᵋ¹.
[2] *Annual Book of ASTM Standards,* Vol 04.02.
[3] *Annual Book of ASTM Standards,* Vol 04.01.

C 138

the requirements of Test Method C 29/C 29M. When measuring bowls of air meters are used, they shall conform to the requirements of Test Method C 231, and shall be calibrated for volume as described in Test Method C 29/C 29M. The top rim of the air meter bowls shall be smooth and plane within 0.01 in. (0.25 mm).

NOTE 3—The metal should not be readily subject to attack by cement paste. However, reactive materials such as aluminum alloys may be used in instances where as a consequence of an initial reaction, a surface film is rapidly formed which protects the metal against further corrosion.

NOTE 4—The top rim is satisfactorily plane if a 0.01-in. (0.25-mm) feeler gage cannot be inserted between the rim and a piece of ¼-in. (6-mm) or thicker plate glass laid over the top of the measure.

4.5 *Strike-Off Plate*—A flat rectangular metal plate at least ¼ in. (6 mm) thick or a glass or acrylic plate at least ½ in. (12 mm) thick with a length and width at least 2 in. (50 mm) greater than the diameter of the measure with which it is to be used. The edges of the plate shall be straight and smooth within a tolerance of ¹⁄₁₆ in. (1.5 mm).

4.6 *Mallet*—A mallet (with a rubber or rawhide head) weighing approximately 1.25 ± 0.50 lb (0.57 ± 0.23 kg) for use with measures of 0.5 ft³ (14 dm³) or smaller, and a mallet weighing approximately 2.25 ± 0.50 lb (1.02 ± 0.23 kg) for use with measures larger than 0.5 ft³.

5. Sample

5.1 Obtain the sample of freshly mixed concrete in accordance with Practice C 172.

6. Procedure

6.1 Compact the concrete in measures smaller than 0.4 ft³ (11 L) by rodding because of the danger of excessive loss of entrained air. For measures 0.4 ft³ or larger, base the selection of the method of consolidation on the slump, unless the method is stated in the specifications under which the work is being performed. The methods of consolidation are rodding and internal vibration. Rod concretes with a slump greater than 3 in. (75 mm). Rod or vibrate concrete with a slump of 1 to 3 in. (25 to 75 mm). Consolidate concretes with a slump less than 1 in. (25 mm) by vibration.

NOTE 5—The nonplastic concrete, such as is commonly used in the manufacture of pipe and unit masonry, is not covered by this method.

6.2 *Rodding*—Place the concrete in the measure in three layers of approximately equal volume. Rod each layer with 25 strokes of the tamping rod when nominal 0.5-ft³ (14-L) or smaller measures are used, 50 strokes when nominal 1-ft³ (28-L) measures are used, and one stroke per 3 in.² (20 cm³) of surface for larger measures. Rod the bottom layer throughout its depth but the rod shall not forcibly strike the bottom of the measure. Distribute the strokes uniformly over the cross section of the measure and for the top two layers, penetrate about 1 in. (25 mm) into the underlying layer. After each layer is rodded, tap the sides of the measure smartly 10 to 15 times with the appropriate mallet (see 4.6) to close any voids left by the tamping rod and to release any large bubbles of air that may have been trapped. Add the final layer so as to avoid overfilling.

6.3 *Internal Vibration*—Fill and vibrate the measure in two approximately equal layers. Place all of the concrete for each layer in the measure before starting vibration of that layer. Insert the vibrator at three different points for each layer. In compacting the bottom layer, do not allow the vibrator to rest on or touch the bottom or sides of the measure. In compacting the final layer, the vibrator shall penetrate into the underlying layer approximately 1 in. (25 mm). Take care that the vibrator is withdrawn in such a manner that no air pockets are left in the specimen. The duration of vibration required will depend upon the workability of the concrete and the effectiveness of the vibrator (Note 6). Continue vibration only long enough to achieve proper consolidation of the concrete (Note 7). Observe a constant duration of vibration for the particular kind of concrete, vibrator, and measure involved.

NOTE 6—Usually, sufficient vibration has been applied as soon as the surface of the concrete becomes relatively smooth.

NOTE 7—Overvibration may cause segregation and loss of appreciable quantities of intentionally entrained air.

6.4 On completion of consolidation the measure must not contain a substantial excess or deficiency of concrete. An excess of concrete protruding approximately ⅛ in. (3 mm) above the top of the mold is optimum. A small quantity of concrete may be added to correct a deficiency. If the measure contains a great excess of concrete at completion of consolidation, remove a representative portion of the excess concrete with a trowel or scoop immediately following completion of consolidation and before the measure is struck-off.

6.5 *Strike-Off*—After consolidation, strike-off the top surface of the concrete and finish it smoothly with the flat strike-off plate using great care to leave the measure just level full. The strike-off is best accomplished by pressing the strike-off plate on the top surface of the measure to cover about two thirds of the surface and withdrawing the plate with a sawing motion to finish only the area originally covered. Then place the plate on the top of the measure to cover the original two thirds of the surface and advance it with a vertical pressure and a sawing motion to cover the whole surface of the measure. Several final strokes with the inclined edge of the plate will produce a smooth finished surface.

6.6 *Cleaning and Weighing*—After strike-off, clean all excess concrete from the exterior of the measure and determine the net weight of the concrete in the measure to an accuracy consistent with the requirements of 4.1.

7. Calculation

7.1 *Unit Weight*—Calculate the net weight of the concrete in pounds or kilograms by subtracting the weight of the measure from the gross weight. Calculate the unit weight, W, by dividing the net weight by the volume of the measure used, determined according to Test Method C 29/C 29M.

7.2 *Yield*—Calculate the yield as follows:

$$Y_f(\text{ft}^3) = W_1/W$$

or,

$$Y(\text{yd}^3) = W_1/(27\ W)$$

or,

$$Y(\text{m}^3) = W_1/W$$

7.3 *Relative Yield*—Relative yield is the ratio of the actual volume of concrete obtained to the volume as designed for the batch calculated as follows:

$$R_y = Y/Y_d$$

NOTE 8—A value for R_y greater than 1.00 indicates an excess of concrete being produced whereas a value less than this indicates the batch to be "short" of its designed volume.

7.4 *Cement Content*—Calculate the actual cement content as follows:

$$N = N_t/Y$$

7.5 *Air Content*—Calculate the air content as follows:

$$A = [(T - W)/T] \times 100$$

or,

$$A = [(Y_f - V)/Y_f] \times 100 \text{ (inch-pound units)}$$

or,

$$A = [(Y - V)/Y] \times 100 \text{ (SI units)}$$

8. Precision and Bias

8.1 Data are being compiled and developed that will be suitable for use in developing precision and bias statements for this test method.

9. Keywords

9.1 air content; cement content; concrete; relative yield; unit weight; yield

AMERICAN SOCIETY FOR TESTING AND MATERIALS
100 Barr Harbor Dr., West Conshohocken, PA 19428
Reprinted from the Annual Book of ASTM Standards. Copyright ASTM
If not listed in the current combined index, will appear in the next edition.

Designation: C 143 – 90a

Standard Test Method for
Slump of Hydraulic Cement Concrete[1]

This standard is issued under the fixed designation C 143; the number immediately following the designation indicates the year of original adoption or, in the case of revision, the year of last revision. A number in parentheses indicates the year of last reapproval. A superscript epsilon (ε) indicates an editorial change since the last revision or reapproval.

This method has been approved for use by agencies of the Department of Defense. Consult the DoD Index of Specifications and Standards for the specific year of issue which has been adopted by the Department of Defense.

1. Scope

1.1 This test method covers determination of slump of concrete, both in the laboratory and in the field.

1.2 The values stated in inch-pound units are to be regarded as the standard. The metric equivalents of inch-pound units may be approximate.

1.3 *This standard may involve hazardous materials, operations, and equipment. This standard does not purport to address all of the safety problems associated with its use. It is the responsibility of the user of this standard to establish appropriate safety and health practices and determine the applicability of regulatory limitations prior to use.*

2. Referenced Document

2.1 *ASTM Standard:*
C 172 Practice for Sampling Freshly Mixed Concrete[2]

3. Summary of Test Method

3.1 A sample of freshly mixed concrete is placed and compacted by rodding in a mold shaped as the frustum of a cone. The mold is raised, and the concrete allowed to subside. The distance between the original and displaced position of the center of the top surface of the concrete is measured and reported as the slump of the concrete.

4. Significance and Use

4.1 This test method is intended to provide the user with a procedure to determine slump of plastic hydraulic cement concretes.

NOTE 1—This test method was originally developed to provide a technique to monitor the consistency of unhardened concrete. Under laboratory conditions, with strict control of all concrete materials, the slump is generally found to increase proportionally with the water content of a given concrete mixture, and thus to be inversely related to concrete strength. Under field conditions, however, such a strength relationship is not clearly and consistently shown. Care should therefore be taken in relating slump results obtained under field conditions to strength.

4.2 This test method is considered applicable to plastic concrete having coarse aggregate up to 1 1/2 in. (37.5 mm) in size. If the coarse aggregate is larger than 1 1/2 in. (37.5 mm) in size, the test method is applicable when it is made on the fraction of concrete passing a 1 1/2-in. (37.5-mm) sieve, with the larger aggregate being removed in accordance with the section titled "Additional Procedures for Large Maximum Size Aggregate Concrete" in Practice C 172.

4.3 This test method is not considered applicable to non-plastic and non-cohesive concrete.

NOTE 2—Concretes having slumps less than 1/2 in. (13 mm) may not be adequately plastic and concretes having slumps greater than about 9 in. (230 mm) may not be adequately cohesive for this test to have significance. Caution should be exercised in interpreting such results.

5. Apparatus

5.1 *Mold*—The test specimen shall be formed in a mold made of metal not readily attacked by the cement paste. The metal shall not be thinner than No. 16 gage (BWG) and if formed by the spinning process, there shall be no point on the mold at which the thickness is less than 0.045 in. (1.14 mm). The mold shall be in the form of the lateral surface of the frustum of a cone with the base 8 in. (203 mm) in diameter, the top 4 in. (102 mm) in diameter, and the height 12 in. (305 mm). Individual diameters and heights shall be within ±1/8 in. (3.2 mm) of the prescribed dimensions. The base and the top shall be open and parallel to each other and at right angles to the axis of the cone. The mold shall be provided with foot pieces and handles similar to those shown in Fig. 1. The mold may be constructed either with or without a seam. When a seam is required, it should be essentially as shown in Fig. 1. The interior of the mold shall be relatively smooth and free from projections such as protruding rivets. The mold shall be free from dents. A mold which clamps to a nonabsorbent base plate is acceptable instead of the one illustrated provided the clamping arrangement is such that it can be fully released without movement of the mold.

5.2 *Tamping Rod*—The tamping rod shall be a round, straight steel rod 5/8 in. (16 mm) in diameter and approximately 24 in. (600 mm) in length, having the tamping end rounded to a hemispherical tip the diameter of which is 5/8 in.

6. Sample

6.1 The sample of concrete from which test specimens are made shall be representative of the entire batch. It shall be obtained in accordance with Practice C 172.

7. Procedure

7.1 Dampen the mold and place it on a flat, moist, nonabsorbent (rigid) surface. It shall be held firmly in place during filling by the operator standing on the two foot pieces.

---

[1] This test method is under the jurisdiction of ASTM Committee C-9 on Concrete and Concrete Aggregates and is the direct responsibility of Subcommittee C09.03.03 on Methods of Testing Fresh Concrete.
Current edition approved July 9, 1990. Published September 1990. Originally published as D 138 – 22 T. Last previous edition C 143 – 90.
[2] *Annual Book of ASTM Standards*, Vol 04.02.

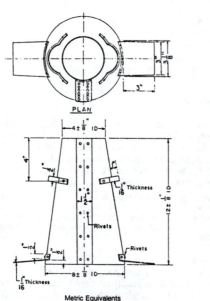

PLAN

Metric Equivalents

in.	1/16	1/8	1/2	1	1½	3	3½	4	8	12
mm	1.6	3.2	12.7	25.4	38.1	76.2	79.4	102	203	305

FIG. 1   Mold for Slump Test

From the sample of concrete obtained in accordance with Section 6, immediately fill the mold in three layers, each approximately one third the volume of the mold.

NOTE 3—One third of the volume of the slump mold fills it to a depth of 2⅝ in. (67 mm); two thirds of the volume fills it to a depth of 6⅛ in. (155 mm).

7.2 Rod each layer with 25 strokes of the tamping rod. Uniformly distribute the strokes over the cross section of each layer. For the bottom layer this will necessitate inclining the rod slightly and making approximately half of the strokes near the perimeter, and then progressing with vertical strokes spirally toward the center. Rod the bottom layer throughout its depth. Rod the second layer and the top layer each throughout its depth, so that the strokes just penetrate into the underlying layer.

7.3 In filling and rodding the top layer, heap the concrete above the mold before rodding is started. If the rodding operation results in subsidence of the concrete below the top edge of the mold, add additional concrete to keep an excess of concrete above the top of the mold at all times. After the top layer has been rodded, strike off the surface of the

🔩 C 143

concrete by means of a screeding and rolling motion of the tamping rod. Remove the mold immediately from the concrete by raising it carefully in a vertical direction. Raise the mold a distance of 12 in. (300 mm) in 5 ± 2 s by a steady upward lift with no lateral or torsional motion. Complete the entire test from the start of the filling through removal of the mold without interruption and complete it within an elapsed time of 2½ min.

7.4 Immediately measure the slump by determining the vertical difference between the top of the mold and the displaced original center of the top surface of the specimen. If a decided falling away or shearing off of concrete from one side or portion of the mass occurs (Note 4), disregard the test and make a new test on another portion of the sample.

NOTE 4—If two consecutive tests on a sample of concrete show a falling away or shearing off of a portion of the concrete from the mass of the specimen, the concrete probably lacks necessary plasticity and cohesiveness for the slump test to be applicable.

8. Report

8.1 Record the slump in terms of inches (millimetres) to the nearest ¼ in. (6 mm) of subsidence of the specimen during the test as follows:

Slump = 12 − inches of height after subsidence

9. Precision and Bias

9.1 *Precision*

9.1.1 *Interlaboratory Test Method*—No interlaboratory test program has been run on this test method. Since it is not possible to provide equivalent concretes at various test sites free of errors from sources other than the slump measurement, a multilaboratory precision statement would not be meaningful.

9.1.2 *Multi-Operator Test Results*—Extensive field data[3] allow a statement regarding the multi-operator precision of this test method.

Test range	1.5 to 2.76 in. (38 to 70 mm)
Total number of samples	2304
Pooled Repeatability	
Standard deviation (1S)	0.30 in. (8 mm)
95 % Repeatability	
Limit (D2S)	0.83 in. (21 mm)

Therefore, results of two properly conducted tests by different operators in the same laboratory on the same material should not differ by more than 0.83 in. (21 mm). Due to the limited slump range in the concrete used in this test program, caution should be exercised in applying these precision values.

9.2 *Bias*—This test method has no bias since slump is defined only in terms of this test method.

---

[3] Baker, W. M., and McMahon, T. F., "Quality Assurance of Portland Cement Concrete," *Public Roads*, Vol 35, No. 8, 1969.

⬤ C 143

AMERICAN SOCIETY FOR TESTING AND MATERIALS
1916 Race St. Philadelphia, Pa 19103
Reprinted from the Annual Book of ASTM Standards. Copyright ASTM
If not listed in the current combined index, will appear in the next edition.

Standard Practice for
Sampling Freshly Mixed Concrete[1]

This standard is issued under the fixed designation C 172; the number immediately following the designation indicates the year of original adoption or, in the case of revision, the year of last revision. A number in parentheses indicates the year of last reapproval. A superscript epsilon (ϵ) indicates an editorial change since the last revision or reapproval.

This standard has been approved for use by agencies of the Department of Defense. Consult the DoD Index of Specifications and Standards for the specific year of issue which has been adopted by the Department of Defense.

1. Scope

1.1 This practice covers procedures for obtaining representative samples of fresh concrete as delivered to the project site on which tests are to be performed to determine compliance with quality requirements of the specifications under which the concrete is furnished (Note 1). The practice includes sampling from stationary, paving and truck mixers, and from agitating and nonagitating equipment used to transport central-mixed concrete.

1.2 The values stated in inch-pound units are to be regarded as the standard. The metric equivalents of inch-pound units may be approximate.

NOTE 1—Composite samples are required by this practice, unless specifically excepted by procedures governing the tests to be performed such as tests to determine uniformity of consistency and mixer efficiency. Procedures used to select the specific test batches are not described in this practice, but it is recommended that random sampling be used to determine over-all specification compliance.

1.3 This practice also covers the procedures to be used for preparing a sample of concrete for further testing where it is desirable or necessary to remove the aggregate larger than a designated size. This removal of larger aggregate particles is preferably accomplished by wet-sieving.

2. Referenced Document

2.1 *ASTM Standard:*
E 11 Specification for Wire-Cloth Sieves for Testing Purposes[2]

3. Sampling

3.1 The elapsed time between obtaining the first and final portions of the composite sample shall be as short as possible, but in no instance shall it exceed 15 min.

3.1.1 Transport the individual samples to the place where fresh concrete tests are to be performed or where test specimens are to be molded. They shall be combined and remixed with a shovel the minimum amount necessary to ensure uniformity and compliance with the minimum time limits specified in 3.1.2.

3.1.2 Start tests for slump or air content, or both, within 5 min after obtaining the final portion of the composite sample. Complete these tests as expeditiously as possible.

Start molding specimens for strength tests within 15 min after fabricating the composite sample. Keep the elapsed time between obtaining and using the sample as short as possible and protect the sample from the sun, wind, and other sources of rapid evaporation, and from contamination.

4. Procedure

4.1 *Size of Sample*—Make the samples to be used for strength tests a minimum of 1 ft³ (28 L). Smaller samples may be permitted for routine air content and slump tests and the size shall be dictated by the maximum aggregate size.

4.2 The procedures used in sampling shall include the use of every precaution that will assist in obtaining samples that are truly representative of the nature and condition of concrete sampled as follows:

NOTE 2—Sampling should normally be performed as the concrete is delivered from the mixer to the conveying vehicle used to transport the concrete to the forms; however, specifications may require other points of sampling, such as the discharge of a concrete pump.

4.2.1 *Sampling from Stationary Mixers, Except Paving Mixers*—Sample the concrete by collecting two or more portions taken at regularly spaced intervals during discharge of the middle of the batch. Obtain these portions within the time limit specified in Section 3. Composite the portions into one sample for testing purposes. Do not obtain portions of the composite sample from the very first or last part of the batch discharge. Perform sampling by passing a receptacle completely through the discharge stream, or by completely diverting the discharge into a sample container. If discharge of the concrete is too rapid to divert the complete discharge stream, discharge the concrete into a container or transportation unit sufficiently large to accommodate the entire batch and then accomplish the sampling in the same manner as given above. Take care not to restrict the flow of concrete from the mixer, container, or transportation unit so as to cause segregation. These requirements apply to both tilting and nontilting mixers.

4.2.2 *Sampling from Paving Mixers*—Sample the concrete after the contents of the paving mixer have been discharged. Obtain samples from at least five different portions of the pile and then composite into one sample for test purposes. Avoid contamination with subgrade material or prolonged contact with and absorptive subgrade. To preclude contamination or absorption by the subgrade, sample the concrete by placing three shallow containers on the subgrade and discharging the concrete across the container. Composite the samples so obtained into one sample for test purposes. The containers shall be of a size sufficient

---

[1] This practice is under the jurisdiction of ASTM Committee C-9 on Concrete and Concrete Aggregates and is the direct responsibility of Subcommittee C09.03.03 on Methods of Testing Fresh Concrete.

Current edition approved April 27, 1990. Published June 1990. Originally published as C 172 – 42. Last previous edition C 172 – 82.

[2] *Annual Book of ASTM Standards*, Vols 04.02 and 14.02.

C 172

to provide a composite sample size that is in agreement with the maximum aggregate size.

NOTE 3—In some instances, the containers may have to be supported above the subgrade to prevent displacement during discharge.

4.2.3 *Sampling from Revolving Drum Truck Mixers or Agitators*—Sample the concrete at two or more regularly spaced intervals during discharge of the middle portion of the batch. Take the samples so obtained within the time limit specified in Section 3 and composite them into one sample for test purposes. In any case do not obtain samples until after all of the water has been added to the mixer; also do not obtain samples from the very first or last portions of the batch discharge. Sample by repeatedly passing a receptacle through the entire discharge stream or by completely diverting the discharge into a sample container. Regulate the rate of discharge of the batch by the rate of revolution of the drum and not by the size of the gate opening.

4.2.4 *Sampling from Open-Top Truck Mixers, Agitators, Nonagitating Equipment, or Other Types of Open-Top Containers*—Take samples by whichever of the procedures described in 4.2.1, 4.2.2, or 4.2.3 is most applicable under the given conditions.

5. Additional Procedure for Large Maximum Size Aggregate Concrete

5.1 When the concrete contains aggregate larger than that appropriate for the size of the molds or equipment to be used, wet-sieve the sample as described below except make unit-weight tests for use in yield computations on the full mix.

NOTE 4—The effect of wet-sieving on the test results should be considered. For example, wet-sieving causes the loss of a small amount of air due to additional handling. The air content of the wet-sieved fraction of concrete is greater than that of the total concrete because the larger size aggregate which is removed does not contain air. The apparent strength of wet-sieved concrete in smaller specimens is usually greater than that of the total concrete in larger appropriate size specimens. The effect of these differences may need to be considered or determined by supplementary testing for quality control or test result evaluation purposes.

5.2 *Definition*:

5.2.1 *wet-sieving concrete*—the process of removing aggregate larger than a designated size from the fresh concrete by sieving it on a sieve of the designated size.

5.3 *Apparatus*:

5.3.1 *Sieves*, as designated, conforming to Specification E 11.

5.3.2 *Wet-Sieving Equipment*—Equipment for wet-sieving concrete shall be a sieve as noted in 5.3.1 of suitable size and conveniently arranged and supported so that one can shake it rapidly by either hand or mechanical means. Generally, a horizontal back and forth motion is preferred. The equipment shall be capable of rapidly and effectively removing the designated size of aggregate.

5.3.3 *Hand Tools*—Shovels, hand scoops, plastering trowels, and rubber gloves as required.

5.4 *Procedure*:

5.4.1 *Wet-Sieving*—After sampling the concrete, pass the concrete over the designated sieve and remove and discard the aggregate retained. This shall be done before remixing. Shake or vibrate the sieve by hand or mechanical means until no undersize material remains on the sieve. Mortar adhering to the aggregate retained on the sieve shall not be wiped from it before it is discarded. Place only enough concrete on the sieve at any one time so that after sieving, the thickness of the layer of retained aggregate is not more than one particle thick. The concrete which passes the sieve shall fall into a batch pan of suitable size which has been dampened before use or onto a clean, moist, nonabsorbent surface. Scrape any mortar adhering to the sides of the wet-sieving equipment into the batch. After removing the larger aggregate particles by wet-sieving remix the batch with a shovel the minimum amount necessary to ensure uniformity and proceed testing immediately.

ASTM Designation: C 173 – 94a$^{\epsilon 1}$

AMERICAN SOCIETY FOR TESTING AND MATERIALS
1916 Race St. Philadelphia, Pa 19103
Reprinted from the Annual Book of ASTM Standards. Copyright ASTM
If not listed in the current combined index, will appear in the next edition.

Standard Test Method for
Air Content of Freshly Mixed Concrete by the Volumetric Method[1]

This standard is issued under the fixed designation C 173; the number immediately following the designation indicates the year of original adoption or, in the case of revision, the year of last revision. A number in parentheses indicates the year of last reapproval. A superscript epsilon (ϵ) indicates an editorial change since the last revision or reapproval.

This test method has been approved for use by agencies of the Department of Defense. Consult the DoD Index of Specifications and Standards for the specific year of issue which has been adopted by the Department of Defense.

$^{\epsilon 1}$ NOTE—Editorial corrections were made in March 1995.

1. Scope

1.1 This test method covers determination of the air content of freshly mixed concrete containing any type of aggregate, whether it be dense, cellular, or lightweight.

1.2 The values stated in inch-pound units are to be regarded as the standard. The values given in parentheses are for information only.

1.3 *This standard does not purport to address all of the safety concerns, if any, associated with its use. It is the responsibility of the user of this standard to establish appropriate safety and health practices and determine the applicability of regulatory limitations prior to use.*

2. Referenced Documents

2.1 *ASTM Standards:*
C 29/C 29M Test Method for Unit Weight and Voids in Aggregate[2]
C 138 Test Method for Unit Weight, Yield, and Air Content (Gravimetric) of Concrete[2]
C 172 Practice for Sampling Freshly Mixed Concrete[2]
C 231 Test Method for Air Content of Freshly Mixed Concrete by the Pressure Method[2]
C 670 Practice for Preparing Precision and Bias Statements for Test Methods for Construction Materials[2]

3. Significance and Use

3.1 This test covers the determination of the air content of freshly mixed concrete. It measures the air contained in the mortar fraction of the concrete, but is not affected by air that may be present inside porous aggregate particles.

3.1.1 Therefore, this is the appropriate test to determine the air content of concretes containing lightweight aggregates, air-cooled slag, and highly porous or vesicular natural aggregates.

3.2 This test method may underestimate the air content of concretes containing more than 600 lb/yd^3 (350 kg/m^3) of cementitious material because it may take up to 60 min of repeated rolling and standing to obtain a stable reading.

3.3 The air content of hardened concrete may be either higher or lower than that determined by this test method. This depends upon the methods and amounts of consolidation effort applied to the concrete from which the hardened concrete specimen is taken; uniformity and stability of the air bubbles in the fresh and hardened concrete; accuracy of the microscopic examination, if used; time of comparison; environmental exposure; stage in the delivery, placement and consolidation processes at which the air content of the unhardened concrete is determined, that is, before or after the concrete goes through a pump; and other factors.

4. Apparatus

4.1 *Airmeter*—An airmeter consisting of a bowl and a top section (Fig. 1) conforming to the following requirements:

4.1.1 The bowl and top sections shall be of sufficient thickness and rigidity to withstand rough field use. The material shall not be attacked by high pH cement paste, deform when stored at high temperatures in closed spaces or become brittle or crack at low temperatures.

4.1.2 *Bowl*—The bowl shall have a diameter equal to 1 to 1.25 times the height and be constructed with a flange at or near the top surface. Bowls shall not have a capacity of less than 0.075 ft^3 (2.1 L).

4.1.3 *Top Section*—The top section shall have a capacity at least 20 % larger than the bowl and shall be equipped with a flexible gasket and a device to attach the top section to the bowl and make a watertight connection. The top section shall be equipped with a transparent scale, graduated in increments not greater than 0.5 % from 0 at the top to 9 %, or more, of the volume of the bowl. Graduations shall be accurate to ±0.1 % by volume of the bowl. The upper end of the neck shall have a water tight cap that will maintain a seal when the meter is inverted and rolled.

4.2 *Funnel*—A funnel with a spout of a size permitting it to be inserted through the neck of the top section and long enough to extend to a point just above the bottom of the top section. The discharge end of the spout shall be so constructed that when water is added to the container there will be a minimum disturbance of the concrete.

4.3 *Tamping Rod*—A round, straight ⅝ in. (16 mm) diameter rod at least 12 in. (300 mm) long with both ends rounded to a hemispherical tip of the same diameter. The rod shall be made of steel, high density polyethylene or other plastic of equal or greater abrasion resistance.

---

[1] This test method is under the jurisdiction of ASTM Committee C-9 on Concrete and Concrete Aggregates and is the direct responsibility of Subcommittee C09.60 on Fresh Concrete Testing.
Current edition approved Sept. 15, 1994. Published November 1994. Originally published as C 173 – 42. Last previous edition C 173 – 94.
[2] *Annual Book of ASTM Standards*, Vol 04.02.

C 173

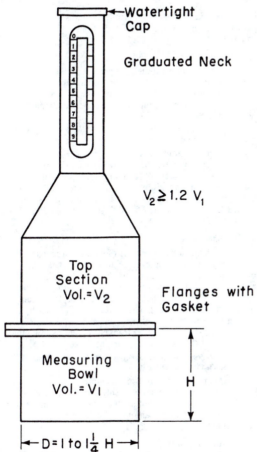

Watertight Cap

Graduated Neck

$V_2 \geq 1.2\ V_1$

Top Section Vol.= V_2

Flanges with Gasket

Measuring Bowl Vol.= V_1

H

$D = 1\ to\ 1\frac{1}{4}\ H$

FIG. 1 Apparatus for Measuring Air Content of Fresh Concrete by Volumetric Method

4.4 *Strike-off Bar*—A flat, straight steel bar at least ⅛ by ¾ by 12 in. (3 by 20 by 300 mm) or a flat, straight bar at least ¼ by ¾ by 12 in. (6 by 20 by 300 mm) high density polyethylene or other plastic of equal or greater abrasion resistance.

4.5 *Calibrated Cup*—A metal or plastic cup either having a capacity of or being graduated in increments equal to 1.03 ± 0.04 % of the volume of the bowl of the air meter.

NOTE 1—The volume of the calibrated cup is slightly larger than 1.0 % of the volume of the bowl to compensate for the volume contraction that takes place when 70 % isopropyl alcohol is mixed with water. Other alcohols or defoaming agents could be used if calculations show that their use will result in an error in indicated air content less than 0.1 %. The calibrated cup should not be used to determine the accuracy of the graduations on the neck of the top section.

4.6 *Syringe*—A small rubber bulb syringe having a capacity at least that of the calibrated cup.

4.7 *Pouring Vessel*—A container of approximately 1 qt or 1 L capacity.

4.8 *Scoop*—A small metal scoop.

4.9 *Isopropyl Alcohol*—Use 70 % by volume isopropyl alcohol (approximately 65 % by weight) (Notes 1 and 2).

NOTE 2—Seventy percent isopropyl alcohol is commonly available as rubbing alcohol. More concentrated grades can be diluted with water to the required concentration.

4.10 *Mallet*—A mallet (with a rubber or rawhide head) weighing approximately 1.25 ± 0.50 lb (0.57 ± 0.23 kg).

5. Calibration

5.1 Calibrate the meter and calibrated cup initially and annually or whenever there is reason to suspect damage or deformation of the meter or calibrated cup.

5.2 Determine the volume of the bowl with an accuracy of at least 0.1 % by weighing the amount of water required to fill it at room temperature, and dividing this weight by the unit weight of water at the same temperature. Follow the calibration procedure outlined in Test Method C 29/C 29M.

5.3 Determine the accuracy of the graduations on the neck of the top section of the airmeter by filling the assembled measuring bowl and top section with water to the level of the mark for highest air content graduation.

5.3.1 Add water in increments of 1.0 % of the volume of the bowl to check accuracy throughout the graduated range of air content. The error at any point throughout the graduated range shall not exceed 0.1 % of air.

5.4 Determine the volume of the calibrated cup using water at 70°F (21.1°C) by the method outlined in 5.2. A quick check can be made by adding one or more calibrated cups of water to the assembled apparatus and observing the increase in the height of the water column after filling to a given level.

6. Sampling

6.1 Obtain the sample of freshly mixed concrete in accordance with Practice C 172. If the concrete contains coarse aggregate particles that would be retained on a 1½ in. (37.5 mm) sieve, wet sieve a representative sample over a 1 in. (25 mm) sieve to yield somewhat more than enough material to fill the measuring bowl. The wet sieving procedure is described in Practice C 172. Carry out the wet sieving operation with the minimum practicable disturbance of the mortar. Make no attempt to wipe adhering mortar from coarse aggregate particles retained on the sieve.

7. Procedure

7.1 *Rodding and Tapping*—Using the scoop, fill the bowl with freshly mixed concrete in three layers of equal depth. Rod each layer 25 times with the tamping rod. After each layer is rodded, tap the sides of the measure 10 to 15 times with the mallet to close any voids left by the tamping rod and to release any large bubbles of air that may have been trapped.

7.2 *Striking Off*—After rodding and tapping of the third layer, strike off the excess concrete with the strike-off bar until the surface is flush with the top of the bowl. Wipe the flange of the bowl clean.

7.3 *Adding Water*—Attach the top section into position on the bowl, insert the funnel, and add water until it appears in the neck. Remove the funnel (Note 3). Using the rubber syringe, adjust the water level until the bottom of the

C 173

meniscus is level with the zero mark. Attach and tighten the watertight cap.

NOTE 3—When filling the air meter with water, the addition of up to 1 pt (470 mL) of alcohol facilitates the removal of air from high air content or high cement content concrete.

7.4 Displace the volume of air in the concrete specimen using these procedures:

7.4.1 *Inverting and Agitating*—Repeatedly invert and agitate the unit for a minimum of 45 s to free concrete from the base. To prevent aggregate from lodging in the neck of the unit do not keep it inverted for more than five s at a time (Note 4).

NOTE 4—This procedure is intended to free the concrete from the base. When the concrete has broken free, the aggregate can be heard moving in the airmeter.

7.4.2 *Rolling and Rocking*—After completing the inverting and agitating procedure, tilt the meter approximately 45 degrees and vigorously roll and rock the unit for approximately 1 min, keeping the neck elevated at all times. Set the unit upright and allow it to stand while the air rises to the top until the liquid level stabilizes. The liquid level is considered stable when it does not change more than 0.1 % within a one min period. If the liquid level is obscured by foam, use the rubber syringe to add sufficient alcohol, in one calibrated cup increments to establish a readable liquid level. Record the number of calibrated cups of alcohol used (Note 5). Read the liquid level.

NOTE 5—It may require more than 20 min for the liquid level to stabilize when moderately high cement content concrete contains more than 6 % air.

7.4.3 Repeat the one minute rolling and rocking procedure until two consecutive readings do not change by more than 0.25 % air.

7.5 *Dispelling Foam*—Remove the cap. Using the syringe, add sufficient isopropyl alcohol, in one calibrated cup increments, to dispel as much of the foam as is practicable. Record the number of calibrated cups of alcohol used.

7.6 *Reading*—Make a direct reading of the liquid in the neck, reading to the bottom of the meniscus, and estimating to the nearest 0.25 % air.

7.7 Disassemble the apparatus and examine the contents to be sure that there are no portions of undisturbed, tightly packed concrete in the base. If portions of undisturbed concrete are found, the test is invalid.

8. Calculation

8.1 Calculate the air content, in percent, of the concrete in the measuring bowl by adding the reading from 7.6 to the amount of alcohol used in accordance with 7.5 and 7.4.2 (Note 6). This is the air content of the concrete sample to the nearest 0.25 %.

NOTE 6—Alcohol added, if any, in initially filling the meter, in 7.3 is not added to the reading from 7.6.

8.2 When the sample tested represents that portion of the mixture obtained by wet sieving over a 1-in. (25-mm) sieve, calculate the air content of the mortar or of the full mixture using the formulas given in Test Method C 231. Use appropriate quantities coarser or finer than the 1-in. sieve instead of the 1½-in. (37.5 mm) sieve specified in Test Method C 231.

9. Precision and Bias

9.1 The standard deviation is essentially proportional to the average for different levels of air content. The following precision statement is based on 979 tests made in six field experiments by the West Virginia D.O.T. The multi-operator coefficient of variation has been found to be 11 percent of the measured air content. Therefore, results of tests by two different operators on specimens taken from a single concrete sample should not differ from each other by more than 32 percent of their average air content (Note 7).

NOTE 7—These numbers represent, respectively, the 1s % and d2s % limits described in Practice C 670.

9.2 This test method provides volumetric procedures for determining the air content of freshly mixed concrete. When conducted properly, this test method has no bias because the value of the air content can only be defined in terms of the test method.

10. Keywords

10.1 air content; calibration; concrete, correction factor; freshly mixed concrete; measuring bowl; meter; volumetric method

AMERICAN SOCIETY FOR TESTING AND MATERIALS
1916 Race St. Philadelphia, Pa 19103
Reprinted from the Annual Book of ASTM Standards. Copyright ASTM
If not listed in the current combined index, will appear in the next edition.

Standard Test Method for
Air Content of Freshly Mixed Concrete
by the Pressure Method[1]

This standard is issued under the fixed designation C 231; the number immediately following the designation indicates the year of original adoption or, in the case of revision, the year of last revision. A number in parentheses indicates the year of last reapproval. A superscript epsilon (ϵ) indicates an editorial change since the last revision or reapproval.

This test method has been approved for use by agencies of the Department of Defense. Consult the DoD Index of Specifications and Standards for the specific year of issue which has been adopted by the Department of Defense.

1. Scope

1.1 This test method covers determination of the air content of freshly mixed concrete from observation of the change in volume of concrete with a change in pressure.

1.2 This test method is intended for use with concretes and mortars made with relatively dense aggregates for which the aggregate correction factor can be satisfactorily determined by the technique described in Section 6. It is not applicable to concretes made with lightweight aggregates, air-cooled blast-furnace slag, or aggregates of high porosity. In these cases, Test Method C 173 should be used. This test method is also not applicable to nonplastic concrete such as is commonly used in the manufacture of pipe and concrete masonry units.

1.3 The values stated in inch-pound units are to be regarded as the standard.

1.4 *This standard does not purport to address all of the safety problems, if any, associated with its use. It is the responsibility of the user of this standard to establish appropriate safety and health practices and determine the applicability of regulatory limitations prior to use. See Note A1.7 for a specific caution statement.*

2. Referenced Documents

2.1 *ASTM Standards:*
C 138 Test Method for Unit Weight, Yield, and Air Content (Gravimetric) of Concrete[2]
C 172 Practice for Sampling Freshly Mixed Concrete[2]
C 173 Test Method for Air Content of Freshly Mixed Concrete by the Volumetric Method[2]
C 192 Practice for Making and Curing Concrete Test Specimens in the Laboratory[2]
C 670 Practice for Preparing Precision and Bias Statements for Test Methods of Construction Materials[2]
E 177 Practice for Use of the Terms Precision and Bias in ASTM Test Methods[3]

3. Significance and Use

3.1 This test method covers the determination of the air content of freshly mixed concrete. The test is intended to determine the air content of freshly mixed concrete exclusive of any air that may be inside voids within aggregate particles. For this reason, it is applicable to concrete made with relatively dense aggregate particles and requires determination of the aggregate correction factor (see 6.1 and 9.1).

3.2 This test method and Test Method C 138 and C 173 provide pressure, gravimetric, and volumetric procedures, respectively, for determining the air content of freshly mixed concrete. The pressure procedure of this test method gives substantially the same air contents as the other two test methods for concretes made with dense aggregates.

3.3 The air content of hardened concrete may be either higher or lower than that determined by this test method. This depends upon the methods and amount of consolidation effort applied to the concrete from which the hardened concrete specimen is taken; uniformity and stability of the air bubbles in the fresh and hardened concrete; accuracy of the microscopic examination, if used; time of comparison; environmental exposure; stage in the delivery, placement and consolidation processes at which the air content of the unhardened concrete is determined, that is, before or after the concrete goes through a pump; and other factors.

4. Apparatus

4.1 *Air Meters*—There are available satisfactory apparatus of two basic operational designs employing the principle of Boyle's law. For purposes of reference herein these are designated Meter Type A and Meter Type B.

4.1.1 *Meter Type A*—An air meter consisting of a measuring bowl and cover assembly (see Fig. 1) conforming to the requirements of 4.2 and 4.3. The operational principle of this meter consists of introducing water to a predetermined height above a sample of concrete of known volume, and the application of a predetermined air pressure over the water. The determination consists of the reduction in volume of the air in the concrete sample by observing the amount the water level is lowered under the applied pressure, the latter amount being calibrated in terms of percent of air in the concrete sample.

4.1.2 *Meter Type B*—An air meter consisting of a measuring bowl and cover assembly (see Fig. 2) conforming to the requirements of 4.2 and 4.3. The operational principle of this meter consists of equalizing a known volume of air at a known pressure in a sealed air chamber with the unknown volume of air in the concrete sample, the dial on the pressure gage being calibrated in terms of percent air for the observed

[1] This test method is under the jurisdiction of ASTM Committee C-9 on Concrete and Concrete Aggregates, and is the direct responsibility of Subcommittee C09.03.03 on Methods of Testing Fresh Concrete.
Current edition approved Nov. 15, 1991. Published January 1992. Originally published as C 231 – 49 T. Last previous edition C 231 – 91a.
[2] *Annual Book of ASTM Standards*, Vol 04.02.
[3] *Annual Book of ASTM Standards*, Vols 04.01, 04.02, and 14.02.

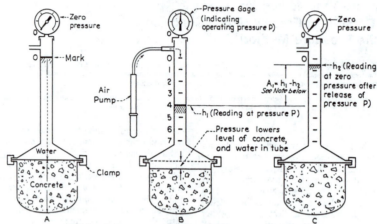

Note: $A_l = h_1 - h_2$ when bowl contains concrete as shown in this figure; when bowl contains only aggregate and water, $h_1 - h_2 = G$ (aggregate correction factor). $A_l - G = A$ (entrained air content of concrete)

FIG. 1   Illustration of the Pressure Method for Air Content—Type-A Meter

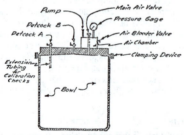

FIG. 2   Schematic Diagram—Type-B Meter

pressure at which equalization takes place. Working pressures of 7.5 to 30.0 psi (51 to 207 kPa) have been used satisfactorily.

4.2 *Measuring Bowl*—The measuring bowl shall be essentially cylindrical in shape, made of steel, hard metal, or other hard material not readily attacked by the cement paste, having a minimum diameter equal to 0.75 to 1.25 times the height, and a capacity of at least 0.20 ft³ (0.006 m³). It shall be flanged or otherwise constructed to provide for a pressure tight fit between bowl and cover assembly. The interior surfaces of the bowl and surfaces of rims, flanges, and other component fitted parts shall be machined smooth. The measuring bowl and cover assembly shall be sufficiently rigid to limit the expansion factor, D, of the apparatus assembly (Annex A1.5) to not more than 0.1 % of air content on the indicator scale when under normal operating pressure.

4.3 *Cover Assembly*:

4.3.1 The cover assembly shall be made of steel, hard metal, or other hard material not readily attacked by the cement paste. It shall be flanged or otherwise constructed to provide for a pressure-tight fit between bowl and cover assembly and shall have machined smooth interior surfaces

contoured to provide an air space above the level of the top of the measuring bowl. The cover shall be sufficiently rigid to limit the expansion factor of the apparatus assembly as prescribed in 4.2.

4.3.2 The cover assembly shall be fitted with a means of direct reading of the air content. The cover for the Type A meter shall be fitted with a standpipe, which may be a transparent graduated tube or may be a metal tube of uniform bore with a glass water gage attached. In the Type B meter, the dial of the pressure gage shall be calibrated to indicate the percent of air. Graduations shall be provided for a range in air content of at least 8 % easily readable to 0.1 % as determined by the proper air pressure calibration test.

4.3.3 The cover assembly shall be fitted with air valves, air bleeder valves, and petcocks for bleeding off or through which water may be introduced as necessary for the particular meter design. Suitable means for clamping the cover to the bowl shall be provided to make a pressure-tight seal without entrapping air at the joint between the flanges of the cover and bowl. A suitable hand pump shall be provided with the cover either as an attachment or as an accessory.

4.4 *Calibration Vessel*—A measure having an internal volume equal to a percent of the volume of the measuring bowl corresponding to the approximate percent of air in the concrete to be tested; or, if smaller, it shall be possible to check calibration of the meter indicator at the approximate percent of air in the concrete to be tested by repeated filling of the measure. When the design of the meter requires placing the calibration vessel within the measuring bowl to check calibration, the measure shall be cylindrical in shape and of an inside depth ½ in. (13 mm) less than that of the bowl. A satisfactory measure of this type may be machined from No. 16 gage brass tubing, of a diameter to provide the volume desired, to which a brass disk ½ in. in thickness is soldered to form an end. When design of the meter requires withdrawing of water from the water-filled bowl and cover

C 231

assembly to check calibration, the measure may be an integral part of the cover assembly or may be a separate cylindrical measure similar to the above described cylinder.

4.5 The designs of various available types of airmeters are such that they differ in operating techniques and therefore, all of the items described in 4.6 through 4.16 may not be required. The items required shall be those necessary for use with the particular design of apparatus used to satisfactorily determine air content in accordance with the procedures prescribed herein.

4.6 *Coil Spring or Other Device for Holding Calibration Cylinder in Place.*

4.7 *Spray Tube*—A brass tube of appropriate diameter, which may be an integral part of the cover assembly or which may be provided separately. It shall be so constructed that when water is added to the container, it is sprayed to the walls of the cover in such a manner as to flow down the sides causing a minimum of disturbance to the concrete.

4.8 *Trowel*—A standard brick mason's trowel.

4.9 *Tamping Rod*—The tamping rod shall be a round straight steel rod ⅝ in. (16 mm) in diameter and not less than approximately 16 in. (400 mm) in length, having the tamping end rounded to hemispherical tip the diameter of which is ⅝ in. (16 mm).

4.10 *Mallet*—A mallet (with a rubber or rawhide head) weighing approximately 1.25 ± 0.50 lb (0.57 ± 0.23 kg) for use with measures of 0.5 ft³ (14 dm³) or smaller, and a mallet weighing approximately 2.25 ± 0.50 lb (1.02 ± 0.23 kg) for use with measures larger than 0.5 ft³.

4.11 *Strike-Off Bar*—A flat straight bar of steel or other suitable metal at least ⅛ in. (3 mm) thick and ¾ in. (20 mm) wide by 12 in. (300 mm) long.

4.12 *Strike-Off Plate*—A flat rectangular metal plate at least ¼ in. (6 mm) thick or a glass or acrylic plate at least ½ in. (12 mm) thick with a length and width at least 2 in. (50 mm) greater than the diameter of the measure with which it is to be used. The edges of the plate shall be straight and smooth within a tolerance of 1/16 in. (1.5 mm).

4.13 *Funnel*, with the spout fitting into spray tube.

4.14 *Measure for Water*, having the necessary capacity to fill the indicator with water from the top of the concrete to the zero mark.

4.15 *Vibrator*, as described in Practice C 192.

4.16 *Sieves*, 1½-in. (37.5-mm) with not less than 2 ft² (0.19 m²) of sieving area.

5. Calibration of Apparatus

5.1 Make calibration tests in accordance with procedures prescribed in the annex. Rough handling will affect the calibration of both Types A and B meters. Changes in barometric pressure will affect the calibration of Type A meter but not Type B meter. The steps described A1.2 to A1.6, as applicable to the meter type under consideration, are prerequisites for the final calibration test to determine the operating pressure, *P*, on the pressure gage of the Type A meter as described in A1.7, or to determine the accuracy of the graduations indicating air content on the dial face of the pressure gage of the Type B meter. Normally the steps in A1.2 to A1.6 need be made only once (at the time of initial calibration), or only occasionally to check volume constancy of the calibration cylinder and measuring bowl. On the other

hand, the calibration test described in A1.7 and A1.9, as applicable to the meter type being checked, must be made as frequently as necessary to ensure that the proper gage pressure, *P*, is being used for the Type A meter or that the correct air contents are being indicated on the pressure gage air content scale for the Type B meter. A change in elevation of more than 600 ft (183 m) from the location at which a Type-A meter was last calibrated will require recalibration in accordance with A1.7.

6. Determination of Aggregate Correction Factor

6.1 *Procedure*—Determine the aggregate correction factor on a combined sample of fine and coarse aggregate as directed in 6.2 to 6.4. It is determined independently by applying the calibrated pressure to a sample of inundated fine and coarse aggregate in approximately the same moisture condition, amount, and proportions occurring in the concrete sample under test.

6.2 *Aggregate Sample Size*—Calculate the weights of fine and coarse aggregate present in the sample of fresh concrete whose air content is to be determined, as follows:

$$F_s = (S/B) \times F_b \tag{1}$$
$$C_s = (S/B) \times C_b \tag{2}$$

where:

F_s = weight of fine aggregate in concrete sample under test, lb (kg),

S = volume of concrete sample (same as volume of measuring bowl), ft³ (m³),

B = volume of concrete produced per batch (Note 1), ft³ (m³),

F_b = total weight of fine aggregate in the moisture condition used in batch, lb (kg),

C_s = weight of coarse aggregate in concrete sample under test, lb (kg), and

C_b = total weight of coarse aggregate in the moisture condition used in batch, lb (kg).

NOTE 1—The volume of concrete produced per batch can be determined in accordance with applicable provisions of Test Method C 138.

NOTE 2—The term "weight" is temporarily used in this standard because of established trade usage. The word is used to mean both "force" and "mass," and care must be taken to determine which is meant in each case (SI unit for force = newton and for mass = kilogram).

6.3 *Placement of Aggregate in Measuring Bowl*—Mix representative samples of fine aggregate F_s and coarse aggregate C_s, and place in the measuring bowl filled one-third full with water. Place the mixed aggregate, a small amount at a time, into the measuring bowl; if necessary, add additional water so as to inundate all of the aggregate. Add each scoopful in a manner that will entrap as little air as possible and remove accumulations of foam promptly. Tap the sides of the bowl and lightly rod the upper 1 in. (25 mm) of the aggregate about ten times. Stir after each addition of aggregate to eliminate entrapped air.

6.4 *Aggregate Correction Factor Determination*:

6.4.1 *Initial Procedure for Types A and B Meters*—When all of the aggregate has been placed in the measuring bowl, remove excess foam and keep the aggregate inundated for a period of time approximately equal to the time between introduction of the water into the mixer and the time of performing the test for air content before proceeding with the determination as directed in 6.4.2 or 6.4.3.

6.4.2 *Type A Meter*—Complete the test as described in 8.2.1 and 8.2.2. The aggregate correction factor, G, is equal to $h_1 - h_2$ (see Fig. 1) (Note 3).

6.4.3 *Type B Meter*—Perform the procedures as described in 8.3.1. Remove a volume of water from the assembled and filled apparatus approximately equivalent to the volume of air that would be contained in a typical concrete sample of a size equal to the volume of the bowl. Remove the water in the manner described in A1.9 for the calibration tests. Complete the test as described in 8.3.2. The aggregate correction factor, G, is equal to the reading on the air-content scale minus the volume of water removed from the bowl expressed as a percent of the volume of the bowl (see Fig. 1).

NOTE 3—The aggregate correction factor will vary with different aggregates. It can be determined only by test, since apparently it is not directly related to absorption of the particles. The test can be easily made and must not be ignored. Ordinarily the factor will remain reasonably constant for given aggregates, but an occasional check test is recommended.

7. Preparation of Concrete Test Sample

7.1 Obtain the sample of freshly mixed concrete in accordance with applicable procedures of Practice C 172. If the concrete contains coarse aggregate particles that would be retained on a 2-in. (50-mm) sieve, wet-sieve a sufficient amount of the representative sample over a 1½-in. (37.5-mm) sieve, as described in Practice C 172, to yield somewhat more than enough material to fill the measuring bowl of the size selected for use. Carry out the wet-sieving operation with the minimum practicable disturbance of the mortar. Make no attempt to wipe adhering mortar from coarse aggregate particles retained on the sieve.

8. Procedure for Determining Air Content of Concrete

8.1 *Placement and Consolidation of Sample*:

8.1.1 Dampen the interior of the measuring bowl and place it on a flat, level, firm surface. Place a representative sample of the concrete, prepared as described in Section 7, in the measuring bowl in equal layers. Consolidate each layer by the rodding procedure (8.1.2) or by vibration (8.1.3). Strike-off the finally consolidated layer (8.1.4). Rod concretes with a slump greater than 3 in. (75 mm). Rod or vibrate concrete with a slump of 1 to 3 in. (25 to 75 mm). Consolidate concretes with a slump less than 1 in. (25 mm) by vibration.

8.1.2 *Rodding*—Place the concrete in the measuring bowl in three layers of approximately equal volume. Consolidate each layer of concrete by 25 strokes of the tamping rod evenly distributed over the cross section. After each layer is rodded, tap the sides of the measure smartly 10 to 15 times with the mallet to close any voids left by the tamping rod and to release any large bubbles of air that may have been trapped. Rod the bottom layer throughout its depth, but the rod shall not forcibly strike the bottom of the measure. In rodding the second and final layers, use only enough force to cause the rod to penetrate the surface of the previous layer about 1 in. (25 mm). Add the final layer of concrete in a manner to avoid excessive overfilling (8.1.4).

8.1.3 *Vibration*—Place the concrete in the measuring

bowl in two layers of approximately equal volume. Place all of the concrete for each layer before starting vibration of that layer. Consolidate each layer by three insertions of the vibrator evenly distributed over the cross section. Add the final layer in a manner to avoid excessive overfilling (8.1.4). In consolidating the bottom layer, do not allow the vibrator to rest on or touch the bottom or sides of the measuring bowl. Take care in withdrawing the vibrator to ensure that no air pockets are left in the specimen. Observe a standard duration of vibration for the particular kind of concrete, vibrator, and measuring bowl involved. The duration of vibration required will depend upon the workability of the concrete and the effectiveness of the vibrator. Continue vibration only long enough to achieve proper consolidation of the concrete. Overvibration may cause segregation and loss of intentionally entrained air. Usually, sufficient vibration has been applied as soon as the surface of the concrete becomes relatively smooth and has a glazed appearance. Never continue vibration long enough to cause escape of froth from the sample.

8.1.4 *Strike Off*—After consolidation of the concrete, strike off the top surface by sliding the strike-off bar across the top flange or rim of the measuring bowl with a sawing motion until the bowl is just level full. On completion of consolidation, the bowl must not contain a great excess or deficiency of concrete. Removal of approximately ⅛ in. (3 mm) during strike off is optimum. A small quantity of representative concrete may be added to correct a deficiency. If the measure contains a great excess, remove a representative portion of concrete with a trowel or scoop before the measure is struck off. When a strike-off plate is used, strike off concrete as prescribed in Test Method C 138.

NOTE 4—The use of the strike-off plate on cast aluminum or other relatively soft metal air meter bases may cause rapid wear of the rim and require frequent maintenance, calibration, and ultimately, replacement.

8.1.5 *Application of Test Method*—Any portion of the test method not specifically designated as pertaining to Type A or Type B meter shall apply to both types.

8.2 *Procedure—Type A Meter*:

8.2.1 *Preparation for Test*—Thoroughly clean the flanges or rims of the bowl and of the cover assembly so that when the cover is clamped in place a pressure-tight seal will be obtained. Assemble the apparatus and add water over the concrete by means of the tube until it rises to about the halfway mark in the standpipe. Incline the apparatus assembly about 30° from vertical and, using the bottom of the bowl as a pivot, describe several complete circles with the upper end of the column, simultaneously tapping the cover lightly to remove any entrapped air bubbles above the concrete sample. Return the apparatus assembly to a vertical position and fill the water column slightly above the zero mark, while lightly tapping the sides of the bowl. Bring the water level to the zero mark of the graduated tube before closing the vent at the top of the water column (see Fig. 1 A).

NOTE 5—Some Type A meters have a calibrated starting fill mark above the zero mark. Generally, this starting mark should not be used since, as noted in 8.2.3, the apparent air content is the difference between the water level reading H, at pressure P and the water level h_2 at zero pressure after release of pressure P.

8.2.2 The internal surface of the cover assembly shall be kept clean and free from oil or grease; the surface shall be wet to prevent adherence of air bubbles that might be difficult to dislodge after assembly of the apparatus.

8.2.3 *Test Procedure*—Apply slightly more than the desired test pressure, P, (about 0.2 psi (1380 Pa) more) to the concrete by means of the small hand pump. To relieve local restraints, tap the sides of the measure sharply to and, when the pressure gage indicates the exact test pressure, P, as determined in accordance with A1.7, read the water level, h_1, and record to the nearest division or half-division on the graduated precision-bore tube or gage glass of the standpipe (see Fig. 1 B). For extremely harsh mixes it may be necessary to tap the bowl vigorously until further tapping produces no change in the indicated air content. Gradually release the air pressure through the vent at the top of the water column and tap the sides of the bowl lightly for about 1 min. Record the water level, h_2, to the nearest division or half-division (see Fig. 1 C). Calculate the apparent air content as follows:

$$A_1 = h_1 - h_2 \qquad (3)$$

where:

A_1 = apparent air content,
h_1 = water level reading at pressure, P (see Note 6), and
h_2 = water level reading at zero pressure after release of pressure, P.

8.2.4 *Check Test*—Repeat the steps described in 8.2.3 without adding water to reestablish the water level at the zero mark. The two consecutive determinations of apparent air content should check within 0.2 % of air and shall be averaged to give the value A_1 to be used in calculating the air content, A_s, in accordance with Section 9.

8.2.5 In the event the air content exceeds the range of the meter when it is operated at the normal test pressure P, reduce the test pressure to the alternative test pressure P_1 and repeat the steps outlined in 8.2.2 and 8.2.3.

NOTE 6—See A1.7 for exact calibration procedures. An approximate value of the alternative pressure, P_1, such that the apparent air content will equal twice the meter reading can be computed from the following relationship:

$$P_1 = P_a P/(2P_a + P) \qquad (4)$$

where:

P_1 = alternative test pressure, psi (or kPa),
P_a = atmospheric pressure, psi (approximately 14.7 psi (101 kPa) but will vary with altitude and weather conditions) (or kPa), and
P = normal test or operating gage pressure, psi (or kPa).

8.3 *Procedure—Type B Meter*

8.3.1 *Preparation for Test*—Thoroughly clean the flanges or rims of the bowl and the cover assembly so that when the cover is clamped in place a pressure-tight seal will be obtained. Assemble the apparatus. Close the air valve between the air chamber and the measuring bowl and open both petcocks on the holes through the cover. Using a rubber syringe, inject water through one petcock until water emerges from the opposite petcock. Jar the meter gently until all air is expelled from this same petcock.

8.3.2 *Test Procedure*—Close the airbleeder valve on the air chamber and pump air into the air chamber until the gage hand is on the initial pressure line. Allow a few seconds for the compressed air to cool to normal temperature. Stabilize the gage hand at the initial pressure line by pumping or bleeding-off air as necessary, tapping the gage lightly by hand. Close both petcocks on the holes through the cover.

Open the air valve between the air chamber and the measuring bowl. Tap the sides of the measuring bowl smartly with the mallet to relieve local restraints. Lightly tap the pressure gage by hand to stabilize the gage hand. Read the percentage of air on the dial of the pressure gage. Failure to close the main air valve before releasing the pressure from either the container or the air chamber will result in water being drawn into the air chamber, thus introducing error in subsequent measurements. In the event water enters the air chamber it must be bled from the air chamber through the bleeder valve followed by several strokes of the pump to blow out the last traces of water. Release the pressure by opening both petcocks (Fig. 1, A and B) before removing the cover.

9. Calculation

9.1 *Air Content of Sample Tested*—Calculate the air content of the concrete in the measuring bowl as follows:

$$A_s = A_1 - G \qquad (5)$$

where:

A_s = air content of the sample tested, %,
A_1 = apparent air content of the sample tested, % (see 7.2.2 and 8.3.2), and
G = aggregate correction factor, % (Section 6).

9.2 *Air Content of Full Mixture*—When the sample tested represents that portion of the mixture that is obtained by wet sieving to remove aggregate particles larger than a 1½-in. (37.5-mm) sieve, the air content of the full mixture may be calculated as follows:

$$A_t = 100 A_s V_c/(100 V_t - A_s V_a) \qquad (6)$$

where (Note 7):

A_t = air content of the full mixture, %,
V_c = absolute volume of the ingredients of the mixture passing a 1½-in. sieve, airfree, as determined from the original batch weights, ft^3 (m^3),
V_t = absolute volume of all ingredients of the mixture, airfree, ft^3 (m^3), and
V_a = absolute volume of the aggregate in the mixture coarser than a 1½-in. sieve, as determined from original batch weights, ft^3 (m^3).

9.3 *Air Content of the Mortar Fraction*—When it is desired to know the air content of the mortar fraction of the mixture, calculate it as follows:

$$A_m = 100 A_s V_c /[100 V_m + A_s(V_c - V_m)] \qquad (7)$$

where (Note 7):

A_m = air content of the mortar fraction, %, and
V_m = absolute volume of the ingredients of the mortar fraction of the mixture, airfree, ft^3 (m^3).

NOTE 7—The values for use in Eqs 6 and 7 are most conveniently obtained from data on the concrete mixture tabulated as follows for a batch of any size:

	Absolute Volume, ft^3 (m^3)	
Cement	___	
Water	___	
Fine aggregate	___	V_m } V_c
Coarse aggregate (No. 4 (4.75-mm) to 1½-in. (37.5-mm))	___	
Coarse aggregate (1½-in.)	___	V_a
Total	___	V_t

◆ C 231

10. Precision and Bias

10.1 *Precision:*

10.1.1 *Single-Operator Precision*—The single-operator standard deviation cannot be established because the sampling requirements for this test, as established in Practice C 172, do not allow a single operator time to conduct more than one test on a sample.

10.1.2 *Multilaboratory Precision*—The multilaboratory standard deviation has not been established.

10.1.3 *Multioperator Precision*—The multioperator standard deviation of a single test result has been found to be 0.28 % air by volume of concrete for Type A air meters as long as the air content does not exceed 7 %. Therefore results of two tests properly conducted by different operators but on the same material should not differ by more than 0.8 % air by volume of concrete (see Practice E 177, Notes 8 and 9).

NOTE 8—These numbers represent, respectively, the (1s) and (d2s) limits as described in Practice C 670. The precision statements are based on the variations in tests on three different concretes, each tested by eleven different operators.[4]

NOTE 9—The precision of this test method using Type B air meters has not been determined.

10.2 *Bias*—This test method has no bias because the air content of freshly mixed concrete can only be defined in terms of the test methods.

11. Keywords

11.1 air content; calibration; concrete; correction factor; measuring bowl; meter; pressure; pump; unit weight

---

[4] Reidenour, D. R., and Howe, R. H., "Air Content of Plastic and Hardened Concrete," presented at the 2nd International Conference on "Durability of Building Materials and Components" Sept. 14–16, 1981. Reprints compiled by: G. Frohnsdorff and B. Horner, National Institute for Standards and Technology, Gaithersburg, MD 20899, formerly National Bureau of Standards, Washington, DC 20234.

ANNEX

Mandatory Information

A1. CALIBRATION OF APPARATUS

A1.1 Calibration tests shall be performed in accordance with the following procedures as applicable to the meter type being employed.

A1.2 *Calibration of the Calibration Vessel*—Determine accurately the weight of water, w, required to fill the calibration vessel, using a scale accurate to 0.1 % of the weight of the vessel filled with water. This step shall be performed for Type A and B meters.

A1.3 *Calibration of the Measuring Bowl*—Determine the weight of water, W, required to fill the measuring bowl, using a scale accurate to 0.1 % of the weight of the bowl filled with water. Slide a glass plate carefully over the flange of the bowl in a manner to ensure that the bowl is completely filled with water. A thin film of cup grease smeared on the flange of the bowl will make a watertight joint between the glass plate and the top of the bowl. This step shall be performed for Type A and B meters.

A1.4 *Effective Volume of the Calibration Vessel, R*—The constant R represents the effective volume of the calibration vessel expressed as a percentage of the volume of the measuring bowl.

A1.4.1 For meter Types A, calculate R as follows (Note A1):

$$R = 0.98 \, w/W \qquad (A1.1)$$

where:

w = weight of water required to fill the calibration vessel, and

W = weight of water required to fill the measuring bowl.

NOTE A1.1—The factor 0.98 is used to correct for the reduction in the volume of air in the calibration vessel when it is compressed by a depth of water equal to the depth of the measuring bowl. This factor is approximately 0.98 for an 8-in. (203-mm) deep measuring bowl at sea level. Its value decreases to approximately 0.975 at 5000 ft (1524 m) above sea level and 0.970 at 13 000 ft (3962 m) above sea level. The

value of this constant will decrease by about 0.01 for each 4-in. (102-mm) increase in bowl depth. The depth of the measuring bowl and atmospheric pressure do not affect the effective volume of the calibration vessel for meter Types B.

A1.4.2 For meter Types B calculate R as follows (Note A1.1):

$$R = w/W \qquad (A1.2)$$

A1.5 *Determination of, or Check of, Allowance for Expansion Factor, D:*

A1.5.1 For meter assemblies of Type A determine the expansion factor, D (Note A1.2) by filling the apparatus with water only (making certain that all entrapped air has been removed and the water level is exactly on the zero mark (Note A1.3) and applying an air pressure approximately equal to the operating pressure, P, determined by the calibration test described in A1.7. The amount the water column lowers will be the equivalent expansion factor, D, for that particular apparatus and pressure (Note A1.5).

NOTE A1.2—Although the bowl, cover, and clamping mechanism of the apparatus must of necessity be sturdily constructed so that it will be pressure-tight, the application of internal pressure will result in a small increase in volume. This expansion will not affect the test results because, with the procedure described in Sections 6 and 8, the amount of expansion is the same for the test for air in concrete as for the test for aggregate correction factor on combined fine and coarse aggregates, and is thereby automatically cancelled. However, it does enter into the calibration test to determine the air pressure to be used in testing fresh concrete.

NOTE A1.3—The water columns on some meters of Type-A design are marked with an initial water level and a zero mark, the difference between the two marks being the allowance for the expansion factor. This allowance should be checked in the same manner as for meters not so marked and in such a case, the expansion factor should be omitted in computing the calibration readings in A1.7.

NOTE A1.4—It will be sufficiently accurate for this purpose to use an approximate value for P determined by making a preliminary calibra-

C 231

tion test as described in A1.7 except that an approximate value for the calibration factor, K, should be used. For this test $K = 0.98 R$ which is the same as Eq A1.2 except that the expansion reading, D, as yet unknown, is assumed to be zero.

A1.5.2 For meters of Type B design, the allowance for the expansion factor, D, is included in the difference between the initial pressure indicated on the pressure gage and the zero percent mark on the air-content scale on the pressure gage. This allowance shall be checked by filling the apparatus with water (making certain that all entrapped air has been removed), pumping air into the air chamber until the gage hand is stabilized at the indicated initial pressure line, and then releasing the air to the measuring bowl (Note A1.5). If the initial pressure line is correctly positioned, the gage should read zero percent. The initial pressure line shall be adjusted if two or more determinations show the same variation from zero percent and the test repeated to check the adjusted initial pressure line.

NOTE A1.5—This procedure may be accomplished in conjunction with the calibration test described in A1.9.

A1.6 *Calibration Reading, K*—The calibration reading, K, is the final meter reading to be obtained when the meter is operated at the correct calibration pressure.

A1.6.1 For meter Types A, the calibration reading, K, is as follows:

$$K = R + D \qquad (A1.3)$$

where:
R = effective volume of the calibration vessel (A4.1), and
D = expansion factor (A5.1, Note A1.6).

A1.6.2 For meter Types B the calibration reading, K, equals the effective volume of the calibration vessel (A4.2) as follows:

$$K = R \qquad (A1.4)$$

NOTE A1.6—If the water column indicator is graduated to include an initial water level and a zero mark, the difference between the two marks being equivalent to the expansion factor, the term D shall be omitted from Eq A1.3.

A1.7 *Calibration Test to Determine Operating Pressure, P, on Pressure Gage, Type A Meter*—If the rim of the calibration cylinder contains no recesses or projections, fit it with three or more spacers equally spaced around the circumference. Invert the cylinder and place it at the center of the dry bottom of the measuring bowl. The spacers will provide an opening for flow of water into the calibration cylinder when pressure is applied. Secure the inverted cylinder against displacement and carefully lower the cover assembly. After the cover is clamped in place, carefully adjust the apparatus assembly to a vertical position and add water at air temperature, by means of the tube and funnel, until it rises above the zero mark on the standpipe. Close the vent and pump air into the apparatus to the approximate operating pressure. Incline the assembly about 30° from vertical and, using the bottom of the bowl as a pivot, describe several complete circles with the upper end of the standpipe, simultaneously tapping the cover and sides of the bowl lightly to remove any entrapped air adhering to the inner surfaces of the apparatus. Return the apparatus to a vertical position, gradually release the pressure (to avoid loss of air from the calibration vessel), and open the vent. Bring the

water level exactly to the zero mark by bleeding water through the petcock in the top of the conical cover. After closing the vent, apply pressure until the water level has dropped an amount equivalent to about 0.1 to 0.2 % of air more than the value of the calibration reading, K, determined as described in A1.6. To relieve local restraints, lightly tap the sides of the bowl, and when the water level is exactly at the value of the calibration reading, K, read the pressure, P, indicated by the gage and record to the nearest 0.1 psi (690 Pa). Gradually release the pressure and open the vent to determine whether the water level returns to the zero mark when the sides of the bowl are tapped lightly (failure to do so indicates loss of air from the calibration vessel or loss of water due to a leak in the assembly). If the water levels fails to return to within 0.05 % air of the zero mark and no leakage beyond a few drops of water is found, some air probably was lost from the calibration cylinder. In this case, repeat the calibration procedure step by step from the beginning of this paragraph. If the leakage is more than a few drops of water, tighten the leaking joint before repeating the calibration procedure. Check the indicated pressure reading promptly by bringing the water level exactly to the zero mark, closing the vent, and applying the pressure, P, just determined. Tap the gage lightly with a finger. When the gage indicates the exact pressure, P, the water column should read the value of the calibration factor, K, used in the first pressure application within about 0.05 % of air.

NOTE A1.7—Caution: The apparatus assembly must not be moved from the vertical position until pressure has been applied which will force water about one third of the way up into the calibration cylinder. Any loss of air from this cylinder will nullify the calibration.

A1.8 *Calibration Test to Determine Alternative Operating Pressure P_1—Meter Type A*—The range of air contents which can be measured with a given meter can be doubled by determining an alternative operating pressure P_1 such that the meter reads half of the calibration reading, K, (Eq A1.3). Exact calibration will require determination of the expansion factor at the reduced pressure in A1.5. For most purposes the change in expansion factor can be disregarded and the alternative operating pressure determined during the determination of the regular operating pressure in A1.7.

A1.9 *Calibration Test to Check the Air Content Graduations on the Pressure Gage, Type B Meter*—Fill the measuring bowl with water as described in A1.3. Screw the short piece of tubing or pipe furnished with the apparatus into the threaded petcock hole on the underside of the cover assembly. Assemble the apparatus. Close the air valve between the air chamber and the measuring bowl and open the two petcocks on holes through the cover assembly. Add water through the petcock on the cover assembly having the extension below until all air is expelled from the second petcock. Pump air into the air chamber until the pressure reaches the indicated initial pressure line. Allow a few seconds for the compressed air to cool to normal temperature. Stabilize the gage hand at the initial pressure line by pumping or bleeding off air as necessary, tapping the gage lightly. Close the petcock not provided with the tube or pipe extension on the under side of the cover. Remove water from the assembly to the calibrating vessel controlling the flow, depending on the particular meter design, by opening the petcock provided with the tube or pipe extension and

⑩ C 231

cracking the air valve between the air chamber and the measuring bowl, or by opening the air valve and using the petcock to control flow. Perform the calibration at an air content which is within the normal range of use. If the calibration vessel (A1.2) has a capacity within the normal range of use, remove exactly that amount of water. With some meters the calibrating vessel is quite small and it will be necessary to remove several times that volume to obtain an air content within the normal range of use. In this instance, carefully collect the water in an auxiliary container and determine the amount removed by weighing to the nearest 0.1 %. Calculate the correct air content, R, by using Eq A1.2. Release the air from the apparatus at the petcock not used for filling the calibration vessel and if the apparatus employs an auxiliary tube for filling the calibration container, open the petcock to which the tube is connected to drain the tube back into the measuring bowl (Note A1.7). At this point of procedure the measuring bowl contains the percentage of air determined by the calibration test of the calibrating vessel. Pump air into the air chamber until the pressure reaches the initial pressure line marked on the pressure gage, close both petcocks in the cover assembly, and then open the valve between the air chamber and the measuring bowl. The indicated air content on the pressure gage dial should correspond to the percentage of air determined to be in the measuring bowl. If two or more determinations show the same variation from the correct air content, the dial hand shall be reset to the correct air content and the test repeated until the gage reading corresponds to the calibrated air content within 0.1 %. If the dial hand was reset to obtain the correct air content, recheck the initial pressure mark as in A1.5.2. If a new initial pressure reading is required, repeat the calibration to check the accuracy of the graduation on the pressure gage described earlier in this section. If difficulty is encountered in obtaining consistent readings, check for leaks, for the presence of water inside the air chamber (see Fig. 2), or the presence of air bubbles clinging to the inside surfaces of the meter from the use of cool aerated water. In this latter instance use deaerated water which can be obtained by cooling hot water to room temperature.

Note A1.8—If the calibrating vessel is an integral part of the cover assembly, the petcock used in filling the vessel should be closed immediately after filling the calibration vessel and not opened until the test is complete.

AMERICAN SOCIETY FOR TESTING AND MATERIALS
100 Barr Harbor Dr., West Conshohocken, PA 19428
Reprinted from the Annual Book of ASTM Standards. Copyright ASTM
If not listed in the current combined index, will appear in the next edition.

Designation: C 496 – 96

Standard Test Method for
Splitting Tensile Strength of Cylindrical Concrete Specimens[1]

This standard is issued under the fixed designation C 496; the number immediately following the designation indicates the year of original adoption or, in the case of revision, the year of last revision. A number in parentheses indicates the year of last reapproval. A superscript epsilon (ϵ) indicates an editorial change since the last revision or reapproval.

This test method has been approved for use by agencies of the Department of Defense. Consult the DoD Index of Specifications and Standards for the specific year of issue which has been adopted by the Department of Defense.

1. Scope

1.1 This test method covers the determination of the splitting tensile strength of cylindrical concrete specimens, such as molded cylinders and drilled cores.

NOTE 1—For methods of molding cylindrical concrete specimens, see Practice C 192 and Practice C 31. For methods of obtaining drilled cores see Test Method C 42.

1.2 The values stated in inch-pound units are to be regarded as the standard.

1.3 *This standard does not purport to address all of the safety concerns, if any, associated with its use. It is the responsibility of the user of this standard to establish appropriate safety and health practices and determine the applicability of regulatory limitations prior to use.*

2. Referenced Documents

2.1 *ASTM Standards:*
C 31 Practice for Making and Curing Concrete Test Specimens in the Field[2]
C 39 Test Method for Compressive Strength of Cylindrical Concrete Specimens[2]
C 42 Test Method for Obtaining and Testing Drilled Cores and Sawed Beams of Concrete[2]
C 192 Practice for Making and Curing Concrete Test Specimens in the Laboratory[2]
C 670 Practice for Preparing Precision and Bias Statements for Test Methods for Construction Materials[2]

3. Summary of Test Method

3.1 This test method consists of applying a diametral compressive force along the length of a cylindrical concrete specimen at a rate that is within a prescribed range until failure occurs. This loading induces tensile stresses on the plane containing the applied load and relatively high compressive stresses in the area immediately around the applied load. Tensile failure occurs rather than compressive failure because the areas of load application are in a state of triaxial compression, thereby allowing them to withstand much higher compressive stresses than would be indicated by a uniaxial compressive strength test result.

3.2 Thin, plywood bearing strips are used so that the load

is applied uniformly along the length of the cylinder.

3.3 The maximum load sustained by the specimen is divided by appropriate geometrical factors to obtain the splitting tensile strength.

4. Significance and Use

4.1 Splitting tensile strength is simpler to determine than direct tensile strength.

4.2 Splitting tensile strength is used to evaluate the shear resistance provided by concrete in reinforced lightweight aggregate concrete members.

5. Apparatus

5.1 *Testing Machine*—The testing machine shall conform to the requirements of Test Method C 39 and may be of any type of sufficient capacity that will provide the rate of loading prescribed in 7.5.

5.2 *Supplementary Bearing Bar or Plate*—If the diameter or the largest dimension of the upper bearing face or the lower bearing block is less than the length of the cylinder to be tested, a supplementary bearing bar or plate of machined steel shall be used. The surfaces of the bar or plate shall be machined to within ± 0.001 in. (0.025 mm) of planeness, as measured on any line of contact of the bearing area. It shall have a width of at least 2 in. (51 mm), and a thickness not less than the distance from the edge of the spherical or rectangular bearing block to the end of the cylinder. The bar or plate shall be used in such manner that the load will be applied over the entire length of the specimen.

5.3 *Bearing Strips*—Two bearing strips of nominal ⅛ in. (3.2 mm) thick plywood, free of imperfections, approximately 1 in. (25 mm) wide, and of a length equal to, or slightly longer than, that of the specimen shall be provided for each specimen. The bearing strips shall be placed between the specimen and both the upper and lower bearing blocks of the testing machine or between the specimen and supplemental bars or plates, if used (see 5.2). Bearing strips shall not be reused.

6. Test Specimens

6.1 The test specimens shall conform to the size, molding, and curing requirements set forth in either Practice C 31 (field specimens) or Practice C 192 (laboratory specimens). Drilled cores shall conform to the size and moisture-conditioning requirements set forth in Test Method C 42. Moist-cured specimens, during the period between their removal from the curing environment and testing, shall be kept moist by a wet burlap or blanket covering, and shall be tested in a moist condition as soon as practicable.

6.2 The following curing procedure shall be used for

---

[1] This test method is under the jurisdiction of ASTM Committee C-9 on Concrete and Concrete Aggregates and is the direct responsibility of Subcommittee C09.61 on Testing Concrete for Strength.
Current edition approved Jan. 10, 1996. Published March 1996. Originally published as C 496 – 62. Last previous edition C 496 – 90.
[2] *Annual Book of ASTM Standards*, Vol 04.02.

〈ISM〉 C 496

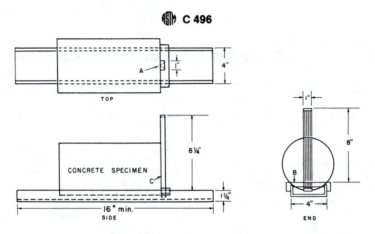

FIG. 1   General Views of a Suitable Apparatus for Marking End Diameters Used for Alignment of Specimen in Testing Machine

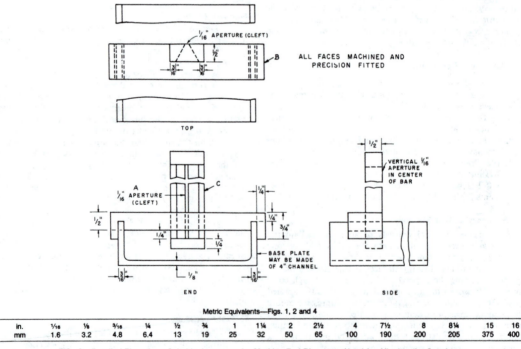

Metric Equivalents—Figs. 1, 2 and 4

in.	1/16	1/8	3/16	1/4	1/2	3/4	1	1 1/4	2	2 1/2	4	7 1/2	8	8 1/4	15	16
mm	1.6	3.2	4.8	6.4	13	19	25	32	50	65	100	190	200	205	375	400

FIG. 2   Detailed Plans for a Suitable Apparatus for Marking End Diameters Used for Aligning the Specimen

evaluations of light-weight concrete: specimens tested at 28 days shall be in an air-dry condition after 7 days moist curing followed by 21 days drying at 73 ± 3°F (23.0 ± 1.7°C) and 50 ± 5 % relative humidity.

7. Procedure

7.1 *Marking*—Draw diametral lines on each end of the specimen using a suitable device that will ensure that they are in the same axial plane (see Figs. 1, 2 and Note 2), or as an alternative, use the aligning jig shown in Fig. 3 (Note 3).

NOTE 2—Figures 1 and 2 show a suitable device for drawing diametral lines on each end of the specimen in the same axial plane. The device consists of three parts as follows:

(*1*) A length of 4-in. (100-mm) steel channel, the flanges of which have been machined flat,

(*2*) A section of a tee bar, *B*, that is grooved to fit smoothly over the flanges of the channel and that includes a rectangular notch for

C 496

FIG. 3   Jig for Aligning Concrete Cylinder and Bearing Strips

positioning the vertical member of the tee bar assembly, and

(3) A vertical bar, C, containing a longitudinal aperture (cleft), A, for guiding a pencil,

The tee bar assembly is not fastened to the channel and is positioned at either end of the channel without disturbing the position of the specimen when marking the diametral lines.

NOTE 3—Figure 4 is a detailed drawing of the aligning jig shown in Fig. 3 for achieving the same purpose as marking the diametral lines. The device consists of:

(1) A base for holding the lower bearing strip and cylinder,

(2) A supplementary bearing bar conforming to the requirements in Section 5 as to critical dimensions and planeness, and

(3) Two uprights to serve for positioning the test cylinder, bearing strips, and supplementary bearing bar.

7.2 *Measurements*—Determine the diameter of the test specimen to the nearest 0.01 in. (0.25 mm) by averaging three diameters measured near the ends and the middle of the specimen and lying in the plane containing the lines marked on the two ends. Determine the length of the specimen to the nearest 0.1 in. (2.5 mm) by averaging at least two length measurements taken in the plane containing the lines marked on the two ends.

7.3 *Positioning Using Marked Diametral Lines*—Center one of the plywood strips along the center of the lower bearing block. Place the specimen on the plywood strip and align so that the lines marked on the ends of the specimen

are vertical and centered over the plywood strip. Place a second plywood strip lengthwise on the cylinder, centered on the lines marked on the ends of the cylinder. Position the assembly to ensure the following conditions:

7.3.1 The projection of the plane of the two lines marked on the ends of the specimen intersects the center of the upper bearing plate, and

7.3.2 The supplementary bearing bar or plate, when used, and the center of the specimen are directly beneath the center of thrust of the spherical bearing block (see Fig. 5).

7.4 *Positioning by Use of Aligning Jig*—Position the bearing strips, test cylinder, and supplementary bearing bar by means of the aligning jig as illustrated in Fig. 3 and center the jig so that the supplementary bearing bar and the center of the specimen are directly beneath the center of thrust of the spherical bearing block.

7.5 *Rate of Loading*—Apply the load continuously and without shock, at a constant rate within the range 100 to 200 psi/min (689 to 1380 kPa/min) splitting tensile stress until failure of the specimen (Note 4). Record the maximum applied load indicated by the testing machine at failure. Note the type of failure and the appearance of the concrete.

NOTE 4—The relationship between splitting tensile stress and applied load is shown in Section 8. The required loading range in splitting tensile stress corresponds to applied total load in the range of 11 300 to 22 600 lbf (50 to 100 kN)/min for 6 by 12-in. (152 by 305-mm) cylinders.

8. Calculation

8.1 Calculate the splitting tensile strength of the specimen as follows:

$$T = 2P/\pi ld$$

where

T = splitting tensile strength, psi (kPa),

P = maximum applied load indicated by the testing machine, lbf (kN),

l = length, in. (m), and

d = diameter, in. (m).

9. Report

9.1 Report the following information:

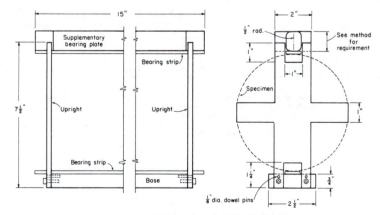

FIG. 4   Detailed Plans for a Suitable Aligning Jig

C 496

FIG. 5   Specimen Positioned in a Testing Machine for Determination of Splitting Tensile Strength

9.1.1 Identification number,

9.1.2 Diameter and length, in. (m),

9.1.3 Maximum load, lbf (kN),

9.1.4 Splitting tensile strength calculated to the nearest 5 psi (35 kPa),

9.1.5 Estimated proportion of coarse aggregate fractured during test,

9.1.6 Age of specimen,

9.1.7 Curing history,

9.1.8 Defects in specimen,

9.1.9 Type of fracture, and

9.1.10 Type of specimen.

10. Precision and Bias

10.1 *Precision*—An interlaboratory study of this test method has not been performed. Available research data,[3]

---

[3] Wright, P. J. F., "Comments on an Indirect Tensile Test on Concrete Cylinders," Magazine of Concrete Research, Vol 7, No. 20, July 1955, pp. 87–95.

however, suggests that the within batch coefficient of variation is 5 % (see Note 5) for 6 × 12-in. (152 × 305-mm) cylindrical specimens with an average splitting tensile strength of 405 psi (2.8 MPa). Results of two properly conducted tests on the same material, therefore, should not differ by more than 14 % (see Note 5) of their average for splitting tensile strengths of about 400 psi (2.8 MPa).

NOTE 5—These numbers represent, respectively, the (1s %) and (d2s %) limits as defined in Practice C 670.

10.2 *Bias*—The test method has no bias because the splitting tensile strength can be defined only in terms of this test method.

11. Keywords

11.1 cylindrical concrete specimens; splitting tension; tensile strength

Designation: C 617 – 94

AMERICAN SOCIETY FOR TESTING AND MATERIALS
1916 Race St. Philadelphia, Pa 19103
Reprinted from the Annual Book of ASTM Standards. Copyright ASTM
If not listed in the current combined index, will appear in the next edition.

Standard Practice for
Capping Cylindrical Concrete Specimens[1]

This standard is issued under the fixed designation C 617; the number immediately following the designation indicates the year of original adoption or, in the case of revision, the year of last revision. A number in parentheses indicates the year of last reapproval. A superscript epsilon (ϵ) indicates an editorial change since the last revision or reapproval.

This practice has been approved for use by agencies of the Department of Defense. Consult the DoD Index of Specifications and Standards for the specific year of issue which has been adopted by the Department of Defense.

1. Scope

1.1 This practice covers apparatus, materials, and procedures for capping freshly molded concrete cylinders with neat cement and hardened cylinders and drilled concrete cores with high-strength gypsum plaster or sulfur mortar.

1.2 The values stated in inch-pound units are to be regarded as the standard. The SI equivalents of inch-pound units may be approximate.

1.3 *This standard does not purport to address all of the safety concerns, if any, associated with its use. It is the responsibility of the user of this standard to establish appropriate safety and health practices and determine the applicability of regulatory limitations prior to use.* For specific precaution statements see 4.3 and 6.2.3.1.

2. Referenced Documents

2.1 *ASTM Standards:*
C 109 Test Method for Compressive Strength of Hydraulic Cement Mortars (Using 2-in. or 50-mm Cube Specimens)[2]
C 150 Specification for Portland Cement[2]
C 472 Test Methods for Physical Testing of Gypsum, Gypsum Plasters and Gypsum Concrete[2]
C 595 Specification for Blended Hydraulic Cements[2]
C 1231 Practice for Use of Unbounded Caps in Determination of Compressive Strength of Hardened Concrete Cylinders[3]
2.2 *ANSI Standard:*
B46.1 Standard for Surface Texture (Surface, Roughness, Waviness and Lay)[4]

3. Significance and Use

3.1 This practice describes procedures for providing plane surfaces on the ends of freshly molded concrete cylinders, hardened cylinders, or drilled concrete cores when the end surfaces do not conform with the planeness and perpendicularity requirements of applicable standards. Practice C 1231 describes alternative procedures using unbonded caps or pad caps.

4. Capping Equipment

4.1 *Capping Plates*—Neat cement caps and high-strength gypsum-plaster caps shall be formed against a glass plate at least ¼ in. (6 mm) thick, a machined metal plate at least 0.45 in. (11 mm) thick, or a polished plate of granite or diabase at least 3 in. (76 mm) thick. Sulfur mortar caps shall be formed against similar metal or stone plates except that the recessed area which receives molten sulfur shall not be deeper than ½ in. (12 mm). In all cases, plates shall be at least 1 in. (25 mm) greater in diameter than the test specimen and the working surfaces shall not depart from a plane by more than 0.002 in. (0.05 mm) in 6 in. (152 mm). The surface roughness of newly finished metal plates shall not exceed that set forth in Table 4 of American National Standard B46.1, or 125 µin. (3.2 µm) for any type of surface and direction of lay. The surface, when new, shall be free of gouges, grooves, or indentations beyond those caused by the finishing operation. Metal plates that have been in use shall be free of gouges, grooves, and indentations greater than 0.010 in. (0.25 mm) deep or greater than 0.05 in.^{2} (32 mm^2) in surface area.

NOTE 1—A Rockwell hardness of 48 HRC is suggested for capping plates of devices used to form sulfur mortar caps.

4.2 *Alignment Devices*—Suitable alignment devices, such as guide bars or bull's-eye levels, shall be used in conjunction with capping plates to ensure that no single cap will depart from perpendicularity to the axis of a cylindrical specimen by more than 0.5° (approximately equivalent to ⅛ in. in 12 in. (3.2 mm in 305 mm)). The same requirement is applicable to the relationship between the axis of the alignment device and the surface of a capping plate when guide bars are used. In addition, the location of each bar with respect to its plate must be such that no cap will be off-centered on a test specimen by more than ¹⁄₁₆ in. (2 mm).

4.3 *Melting Pots for Sulfur Mortars*—Pots used for melting sulfur mortars shall be equipped with automatic temperature controls and shall be made of metal or lined with a material that is nonreactive with molten sulfur.

4.3.1 **Caution:** Melting pots equipped with peripheral heating will ensure against accidents during reheating of cooled sulfur mixture that have a crusted-over surface. When using melting pots not so equipped, a build-up of pressure under the hardened surface crust on subsequent reheating may be avoided by use of a metal rod that contacts the bottom of the pot and projects above the surface of the fluid sulfur mix as it cools. The rod should be of sufficient size to conduct enough heat to the top on reheating to melt a ring around the rod first and thus avoid the development of pressure. A large metal ladle can be substituted for the rod.

---

[1] This practice is under the jurisdiction of ASTM Committee C-9 on Concrete and Concrete Aggregates and is the direct responsibility of Subcommittee C09.61 on Testing Concrete for Strength.
Current edition approved March 15, 1994. Published May 1994. Originally published as C 617 – 68. Last previous edition C 617 – 87.
[2] *Annual Book of ASTM Standards*, Vol 04.01.
[3] *Annual Book of ASTM Standards*, Vol 04.02.
[4] Available from American Society of Mechanical Engineers, 345 E. 47th Street, New York, NY 10017.

₵₮₥ C 617

4.3.1.1 Use sulfur melting pots in a hood to exhaust the fumes to outdoors. Heating over an open flame is dangerous because the flash point of sulfur is approximately 440°F (227°C) and the mixture can ignite due to overheating. Should the mixture start to burn, covering will snuff out the flame. The pot should be recharged with fresh material after the flame has been extinguished.

5. Capping Materials

5.1 All capping material shall conform to the strength and thickness requirements of Table 1.

5.1.1 The compressive strength of capping materials shall be determined by testing 2 in. cubes following the procedure described in Test Method C 109. Except for sulfur mortars, molding procedures shall be as in Test Method C 109 unless other procedures are required to eliminate large entrapped air voids. See Test Methods C 472 for alternative compaction procedures. Cure cubes in the same environment for the same length of time as the material used to cap specimens.

5.1.2 The strength of the capping material shall be determined on receipt of a new lot and at intervals not exceeding three months. If a given lot of the capping material fails to conform to the strength requirements, it shall not be used, and strength tests of the replacement material shall be made weekly until four consecutive determinations conform to specification requirements.

5.2 *Neat Hydraulic Cement Paste:*

5.2.1 Make qualification tests of the neat hydraulic cement paste prior to use for capping to establish the effects of water-cement ratio and age on compressive strength of 2 in. (50 mm) cubes.

NOTE 2—The cements used generally conform to Specification C 150 Types I, II or III; however, Specification C 595 blended cements, calcium aluminate or other hydraulic cements producing acceptable strength may be used.

5.2.2 Mix the neat cement paste to the desired consistency at a water-cement ratio equal to or less than that required to produce the required strength, generally 2 to 4 h before the paste is to be used (Note 3). Remix as necessary to maintain acceptable consistency (Note 4). Some retempering of the paste is acceptable if the required water-cement ratio is not exceeded. Optimum consistency is generally produced at water-cement ratios of 0.32 to 0.36 by mass for Type I and Type II cements and 0.35 to 0.39 by mass for Type III cements.

NOTE 3—Freshly mixed pastes tend to bleed, shrink, and make unacceptable caps. The 2 to 4 h period is generally appropriate for portland cements.

TABLE 1 Compressive Strength and Maximum Thickness of Capping Materials

Cylinder Compressive Strength psi (MPa)	Minimum Strength of Capping Material	Maximum Average Thickness of Cap	Maximum Thickness Any Part of Cap
500 to 7000 psi (3.5 to 50 MPa)	5000 psi (35 MPa) or cylinder strength whichever is greater	¼ in. (6 mm)	⁵⁄₁₆ in. (8 mm)
greater than 7000 psi (50 MPa)	Compressive strength not less than cylinder strength	⅛ in. (3 mm)	³⁄₁₆ in. (5 mm)

NOTE 4—The required consistency of the paste is determined by the appearance of the cap when it is stripped. Fluid paste results in streaks in the cap. Stiff paste results in thick caps.

5.3 *High-Strength Gypsum Cement Paste:*

5.3.1 No fillers or extenders may be added to neat high-strength gypsum cement paste subsequent to the manufacture of the cement. (Note 5) Qualification tests shall be made to determine the effects of water-cement ratio and age on compressive strength of 2 in. (50 mm) cubes. Retarders may be used to extend working time, but their effects on required water-cement ratio and strength must be determined. (Note 6)

NOTE 5—Low-strength molding plaster, plaster of paris, or mixtures of plaster of paris and portland cement are unsuitable for capping.

NOTE 6—The water-gypsum cement ratio should be between 0.26 and 0.30. Use of low water-cement ratios and vigorous mixing usually permit development of 5000 psi (35 MPa) at ages of 1 or 2 h. Higher water-gypsum cement ratios extend working time, but reduce strength.

5.3.2 Mix the neat gypsum cement paste at the desired water-cement ratio and use it promptly since it sets rapidly.

5.4 *Sulfur Mortar:*

5.4.1 Proprietary or laboratory-prepared sulfur mortars may be used if allowed to harden a minimum of 2 h before testing.

NOTE 7—Allowing caps to harden overnight is desirable on concrete specimens with strength greater than 5000 psi (35 MPa).

5.4.2 *Determination of Compressive Strength*—Prepare test specimens using a cube mold and base plate conforming to the requirements of Test Method C 109 and a metal cover plate conforming in principle to the design shown in Fig. 1 (Note 8). Bring the various parts of the apparatus to a temperature of 68 to 86°F (20 to 30°C), lightly coat the surfaces that will be in contact with the sulfur mortar with mineral oil, and assemble near the melting pot. Bring the temperature of the molten-sulfur mortar in the pot within a range of 265 to 290°F (129 to 143°C), stir thoroughly, and begin casting cubes. Using a ladle, or other suitable pouring device, quickly fill each of the three compartments until the molten material reaches the top of the filling hole. Allow sufficient time for maximum shrinkage, due to cooling, and solidification to occur (approximately 15 min) and refill each hole with molten material (Note 9). After solidification is complete, remove the cubes from the mold without breaking off the knob formed by the filling hole in the cover plate. Remove oil, sharp edges, and fins from the cubes and check the planeness of the bearing surfaces in the manner described in Test Method C 109. After storage at room temperature to the desired age, but not less than 2 h, test cubes in compression following the procedure described in Test Method C 109, and calculate the compressive strength.

NOTE 8—If desired, a plane phenol formaldehyde (bakelite) plate of ⅛-in. (3-mm) thickness, provided with three appropriately spaced filling holes, may be inserted between the cover plate and the mold to slow the rate of cooling of test specimens.

NOTE 9—The second filling helps to prevent the formation of a large void or shrinkage pipe in the body of a cube. However, such defects may occur no matter how much care is exercised, and it therefore is advisable to inspect the interior of tested sulfur mortar cubes for homogeneity whenever the strength values obtained are significantly lower than anticipated.

C 617

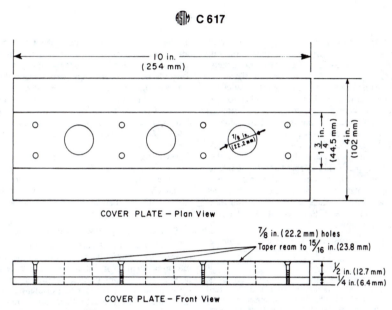

COVER PLATE – Plan View

$\frac{7}{8}$ in. (22.2 mm) holes

Taper ream to $\frac{15}{16}$ in. (23.8 mm)

$\frac{1}{2}$ in. (12.7 mm)

$\frac{1}{4}$ in. (6.4 mm)

COVER PLATE – Front View

FIG. 1   Sketch of Cover Plate for 2-in. (50-mm) Cube Mold

6. Capping Procedures

6.1 *Freshly Molded Cylinders*—Use only neat portland cement pastes (Note 10) to cap freshly molded cylinders. Make caps as thin as practicable. Do not apply the neat paste to the exposed end until the concrete has ceased settling in the molds, generally from 2 to 4 h after molding. During the molding of the cylinder, strike off the upper end even with or slightly below the plane of the rim of the mold. Remove free water and laitance from the top of the specimen immediately before capping. Form the cap by placing a conical mound of paste on the specimen and then gently pressing a freshly oiled capping plate on the conical mound until the plate contacts the rim of the mold. A very slight twisting motion may be required to extrude excess paste and minimize air voids in the paste. The capping plate must not rock during this operation. Carefully cover the capping plate and mold with a double layer of damp burlap and a polyethylene sheet to prevent drying. Removal of the capping plate after hardening may be accomplished by tapping the edge with a rawhide hammer in a direction parallel to the plane of the cap.

NOTE 10—Type I neat cement caps generally require at least 6 days to develop acceptable strength and Type III neat cement caps at least 2 days. Dry concrete specimens will absorb water from freshly mixed neat cement paste and produce unsatisfactory caps. Neat cement paste caps will shrink and crack on drying and, therefore, should be used only for specimens that are to be moist cured continuously until time of testing.

NOTE 11—High-strength gypsum caps soften and deteriorate on contact with water and cannot be used on freshly mixed concrete or stored in a moist room for more than very brief periods.

6.2 *Hardened Concrete Specimens:*

6.2.1 *General*—If an end of a specimen has a coating or deposit of oily or waxy materials that would interfere with the bond of the cap, remove such coatings or deposits. If necessary, the ends of a specimen may be slightly roughened

with a steel file or wire brush to produce proper adhesion of the cap. If desired, capping plates may be coated with a thin layer of mineral oil or grease to prevent the capping material from adhering to the surface of the plate.

6.2.2 *Capping with High-Strength Gypsum Plaster or Neat Cement Paste*—Mix the paste as described in Section 5. Do not exceed the water-cement ratio determined in qualification tests. Form the caps as described in 6.1 using capping plates described in 4.1 to achieve the alignment required in 4.2 (Note 12). Generally, capping plates may be removed within 45 min with gypsum cement pastes and after 12 h with neat cement paste, without visibly damaging the cap.

NOTE 12—A number of methods have been used to obtain the desired perpendicularity of the cap to the axis of the cylinder. A mound of paste can be placed on a capping plate and the specimen lowered into it. A bull's-eye level on the top of the cylinder helps obtain alignment. A mound of paste can be placed on top of the cylinder and a capping plate pressed into it, again using the bull's-eye level. A better system is to make a half-height mold with a vertical split so that it can be slipped over the hardened cylinder. A clamp is used to position the mold and to ensure the required cap thickness. The mound of paste can then be placed either on a capping plate or on top of the cylinder and pressed until the plate contacts the mold. As noted earlier, very stiff paste may require excessive pressure and produce thick or defective caps.

6.2.3 *Capping with Sulfur Mortar*—Prepare sulfur mortar for use by heating to about 265 to 295°F (129 to 143°C), as periodically determined by an all-metal thermometer inserted near the center of the mass. Recharge the pot with fresh material at frequent enough intervals to ensure that the oldest material in the pot has not been used more than five times (Note 13). Fresh sulfur mortar must be dry at the time it is placed in the pot as dampness may cause foaming. Keep water away from molten sulfur mortar for the same reason. The capping plate or device should be warmed before use to slow the rate of hardening and permit the production of thin caps. Oil the capping plate lightly and stir the molten sulfur

ⓈⓂ C 617

mortar immediately prior to pouring each cap. The ends of moist cured specimens shall be dry enough at the time of capping to preclude the formation of steam or foam pockets under or in the cap larger than ¼ in. (6 mm) in diameter. Replace caps with steam pockets or voids larger than ¼ in. (6 mm) (Note 14). To ensure that the cap is bonded to the surface of the specimen, the end of the specimen shall not be oiled prior to the application of the cap. When using a vertical device, pour the mortar onto the surface of the capping plate, lift the cylinder above the plate and contact the cylinder sides with the guides, slide the cylinder down the guides onto the capping plate while keeping constant contact with the alignment guides. The cylinder end should continue to rest on the capping plate with cylinder sides in positive contact with the alignment guides until the mortar has hardened. Use sufficient material to cover the cylinder end after the sulfur mortar solidifies.

NOTE 13—Reuse of material must be restricted in order to minimize loss of strength and pourability occasioned by contamination of the mortar with oil and miscellaneous debris, and loss of sulfur through volatilization.

NOTE 14—Periodically, the sulfur mortar cap should be examined after testing for air or steam pockets in the cap. Before testing, the cap can be tapped with a coin or rubbed with a light metal implement to see if a hollow sound can be detected. Caps with hollow areas should be removed and recapped.

6.2.3.1 **Caution:** Hydrogen sulfide gas may be produced during capping when sulfur mortar is contaminated with organic materials such as paraffin or oil. The gas is colorless and has a notoriously bad odor of rotten eggs; however, the odor should not be relied upon as a warning sign, since the sensitivity to the odor disappears rapidly on exposure. High concentrations are lethal and less concentrated dosages may produce nausea, stomach distress, dizziness, headache, or irritation of the eyes. For this and other reasons, the melting pot must be located under a hood with an exhaust fan and that capping area must be well ventilated.

6.2.4 *Daily Check*—During each day's capping operation, check the planeness of the caps on at least three specimens representing the start, middle, and end of the run, with a straight-edge and feeler gage, making a minimum of three measurements on different diameters to ensure that the surfaces of the caps do not depart from a plane by more than 0.002 in. (0.05 mm). Check also for hollow areas (Note 14).

7. Protection of Specimens After Capping

7.1 Maintain moist cured specimens in a moist condition between the completion of capping and the time of testing by returning them to moist storage or wrapping them with a double layer of wet burlap. Do not store specimens with gypsum plaster caps immersed in water or for more than 4 h in a moist room. Protect plaster caps from dripping water.

7.2 Do not test capped specimens before the capping material has sufficient time to develop the strength required in 5.1. Additionally, sulfur mortar and gypsum cement capped specimens shall not be tested at ages less than 2 h after completion of capping.

AMERICAN SOCIETY FOR TESTING AND MATERIALS
1916 Race St., Philadelphia, Pa. 19103
Reprinted from the Annual Book of ASTM Standards, Copyright ASTM
If not listed in the current combined index, will appear in the next edition.

Standard Test Method for
TEMPERATURE OF FRESHLY MIXED PORTLAND CEMENT CONCRETE[1]

This standard is issued under the fixed designation C 1064; the number immediately following the designation indicates the year of original adoption or, in the case of revision, the year of last revision. A number in parentheses indicates the year of last reapproval. A superscript epsilon (ϵ) indicates an editorial change since the last revision or reapproval.

1. Scope

1.1 This test method covers the determination of temperature of freshly mixed portland cement concrete.

1.2 The values stated in inch-pound units are to be regarded as the standard.

1.3 *This standard may involve hazardous materials, operations, and equipment. This standard does not purport to address all of the safety problems associated with its use. It is the responsibility of whoever uses this standard to consult and establish appropriate safety and health practices and determine the applicability of regulatory limitations prior to use.*

2. Referenced Documents

2.1 *ASTM Standards:*
C 172 Method for Sampling Freshly Mixed Concrete[2]
E 1 Specification for ASTM Thermometers[3]
E 77 Method for Verification and Calibration of Liquid-in-Glass Thermometers[3]
2.2 *NBS Standard:*
N.B.S. Monograph 150 Liquid-in-Glass Thermometry[4]

3. Significance and Use

3.1 This test method provides a means for measuring the temperature of freshly mixed concrete. It may be used to verify conformance to a specified requirement for temperature of concrete.

3.2 Concrete containing aggregate of a nominal maximum size greater than 3 in. (75 mm) may require up to 20 min for the transfer of heat from aggregate to mortar. (See ACI Committee 207.1R Report.[5])

4. Apparatus

4.1 *Container*—The container shall be made of nonabsorptive material and large enough to provide at least 3 in. (75 mm) of concrete in all directions around the sensor of the temperature measuring device; concrete cover must also be at least three times the nominal maximum size of the coarse aggregate.

4.2 *Temperature Measuring Device*—The temperature measuring device shall be capable of measuring the temperature of the freshly mixed concrete to ±1°F (±0.5°C) throughout the entire temperature range likely to be encountered in the fresh concrete. ASTM liquid-in-glass thermometers having a range from 0 to 120°F (−18 to 49°C) and conforming to the requirements for ASTM thermometer No. 36°C as prescribed in Specification E 1 are satisfactory. Other thermometers of the required accuracy, including the metal immersion type, are acceptable.

4.3 Partial immersion liquid-in-glass thermometers (and possibly other types) shall have a permanent mark to which the device must be immersed without applying a correction factor.

4.4 *Reference Temperature Measuring De-*

[1] This test method is under the jurisdiction of ASTM Committee C-9 on Concrete and Concrete Aggregates and are the direct responsibility of Subcommittee C09.03.03 on Methods of Testing Fresh Concrete.
Current edition approved July 17, 1986. Published 1986.
[2] *Annual Book of ASTM Standards*, Vol 04.02.
[3] *Annual Book of ASTM Standards*, Vol 14.01.
[4] Available from National Bureau of Standards, U.S. Department of Commerce, Washington, DC 20234.
[5] Available from American Concrete Institute, Box 19150, Redford Station, Detroit, MI 48219. Other related documents also available from American Concrete Institute are Committee Reports 305, (Hot Weather Concreting) and 306 (Cold Weather Concreting).

C 1064

vice—The reference temperature measuring device shall be a liquid-in-glass thermometer readable to 0.5°F (0.2°C) that has been verified and calibrated in accordance with Method E 77. The calibration certificate or report shall be available for inspection.

5. Calibration of Temperature Measuring Device

5.1 Each temperature measuring device used for determining temperature of freshly mixed concrete shall be calibrated annually, or whenever there is a question of accuracy. This calibration shall be performed by comparing the readings on the temperature measuring device at two temperatures at least 30°F (15°C) apart.

5.2 Calibration of the temperature measuring devices may be made in oil or other suitable baths having uniform density if provision is made to:

5.2.1 Maintain the bath temperature constant within 0.5°F (0.2°C) during the period of the test.

5.2.2 Have both the temperature and reference temperature measuring devices maintained in the bath for a minimum of 5 min before reading temperatures.

5.2.3 Continuously circulate the bath liquid to provide a uniform temperature.

5.2.4 Slightly tap thermometers containing liquid to avoid adhesion of the liquid to the glass if the temperature exposure is being reduced.

5.3 If a limiting temperature is specified, calibrate the measuring device at a temperature within ±5°F (2°C) of the limiting temperature permitted.

6. Sampling Concrete

6.1 The temperature of freshly mixed concrete may be measured in the transporting equipment provided the sensor of the temperature measuring device has at least 3 in. (75 mm) of concrete cover in all directions around it.

6.2 Temperature of the freshly mixed concrete may be obtained following concrete placement using the forms as the container.

6.3 If the transporting equipment or placement forms are not used as the container, a sample shall be prepared as follows:

6.3.1 Immediately, prior to sampling the freshly mixed concrete, dampen (with water) the sample container.

6.3.2 Sample the freshly mixed concrete in accordance with Method C 172, except that composite samples are not required if the only purpose for obtaining the sample is to determine temperature.

6.3.3 Place the freshly mixed concrete into the container.

6.3.4 When concrete contains a nominal maximum size of aggregate greater than 3 in. (75 mm), it may require 20 min before the temperature is stabilized after mixing.

7. Procedure

7.1 Place the temperature measuring device in the freshly mixed concrete so that the temperature sensing portion is submerged a minimum of 3 in. (75 mm). Gently press the concrete around the temperature measuring device at the surface of the concrete so that ambient air temperature does not affect the reading.

7.2 Leave the temperature measuring device in the freshly mixed concrete for a minimum period of 2 min or until the temperature reading stabilizes, then read and record the temperature.

7.3 Complete the temperature measurement of the freshly mixed concrete within 5 min after obtaining the sample.

8. Report

8.1 Record the measured temperature of the freshly mixed concrete to the nearest °F (0.5°C).

9. Precision and Bias

9.1 The precision and bias of this test method have not been determined. A precision and bias statement will be included when sufficient test data have been obtained and analyzed.

ASTM **Designation: C 67 – 94**

AMERICAN SOCIETY FOR TESTING AND MATERIALS
1916 Race St. Philadelphia, Pa 19103
Reprinted from the Annual Book of ASTM Standards. Copyright ASTM
If not listed in the current combined index, will appear in the next edition.

American Association State Highway and Transportation
Officials Standard
AASHTO No.: T 32-70

Standard Test Methods of
Sampling and Testing Brick and Structural Clay Tile[1]

This standard is issued under the fixed designation C 67; the number immediately following the designation indicates the year of original adoption or, in the case of revision, the year of last revision. A number in parentheses indicates the year of last reapproval. A superscript epsilon (ε) indicates an editorial change since the last revision or reapproval.

This standard has been approved for use by agencies of the Department of Defense. Consult the DoD Index of Specifications and Standards for the specific year of issue which has been adopted by the Department of Defense.

1. Scope

1.1 These test methods cover procedures for the sampling and testing of brick and structural clay tile. Although not necessarily applicable to all types of units, tests include modulus of rupture, compressive strength, absorption, saturation coefficient, effect of freezing and thawing, efflorescence, initial rate of absorption and determination of weight, size, warpage, length change, and void area. (Additional methods of test pertinent to ceramic glazed facing tile are included in Specification C 126.)

1.2 *This standard does not purport to address all of the safety concerns, if any, associated with its use. It is the responsibility of the user of this standard to establish appropriate safety and health practices and determine the applicability of regulatory limitations prior to use.*

2. Referenced Documents

2.1 *ASTM Standards:*
C 43 Terminology of Structural Clay Products[2]
C 126 Specification for Ceramic Glazed Structural Clay Facing Tile, Facing Brick, and Solid Masonry Units[2]
C 150 Specification for Portland Cement[3]
E 4 Practices for Force Verification of Testing Machines[4]
E 6 Terminology Relating to Methods of Mechanical Testing[4]

3. Terminology

3.1 *Definitions:*
3.1.1 Terminology E 6 and Terminology C 43 shall be considered as applying to the terms used in these test methods.

4. Sampling

4.1 *Selection of Test Specimens*—For the purpose of these tests, full-size brick, tile, or solid masonry units shall be selected by the purchaser or by his authorized representative. Specimens shall be representative of the whole lot of units from which they are selected and shall include specimens representative of the complete range of colors, textures and sizes in the shipment and shall be free of dirt, mud, mortar, or other foreign materials unassociated with the manufacturing process.

4.2 *Number of Specimens:*
4.2.1 *Brick*—For the modulus of rupture, compressive strength, abrasion resistance, and absorption determinations, at least ten individual brick shall be selected for lots of 1 000 000 brick or fraction thereof. For larger lots, five additional specimens shall be selected from each additional 500 000 brick or fraction thereof. Additional specimens may be taken at the discretion of the purchaser.

4.2.2 *Structural Clay Tile*—For the weight determination and for compressive strength and absorption tests, at least five tile shall be selected from each lot of 250 tons (226.8 Mg) or fraction thereof. For larger lots, five additional specimens shall be tested for each 500 tons (453.6 Mg) or fraction thereof. In no case shall less than five tile be taken. Additional specimens may be taken at the discretion of the purchaser.

4.3 *Identification*—Each specimen shall be marked so that it may be identified at any time. Markings shall cover not more than 5 % of the superficial area of the specimen.

4.4 *Weight Determination:*
4.4.1 *Drying*—Dry the test specimens in a ventilated oven at 230 to 239°F (110 to 115°C) for not less than 24 h and until two successive weighings at intervals of 2 h show an increment of loss not greater than 0.2 % of the last previously determined weight of the specimen.

4.4.2 *Cooling*—After drying, cool the specimens in a drying room maintained at a temperature of 75 ± 15°F (24 ± 8°C), with a relative humidity between 30 and 70 %. Store the units free from drafts, unstacked, with separate placement, for a period of at least 4 h. Do not use specimens noticeably warm to the touch for any test requiring dry units.

4.4.2.1 An alternative method of cooling the specimens to approximate room temperature may be used as follows: Store units, unstacked, with separate placement, in a ventilated room for a period of 4 h, with a current of air from an electric fan passing over them for a period of at least 2 h.

4.4.3 *Calculations and Report:*
4.4.3.1 Calculate the weight per unit area of a specimen by dividing the total weight in pounds by the average area in square feet of the two faces of the unit as normally laid in a wall.

4.4.3.2 Report results separately for each unit with the average for five units or more.

4.5 *Removal of Silicone Coatings from Brick Units*—The silicone coatings intended to be removed by this process are any of the various polymeric organic silicone compounds used for water-resistant coatings of brick units. Heat the brick at 950 ± 50°F (510 ± 10°C) in an oxidizing atmosphere

---

[1] These test methods are under the jurisdiction of Committee C-15 on Manufactured Masonry Units and is the direct responsibility of Subcommittee C15.02 on Clay Brick and Structural Clay Tile.
Current edition approved Dec. 15, 1994. Published February 1995. Originally published as C 67 – 37 T and C 112 – 34 T. Last previous edition C 67 – 93a.
[2] *Annual Book of ASTM Standards*, Vol 04.05.
[3] *Annual Book of ASTM Standards*, Vol 04.01.
[4] *Annual Book of ASTM Standards*, Vol 03.01.

for a period of not less than 3 h. The rate of heating and cooling shall not exceed 300°F (149°C) per h.

5. Modulus of Rupture (Flexure Test)

5.1 *Test Specimens*—The test specimens shall consist of whole dry full-size units (see 4.4.1). Five such specimens shall be tested.

5.2 *Procedure:*

5.2.1 Support the test specimen flatwise unless specified and reported otherwise (that is, apply the load in the direction of the depth of the unit) on a span approximately 1 in. (25.4 mm) less than the basic unit length and loaded at midspan. If the specimens have recesses (panels or depressions) place them so that such recesses are on the compression side. Apply the load to the upper surface of the specimen through a steel bearing plate ¼ in. (6.35 mm) in thickness and 1½ in. (38.10 mm) in width and of a length at least equal to the width of the specimen.

5.2.2 Make sure the supports for the test specimen are free to rotate in the longitudinal and transverse directions of the test specimen and adjust them so that they will exert no force in these directions.

5.2.3 *Speed of Testing*—The rate of loading shall not exceed 2000 lbf (8896 N). but this requirement may be considered as being met if the speed of the moving head of the testing machine immediately prior to application of the load is not more than 0.05 in. (1.27 mm)/min.

5.3 *Calculation and Report:*

5.3.1 Calculate the modulus of rupture of each specimen as follows:

$$S = 3W(l/2 - x)/bd^2$$

where:

S = modulus of rupture of the specimen at the plane of failure, lb/in.^{2} (Pa),

W = maximum load indicated by the testing machine, lbf (N),

l = distance between the supports, in. (mm),

b = net width, (face to face minus voids), of the specimen at the plane of failure, in. (mm),

d = depth, (bed surface to bed surface), of the specimen at the plane of failure, in. (mm), and

x = average distance from the midspan of the specimen to the plane of failure measured in the direction of the span along the centerline of the bed surface subjected to tension, in. (mm).

5.3.2 Report the average of the modulus of rupture determinations of all the specimens tested as the modulus of rupture of the lot.

6. Compressive Strength

6.1 *Test Specimens:*

6.1.1 *Brick*—The test specimens shall consist of dry half brick (see 4.4.1), the full height and width of the unit, with a length equal to one half the full length of the unit ±1 in. (25.4 mm), except as described below. If the test specimen, described above, exceeds the testing machine capacity, the test specimens shall consist of dry pieces of brick, the full height and width of the unit, with a length not less than one quarter of the full length of the unit, and with a gross cross-sectional area perpendicular to bearing not less than 14

in.^{2} (90.3 cm^2). Test specimens shall be obtained by any method that will produce, without shattering or cracking, a specimen with approximately plane and parallel ends. Five specimens shall be tested.

6.1.2 *Structural Clay Tile*—Test five dry tile specimens in a bearing bed length equal to the width ± 1 in. (25.4 mm); or test full-size units.

6.2 *Capping Test Specimens:*

6.2.1 All specimens shall be dry and cool within the meaning of 4.4.1 and 4.4.2 before any portion of the capping procedure is carried out.

6.2.2 If the surface which will become bearing surfaces during the compression test are recessed or paneled, fill the depressions with a mortar composed of 1 part by weight of quick-hardening cement conforming to the requirements for Type III cement of Specification C 150, and 2 parts by weight of sand. Age the specimens at least 48 h before capping them. Where the recess exceeds ½ in. (12.7 mm), use a brick or tile slab section or metal plate as a core fill. Cap the test specimens using one of the two procedures described in 6.2.3 and 6.2.4.

6.2.3 *Gypsum Capping*—Coat the two opposite bearing surfaces of each specimen with shellac and allow to dry thoroughly. Bed one of the dry shellacked surfaces of the specimen in a thin coat of neat paste of calcined gypsum (plaster of paris) that has been spread on an oiled nonabsorbent plate, such as glass or machined metal. The casting surface plate shall be plane within 0.003 in. (0.076 mm) in 16 in. (406.4 mm) and sufficiently rigid; and so supported that it will not be measurably deflected during the capping operation. Lightly coat it with oil or other suitable material. Repeat this procedure with the other shellacked surface. Take care that the opposite bearing surfaces so formed will be approximately parallel and perpendicular to the vertical axis of the specimen and the thickness of the caps will be approximately the same and not exceeding ⅛ in. (3.18 mm). Age the caps at least 24 h before testing the specimens.

NOTE 1—A rapid-setting industrial type gypsum, such as Hydrocal or Hydrostone, is frequently used for capping.

6.2.4 *Sulfur-Filler Capping*—Use a mixture containing 40 to 60 weight % sulfur, the remainder being ground fire clay or other suitable inert material passing a No. 100 (150-μm) sieve with or without plasticizer. The casting surface plate requirements shall be as described in 6.2.3. Place four 1-in. (25.4-mm) square steel bars on the surface plate to form a rectangular mold approximately ½ in. (12.7 mm) greater in either inside dimension than the specimen. Heat the sulfur mixture in a thermostatically controlled heating pot to a temperature sufficient to maintain fluidity for a reasonable period of time after contact with the surface being capped. Take care to prevent overheating, and stir the liquid in the pot just before use. Fill the mold to a depth of ¼ in. (6.35 mm) with molten sulfur material. Place the surface of the unit to be capped quickly in the liquid, and hold the specimen so that its vertical axis is at right angles to the capping surface. The thickness of the caps shall be approximately the same. Allow the unit to remain undisturbed until solidification is complete. Allow the caps to cool for a minimum of 2 h before testing the specimens.

6.3 *Procedure:*

C 67

6.3.1 Test brick specimens flatwise (that is, the load shall be applied in the direction of the depth of the brick). Test structural clay tile specimens in a position such that the load is applied in the same direction as in service. Center the specimens under the spherical upper bearing within $\frac{1}{16}$ in. (1.59 mm).

6.3.2 The testing machine shall conform to the requirements of Practices E 4.

6.3.3 The upper bearing shall be a spherically seated, hardened metal block firmly attached at the center of the upper head of the machine. The center of the sphere shall lie at the center of the surface of the block in contact with the specimen. The block shall be closely held in its spherical seat, but shall be free to turn in any direction, and its perimeter shall have at least $\frac{1}{4}$ in. (6.35 mm) clearance from the head to allow for specimens whose bearing surfaces are not exactly parallel. The diameter of the bearing surface shall be at least 5 in. (127.00 mm). Use a hardened metal bearing block beneath the specimen to minimize wear of the lower platen of the machine. The bearing block surfaces intended for contact with the specimen should have a hardness not less than HRC60 (HB 620). These surfaces shall not depart from plane surfaces by more than 0.001 in. (0.03 mm). When the bearing area of the spherical bearing block is not sufficient to cover the area of the specimen, place a steel plate with surfaces machined to true planes within ± 0.001 in. (0.03 mm), and with a thickness equal to at least one third of the distance from the edge of the spherical bearing to the most distant corner between the spherical bearing block and the capped specimen.

6.3.4 *Speed of Testing*—Apply the load, up to one half of the expected maximum load, at any convenient rate, after which, adjust the controls of the machine so that the remaining load is applied at a uniform rate in not less than 1 nor more than 2 min.

6.4 *Calculation and Report:*

6.4.1 Calculate the compressive strength of each specimen as follows:

$$\text{Compressive strength, } C = W/A$$

where:

C = compressive strength of the specimen, lb/in.^{2} (or kg/cm^2) (or Pa·10^4)

W = maximum load, lbf, (or kgf) (or N), indicated by the testing machine, and

A = average of the gross areas of the upper and lower bearing surfaces of the specimen, in.^{2} (or cm^2).

NOTE 2—When compressive strength is to be based on net area (example: clay floor tile), substitute for A in the above formula the net area, in.^{2} (or cm^2), of the fired clay in the section of minimum area perpendicular to the direction of the load.

7. Absorption

7.1 *Accuracy of Weighings:*

7.1.1 *Brick*—The scale or balance used shall have a capacity of not less than 2000 g, and shall be sensitive to 0.5 g.

7.1.2 *Tile*—The balance used shall be sensitive to within 0.2 % of the weight of the smallest specimen tested.

7.2 *Test Specimens:*

7.2.1 *Brick*—The test specimens shall consist of half brick

conforming to the requirements of 6.1.1. Five specimens shall be tested.

7.2.2 *Tile*—The specimens for the absorption test shall consist of five tile or three representative pieces from each of these five tile. If small pieces are used, take two from the shell and one from an interior web, the weight of each piece being not less than 227 g. The specimens shall have had their rough edges or loose particles ground off and, if taken from tile that have been subjected to compressive strength tests, specimens shall be free of cracks due to failure in compression.

7.3 *5-h and 24-h Submersion Tests:*

7.3.1 *Procedure:*

7.3.1.1 Dry and cool the test specimens in accordance with 4.4.1 and 4.4.2 and weigh each one.

7.3.1.2 *Saturation*—Submerge the dry, cooled specimen, without preliminary partial immersion, in clean water (soft, distilled or rain water) at 60 to 86°F (15.5 to 30°C) for the specified time. Remove the specimen, wipe off the surface water with a damp cloth and weigh the specimen. Complete weighing of each specimen within 5 min after removing the specimen from the bath.

7.3.2 *Calculation and Report:*

7.3.2.1 Calculate the absorption of each specimen as follows:

$$\text{Absorption, } \% = 100(W_s - W_d)/W_d$$

where:

W_d = dry weight of the specimen, and

W_s = saturated weight of the specimen after submersion in cold water.

7.3.2.2 Report the average absorption of all the specimens tested as the absorption of the lot.

7.4 *1-h, 2-h, and 5-h Boiling Tests:*

7.4.1 *Test Specimens*—The test specimens shall be the same five specimens used in the 5-h or 24-h cold-water submersion test where required and shall be used in the state of saturation existing at the completion of that test.

7.4.2 *Procedure:*

7.4.2.1 Return the specimen that has been subjected to the cold-water submersion to the bath, and subject it to the boiling test as described in 7.4.2.2.

7.4.2.2 Submerge the specimen in clean water (soft, distilled or rain water) at 60 to 86°F (15.5 to 30°C) in such a manner that water can circulate freely on all sides of the specimen. Heat the water to boiling, within 1 h, boil continuously for specified time, and then allow to cool to 60 to 86°F (15.5 to 30°C) by natural loss of heat. Remove the specimen, wipe off the surface water with a damp cloth, and weigh the specimen. Complete weighing of each specimen within 5 min after removing the specimen from the bath.

7.4.2.3 If the tank is equipped with a drain so that water at 60 to 86°F (15.5 to 30°C) can be passed through the tank continuously and at such a rate that a complete change of water takes place in not more than 2 min, make weighings at the end of 1 h.

7.4.3 *Calculation and Report:*

7.4.3.1 Calculate the absorption of each specimen as follows:

$$\text{Absorption, } \% = 100(W_b - W_d)/W_d$$

where:

W_d = dry weight of the specimen, and

W_b = saturated weight of the specimen after submersion in boiling water.

7.4.3.2 Report the average absorption of all the specimens tested as the absorption of the lot.

7.4.4 *Saturation Coefficient: Calculate the saturation coefficient of each specimen as follows:*

$$\text{Saturation coefficient} = W_{s2} - W_d / W_{bs} - W_d$$

where:

W_d = dry weight of the specimen,

W_{s2} = saturated weight of the specimen after 24-h submersion in cold water, and

W_{bs} = saturated weight of the specimen after 5-h submersion in boiling water.

8. Freezing and Thawing

8.1 *Apparatus:*

8.1.1 *Compressor, Freezing Chamber, and Circulator* of such design and capacity that the temperature of the air in the freezing chamber will not exceed 16°F (−9°C) 1 h after introducing the maximum charge of units, initially at a temperature not exceeding 90°F (32°C).

8.1.2 *Trays and Containers,* shallow, metal, having an inside depth of 1½ ± ½ in. (38.1 ± 12.7 mm), and of suitable strength and size so that the tray with a charge of frozen units can be removed from the freezing chamber by one man.

8.1.3 *Balance,* having a capacity of not less than 2000 g and sensitive to 0.5 g.

8.1.4 *Drying Oven* that provides a free circulation of air through the oven and is capable of maintaining a temperature between 230 and 239°F (110 and 115°C).

8.1.5 *Thawing Tank* of such dimensions as to permit complete submersion of the specimens in their trays. Adequate means shall be provided so that the water in the tank may be kept at a temperature of 75 ± 10°F (24 ± 5.5°C).

8.1.6 *Drying Room,* maintained at a temperature of 75 ± 15°F (24 ± 8°C), with a relative humidity between 30 and 70 %, and free from drafts.

8.2 *Test Specimens:*

8.2.1 *Brick*—The test specimens shall consist of half brick with approximately plane and parallel ends. If necessary, the rough ends may be smoothed by trimming off a thin section with a masonry saw. The specimens shall be free from shattering or unsoundness, visually observed, resulting from the flexure or from the absorption tests. Additionally, prepare specimens by removing all loosely adhering particles, sand or edge shards from the surface or cores. Test five specimens.

8.2.2 *Structural Clay Tile*—The test specimens shall consist of five tile or of a cell not less than 4 in. (101.6 mm) in length sawed from each of the five tile.

8.3 *Procedure:*

8.3.1 Dry and cool the test specimens as prescribed in 4.4.1 and 4.4.2 and weigh and record the dry weight of each.

8.3.2 Carefully examine each specimen for cracks. A crack is defined as a fissure or separation visible to a person with normal vision from a distance of one foot under an illumination of not less than 50 fc. Mark each crack its full length with an indelible felt marking pen.

8.3.3 Submerge the test specimens in the water of the thawing tank for 4 ± ½ h.

8.3.4 Remove the specimens from the thawing tank and stand them in the freezing trays with one of their head faces down. Head face is defined as the end surfaces of a whole rectangular brick (which have the smallest area). A space of at least ½ in. (12.7 mm) shall separate the specimens as placed in the tray. Pour sufficient water into the trays so that each specimen stands in ½ in. depth of water and then place the trays and their contents in the freezing chamber for 20 ± 1 h.

8.3.5 Remove the trays from the freezing chamber after 20 ± 1 h and totally immerse them and their contents in the water of the thawing tank for 4 ± ½ h.

8.3.6 Freeze the test specimens by the procedure in 8.3.4 one cycle each day of the normal work week. Following the 4 ± ½ h thawing after the last freeze-thaw cycle of the normal work week, remove the specimens from the trays and store them for 44 ± 1 h in the drying room. Do not stack or pile units. Provide a space of at least 1 in. (25.4 mm) between all specimens. Following this period of air drying, inspect the specimens, submerge them in the water of the thawing tank for 4 ± ½ h, and again subject them to a normal week of freezing and thawing cycles in accordance with 8.3.4 and 8.3.5. If a laboratory has personnel available for testing 7 days a week, the requirement for storing the specimens for 44 ± 1 h in the drying room following the 4 ± ½ h thawing after the last freezing cycle of the week may be waived. The specimens may then be subjected to 50 cycles of freezing and thawing on 50 consecutive days. When a normal 5-day work week is interrupted, put specimens into a drying cycle which may extend past the 44 ± 1 h drying time outlined in the procedures of this section.

8.3.7 Continue the alternations of drying and submersion in water for 4 ± ½ h, followed by 5 cycles of freezing and thawing or the number of cycles needed to complete a normal work week, until a total of 50 cycles of freezing and thawing has been completed. Stop the test if the test specimen has been broken or appears to have lost more than 3 % of its original weight as judged by visual inspection.

8.3.8 After completion of 50 cycles, or when the test specimen has been withdrawn from test as a result of disintegration, dry and weigh the specimen as prescribed in 8.3.1.

8.4 *Calculations, Examination, Rating and Report:*

8.4.1 *Calculation*—Calculate the loss in weight as a percentage of the original weight of the dried specimen.

8.4.2 *Examination*—Reexamine the surface of the specimens for cracks (see 8.3.2) and record the presence of any new cracks developed during the freezing-thawing testing procedure. Measure and record the length of the new cracks.

8.4.3 *Rating*—A specimen is considered to fail the freezing and thawing test under any one of three circumstances:

8.4.3.1 Weight Loss—A weight loss of greater than 0.5 %.

8.4.3.2 Breakage—The specimen separates into two or more significant pieces, or

8.4.3.3 Cracking—A specimen develops a crack during the freezing and thawing procedure that exceeds in length the minimum dimension of the specimen.

If none of the above circumstances occur, the specimens are considered to pass the freezing and thawing test.

8.4.4 *Report*—The report shall state whether the sample

⏣ C 67

passed or failed the test. Any failures shall include the rating and the reason for classification as a failure and the number of cycles causing failure in the event failure occurs prior to 50 cycles.

9. Initial Rate of Absorption (Suction) (Laboratory Test)

9.1 *Apparatus:*

9.1.1 *Trays or Containers*—Watertight trays or containers, having an inside depth of not less than ½ in. (12.7 mm), and of such length and width that an area of not less than 300 in.² (1935.5 cm.²) of water surface is provided. The bottom of the tray shall provide a plane, horizontal upper surface, when suitably supported, so that an area not less than 8 in. (203.2 mm) in length by 6 in. (152.4 mm) in width will be level when tested by a spirit level.

9.1.2 *Supports for Brick*—Two noncorrodible metal supports consisting of bars between 5 and 6 in. (127.00 and 152.5 mm) in length, having triangular, half-round, or rectangular cross sections such that the thickness (height) will be approximately ¼ in. (6.35 mm). The thickness of the two bars shall agree within 0.001 in. (0.03 mm) and, if the bars are rectangular in cross section, their width shall not exceed ⁵⁄₁₆ in. (1.94 mm).

9.1.3 *Means for Maintaining Constant Water Level*—Suitable means for controlling the water level above the upper surface of the supports for the brick within ± 0.01 in. (0.25 mm) (see Note 3), including means for adding water to the tray at a rate corresponding to the rate of removal by the brick undergoing test (see Note 4). For use in checking the adequacy of the method of controlling the rate of flow of the added water, a reference brick or half brick shall be provided whose displacement in ⅛ in. (3.18 mm) of water corresponds to the brick or half brick to be tested within ± 2.5 %. Completely submerge the reference brick in water for not less than 3 h preceding its use.

NOTE 3—A suitable means for obtaining accuracy in control of the water level may be provided by attaching to the end of one of the bars two stiff metal wires that project upward and return, terminating in points; one of which is ⅛ − 0.01 in. (3.18 − 0.25 mm) and the other ⅛ + 0.01 in. (3.18 + 0.25 mm) above the upper surface or edge of the bar. Such precise adjustment is obtainable by the use of depth plates or a micrometer microscope. When the water level with respect to the upper surface or edge of the bar is adjusted so that the lower point dimples the water surface when viewed by reflected light and the upper point is not in contact with the water, the water level is within the limits specified. Any other suitable means for fixing and maintaining a constant depth of immersion may be used if equivalent accuracy is obtained. As an example of such other suitable means, there may be mentioned the use of rigid supports movable with respect to the water level.

NOTE 4—A rubber tube leading from a siphon or gravity feed and closed by a spring clip will provide a suitable manual control. The so-called "chicken-feed" devices as a rule lack sensitivity and do not operate with the very small changes in water level permissible in this test.

9.1.4 *Balance*, having a capacity of not less than 3000 g, and sensitive to 0.5 g.

9.1.5 *Drying Oven*, conforming to the requirements of 8.1.4.

9.1.6 *Constant-Temperature Room*, maintained at a temperature of 70 ± 2.5°F (21 ± 1.4°C).

9.1.7 *Timing Device*—A suitable timing device, preferably a stop watch or stop clock, which shall indicate a time of 1 min to the nearest 1 s.

9.2 *Test Specimens*, consisting of whole brick. Five specimens shall be tested.

9.3 *Procedure:*

9.3.1 Dry and cool the test specimens in accordance with one of the following procedures.

9.3.1.1 *Oven-dried Procedure*—Dry and cool the test specimens in accordance with 4.4.1 and 4.4.2.

9.3.1.2 *Ambient Air-dried Procedure*—Store units unstacked, with separate placement in a ventilated room maintained at a temperature of 75 ± 15°F (24 ± 8°C) with a relative humidity between 30 % and 70 % for a period of 4 h, with a current of air from an electric fan passing over them for a period of at least 2 h. Continue until two successive weighings at intervals of 2 h show an increment of loss not greater than 0.2 % of the last previously determined weight of the specimen.

9.3.2 Measure to the nearest 0.05 in. (1.27 mm) the length and width of the flatwise surface of the test specimen of rectangular units or determine the area of other shapes to similar accuracy that will be in contact with the water. Weigh the specimen to the nearest 0.5 g.

9.3.3 Adjust the position of the tray for the absorption test so that the upper surface of its bottom will be level when tested by a spirit level, and set the saturated reference brick (9.1.3) in place on top of the supports. Add water until the water level is ⅛ ± 0.01 in. (3.18 ± 0.25 mm) above the top of the supports. When testing tile with scored bed surfaces, the depth of water level is ⅛ ± 0.01 in. plus the depth of scores.

9.3.4 After removal of the reference brick, set the test brick in place flatwise, counting zero time as the moment of contact of the brick with the water. During the period of contact (1 min ± 1 s) keep the water level within the prescribed limits by adding water as required. At the end of 1 min ± 1 s, lift the brick from contact with the water, wipe off the surface water with a damp cloth, and reweigh the brick to the nearest 0.5 g. Wiping shall be completed within 10 s of removal from contact with the water, and weighing shall be completed within 2 min.

NOTE 5—Place the brick in contact with the water quickly, but without splashing. Set the brick in position with a rocking motion to avoid the entrapping of air on its under surface. Test brick with frogs or depressions in one flatwise surface with the frog or depression uppermost.

9.4 *Calculation and Report:*

9.4.1 The difference in weight in grams between the initial and final weighings is the weight in grams of water absorbed by the brick during 1-min contact with the water. If the area of its flatwise surface (length times width) does not differ more than ± 0.75 in.² (4.84 cm²) (±2.5 %) from 30 in.² (193.55 cm²), report the gain in weight in grams as the initial rate of absorption in 1 min.

9.4.2 If the area of its flatwise surface differs more than ± 0.75 in.² (4.84 cm²) (±2.5 %) from 30 in.² (193.55 cm²), calculate the equivalent gain in weight from 30 in.² (193.55 cm²) as follows:

$$X = 30\,W/LB \quad (\text{metric } X = 193.55\,W/LB)$$

where:

X = gain in weight corrected to basis of 30 in.² (193.55 cm²) flatwise area,

W = actual gain in weight of specimen, g,

C 67

L = length of specimen, in., (cm), and
B = width of specimen, in., (cm).

9.4.3 Report the corrected gain in weight, X, as the initial rate of absorption in 1 min.

9.4.4 If the test specimen is a cored brick, calculate the net area and substitute for LB in the equation given in 9.4.2. Report the corrected gain in weight as the initial rate of absorption in 1 min.

9.4.5 If specimen is non-prismatic, calculate the net area by suitable geometric means and substitute for LB in the equation given in 9.4.2.

9.4.6 Report the method of drying as oven-dried (in accordance with 9.3.1.1) or ambient air-dried (in acordance with 9.3.1.2).

10. Efflorescence

10.1 *Apparatus:*

10.1.1 *Trays and Containers*—Watertight shallow pans or trays made of corrosion-resistant metal or other material that will not provide soluble salts when in contact with distilled water containing leachings from brick. The pan shall be of such dimensions that it will provide not less than a 1-in. (25.4-mm) depth of water. Unless the pan provides an area such that the total volume of water is large in comparison with the amount evaporated each day, suitable apparatus shall be provided for keeping a constant level of water in the pan.

10.1.2 *Drying Room*, conforming to the requirements of 8.1.6.

10.1.3 *Drying Oven*, conforming to the requirements of 8.1.4.

10.2 *Test Specimens:*

10.2.1 The sample shall consist of ten full-size brick.

10.2.2 The ten specimens shall be sorted into five pairs so that both specimens of each pair will have the same appearance as nearly as possible.

10.3 *Preparation of Specimens*—Remove by brushing any adhering dirt that might be mistaken for efflorescence. Dry the specimens and cool them as prescribed in 4.4.1 and 4.4.2.

10.4 *Procedure:*

10.4.1 Set one specimen from each of the five pairs, on end, partially immersed in distilled water to a depth of approximately 1 in. (25.4 mm) for 7 days in the drying room. When several specimens are tested in the same container, separate the individual specimens by a spacing of at least 2 in. (50.8 mm).

NOTE 6—Do not test specimens from different sources simultaneously in the same container, because specimens with a considerable content of soluble salts may contaminate salt-free specimens.

NOTE 7—Empty and clean the pans or trays after each test.

10.4.2 Store the second specimen from each of the five pairs in the drying room without contact with water.

10.4.3 At the end of 7 days, inspect the first set of specimens and then dry both sets in the drying oven for 24 h.

10.5 *Examination and Rating*—After drying, examine and compare each pair of specimens, observing the top and all four faces of each specimen from a distance of 10 ft. (3 m) under an illumination of not less than 50 footcandles (538.2 lm/m^2) by an observer with normal vision. If under these conditions no difference is noted, report the rating as "not effloresced." If a perceptible difference due to efflorescence is noted under these conditions, report the rating as "effloresced." Record the appearance and distribution of the efflorescence.

11. Measurement of Size

11.1 *Apparatus*—Either a 1-ft (or metric) steel rule, graduated in $^1/_{32}$-in. (or 1-mm) divisions, or a gage or caliper having a scale ranging from 1 to 12 in. (25 to 300 mm), and having parallel jaws, shall be used for measuring the individual units. Steel rules or calipers of corresponding accuracy and size required shall be used for measurement of larger brick, solid masonry units and tile.

11.2 *Test Specimens*—Measure ten dry full-size units. These units shall be representative of the shipment and shall include the extremes of color range and size as determined by visual inspection of the shipment. (The same samples may be used for determining efflorescence and other properties.)

11.3 *Individual Measurements of Width, Length, and Height*—Measure the width across both ends and both beds from the midpoints of the edges bounding the faces. Record these four measurements to the nearest $^1/_{32}$ in. (1 mm) and record the average to the nearest $^1/_{64}$ in. (0.5 mm) as the width. Measure the length along both beds and along both faces from the midpoints of the edges bounding the ends. Record these four measurements to the nearest $^1/_{32}$ in. (1 mm) and record the average to the nearest $^1/_{64}$ in. (0.5 mm) as the length. Measure the height across both faces and both ends from the midpoints of the edges bounding the beds. Record these four measurements to the nearest $^1/_{32}$ in. (1 mm) and record the average to the nearest $^1/_{64}$ in. (0.5 mm) as the height. Use the apparatus described in 11.1. Retest by the same method when required.

12. Measurement of Warpage

12.1 *Apparatus:*

12.1.1 *Steel Straightedge:*

12.1.2 *Rule or Measuring Wedge*—A steel rule graduated from one end in $^1/_{32}$-in. (or 1-mm) divisions, or alternatively, a steel measuring wedge 2.5 in. (60 mm) in length by 0.5 in. (12.5 mm) in width by 0.5 in. (12.5 mm) in thickness at one end and tapered, starting at a line 0.5 in. (12.5 mm) from one end, to zero thickness at the other end. The wedge shall be graduated in $^1/_{32}$-in. (or 1-mm) divisions and numbered to show the thickness of the wedge between the base, AB, and the slope, AC, Fig. 1.

12.1.3 *Flat Surface*, of steel or glass, not less than 12 by 12 in. (305 by 305 mm) and plane to within 0.001 in. (0.025 mm).

12.2 *Sampling*—Use the sample of ten units selected for determination of size.

12.3 *Preparation of Samples*—Test the specimens as received, except remove any adhering dirt by brushing.

12.4 *Procedure:*

12.4.1 *Concave Surfaces*—Where the warpage to be measured is of a surface and is concave, place the straightedge lengthwise or diagonally along the surface to be measured, selecting the location that gives the greatest departure from straightness. Select the greatest distance from the unit surface to the straightedge. Using the steel rule or wedge, measure this distance to the nearest $^1/_{32}$ in. (1 mm), and record as the

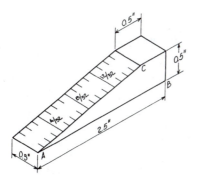

FIG. 1 Measuring Wedge

concave warpage of the surface.

12.4.2 *Concave Edges*—Where the warpage to be measured is of an edge and is concave, place the straightedge between the ends of the concave edge to be measured. Select the greatest distance from the unit edge to the straightedge. Using the steel rule or wedge, measure this distance to the nearest 1/32 in. (1 mm), and record as the concave warpage of the edge.

12.4.3 *Convex Surfaces*—When the warpage to be measured is of a surface and is convex, place the unit with the convex surface in contact with a plane surface and with the corners approximately equidistant from the plane surface. Using the steel rule or wedge, measure the distance to the nearest 1/32 in. (1 mm) of each of the four corners from the plane surface. Record the average of the four measurements as the convex warpage of the unit.

12.4.4 *Convex Edges*—Where the warpage to be measured is of an edge and is convex, place the straightedge between the ends of the convex edge. Select the greatest distance from the unit edge to the straightedge. Using the steel rule or wedge, measure this distance to the nearest 1/32 in. (1 mm) and record as the convex warpage of the edge.

13. Measurement of Length Change

13.1 *Apparatus*—A *dial micrometer* or other suitable measuring device graduated to read in 0.0001-in. (or 0.001-mm) increments, mounted on a stand suitable for holding the specimen in such a manner that reproducible results can be obtained, shall be used for measuring specimen length. Provisions shall be made to permit changing the position of the dial micrometer on its mounting rod so as to accommodate large variations in specimen size. The base of the stand and the tip of the dial micrometer shall have a conical depression to accept a 1/4-in. (6.35-mm) steel ball. A suitable reference instrument shall be provided for checking the measuring device.

13.2 *Preparation of Specimen*—Remove the ends of deeply textured specimens to the depth of the texture by cutting perpendicular to the length and parallel to each other. Drill a hole in each end of the specimen with a 1/4-in. (6.35-mm) carbide drill. Drill these holes at the intersection of the two diagonals from the corners. Place 1/4-in. (6.35-mm) steel balls in these depressions by cementing in place with a calcium aluminate cement. Any equivalent method

for establishing the reference length is permissible.

13.3 *Procedure*—Mark the specimen for identification and measure to the nearest 0.0001 in. (or 0.001 mm) in a controlled environment and make subsequent measurements in the same controlled environment, ± 2°F and ± 5 % relative humidity. Record the temperature and relative humidity. Apply a reference mark to the specimen for orientation in the measuring device. Check the measuring device with the reference instrument before each series of measurements.

14. Initial Rate of Absorption (Suction)—Field Test

14.1 *Scope*—This test method is intended to serve as a volumetric means of determining the initial rate of absorption (IRA) of any size brick when weighing determination, described in Section 9 of this standard, is impractical. This test method is applicable to assess the need for wetting the brick. This test method is performed on specimens taken from the field with no modification of moisture content, therefore, the IRA determined by this test method may differ from the IRA determined by the laboratory test method in Section 9, which requires drying the specimens.

14.2 *Apparatus:*

14.2.1 *Absorption Test Pan*—A watertight, rectangular pan, constructed of noncorroding material, with a flat, rigid bottom and inside depth of about 1½ in. (38.1 mm). The inside length and width of the pan shall exceed the length and width of the tested brick by a minimum of 3 in. (76.2 mm) but not more than 5 in. (127.0 mm).

14.2.2 *Brick Supports*—Two noncorroding rectangular bars, ¼ in. (6.4 mm) in height and width and 1 in. (25.4 mm) shorter than the inside width of the pan in length. The brick supports can be placed on the bottom of the pan just before the test or permanently affixed to the bottom of the pan. The space between the supports should be about 4 in. (101.6 mm) shorter than the length of the tested brick. A device indicating the desired water level can be permanently attached to the end of one of the brick supports or suspended from the top of the pan (see Figs. 2a and b). Any other device of equivalent accuracy for controlling the required water level, ⅛ in. (3.2 mm) above the brick supports, can be used in place of that depicted in Fig. 2.

14.2.3 *Timing Device*—A suitable timing device that shall indicate a time of 1 min to the nearest 1 s.

14.2.4 *Squeeze Bottle*—A plastic squeeze bottle, 100 mL capacity.

14.2.5 *Graduated Cylinder*—A plastic or glass graduated

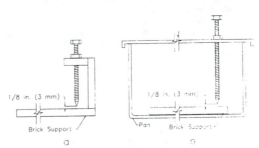

FIG. 2 Water Level Indicators

measuring cylinder, 100 mL capacity.

14.3 *Test Specimens*—Select six whole brick in accordance with the requirements of Paragraph 4.1.

14.4 *Procedure:*

14.4.1 Completely immerse one brick specimen in a container of water for 2 h.

14.4.2 Measure to the nearest $1/16$ in. (1.6 mm) the length and width of the five remaining specimens at the surface that will be in contact with water. If the test specimens are cored, determine the area of the cores at the same surface.

14.4.3 Pre-wet and drain the absorption pan and place it on a flat, level surface.

14.4.4 Remove the pre-wetted specimen from the container, shake off the surface water, and place the specimen on brick supports in the pan. Pour water into the pan until the water reaches a level $1/8$ in. (3.2 mm) above the brick supports. (If using a pointed level water indicator, pour water into the pan until the water makes a minimum contact (dimpling effect).) Remove the pre-wetted brick, and tilt the brick sharply so that one corner serves as a drip point for clinging surface water to return to the pan. A gentle shake of the brick may be necessary to make the last drop fall. Put the pre-wetted brick back into the container of water.

14.4.5 Using the graduated cylinder, fill the squeeze bottle with exactly 100 mL of water.

14.4.6 Set the first test specimen squarely on the brick supports, counting zero time as the moment the brick contacts the water. At the end of 1 min ± 1 s lift the test specimen from water and tilt the brick sharply so that one corner serves as a drip point for clinging surface water to return to the pan. A gentle shake of the brick may be necessary to make the last drop fall.

14.4.6.1 Continue setting the remaining test specimens into the pan in the same way until all five specimens are tested. During the test add water to the pan, using the squeeze bottle, to keep the water level approximately constant at the $1/8$ in. depth. Refill the squeeze bottle with 100 mL of water when empty, recording each refill.

14.4.6.2 After the last specimen is tested, place the pre-wetted brick back in the pan and restore the original level with water from the squeeze bottle.

NOTE 8—Place the brick in contact with the water quickly, but without splashing. Set the brick in position with a rocking motion to avoid the entrapping of air on its under surface. Test brick with frogs or depressions in one flatwise surface with the frog or depression uppermost.

14.4.7 Using the graduated cylinder, measure the volume of water remaining in the squeeze bottle.

14.5 *Calculation and Report:*

14.5.1 The number of refills plus the first full bottle, times 100 mL, minus the volume of water remaining in the squeeze bottle, is the total measured volume of water in millilitres absorbed by the five specimens.

$$V_t = 100 (n + 1) - V_r$$

where:

V_t = total measured volume of water absorbed by all tested specimens, mL,

n = the number of squeeze bottle refills, and

V_r = the volume of water remaining in the squeeze bottle, mL.

14.5.2 When the average net surface area in contact with water of a single specimen (sum of net surface areas divided by the number of specimens) differs by ±0.75 in.² (4.84 cm²) or less from 30 in.² (193.5 cm²), report the total measured absorbed volume of water divided by five, the number of tested specimens, as the IRA (Field) in g/min/30 in.².

$$\text{IRA (Field)} = \frac{V_t}{5}$$

14.5.3 If the average net surface area in contact with water differs by more than ±0.75 in.² (4.84 cm²) from 30 in.² (193.5 cm²), calculate the equivalent volume in 1 min for 30 in.² (193.5 cm²) of surface as follows:

$$V_c = \frac{30\ V_t}{A_n} \left(\text{metric } V_c = \frac{193.5\ V_t}{A_n}\right)$$

where:

V_c = average volume of absorbed water by a specimen, corrected to basis of 30 in.² (193.5 cm²) of surface, mL, and

A_n = sum of net surface areas in contact with water of all tested specimens, in.² (cm²).

14.5.4 *Report*—Report the corrected volume (V_c) as the IRA (Field) in g/l min/30 in.².

14.6 *Precision and Bias*—Insufficient data is currently available for a precision and bias statement.

15. Measurement of Void Area in Cored Units

15.1 *Apparatus:*

15.1.1 *Steel Rule or Calipers*—As described in 11.1.

15.1.2 *Graduated Cylinder*—A glass cylinder with a capacity of 500 mL and graduated in 1-mL increments.

15.1.3 *Paper*—A sheet of smooth, hard-finish paper not less than 24 by 24 in. (610 by 610 mm).

15.1.4 *Sand*—500 mL of clean, dry sand.

15.1.5 *Steel Straightedge.*

15.1.6 *Flat Surface*—A level, flat, smooth, clean dry surface.

15.1.7 *Brush*—A soft-bristle brush.

15.1.8 *Neoprene Mat*—24 by 24 in. (610 by 610 mm) open-cell neoprene sponge $1/4$ in. (6.4 mm) in thickness.

15.2 *Test Specimens*—Use of a sample of ten units selected as described for the determination of size (The samples taken for the determination of size may be used).

15.3 *Preparation of Samples*—Test the specimens as received, except remove any adhering dirt by brushing.

15.4 *Procedure:*

15.4.1 Measure and record the length, width, and depth of the unit as described for the determination of size.

15.4.2 Place the unit to be tested bed down (cores vertical) on the sheet of paper that has been spread over the neoprene mat on the flat surface.

15.4.3 Fill the cores with sand, allowing the sand to fall naturally. Do not work the sand into the cores. Using the steel straightedge, bring the level of the sand in the cores down to the top of the unit. With the brush, remove all excess sand from the top of the unit and from the paper sheet.

15.4.4 Lifting the unit up, allow all of the sand in the cores to fall on the sheet of paper.

15.4.5 Transfer the sand from the sheet of paper to the

ASTM C 67

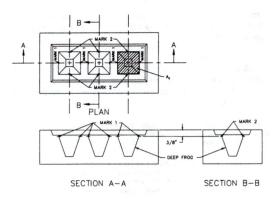

SECTION A–A   SECTION B–B

FIG. 3   Deep Frogged Units

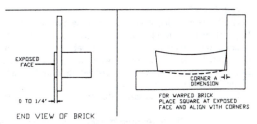

FIG. 4   Location of Carpenter's Square

graduated cylinder allowing the sand to fall naturally. Do not shake or vibrate the cylinder. Level the sand in the cylinder. Read and record the sand level to the nearest 1 mL.

15.5 *Calculation and Report:*

15.5.1 Determine the percentage of void as follows:

$$\% \text{ Void area} = \frac{V_s}{V_u} \times \frac{1}{16.4} \times 100$$

where:

V_s = amount of Sand recorded in 15.4.5, mL, and
V_u = length × width × depth recorded in 15.4.1, in.^{3}.

15.5.2 Report the results of the equation in 15.5.1 as the units percentage of void area.

16. Measurement of Void Area In Deep Frogged Units

Note 9—The area measured corresponds to a section located ⅜ in. (9.5 mm) distant from the voided bed of the units.

16.1 *Apparatus:*

16.1.1 *Steel Rule or Gage or Calipers (inside and outside)*—as described in 11.1.

16.1.2 *Steel Straightedge.*

16.1.3 *Marking Pen or Scribe.*

16.2 *Test Specimens*—Use a sample of 10 units selected as described for the determination of size. (The samples taken for the determination of size may be used.)

16.3 *Preparation of Sample*—Test the specimens as received except remove any adhering dirt by brushing.

16.4 *Procedure:*

16.4.1 Measure the length along both faces and the width along both ends at a distance of ⅜ in. (9.5 mm) down from the bed containing the deep frogs. Record the measurements to the nearest ¹⁄₃₂ in. (1 mm). Record the average of the two length measurements to the nearest ¹⁄₃₂ in. (1 mm) as the length of the unit and the average of the two width measurements to the nearest ¹⁄₃₂ in. (1 mm) as the width of the unit.

16.4.2 With the steel straightedge parallel to the length of the unit and centered over the deep frog or frogs, inscribe a mark on both faces of the frog ⅜ in. (9.5 mm) below the underside of the steel straightedge (mark 1 on Fig. 3). With the steel straightedge parallel to the width of the unit and centered over the deep frog, inscribe a mark on both faces of

each frog ⅜ in. (9.5 mm) below the underside of the steel straightedge (mark 2 on Fig. 3).

16.4.3 Measure and record to the nearest ¹⁄₃₂ in. (1 mm) the distance between the inscribed marks on a line parallel to the length of the unit for each frog, and measure and record to the nearest ¹⁄₃₂ in. (1 mm) the distance between the inscribed marks on a line parallel to the width of the unit for each frog.

16.5 *Calculations and Report:*

16.5.1 Using the recorded length and width measurements calculate the gross area of the unit (A_u) in the plane of the unit ⅜ in. (9.5 mm) down from the frogged bed.

16.5.2 Using the distance between the inscribed marks calculate the inside area of each deep frog (A_f) in the plane of the unit ⅜ in. (9.5 mm) down from the frogged bed (see Fig. 3).

16.5.3 Determine the percentage of void as follows:

$$\% \text{ Void area} = \frac{\Sigma A_f \times 100}{A_u}$$

where:

ΣA_f = sum of the inside area of the deep frogs
A_u = gross area of unit

16.5.4 Report the results of the equation in 16.5.3 as the unit's percentage of void area.

17. Measurement of Out of Square

17.1 *Apparatus:*

17.1.1 *Steel Rule or Calipers*, as described in 11.1.

17.1.2 *Steel Carpenter's Square.*

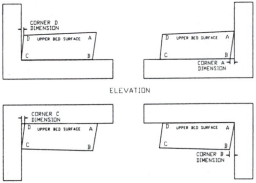

FIG. 5   Out-of-Square Measurements

◍ **C 67**

17.2 *Procedure:*

17.2.1 Place one leg of a carpenter's square adjacent to the length of the unit when laid as a stretcher. Align the leg of the square parallel to the length of the unit by having the corners of the face of the unit in contact with the leg of the square. Locate the square parallel to and at or within ¼ in. (6.4 mm) of the face to be exposed. See Fig. 4.

17.2.2 Measure the deviation due to the departure from the 90° angle at each corner of the exposed face of the unit. Record the measurement to the nearest 1/32 in. (0.8 mm) for each corner. See Fig. 5.

18. Keywords

18.1 absorption; compressive strength; efflorescence; freezing and thawing; initial rate of absorption; length change; modulus of rupture; out-of-square; sampling; size; void area; warpage

AMERICAN SOCIETY FOR TESTING AND MATERIALS
100 Barr Harbor Dr., West Conshohocken, PA 19428
Reprinted from the Annual Book of ASTM Standards. Copyright ASTM
If not listed in the current combined index, will appear in the next edition.

Standard Specification for
Loadbearing Concrete Masonry Units[1]

This standard is issued under the fixed designation C 90; the number immediately following the designation indicates the year of original adoption or, in the case of revision, the year of last revision. A number in parentheses indicates the year of last reapproval. A superscript epsilon (ε) indicates an editorial change since the last revision or reapproval.

This standard has been approved for use by agencies of the Department of Defense. Consult the DoD Index of Specifications and Standards for the specific year of issue which has been adopted by the Department of Defense.

1. Scope

1.1 This specification covers hollow and solid (see 5.4 and 5.5) concrete masonry units made from portland cement, water, and mineral aggregates with or without the inclusion of other materials. There are three classes of concrete masonry units: (1) normal weight, (2) medium weight, and (3) lightweight. There are two types of concrete masonry units: (1) Type I, moisture-controlled, and (2) Type II, nonmoisture-controlled. These units are suitable for both loadbearing and nonloadbearing applications.

1.2 Concrete masonry units covered by this specification are made from lightweight or normal weight aggregates, or both.

1.3 The values stated in inch-pound units are to be regarded as the standard. The values given in parentheses are for information only.

NOTE 1—When particular features are desired such as surface textures for appearance or bond, finish, color, or particular properties such as weight classification, higher compressive strength, fire resistance, thermal performance or acoustical performance, these features should be specified separately by the purchaser. Local suppliers should be consulted as to the availability of units having the desired features.

2. Referenced Documents

2.1 *ASTM Standards:*
C 33 Specification for Concrete Aggregates[2]
C 140 Test Methods of Sampling and Testing Concrete Masonry Units[3]
C 150 Specification for Portland Cement[4]
C 331 Specification for Lightweight Aggregates for Concrete Masonry Units[2]
C 426 Test Method for Drying Shrinkage of Concrete Masonry Units[3]
C 595/C 595M Specification for Blended Hydraulic Cements[2]
C 618 Specification for Coal Fly Ash and Raw or Calcined Natural Pozzolan for Use as a Mineral Admixture in Concrete[2]
C 989 Specification for Ground Granulated Blast-Furnace Slag for Use in Concrete and Mortars[2]

E 72 Methods for Conducting Strength Tests of Panels for Building Construction[5]
E 447 Test Methods for Compressive Strength of Masonry Prisms[3]
E 519 Test Method for Diagonal Tension (Shear) in Masonry Assemblages[3]

3. Classification

3.1 *Types*—Two types of concrete masonry units are covered as follows:

3.1.1 *Type I, Moisture-Controlled Units*—Units designated as Type I shall conform to the requirements of this specification.

3.1.2 *Type II, Nonmoisture-Controlled Units*—Units designated as Type II shall conform to the requirements of this specification, except the requirements of Table 1.

4. Materials

4.1 *Cementitious Materials*—Materials shall conform to the following applicable specifications:

4.1.1 *Portland Cement*—Specification C 150.

4.1.2 *Modified Portland Cement*—Portland cement conforming to Specification C 150, modified as follows:

4.1.2.1 *Limestone*—Calcium carbonate, with a minimum 85 % $CaCO_3$ content, may be added to the cement, provided these requirements of Specification C 150 as modified are met:

(1) Limitation on Insoluble Residue—1.5 %.

(2) Limitation on Air Content of Mortar—Volume percent, 22 % max.

(3) Limitation on Loss on Ignition—7 %.

4.1.3 *Blended Cements*—Specification C 595.

4.1.4 *Pozzolans*—Specification C 618.

4.1.5 *Blast Furnace Slag Cement*—Specification C 989.

4.2 *Aggregates*—Aggregates shall conform to the following specifications, except that grading requirements shall not necessarily apply:

4.2.1 *Normal Weight Aggregates*—Specification C 33.

4.2.2 *Lightweight Aggregates*—Specification C 331.

4.3 *Other Constituents*—Air-entraining agents, coloring pigments, integral water repellents, finely ground silica, and other constituents shall be previously established as suitable for use in concrete masonry units and shall conform to applicable ASTM standards or shall be shown by test or experience not to be detrimental to the durability of the

---

[1] This specification is under the jurisdiction of ASTM Committee C-15 on Manufactured Masonry Units and is the direct responsibility of Subcommittee C15.03 on Concrete Masonry Units and Related Units.
Current edition approved Jan. 10, 1996. Published April 1996. Originally published as C 90 – 31T. Last previous edition C 90 – 95.
[2] *Annual Book of ASTM Standards*, Vol 04.02.
[3] *Annual Book of ASTM Standards*, Vol 04.05.
[4] *Annual Book of ASTM Standards*, Vol 04.01.

[5] *Annual Book of ASTM Standards*, Vol 04.07.

⬨ C 90

TABLE 1   Moisture Content Requirements for Type I Units

Total Linear Drying Shrinkage, %	Moisture Content, max, % of Total Absorption (Average of 3 Units)		
	Humidity[A] Conditions at Job Site or Point of Use		
	Humid[B]	Intermediate[C]	Arid[D]
Less than 0.03	45	40	35
0.03 to less than 0.045	40	35	30
0.045 to 0.065, max	35	30	25

[A] See Appendix X1 for map of mean annual relative humidity.
[B] Mean annual relative humidity above 75 %.
[C] Mean annual relative humidity 50 to 75 %.
[D] Mean annual relative humidity less than 50 %.

TABLE 2   Minimum Thickness of Face Shells and Webs

Nominal Width (W) of Units, in. (mm)	Face Shell Thickness (FST), min, in. (mm)[A]	Web Thickness (WT)	
		Webs[A] min, in. (mm)	Equivalent Web Thickness, min, in./linear ft[B,C] (mm/linear m)
3 (76.2) and 4 (102)	¾ (19)	¾ (19)	1⅝ (136)
6 (152)	1 (25)[D]	1 (25)	2¼ (188)
8 (203)	1¼ (32)[D]	1 (25)	2¼ (188)
10 (254)	1⅜ (35)[D]	1⅛ (29)	2½ (209)
	1¼ (32)[D,E]		
12 (305)	1½ (38)	1⅛ (29)	2½ (209)
	1¼ (32)[D,E]		

[A] Average of measurements on 3 units taken at the thinnest point when measured as described in Test Methods C 140. When this standard is used for split face units, a maximum of 10 % of a split face shell area may have thickness less than those shown, but not less than ¾ inch (19.1 mm). When the units are solid grouted the 10 % limit does not apply.
[B] Average of measurements on 3 units taken at the thinnest point when measured as described in Test Methods C 140. The minimum web thickness for units with webs closer than 1 in. (25.4 mm) apart shall be ¾ in. (19.1 mm).
[C] Sum of the measured thicknesses of all webs in the unit, multiplied by 12 and divided by the length of the unit. Equivalent web thickness does not apply to the portion of the unit to be filled with grout. The length of that portion shall be deducted from the overall length of the unit for the calculation of the equivalent web thickness.
[D] For solid grouted masonry construction, minimum face shell thickness shall be not less than ⅝ in. (16 mm).
[E] This face shell thickness (FST) is applicable where allowable design load is reduced in proportion to the reduction in thickness from basic face shell thicknesses shown, except that allowable design loads on solid grouted units shall not be reduced.

concrete masonry units or any material customarily used in masonry construction.

5. Physical Requirements

5.1 At the time of delivery to the purchaser, all units shall conform to the physical requirements prescribed in Tables 2 and 3.

5.2 At the time of delivery to the purchaser, Type I units shall conform to the requirements prescribed in Table 1.

5.3 At the time of delivery to the purchaser, the linear shrinkage of Type II units shall not exceed 0.065 %.

NOTE 2—The purchaser is the public body or authority, association, corporation, partnership, or individual entering into a contract or agreement to purchase or install, or both, concrete masonry units. The time of delivery to the purchaser is FOB plant when the purchaser or the purchaser's agent transports the concrete masonry units, or at the time unloaded at the worksite if the manufacturer or the manufacturer's agent transports the concrete masonry units.

5.4 *Hollow Units:*

5.4.1 Face shell thickness (FST) and web thickness (WT) shall conform to the requirements prescribed in Table 2.

NOTE 3—Web thickness (WT) not conforming to the requirements prescribed in Table 2 may be approved, provided equivalent structural capability has been established when tested in accordance with the applicable provisions of Methods E 72, Test Method E 519, Test Methods E 447, or other applicable tests and the appropriate design criteria developed is in accordance with applicable building codes.

5.5 *Solid Units:*

5.5.1 The net cross-sectional area of solid units in every plane parallel to the bearing surface shall be not less than 75 % of the gross cross-sectional area measured in the same plane.

5.6 *End Flanges:*

5.6.1 For units having end flanges, the thickness of each flange shall not be less than the minimum face shell thickness.

NOTE 4—Flanges beveled at the ends for mortarless head joint applications that will be filled with grout are exempt from this requirement. Flanges which are specially shaped for mortarless head joint applications which have been shown by testing or field experience to provide equivalent performance are exempt from this requirement.

6. Permissible Variations in Dimensions

6.1 Overall dimensions for width, height, and length shall differ by not more than ±⅛ in. (3.2 mm) from the specified standard dimensions.

6.2 Permissible variations in dimensions for architectural features such as scores, dummy joints, flutes, and ribs shall be ⅙ in. (1.6 mm) from the specified standard dimensions. These requirements do not apply to split faces.

NOTE 5—Standard dimensions of units are the manufacturer's designated dimension. Nominal dimensions of units are equal to the standard dimensions plus the thickness of one mortar joint.

7. Finish and Appearance

7.1 All units shall be sound and free of cracks or other defects that would interfere with the proper placement of the unit or would significantly impair the strength or permanence of the construction. Minor cracks incidental to the usual method of manufacture or minor chipping resulting from customary methods of handling in shipment and delivery are not grounds for rejection.

7.2 Where units are to be used in exposed wall construc-

TABLE 3   Strength and Absorption Requirements

Compressive Strength,[A] min, psi (MPa)		Water Absorption, max, lb/ft³ (kg/m³) (Average of 3 Units)		
Average Net Area		Weight Classification—Oven-Dry Weight of Concrete, lb/ft³ (kg/m³)		
Average of 3 Units	Individual Unit	Lightweight, less than 105 (1680)	Medium Weight, 105 to less than 125 (1680–2000)	Normal Weight, 125 (2000) or more
1900 (13.1)	1700 (11.7)	18 (288)	15 (240)	13 (208)

[A] Higher compressive strengths may be specified where required by design. Consult with local suppliers to determine availability of units of higher compressive strength.

⟨ASTM⟩ C 90

tion, the face or faces that are to be exposed shall not show chips or cracks, not otherwise permitted, or other imperfections when viewed from a distance of not less than 20 ft (6.1 m) under diffused lighting.

7.2.1 Five percent of a shipment containing chips not larger than 1 in. (25.4 mm) in any dimension, or cracks not wider than 0.02 in. (0.5 mm) and not longer than 25 % of the nominal height of the unit is permitted.

7.3 The color and texture of units shall be specified by the purchaser. The finished surfaces that will be exposed in place shall conform to an approved sample consisting of not less than four units, representing the range of texture and color permitted.

8. Sampling and Testing

8.1 The purchaser or authorized representative shall be accorded proper facilities to inspect and sample the units at the place of manufacture from the lots ready for delivery.

8.2 Sample and test units in accordance with Test Methods C 140.

8.3 Total linear drying shrinkage shall be based on tests of concrete masonry units made with the same materials,

concrete mix design, manufacturing process, and curing method, conducted in accordance with Test Method C 426 and not more than 24 months prior to delivery.

9. Rejection

9.1 If the samples tested from a shipment fail to conform to the specified requirements, the manufacturer may sort it, and new specimens shall be selected by the purchaser from the retained lot and tested at the expense of the manufacturer. If the second set of specimens fails to conform to the specified requirements, the entire lot shall be rejected.

NOTE 6—Unless otherwise specified in the purchase order, the cost of tests is typically borne as follows: (1) if the results of the tests show that the units do not conform to the requirements of this specification, the cost is typically borne by the seller; (2) if the results of the tests show that the units conform to the specification requirements, the cost is typically borne by the purchaser.

10. Keywords

10.1 absorption; climatic map; concrete masonry units; equivalent web thickness; face shell; flange; lightweight; linear shrinkage; loadbearing; medium weight; moisture-controlled; normal weight; webs

APPENDIX

(Nonmandatory Information)

X1. CLIMATIC MAP

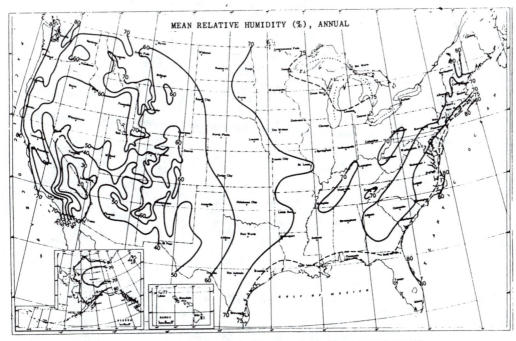

NOTE—Based on 1:30 AM and PM and 7:30 AM and PM Eastern Standard Time, observations for 20 years or more through 1964.

FIG. X1.1   Selected Climatic Maps of the United States

伽⑪ C 90

X2. WATER PENETRATION RESISTANCE

X2.1 Exterior walls are often subjected to moisture penetration from one or more sources. For example, basement walls may be exposed to water from saturated soil. Above-grade exterior walls are usually exposed to wind-driven rain. To prevent water penetration, proper detailing, construction, flashing, and drainage should be provided. Proper water penetration resistant treatments should be applied to the walls. While it is not within the scope of Specification C 90 to include information on resistance to water penetration, such information and guidelines are available from other organizations.

ASTM Designation: C 109/C 109M – 95

AMERICAN SOCIETY FOR TESTING AND MATERIALS
1916 Race St. Philadelphia, Pa 19103
Reprinted from the Annual Book of ASTM Standards. Copyright ASTM
If not listed in the current combined index, will appear in the next edition.

Standard Test Method for
Compressive Strength of Hydraulic Cement Mortars
(Using 2-in. or [50-mm] Cube Specimens)[1]

This standard is issued under the fixed designation C 109/C 109M; the number immediately following the designation indicates the year of original adoption or, in the case of revision, the year of last revision. A number in parentheses indicates the year of last reapproval. A superscript epsilon (ε) indicates an editorial change since the last revision or reapproval.

This test method has been approved for use by agencies of the Department of Defense. Consult the DoD Index of Specifications and Standards for the specific year of issue which has been adopted by the Department of Defense.

1. Scope

1.1 This test method covers determination of the compressive strength of hydraulic cement mortars, using 2-in. or [50-mm] cube specimens.

NOTE 1—Test Method C 349 provides an alternative procedure for this determination (not to be used for acceptance tests).

1.2 This test method covers the application of the test using either inch-pound or SI units. The values stated in either system shall be regarded separately as standard. Within the text, the SI units are shown in brackets. The values stated in each system are not exact equivalents; therefore, each system shall be used independently of the other. Combining values from the two systems may result in nonconformance with the specification.

1.3 *This standard does not purport to address all of the safety concerns, if any, associated with its use. It is the responsibility of the user of this standard to establish appropriate safety and health practices and determine the applicability of regulatory limitations prior to use.*

2. Referenced Documents

2.1 *ASTM Standards:*
C 230 Specification for Flow Table for Use in Tests of Hydraulic Cement[2]
C 305 Practice for Mechanical Mixing of Hydraulic Cement Pastes and Mortars of Plastic Consistency[2]
C 349 Test Method for Compressive Strength of Hydraulic Cement Mortars (Using Portions of Prisms Broken in Flexure)[2]
C 511 Specification for Moist Cabinets, Moist Rooms and Water Storage Tanks Used in the Testing of Hydraulic Cements and Concretes[2]
C 670 Practice for Preparing Precision and Bias Statements for Test Methods for Construction Materials[3]
C 778 Specification for Standard Sand[2]
C 1005 Specification for Weights and Weighing Devices for Use in Physical Testing of Hydraulic Cements[2]

3. Summary of Test Method

3.1 The mortar used consists of 1 part cement and 2.75 parts of sand proportioned by mass. Portland or air-entraining portland cements are mixed at specified water/cement ratios. Water content for other cements is that sufficient to obtain a flow of 110 ± 5 in 25 drops of the flow table. Two-inch or [50-mm] test cubes are compacted by tamping in two layers. The cubes are cured one day in the molds and stripped and immersed in lime water until tested.

4. Significance and Use

4.1 This test method provides a means of determining the compressive strength of hydraulic cement and other mortars and results may be used to determine compliance with specifications. Further, this test method is referenced by numerous other specifications and test methods. Caution must be exercised in using the results of this test method to predict the strength of concretes.

5. Apparatus

5.1 *Weights and Weighing Devices*, shall conform to the requirements of Specification C 1005. The weighing device shall be evaluated for precision and bias at a total load of 2000 g.

5.2 *Glass Graduates*, of suitable capacities (preferably large enough to measure the mixing water in a single operation) to deliver the indicated volume at 20°C. The permissible variation shall be ±2 mL. These graduates shall be subdivided to at least 5 mL, except that the graduation lines may be omitted for the lowest 10 mL for a 250-mL graduate and for the lowest 25 mL of a 500-mL graduate. The main graduation lines shall be circles and shall be numbered. The least graduations shall extend at least one seventh of the way around, and intermediate graduations shall extend at least one fifth of the way around.

5.3 *Specimen Molds*, for the 2-in. or [50-mm] cube specimens shall be tight fitting. The molds shall have not more than three cube compartments and shall be separable into not more than two parts. The parts of the molds when assembled shall be positively held together. The molds shall be made of hard metal not attacked by the cement mortar. For new molds the Rockwell hardness number of the metal shall be not less than 55 HRB. The sides of the molds shall be sufficiently rigid to prevent spreading or warping. The interior faces of the molds shall be plane surfaces and shall conform to the tolerances of Table 1.

5.4 *Mixer, Bowl and Paddle*, an electrically driven mechanical mixer of the type equipped with paddle and mixing bowl, as specified in Practice C 305.

---
[1] This test method is under the jurisdiction of ASTM Committee C-1 on Cement and is the direct responsibility of Subcommittee C01.27 on Strength.
Current edition approved March 15, 1995. Published July 1995. Originally published as C 109 – 34 T. Last previous edition C 109 – 94a.
[2] *Annual Book of ASTM Standards*, Vol 04.01.
[3] *Annual Book of ASTM Standards*, Vol 04.02.

C 109/C 109M

TABLE 1 Permissible Variations of Specimen Molds

Parameter	2-in. Cube Molds		[50-mm] Cube Molds	
	New	In Use	New	In Use
Planeness of sides	<0.001 in.	<0.002 in.	[<0.025 mm]	[<0.05 mm]
Distance between opposite sides	2 in. ± 0.005	2 in. ± 0.02	[50 mm ± 0.13 mm]	[50 mm ± 0.50 mm]
Height of each compartment	2 in. + 0.01 in. to − 0.005 in.	2 in. + 0.01 in. to − 0.015 in.	[50 mm + 0.25 mm to − 0.13 mm]	[50 mm + 0.25 mm to − 0.38 mm]
Angle between adjacent faces[A]	90 ± 0.5°	90 ± 0.5°	90 ± 0.5°	90 ± 0.5°

[A] Measured at points slightly removed from the intersection. Measured separately for each compartment between all the interior faces and the adjacent face and between interior faces and top and bottom planes of the mold.

5.5 *Flow Table and Flow Mold,* conforming to the requirements of Specification C 230.

5.6 *Tamper,* a nonabsorptive, nonabrasive, nonbrittle material such as a rubber compound having a Shore A durometer hardness of 80 ± 10 or seasoned oak wood rendered nonabsorptive by immersion for 15 min in paraffin at approximately 392°F or [200°C], shall have a cross section of about ½ by 1 in. or [13 by 25 mm] and a convenient length of about 5 to 6 in. or [120 to 150 mm]. The tamping face shall be flat and at right angles to the length of the tamper.

5.7 *Trowel,* having a steel blade 4 to 6 in. [100 to 150 mm] in length, with straight edges.

5.8 *Moist Cabinet or Room,* conforming to the requirements of Specification C 511.

5.9 *Testing Machine,* either the hydraulic or the screw type, with sufficient opening between the upper bearing surface and the lower bearing surface of the machine to permit the use of verifying apparatus. The load applied to the test specimen shall be indicated with an accuracy of ±1.0 %. If the load applied by the compression machine is registered on a dial, the dial shall be provided with a graduated scale that can be read to at least the nearest 0.1 % of the full scale load (Note 2). The dial shall be readable within 1 % of the indicated load at any given load level within the loading range. In no case shall the loading range of a dial be considered to include loads below the value that is 100 times the smallest change of load that can be read on the scale. The scale shall be provided with a graduation line equal to zero and so numbered. The dial pointer shall be of sufficient length to reach the graduation marks; the width of the end of the pointer shall not exceed the clear distance between the smallest graduations. Each dial shall be equipped with a zero adjustment that is easily accessible from the outside of the dial case, and with a suitable device that at all times until reset, will indicate to within 1 % accuracy the maximum load applied to the specimen.

5.9.1 If the testing machine load is indicated in digital form, the numerical display must be large enough to be easily read. The numerical increment must be equal to or less than 0.10 % of the full scale load of a given loading range. In no case shall the verified loading range include loads less than the minimum numerical increment multiplied by 100. The accuracy of the indicated load must be within 1.0 % for any value displayed within the verified loading range. Provision must be made for adjusting to indicate true zero at zero load. There shall be provided a maximum load indicator that at all times until reset will indicate within 1 % system accuracy the maximum load applied to the specimen.

NOTE 2—As close as can be read is considered 1/50 in. or [0.5 mm] along the arc described by the end of the pointer. Also, one half of the scale interval is about as close as can reasonably be read when the spacing on the load indicating mechanism is between 1/25 in. or [1 mm] and 1/16 in. or [1.6 mm]. When the spacing is between 1/16 in. or [1.6 mm] and ⅛ in. or [3.2 mm], one third of the scale interval can be read with reasonable certainty. When the spacing is ⅛ in. or [3.2 mm] or more, one fourth of the scale interval can be read with reasonable certainty.

5.9.2 The upper bearing shall be a spherically seated, hardened metal block firmly attached at the center of the upper head of the machine. The center of the sphere shall lie at the center of the surface of the block in contact with the specimen. The block shall be closely held in its spherical seat, but shall be free to tilt in any direction. The diagonal or diameter (Note 3) of the bearing surface shall be only slightly greater than the diagonal of the face of the 2-in. or [50-mm] cube in order to facilitate accurate centering of the specimen. A hardened metal bearing block shall be used beneath the specimen to minimize wear of the lower platen of the machine. The bearing block surfaces intended for contact with the specimen shall have a Rockwell hardness number not less than 60 HRC. These surfaces shall not depart from plane surfaces by more than 0.0005 in. or [0.013 mm] when the blocks are new and shall be maintained within a permissible variation of 0.001 in. or [0.025 mm].

NOTE 3—A diameter of 3⅛ in. or [79.4 mm], is satisfactory, provided that the lower bearing block has a diameter slightly greater than the diagonal of the face of the 2-in. or [50-mm] cube but not more than 2.9 in. or [74 mm], and is centered with respect to the upper bearing block and held in position by suitable means.

6. Materials

6.1 *Graded Standard Sand:*

6.1.1 The sand (Note 4) used for making test specimens shall be natural silica sand conforming to the requirements for graded standard sand in Specification C 778.

NOTE 4—*Segregation of Graded Sand*—The graded standard sand should be handled in such a manner as to prevent segregation, since variations in the grading of the sand cause variations in the consistency of the mortar. In emptying bins or sacks, care should be exercised to prevent the formation of mounds of sand or craters in the sand, down the slopes of which the coarser particles will roll. Bins should be of sufficient size to permit these precautions. Devices for drawing the sand from bins by gravity should not be used.

7. Temperature and Humidity

7.1 *Temperature*—The temperature of the air in the vicinity of the mixing slab, the dry materials, molds, base plates, and mixing bowl, shall be maintained between 68 and 81.5°F or [20 and 27.5°C]. The temperature of the mixing water, moist closet or moist room, and water in the storage tank shall be set at 73.4°F or [23°C] and shall not vary from

C 109/C 109M

this temperature by more than ±3°F or [±1.7°C].

7.2 *Humidity*—The relative humidity of the laboratory shall be not less than 50 %. The moist closet or moist room shall conform to the requirements of Specification C 511.

8. Test Specimens

8.1 Make two or three specimens from a batch of mortar for each period of test or test age.

9. Preparation of Specimen Molds

9.1 Apply a thin coating of release agent to the interior faces of the mold and non-absorptive base plates. Apply oils and greases using an impregnated cloth or other suitable means. Wipe the mold faces and the base plate with a cloth as necessary to remove any excess release agent and to achieve a thin, even coating on the interior surfaces. When using an aerosol lubricant, spray the release agent directly onto the mold faces and base plate from a distance of 6 to 8 in. or [150 to 200 mm] to achieve complete coverage. After spraying, wipe the surface with a cloth as necessary to remove any excess aerosol lubricant. The residue coating should be just sufficient to allow a distinct finger print to remain following light finger pressure (Note 5).

9.2 Seal the surfaces where the halves of the mold join by applying a coating of light cup grease such as petrolatum. The amount should be sufficient to extrude slightly when the two halves are tightened together. Remove any excess grease with a cloth.

9.3 After placing the mold on its base plate (and attaching, if clamp-type) carefully remove with a dry cloth any excess oil or grease from the surface of the mold and the base plate to which watertight sealant is to be applied. As a sealant, use paraffin, microcrystalline wax, or a mixture of three parts paraffin to five parts rosin by mass. Liquify the sealant by heating between 230 and 248°F or [110 and 120°C]. Effect a watertight seal by applying the liquefied sealant at the outside contact lines between the mold and its base plate.

NOTE 5—Because aerosol lubricants evaporate, molds should be checked for a sufficient coating of lubricant immediately prior to use. If an extended period of time has elapsed since treatment, retreatment may be necessary.

NOTE 6—*Watertight Molds*—The mixture of paraffin and rosin specified for sealing the joints between molds and base plates may be found difficult to remove when molds are being cleaned. Use of straight paraffin is permissible if a watertight joint is secured, but due to the low strength of paraffin it should be used only when the mold is not held to the base plate by the paraffin alone. A watertight joint may be secured with paraffin alone by slightly warming the mold and base plate before brushing the joint. Molds so treated should be allowed to return to the specified temperature before use.

10. Procedure

10.1 *Composition of Mortars:*

10.1.1 The proportions of materials for the standard mortar shall be one part of cement to 2.75 parts of graded standard sand by weight. Use a water-cement ratio of 0.485 for all portland cements and 0.460 for all air-entraining portland cements. The amount of mixing water for other than portland and air-entraining portland cements shall be such as to produce a flow of 110 ± 5 as determined in

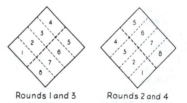

| Rounds 1 and 3 | Rounds 2 and 4 |

FIG. 1 Order of Tamping in Molding of Test Specimens

accordance with 10.3 and shall be expressed as weight percent of cement.

10.1.2 The quantities of materials to be mixed at one time in the batch of mortar for making six and nine test specimens shall be as follows:

	Number of Specimens	
	6	9
Cement, g	500	740
Sand, g	1375	2035
Water, mL		
Portland (0.485)	242	359
Air-entraining portland (0.460)	230	340
Other (to flow of 110 ± 5)	. . .	. . .

10.2 *Preparation of Mortar:*

10.2.1 Mechanically mix in accordance with the procedure given in Practice C 305.

10.3 *Determination of Flow:*

10.3.1 Carefully wipe the flow-table top clean and dry, and place the flow mold at the center. Place a layer of mortar about 1 in. or [25 mm] in thickness in the mold and tamp 20 times with the tamper. The tamping pressure shall be just sufficient to ensure uniform filling of the mold. Then fill the mold with mortar and tamp as specified for the first layer. Cut off the mortar to a plane surface, flush with the top of the mold, by drawing the straight edge of a trowel (held nearly perpendicular to the mold) with a sawing motion across the top of the mold. Wipe the table top clean and dry, being especially careful to remove any water from around the edge of the flow mold. Lift the mold away from the mortar 1 min after completing the mixing operation. Immediately, drop the table through a height of ½ in. or [13 mm] 25 times in 15 s. Using the calipers, determine the flow by measuring the diameters of the mortar along the lines scribed in the table top, adding the four readings. The total of the four readings from the calipers equals the percent increase of the original diameter of the mortar.

10.3.2 For portland and air-entraining portland cements, merely record the flow.

10.3.3 In the case of cements other than portland or air-entraining portland cements, make trial mortars with varying percentages of water until the specified flow is obtained. Make each trial with fresh mortar.

10.4 *Molding Test Specimens:*

10.4.1 Immediately following completion of the flow test, return the mortar from the flow table to the mixing bowl. Quickly scrape the bowl sides and transfer into the batch the mortar that may have collected on the side of the bowl and then remix the entire batch 15 s at medium speed. Upon completion of mixing, the mixing paddle shall be shaken to remove excess mortar into the mixing bowl.

C 109/C 109M

10.4.2 When a duplicate batch is to be made immediately for additional specimens, the flow test may be omitted and the mortar allowed to stand in the mixing bowl 90 s without covering. During the last 15 s of this interval, quickly scrape the bowl sides and transfer into the batch the mortar that may have collected on the side of the bowl. Then remix for 15 s at medium speed.

10.4.3 Start molding the specimens within a total elapsed time of not more than 2 min and 30 s after completion of the original mixing of the mortar batch. Place a layer of mortar about 1 in. or [25 mm] (approximately one half of the depth of the mold) in all of the cube compartments. Tamp the mortar in each cube compartment 32 times in about 10 s in 4 rounds, each round to be at right angles to the other and consisting of eight adjoining strokes over the surface of the specimen, as illustrated in Fig. 1. The tamping pressure shall be just sufficient to ensure uniform filling of the molds. The 4 rounds of tamping (32 strokes) of the mortar shall be completed in one cube before going to the next. When the tamping of the first layer in all of the cube compartments is completed, fill the compartments with the remaining mortar and then tamp as specified for the first layer. During tamping of the second layer bring in the mortar forced out onto the tops of the molds after each round of tamping by means of the gloved fingers and the tamper upon completion of each round and before starting the next round of tamping. On completion of the tamping, the tops of all cubes should extend slightly above the tops of the molds. Bring in the mortar that has been forced out onto the tops of the molds with a trowel and smooth off the cubes by drawing the flat side of the trowel (with the leading edge slightly raised) once across the top of each cube at right angles to the length of the mold. Then, for the purpose of leveling the mortar and making the mortar that protrudes above the top of the mold of more uniform thickness, draw the flat side of the trowel (with the leading edge slightly raised) lightly once along the length of the mold. Cut off the mortar to a plane surface flush with the top of the mold by drawing the straight edge of the trowel (held nearly perpendicular to the mold) with a sawing motion over the length of the mold.

10.5 *Storage of Test Specimens*—Immediately upon completion of molding, place the test specimens in the moist closet or moist room. Keep all test specimens, immediately after molding, in the molds on the base plates in the moist closet or moist room from 20 to 24 h with their upper surfaces exposed to the moist air but protected from dripping water. If the specimens are removed from the molds before 24 h, keep them on the shelves of the moist closet or moist room until they are 24-h old, and then immerse the specimens, except those for the 24-h test, in saturated lime water in storage tanks constructed of noncorroding materials. Keep the storage water clean by changing as required.

10.6 *Determination of Compressive Strength:*

10.6.1 Test the specimens immediately after their removal from the moist closet in the case of 24-h specimens, and from storage water in the case of all other specimens. All test specimens for a given test age shall be broken within the permissible tolerance prescribed as follows:

TABLE 2 Precision

	Test Age, Days	Coefficient of Variation 1s %[A]	Acceptable Range of Test Results d2s %[A]
Portland Cements Constant water-cement ratio:			
Single-lab	3	4.0	11.3
	7	3.6	10.2
Av		3.8	10.7
Multi-lab	3	6.8	19.2
	7	6.4	18.1
Av		6.6	18.7
Blended Cements Constant flow mortar:			
Single-lab	3	4.0	11.3
	7	3.8	10.7
	28	3.4	9.6
Av		3.8	10.7
Multi-lab	3	7.8	22.1
	7	7.6	21.5
	28	7.4	20.9
Av		7.6	21.5
Masonry Cements Constant flow mortar:			
Single-lab	7	7.9	22.3
	28	7.5	21.2
Av		7.7	21.8
Multi-lab	7	11.8	33.4
	28	12.0	33.9
Av		11.9	33.7

[A] These numbers represent, respectively, the (1s %) and (d2s %) limits as described in Practice C 670.

Test Age	Permissible Tolerance
24 h	±½ h
3 days	±1 h
7 days	±3 h
28 days	±12 h

If more than one specimen at a time is removed from the moist closet for the 24-h tests, keep these specimens covered with a damp cloth until time of testing. If more than one specimen at a time is removed from the storage water for testing, keep these specimens in water at a temperature of 73.4 ± 3°F or [23 ± 1.7°C] and of sufficient depth to completely immerse each specimen until time of testing.

10.6.2 Wipe each specimen to a surface-dry condition, and remove any loose sand grains or incrustations from the faces that will be in contact with the bearing blocks of the testing machine. Check these faces by applying a straightedge (Note 7). If there is appreciable curvature, grind the face or faces to plane surfaces or discard the specimen. A periodic check of the cross-sectional area of the specimens should be made.

NOTE 7—*Specimen Faces*—Results much lower than the true strength will be obtained by loading faces of the cube specimen that are not truly plane surfaces. Therefore, it is essential that specimen molds be kept scrupulously clean, as otherwise, large irregularities in the surfaces will occur. Instruments for cleaning molds should always be softer than the metal in the molds to prevent wear. In case grinding specimen faces is necessary, it can be accomplished best by rubbing the specimen on a sheet of fine emery paper or cloth glued to a plane surface, using only a moderate pressure. Such grinding is tedious for more than a few thousandths of an inch (hundredths of a millimetre); where more than this is found necessary, it is recommended that the specimen be discarded.

🏛 C 109/C 109M

10.6.3 Apply the load to specimen faces that were in contact with the true plane surfaces of the mold. Carefully place the specimen in the testing machine below the center of the upper bearing block. Prior to the testing of each cube, it shall be ascertained that the sperically seated block is free to tilt. Use no cushioning or bedding materials. An initial loading up to one half of the expected maximum loads for specimens having expected maximum loads of more than 3000 lbf or [15 kN] may be applied at any convenient rate. Apply no initial loading to specimens having expected maximum loads of less than 3000 lbf or [15 kN]. Adjust the rate of load application so that the remainder of the load (or the entire load in the case of expected maximum loads of less than 3000 lbf or [15 kN]) is applied, without interruption, to failure at such a rate that the maximum load will be reached in not less than 20 nor more than 80 s from start of loading. Make no adjustment in the controls of the testing machine while a specimen is yielding before failure.

NOTE 8—It is advisable to apply only a very light coating of a good quality, light mineral oil to the spherical seat of the upper platen.

11. Calculation

11.1 Record the total maximum load indicated by the testing machine, and calculate the compressive strength as follows:

$$fm = P/A$$

where:
fm = compressive strength in psi or [MPa],
P = total maximum load in lbf or [N], and
A = area of loaded surface in^2 or [mm^2].
Either 2-in. or [50-mm] cube specimens may be used for the determination of compressive strength, whether inch-pound or SI units are used. However, consistent units for load and area must be used to calculate strength in the units selected. If the cross-sectional area of a specimen varies more than 1.5 % from the nominal, use the actual area for the calculation of the compressive strength. The compressive strength of all acceptable test specimens (see Section 12) made from the same sample and tested at the same period shall be averaged and reported to the nearest 10 psi [0.1 MPa].

12. Report

12.1 Report the flow to the nearest 1 % and the water used to the nearest 0.1 %. Average compressive strength of all specimens from the same sample shall be reported to the nearest 10 psi [0.1 MPa].

13. Faulty Specimens and Retests

13.1 In determining the compressive strength, do not consider specimens that are manifestly faulty.

13.2 The maximum permissible range between specimens from the same mortar batch, at the same test age is 8.7 % of the average when three cubes represent a test age and 7.6 % when two cubes represent a test age (Note 9).

NOTE 9—The probability of exceeding these ranges is 1 in 100 when the within-batch coefficient of variation is 2.1 %. The 2.1 % is an average for laboratories participating in the portland cement and masonry cement reference sample programs of the Cement and Concrete Reference Laboratory.

13.3 If the range of three specimens exceeds the maximum in 13.2, discard the result which differs most from the average and check the range of the remaining two specimens. Make a retest of the sample if less than two specimens remain after disgarding faulty specimens or disgarding tests that fail to comply with the maximum permissible range of two specimens.

NOTE 10—Reliable strength results depend upon careful observance of all of the specified requirements and procedures. Erratic results at a given test period indicate that some of the requirements and procedures have not been carefully observed; for example, those covering the testing of the specimens as prescribed in 10.6.2 and 10.6.3. Improper centering of specimens resulting in oblique fractures or lateral movement of one of the heads of the testing machine during loading will cause lower strength results.

14. Precision and Bias

14.1 *Precision*—The precision statements for this test method are listed in Table 2 and are based on results from the Cement and Concrete Reference Laboratory Reference Sample Program. They are developed from data where a test result is the average of compressive strength tests of three cubes molded from a single batch of mortar and tested at the same age. A significant change in precision will not be noted when a test result is the average of two cubes rather than three.

14.2 These precision statements are applicable to mortars made with cements mixed, and tested at the ages as noted. The appropriate limits are likely, somewhat larger for tests at younger ages and slightly smaller for tests at older ages.

14.3 *Bias*—The procedure in this test method has no bias because the value of compressive strength is defined in terms of the test method.

15. Keywords

15.1 compressive strength; hydraulic cement mortar; hydraulic cement strength; mortar strength; strength

ASTM Designation: C 140 – 96

AMERICAN SOCIETY FOR TESTING AND MATERIALS
100 Barr Harbor Dr., West Conshohocken, PA 19428
Reprinted from the Annual Book of ASTM Standards. Copyright ASTM
If not listed in the current combined index, will appear in the next edition.

Standard Test Methods of
Sampling and Testing Concrete Masonry Units[1]

This standard is issued under the fixed designation C 140; the number immediately following the designation indicates the year of original adoption or, in the case of revision, the year of last revision. A number in parentheses indicates the year of last reapproval. A superscript epsilon (ϵ) indicates an editorial change since the last revision or reapproval.

This standard has been approved for use by agencies of the Department of Defense. Consult the DoD Index of Specifications and Standards for the specific year of issue which has been approved by the Department of Defense.

1. Scope

1.1 These test methods cover the sampling and testing of concrete masonry units for dimensions, compressive strength, absorption, unit weight (density), and moisture content. Flexural load testing and ballast weight determination of concrete roof pavers are also covered.

1.2 The values stated in inch-pound units are to be regarded as the standard. The values given in parentheses are for information only.

1.3 *This standard does not purport to address all of the safety concerns, if any, associated with its use. It is the responsibility of the user of this standard to establish appropriate safety and health practices and determine the applicability of regulatory limitations prior to use.*

2. Referenced Documents

2.1 *ASTM Standards:*
E 4 Practices for Force Verification of Testing Machines[2]
E 6 Terminology Relating to Methods of Mechanical Testing[2]

3. Terminology

3.1 *Definitions*—For definitions of terms listed in these test methods, refer to Terminology E 6.

4. Sampling

4.1 *Selection of Test Specimens:*

4.1.1 For purposes of test, full-size concrete masonry units shall be selected by the purchaser or authorized representative. The selected specimens shall be of similar configuration and dimensions. Specimens shall be representative of the whole lot of units from which they are selected. If test specimens are selected at the work site, units for moisture content tests shall be sampled upon delivery to the purchaser and placed in a sealed container until the received weight (W_r) is determined in accordance with 4.3.2.

4.1.2 The term "lot" refers to any number of concrete masonry units of any configuration or dimension manufactured by the producer using the same materials, concrete mix design, manufacturing process, and curing method.

4.2 *Number of Specimens:*

4.2.1 For the compressive strength, absorption, unit weight (density), and moisture content determinations, six units shall be selected from each lot of 10 000 units or fraction thereof and 12 units from each lot of more than 10 000 and less than 100 000 units. For lots of more than 100 000 units, six units shall be selected from each 50 000 units or fraction thereof contained in the lot. Additional specimens may be taken at the discretion of the purchaser.

4.3 *Identification:*

4.3.1 Mark each specimen so that it may be identified at any time. Markings shall cover not more than 5 % of the superficial area of the specimen.

4.3.2 Weigh units for moisture content tests immediately after sampling and marking and record as W_r (received weight).

5. Measurement of Dimensions

5.1 *Apparatus:*

5.1.1 Measure overall dimensions with a steel scale graduated in 1/32-in. (1-mm) divisions. Face shell and web thicknesses shall be measured with a caliper rule graduated in 1/64-in. (0.4-mm) divisions and having parallel jaws not less than 1/2 in. (12.7 mm) nor more than 1 in. (25.4 mm) in length.

5.2 *Specimens*—Three full-size units shall be measured for width, height, and length, and minimum thicknesses of face shells and webs.

NOTE 1—The same specimens may be used in other tests.

5.3 *Measurements:*

5.3.1 For each unit, measure and record the width (W) across the top and bottom bearing surfaces at mid-length, height (H) at mid-length of each face, and length (L) at mid-height of each face.

5.3.2 For each unit, measure face shell thicknesses (FST) and web thicknesses (WT) at the thinnest point of each such element 1/2 in. (12.7 mm) above the mortar-bed plane and record to the nearest division of the scale or caliper. Where the thinnest point of opposite face shells differ in thickness by less than 1/8 in. (3.2 mm), average their measurements to determine the minimum face shell thickness for that unit. Disregard sash grooves, dummy joints, and similar details in the measurements.

6. Compressive Strength

6.1 *Apparatus:*

6.1.1 *Testing Machine*—The testing machine shall conform to the requirements prescribed in Practices E 4. The machine shall be equipped with two steel bearing blocks (Note 2), one of which is a spherically seated block that will

[1] These test methods are under the jurisdiction of ASTM Committee C-15 on Manufactured Masonry Units and are the direct responsibility of Subcommittee C15.03 on Concrete Masonry Units and Related Units.
Current edition approved Jan. 10, 1996. Published April 1996. Originally published as C 140 – 38 T. Last previous edition C 140 – 95a.
[2] *Annual Book of ASTM Standards*, Vol 03.01.

⚡ C 140

transmit load to the upper surface of the masonry specimen, and the other a plane rigid block on which the specimen will rest. When the bearing area of the steel blocks is not sufficient to cover the bearing area of the masonry specimen, steel bearing plates meeting the requirements of 6.1.2 shall be placed between the bearing blocks and the capped specimen after the centroid of the masonry bearing surface has been aligned with the center of thrust of the bearing blocks (see 6.4.1).

6.1.2 *Steel Bearing Blocks and Plates*—The surfaces of the steel bearing blocks and plates shall not depart from a plane by more than 0.001 in. (0.025 mm) in any 6-in. (152.4-mm) dimension. The center of the sphere of the spherically seated upper bearing block shall coincide with the center of its bearing face. If a bearing plate is used, the center of the sphere of the spherically seated bearing block shall lie on a line passing vertically through the centroid of the specimen bearing face. The spherically seated block shall be held closely in its seat but shall be free to turn in any direction. The diameter of the face of the bearing blocks shall be at least 6 in. (152.4 mm). When steel plates are employed between the steel bearing blocks and the masonry specimen (see 6.4.1), the plates shall have a thickness equal to at least one half of the distance from the edge of the bearing block to the most distant corner of the specimen. In no case shall the plate thickness be less than 1 in. (25.4 mm).

NOTE 2—It is desirable that the bearing faces of blocks and plates used for compression testing of concrete masonry have a Rockwell hardness of not less than HRC 60 (BHN 620).

6.2 *Test Specimens:*

6.2.1 Three specimens shall be tested within 72 h after delivery to the laboratory, during which time they shall be stored continuously in air at a temperature of 75 ± 15°F (24 ± 8°C) and a relative humidity of less than 80 % and shall not be subjected to oven drying. Specimens shall be full-sized units except as modified in 6.2.2 through 6.2.4.

NOTE 3—In this test method, net area (other than certain solid units, see 9.4) is determined from specimens other than those subjected to compression testing. The compressive strength method is based on the assumption that units used for determining net volume (absorption specimens) have the same net volume as units used for compression testing. Sampled split face units, which have irregular surfaces, should be divided at the time they are sampled from the lot, such that the absorption test specimens have a net volume that is visually representative and a weight that is representative of the compression test specimens.

6.2.2 Unsupported projections having a length greater than the thickness of the projection shall be removed by saw-cutting. For units with recessed webs, the face shell projecting above the web shall be removed by saw-cutting to provide a full bearing surface over the net cross section of the unit. Where the resulting unit height would be reduced by more than one-third of the original unit height, the unit shall be coupon tested in accordance with 6.2.4.

6.2.3 When compression testing full-sized units that are too large for the test machine's bearing block and platens or are beyond the load capacity of the test machine, saw-cut the units to properly size them to conform to the capabilities of the testing machine. The resulting specimen shall have no face shell projections or irregular webs and shall be fully enclosed in a four-sided cell or cells. The compressive

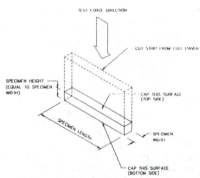

FIG. 1   Compressive Strength Test Setup

strength of the segment shall be considered to be the compressive strength of the whole unit.

6.2.4 When compression testing units of unusual size and shape (such as, but not limited to, bond beam units, open end units, and pilaster units), the specimens shall be sawed to remove any face shell projections. The resulting specimen shall be a cell or cells containing four sides that will ensure a 100 % bearing surface. Where saw-cutting will not result in an enclosed four-sided unit, the specimen shall be a coupon cut from a face shell of each unit. The coupon size shall have a height to thickness ratio of 2 to 1 before capping and a length to thickness ratio of 4 to 1. The coupon shall be cut from the unit such that the coupon height dimension is in the same direction as the unit height dimension. The compressive strength of the coupon shall be the net area compressive strength of the whole unit.

6.2.5 For concrete roof paver compressive strength tests, cut three test specimens from three whole paver units. Each specimen shall consist of a strip of paver with specimen height equal to specimen width. Where a unit contains supporting ribs, obtain specimens by cutting perpendicular to the direction of the ribs so as to avoid inclusion of bevelled or recessed surfaces at top or bottom edges (see Fig. 1).

6.2.6 Sawing shall be performed in an accurate, competent manner subjecting the specimen to as little saw vibration as possible. Use a diamond saw blade of proper hardness. If the specimen is wetted during sawing, dry the specimen for not less than 24 h in a ventilated oven at 212 to 239°F (100 to 114°C) or dry to equilibrium in normal room air before testing.

6.2.7 If compression test specimens have been saw-cut from full-size units in accordance with the provisions of 6.2.2 through 6.2.5 and the net area of the compression test specimens can not be determined by 9.4.1, saw-cut an additional three units to the dimensions and configuration of the three compression test specimens. The average net area for the saw-cut compression specimens shall be taken as the average net area of the additional three saw-cut units calculated as required in 9.4. Calculated net volumes of saw-cut specimens shall not be used in calculating equivalent thickness.

6.3 *Capping Test Specimens:*

6.3.1 Cap bearing surfaces of units by one of the methods in 6.3.2 or 6.3.3.

⚙ C 140

6.3.2 *Sulfur and Granular Materials*—Spread evenly on a nonabsorbent capping surface that has been lightly coated with oil (Note 4) or sprayed with a TFE-fluorocarbon coating. Use proprietary or laboratory prepared mixtures of 40 to 60 % sulfur by weight, the remainder being ground fire clay or other suitable inert material passing a No. 100 (150-μm) sieve with or without a plasticizer. Heat the sulfur mixture in a thermostatically controlled heating pot to a temperature sufficient to maintain fluidity after contact with the capping surface. Take care to prevent overheating, and stir the liquid in the pot just before use. The capping surface shall be plane within 0.003 in. (0.08 mm) in 16 in. (406.4 mm) and shall be sufficiently rigid and supported so as not to be measurably deflected during the capping operation. Place four 1-in. (25-mm) square steel bars on the *capping* surface plate to form a rectangular mold approximately ½ in. (12.7 mm) greater in either inside dimension than the masonry unit. Fill the mold to a depth of ¼ in. (6.4 mm) with molten sulfur material. Bring the surface of the unit to be capped quickly into contact with the liquid, and insert the specimen, holding it so that its axis is at right angles to the surface of the capping liquid. Allow the unit to remain undisturbed until solidification is complete. Allow the caps to cool for a minimum of 2 h before testing the specimens. Patching of caps shall not be permitted. Remove imperfect caps and replace with new ones.

NOTE 4—The use of oil on capping plates may be omitted if it is found that plate and unit can be separated without damaging the cap.

6.3.3 *Gypsum Cement Capping*—Spread evenly on a nonabsorbent capping surface that has been lightly coated with oil (Note 4) or sprayed with a TFE-fluorocarbon coating, a neat paste of special high-strength gypsum cement (Note 5) and water. Such gypsum cement, when gaged with water at the capping consistency, shall have a compressive strength at a 2-h age of not less than 3500 psi (24.1 MPa) when tested as 2-in. (50.8-mm) cubes. The casting surface plate shall conform to the requirements described in 6.3.2. Bring the surface of the unit to be capped into contact with the capping paste; firmly press down the specimen with a single motion, holding it so that its axis is at right angles to the capping surface. The average thickness of the cap shall not exceed ⅛ in. (3.2 mm). Patching of caps shall not be permitted. Remove imperfect caps and replace with new ones. Age the caps for at least 2 h before testing the specimens.

NOTE 5—The following two gypsum cements are considered to be in this classification: Hydrostone[3] and Hydrocal white gypsum cement.[3] Other cements should not be used unless shown by test to meet the strength requirement.

6.4 *Procedure:*

6.4.1 *Position of Specimens*—Test specimens with the centroid of their bearing surfaces aligned vertically with the center of thrust of the spherically seated steel bearing block of the testing machine (Note 6). Except for special units intended for use with their cores in a horizontal direction, test all hollow concrete masonry units with their cores in a vertical direction. Test masonry units that are 100 % solid and special hollow units intended for use with their hollow

---

[3] These gypsum cements are widely available commercially.

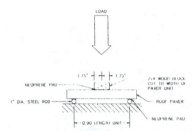

FIG. 2   Flexural Strength Test Setup

cores in a horizontal direction in the same direction as in service.

NOTE 6—For those masonry units that are symmetrical about an axis, the location of that axis can be determined geometrically by dividing the dimension perpendicular to that axis (but in the same plane) by two. For those masonry units that are nonsymmetrical about an axis, the location of that axis can be determined by balancing the masonry unit on a knife edge or a metal rod placed parallel to that axis. If a metal rod is used, the rod shall be straight, cylindrical (able to roll freely on a flat surface), have a diameter of not less than ¼ in. (6.4 mm) and not more than ¾ in. (19.1 mm), and its length shall be sufficient to extend past each end of the specimen when placed upon it. The metal rod shall be placed on a smooth, flat, level surface. One determined, the centroidal axis shall be marked on the end of the unit using a pencil or marker having a marking width of not greater than 0.05 in. (1.3 mm).

6.4.2 *Speed of Testing*—Apply the load up to one half of the expected maximum load at any convenient rate, after which adjust the controls of the machine as required to give a uniform rate of travel of the moving head such that the remaining load is applied in not less than 1 nor more than 2 min.

6.4.3 *Maximum Load*—Record the maximum compressive load in pounds (newtons) as P_{max}.

7. Flexural Load on Concrete Roof Pavers

7.1 Three full-size units shall be tested.

7.2 *Capping*—Units with wearing (top) surfaces containing recesses or other irregularities shall have such recesses capped flush with the uppermost surface by either the sulfur and granular method or the gypsum cement casting method in accordance with 6.3.

7.3 *Testing*—The testing arrangement shall be as shown in Fig. 2. The load from the upper bearing block of the testing machine shall be applied through the centroid of the concrete roof paver by the bearing assembly illustrated. The flexural length of the paver units is taken as the end to end plan dimension of the units.

8. Absorption

8.1 *Apparatus*—The balance used shall be sensitive to within 0.5 % of the weight of the smallest specimen tested.

8.2 *Test Specimens*—Three full-size units that have been marked, weighed, and recorded in accordance with 4.3.2 shall be used.

8.3 *Procedure:*

8.3.1 *Saturation*—Immerse the test specimens in water at a temperature of 60 to 80°F (15.6 to 26.7°C) for 24 h. Weigh the specimens while suspended by a metal wire and completely submerged in water and record W_i (immersed

🔷 C 140

weight). Remove from the water and allow to drain for 1 min by placing them on a ⅜-in. (9.5-mm) or coarser wire mesh, removing visible surface water with a damp cloth; weigh and record as W_s (saturated weight).

8.3.2 *Drying*—Subsequent to saturation, dry all specimens in a ventilated oven at 212 to 239°F (100 to 115°C) for not less than 24 h and until two successive weighings at intervals of 2 h show an increment of loss not greater than 0.2 % of the last previously determined weight of the specimen. Record weight of dried specimens as W_d (oven-dry weight).

9. Calculations

9.1 *Absorption*—Calculate absorption as follows:

$$\text{Absorption, lb/ft}^3 = [(W_s - W_d)/(W_s - W_i)] \times 62.4$$
$$\text{Absorption, kg/m}^3 = [(W_s - W_d)/(W_s - W_i)] \times 1000 \quad (1)$$
$$\text{Absorption, \%} = [(W_s - W_d)/W_d] \times 100$$

where:
W_s = saturated weight of unit, lb (kg) (see 8.3.1),
W_i = immersed weight of unit, lb (kg) (see 8.3.1), and
W_d = oven-dry weight of unit, lb (kg) (see 8.3.2).

9.2 *Moisture Content*—Calculate the moisture content as follows:

$$\text{Moisture Content, \% of total absorption}$$
$$= [(W_r - W_d)/(W_s - W_d)] \times 100 \quad (2)$$

where:
W_r = received weight of unit, lb (kg) (see 4.3.2),
W_d = oven-dry weight of unit, lb (kg) (see 8.3.2), and
W_s = saturated weight of unit, lb (kg) (see 8.3.1).

9.3 *Density*—Calculate oven-dry density as follows:

$$\text{Density } (D), \text{lb/ft}^3 = [W_d/(W_s - W_i)] \times 62.4$$
$$\text{Density } (D), \text{kg/m}^3 = [W_d/(W_s - W_i)] \times 1000 \quad (3)$$

where:
W_d = oven-dry weight of unit, lb (kg) (see 8.3.2),
W_s = saturated weight of unit, lb (kg) (see 8.3.1), and
W_i = immersed weight of unit, lb (kg) (see 8.3.1).

9.4 *Average Net Area*—Calculate average net area as follows:

$$\text{Net Volume } (V_n), \text{ft}^3 = W_d/D = (W_s - W_i)/62.4$$
$$\text{Net Volume } (V_n), \text{mm}^3 = W_d/D = (W_s - W_i) \times 10^4$$
$$\text{Average Net Area } (A_n), \text{in.}^2 = (V_n \times 1728)/H \quad (4)$$
$$\text{Average Net Area } (A_n), \text{mm}^2 = V_n/H$$

where:
V_n = net volume of unit, ft³ (mm³),
W_d = oven-dry weight of unit, lb (kg) (see 8.3.2),
D = oven-dry density of unit, lb/ft³ (kg/m³) (see 9.3),
W_s = saturated weight of unit, lb (kg) (see 8.3.1),
W_i = immersed weight of unit, lb (kg) (see 8.3.1),
A_n = average net area of unit, in.² (mm²), and
H = average height of unit, in. (mm) (see 5.3.2).

9.4.1 Except for irregularly shaped units, such as those with split surfaces, calculate the net area of coupons and those units whose net cross-sectional area in every plane parallel to the bearing surface is the gross cross-sectional area measured in the same plane, as follows:

$$\text{Net Area } (A_n), \text{in.}^2 (\text{mm}^2) = L \times W \quad (5)$$

where:

A_n = net area of the coupon or unit, in.² (mm²),
L = average length of the coupon or unit, in. (mm) (see 5.3.1), and
W = average width of the coupon or unit, in. (mm) (see 5.3.1)

9.5 *Gross Area*—Calculate gross area as follows:

$$\text{Gross Area } (A_g), \text{in.}^2 (\text{mm}^2) = L \times W \quad (6)$$

where:
A_g = gross area of the unit, in.² (mm²),
L = average length of the unit, in. (mm) (see 5.3.2), and
W = average width of the unit, in. (mm) (see 5.3.2).

The gross cross-sectional area of a unit is the total area of a section perpendicular to the direction of the load, including areas within cells and reentrant spaces, unless these spaces are to be occupied in the masonry by portions of adjacent masonry.

9.6 *Compressive Strength:*

9.6.1 *Net Area Compressive Strength*—Calculate the net area compressive strength of the unit as follows:

$$\text{Net Area Compressive Strength, psi (MPa)} = P_{max}/A_n \quad (7)$$

where:
P_{max} = maximum compressive load, lb (N) (see 6.4.3), and
A_n = average net area of unit, in.² (mm²) (see 9.4).

9.6.2 *Gross Area Compressive Strength*—Calculate the gross area compressive strength of the unit as follows:

$$\text{Gross Area Compressive Strength, psi (MPa)} = P_{max}/A_g \quad (8)$$

where:
P_{max} = maximum compressive load, lb (N) (see 6.4.3), and
A_g = gross area of unit, in.² (mm²) (see 9.5).

9.7 *Equivalent Web Thickness*—Equivalent web thickness of each unit (in inches per linear foot of specimen) is equal to the sum of the measured thicknesses of all webs in the unit multiplied by 12 and divided by the length of the unit.

NOTE 7—Equivalent web thickness does not apply to the portion of the unit to be filled with grout. The length of that portion should be deducted from the overall length of the unit.

9.8 *Equivalent Thickness*—Equivalent thickness for concrete masonry is defined as the average thickness of solid material in the unit and is calculated as follows:

$$T_e, \text{in.} = [V_n/(L \times H)] \times 1728$$
$$T_e, \text{mm} = [V_n/(L \times H)] \quad (9)$$

where:
T_e = equivalent thickness, in. (mm),
V_n = average net volume of full-size units, ft³ (mm³) (see 9.4),
L = average length of full-size units, in. (mm) (see 5.3.2), and
H = average height of full-size units, in. (mm) (see 5.3.2).

9.9 *Ballast Weight*—For concrete roof pavers, calculate ballast weight as follows:

$$W_b \text{ (lb/ft}^2) = \frac{W_d}{A_g} \times 144$$

$$\quad (10)$$

$$W_b \text{ (kg/m}^2) = \frac{W_d}{A_g} \times 10^6$$

where:
W_b = ballast weight, lb/ft² (kg/m²),

W_d = oven-dry weight of unit, lb (kg) (see 8.3.2), and
A_g = gross area of unit, in.² (mm²) (see 9.5).

10. Report

10.1 A complete report shall include the following:

10.1.1 The net area compressive strength to the nearest 10 psi (69 kPa) separately for each specimen and as the average for three specimens as determined by 9.6.1.

10.1.2 The absorption and density results separately for each unit and as the average for the three units as determined by 9.1 and 9.3.

10.1.3 The average width, height, and length of each specimen as determined by 5.3.2.

10.1.4 The minimum face shell thickness as an average of the minimum face shell thicknesses recorded for each of three specimens as determined by 5.3.2.

10.1.5 The minimum web thickness as an average of the minimum web thicknesses recorded for each of three specimens as determined by 5.3.2.

10.1.6 The equivalent web thickness as an average for three specimens as determined by 9.7.

10.1.7 The equivalent thickness as an average for three specimens as determined by 9.8 when required.

10.1.8 The moisture content as an average for three specimens as determined by 9.2 when required.

10.1.9 *Flexural Strength of Concrete Roof Pavers*—Report the flexural load required to fail a unit separately and as an average for three units.

11. Keywords

11.1 absorption; compressive strength; concrete masonry units; density; equivalent thickness; equivalent web thickness; face shell; moisture content; roof paver; web thickness; webs

ASTM C 140

APPENDIX

(Nonmandatory Information)

XI. WORKSHEET AND TEST REPORT

ASTM C 140 Worksheet   Lab Proj. No.: _____
                                                        Date Received: _____

Client: _____   Testing Agency: _____
Address: _____   Address: _____
           _____   _____
           _____   _____

Job No./Description: _____   Sampling Party: _____

Unit Designation/Description: Specified Overall Dimensions: Width (in.) _____
           _____   Height (in.) _____
           _____   Length (in.) _____

Compression Units
(Determine the following information for each of the three units to be tested in compression.)

	Unit #1	Unit #2	Unit #3		
Width (W) @ Top	_____	_____	_____	in.	
@ Bottom	_____	_____	_____	in.	
Height (H) @ Face 1	_____	_____	_____	in.	
@ Face 2	_____	_____	_____	in.	
Length (L) @ Face 1	_____	_____	_____	in.	
@ Face 2	_____	_____	_____	in.	
Faceshell Thickness (FST)					
@ Face 1	_____	_____	_____	in.	
@ Face 2	_____	_____	_____	in.	
Web Thickness (WT)					
@ Web 1	_____	_____	_____	in.	
@ Web 2	_____	_____	_____	in.	
@ Web 3	_____	_____	_____	in.	Measurements...
@ Web 4	_____	_____	_____	in.	Date _____ By _____
Received Weight (W_R)	_____	_____	_____	lb	Date _____ By _____
Max. Compressive Load (P_{MAX})	_____	_____	_____	lb	Date _____ By _____

Absorption Units
(Determine the following information for each of the three units to be immersed in water for absorption testing.)

	Unit #4	Unit #5	Unit #6		
Width (W) @ Top	_____	_____	_____	in.	
@ Bottom	_____	_____	_____	in.	
Height (H) @ Face 1	_____	_____	_____	in.	
@ Face 2	_____	_____	_____	in.	
Length (L) @ Face 1	_____	_____	_____	in.	Measurements...
@ Face 2	_____	_____	_____	in.	Date _____ By _____
Received Weight (W_R)	_____	_____	_____	lb	Date _____ By _____
Immersed Weight (W_I)	_____	_____	_____	lb	Date _____ By _____
Saturated Weight (W_s)	_____	_____	_____	lb	Date _____ By _____
Oven-Dry Weight (W_D)	_____	_____	_____	lb	Date _____ By _____

FIG. X1.1 Worksheet

⟨⟩ C 140

ASTM C 140 Test Report

Job No.: _____
Report Date: _____

Client: _____
Address: _____
_____
_____

Testing Agency: _____
Address: _____
_____
_____

Job No./Description: _____

Sampling Party: _____

Unit Specification: ASTM C_____

Unit Designation/Description:
_____
_____
_____

Unit Configuration:

```
┌──────────────────────────┐
│                          │
│          (sketch)        │
│                          │
└──────────────────────────┘
```

Summary of Test Results

	Required Values	Tested Values
Net Area Compressive Strength	****	----- psi
Gross Area Compressive Strength	****	----- psi
Density	****	----- pcf
Absorption	****	----- pcf
Minimum Faceshell Thickness	****	----- in.
Minimum Web Thickness	****	----- in.
Equivalent Web Thickness	****	----- in.
Equivalent Thickness	****	----- in.
Max. Variation from Specified Dimensions	****	----- in.
Net Cross-Sectional Area	****	----- in.^{2}
Gross Cross-Sectional Area	****	----- in.^{2}
Percent Solid	****	----- %
Moisture Content	****	----- %

Individual Unit Test Results

	Avg. Width in.	Avg. Height in.	Avg. Length in.	Received Weight lb	Max. Load lb	Cross-Sectional Area Gross in.^{2}	Net in.^{2}	Compressive Strength Gross psi	Net psi
Unit #1	-----	-----	-----	-----	-----	-----	-----	-----	-----
Unit #2	-----	-----	-----	-----	-----	-----	-----	-----	-----
Unit #3	-----	-----	-----	-----	-----	-----	-----	-----	-----
Average	-----	-----	-----	-----	-----	-----	-----	-----	-----

	Avg. Width in.	Avg. Height in.	Avg. Length in.	Received Weight lb	Absorp. pcf	Density pcf	Gross Volume ft^3	Net Volume ft^3	Percent Solid %
Unit #4	-----	-----	-----	-----	-----	-----	-----	-----	-----
Unit #5	-----	-----	-----	-----	-----	-----	-----	-----	-----
Unit #6	-----	-----	-----	-----	-----	-----	-----	-----	-----
Average	-----	-----	-----	-----	-----	-----	-----	-----	-----

Signature of Lab Director
Name of Lab Director
Title of Lab Director

FIG. X1.2   Test Report

C 140

ASTM **Designation: C 144 – 93**

AMERICAN SOCIETY FOR TESTING AND MATERIALS
1916 Race St. Philadelphia, Pa 19103
Reprinted from the Annual Book of ASTM Standards. Copyright ASTM
If not listed in the current combined index, will appear in the next edition.

American Association State Highway and Transportation Officials Standard
AASHTO No.: M 45-70 (1974)

Standard Specification for
Aggregate for Masonry Mortar[1]

This standard is issued under the fixed designation C 144; the number immediately following the designation indicates the year of original adoption or, in the case of revision, the year of last revision. A number in parentheses indicates the year of last reapproval. A superscript epsilon (ε) indicates an editorial change since the last revision or reapproval.

This standard has been approved for use by agencies of the Department of Defense. Consult the DoD Index of Specifications and Standards for the specific year of issue which has been adopted by the Department of Defense.

ε1 NOTE—Section 8 was added editorially in August 1992.

1. Scope

1.1 This specification covers aggregate for use in masonry mortar.

1.2 The following precautionary caveat pertains only to the methods portion, Section 7, of this standard. *This standard does not purport to address all of the safety problems, if any, associated with its use. It is the responsibility of the user of this standard to establish appropriate safety and health practices and determine the applicability of regulatory limitations prior to use.*

2. Referenced Documents

2.1 *ASTM Standards:*
C 40 Test Method for Organic Impurities in Fine Aggregates for Concrete[2]
C 87 Test Method for Effect of Organic Impurities in Fine Aggregate on Strength of Mortar[2]
C 88 Test Method for Soundness of Aggregates by Use of Sodium Sulfate or Magnesium Sulfate[3]
C 117 Test Method for Materials Finer than 75-µm (No. 200) Sieve in Mineral Aggregates by Washing[3]
C 123 Test Method for Lightweight Pieces in Aggregate[3]
C 128 Test Method for Specific Gravity and Absorption of Fine Aggregate[3]
C 136 Test Method for Sieve Analysis of Fine and Coarse Aggregates[3]
C 142 Test Method for Clay Lumps and Friable Particles in Aggregates[3]
C 270 Specification for Mortar for Unit Masonry[4]
C 404 Specification for Aggregates for Masonry Grout[2,4]
D 75 Practice for Sampling Aggregates[3]

3. Materials and Manufacture

3.1 Aggregate for use in masonry mortar shall consist of natural sand or manufactured sand. Manufactured sand is the product obtained by crushing stone, gravel, or air-cooled iron blast-furnace slag specially processed to ensure suitable particle shape as well as gradation.

4. Grading

4.1 Aggregate for use in masonry mortar shall be graded within the following limits, depending upon whether natural sand or manufactured sand is to be used:

| | Percent Passing | |
Sieve Size	Natural Sand	Manufactured Sand
No. 4 (4.75-mm)	100	100
No. 8 (2.36-mm)	95 to 100	95 to 100
No. 16 (1.18-mm)	70 to 100	70 to 100
No. 30 (600-µm)	40 to 75	40 to 75
No. 50 (300-µm)	10 to 35	20 to 40
No. 100 (150-µm)	2 to 15	10 to 25
No. 200 (75-µm)	0 to 5	0 to 10

4.2 The aggregate shall not have more than 50 % retained between any two consecutive sieves of those listed in 4.1 nor more than 25 % between No. 50 (300-µm) and the No. 100 (150-µm) sieve.

4.3 If the fineness modulus varies by more than 0.20 from the value assumed in selecting proportions for the mortar, the aggregate shall be rejected unless suitable adjustments are made in proportions to compensate for the change in grading.

NOTE 1—For heavy construction employing joints thicker than ½ in. (13 mm), a coarser aggregate may be desirable; for such work a fine aggregate conforming to Specification C 404 is satisfactory.

4.4 When an aggregate fails the gradation limits specified in 4.1 and 4.2, it may be used provided the mortar can be prepared to comply with the aggregate ratio, water retention, and compressive strength requirements of the property specifications of Specification C 270.

5. Composition

5.1 *Deleterious Substances*—The amount of deleterious substances in aggregate for masonry mortar, each determined on independent samples complying with the grading requirements of Section 4, shall not exceed the following:

Item	Maximum Permissible Weight Percent
Friable particles	1.0
Lightweight particles, floating on liquid having a specific gravity of 2.0	0.5[A]

[A] This requirement does not apply to blast-furnace slag aggregate.

5.2 *Organic Impurities:*
5.2.1 The aggregate shall be free of injurious amounts of

---

[1] This specification is under the jurisdiction of ASTM Committee C-12 on Mortars for Unit Masonry and is the direct responsibility of Subcommittee C12.04 on Specifications for Aggregates for Mortar.
Current edition approved April 15, 1993. Published June 1993. Originally published as C 144 – 39 T. Last previous edition C 144 – 91ε1.
[2] *Annual Book of ASTM Standards*, Vol 04.02.
[3] *Annual Book of ASTM Standards*, Vols 04.02 and 04.03.
[4] *Annual Book of ASTM Standards*, Vol 04.05.

C 144

organic impurities. Except as herein provided, aggregates subjected to the test for organic impurities and producing a color darker than the standard shall be rejected.

5.2.2 Aggregate failing in the test may be used, provided that the discoloration is due principally to the presence of small quantities of coal, lignite, or similar discrete particles.

5.2.3 Aggregate failing in the test may be used provided that, when tested for the effect of organic impurities on strength of mortar, the relative strength at seven days calculated in accordance with the Procedure Section of Test Method C 87, is not less than 95 %.

6. Soundness

6.1 Except as herein provided, aggregate subjected to five cycles of the soundness test shall show a loss, weighted in accordance with the grading of a sample complying with the limitations set forth in Section 4, not greater than 10 % when sodium sulfate is used or 15 % when magnesium sulfate is used.

6.2 Aggregate failing to meet the requirements of 6.1 may be accepted, provided that mortar of comparable properties made from similar aggregates from the same source has been exposed to weathering, similar to that to be encountered, for a period of more than five years without appreciable disintegration.

7. Methods of Sampling and Testing

7.1 Sample and test the aggregate in accordance with the following ASTM methods, except as otherwise provided in this specification:

7.1.1 *Sampling*—Practice D 75.

7.1.2 *Sieve Analysis and Fineness Modulus*—Method C 136.

7.1.3 *Amount of Material Finer Than No. 200 (75-μm) Sieve*—Test Method C 117.

7.1.4 *Organic Impurities*—Test Method C 40.

7.1.5 *Effect of Organic Impurities on Strength*—Test Method C 87.

7.1.6 *Friable Particles*—Test Method C 142.

7.1.7 *Lightweight Constituents*—Test Method C 123.

7.1.8 *Soundness*—Test Method C 88.

7.1.9 *Density*—Determine the density of the fine aggregate in accordance with Test Method C 128. Use the bulk specific gravity (saturated surface dry-SSD) determined in the calculation of the air content of the mortars, as required by Specification C 270.

8. Keywords

8.1 aggregate; fine aggregate; masonry; mortar; sand; soundness

Standard Specification for
Facing Brick (Solid Masonry Units Made from Clay or Shale)[1]

This standard is issued under the fixed designation C 216; the number immediately following the designation indicates the year of original adoption or, in the case of revision, the year of last revision. A number in parentheses indicates the year of last reapproval. A superscript epsilon (ε) indicates an editorial change since the last revision or reapproval.

This standard has been approved for use by agencies of the Department of Defense. Consult the DoD Index of Specifications and Standards for the specific year of issue which has been adopted by the Department of Defense.

1. Scope

1.1 This specification covers brick intended for use in masonry and supplying structural or facing components, or both, to the structure.

1.2 The property requirements of this standard apply at the time of purchase. The use of results from testing of brick extracted from masonry structures for determining conformance or nonconformance to the property requirements (Section 5) of this standard is beyond the scope of this standard.

1.3 The brick are prismatic units available in a variety of sizes, textures, colors, and shapes. This specification is not intended to provide specifications for paving brick (see Specification C 902).

1.4 Brick are manufactured from clay, shale, or similar naturally occurring earthy substances and subjected to a heat treatment at elevated temperatures (firing). The heat treatment must develop a fired bond between the particulate constituents to provide the strength and durability requirements of this specification (see firing, fired bond, and incipient fusion in Terminology C 43).

1.5 Brick may be shaped during manufacture by molding, pressing, or extrusion, and the shaping method may be used to describe the brick.

1.6 Three types of brick in each of two grades are covered.

1.7 The values stated in inch-pound units are to be regarded as the standard. The values given in parentheses are for information only.

2. Referenced Documents

2.1 *ASTM Standards:*
C 43 Terminology of Structural Clay Products[2]
C 67 Test Methods of Sampling and Testing Brick and Structural Clay Tile[2]
C 902 Specification for Pedestrian and Light Traffic Paving Brick[2]
E 835/E 835M Guide for Modular Coordination of Clay and Concrete Masonry Units[3]

3. Grades

3.1 Grades classify brick according to their resistance to

damage by freezing when wet, as defined in Note 1. Two grades of facing brick are covered and the requirements are shown in Table 1.

3.1.1 *Grade SW*—Brick intended for use where high and uniform resistance to damage caused by cyclic freezing is desired and where the brick may be frozen when saturated with water.

3.1.2 *Grade MW*—Brick which may be used where moderate resistance to cyclic freezing damage is permissible or where the brick may be damp but not saturated with water when freezing occurs.

NOTE 1—The word "saturated," with respect to this standard, refers to the condition of a brick that has absorbed water to an amount equal to that resulting from submersion in room temperature water for 24 h.

4. Types

4.1 Three types of facing brick are covered:

4.1.1 *Type FBS*—Brick for general use in masonry.

4.1.2 *Type FBX*—Brick for general use in masonry where a higher degree of precision and lower permissible variation in size than permitted for Type FBS is required.

4.1.3 *Type FBA*—Brick for general use in masonry selected to produce characteristic architectural effects resulting from nonuniformity in size and texture of the individual units.

4.2 When the type is not specified, the requirements for Type FBS shall govern.

5. Physical Properties

5.1 *Durability*—When Grade is not specified, the requirements for Grade SW shall govern. Unless otherwise specified by the purchaser, brick of Grade SW shall be accepted instead of Grade MW.

5.1.1 *Physical Property Requirements*—The brick shall conform to the physical requirements for the Grade specified as prescribed in Table 1. For the compressive strength requirements in Table 1, test the unit with the compressive force perpendicular to the bed surface of the unit, with the unit in the stretcher position.

5.1.2 *Absorption Alternate*—The saturation coefficient requirement does not apply, provided the cold water absorption of any single unit of a random sample of five brick does not exceed 8 %.

5.1.3 *Freezing and Thawing Alternative*—The requirements for 5 h boiling water absorption and saturation coefficient do not apply, provided a sample of five brick, meeting the strength requirements of Table 1, passes the freezing and thawing test as described in the Rating Section

[1] This specification is under the jurisdiction of ASTM Committee C-15 on Manufactured Masonry Units and is the direct responsibility of Subcommittee C15.02 on Clay Brick and Structural Clay Tile.
Current edition approved June 15, 1995. Published August 1995. Originally published as C 216 – 46. Last previous edition C 216 – 95.
[2] *Annual Book of ASTM Standards*, Vol 04.05.
[3] *Annual Book of ASTM Standards*, Vol 04.07.

C 216

TABLE 1 Physical Requirements

Designation	Minimum Compressive Strength psi, (MPa) gross area		Maximum Water Absorption by 5-h Boiling, %		Maximum Saturation Coefficient[A]	
	Average of 5 brick	Individual	Average of 5 brick	Individual	Average of 5 brick	Individual
Grade SW	3000 (20.7)	2500 (17.2)	17.0	20.0	0.78	0.80
Grade MW	2500 (17.2)	2200 (15.2)	22.0	25.0	0.88	0.90

[A] The saturation coefficient is the ratio of absorption by 24-h submersion in cold water to that after 5-h submersion in boiling water.

TABLE 2 Grade Recommendations for Face Exposures

Exposure	Weathering Index (Explanatory Note 2)	
	Less than 50	50 and greater
In vertical surfaces:		
In contact with earth	MW	SW
Not in contact with earth	MW	SW
In other than vertical surfaces:		
In contact with earth	SW	SW
Not in contact with earth	MW	SW

of the Freezing and Thawing test procedures of Test Methods C 67:

5.1.3.1 *Grade SW—Weight Loss Requirement*—Not greater than 0.5 % loss in dry weight of any individual unit.

NOTE 2—The 50 cycle freezing and thawing test is specified as an alternative only when brick do not conform to either Table 1 requirements for maximum water absorption and saturation coefficient, or to the requirements of the Absorption Alternate in Section 5.1.2.

5.1.4 *Waiver of Absorption and Saturation Coefficient Requirements*—If the brick are intended for use exposed to weather where the weathering index is less than 50 (see Fig. 1), and unless otherwise specified, the requirements given in Table 1 for 5-h boiling water absorption and for saturation coefficient shall not apply, but the minimum average com-

pressive strength requirement of 2500 psi (17.2 MPa) shall apply.

NOTE 3—The effect of weathering on brick is related to the weathering index, which for any locality is the product of the average annual number of *freezing cycle days* and the average annual *winter rainfall* in inches (millimetres), defined as follows.[4]

A Freezing Cycle Day is any day during which the air temperature passes either above or below 32°F (0°C). The average number of freezing cycle days in a year may be taken to equal the difference between the mean number of days during which the minimum temperature was 32°F or below, and the mean number of days during which the maximum temperature was 32°F or below.

Winter Rainfall is the sum, in inches (millimetres), of the mean monthly corrected precipitation (rainfall) occurring during the period between and including the normal date of the first killing frost in the fall and the normal date of the last killing frost in the spring. The winter rainfall for any period is equal to the total precipitation less one tenth of the total fall of snow, sleet, and hail. Rainfall for a portion of a month is prorated.

Fig. 1 indicates general areas of the United States in which brick masonry is subject to severe, moderate, and negligible weathering. The severe weathering region has a weathering index greater than 500. The moderate weathering region has a weathering index of 50 to 500. The

---

[4] Data needed to determine the weathering for any locality may be found or estimated from tables of Local Climatological Data—Annual Summary with Comparative Data available from the National Oceanic and Atmospheric Administration.

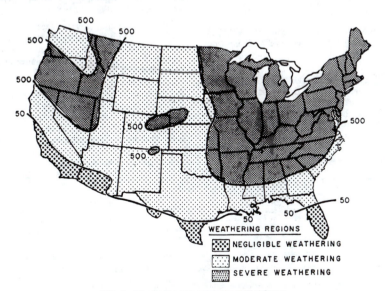

FIG. 1 Weathering Indexes in the United States

negligible weathering region has a weathering index of less than 50. The index for geographic locations near the 50 and 500-in. cycle lines should be determined by analysis of weather bureau local climatological summaries, with due regard to the effect of microclimatic conditions, especially altitude.

The recommended correlation between grade of facing brick, weathering index, and exposure is found in Table 2. The specifier may use these recommendations or use the grade descriptions and physical requirements along with use exposure and local climatological conditions to select grade.

5.2 *Strength*—When brick are required having strengths greater than prescribed by this specification, the purchaser shall specify the desired minimum compressive strength.

5.3 *Initial Rate of Absorption (IRA)*—Test results for IRA shall be determined in accordance with the IRA (Suction) (Laboratory Test) of Test Methods C 67 and shall be furnished at the request of the specifier or purchaser. IRA is not a qualifying condition or property of units in this specification. This property is measured in order to assist in mortar selection and material handling in the construction process. See Note 4.

NOTE 4—*Initial Rate of Absorption (Suction)*—Both laboratory and field investigation have shown that strong and watertight joints between mortar and masonry units are not achieved by ordinary construction methods when the units as laid have excessive initial rates of absorption. Mortar that has stiffened somewhat because of excessive loss of mixing water to a unit may not make complete and intimate contact with the second unit, resulting in poor adhesion, incomplete bond, and water-permeable joints of low strength. IRA of the units is determined by the oven-dried procedure described in the IRA (Suction) (Laboratory Test) of Test Methods C 67. IRA in the field depends on the moisture content of the masonry unit and is determined in accordance with the IRA (Suction)—Field Test of Test Methods C 67. Units having average field IRA exceeding 30 g/min · 30 in.^{2} (30 g/min · 194 cm^2) should have their IRA reduced below 30 g/min · 30 in.^{2} prior to laying. They may be wetted immediately before they are laid, but it is preferable to wet them thoroughly 3 to 24 h prior to their use so as to allow time for moisture to become distributed throughout the unit.

6. Efflorescence

6.1 When the brick are tested in accordance with Test Methods C 67, the rating for efflorescence shall be: "not effloresced."

7. Material and Finish

7.1 Colors and textures produced by application of inorganic coatings to the faces of the brick are permissible with the consent of the purchaser, provided that evidence is furnished of the durability of the coatings. Brick that are colored by flashing or textured by sanding, where the sand does not form a continuous coating, are not considered as surface-colored brick for the purpose of this specification.

NOTE 5—When surface colored brick, other than sanded or flashed, are specified for *exterior* use, the purchaser should require that data be submitted showing that after 50 cycles of freezing thawing there is no observable difference in the applied finish when viewed from a distance of 10 ft (3.0 m) under an illumination of not less than 50 ft-candles (538 lx) by an observer with normal vision.

Service records of the performance of the particular coated brick in exterior locations may be accepted in place of the freezing and thawing test, upon consent of the purchaser.

7.2 The brick shall be free of defects, deficiencies, and surface treatments, including coatings, that would interfere with the proper setting of the brick or significantly impair the strength or performance of the construction.

7.3 If any post-firing coatings or surface treatments are applied by the manufacturer, the manufacturer shall report the type and extent of these coatings or surface treatments in all certificates of compliance with this specification.

7.4 The face or faces that will be exposed in place shall be free of chips that exceed the limits given in Table 3. The aggregate length of chips shall not exceed 10 % of the perimeter of the face of the brick.

NOTE 6—Of all the units that will be exposed in place, a small percentage of the units may have chips that are larger in size than those chips allowed for the majority of the units. This special allowed percentage, listed in the second column from the left of Table 3 ranges up to 5 % for FBX, up to 10 % for FBS Smooth, and up to 15 % for FBS Rough. The remainder of the units that will be exposed in place, listed in the fifth column from the left, must conform to the chip sizes listed in the sixth and seventh columns from the left.

Example: Type FBS Smooth units will conform to the requirements of Table 3 if not more than 10 % of the units have edge chips greater than ¼ in. (6.4 mm) but less than 5/16 in. (7.9 mm) or corner chips greater than ⅜ in. (9.5 mm) but less than ½ in. (12.7 mm) and the remainder of the units, in this maximum case 90 % (100 % − 10 %) do not have edge chips greater than ¼ in. (6.4 mm) in from the edge nor corner chips greater than ⅜ in. (9.5 mm) in from the corner.

7.4.1 Other than chips, the face or faces shall be free of cracks or other imperfections detracting from the appearance of the designated sample when viewed from a distance of 15 ft (4.6 m) for Type FBX and a distance of 20 ft (6.1 m) for Types FBS and FBA.

7.5 Unless otherwise agreed upon between the purchaser and the seller, a delivery of brick may contain not more than 5 % brick, including broken brick, that do not meet the requirements for chippage and tolerances.

7.6 After brick are placed in usage the manufacturer or his agent shall not be held responsible for compliance of brick

TABLE 3 Maximum Permissible Extent of Chippage From the Edges and Corners of Finished Face or Faces onto the Surface

Type	Percentage Allowed[A]	Chippage in in. (mm) in from		Percentage Allowed[A]	Chippage in in. (mm) in from	
		Edge	Corner		Edge	Corner
FBX	5 % or less	⅛–¼ (3.2–6.4)	¼–⅜ (6.4–9.5)	95 to 100 %	0–⅛ (0–3.2)	0–¼ (0–6.4)
FBS[B] (Smooth)	10 % or less	¼–5/16 (6.4–7.9)	⅜–½ (9.5–12.7)	90 to 100 %	0–¼ (0–6.4)	0–⅜ (0–9.5)
FBS[C] (Rough)	15 % or less	5/16–7/16 (7.9–11.1)	½–¾ (12.7–19.1)	85 to 100 %	0–5/16 (0–7.9)	0–½ (0–12.7)
FBA	to meet the designated sample or as specified by the purchaser, but not more restrictive than Type FBS (rough)					

[A] Percentage of exposed brick allowed in the wall with chips measured the listed dimensions in from an edge or corner.

[B] Smooth texture is the unbroken natural die finish.

[C] Rough texture is the finish produced when the face is sanded, combed, scratched, or scarified or the die skin on the face is entirely broken by mechanical means such as wire-cutting or wire-brushing.

⬡ C 216

TABLE 4 Tolerances on Dimensions

Specified Dimension or Average Brick Size in Job Lot Sample, in. (mm)	Maximum Permissible Variation, in. (mm) plus or minus from:				
	Column A (for Specified Dimension)		Column B (for Average Brick Size in Job Lot Sample)[A]		
	Type FBX	Type FBS	Type FBX	Type FBS Smooth[B]	Type FBS Rough[C]
3 (76) and under	1/16 (1.6)	3/32 (2.4)	1/16 (1.6)	1/16 (1.6)	3/32 (2.4)
Over 3–4 (76 to 102), incl	3/32 (2.4)	1/8 (3.2)	1/16 (1.6)	3/32 (2.4)	1/8 (3.2)
Over 4–6 (102 to 152), incl	1/8 (3.2)	3/16 (4.8)	3/32 (2.4)	3/32 (2.4)	3/16 (4.8)
Over 6–8 (152 to 203), incl	5/32 (4.0)	1/4 (6.4)	3/32 (2.4)	1/8 (3.2)	1/4 (6.4)
Over 8–12 (203 to 305), incl	7/32 (5.6)	5/16 (7.9)	1/8 (3.2)	3/16 (4.8)	5/16 (7.9)
Over 12–16 (305 to 406), incl	9/32 (7.1)	3/8 (9.5)	3/16 (4.8)	1/4 (6.4)	3/8 (9.5)

[A] Lot size shall be determined by agreement between purchaser and seller. If not specified, lot size shall be understood to include all brick of one size and color in the job order.

[B] Type FBS Smooth units have relatively fine texture and smooth edges, including wire cut surfaces. These definitions relate to dimensional tolerances only.

[C] Type FBS Rough units have textured, rounded, or tumbled edges or faces. These definitions apply to dimensional tolerances only.

TABLE 5 Tolerances on Distortion

Maximum Dimension, in. (mm)	Maximum Permissible Distortion, in. (mm)	
	Type FBX	Type FBS
8 (203) and under	1/16 (1.6)	3/32 (2.4)
Over 8–12 (203 to 305), incl	3/32 (2.4)	1/8 (3.2)
Over 12–16 (305 to 406), incl	1/8 (3.2)	5/32 (4.0)

with the requirements of this specification for chippage and dimensional tolerances.

8. Texture and Color

8.1 The color, color range, and texture should be specified by the purchaser. Unless otherwise specified by the purchaser, at least one end of the majority of the individual brick shall have the same general texture and general color tone as the approved sample. The texture of the finished surfaces that will be exposed when in place shall conform to an approved sample consisting of not less than four stretcher brick, each representing the texture desired. The color range shall be indicated by the approved sample.

8.2 Where brick with other than one finished face and one finished end are required (brick with two finished faces or ends, or other types), all such special brick shall be explicitly specified by the purchaser.

NOTE 7—The manufacturer should be consulted for the availability of specialty units suitable for the intended purpose.

9. Size

9.1 Size—The size of brick shall be as specified by the purchaser (see Note 8). In a sample of ten brick selected to represent the extreme range of sizes of brick to be supplied, no brick shall depart from the specified size by more than the individual tolerance for the type specified as prescribed in Table 4, Column A. The average size of the ten brick sample shall be determined, and no brick in the job lot (delivered brick) shall vary from this average size by more than the individual tolerance for the type specified as prescribed in Table 4, Column B. No individual brick in the job lot shall fall outside of the dimensional tolerances of Table 4, Column A. Tolerances on dimensions for Type FBA shall be as specified by the purchaser, but not more restrictive than FBS.

NOTE 8—For a list of modular sizes, see Guide E 835/E 835M. Sizes listed in this standard are not produced in all parts of the United States. Brick names denoting sizes may be regional and, therefore, may not be included in all reference books. Purchasers should ascertain the sizes of brick available in their locality and should specify accordingly, stating the desired dimensions (width by height by length).

9.2 Warpage—Tolerances for distortion or warpage of surfaces or edges intended to be exposed in use of individual brick from a plane surface and from a straight line, respectively, shall not exceed the maximum for the type specified as prescribed in Table 5. Tolerances on distortion for Type FBA shall be as specified by the purchaser.

9.3 Out-of-Square—The maximum permitted dimension for out-of-square of the exposed face of the brick is 1/8 in. (3.2 mm) for Type FBS brick and 3/32 in. (2.4 mm) for Type FBX brick. Tolerances on out-of-square for Type FBA brick shall be specified by the purchaser.

NOTE 9—Linear dimensions and flat surfaces of specially shaped brick shall meet the requirements for size and warpage, respectively, of the specified type. Tolerances for size and warpage of nonlinear dimensions and surfaces, and out-of-square shall be determined by agreement with the manufacturer.

10. Coring and Frogging

10.1 Coring—Unless otherwise specified in the invitation for bids, brick may or may not be cored at the option of the seller. The net cross-sectional area of cored brick in any plane parallel to the surface containing the cores shall be at least 75 % of the gross cross-sectional area measured in the same plane. No part of any hole shall be less than 3/4 in. (19.1 mm) from any edge of the brick.

10.2 Frogging—Unless otherwise specified in the invitation for bids, one bearing face of each brick may have a recess or panel frog and deep frogs. The recess or panel frog shall not exceed 3/8 in. (9.5 mm) in depth and no part of the recess or panel frog shall be less than 3/4 in. (19.1 mm) from any edge of the brick. In brick containing deep frogs, frogs deeper than 3/8 in. (9.5 mm), any cross-section through the deep frogs parallel to the surface containing the deep frogs shall conform to the requirements of 10.1.

11. Sampling and Testing

11.1 For purposes of tests, brick that are representative of the commercial product shall be selected by a competent person appointed by the purchaser, the place or places of

C 216

selection to be designated when the purchase order is placed. The sample or samples shall include specimens representative of the complete range of colors and sizes of the brick supplied or to be supplied. The manufacturer or the seller shall furnish specimens for tests without charge.

11.2 The brick shall be sampled and tested in accordance with Test Methods C 67.

NOTE 10—Unless otherwise specified in the purchase order, the cost of tests is typically borne as follows: If the results of the tests show that the brick do not conform to the requirements of this specification, the cost is typically borne by the seller. If the results of the tests show that the brick do conform to the requirements of this specification, the cost is typically borne by the purchaser.

12. Keywords

12.1 appearance requirements; clay; facing brick; fired masonry units; masonry construction; physical properties; shale; solid brick

AMERICAN SOCIETY FOR TESTING AND MATERIALS
100 Barr Harbor Dr., West Conshohocken, PA 19428
Reprinted from the Annual Book of ASTM Standards. Copyright ASTM
If not listed in the current combined index, will appear in the next edition.

Standard Specification for Mortar for Unit Masonry[1]

This standard is issued under the fixed designation C 270; the number immediately following the designation indicates the year of original adoption or, in the case of revision, the year of last revision. A number in parentheses indicates the year of last reapproval. A superscript epsilon (ε) indicates an editorial change since the last revision or reapproval.

This specification has been approved for use by agencies of the Department of Defense. Consult the DoD Index of Specifications and Standards for the specific year of issue which has been adopted by the Department of Defense.

1. Scope

1.1 This specification covers mortars for use in the construction of non-reinforced and reinforced unit masonry structures. Four types of mortar are covered in each of two alternative specifications: (*1*) proportion specifications and (*2*) property specifications.

1.2 The proportion or property specifications shall govern as specified.

1.3 When neither proportion or property specifications are specified, the proportion specifications shall govern, unless data are presented to and accepted by the specifier to show that mortar meets the requirements of the property specifications.

2. Referenced Documents

2.1 *ASTM Standards:*

C 5 Specification for Quicklime for Structural Purposes[2]

C 91 Specification for Masonry Cement[2]

C 109 Test Method for Compressive Strength of Hydraulic Cement Mortars (Using 2-in. or 50-mm Cube Specimens)[2]

C 144 Specification for Aggregate for Masonry Mortar[3]

C 150 Specification for Portland Cement[2]

C 207 Specification for Hydrated Lime for Masonry Purposes[2]

C 305 Practice for Mechanical Mixing of Hydraulic Cement Pastes and Mortars of Plastic Consistency[2]

C 511 Specification for Moist Cabinets, Moist Rooms, and Water Storage Tanks Used in the Testing of Hydraulic Cements and Concretes[2]

C 595/C 595M Specification for Blended Hydraulic Cements[2]

C 780 Test Method for Preconstruction and Construction Evaluation of Mortars for Plain and Reinforced Unit Masonry[3]

E 514 Test Method for Water Penetration and Leakage Through Masonry[3]

E 518 Test Methods for Flexural Bond Strength of Masonry[3]

2.2 *International Masonry All Weather Council:*[4]

Recommended Practices and Guide Specifications for Cold Weather Masonry Construction; Section 04200, Article 3 of the Guide Specifications, Sixth Edition, July 1977

3. Requirements

3.1 *Proportion Specifications*—Mortar conforming to the proportion specifications shall consist of a mixture of cementitious material, aggregate, and water, all conforming to the requirements of Section 4 and the proportion specifications' requirements of Table 1. See Appendix for a guide for selecting masonry mortars.

3.1.1 Unless otherwise stated, either a cement/lime mortar or a masonry cement mortar may be used. Mortar of known higher strength shall not be indiscriminately substituted where a mortar type of anticipated lower strength is specified.

3.2 *Property Specifications*—Mortar conformance to the property specifications shall be established by tests of laboratory prepared mortar in accordance with Sections 5 and 6.2. The laboratory prepared mortar shall consist of a mixture of cementitious material, aggregate, and water, all conforming to the requirements of Section 4 and the properties of the laboratory prepared mortar shall conform to the requirements of Table 2. See Appendix X1 for a guide for selecting masonry mortars.

3.2.1 No change shall be made in the laboratory established proportions for mortar accepted under the property specifications, except for the quantity of mixing water. Materials with different physical characteristics shall not be utilized in the mortar used in the work unless compliance with the requirements of the property specifications is re-established.

NOTE 1—The required properties of the mortar in Table 2 are for laboratory prepared mortar mixed with a quantity of water to produce a flow of 110 ± 5 %. This quantity of water is not sufficient to produce a mortar with a workable consistency suitable for laying masonry units in the field. Mortar for use in the field must be mixed with the maximum amount of water, consistent with workability, in order to provide sufficient water to satisfy the initial rate of absorption (suction) of the masonry units. The properties of laboratory prepared mortar at a flow of 110 ± 5, as required by this specification, are intended to approximate the flow and properties of field prepared mortar after it has been placed in use and the suction of the masonry units has been satisfied. The properties of field prepared mortar mixed with the greater quantity of water, prior to being placed in contact with the masonry units, will differ

[1] This specification is under the jurisdiction of ASTM Committee C-12 on Mortars for Unit Masonry and is the direct responsibility of Subcommittee C12.03 on Specifications for Mortar.

Current edition approved Feb. 15, 1995. Published April 1995. Originally published as C 270 – 51 T. Last previous edition C 270 – 94.

[2] *Annual Book of ASTM Standards*, Vol 04.01.

[3] *Annual Book of ASTM Standards*, Vol 04.05.

[4] Available from the International Masonry All Weather Council, 823 Fifteenth Street, N. W., Washington, DC 20005.

C 270

TABLE 1   Proportion Specification Requirements

NOTE—Two air-entraining materials shall not be combined in mortar.

Mortar	Type	Portland Cement or Blended Cement	Masonry Cement			Hydrated Lime or Lime Putty	Aggregate Ratio (Measured in Damp, Loose Conditions)
			M	S	N		
Cement-lime	M	1	...	...	...	¼	
	S	1	...	...	...	over ¼ to ½	
	N	1	...	...	...	over ½ to 1¼	
	O	1	...	...	...	over 1¼ to 2½	
Masonry cement	M	1	...	...	1	...	Not less than 2¼ and not more than 3 times the sum of the separate volumes of cementitious materials.
	M	...	1	...	...	...	
	S	½	...	...	1	...	
	S	...	...	1	...	...	
	N	...	...	...	1	...	
	O	...	...	...	1	...	

from the property requirements in Table 2. Therefore, the property requirements in Table 2 cannot be used as requirements for quality control of field prepared mortar. Test Method C 780 may be used for this purpose.

4. Materials

4.1 Materials used as ingredients in the mortar shall conform to the requirements specified in 4.1.1 to 4.1.4.

4.1.1 *Cementitious Materials*—Cementitious materials shall conform to the following ASTM specifications:

4.1.1.1 *Portland Cement*—Types I, IA, II, IIA, III, or IIIA of Specification C 150.

4.1.1.2 *Blended Hydraulic Cements*—Types IS, IS-A, IP, IP-A, I(PM) or I(PM)-A of Specification C 595.

4.1.1.3 *Slag Cement (for Use in Property Specifications Only)*—Types S or SA of Specification C 595.

4.1.1.4 *Masonry Cement*—See Specification C 91.

4.1.1.5 *Quicklime*—See Specification C 5.

4.1.1.6 *Hydrated Lime*—Specification C 207, Types S or SA. Types N or NA limes may be permitted if shown by test or performance record to be not detrimental to the soundness of the mortar.

4.1.2 *Aggregates*—See Specification C 144.

4.1.3 *Water*—Water shall be clean and free of amounts of oils, acids, alkalies, salts, organic materials, or other substances that may be deleterious to mortar or any metal in the wall.

4.1.4 *Admixtures*—Admixtures such as coloring pigments, air-entraining agents, accelerators, retarders, water-repellent agents, antifreeze compounds, and other admixtures shall not be added to mortar unless specified. Calcium chloride, when explicitly provided for in the contract documents, may

be used as an accelerator in amounts not exceeding 2 % by weight of the portland cement content or 1 % by weight of the masonry cement content, or both, of the mortar.

NOTE 2—If calcium chloride is allowed, it should be used with caution as it may have a detrimental effect on metals and on some wall finishes.

5. Test Methods

5.1 *Proportions of Materials for Test Specimens*—Laboratory mixed mortar used for determining conformance to this property specification shall contain construction materials in proportions indicated in project specifications. Measure materials by weight for laboratory mixed batches. Convert proportions, by volume, to proportions, by weight, using a batch factor calculated as follows:

Batch factor = 1440/(80 times total sand volume proportion)

NOTE 3—See the Appendix for examples of material proportioning.

5.1.1 Oven dry and cool to room temperature all sand for laboratory mixed mortars. Sand weight shall be 1440 g for each individual batch of mortar prepared. Add water to obtain flow of 110 ± 5 %. A test batch provides sufficient mortar for completing the water retention test and fabricating three 2-in. cubes for the compressive strength test.

5.2 *Mixing of Mortars*—Mix the mortar in accordance with Practice C 305.

5.3 *Water Retention*—Determine water retention in accordance with Specification C 91, except that the laboratory-mixed mortar shall be of the materials and proportions to be used in the construction.

5.4 *Compressive Strength*—Determine compressive strength in accordance with Test Method C 109. The mortar shall be composed of materials and proportions that are to be

TABLE 2   Property Specification Requirements[A]

Mortar	Type	Average Compressive Strength at 28 Days, Min. psi (MPa)	Water Retention, min, %	Air Content, max, %	Aggregate Ratio (Measured in Damp, Loose Conditions)
Cement-lime	M	2500 (17.2)	75	12	
	S	1800 (12.4)	75	12	
	N	750 (5.2)	75	14[B]	
	O	350 (2.4)	75	14[B]	Not less than 2¼ and not more than 3½ times the sum of the separate volumes of cementitious materials.
Masonry cement	M	2500 (17.2)	75	...[C]	
	S	1800 (12.4)	75	...[C]	
	N	750 (5.2)	75	...[C]	
	O	350 (2.4)	75	...[C]	

[A] Laboratory prepared mortar only (see Note 1).
[B] When structural reinforcement is incorporated in cement-lime mortar, the maximum air content shall be 12 %.
[C] When structural reinforcement is incorporated in masonry cement mortar, the maximum air content shall be 18 %.

used in the construction with mixing water to produce a flow of 110 ± 5.

5.4.1 *Specimen Storage*—Keep mortar cubes for compressive strength tests in the molds on plane plates in a moist room or a cabinet meeting the requirements of Specification C 511, from 48 to 52 h in such a manner that the upper surfaces shall be exposed to the moist air. Remove mortar specimens from the molds and place in a moist cabinet or moist room until tested.

5.5 *Air Content*—Determine air content in accordance with Specification C 91 *except* that the laboratory mixed mortar is to be of the materials and proportions to be used in the construction. Calculate the air content to the nearest 0.1 % as follows:

$$D = \frac{(W_1 + W_2 + W_3 + W_4 + V_w)}{\dfrac{W_1}{P_1} + \dfrac{W_2}{P_2} + \dfrac{W_3}{P_3} + \dfrac{W_4}{P_4} + V_w}$$

$$A = 100 - \frac{W_m}{4D}$$

where:

D = density of air-free mortar, g/cm^3,
W_1 = weight of portland cement, g,
W_2 = weight of hydrated lime, g,
W_3 = weight of masonry cement, g,
W_4 = weight of sand, g,
V_w = millilitres of water used,
P_1 = density of portland cement, g/cm^3,
P_2 = density of hydrated lime, g/cm^3,
P_3 = density of masonry cement, g/cm^3,
P_4 = density of sand, g/cm^3,
A = volume of air, %, and
W_m = weight of 400 mL of mortar, g.

6. Construction Practices

6.1 *Storage of Materials*—Cementitious materials and aggregates shall be stored in such a manner as to prevent deterioration or intrusion of foreign material.

6.2 *Measurement of Materials*—The method of measuring materials for the mortar used in construction shall be such that the specified proportions of the mortar materials can be controlled and accurately maintained.

NOTE 4—The weights per cubic foot of the materials are considered to be as follows:

Material	Weight, lb/ft³ (kg/m³)
Portland cement	94(1505)
Blended cement	Weight printed on bag
Masonry cement	Weight printed on bag
Hydrated lime	40(640)
Lime putty[A]	80(1280)
Sand, damp and loose[B]	80 lb (1280 kg) of dry sand

[A] All quicklime should be slaked in accordance with the manufacturer's directions. All quicklime putty, except pulverized quicklime putty, should be sieved through a No. 20 (850-µm) sieve and allowed to cool until it has reached a temperature of 80°F (26.7°C). Quicklime putty should weigh at least 80 lb/ft³ (1280 kg/m³). Putty that weighs less than this may be used in the proportion

specifications, if the required quantity of extra putty is added to meet the minimum weight requirement.

[B] For the purposes of this specification, a weight of 80 lb of oven-dried sand shall be used. This is, in most cases, equivalent to one cubic foot of loose, damp sand.

6.3 *Mixing Mortars*—All cementitious materials and aggregate shall be mixed between 3 and 5 min in a mechanical batch mixer with the maximum amount of water to produce a workable consistency. Hand mixing of the mortar may be permitted with the written approval of the specifier outlining hand mixing procedures.

NOTE 5—These mixing water requirements differ from those in test methods in Section 5.

6.4 *Tempering Mortars*—Mortars that have stiffened shall be re-tempered by adding water as frequently as needed to restore the required consistency. No mortars shall be used beyond 2½ h after mixing.

6.5 *Climatic Conditions*—Unless superseded by other contractual relationships or the requirements of local building codes, cold weather masonry construction relating to mortar shall comply with the International Masonry All-Weather Council's "Guide Specification for Cold Weather Masonry Construction, Section 04200, Article 3."

NOTE 6—*Limitations*—Mortar type should be correlated with the particular masonry unit to be used because certain mortars are more compatible with certain masonry units.

The specifier should evaluate the interaction of the mortar type and masonry unit specified, that is, masonry units having a high initial rate of absorption will have greater compatibility with mortar of high-water retentivity.

7. Specification Limitations

7.1 Specification C 270 is *not* a specification to determine mortar strengths through field testing.

7.2 Test Method C 780 is acceptable for preconstruction and construction evaluation of mortars for plain and reinforced unit masonry.

7.3 *Tests of Hardened Mortars*—There is no ASTM method for determining the conformance or nonconformance of a mortar to Specification C 270 by tests on hardened mortar samples removed from a structure, but such standards are under development.

NOTE 7—Where necessary, testing of a wall or a masonry prism from the wall is generally more desirable than attempting to test individual components.

NOTE 8—The cost of tests to show initial compliance are typically borne by the seller. The party initiating a change of materials typically bear the cost for recompliance.

Unless otherwise specified, the cost of other tests are typically borne as follows:

If the results of the tests show that the mortar does not conform to the requirements of the specification, the costs are typically borne by the seller.

If the results of the tests show that the mortar does conform to the requirements of the specification, the costs are typically borne by the purchaser.

8. Keywords

8.1 air content; compressive strength; masonry; masonry cement; mortar; portland cement-lime; water retention

C 270

APPENDIXES

(Nonmandatory Information)

X1. SELECTION AND USE OF MORTAR FOR UNIT MASONRY

X1.1 *Scope*—This appendix provides information to allow a more knowledgeable decision in the selection of mortar for a specific use.

X1.2 *Significance and Use*—Masonry mortar is a versatile material capable of satisfying a variety of diverse requirements. The relatively small portion of mortar in masonry significantly influences the total performance. There is no single mortar mix that satisfies all situations. Only an understanding of mortar materials and their properties, singly and collectively, will enable selection of a mortar that will perform satisfactorily for each specific endeavor.

X1.3 *Function:*

X1.3.1 The primary purpose of mortar in masonry is to bond masonry units into an assemblage which acts as an integral element having desired functional performance characteristics. Mortar influences the structural properties of the assemblage while adding to its water resistance.

X1.3.2 Because portland cement concretes and masonry mortars contain some of the same principal ingredients, it is often erroneously assumed that good concrete practice is also good mortar practice. Realistically, mortars differ from concrete in working consistencies, in methods of placement and in the curing environment. Masonry mortar is commonly used to bind masonry units into a single structural element, while concrete is usually a structural element in itself.

X1.3.3 A major distinction between the two materials is illustrated by the manner in which they are handled during construction. Concrete is usually placed in nonabsorbent metal or wooden forms or otherwise treated so that most of the water will be retained. Mortar is usually placed between absorbent masonry units, and as soon as contact is made the mortar loses water to the units. Compressive strength is a prime consideration in concrete, but it is only one of several important factors in mortar.

X.1.4 *Properties:*

X1.4.1 Masonry mortars have two distinct, important sets of properties, those of plastic mortars and those of hardened mortars. Plastic properties determine a mortar's construction suitability, which in turn relate to the properties of the hardened mortar and, hence, of finished structural elements. Properties of plastic mortars that help determine their construction suitability include workability and water retentivity. Properties of hardened mortars that help determine the performance of the finished masonry include bond, durability, elasticity, and compressive strength.

X1.4.2 Many properties of mortar are not quantitatively definable in precise terms because of a lack of measurement standards. For this and other reasons there are no mortar standards wholly based upon performance, thus the continued use of the traditional prescription specification in most situations.

X1.4.3 It is recommended that Test Method C 780 and assemblage testing be considered with proper interpretation to aid in determining the field suitability of a given masonry mortar for an intended use.

X1.5 Plastic Mortars

X1.5.1 *Workability*—Workability is the most important property of plastic mortar. Workable mortar can be spread easily with a trowel into the separations and crevices of the masonry unit. Workable mortar also supports the weight of masonry units when placed and facilitates alignment. It adheres to vertical masonry surfaces and readily extrudes from the mortar joints when the mason applies pressure to bring the unit into alignment. Workability is a combination of several properties, including plasticity, consistency, cohesion, and adhesion, which have defied exact laboratory measurement. The mason can best assess workability by observing the response of the mortar to the trowel.

X1.5.2 Workability is the result of a ball bearing affect of aggregate particles lubricated by the cementing paste. Although largely determined by aggregate grading, material proportions and air content, the final adjustment to workability depends on water content. This can be, and usually is, regulated on the mortar board near the working face of the masonry. The capacity of a masonry mortar to retain satisfactory workability under the influence of masonry unit suction and evaporation rate depends on the water retentivity and setting characteristics of the mortar. Good workability is essential for maximum bond with masonry units.

X1.5.3 *Flow*—Initial flow is a laboratory measured property of mortar that indicates the percent increase in diameter of the base of a truncated cone of mortar when it is placed on a flow table and mechanically raised ½ in. (12.7 mm) and dropped 25 times in 15 s. Flow after suction is another laboratory property which is determined by the same test, but performed on a mortar sample which has had some water removed by a specific applied vacuum. Water retentivity is the ratio of flow after suction to initial flow, expressed in percent.

X1.5.3.1 Construction mortar normally requires a greater flow value than laboratory mortar, and consequently possesses a greater water content. Mortar standards commonly require a minimum water retention of 75 %, based on an initial flow of only 105 to 115 %. Construction mortars normally have initial flows, although infrequently measured, in the range of 130 to 150 % (50–60 mm by cone penetration, as outlined in the annex of Test Method C 780) in order to produce a workability satisfactory to the mason. The lower initial flow requirements for laboratory mortars were arbitrarily set because the low flow mortars more closely indicated the mortar compressive strength in the masonry. This is because most masonry units will remove some water from the mortar once contact is made. While there may be some discernible relationship between bond and compressive strength of mortar, the relationship between mortar flow and tensile bond strength is apparent. For most mortars, and with minor exceptions for all but very low suction masonry units, bond strength increases as flow increases to where detectable

C 270

bleeding begins. Bleeding is defined as migration of free water through the mortar to its surface.

X1.5.4 *Water Retentivity*—Water retentivity is a measure of the ability of a mortar under suction to retain its mixing water. This mortar property gives the mason time to place and adjust a masonry unit without the mortar stiffening. Water retentivity is increased through higher lime or air content, addition of sand fines within allowable gradation limits, or use of water retaining materials.

X1.5.5 *Stiffening Characteristics*—Hardening of plastic mortar relates to the setting characteristics of the mortar, as indicated by resistance to deformation. Initial set as measured in the laboratory for cementitious materials indicates extent of hydration or setting characteristics of neat cement pastes. Too rapid stiffening of the mortar before use is harmful. Mortar in masonry stiffens through loss of water and hardens through normal setting of cement. This transformation may be accelerated by heat or retarded by cold. A consistent rate of stiffening assists the mason in tooling joints.

X1.6 *Hardened Mortars:*

X1.6.1 *Bond*—Bond is probably the most important single physical property of hardened mortar. It is also the most inconstant and unpredictable. Bond actually has three facets; strength, extent and durability. Because many variables affect bond, it is difficult to devise a single laboratory test for each of these categories that will consistently yield reproducible results and which will approximate construction results. These variables include air content and cohesiveness of mortar, elapsed time between spreading mortar and laying masonry unit, suction of masonry unit, water retentivity of mortar, pressure applied to masonry joint during placement and tooling, texture of masonry unit's bedded surfaces, and curing conditions.

X1.6.1.1 The test method for flexural bond strength of masonry as prescribed in Test Method E 518 is presently the most common method for evaluating this property of mortar. Test Method E 518 consists of loading to failure a stack-bond, mortar and unit masonry prism, tested as a simple beam. Test Method E 518 replaced a crossed-brick couplet test. Research on new test methods is currently underway. Presently the bend wrench method of test is under scrutiny as an alternative to Test Method E 518.

X1.6.1.2 Extent of bond may be observed under the microscope. Lack of extent of bond, where severe, may be measured indirectly by testing for relative movement of water through the masonry at the unit-mortar interface, such as prescribed in Test Method E 514. This laboratory test method consists of subjecting a sample wall to a through-the-wall pressure differential and applying water to the high pressure side. Time, location and rate of leakage must be observed and interpreted.

X1.6.1.3 The tensile and compressive strength of mortar far exceeds the bond strength between the mortar and the masonry unit. Mortar joints, therefore, are subject to bond failures at lower tensile or shear stress levels. A lack of bond at the interface of mortar and masonry unit may lead to moisture penetration through those areas. Complete and intimate contact between mortar and masonry unit is essential for good bond. This can best be achieved through use of mortar having proper composition and good work-ability, and being properly placed.

X1.6.1.4 In general, the tensile bond strength of laboratory mortars increase with an increase in cement content. Because of mortar workability, it has been found that Type S mortar generally results with the maximum tensile bond strength that can practically be achieved in the field.

X1.6.2 *Extensibility and Plastic Flow*—Extensibility is maximum unit tensile strain at rupture. It reflects the maximum elongation possible under tensile forces. Low strength mortars, which have lower moduli of elasticity, exhibit greater plastic flow than their high moduli counterparts at equal paste to aggregate ratios. For this reason, mortars with higher strength than necessary should not be used. Plastic flow or creep will impart flexibility to the masonry, permitting slight movement without apparent joint opening.

X1.6.3 *Compressive Strength*—The compressive strength of mortar is sometimes used as a principal criterion for selecting mortar type, since compressive strength is relatively easy to measure, and it commonly relates to some other properties, such as tensile strength and absorption of the mortar.

X1.6.3.1 The compressive strength of mortar depends largely upon the cement content and the water-cement ratio. The accepted laboratory means for measuring compressive strength is to test 2 in. (50.8 mm) cubes of mortar. Because the referenced test in this specification is relatively simple, and because it gives consistent, reproducible results, compressive strength is considered a basis for assessing the compatibility of mortar ingredients. Field testing compressive strength of mortar is accomplished with Test Method C 780 using either 2 in. (50.8 mm) cubes or small cylindrical specimens of mortar.

X1.6.3.2 Perhaps because of the previously noted confusion regarding mortar and concrete, the importance of compressive strength of mortar is over-emphasized. Compressive strength should not be the sole criterion for mortar selection. Bond strength is generally more important, as is good workability and water retentivity, both of which are required for maximum bond. Flexural strength is also important because it measures the ability of a mortar to resist cracking. Often overlooked is the size/shape of mortar joints in that the ultimate compressive load carrying capacity of a typical 3/8 in. (9.5 mm) bed joint will probably be well over twice the value obtained when the mortar is tested as a 2 in. (50.8 mm) cube. Mortars should typically be weaker than the masonry units, so that any cracks will occur in the mortar joints where they can more easily be repaired.

X.1.6.3.3 Compressive strength of mortar increases with an increase in cement content and decreases with an increase in lime, sand, water or air content. Retempering is associated with a decrease in mortar compressive strength. The amount of the reduction increases with water addition and time between mixing and retempering. It is frequently desirable to sacrifice some compressive strength of the mortar in favor of improved bond, consequently retempering within reasonable time limits is recommended to improve bond.

X1.6.4 *Durability*—The durability of relatively dry masonry which resists water penetration is not a serious problem. The coupling of mortars with certain masonry units, and design without exposure considerations, can lead

C 270

to unit or mortar durability problems. It is generally conceded that masonry walls, heated on one side, will stand many years before requiring maintenance, an indication of mortar's potential longevity. Parapets or other walls exposed on both sides represent an extreme exposure, thus requiring more durable mortar.

X1.6.4.1 Mortar, when tested in the laboratory for durability, is subjected to repeated cycles of freezing and thawing. Unless a masonry assemblage is allowed to become nearly saturated, there is little danger of substantial damage due to freezing. An increase in air content will generally increase the durability of masonry mortar. Durability is adversely affected by oversanded or overtempered mortars as well as use of highly absorbent masonry units.

X1.7 *Composition and Its Effect on Properties:*

X1.7.1 Essentially, mortars contain cementitious materials, aggregate and water. Sometimes admixtures are used also.

X1.7.2 Each of the principal constituents of mortar makes a definite contribution to its performance. Portland cement contributes to strength and durability. Lime, in its hydroxide state, provides workability, water retentivity, and elasticity. Both portland cement and lime contribute to bond strength. Instead of portland cement-lime combinations, masonry cement is frequently used. Sand acts as a filler and enables the unset mortar to retain its shape and thickness under the weight of subsequent courses of masonry. Water is the mixing agent which gives fluidity and causes cement hydration to take place.

X1.7.3 Mortar should be composed of materials which will produce the best combination of mortar properties for the intended service conditions.

X1.7.4 *Cementitious Materials Based on Hydration*—Portland cement, a hydraulic cement, is the principal cementitious ingredient in most masonry mortars. Portland cement contributes strength to masonry mortar, particularly early strength, which is essential for speed of construction. Straight portland cement mortars are not used because they lack plasticity, have low water retentivity, and are harsh and less workable than portland cement-lime or masonry cement mortars.

X1.7.4.1 Masonry cement is a proprietary product usually containing portland cement and fines, such as ground limestone or other materials in various proportions, plus additives such as air entraining and water repellency agents.

X1.7.5 *Cementitious Materials Based on Carbonation*—Hydrated lime contributes to workability, water retentivity, and elasticity. Lime mortars carbonate gradually under the influence of carbon dioxide in the air, a process slowed by cold, wet weather. Because of this, complete hardening occurs very slowly over a long period of time. This allows healing, the recementing of small hairline cracks.

X1.7.5.1 Lime goes into solution when water is present and migrates through the masonry where it can be deposited in cracks and crevices as water evaporates. This could also cause some leaching, especially at early ages. Successive deposits may eventually fill the cracks. Such autogenous healing will tend to reduce water permeance.

X1.7.5.2 Portland cement will produce approximately 25 percent of its weight in calcium hydroxide at complete hydration. This calcium hydroxide performs the same as

lime during carbonation, solubilizing, and redepositing.

X1.7.6 *Aggregates*—Aggregates for mortar consist of natural or manufactured sand and are the largest volume and weight constituent of the mortar. Sand acts as an inert filler, providing economy, workability and reduced shrinkage, while influencing compressive strength. An increase in sand content increases the setting time of a masonry mortar, but reduces potential cracking due to shrinkage of the mortar joint. The special or standard sand required for certain laboratory mortar tests may produce quite different test results from sand that is used in the construction mortar.

X1.7.6.1 Well graded aggregate reduces separation of materials in plastic mortar, which reduces bleeding and improves workability. Sands deficient in fines produce harsh mortars, while sands with excessive fines produce weak mortars and increase shrinkage. High lime or high air content mortars can carry more sand, even with poorly graded aggregates, and still provide adequate workability.

X1.7.6.2 Field sands deficient in fines can result in the cementitious material acting as fines. Excess fines in the sand, however, is more common and can result in oversanding, since workability is not substantially affected by such excess.

X1.7.6.3 Unfortunately, aggregates are frequently selected on the basis of availability and cost rather than grading. Mortar properties are not seriously affected by some variation in grading, but quality is improved by more attention to aggregate selection. Often gradation can be easily and sometimes inexpensively altered by adding fine or coarse sands. Frequently the most feasible method requires proportioning the mortar mix to suit the available sand within permissible aggregate ratio tolerances, rather than requiring sand to meet a particular gradation.

X.1.7.7 *Water*—Water performs three functions. It contributes to workability, hydrates cement, and facilitates carbonation of lime. The amount of water needed depends primarily on the ingredients of the mortar. Water should be clean and free from injurious amounts of any substances that may be deleterious to mortar or metal in the masonry. Usually, potable water is acceptable.

X1.7.7.1 Water content is possibly the most misunderstood aspect of masonry mortar, probably due to the confusion between mortar and concrete requirements. Water requirement for mortar is quite different from that for concrete where a low water/cement ratio is desirable. Mortars should contain the maximum amount of water consistent with optimum workability. Mortar should also be retempered to replace water lost by evaporation.

X1.7.8 *Admixtures*—Admixtures for masonry mortars are available in a wide variety and affect the properties of fresh or hardened mortar physically or chemically. Some chemical additions are essential in the manufacture of basic mortar materials. The inclusion of an additive is also necessary for the production of ready mixed mortars. Undoubtedly there are also some special situations where the use of admixtures may be advantageous when added at the job site mixer. In general, however, such use of admixtures is not recommended. Careful selection of the mortar mix, use of quality materials, and good practice will usually result in sound masonry. Improprieties cannot be corrected by admixtures, some of which are definitely harmful.

C 270

X1.7.8.1 Admixtures are usually commercially prepared products and their compositions are not generally disclosed. Admixtures are functionally classified as agents promoting air entrainment, water retentivity, workability, accelerated set, and so on. Limited data are available regarding the effect of proprietary admixtures on mortar bond, compressive strength, or water permeance of masonry. Field experience indicates that detrimental results have frequently occurred. For these reasons, admixtures should be used in the field only after it has been established by laboratory test under conditions duplicating their intended use, and experience, that they improve the masonry.

X1.7.8.2 Use of an air entraining admixture, along with the limits on air content in a field mortar, still continues to create controversy. Most masonry cements, all Type "A" portland cements and all Type "A" limes incorporate air entraining additions during their manufacture to provide required minimum as well as maximum levels of air in a laboratory mortar. Such materials should never be combined, nor should admixtures which increase the entrained air content of the mortar be added in the field, except under the most special of circumstances.

X1.7.8.3 The uncontrolled use of air entraining agents should be prohibited. At high air levels, a definite inverse relationship exists between air content and tensile bond strength of mortar as measured in the laboratory. In general, any increase in air content is accompanied by a decrease in bond as well as compressive strength. Data on masonry grouts indicate that lower bond strength between grout and reinforcing steel is associated with high air content. Most highly air entrained mortar systems can utilize higher sand contents without losing workability, which could be detrimental to the masonry if excessive sand were used. The use of any mortar containing air entraining materials, where resulting levels of air are high or unknown, should be based on a knowledge of local performance or on laboratory tests of mortar and masonry assemblages.

X1.7.8.4 Air can be removed from plastic mortar containing air entraining material by use of a defoamer, although its use in the field is strongly discouraged.

X1.7.8.5 Color can be added to mortar using selected aggregates or inorganic pigments. Inorganic pigments should be of mineral oxide composition and should not exceed 10 % of the weight of portland cement, with carbon black limited to 2 %, to avoid excessive strength reduction of the mortar. Pigments should be carefully chosen and used in the smallest amount that will produce the desired color. To minimize variations from batch to batch it is advisable to purchase cementitious materials to which coloring has been added at the plant or to use preweighed individual packets of coloring compounds for each batch of mortar, and to mix the mortar in batches large enough to permit accurate batching. Mortar mixing procedures should remain constant for color consistency.

X1.8 *Kinds of Mortars:*

X1.8.1 *History*—History records that burned gypsum and sand mortars were used in Egypt at least as early as 2690 B.C. Later in ancient Greece and Rome, mortars were produced from various materials such as burned lime, volcanic tuff, and sand. When the first settlements appeared in North America, a relatively weak product was still being made from lime and sand. The common use of portland cement in mortar began in the early part of the twentieth century and led to greatly strengthened mortar, either when portland cement was used alone or in combination with lime. Modern mortar is still made from portland cement and hydrated lime, in addition to mortars made from masonry cement.

X1.8.2 *Portland Cement-Hydrated Lime*—Cement-lime mortars have a wide range of properties. At one extreme, a straight portland cement and sand mortar would have high compressive strength and low water retentivity. A wall containing such a mortar would be strong but vulnerable to cracking and rain penetration. At the other extreme, a straight lime and sand mortar would have low compressive strength and high water retentivity. A wall containing such a mortar would have lower strength, particularly early strength, but greater resistance to cracking and rain penetration. Between the two extremes, various combinations of cement and lime provide a balance with a wide variety of properties, the high strength and early setting characteristics of cement modified by the excellent workability and water retentivity of lime. Selective proportions are found in this specification.

X1.8.3 *Masonry Cement*—Masonry cement mortars generally have excellent workability. Microscopic bubbles of entrained air contribute to the ball bearing action and provide a part of this workability. Freeze-thaw durability of masonry cement mortars in the laboratory is outstanding. Three types of masonry cement are recognized by Specification C 91. These masonry cements are formulated to produce mortars conforming to either the proportion or the property specifications of this specification. Such masonry cements provide the total cementitious material in a single bag to which sand and water are added at the mixer. A consistent appearance of mortar made from masonry cements should be easier to obtain because all the cementitious ingredients are proportioned, and ground or blended together before being packaged.

X1.8.4 *Portland Cement-Masonry Cement*—The addition of portland cement to Type N masonry cement mortars also allow qualification as Types M and S Mortars in this specification.

X1.8.5 *Prebatched or Premixed*—Recently, prebatched or premixed mortars have been made readily available in two options. One is a wet, ready mixed combination of hydrated lime or lime putty, sand, and water delivered to the construction project, and when mixed with cement and additional water is ready for use. The other is dry, packaged mortar mixtures requiring only the addition of water and mixing. Special attention should be given to the dry system, in that resulting mortars may have to be mixed for a longer period of time to overcome the water affinity of oven dry sand and subsequent workability loss in the mortar. The use of ready mixed mortar is also on the increase. These are mixtures consisting of cementitious materials, aggregates, and admixtures, batched and mixed at a central location, and delivered to the construction project with suitable workability characteristics for a period in excess of 2½ h after mixing. Systems utilizing continuous batching of mortar are also available.

X1.9 *Related Items That Have an Effect on Properties:*

X1.9.1 The factors influencing the successful conclusion of any project with the desired performance characteristics are the design, material, procedure and craftsmanship selected and used.

X1.9.2 The supervision, inspecting and testing necessary for compliance with requirements should be appropriate and predetermined.

X1.9.3 *Masonry Units*—Masonry units are absorptive by nature, with the result that water is extracted from the mortar as soon as the masonry unit and the mortar come into contact. The amount of water removal and its consequences effect the strength of the mortar, the properties of the boundary between the mortar and the masonry units, and thus the strength, as well as other properties, of the masonry assemblage.

X1.9.3.1 The suction exerted by the masonry unit is a very important external factor which affects the fresh mortar and initiates the development of bond. Masonry units vary widely in initial rate of absorption (suction). It is therefore necessary that the mortar chosen have properties that will provide compatibility with the properties of the masonry unit being used, as well as environmental conditions that exist during construction and the construction practices peculiar to the job.

X1.9.3.2 Mortar generally bonds best to masonry units having moderate initial rates of absorption (IRA), from 5 to 25 g/min · 30 in.^{2} (194 cm^2), at the time of laying. More than adequate bond can be obtained, however, with many units having IRA's less than or greater than these values.

X1.9.3.3 The extraction of too much or too little of the available water in the mortar tends to reduce the bond between the masonry unit and the mortar. A loss of too much water from the mortar can be caused by low water retentivity mortar, high suction masonry units, or dry, windy conditions. When this occurs, the mortar is incapable of forming a complete bond when the next unit is placed. Where lowering the suction by prewetting the units is not proper or possible, the time lapse between spreading the mortar and laying of a masonry unit should be kept to a minimum. When a very low suction masonry unit is used, the unit tends to float and bond is difficult to accomplish. There is no available means of increasing the suction of a low suction masonry unit, and thus the time lapse between spreading the mortar and placing the unit may have to be increased.

X1.9.3.4 Mortars having higher water retentivity are desirable for use in summer or with masonry units having high suction. Mortars having lower water retentivity are desirable for use in winter or with masonry units having low suction.

X1.9.3.5 Shrinkage or swelling of the masonry unit or mortar once contact has been achieved affects the quality of the mortar joint. Protection should be provided to prevent excessive wetting, drying, heating or cooling, until the mortar has at least achieved final set.

X1.9.3.6 Mortar bond is less to surfaces having an unbroken die skin or sanded finish than it is to roughened surfaces such as a wire cut or textured finish.

X1.9.4 *Construction Practice*—Careful attention to good practice on the construction site is essential to achieve quality. Cementitious materials and aggregate should be protected from rain and ground moisture and air borne contaminants.

X1.9.4.1 Proper batching procedures include use of a

known volume container (such as a one cubic foot batching box) for measuring sand. When necessary, sand quantities should be adjusted to provide for bulking of the sand. Shovel measuring cannot be expected to produce mortar of consistent quality. Alternatively, a combination volumetric measure calibration of a mixer followed by full bag cementitious additions and shovel additions of sand to achieve the same volume of mortar in the mixer with subsequent batches, should prove adequate.

X1.9.4.2 Good mixing results can be obtained where about three-fourths of the required water, one-half of the sand, and all of the cementitious materials are briefly mixed together. The balance of the sand is then charged and the remaining water added. The mixer should be charged to its full design capacity for each batch and completely emptied before charging the next batch.

X1.9.4.3 Mixing time in a paddle mixer should usually be a minimum of 3 and a maximum of 5 min. after the last mixing water has been added, to insure homogeneity and workability of the mortar. Overmixing results in changing the air content of the mortar. Worn paddles and rubber scrapers will greatly influence the mixing efficiency. Concern for quality suggests use of an automatic timer on the mixing machine. Mixing time should not be determined by the demand of the working force.

X1.9.4.4 Since all mortar is not used immediately after mixing, evaporation may require the addition of water, retempering the mortar, to restore its original consistency. The addition of water to mortar within specified time limits should not be prohibited. Although compressive strength of the mortar is reduced slightly by retempering, bond strength is usually increased. For this reason, retempering should be required to replace water lost by evaporation. Because retempering is harmful only after mortar has begun to set, all site prepared mortar should be placed in final position as soon as possible, but always within 2½ h after the original mixing, or the mortar discarded.

X1.9.4.5 Weather conditions also should be considered when selecting mortar. During warm, dry, windy, summer weather, mortar must have a high water retentivity to minimize the effect of water lost by evaporation. In winter, a lower water retentivity has merit because it facilitates water loss from the mortar to the units prior to a freeze. To minimize the risk of reduced bond in cold weather, the masonry units being used as well as the surface on which the mortar is placed should both be brought to a temperature at least above 32°F (0°C) before any work commences.[5]

X1.9.5 *Workmanship*—Workmanship has a substantial effect on strength and extent of bond. The time lapse between spreading mortar and placing masonry units should be kept to a minimum because the flow will be reduced through suction of the unit on which it is first placed. This time lapse should normally not exceed one minute. Reduce this time lapse for hot, dry and windy conditions, or with use of highly absorptive masonry units. If excessive time elapses before a unit is placed on the mortar, bond will be reduced. Elimination of deep furrows in horizontal bed joints and

---

[5] For more inclusive suggestions, see "Recommended Practices for Cold Weather Masonry Construction" available from the International Masonry Industry All-Weather Council.

⏥ C 270

TABLE X1.1 Guide for the Selection of Masonry Mortars[A]

Location	Building Segment	Mortar Type	
		Recommended	Alternative
Exterior, above grade	load-bearing wall	N	S or M
	non-load bearing wall	O[B]	N or S
	parapet wall	N	S
Exterior, at or below grade	foundation wall, retaining wall, manholes, sewers, pavements, walks, and patios	S[C]	M or N[C]
Interior	load-bearing wall	N	S or M
	non-bearing partitions	O	N
Interior or Exterior	tuck pointing	see X3	see X3

[A] This table does not provide for many specialized mortar uses, such as chimney, reinforced masonry, and acid-resistant mortars.

[B] Type O mortar is recommended for use where the masonry is unlikely to be frozen when saturated, or unlikely to be subjected to high winds or other significant lateral loads. Type N or S mortar should be used in other cases.

[C] Masonry exposed to weather in a nominally horizontal surface is extremely vulnerable to weathering. Mortar for such masonry should be selected with due caution.

providing full head joints are essential. Any metal embedded in mortar should be completely surrounded by mortar.

X1.9.5.1 Once the mortar between adjacent units has begun to stiffen, tapping or otherwise attempting to move masonry units is highly detrimental to bond and should be prohibited. The movement breaks the bond between the mortar and the masonry unit, and the mortar will not be sufficiently plastic to re-establish adherence to the masonry unit.

X1.9.5.2 Tooling of the mortar joint should be done when its surface is thumb-print hard utilizing a jointer having a diameter slightly larger than the mortar joint width. Joint configurations other than concave can result in increased water permeance of the masonry assemblage. Striking joints with the same degree of hardness produces uniform joint appearance. Finishing is not only for appearance, but to seal the interface between mortar and masonry unit, while densifying the surface of the mortar joint.

X1.9.5.3 The benefits of the finishing operation should be protected from improper cleaning of the masonry. Use of strong chemical or harsh physical methods of cleaning may be detrimental to the mortar. Colored mortars are especially susceptible to damage from such cleaning. Most chemicals used in cleaning attack the cementitious materials within the mortar system, as well as enlarge cracks between mortar and masonry unit.

X1.9.5.4 With very rapid drying under hot, dry and windy conditions, very light wetting of the in-place masonry, such as fog spray, can improve its quality. Curing of mortar by the addition of considerable water to the masonry assemblage, however, could prove to be more detrimental than curing of mortar by retention of water in the system from its construction. The addition of excess moisture might saturate the masonry, creating movements which decrease the adhesion between mortar and masonry unit.

X1.10 *Summary:*

X1.10.1 No one combination of ingredients provides a mortar possessing an optimum in all desirable properties. Factors that improve one property generally do so at the expense of others. Testing of mortars in the laboratory by this specification's referenced methods, and in the field by Test Method C 780 is beneficial. Some physical properties of mortar, however, are of equal or greater significance to masonry performance than those properties commonly specified. When selecting a mortar, evaluate all properties, and then select the mortar providing the best compromise for the particular requirements.

X1.10.2 Bond is probably the most important single property of a conventional mortar. Many variables affect bond. To obtain optimum bond, use a mortar with properties that are compatible with the masonry units to be used. To increase tensile bond strength in general, increase the cement content of the mortar (see X1.6.1.4); keep air content of the mortar to a minimum; use mortars having high water retentivity; mix mortar to the water content compatible with workability; allow retempering of the mortar; use masonry units having moderate initial rates of absorption when laid (see X1.9.3.2); bond mortar to a rough surface rather than to a die skin surface; minimize time between spreading mortar and placing masonry units; apply pressure in forming the mortar joint; and do not subsequently disturb laid units.

X1.10.3 Table X1.1 is a general guide for the selection of mortar type for various masonry wall construction. Selection of mortar type should also be based on the type of masonry units to be used as well as the applicable building code and engineering practice standard requirements, such as allowable design stresses, and lateral support.

X2. EFFLORESCENCE

X2.1 Efflorescence is a crystalline deposit, usually white, of water soluble salts on the surface of masonry. The principal objection to efflorescence is the appearance of the salts and the nuisance of their removal. Under certain circumstances, particularly when exterior coatings are present, salts can be deposited below the surface of the masonry units. When this cryptoflorescence occurs, the force of crystallization can cause disintegration of the masonry.

X2.2 A combination of circumstances is necessary for the formation of efflorescence. First, there must be a source of soluble salts. Second, there must be moisture present to pick up the soluble salts and carry them to the surface. Third, evaporation or hydrostatic pressure must cause the solution to migrate. If any one of these conditions is eliminated,

⚔️ C 270

efflorescence will not occur.

X2.3 Salts may be found in the masonry units, mortar components, admixtures or other secondary sources. Water-soluble salts that appear in chemical analyses as only a few tenths of one percent are sufficient to cause efflorescence when leached out and concentrated on the surface. The amount and character of the deposits vary according to the nature of the soluble materials and the atmospheric conditions. A test for the efflorescence of individual masonry units is contained within ASTM Standards. Preferable testing of a masonry assemblage or combined components is currently under research.

X2.4 The probability of efflorescence in masonry as related directly to materials may be reduced by the restrictive selection of materials. Masonry units with a rating of "not effloresced" are the least likely to contribute towards efflorescence. The potential for efflorescence decreases as the alkali content of cement decreases. Admixtures should not be used in the field. Washed sand and clean, potable water should be used.

X2.5 Moisture can enter masonry in a number of ways.

Attention must be paid to the design and installation of flashing, vapor barriers, coping and caulking to minimize penetration of rainwater into the masonry. During construction, masonry materials and unfinished walls should be protected from rain and construction applied water. Full bed and head joints, along with a compacting finish on a concave mortar joint, will reduce water penetration. Condensation occurring within the masonry is a further source of water.

X2.6 Although selection of masonry construction materials having a minimum of soluble salts is desirable, the prevention of moisture migration through the wall holds the greatest potential in minimizing efflorescence. Design of masonry using the principle of pressure equalization between the outside and a void space within the wall will greatly reduce the chances of water penetration and subsequently efflorescence.

X2.7 Removal of efflorescence from the face of the masonry can frequently be achieved by dry brushing. Since many salts are highly soluble in water, they will disappear of their own accord under normal weathering processes. Some salts, however, may require harsh physical or even chemical treatment, if they are to be removed.

X3. TUCK POINTING MORTAR

X3.1 *General:*

X3.1.1 Tuck pointing mortars are replacement mortars used at or near the surface of the masonry wall to restore integrity or improve appearance. Mortars made without portland cement may require special considerations in selecting tuck pointing mortars.

X3.1.2 If the entire wall is not to be tuck pointed, the color and texture should closely match those of the original mortar. An exact match is virtually impossible to achieve.

X3.2 *Materials:*

X3.2.1 Use cementitious materials that conform to the requirements of this specification (C 270).

X3.2.2 Use sand that conforms to the requirements of this specification (C 270). Sand may be selected to have color,

size, and gradation similar to that of the original mortar, if color and texture are important.

X3.3 *Selection Guide*—Use tuck pointing mortar of the same or weaker composition as the original mortar.

X3.4 *Materials*—Mortar shall be specified as one of the following:

X3.4.1 The proportion specification of C 270, Type _____.

X3.4.2 *Type K*—One part portland cement and 2½ to 4 parts hydrated lime. Aggregate Ratio of 2¼ to 3 times sum of volume of cement and lime.

NOTE—Type K mortar proportions were referenced in this specification (C 270) prior to 1982.

X3.5 *Mixing:*

X3.5.1 Dry mix all solid materials.

X3.5.2 Add sufficient water to produce a damp mix that will retain its shape when pressed into a ball by hand. Mix from 3 to 7 min., preferably with a mechanical mixer.

X3.5.3 Let mortar stand for not less than 1 h nor more than 1½ h for prehydration.

X3.5.4 Add sufficient water to bring the mortar to the proper consistency for tuck pointing, somewhat drier than mortar used for laying the units.

X3.5.5 Use the mortar within 2½ h of its initial mixing. Permit tempering of the mortar within this time interval.

TABLE X3.1   Guide for Selection of Tuck Pointing Mortar[A]

Location or Service	Mortar Type	
	Recommended	Alternate
interior	O	K,N
exterior, above grade exposed on one side, unlikely to be frozen when saturated, not subject to high wind or other significant lateral load	O	N,K
exterior, other than above	N	O

[A] In some applications structural concerns may dictate the use of mortars other than those recommended. This table is not applicable to pavement applications.

C 270

X4. EXAMPLES OF MATERIAL PROPORTIONING FOR TEST BATCHES OF MORTAR

X4.1 *Example A*—A mortar consisting of one part portland cement, 1¼ parts lime, and 6¾ parts of sand[A] is to be tested. The weights of the materials used in the mortar are calculated as follows:

Batch factor = 1440/(80 × 6.75) = 2.67

Weight of portland cement = 1 × 94 × 2.67 = 251
Weight of lime = 1¼ × 40 × 2.67 = 133
Weight of sand = 6¾ × 80 × 2.67 = 1440

	Portland Cement	Lime	Sand
Proportions by volume	1	1¼	6¾
Unit weight (lb/ft³)	94	40	80
Batch factor	2.67	2.67	2.67
Weight of material[B] (in g)	251	133	1440

[A] Total sand content is calculated as: (1 volume part of portland cement plus 1¼ volume parts of hydrated lime) times three = 6¾ parts of sand.
[B] Weight of material = volume proportion times unit weight times batch factor.

X4.2 *Example B*—A mortar consisting of one part masonry cement, three parts sand[C] is to be tested. The weights of the materials used in the mortar are calculated as follows:

Batch factor = 1440/(80 × 3) = 6.00

Weight of masonry cement = 1 × 70 × 6.00 = 420
Weight of sand = 3 × 80 × 6.00 = 1440

	Masonry Cement	Sand
Proportions by volume	1	3
Unit weight (lb/ft³) (Weight printed on bag for masonry cement)	70	80
Batch factor	6.00	6.00
Weight of material[B] (in g)	420	1440

[C] Total sand content is calculated as: (1 volume part of masonry cement) times three = 3 parts of sand.

Standard Specification for
Grout for Masonry[1]

This standard is issued under the fixed designation C 476; the number immediately following the designation indicates the year of original adoption or, in the case of revision, the year of last revision. A number in parentheses indicates the year of last reapproval. A superscript epsilon (ε) indicates an editorial change since the last revision or reapproval.

This specification has been approved for use by agencies of the Department of Defense. Consult the DoD Index of Specifications and Standards for the specific year of issue which has been adopted by the Department of Defense.

1. Scope

1.1 This specification covers two types of grout, fine and coarse grout, for use in the construction of masonry structures Grout is specified by: (1) proportions or (2) strength requirements.

1.2 The text of this specification references notes and footnotes that provide explanatory material. These notes and footnotes (excluding those in tables and figures) shall not be considered as requirements of this specification.

2. Referenced Documents

2.1 *ASTM Standards:*
C 5 Specification for Quicklime for Structural Purposes[2]
C 150 Specification for Portland Cement[2]
C 207 Specification for Hydrated Lime for Masonry Purposes[2]
C 260 Specification for Air-Entraining Admixtures for Concrete[3]
C 404 Specification for Aggregates for Masonry Grout[4]
C 595/C 595M Specification for Blended Hydraulic Cements[2]
C 1019 Test Method of Sampling and Testing Grout[4]

3. Materials

3.1 Materials used as ingredients in grout shall conform to the requirements specified in 3.1.1 to 3.1.8.

3.1.1 *Cementitious Materials*—Cementitious materials shall conform to one of the following specifications:

3.1.1.1 *Portland Cement*—Type I, IA, II, IIA, III, and IIIA of Specification C 150.

3.1.1.2 *Blended Cements*—Type IS, IS(MS), IS-A, IS-A(MS), IP, or IP-A of Specification C 595/C 595M.

3.1.1.3 *Quicklime*—Specification C 5.

3.1.1.4 *Hydrated Lime*—Type S of Specification C 207.

3.1.2 *Air-Entraining Admixtures*—Air-entraining admixtures shall conform to Specification C 260.

3.1.3 *Aggregates*—Aggregates shall conform to Specification C 404.

3.1.4 *Water*—Water shall be clean and potable.

3.1.5 *Admixtures*—Integral waterproofing compounds,

accelerators, or other admixtures not mentioned definitely in the specification shall not be used in grout for use in reinforced masonry without approval from the purchaser.

3.1.6 *Pumping Aids*—Pumping aids are permitted to be used in cases where the brand, quality, and quantity are approved in writing by the purchaser or are definitely stipulated in the specification.

3.1.7 *Antifreeze Compounds*—No antifreeze liquids, salts, or other substances shall be used in grout to lower the freezing point.

3.1.8 *Storage of Materials*—Cementitious materials and aggregates shall be stored in such a manner as to prevent deterioration or intrusion of foreign material or moisture. Any material that has become unsuitable for good construction shall not be used.

NOTE 1—If the grout is to be used to bond masonry units to reinforcing bars, the use of air-entraining materials or air-entraining admixtures is not recommended.

4. Measurement and Mixing

4.1 *Measurement of Materials*—The method of measuring materials for the grout used in construction shall be such that the specified proportions of the grout materials can be controlled and accurately maintained.

NOTE 2—The weights per cubic foot of the materials are as follows:

Material	Weight, lb/ft³ (kg/m³)
Portland cement	94 (1504)
Blended cement	weight printed on bag
Hydrated lime	40 (640)
Lime putty [A]	80 (1281)
Sand, damp and loose	80 (1281) of dry sand

[A] All quicklime should be slaked in accordance with the manufacturer's directions. All quicklime putty, except pulverized quicklime putty, should be sieved through a No. 20 (850-μm) sieve and allowed to cool until it has reached a temperature of 80°F(26.7°C). Quicklime putty should weigh at least 80 lb/ft.³ Putty that weighs less than this may be used in the proportion specifications if the required quantity of extra is added to meet the minimum weight requirements.

4.2 *Mixing of Materials*—Grout shall consist of cementitious material and aggregate (conforming to the requirements specified in Section 2) that have been mixed thoroughly for a minimum of 5 min in a mechanical mixer (Note 3) with sufficient water to bring the mixture to the desired consistency.

NOTE 3—Hand mixing of the grout may be permitted on small jobs, with the written approval of the purchaser outlining the hand mixing procedure.

---

[1] This specification is under the jurisdiction of ASTM Committee C-12 on Mortars for Unit Masonry and is the direct responsibility of Subcommittee C12.05 on Grout and Grout Admixtures for Masonary.
Current edition approved Nov. 10, 1995. Published January 1996. Originally published as C 476 – 61 T. Last previous edition C 476 – 91.
[2] *Annual Book of ASTM Standards,* Vol 04.01.
[3] *Annual Book of ASTM Standards,* Vol 04.02.
[4] *Annual Book of ASTM Standards,* Vol 04.05.

ⓐⓢⓣⓜ C 476

TABLE 1 Grout Proportions by Volume

Type	Parts by Volume of Portland Cement or Blended Cement	Parts by Volume of Hydrated Lime or Lime Putty	Aggregate, Measured in a Damp, Loose Condition	
			Fine	Coarse
Fine grout	1	0–1/10	2¼–3 times the sum of the volumes of the cementitious materials	. . .
Coarse grout	1	0–1/10	2¼–3 times the sum of the volumes of the cementitious materials	1–2 times the sum of the volumes of the cementitious materials

5. Grout

5.1 Grout type shall be specified and shall meet one of the following:

5.1.1 Fine grout shall be manufactured with fine aggregates (Specification C 404).

5.1.2 Course grout shall be manufactured with a combination of coarse and fine aggregates (Specification C 404).

NOTE 4—Building Code provisions and grout space dimensions should be reviewed in selecting grout type or types.

5.2 The grout shall be either proportioned in accordance with the requirements of Table 1 or the compressive strength of grout shall be specified. When compressive strength is specified, the grout shall have a minimum compressive strength of 2000 psi at 28 days and shall be sampled and tested in accordance with Test Method C 1019.

NOTE 5—Building Code provisions should be reviewed in selecting the specified compressive strength of grout.

6. Keywords

6.1 aggregates; cement; compressive strength; grout; masonry; portland cement; proportions

ASTM Designation: C 1019 – 89a (Reapproved 1993)ᵉ¹

AMERICAN SOCIETY FOR TESTING AND MATERIALS
1916 Race St. Philadelphia, Pa 19103
Reprinted from the Annual Book of ASTM Standards. Copyright ASTM
If not listed in the current combined index, will appear in the next edition.

Standard Test Method for
Sampling and Testing Grout[1]

This standard is issued under the fixed designation C 1019; the number immediately following the designation indicates the year of original adoption or, in the case of revision, the year of last revision. A number in parentheses indicates the year of last reapproval. A superscript epsilon (ε) indicates an editorial change since the last revision or reapproval.

ᵉ¹ NOTE—Section 11 was added editorially in June 1993.

1. Scope

1.1 This test method covers procedures for both field and laboratory sampling and compression testing of grout used in masonry construction.

1.2 The values stated in inch-pound units are to be regarded as the standard.

1.3 *This standard does not purport to address all of the safety problems, if any, associated with its use. It is the responsibility of the user of this standard to establish appropriate safety and health practices and determine the applicability of regulatory limitations prior to use.*

2. Referenced Documents

2.1 *ASTM Standards:*

C 39 Test Method for Compressive Strength of Cylindrical Concrete Specimens[2]

C 143 Test Method for Slump of Hydraulic Cement Concrete[2]

C 511 Specification for Moist Cabinets, Moist Rooms, and Water Storage Tanks Used in the Testing of Hydraulic Cements and Concretes[3]

C 617 Practice for Capping Cylindrical Concrete Specimens[2]

3. Significance and Use

3.1 Grout used in masonry is a fluid mixture of cementitious materials and aggregate with a high water content for ease of placement.

3.1.1 During construction, grout is placed within or between absorptive masonry units. Excess water must be removed from grout specimens in order to provide compressive strength test results more nearly indicative of the grout strength in the wall. In this test method, molds are made from masonry units having the same absorption and moisture content characteristics as those being used in the construction.

3.2 This test method can be used to either help select grout proportions by comparing test values or as a quality control test for uniformity of grout preparation during construction.

3.3 The physical exposure condition and curing of the grout are not exactly reproduced, but this test method does subject the grout specimens to absorption conditions similar to those experienced by grout in the wall. Test results of grout specimens taken from a wall should not be compared to test results obtained with this test method.

4. Apparatus

4.1 *Maximum-Minimum Thermometer.*

4.2 *Straightedge,* a steel straightedge not less than 6 in. (152.4 mm) long and not less than 1/16 in. (1.6 mm) in thickness.

4.3 *Tamping Rod,* a nonabsorbent rod, either round or square in cross section nominally 5/8 in. (15.9 mm) in dimension with ends rounded to hemispherical tips of the same diameter. The rod shall be a minimum length of 12 in. (304.8 mm).

4.4 *Wooden Blocks,* wooden squares with side dimensions equal to one half the desired grout specimen height, within a tolerance of 5 %, and of sufficient quantity or thickness to yield the desired grout specimen height, as shown in Figs. 1 and 2.

NOTE 1—Certain species of wood contain sugars which cause retardation of cement. In order to prevent this from occurring, new wooden blocks shall be soaked in limewater for 24 h, sealed with varnish or wax, or covered with an impermeable material prior to use.

5. Sampling

5.1 *Size of Sample*—Grout samples to be used for slump and compressive strength tests shall be a minimum of 1/2 ft³ (0.014 m³).

5.2 *Field Sample*—Take grout samples as the grout is being placed into the wall. Field samples may be taken at any time except for the first and last 10 % of the batch volume.

NOTE 2—Frequency of sampling and age of test is to be determined by the specifier of this test method and is usually found in the contract documents.

6. Test Specimen and Sample

6.1 Each grout specimen shall have a square cross-section, nominally 3 in. (76.2 mm) or larger on the sides and twice as high as its width. Dimensional tolerances shall be within 5 % of the nominal width selected.

6.2 Three specimens shall constitute one sample to be tested at each age of test.

7. Procedure

7.1 Select a level location where the molds can remain undisturbed for 48 h.

7.2 *Mold Construction:*

---

[1] This method is under the jurisdiction of ASTM Committee C-12 on Mortars for Unit Masonry and is the direct responsibility of Subcommittee C12.02 on Research and Methods of Test.

Current edition approved March 31 and May 26, 1989. Published July 1989. Originally published as C 1019 – 84. Last previous edition C 1019 – 84.

[2] *Annual Book of ASTM Standards,* Vol 04.02.

[3] *Annual Book of ASTM Standards,* Vol 04.01.

C 1019

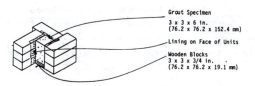

Grout Specimen
3 x 3 x 6 in.
(76.2 x 76.2 x 152.4 mm)

Lining on Face of Units

Wooden Blocks
3 x 3 x 3/4 in.
(76.2 x 76.2 x 19.1 mm)

NOTE—Front masonry unit stack not shown to allow view of specimen.

FIG. 1   Grout Mold (Units 6 in. (152.4 mm) or Less in Height, 2¼ in. (57.2 mm) High Brick Shown)

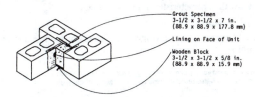

Grout Specimen
3-1/2 x 3-1/2 x 7 in.
(88.9 x 88.9 x 177.8 mm)

Lining on Face of Unit

Wooden Block
3-1/2 x 3-1/2 x 5/8 in.
(88.9 x 88.9 x 15.9 mm)

NOTE—Front masonry unit not shown to allow view of specimen.

FIG. 2   Grout Mold (Units Greater than 6 in. (152.4 mm) High, 8 in. (203.2 mm) High Concrete Masonry Unit Shown)

7.2.1 The mold space should simulate the grout location in the wall. If the grout is placed between two different types of masonry units, both types should be used to construct the mold.

7.2.2 Form a space with a square cross-section, nominally 3 in. (76.2 mm) or larger on each side and twice as high as its width, by stacking masonry units of the same type and moisture condition as those being used in the construction. Place wooden blocks, cut to proper size and of the proper thickness or quantity, at the bottom of the space to achieve the necessary height of specimen. Tolerance on space and specimen dimensions shall be within 5 % of the specimen width. See Figs. 1 and 2 and accompanying notes.

NOTE 3—Other methods of obtaining grout specimens and specimens of different geometry have been employed in grout testing, but are not covered by this test method. Since test results will vary with methods of forming and specimen geometry, comparison of test results should be confined to a single specimen shape and method of forming.

7.2.3 Line the masonry surfaces that will be in contact with the grout specimen with a permeable material, such as paper towel, to prevent bond to the masonry units.

NOTE 4—The lining is used to aid in stripping the grout specimen from the mold. Proper installation of the lining prevents irregularly sized specimens and varying test results.

7.3 Measure and record the slump of the grout in accordance with the requirements of Test Method C 143.

7.4 Fill the mold with grout in two layers. Rod each layer 15 times with the tamping rod. Rod the bottom layer through its depth. Slightly overfill the mold. Rod the second layer with the tamping rod penetrating ½ in. (12.7 mm) into the lower layer. Distribute the strokes uniformly over the cross section of the mold.

7.5 Level the top surface of the specimen with a straight-edge and cover immediately with a damp absorbent material such as cloth or paper towel. Keep the top surface of the

sample damp by wetting the absorbent material and do not disturb the specimen for 48 h.

7.6 Protect the sample from freezing and variations in temperature. Store an indicating maximum-minimum thermometer with the sample and record the maximum and minimum temperatures experienced prior to the time the specimens are placed in the moist room.

7.7 Remove the masonry units after 48 h.

7.7.1 Transport field specimens to the laboratory, keeping the specimens damp and in a protective container.

7.8 Store in a moist room conforming to Specification C 511.

7.9 Cap the specimens in accordance with the applicable requirements of Practice C 617.

NOTE 5—Practice C 617 refers to capping cylindrical specimens; therefore, the alignment devices may need to be modified to ensure proper use with the rectangular prism specimens of this method. All other sections of Practice C 617 are applicable.

7.10 Measure and record the width of each face at mid-height. Measure and record the height of each face at mid-width. Measure and record the amount out of plumb at mid-width of each face.

7.11 Test the specimens in a damp condition in accordance with the applicable requirements of Test Method C 39.

8. Calculations

8.1 Determine the average cross-sectional area by measuring the width of each face at its mid-height, calculating the average width of opposite faces, and multiplying the averages.

8.2 Calculate the compressive strength by dividing the maximum load by the average cross-sectional area and express the result to the nearest 10 psi (69 kPa).

9. Report

9.1 The report shall include the following:

9.1.1 Mix design,

9.1.2 Slump of the grout,

9.1.3 Type and number of units used to form mold for specimens,

9.1.4 Description of the specimens—dimensions, amount out of plumb in percent,

9.1.5 Curing history, including maximum and minimum temperatures, and age of specimen when transported to laboratory and when tested,

9.1.6 Maximum load and compressive strength of each specimen and average compressive strength of the sample, and

9.1.7 Description of failure.

10. Precision and Bias

10.1 *General:*

10.1.1 The masonry units used to form the mold have different absorption rates and will remove slightly different amounts of water from each specimen. Thus the standard deviation for this test method is higher than that using a nonabsorbent mold.

10.1.2 The standard deviation from field samples of grout will be higher than that for laboratory samples. There is less control of grout ingredients, conditions of units for mold

🖏 C 1019

TABLE 1	Statistics of Laboratory-Prepared Samples		
Number of Specimens	Mean, psi (MPa)	Standard Deviation, psi (MPa)	Coefficient of Variation, %
5	3784 (26.1)	306 (2.11)	8.1
5	2494 (17.2)	220 (1.52)	8.8
5	3178 (21.9)	634 (4.37)	20.0
6	5480 (37.8)	899 (6.2)	16.4
10	5350 (36.9)	826 (5.7)	15.4
12	3872 (26.7)	333 (2.30)	8.6

TABLE 2	Statistics of Field-Prepared Samples		
Number of Specimens	Mean, psi (MPa)	Standard Deviation, psi (MPa)	Coefficient of Variation, %
3	3583 (24.7)	118 (0.81)	3.3
6	5455 (37.6)	324 (2.23)	5.9
6	3992 (27.5)	228 (1.57)	5.7

construction, and initial curing environment in field-prepared samples.

10.2 Limited test data are available for analysis at this time. A more detailed statement will be provided later. The following summary of available data is provided for review.

10.2.1 *Laboratory Samples*—The coefficients of variation for a series of laboratory samples of three specimens each ranged from 5.8 % with a mean value of 6452 psi (44.45 MPa) to 24.6 % with a mean value of 1373 psi (9.47 MPa) averaging 14.4 %. The standard deviation ranged from 211 psi (1.46 MPa) to 505 psi (3.48 MPa). Samples with a larger number of specimens had the characteristics found in Table 1.

10.2.2 *Field Samples*—Test reports from one project show the characteristics found in Table 2.

11. Keywords

11.1 cementitious; compressive strength; grout; masonry units

Standard Practice for Selecting Proportions for Normal, Heavyweight, and Mass Concrete (ACI 211.1-91)

Reported by ACI Committee 211

Donald E. Dixon,
Chairman

Jack R. Prestrera,
Secretary

George R. U. Burg,[*]
Chairman, Subcommittee A

Edward A. Abdun-Nur[*]
Stanley G. Barton
Leonard W. Bell[*]
Stanley J. Blas, Jr.
Ramon L. Carraquillo
Peggy M. Carraquillo
Alan C. Carter
Martyn T. Conrey
James E. Cook
Russel A. Cook[*]
William A. Cordon
Wayne J. Costa

David A. Crocker
Kenneth W. Day
Calvin L. Dodl
Thomas A. Fox
Donald A. Graham
George W. Hollon
William W. Hotaling, Jr.
Robert S. Jenkins
Paul Klieger
Frank J. Lahm
Stanley H. Lee
Gary R. Mass[*]

Mark A. Mearing
Richard C. Meininger[*]
Richard W. Narva
Leo P. Nicholson
James E. Oliverson
James S. Pierce
Sandor Popovics[*]
Steven A. Ragan
Harry C. Robinson
Jere H. Rose[*]
James A. Scherocman
James M. Shilstone[*]

George B. Southworth
Alfred B. Spamer
Paul R. Stodola
Michael A. Taylor
Stanely J. Vigalitte
William H. Voelker
Jack W. Weber[*]
Dean J. White II
Milton H. Willis, Jr.
Francis C. Wilson
Robert Yuan

Committee Members Voting on 1991 Revision

Gary R. Mass[†]
Chairman

George R. U. Burg[†]
Chairman, Subcommittee A

Edward A. Abdun-Nur[†]
William L. Barringer[†]
Stanley G. Barton
Leonard W. Bell[†]
James E. Bennett, Jr.
J. Floyd Best
Ramon L. Carrasquillo
James E. Cook[†]
Russell A. Cook

David A. Crocker
Luis H. Diaz
Donald E. Dixon[†]
Calvin L. Dodl
Thomas A. Fox
George W. Hollon
Tarif M. Jaber
Stephen M. Lane
Stanley H. Lee

Richard C. Meininger[†]
James E. Oliverson
James S. Pierce
Sandor Popovics
Steven A. Ragan
Jere H. Rose[†]
Donald L. Schlegel
James M. Shilstone, Sr.
Paul R. Stodola

William S. Sypher
Ava Szypula
Jimmie L. Thompson[†]
Stanley J. Virgalitte
Woodward L. Vogt
Jack W. Weber
Dean J. White, III
Marshall S. Williams
John R. Wilson[†]

Describes, with examples, two methods for selecting and adjusting proportions for normal weight concrete, both with and without chemical admixtures, pozzolanic, and slag materials. One method is based on an estimated weight of the concrete per unit volume; the other is based on calculations of the absolute volume occupied by the concrete ingredients. The procedures take into consideration the requirements for placeability, consistency, strength, and durability. Example calculations are shown for both methods, including adjustments based on the characteristics of the first trial batch.

The proportioning of heavyweight concrete for such purposes as radiation shielding and bridge counterweight structures is described in an appendix. This appendix uses the absolute volume method, which is generally accepted and is more convenient for heavyweight concrete.

There is also an appendix that provides information on the proportioning of mass concrete. The absolute volume method is used because of its general acceptance.

Keywords: absorption; admixtures; aggregates; blast-furnace slag; cementitious materials; concrete durability; concretes; consistency; durability; exposure; fine aggregates; fly ash; heavyweight aggregates; heavyweight concretes; mass concrete; mix proportioning; pozzolans; quality control; radiation shielding; silica fume; slump tests; volume; water-cement ratio; water-cementitious ratio; workability.

CONTENTS

* Members of Subcommittee A who prepared this standard. The committee acknowledges the significant contribution of William L. Barringer to the work of the subcommittee.

† Members of Subcommittee A who prepared the 1991 revision.

This standard supersedes ACI 211.1-89. It was revised by the Expedited Standardization procedure, effective Nov. 1, 1991. This revision incorporates provisions related to the use of the mineral admixture silica fume in concrete. Chapter 4 has been expanded to cover in detail the effects of the use of silica fume on the proportions of concrete mixtures. Editorial changes have also been made in Chapters 2 through 4, and Chapters 6 through 8.

Reprinted with permission of the American Concrete Institute.

CHAPTER 1 -- SCOPE

1.1 This Standard Practice describes methods for selecting proportions for hydraulic cement concrete made with and without other cementitious materials and chemical admixtures. This concrete consists of normal and/or high-density aggregates (as distinguished from lightweight aggregates) with a workability suitable for usual cast-in-place construction (as distinguished from special mixtures for concrete products manufacture). Also included is a description of methods used for selecting proportions for mass concrete. Hydraulic cements referred to in this Standard Practice are portland cement (ASTM C 150) and blended cement (ASTM C 595). The Standard does not include proportioning with condensed silica fume.

1.2 The methods provide a first approximation of proportions intended to be checked by trial batches in the laboratory or field and adjusted, as necessary, to produce the desired characteristics of the concrete.

1.3 U.S. customary units are used in the main body of the text. Adaption for the metric system is provided in Appendix 1 and demonstrated in an example problem in Appendix 2.

1.4 Test methods mentioned in the text are listed in Appendix 3.

CHAPTER 2 -- INTRODUCTION

2.1 Concrete is composed principally of aggregates, a portland or blended cement, and water, and may contain other cementitious materials and/or chemical admixtures. It will contain some amount of entrapped air and may also contain purposely entrained air obtained by use of an admixture or air-entraining cement. Chemical admixtures are frequently used to accelerate, retard, improve workability, reduce mixing water requirements, increase strength, or alter other properties of the concrete (see ACI 212.3R). De-

pending upon the type and amount, certain cementitious materials such as fly ash, (see ACI 226.3R) natural pozzolans, ground granulated blast-furnace (GGBF) slag (see ACI 226.1R), and silica fume may be used in conjunction with portland or blended cement for economy or to provide specific properties such as reduced early heat of hydration, improved late-age strength development, or increased resistance to alkali-aggregate reaction and sulfate attack, decreased permeability, and resistance to the intrusion of aggressive solutions (See ACI 225R and ACI 226.1R).

2.2 The selection of concrete proportions involves a balance between economy and requirements for placeability, strength, durability, density, and appearance. The required characteristics are governed by the use to which the concrete will be put and by conditions expected to be encountered at the time of placement. These characteristics should be listed in the job specifications.

2.3 The ability to tailor concrete properties to job needs reflects technological developments that have taken place, for the most part, since the early 1900s. The use of water-cement ratio as a tool for estimating strength was recognized about 1918. The remarkable improvement in durability resulting from the entrainment of air was recognized in the early 1940s. These two significant developments in concrete technology have been augmented by extensive research and development in many related areas, including the use of admixtures to counteract possible deficiencies, develop special properties, or achieve economy (ACI 212.2R). It is beyond the scope of this discussion to review the theories of concrete proportioning that have provided the background and sound technical basis for the relatively simple methods of this Standard Practice. More detailed information can be obtained from the list of references in Chapter 8.

2.4 Proportions calculated by any method must always be considered subject to revision on the basis of experience with trial batches. Depending on the circumstances, the trial mixtures may be prepared in a laboratory, or, perhaps preferably, as full-size field batches. The latter procedure, when feasible, avoids possible pitfalls of assuming that data from small batches mixed in a laboratory environment will predict performance under field conditions. When using maximum-size aggregates larger than 2 in., laboratory trial batches should be verified and adjusted in the field using mixes of the size and type to be used during construction. Trial batch procedures and background testing are described in Appendix 3.

2.5 Frequently, existing concrete proportions not containing chemical admixtures and/or materials other than hydraulic cement are reproportioned to include these materials or a different cement. The performance of the reproportioned concrete should be verified by trial batches in the laboratory or field.

CHAPTER 3 -- BASIC RELATIONSHIP

3.1 Concrete proportions must be selected to provide

necessary placeability, density, strength, and durability for the particular application. In addition, when mass concrete is being proportioned, consideration must be given to generation of heat. Well-established relationships governing these properties are discussed next.

3.2 *Placeability* -- Placeability (including satisfactory finishing properties) encompasses traits loosely accumulated in the terms "workability" and "consistency." For the purpose of this discussion, workability is considered to be that property of concrete that determines its capacity to be placed and consolidated properly and to be finished without harmful segregation. It embodies such concepts as moldability, cohesiveness, and compactability. Workability is affected by: the grading, particle shape, and proportions of aggregate; the amount and qualities of cement and other cementitious materials; the presence of entrained air and chemical admixtures; and the consistency of the mixture. Procedures in this Standard Practice permit these factors to be taken into account to achieve satisfactory placeability economically.

3.3 *Consistency* -- Loosely defined, consistency is the relative mobility of the concrete mixture. It is measured in terms of slump -- the higher the slump the more mobile the mixture -- and it affects the ease with which the concrete will flow during placement. It is related to but not synonymous with workability. In properly proportioned concrete, the unit water content required to produce a given slump will depend on several factors. Water requirement increases as aggregates become more angular and rough textured (but this disadvantage may be offset by improvements in other characteristics such as bond to cement paste). Required mixing water decreases as the maximum size of well-graded aggregate is increased. It also decreases with the entrainment of air. Mixing water requirements usually are reduced significantly by certain chemical water-reducing admixtures.

3.4 *Strength* -- Although strength is an important characteristic of concrete, other characteristics such as durability, permeability, and wear resistance are often equally or more important. Strength at the age of 28 days is frequently used as a parameter for the structural design, concrete proportioning, and evaluation of concrete. These may be related to strength in a general way, but are also affected by factors not significantly associated with strength. In mass concrete, mixtures are generally proportioned to provide the design strength at an age greater than 28 days. However, proportioning of mass concrete should also provide for adequate early strength as may be necessary for form removal and form anchorage.

3.5 *Water-cement or water-cementitious ratio [w/c or w/(c + p)]* -- For a given set of materials and conditions, concrete strength is determined by the net quantity of water used per unit quantity of cement or total cementitious materials. The net water content excludes water absorbed by the aggregates. Differences in strength for a given water-cement ratio w/c or water-cementitious materials ratio $w/(c + p)$ may result from changes in: maximum size of aggregate; grading, surface texture, shape, strength, and

stiffness of aggregate particles; differences in cement types and sources; air content; and the use of chemical admixtures that affect the cement hydration process or develop cementitious properties themselves. To the extent that these effects are predictable in the general sense, they are taken into account in this Standard Practice. In view of their number and complexity, it should be obvious that accurate predictions of strength must be based on trial batches or experience with the materials to be used.

3.6 *Durability* -- Concrete must be able to endure those exposures that may deprive it of its serviceability -- freezing and thawing, wetting and drying, heating and cooling, chemicals, deicing agents, and the like. Resistance to some of these may be enhanced by use of special ingredients: low-alkali cement, pozzolans, GGBF slag, silica fume, or aggregate selected to prevent harmful expansion to the alkali-aggregate reaction that occurs in some areas when concrete is exposed in a moist environment; sulfate-resisting cement, GGBF slag, silica fume, or other pozzolans for concrete exposed to seawater or sulfate-bearing soils; or aggregate composed of hard minerals and free of excessive soft particles where resistance to surface abrasion is required. Use of low water-cement or cementitious materials ratio *[w/c or w/(c + p)]* will prolong the life of concrete by reducing the penetration of aggressive liquids. Resistance to severe weathering, particularly freezing and thawing, and to salts used for ice removal is greatly improved by incorporation of a proper distribution of entrained air. Entrained air should be used in all exposed concrete in climates where freezing occurs. (See ACI 201.2R for further details).

3.7 *Density* -- For certain applications, concrete may be used primarily for its weight characteristic. Examples of applications are counterweights on lift bridges, weights for sinking oil pipelines under water, shielding from radiation, and insulation from sound. By using special aggregates, placeable concrete of densities as high as 350 lb/ft^3 can be obtained--see Appendix 4.

3.8 *Generation of heat* -- A major concern in proportioning mass concrete is the size and shape of the completed structure or portion thereof. Concrete placements large enough to require that measures be taken to control the generation of heat and resultant volume change within the mass will require consideration of temperature control measures. As a rough guide, hydration of cement will generate a concrete temperature rise of 10 to 15 F per 100 lb of portland cement/yd^3 in 18 to 72 hours. If the temperature rise of the concrete mass is not held to a minimum and the heat is allowed to dissipate at a reasonable rate, or if the concrete is subjected to severe temperature differential or thermal gradient, cracking is likely to occur. Temperature control measures can include a relatively low initial placing temperature, reduced quantities of cementitious materials, circulation of chilled water, and, at times, insulation of concrete surfaces as may be required to adjust for these various concrete conditions and exposures. It should be emphasized that mass concrete is not necessarily large-aggregate concrete and that concern about generation of an excessive amount of heat in concrete is not confined to massive dam or foundation structures. Many large structural elements may be massive enough that heat generation should be considered, particularly when the minimum cross-sectional dimensions of a solid concrete member approach or exceed 2 to 3 ft or when cement contents above 600 lb/yd^3 are being used.

CHAPTER 4--EFFECTS OF CHEMICAL ADMIXTURES, POZZOLANIC, AND OTHER MATERIALS ON CONCRETE PROPORTIONS

4.1 *Admixtures* -- By definition (ACI 116R), an admixture is "a material other than water, aggregates, hydraulic cement, and fiber reinforcement used as an ingredient of concrete or mortar and added to the batch immediately before or during its mixing." Consequently, the term embraces an extremely broad field of materials and products, some of which are widely used while others have limited application. Because of this, this Standard Practice is restricted to the effects on concrete proportioning of air-entraining admixtures, chemical admixtures, fly ashes, natural pozzolans, and ground granulated blast-furnace slags (GGBF slag).

4.2 *Air-entraining admixture* -- Air-entrained concrete is almost always achieved through the use of an air-entraining admixture, ASTM C 260, as opposed to the earlier practice in which an air-entraining additive is interground with the cement. The use of an air-entraining admixture gives the concrete producer the flexibility to adjust the entrained air content to compensate for the many conditions affecting the amount of air entrained in concrete, such as: characteristics of aggregates, nature and proportions of constituents of the concrete admixtures, type and duration of mixing, consistency, temperature, cement fineness and chemistry, use of other cementitious materials or chemical admixtures, etc. Because of the lubrication effect of the entrained air bubbles on the mixture and because of the size and grading of the air voids, air-entrained concrete usually contains up to 10 percent less water than non-air-entrained concrete of equal slump. This reduction in the volume of mixing water as well as the volume of entrained and entrapped air must be considered in proportioning.

4.3 *Chemical admixtures* -- Since strength and other important concrete qualities such as durability, shrinkage, and cracking are related to the total water content and the w/c or $w/(c + p)$, water-reducing admixtures are often used to improve concrete quality. Further, since less cement can be used with reduced water content to achieve the same w/c or $w/(c + p)$ or strength, water-reducing and set-controlling admixtures are used widely for reasons of economy (ACI 212.2R).

Chemical admixtures conforming to ASTM C 494, Types A through G, are of many formulations and their purpose or purposes for use in concrete are as follows:

Type A -- Water-reducing
Type B -- Retarding
Type C -- Accelerating
Type D -- Water-reducing and retarding
Type E -- Water-reducing, and accelerating
Type F -- Water-reducing, high-range
Type G -- Water-reducing, high-range, and retarding

The manufacturer or manufacturer's literature should be consulted to determine the required dosage rate for each specific chemical admixture or combination of admixtures. Chemical admixtures have tendencies, when used in large doses, to induce strong side-effects such as excessive retardation and, possibly, increased air entrainment, in accordance with ASTM C 1017. Types A, B, and D, when used by themselves, are generally used in small doses (2 to 7 oz/100 lb of cementitious materials), so the water added to the mixture in the form of the admixture itself can be ignored. Types C, E, F, and G are most often used in large quantities (10 to 90 oz/100 lb of cementitious materials) so their water content should be taken into account when calculating the total unit water content and the w/c or $w/(c + p)$. When Types A, B, and D admixtures are used at higher than normal dosage rates in combination or in an admixture system with an accelerating admixture (Type C or E), their water content should also be taken into account.

Although chemical admixtures are of many formulations, their effect on water demand at recommended dosages is governed by the requirements of ASTM C 494. Recommended dosage rates are normally established by the manufacturer of the admixture or by the user after extensive tests. When used at normal dosage rates, Type A water-reducing, Type D water-reducing and retarding, and Type E water-reducing and accelerating admixtures ordinarily reduce mixing-water requirements 5 to 8 percent, while Type F water-reducing, high-range, and Type G water-reducing, high-range, and retarding admixtures reduce water requirements 12 to 25 percent or more. Types F and G water-reducing, high-range admixtures (HRWR) are often called "superplasticizers."

High-range, water-reducing admixtures are often used to produce flowing concrete with slumps between about 7½ or more with no increase in water demand other than that contained in the admixture itself. Types A, B, or D admixtures at high dosage rates, in combination with Types C or E (for acceleration), may also be used to produce the same effect. When flowing concrete is so produced, it is sometimes possible to increase the amount of coarse aggregate to take advantage of the fluidity of the concrete to flow into place in constricted areas of heavy reinforcement. Flowing concrete has a tendency to segregate; therefore, care must be taken to achieve a proper volume of mortar in the concrete required for cohesion without making the concrete undesirably sticky.

ASTM C 494 lists seven types of chemical admixtures as to their expected performance in concrete. It does not classify chemical admixtures as to their composition. ACI 212.2R lists five general classes of materials used to formulate most water-reducing, set-controlling chemical admixtures. This report, as well as ACI 301 and ACI 318, should be reviewed to determine when restrictions should be placed upon the use of certain admixtures for a given class of concrete. For example, admixtures containing purposely added calcium chloride have been found to accelerate the potential for stress-corrosion of tensioned cables imbedded in concrete when moisture and oxygen are available.

4.4 *Other cementitious materials* -- Cementitious materials other than hydraulic cement are often used in concrete in combination with portland or blended cement for economy, reduction of heat of hydration, improved workability, improved strength and/or improved durability under the anticipated service environment. These materials include fly ash, natural pozzolans (ASTM C 618), GGBF slag (ASTM C 989), and silica fune. Not all of these materials will provide all of the benefits listed.

As defined in ASTM C 618, pozzolans are: "Siliceous or siliceous and aluminous materials which in themselves possess little or no cementitious value, but will, in finely divided form and in the presence of moisture, chemically react with calcium hydroxide at ordinary temperatures to form compounds possessing cementitious properties ... " Fly ash is the "finely divided residue that results from the combustion of ground or powdered coal ... " Fly ash used in concrete is classified into two categories: Class F, which has pozzolanic properties, and Class C, which, in addition to having pozzolanic properties, also has some cemetitious properties in that this material may be self-setting when mixed with water. Class C fly ash may contain lime (CaO) amounts higher than 10 percent. The use of fly ash in concrete is more fully described and discussed in ACI 226.3R.

Blast-furnace slag is a by-product of the production of pig iron. When this slag is rapidly quenched and ground, it will possess latent cementitious properties. After processing, the material is known as GGBF slag, whose hydraulic properties may vary and can be separated into grades noted in ASTM C 989. The grade classification gives guidance on the relative strength potential of 50 percent GGBF slag mortars to the reference portland cement at 7 and 28 days. GGBF slag grades are 80, 100, and 120, in order of increasing strength potential.

Silica fume,* as used in concrete, is a by-product resulting from the reduction of high-purity quartz with coal and wood chips in an electric arc furnace during the production of silicon metal or ferrosilicon alloys. The silica fume, which condenses from the gases escaping from the furnaces, has a very high content of amorphous silicon dioxide and consists of very fine spherical particles.

Uses of silica fume in concrete fall into three general categories:

a.   Production of low permeability concrete with enhanced durability.
b.   Production of high-strength concrete.
c.   As a cement replacement (The current economics of cement costs versus silica fume costs do not usually

make this a viable use for silica fume in the U.S.).

Silica fume typically has a specific gravity of about 2.2. The lower specific gravity of silica fume compared with that of portland cement means that when replacement is based on weight (mass), a larger volume of silica fume is added than the volume of cement removed. Thus, the volume of cementitious paste increases and there is actually a lowering of the water-cementitious materials ratio on a volume basis.

The particle-size distribution of a typical silica fume shows that most particles are smaller than one micrometer (1 μm with an average diameter of about 0.1 μm, which is approximately one hundred times smaller than the average size cement particle).

The extreme fineness and high silica content of silica fume make it a highly effective pozzolanic material. The silica fume reacts pozzolanically with the calcium hydroxide produced during the hydration of cement to form the stable cementitious compound, calcium silicate hydrate (CSH).

Silica fume has been successfully used to produce very high strength (over 18,000 psi), low permeability, and chemically resistant concretes. Such concretes contain up to 25 percent silica fume by weight (mass) of cement. The use of this high amount of silica fume generally makes the concrete difficult to work. The mixing water demand of a given concrete mixture incorporating silica fume increases with increasing amounts of silica fume.

To maximize the full strength-producing potential of silica fume in concrete, it should always be used with a water-reducing admixture, preferably a high-range, water-reducing (HRWR) admixture. the dosage of the HRWR will depend on the percentages of silica fume and the type of HRWR used.

When proportioning concrete containing silica fume, the following should be considered:

a.   Mixing -- The amount of mixing will depend on the percentage of silica fume used and the mixing conditions. Mixing time may need to be increased to achieve thorough distribution when using large quantities of silica fume with low water content concrete. The use of HRWR assists greatly in achieving uniform dispersion.

b.   Air-entrainment -- The amount of air-entraining admixture to produce a required volume of air in concrete may increase with increasing amounts of silica fume due to the very high surface area of the silica fume and the presence of any carbon within the silica fume. Air entrainment is not usually used in high strength concretes unless they are expected to be exposed to freezing and thawing when saturated with water or to deicing salts.

c.   Workability -- Fresh concrete containing silica fume is generally more cohesive and less prone to segregation than concrete without silica fume. This increase in cohesiveness and reduction to bleeding can provide improved pumping properties. Concrete containing silica fume in excess of 10 percent by

---

* Other names that have been used include silica dust, condensed or pre-compacted silica fume, and micro silica; the most appropriate is silica fume.

weight (mass) of the cementitious materials may become sticky. It may be necessary to increase the slump 2 to 5 in. to maintain the same workability for a given length of time.

d. Bleeding -- Concrete containing silica fume exhibits reduced bleeding. This reduced bleeding is primarily caused by the high surface area of the silica fume particles, resulting in very little water being left in the mixture for bleeding. As the result of reduced bleeding of concrete containing silica fume, there is a greater tendency for plastic shrinkage cracking to occur.

Typically, the materials listed previously are introduced into the concrete mixer separately. In some cases, however, these same materials may be blended with portland cement in fixed proportions to produce a blended cement, ASTM C 595. Like air-entraining admixtures added to the concrete at the time of batching, the addition of GGBF slag also gives the producer flexibility to achieve desired concrete performance.

When proportioning concrete containing a separately batched, cementitious material such as fly ash, natural pozzolan, GGBF slag, or silica fume, a number of factors must be considered. These include:

a. Chemical activity of the cementitious material and its effect on concrete strength at various ages.
b. Effect on the mixing-water demand needed for workability and placeability.
c. Density (or specific gravity) of the material and its effect on the volume of concrete produced in the batch.
d. Effect on the dosage rate of chemical admixtures and/or air-entraining admixtures used in the mixture.
e. Effect of combinations of materials on other critical properties of the concrete, such as time of set under ambient temperature conditions, heat of hydration, rate of strength development, and durability.
f. Amount of cementitious materials and cement needed to meet the requirements for the particular concrete.

4.4.1 Methods for proportioning and evaluating concrete mixtures containing these supplementary cementitious materials must be based on trial mixtures using a range of ingredient proportions. By evaluating their effect on strength, water requirement, time of set, and other important properties, the optimum amount of cementitious materials can be determined. In the absence of prior information and in the interest of preparing estimated proportions for a first trial batch or a series of trial batches in accordance with ASTM C 192, the following general ranges are given based on the percentage of the ingredients by the total weight of cementitious material used in the batch for structural concrete:

Class F fly ash -- 15 to 25 percent

Class C fly ash -- 15 to 35 percent
Natural pozzolans -- 10 to 20 percent
Ground granulated blast-furnace slag -- 25 to 70 percent
Silica fume -- 5 to 15 percent

For special projects, or to provide certain special required properties, the quantity of the materials used per yd^3 of concrete may be different from that shown above.

In cases where high early strengths are required, the total weight of cementitious material may be greater than would be needed if portland cement were the only cementitious material. Where high early strength is not required higher percentages of fly ash are frequently used.

Often, it is found that with the use of fly ash and GGBF slag, the amount of mixing water required to obtain the desired slump and workability of concrete may be lower than that used in a portland cement mixture using only portland cement. When silica fume is used, more mixing water is usually required than when using only portland cement. In calculating the amount of chemical admixtures to dispense for a given batch of concrete, the dosage should generally be applied to the total amount of cementitious material. Under these conditions the reduction in mixing water for conventional water-reducing admixtures (Types A, D, and E) should be at least 5 percent, and for water-reducing, high-range admixtures at least 12 percent. When GGBF slag is used in concrete mixtures containing some high-range water-reducing admixtures, the admixture dosage may be reduced by approximately 25 percent compared to mixtures containing only portland cement.

4.4.2 Due to differences in their specific gravities, a given weight of a supplementary cementitious material will not occupy the same volume as an equal weight of portland cement. The specific gravity of blended cements will be less than that of portland cement. Thus, when using either blended cements or supplementary cementitious materials, the yield of the concrete mixture should be adjusted using the actual specific gravities of the materials used.

4.4.3 Class C fly ash, normally of extremely low carbon content, usually has little or no effect on entrained air or on the air-entraining admixture dosage rate. Many Class F fly ashes may require a higher dosage of air-entraining admixture to obtain specified air contents; if carbon content is high, the dosage rate may be several times that of non-fly ash concrete. The dosage required may also be quite variable. The entrained air content of concrete containing high carbon-content fly ash may be difficult to obtain and maintain. Other cementitious materials may be treated the same as cement in determining the proper quantity of air-entraining admixtures per yd^3 of concrete or per 100 lb of cementitious material used.

4.4.4 Concrete containing a proposed blend of cement, other cementitious materials, and admixtures should be tested to determine the time required for setting at various temperatures. The use of most supplementary cementitious materials generally slows the time-of-set of the concrete, and this period may be prolonged by higher percentages of these materials in the cementitious blend, cold weather, and the presence of chemical admixtures not formulated especially for acceleration.

Because of the possible adverse effects on finishing time and consequent labor costs, in some cold climates the proportion of other cementitious materials in the blend may have to be reduced below the optimum amount for strength considerations. Some Class C fly ashes may affect setting time while some other cementitious materials may have little effect on setting time. Any reduction in cement content will reduce heat generation and normally prolong the setting time.

CHAPTER 5 -- BACKGROUND DATA

5.1 To the extent possible, selection of concrete proportions should be based on test data or experience with the materials actually to be used. Where such background is limited or not available, estimates given in this recommended practice may be employed.

5.2 The following information for available materials will be useful:

5.2.1 Sieve analyses of fine and coarse aggregates.

5.2.2 Unit weight of coarse aggregate.

5.2.3 Bulk specific gravities and absorptions of aggregates.

5.2.4 Mixing-water requirements of concrete developed from experience with available aggregates.

5.2.5 Relationships between strength and water-cement ratio or ratio of water-to-cement plus other cementitious materials, for available combinations of cements, other cementitious materials if considered, and aggregates.

5.2.6 Specific gravities of portland cement and other cementitious materials, if used.

5.2.7 Optimum combination of coarse aggregates to meet the maximum density gradings for mass concrete as discussed in Section 5.3.2.1 of Appendix 5.

5.3 Estimates from Tables 6.3.3 and 6.3.4, respectively, may be used when items in Section 5.2.4 and Section 6.3.5 are not available. As will be shown, proportions can be estimated without the knowledge of aggregate-specific gravity and absorption, Section 5.2.3.

CHAPTER 6 -- PROCEDURE

6.1 The procedure for selection of mix proportions given in this section is applicable to normal weight concrete. Although the same basic data and procedures can be used in proportioning heavyweight and mass concretes, additional information and sample computations for these types of concrete are given in Appendixes 4 and 5, respectively.

6.2 Estimating the required batch weights for the concrete involves a sequence of logical, straightforward steps which, in effect, fit the characteristics of the available materials into a mixture suitable for the work. The question of suitability is frequently not left to the individual selecting

the proportions. The job specifications may dictate some or all of the following:

6.2.1 Maximum water-cement or water-cementitious material ratio.

6.2.2 Minimum cement content.

6.2.3 Air content.

6.2.4 Slump.

6.2.5 Maximum size of aggregate.

6.2.6 Strength.

6.2.7 Other requirements relating to such things as strength overdesign, admixtures, and special types of cement, other cementitious materials, or aggregate.

6.3 Regardless of whether the concrete characteristics are prescribed by the specifications or are left to the individual selecting the proportions, establishment of batch weights per yd^3 of concrete can be best accomplished in the following sequence:

6.3.1 *Step 1. Choice of slump* -- If slump is not specified, a value appropriate for the work can be selected from Table 6.3.1. The slump ranges shown apply when vibration is used to consolidate the concrete. Mixes of the stiffest consistency that can be placed efficiently should be used.

Table 6.3.1 — Recommended slumps for various types of construction*

Types of construction	Slump, in.	
	Maximum'	Minimum
Reinforced foundation walls and footings	3	1
Plain footings, caissons, and substructure walls	3	1
Beams and reinforced walls	4	1
Building columns	4	1
Pavements and slabs	3	1
Mass concrete	2	1

*Slump may be increased when chemical admixtures are used, provided that the admixture-treated concrete has the same or lower water-cement or water-cementitious material ratio and does not exhibit segregation potential or excessive bleeding.
'May be increased 1 in. for methods of consolidation other than vibration.

6.3.2 *Step 2. Choice of maximum size of aggregate* -- Large nominal maximum sizes of well graded aggregates have less voids than smaller sizes. Hence, concretes with the larger-sized aggregates require less mortar per unit volume of concrete. Generally, the nominal maximum size of aggregate should be the largest that is economically available and consistent with dimensions of the structure. In no event should the nominal maximum size exceed one-fifth of the narrowest dimension between sides of forms, one-third the depth of slabs, nor three-fourths of the minimum clear spacing between individual reinforcing bars, bundles of bars, or pretensioning strands. These limitations are sometimes waived if workability and methods of consolidation are such that the concrete can be placed without honeycomb or void. In areas congested with reinforcing steel, post-tension ducts or conduits, the proportioner should select a nominal maximum size of the aggregate so concrete can be placed without excessive segregation, pockets, or voids. When high strength concrete is desired, best results may be obtained with reduced nominal maximum sizes of aggregate since these produce higher strengths at a given water-cement ratio.

Table 6.3.3 — Approximate mixing water and air content requirements for different slumps and nominal maximum sizes of aggregates

Slump, in.	Water, lb/yd³ of concrete for indicated nominal maximum sizes of aggregate							
	⅜ in.*	½ in.*	¾ in.*	1 in.*	1-½ in.*	2 in.*'	3 in.ᶜ	6 in.ᶜ
Non-air-entrained concrete								
1 to 2	350	335	315	300	275	260	220	190
3 to 4	385	365	340	325	300	285	245	210
6 to 7	410	385	360	340	315	300	270	—
More than 7*	—	—	—	—	—	—	—	—
Approximate amount of entrapped air in non-air-entrained concrete, percent	3	2.5	2	1.5	1	0.5	0.3	0.2
Air-entrained concrete								
1 to 2	305	295	280	270	250	240	205	180
3 to 4	340	325	305	295	275	265	225	200
6 to 7	365	345	325	310	290	280	260	—
More than 7*	—	—	—	—	—	—	—	—
Recommended averages¹ total air content, percent for level of exposure:								
Mild exposure	4.5	4.0	3.5	3.0	2.5	2.0	1.5**ᶜ	1.0**ᶜ
Moderate exposure	6.0	5.5	5.0	4.5	4.5	4.0	3.5**ᶜ	3.0**ᶜ
Severe exposureᶜ	7.5	7.0	6.0	6.0	5.5	5.0	4.5**ᶜ	4.0**ᶜ

*The quantities of mixing water given for air-entrained concrete are based on typical total air content requirements as shown for "moderate exposure" in the table above. These quantities of mixing water are for use in computing cement contents for trial batches at 68 to 77 F. They are maximum for reasonably well-shaped angular aggregates graded within limits of accepted specifications. Rounded aggregate will generally require 30 lb less water for non-air-entrained and 25 lb less for air-entrained concretes. The use of water-reducing chemical admixtures, ASTM C 494, may also reduce mixing water by 5 percent or more. The volume of the liquid admixtures is included as part of the total volume of the mixing water. The slump values of more than 7 in. are only obtained through the use of water-reducing chemical admixture; they are for concrete containing nominal maximum size aggregate not larger than 1 in.

'The slump values for concrete containing aggregate larger than 1½ in. are based on slump tests made after removal of particles larger than 1½ in. by wet-screening.

ᶜThese quantities of mixing water are for use in computing cement factors for trail batches when 3 in. or 6 in. nominal maximum size aggregate is used. They are average for reasonably well-shaped coarse aggregates, well-graded from coarse to fine.

¹Additional recommendations on air-content and necessary tolerances on air content for control in the field are given in a number of ACI documents, including ACI 201, 345, 318, 301, and 302. ASTM C 94 for ready-mixed concrete also gives air-content limits. The requirements in other documents may not always agree exactly, so in proportioning concrete consideration must be given to selecting an air content that will meet the needs of the job and also meet the applicable specifications.

**For concrete containing large aggregates that will be wet-screened over the 1½ in. sieve prior to testing for air content, the percentage of air expected in the 1½ in. minus material should be as tabulated in the 1½ in. column. However, initial proportioning calculations should include the air content as a pecent of the whole.

ᶜWhen using large aggregate in low cement factor concrete, air entrainment need not be detrimental to strength. In most cases mixing water requirement is reduced sufficiently to improve the water-cement ratio and to thus compensate for the strength-reducing effect of air-entrained concrete. Generally, therefore, for these large nominal maximum sizes of aggregate, air contents recommended for extreme exposure should be considered even though there may be little or no exposure to moisture and freezing.

ᶜThese values are based on the criteria that 9 percent air is needed in the mortar phase of the concrete. If the mortar volume will be substantially different from that determined in this recommended practice, it may be desirable to calculate the needed air content by taking 9 percent of the actual mortar volume.

6.3.3 *Step 3. Estimation of mixing water and air content* -- The quantity of water per unit volume of concrete required to produce a given slump is dependent on: the nominal maximum size, particle shape, and grading of the aggregates; the concrete temperature; the amount of entrained air; and use of chemical admixtures. Slump is not greatly affected by the quantity of cement or cementitious materials within normal use levels (under favorable circumstances the use of some finely divided mineral admixtures may lower water requirements slightly -- see ACI 212.1R). Table 6.3.3 provides estimates of required mixing water for concrete made with various maximum sizes of aggregate, with and without air entrainment. Depending on aggregate texture and shape, mixing water requirements may be somewhat above or below the tabulated values, but they are sufficiently accurate for the first estimate. The differences in water demand are not necessarily reflected in strength since other compensating factors may be involved. A rounded and an angular coarse aggregate, both well and similarly graded and of good quality, can be expected to produce concrete of about the same compressive strength for the same cement factor in spite of differences in w/c or $w/(c + p)$ resulting from the different mixing water requirements.

Particle shape is not necessarily an indicator that an aggregate will be either above or below in its strength-producing capacity.

Chemical admixtures -- Chemical admixtures are used to modify the properties of concrete to make it more workable, durable, and/or economical; increase or decrease the time of set; accelerate strength gain; and/or control temperature gain. Chemical admixtures should be used only after an appropriate evaluation has been conducted to show that the desired effects have been accomplished in the particular concrete under the conditions of intended use. Water-reducing and/or set-controlling admixtures conforming to the requirements of ASTM C 494, when used singularly or in combination with other chemical admixtures, will reduce significantly the quantity of water per unit volume of concrete. The use of some chemical admixtures, even at the same slump, will improve such qualities as workability, finishability, pumpability, durability, and compressive and flexural strength. Significant volume of liquid admixtures should be considered as part of the mixing water. The slumps shown in Table 6.3.1, "Recommended Slumps for Various Types of Construction," may be increased when chemical admixtures are used, providing the admixture-treated concrete has the same or a lower water-cement ratio and does not exhibit segregation potential and excessive bleeding. When only used to increase slump, chemical admixtures may not improve any of the properties of the concrete.

Table 6.3.3 indicates the approximate amount of entrapped air to be expected in non-air-entrained concrete in the upper part of the table and shows the recommended average air content for air-entrained concrete in the lower part of the table. If air entrainment is needed or desired, three levels of air content are given for each aggregate size depending on the purpose of the entrained air and the severity of exposure if entrained air is needed for durability.

Mild exposure -- When air entrainment is desired for a beneficial effect other than durability, such as to improve workability or cohesion or in low cement factor concrete to improve strength, air contents lower than those needed for durability can be used. This exposure includes indoor or outdoor service in a climate where concrete will not be exposed to freezing or to deicing agents.

Moderate exposure -- Service in a climate where freezing is expected but where the concrete will not be continually exposed to moisture or free water for long periods prior to freezing and will not be exposed to deicing agents or other aggressive chemicals. Examples include: exterior beams, columns, walls, girders, or slabs that are not in contact with wet soil and are so located that they will not receive direct applications of deicing salts.

Severe exposure -- Concrete that is exposed to deicing chemicals or other aggressive agents or where the concrete may become highly saturated by continued contact with moisture or free water prior to freezing. Examples include: pavements, bridge decks, curbs, gutters, sidewalks, canal linings, or exterior water tanks or sumps.

The use of normal amounts of air entrainment in concrete with a specified strength near or about 5000 psi may not be possible due to the fact that each added percent of air lowers the maximum strength obtainable with a given combination of materials.[1] In these cases the exposure to water, deicing salts, and freezing temperatures should be carefully evaluated. If a member is not continually wet and will not be exposed to deicing salts, lower air-content values such as those given in Table 6.3.3 for moderate exposure are appropriate even though the concrete is exposed to freezing and thawing temperatures. However, for an exposure condition where the member may be saturated prior to freezing, the use of air entrainment should not be sacrificed for strength. In certain applications, it may be found that the content of entrained air is lower than that specified, despite the use of usually satisfactory levels of air-entraining admixture. This happens occasionally, for example, when very high cement contents are involved. In such cases, the achievement of required durability may be demonstrated by satisfactory results of examination of air-void structure in the paste of the hardened concrete.

When trial batches are used to establish strength relationships or verify strength-producing capability of a mixture, the least favorable combination of mixing water and

air content should be used. The air content should be the maximum permitted or likely to occur, and the concrete should be gaged to the highest permissible slump. This will avoid developing an over-optimistic estimate of strength on the assumption that average rather than extreme conditions will prevail in the field. If the concrete obtained in the field has a lower slump and/or air content, the proportions of ingredients should be adjusted to maintain required yield. For additional information on air content recommendations, see ACI 201.2R, 301, and 302.1R.

6.3.4 *Step 4. Selection of water-cement or water-cementitious materials ratio* -- The required w/c or $w/(c + p)$ is determined not only by strength requirements but also by factors such as durability. Since different aggregates, cements, and cementitious materials generally produce different strengths at the same w/c or $w/(c + p)$, it is highly desirable to have or to develop the relationship between strength and w/c or $w/(c + p)$ for the materials actually to be used. In the absence of such data, approximate and relatively conservative values for concrete containing Type I portland cement can be taken from Table 6.3.4(a). With typical materials, the tabulated w/c or $w/(c + p)$ should produce the strengths shown, based on 28-day tests of specimens cured under standard laboratory conditions. The average strength selected must, of course, exceed the specific strength by a sufficient margin to keep the number of low tests within specific limits -- see ACI 214 and ACI 318.

Table 6.3.4(a) — Relationship between water-cement or water-cementitious materials ratio and compressive strength of concrete

Compressive strength at 28 days, psi*	Water-cement ratio, by weight	
	Non-air-entrained concrete	Air-entrained concrete
6000	0.41	—
5000	0.48	0.40
4000	0.57	0.48
3000	0.68	0.59
2000	0.82	0.74

*Values are estimated average strengths for concrete containing not more than 2 percent air for non-air-entrained concrete and 6 percent total air content for air-entrained concrete. For a constant w/c or $w/(c+p)$, the strength of concrete is reduced as the air content is increased. 28-day strength values may be conservative and may change when various cementitious materials are used. The rate at which the 28-day strength is developed may also change.

Strength is based on 6 × 12 in. cylinders moist-cured for 28 days in accordance with the sections on "Initial Curing" and "Curing of Cylinders for Checking the Adequacy of Laboratory Mixture Proportions for Strength or as the Basis for Acceptance or for Quality Control" of ASTM method C 31 for Making and Curing Concrete Specimens in the Field. These are cylinders cured moist at 73.4 ± 3 F (23 ± 1.7 C) prior to testing.

The relationship in this table assumes a nominal maximum aggregate size of about ¾ to 1 in. For a given source of aggregate, strength produced at a given w/c or $w/(c+p)$ will increase as nominal maximum size of aggregate decreases: see Sections 3.4 and 6.3.2.

For severe conditions of exposure, the w/c or $w/(c + p)$ ratio should be kept low even though strength requirements may be met with a higher value. Table 6.3.4(b) gives limiting values.

When natural pozzolans, fly ash, GGBF slag, and silica fume, hereafter referred to as pozzolanic materials, are used in concrete, a water-to-cement plus pozzolanic materials ratio (or water-to-cement plus other cementitious materials ratio) by weight must be considered in place of the traditional water-cement ratio by weight. There are two ap-

Table 6.3.4(b) — Maximum permissible water-cement or water-cementitious materials ratios for concrete in severe exposures*

Type of structure	Structure wet continuously or frequently and exposed to freezing and thawing[†]	Structure exposed to sea water or sulfates
Thin sections (railings, curbs, sills, ledges, ornamental work) and sections with less than 1 in. cover over steel	0.45	0.40[‡]
All other structures	0.50	0.45[‡]

*Based on report of ACI Committee 201. Cementitious materials other than cement should conform to ASTM C 618 and C 989.
[†]Concrete should also be air-entrained.
[‡]If sulfate resisting cement (Type II or Type V of ASTM C 150) is used, permissible water-cement or water-cementitious materials ratio may be increased by 0.05.

proaches normally used in determining the $w/(c + p)$ ratio that will be considered equivalent to the w/c of a mixture containing only portland cement: (1) equivalent weight of pozzolanic materials or (2) equivalent absolute volume of pozzolanic materials in the mixture. For the first approach, the weight equivalency, the total weight of pozzolanic materials remains the same [that is, $w/(c + p) = w/c$ directly]: but the total absolute volume of cement plus pozzolanic materials will normally be slightly greater. With the second approach, using the Eq. (6.3.4.2), a $w/(c + p)$ by weight is calculated that maintains the same absolute volume relationship but that will reduce the total weight of cementitious material since the specific gravities of pozzolanic materials are normally less than that of cement.

The equations for converting a target water-cement ratio w/c to a weight ratio of water to cement plus pozzolanic materials $w/(c + p)$ by (1) weight equivalency or (2) volume equivalency are as follows:

Eq. (6.3.4.1)--Weight equivalency

$$\frac{w}{c+p} \text{ weight ratio, weight equivalency} = \frac{w}{c}$$

where

$$\frac{w}{c+p} = \text{weight of water divided by weight}$$
$$\text{of cement + pozzolanic materials}$$

$$\frac{w}{c} = \text{target water--cement ratio by weight}$$

When the weight equivalency approach is used, the percentage or fraction of pozzolanic materials used in the cementitious material is usually expressed by weight. That is, F_w, the pozzolanic materials percentage by weight of total

cement plus pozzolanic materials, expressed as a decimal factor, is

$$F_w = \frac{p}{c+p}$$

where

F_w = pozzolanic materials percentage by weight, expressed as a decimal factor
p = weight of pozzolanic materials
c = weight of cement

(Note: If only the desired pozzolanic materials percentage factor by absolute volume F_v, is known, it can be converted to F_w as follows

$$F_w = \frac{1}{1 + \left(\dfrac{3.15}{G_p}\right)\left(\dfrac{1}{F_v}-1\right)}$$

where

F_v = pozzolanic materials percentage by absolute volume of the total absolute volume of cement plus pozzolanic materials expressed as a decimal factor
G_p = specific gravity of pozzolanic materials
3.15 = specific gravity of portland cement [use actual value if known to be different])

Example 6.3.4.1 -- Weight equivalency

If a water-cement ratio of 0.60 is required and a fly ash pozzolan is to be used as 20 percent of the cementitous material in the mixture by weight ($F_w = 0.20$), then the required water-to-cement plus pozzolanic material ratio on a weight equivalency basis is

$$\frac{w}{c+p} = \frac{w}{c} = 0.60, \text{ and}$$

$$F_w = \frac{p}{c+p} = 0.20$$

Assuming an estimated mixing-water requirement of 270 lb/yd³, then the required weight of cement + pozzolan is 270 ÷ 0.60 = 450 lb; and the weight of pozzolan is (0.20)(450) = 90 lb. The weight of cement is, therefore, 450 - 90 = 360 lb. If instead of 20 percent fly ash by weight, 20 percent by absolute volume of cement plus pozzolan was specified (F_v = 0.20), the corresponding weight factor is computed as follows for a fly ash with an assumed gravity of 2.40:

$$F_w = \cfrac{1}{1 + \left(\cfrac{3.15}{G_P}\right)\left(\cfrac{1}{F_v} - 1\right)}$$

$$\cfrac{1}{1 + \left(\cfrac{3.15}{2.40}\right)\left(\cfrac{1}{0.2} - 1\right)}$$

$$F_w = \frac{1}{1 + (1.31)(4)} = \frac{1}{1 + 5.24} = \frac{1}{6.24} = 0.16$$

In this case 20 percent by absolute volume is 16 percent by weight, and the weight of pozzolan in the batch would be $(0.16)(450) = 72$ lb, and the weight of cement $450 - 72 = 378$ lb.

Eq. (6.3.4.2) -- Absolute volume equivalency

$$\frac{w}{c + p} \text{ weight ratio, absolute}$$

$$\text{volume equivalency} =$$

$$\cfrac{3.15\dfrac{w}{c}}{3.15(1 - F_v) + G_p(F_v)}$$

where
$\dfrac{w}{c + p}$ = weight of water divided by weight of cement + pozzolanic materials

$\dfrac{w}{c}$ = target water-cement ratio by weight

3.15 = specific gravity of portland cement (use actual value if known to be different)

F_v = pozzolan percentage by absolute volume of the total absolute volume of cement plus pozzolan, expressed as a decimal factor

(Note: If only the desired pozzolan percentage by weight F_w is known, it can be converted to F_v as follows

$$F_v = \cfrac{1}{1 + \left(\cfrac{G_p}{3.15}\right)\left(\cfrac{1}{F_w} - 1\right)}$$

where these symbols are the same as defined previously.)

Example 6.3.4.2 -- Absolute volume equivalency
Use the same basic data as Example 6.3.4.1, but it should be specified that the equivalent water-to-cement plus pozzolan ratio be established on the basis of absolute volume, which will maintain, in the mixture, the same ratio of volume of water to volume of cementitious material when changing from cement only to cement plus pozzolan. Again the required water-cement ratio is 0.60, and it is assumed initially that it is desired to use 20 percent by absolute volume of fly ash ($F_v = 0.20$). The specific gravity of the fly ash is assumed to be 2.40 in this example

$$\frac{w}{c+p} = \frac{3.15\left(\dfrac{w}{c}\right)}{3.15(1 - F_v) + G_p(F_v)}$$

$$= \frac{(3.15)(0.60)}{(3.15)(0.80) + (2.40)(0.20)}$$

$$+ \frac{1.89}{2.52 + 0.48} = \frac{1.89}{3.00} = 0.63$$

So the target weight ratio to maintain an absolute volume equivalency is $w/(c + p) = 0.63$. If the mixing water is again 270 lb/yd$_3$, then the required weight of cement + pozzolan is $270 \div 0.63 = 429$ lb; and, since the corresponding weight percentage factor for $F_v = 0.20$ is $F_w = 0.16$ as calculated in Example 6.3.4.1, the weight of fly ash to be used is $(0.16)(429) = 69$ lb and the weight of cement is $429 - 69 = 360$ lb. The volume equivalency procedure provides lower weights of cementitious materials. Checking the absolute volumes

$$fly\ ash = \frac{69}{(2.40)(62.4)} = 0.461 ft^3$$

$$cement = \frac{360}{(3.15)(62.4)} = 1.832 ft^3$$

$$total = 0.461 + 1.832 = 2.293 ft^3$$

$$\begin{array}{l}percent\ pozzolan \\ by\ volume\end{array} = \frac{0.461}{2.293} \times 100 = 20\ percent$$

If, instead of 20 percent fly ash by volume ($F_v = 0.20$), a weight percentage of 20 percent was specified ($F_w = 0.20$), it could be converted to F_v using $G_p = 2.40$ and the appropriate formula

$$F_v = \cfrac{1}{1 + \left(\cfrac{G_p}{3.15}\right)\left(\cfrac{1}{F_w} - 1\right)}$$

$$F_v = \cfrac{1}{1 + \left(\cfrac{2.40}{3.15}\right)\left(\cfrac{1}{0.2} - 1\right)}$$

$$F_v = \frac{1}{1 + (0.762)(4)} = \frac{1}{4.048} = 0.247$$

In this case 20 percent by weight is almost 25 percent by

absolute volume. The equivalent $w/(c + p)$ ratio by volume will have to be recomputed for this condition since F_v has been changed from that originally assumed in this example

$$\frac{w}{c + p} = \frac{3.15\left(\dfrac{w}{c}\right)}{3.15(1 - F_v) + G_p(F_v)}$$

$$= \frac{(3.15)(0.60)}{3.15(0.75) + 2.40(0.25)}$$

$$= \frac{1.89}{2.36 + 0.60} = \frac{1.89}{2.96} = 0.64$$

Total cementitious material would be $270 \div 0.64 = 422$ lb. Of this weight 20 percent ($F_w = 0.20$) would be fly ash; $(422)(0.20) = 84$ lb of fly ash and $422 - 84 = 338$ lb of cement.

6.3.5 *Step 5. Calculation of cement content* -- The amount of cement per unit volume of concrete is fixed by the determinations made in Steps 3 and 4 above. The required cement is equal to the estimated mixing-water content (Step 3) divided by the water-cement ratio (Step 4). If, however, the specification includes a separate minimum limit on cement in addition to requirements for strength and durability, the mixture must be based on whichever criterion leads to the larger amount of cement.

The use of pozzolanic or chemical admixtures will affect properties of both the fresh and hardened concrete. See ACI 212.

6.3.6 *Step 6. Estimation of coarse aggregate content* -- Aggregates of essentially the same nominal maximum size and grading will produce concrete of satisfactory workability when a given volume of coarse aggregate, on an oven-dry-rodded basis, is used per unit volume of concrete. Appropriate values for this aggregate volume are given in Table 6.3.6. It can be seen that, for equal workability, the volume of coarse aggregate in a unit volume of concrete is dependent only on its nominal maximum size and the fine-

ness modulus of the fine aggregate. Differences in the amount of mortar required for workability with different aggregates, due to differences in particle shape and grading, are compensated for automatically by differences in oven-dry-rodded void content.

The volume of aggregate in ft^3, on an oven-dry-rodded basis, for a yd^3 of concrete is equal to the value from Table 6.3.6 multiplied by 27. This volume is converted to dry weight of coarse aggregate required in a yd^3 of concrete by multiplying it by the oven-dry-rodded weight per ft^3 of the coarse aggregate.

6.3.6.1 For more workable concrete, which is sometimes required when placement is by pump or when concrete must be worked around congested reinforcing steel, it may be desirable to reduce the estimated coarse aggregate content determined using Table 6.3.6 by up to 10 percent. However, caution must be exercised to assure that the resulting slump, water-cement or water-cementitious materials ratio, and strength properties of the concrete are consistent with the recommendations in Sections 6.3.1 and 6.3.4 and meet applicable project specification requirements.

6.3.7 *Step 7. Estimation of fine aggregate content* -- At completion of Step 6, all ingredients of the concrete have been estimated except the fine aggregate. Its quantity is determined by difference. Either of two procedures may be employed: the weight method (Section 6.3.7.1) or the absolute volume method (Section 6.3.7.2).

6.3.7.1 If the weight of the concrete per unit volume is assumed or can be estimated from experience, the required weight of fine aggregate is simply the difference between the weight of fresh concrete and the total weight of the other ingredients. Often the unit weight of concrete is known with reasonable accuracy from previous experience with the materials. In the absence of such information, Table 6.3.7.1 can be used to make a first estimate. Even if the estimate of concrete weight per yd^3 is rough, mixture proportions will be sufficiently accurate to permit easy adjustment on the basis of trial batches as will be shown in the examples.

Table 6.3.6 — Volume of coarse aggregate per unit of volume of concrete

Nominal maximum size of aggregate, in.	Volume of oven-dry-rodded coarse aggregate* per unit volume of concrete for different fineness moduli of fine aggregate'			
	2.40	2.60	2.80	3.00
⅜	0.50	0.48	0.46	0.44
½	0.59	0.57	0.55	0.53
¾	0.66	0.64	0.62	0.60
1	0.71	0.69	0.67	0.65
1½	0.75	0.73	0.71	0.69
2	0.78	0.76	0.74	0.72
3	0.82	0.80	0.78	0.76
6	0.87	0.85	0.83	0.81

*Volumes are based on aggregates in oven-dry-rodded condition as described in ASTM C 29.

These volumes are selected from empirical relationships to produce concrete with a degree of workability suitable for usual reinforced construction. For less workable concrete, such as required for concrete pavement construction, they may be increased about 10 percent. For more workable concrete see Section 6.3.6.1.

'See ASTM C 136 for calculation of fineness modulus.

Table 6.3.7.1 — First estimate of weight of fresh concrete

Nominal maximum size of aggregate, in.	First estimate of concrete weight, lb/yd³*	
	Non-air-entrained concrete	Air-entrained concrete
⅜	3840	3710
½	3890	3760
¾	3960	3840
1	4010	3850
1½	4070	3910
2	4120	3950
3	4200	4040
6	4260	4110

*Values calculated by Eq. (6-1) for concrete of medium richness (550 lb of cement per yd³) and medium slump with aggregate specific gravity of 2.7. Water requirements based on values for 3 to 4 in. slump in Table 6.3.3. If desired, the estimated weight may be refined as follows if necessary information is available: for each 10 lb difference in mixing water from the Table 6.3.3 values for 3 to 4 in. slump, correct the weight per yd³ 15 lb in the opposite direction; for each 100 lb difference in cement content from 550 lb, correct the weight per yd³ 15 lb in the same direction; for each 0.1 by which aggregate specific gravity deviates from 2.7, correct the concrete weight 100 lb in the same direction. For air-entrained concrete the air content for severe exposure from Table 6.3.3 was used. The weight can be increased 1 percent for each percent reduction in air content from that amount.

If a theoretically exact calculation of fresh concrete weight per yd³ is desired, the following formula can be used

$$U = 16.85\, G_a\, (100 - A) \\ + c(1 - G_a/G_c) - w(G_a - 1)$$
$$(6\text{-}1)$$

where

U = weight in lb of fresh concrete per yd³
G_a = weighted average specific gravity of combined fine and coarse aggregate, bulk SSD*
G_c = specific gravity of cement (generally 3.15)
A = air content, percent
w = mixing water requirement, lb/yd³
c = cement requirement, lb/yd³

6.3.7.2 A more exact procedure for calculating the required amount of fine aggregate involves the use of volumes displaced by the ingredients. In this case, the total volume displaced by the known ingredients--water, air, cementitious materials, and coarse aggregate--is subtracted from the unit volume of concrete to obtain the required volume of fine aggregate. The volume occupied in concrete by any ingredient is equal to its weight divided by the density of that material (the latter being the product of the unit weight of water and the specific gravity of the material).

6.3.8 *Step 8. Adjustments for aggregate moisture* -- The aggregate quantities actually to be weighed out for the concrete must allow for moisture in the aggregates. Generally, the aggregates will be moist and their dry weights should be increased by the percentage of water they contain, both absorbed and surface. The mixing water added to the batch must be reduced by an amount equal to the free moisture contributed by the aggregate -- i.e., total moisture minus absorption.

6.3.8.1 In some cases, it may be necessary to batch an aggregate in a dry condition. If the absorption (normally measured by soaking one day) is higher than approximately one percent, and if the pore structure within the aggregate particles is such that a significant fraction of the absorption occurs during the time prior to initial set, there may be a noticeable increase in the rate of slump loss due to an effective decrease in mixing water. Also, the effective water-cement ratio would be decreased for any water absorbed by the aggregate prior to set; this, of course, assumes that cement particles are not carried into aggregate particle pores.

6.3.8.2 Laboratory trial batch procedures according to ASTM C 192 allow the batching of laboratory air-dried aggregates if their absorption is less than 1.0 percent with an allowance for the amount of water that will be absorbed from the unset concrete. It is suggested by ASTM

C 192 that the amount absorbed may be assumed to be 80 percent of the difference between the actual amount of water in the pores of the aggregate in their air-dry state and the nominal 24-hr absorption determined by ASTM C 127 or C 128. However, for higher-absorption aggregates, ASTM C 192 requires preconditioning of aggregates to satisfy absorption with adjustments in aggregate weight based on total moisture content and adjustment to include surface moisture as a part of the required amount of mixing water.

6.3.9 *Step 9. Trial batch adjustments* -- The calculated mixture proportions should be checked by means of trial batches prepared and tested in accordance with ASTM C 192 or full-sized field batches. Only sufficient water should be used to produce the required slump regardless of the amount assumed in selecting the trial proportions. The concrete should be checked for unit weight and yield (ASTM C 138) and for air content (ASTM C 138, C 173, or C 231). It should also be carefully observed for proper workability, freedom from segregation, and finishing properties. Appropriate adjustments should be made in the proportions for subsequent batches in accordance with the following procedure.

6.3.9.1 Re-estimate the required mixing water per yd³ of concrete by multiplying the net mixing water content of the trial batch by 27 and dividing the product by the yield of the trial batch in ft³. If the slump of the trial batch was not correct, increase or decrease the re-estimated amount of water by 10 lb for each 1 in. required increase or decrease in slump.

6.3.9.2 If the desired air content (for air-entrained concrete) was not achieved, re-estimate the admixture content required for proper air content and reduce or increase the mixing-water content of Paragraph 6.3.9.1 by 5 lb for each 1 percent by which the air content is to be increased or decreased from that of the previous trial batch.

6.3.9.3 If estimated weight per yd³ of fresh concrete is the basis for proportioning, re-estimate that weight by multiplying the unit weight in lb/ft³ of the trial batch by 27 and reducing or increasing the result by the anticipated percentage increase or decrease in air content of the adjusted batch from the first trial batch.

6.3.9.4 Calculate new batch weights starting with Step 4 (Paragraph 6.3.4), modifying the volume of coarse aggregate from Table 6.3.6 if necessary to provide proper workability.

CHAPTER 7 -- SAMPLE COMPUTATIONS

7.1 Two example problems will be used to illustrate application of the proportioning procedures. The following conditions are assumed:

7.1.1 Type I non-air-entraining cement will be used and its specific gravity is assumed to be 3.15.†

---

* SSD indicates saturated-surface-dry basis used in considering aggregate displacement. The aggregate specific gravity used in calculations must be consistent with the moisture condition assumed in the basic aggregate batch weights -- i.e., bulk dry if aggregate weights are stated on a dry basis, and bulk SSD if weights are stated on a saturated-surface-dry basis.

---

† The specific gravity values are not used if proportions are selected to provide a weight of concrete assumed to occupy 1 yd³.

7.1.2 Coarse and fine aggregates in each case are of satisfactory quality and are graded within limits of generally accepted specifications. See ASTM C 33.

7.1.3 The coarse aggregate has a bulk specific gravity of 2.68* and an absorption of 0.5 percent.

7.1.4 The fine aggregate has a bulk specific gravity of 2.64,* an absorption of 0.7 percent, and a fineness modulus of 2.8.

7.2 *Example 1* -- Concrete is required for a portion of a structure that will be below ground level in a location where it will not be exposed to severe weathering or sulfate attack. Structural considerations require it to have an average 28-day compressive strength of 3500 psi.† On the basis of information in Table 6.3.1, as well as previous experience, it is determined that under the conditions of placement to be employed, a slump of 3 to 4 in. should be used and that the available No. 4 to 1½-in. coarse aggregate will be suitable. The dry-rodded weight of coarse aggregate is found to be 100 lb/ft³. Employing the sequence outlined in Section 6, the quantities of ingredients per yd³ of concrete are calculated as follows:

7.2.1 *Step 1* -- As indicated previously, the desired slump is 3 to 4 in.

7.2.2 *Step 2* -- The locally available aggregate, graded from No. 4 to 1½ in., has been indicated as suitable.

7.2.3 *Step 3* -- Since the structure will not be exposed to severe weathering, non-air-entrained concrete will be used. The approximate amount of mixing water to produce 3 to 4-in. slump in non-air-entrained concrete with 1½-in aggregate is found from Table 6.3.3 to be 300 lb/yd³. Estimated entrapped air is shown as 1 percent.

7.2.4 *Step 4* -- From Table 6.3.4(a), the water-cement ratio needed to produce a strength of 3500 psi in non-air-entrained concrete is found to be about 0.62.

7.2.5 *Step 5* -- From the information derived in Steps 3 and 4, the required cement content is found to be 300/0.62 = 484 lb/yd³.

7.2.6 *Step 6* -- The quantity of coarse aggregate is estimated from Table 6.3.6. For a fine aggregate having a fineness modulus of 2.8 and a 1½ in. nominal maximum size of coarse aggregate, the table indicates that 0.71 ft³ of coarse aggregate, on a dry-rodded basis, may be used in each ft³ of concrete. For each yd³, therefore, the coarse aggregate will be 27 x 0.71 = 19.17 ft³. Since it weighs 100 lb per ft³, the dry weight of coarse aggregate is 1917 lb.

7.2.7 *Step 7* -- With the quantities of water, cement, and coarse aggregate established, the remaining material comprising the yd³ of concrete must consist of fine aggregate and whatever air will be entrapped. The required fine aggregate may be determined on the basis of either weight or absolute volume as shown:

7.2.7.1 *Weight basis* -- From Table 6.3.7.1, the weight of a yd³ of non-air-entrained concrete made with ag-

gregate having a nominal maximum size of 1½ in. is estimated to be 4070 lb. (For a first trial batch, exact adjustments of this value for usual differences in slump, cement factor, and aggregate specific gravity are not critical.) Weights already known are:

Water, net mixing	300 lb
Cement	484 lb
Coarse aggregate	1917 lb (dry)‡
Total	2701 lb

The weight of fine aggregate, therefore, is estimated to be

$$4070 - 2701 = 1369 \text{ lb (dry)‡}$$

7.2.7.2 *Absolute volume basis* -- With the quantities of cement, water, and coarse aggregate established, and the approximate entrapped air content (as opposed to purposely entrained air) taken from Table 6.3.3, the fine aggregate content can be calculated as follows:

$$\text{Volume of water} = \frac{300}{62.4} = 4.81 \text{ ft}^3$$

$$\text{Solid volume of cement} = \frac{484}{3.15 \times 62.4} = 2.46 \text{ ft}^3$$

$$\text{Solid volume of coarse aggregate} = \frac{1917}{2.68 \times 62.4} = 11.46 \text{ ft}^3$$

$$\text{Volume of entrapped air} = 0.01 \times 27 = 0.27 \text{ ft}^3$$

$$\text{Total solid volume of ingredients except fine aggregate} = 19.00 \text{ ft}^3$$

$$\text{Solid volume of fine aggregate required} = 27 - 19.00 = 8.00 \text{ ft}^3$$

$$\text{Required weight of dry aggregate} = 8.00 \times 2.64 \times 62.4 = 1318 \text{ lb}$$

7.2.7.3 Batch weights per yd³ of concrete calculated on the two bases are compared as follows:

	Based on estimated concrete weight, lb	Based on absolute volume of ingredients, lb
Water, net mixing	300	300
Cement	484	484
Coarse aggregate, dry	1917	1917
Fine aggregate, dry	1369	1318

---

* The specific gravity values are not used if proportions are selected to provide a weight of concrete assumed to occupy 1 yd³.

† This is not the specified strength used for structural design but a higher figure expected to be produced on the average. For the method of determining the amount by which average strength should exceed design strength, see ACI 214.

‡ Aggregate absorption of 0.5 percent is disregarded since its magnitude is unconsequential in relocation to other approximations.

7.2.8 *Step 8* -- Tests indicate total moisture of 2 percent in the coarse aggregate and 6 percent in the fine aggregate. If the trial batch proportions based on assumed concrete weight are used, the adjusted aggregate weights become:

Coarse aggregate, wet	1917 (1.02) = 1955 lb
Fine aggregate, wet	1369 (1.06) = 1451 lb

Absorbed water does not become part of the mixing water and must be excluded from the adjustment in added water. Thus, surface water contributed by the coarse aggregate amounts to 2 - 0.5 = 1.5 percent; that contributed by the fine aggregate to 6 - 0.7 = 5.3 percent. The estimated requirement for added water, therefore, becomes

$$300 - 1917(0.015) - 1369(0.053) = 199 \text{ lb}$$

The estimated batch weights for a yd³ of concrete are:

Water, to be added	199 lb
Cement	484 lb
Coarse aggregate, wet	1955 lb
Fine aggregate, wet	1451 lb

7.2.9 *Step 9* -- For the laboratory trial batch, it was found convenient to scale the weights down to produce 0.03 yd³ or 0.81 ft³ of concrete. Although the calculated quantity of water to be added was 5.97 lb, the amount actually used in an effort to obtain the desired 3 to 4 in. slump is 7.00 lb. The batch as mixed therefore consists of:

Water, to be added	7.00 lb
Cement	14.52 lb
Coarse aggregate, wet	58.65 lb
Fine aggregate, wet	43.53 lb
Total	123.70 lb

The concrete has a measured slump of 2 in. and unit weight of 149.0 lb per ft³. It is judged to be satisfactory from the standpoint of workability and finishing properties. To provide proper yield and other characteristics for future batches, the following adjustments are made:

7.2.9.1 Since the yield of the trial batch was

$$123.70/149.0 = 0.830 \text{ ft}^3$$

and the mixing water content was 7.00 (added) + 0.86 on coarse aggregate + 2.18 on fine aggregate = 10.04 lb, the mixing water required for a yd³ of concrete with the same slump as the trial batch should be

$$10.04 \times 27/0.830 = 327 \text{ lb}$$

As indicated in Paragraph 6.3.9.1, this amount must be increased another 15 lb to raise the slump from the measured 2 in. to the desired 3 to 4 in. range, bringing the

net mixing water to 342 lb.

7.2.9.2 With the increased mixing water, additional cement will be required to provide the desired water-cement ratio of 0.62. The new cement content becomes

$$342/0.62 = 552 \text{ lb}$$

7.2.9.3 Since workability was found to be satisfactory, the quantity of coarse aggregate per unit volume of concrete will be maintained the same as in the trial batch. The amount of coarse aggregate per yd³ becomes

$$\frac{58.65}{0.83} \times 27 = 1908 \text{ } lb \text{ } wet$$

which is

$$\frac{1908}{1.02} = 1871 \text{ } lb \text{ } dry$$

and

$$1871 (1.005) = 1880 \text{ SSD*}$$

7.2.9.4 The new estimate for the weight of a yd³ of concrete is 149.0 x 27 = 4023 lb. The amount of fine aggregate required is therefore

$$4023 - (342 + 552 + 1880) = 1249 \text{ lb SSD}$$

or

$$1249/1.007 = 1240 \text{ lb dry}$$

The adjusted basic batch weights per yd³ of concrete are:

Water, net mixing	342 lb
Cement	522 lb
Coarse aggregate, dry	1871 lb
Fine aggregate, dry	1240 lb

7.2.10 Adjustments of proportions determined on an absolute volume basis follow a procedure similar to that just outlined. The steps will be given without detailed explanation:

7.2.10.1 Quantities used in nominal 0.81 ft³ batch are:

Water, added	7.00 lb
Cement	14.52 lb
Coarse aggregate, wet	58.65 lb
Fine aggregate, wet	41.91 lb
Total	122.08 lb

Measured slump 2 in.; unit weight 149.0 lb/ft³; yield 122.08/149.0 = 0.819 ft³, workability o.k.

7.2.10.2 Re-estimated water for same slump as

---

* Saturated-surface-dry

trial batch

$$\frac{27(7.00 + 0.86 + 2.09)}{0.819} = 328 \; lb$$

Mixing water required for slump of 3 to 4 in.

$$328 + 15 = 343 \; lb$$

7.2.10.3 Adjusted cement content for increased water

$$343/0.62 = 553 \; lb$$

7.2.10.4 Adjusted coarse aggregate requirement

$$\frac{58.65}{0.819} \; x \; 27 = 1934 \; lb \; wet$$

or

$$1934/1.02 = 1896 \; lb \; dry$$

7.2.10.5 The volume of ingredients other than air in the original trial batch was

Water	$\dfrac{9.95}{62.4}$	=	0.159 ft³
Cement	$\dfrac{14.52}{3.15 \; x \; 62.4}$	=	0.074 ft³
Coarse aggregate	$\dfrac{57.50}{2.68 \; x \; 62.4}$	=	0.344 ft³
Fine aggregate	$\dfrac{39.54}{2.64 \; x \; 62.4}$	=	0.240 ft³
Total		=	0.817 ft³

Since the yield was 0.819 ft³, the air content was

$$\frac{0.819 - 0.817}{0.819} = 0.2 \; percent$$

With the proportions of all components except fine aggregate established, the determination of adjusted yd³ batch quantities can be completed as follows:

Volume of water	=	$\dfrac{343}{62.4}$ =	5.50 ft³
Volume of cement	=	$\dfrac{553}{3.15 \; x \; 62.4}$ =	2.81 ft³
Volume of air	=	0.002 x 27 =	0.05 ft³

Volume of coarse aggregate	=	$\dfrac{1896}{2.68 \; x \; 62.4}$ =	11.34 ft³
Total volume exclusive of fine aggregate		=	19.70 ft³
Volume of fine aggregate required	=	27 - 19.70 =	7.30 ft³
Weight of fine aggregate (dry basis)	=	7.30 x 2.64 x 62.4 =	1203 lb

The adjusted basic batch weights per yd³ of concrete are then:

Water, net mixing	343 lb
Cement	553 lb
Coarse aggregate, dry	1896 lb
Fine aggregate, dry	1203 lb

These differ only slightly from those given in Paragraph 7.2.9.4 for the method of assumed concrete weight. Further trials or experience might indicate small additional adjustments for either method.

7.3 *Example 2* -- Concrete is required for a heavy bridge pier that will be exposed to fresh water in a severe climate. An average 28-day compressive strength of 3000 psi will be required. Placement conditions permit a slump of 1 to 2 in. and the use of large aggregate, but the only economically available coarse aggregate of satisfactory quality is graded from No. 4 to 1 in. and this will be used. Its dry-rodded weight is found to be 95 lb/ft³. Other characteristics are as indicated in Section 7.1.

The calculations will be shown in skeleton form only. Note that confusion is avoided if all steps of Section 6 are followed even when they appear repetitive of specified requirements.

7.3.1 *Step 1* -- The desired slump is 1 to 2 in.

7.3.2 *Step 2* -- The locally available aggregate, graded from No. 4 to 1 in., will be used.

7.3.3 *Step 3* -- Since the structure will be exposed to severe weathering, air-entrained concrete will be used. The approximate amount of mixing water to produce a 1 to 2-in. slump in air-entrained concrete with 1-in. aggregate is found from Table 6.3.3 to be 270 lb/yd³. The recommended air content is 6 percent.

7.3.4 *Step 4* -- From Table 6.3.4(a), the water-cement ratio needed to produce a strength of 3000 psi in air-entrained concrete is estimated to be about 0.59. However, reference to Table 6.3.4(b) reveals that, for the severe weathering exposure anticipated, the water-cement ratio should not exceed 0.50. This lower figure must govern and will be used in the calculations.

7.3.5 *Step 5* -- From the information derived in Steps 3 and 4, the required cement content is found to be 270/0.50

= 540 lb/yd³.

7.3.6 *Step 6* -- The quantity of coarse aggregate is estimated from Table 6.3.6. With a fine aggregate having a fineness modulus of 2.8 and a 1 in. nominal maximum size of coarse aggregate, the table indicates that 0.67 ft³ of coarse aggregate, on a dry-rodded basis, may be used in each ft³ of concrete. For a ft³, therefore, the coarse aggregate will be 27 x 0.67 = 18.09 ft³. Since it weighs 95 lb/ft³, the dry weight of coarse aggregate is 18.09 x 95 = 1719 lb.

7.3.7 *Step 7* -- With the quantities of water, cement, and coarse aggregate established, the remaining material comprising the yd³ of concrete must consist of fine aggregate and air. The required fine aggregate may be determined on the basis of either weight or absolute volume as shown below.

7.3.7.1 *Weight basis* -- From Table 6.3.7.1 the weight of a yd³ of air-entrained concrete made with aggregate of 1 in. maximum size is estimated to be 3850 lb. (For a first trial batch, exact adjustments of this value for differences in slump, cement factor, and aggregate specific gravity are not critical.) Weights already known are:

Water, net mixing	270 lb
Cement	540 lb
Coarse aggregate, dry	1719 lb
Total	2529 lb

The weight of fine aggregate, therefore, is estimated to be

3850 - 2529 = 1321 lb (dry)

7.3.7.2 *Absolute volume basis* -- With the quantities of cement, water, air, and coarse aggregate established, the fine aggregate content can be calculated as follows:

$$\text{Volume of water} = \frac{270}{62.4} = 4.33 \text{ ft}^3$$

$$\text{Solid volume of cement} = \frac{540}{3.15 \times 62.4} = 2.75 \text{ ft}^3$$

$$\text{Solid volume of coarse aggregate} = \frac{1719}{2.68 \times 62.4} = 10.28 \text{ ft}^3$$

$$\text{Volume of air} = 0.06 \times 27 = 1.62 \text{ ft}^3$$

$$\text{Total volume of ingredients except fine aggregate} = 18.98 \text{ ft}^3$$

$$\text{Solid volume of fine aggregate required} = 27 - 18.98 = 8.02 \text{ ft}^3$$

$$\text{Required weight of dry fine aggregate} = 8.02 \times 2.64 \times 62.4 = 1321 \text{ lb}$$

7.3.7.3 Batch weights per yd³ of concrete calculated on the two bases are compared as follows:

	Based on estimated concrete weight, lb	Based on absolute volume of ingredients, lb
Water, net mixing	270	270
Cement	540	540
Coarse aggregate, dry	1719	1719
Fine aggregate, dry	1321	1321

7.3.8 *Step 8* -- Tests indicate total moisture of 3 percent in the coarse aggregate and 5 percent in the fine aggregate. If the trial batch proportions based on assumed concrete weight are used, the adjusted aggregate weights become:

Coarse aggregate, wet	1719(1.03) = 1771 lb
Fine aggregate, wet	1321(1.05) = 1387 lb

Absorbed water does not become part of the mixing water and must be excluded from the adjustment in added water. Thus, surface water contributed by the coarse aggregate amounts to 3 - 0.5 = 2.5 percent; by the fine aggregate 5 - 0.7 = 4.3 percent. The estimated requirement for added water, therefore, becomes

270 - 1719(0.025) - 1321(0.043) = 170 lb

The estimated batch weights for a yd³ of concrete are:

Water, to be added	170 lb
Cement	540 lb
Coarse aggregate, wet	1771 lb
Fine aggregate, wet	1387 lb
Total	3868 lb

7.3.9 *Step 9* -- For the laboratory trial batch, the weights are scaled down to produce 0.03 yd³ or 0.81 ft³ of concrete. Although the calculated quantity of water to be added was 5.10 lb, the amount actually used in an effort to obtain the desired 1 to 2-in. slump is 4.60 lb. The batch as mixed, therefore, consists of:

Water, added	4.60 lb
Cement	16.20 lb
Coarse aggregate, wet	53.13 lb
Fine aggregate, wet	41.61 lb
Total	115.54 lb

The concrete has a measured slump of 2 in., unit weight of 141.8 lb/ft³ and air content of 6.5 percent. It is judged to be slightly oversanded for the easy placement condition involved. To provide proper yield and other characteristics for future batches, the following adjustments are made.

7.3.9.1 Since the yield of the trial batch was

$$115.543/141.8 = 0.815 \text{ ft}^3$$

and the mixing water content was 4.60 (added) + 1.29 on coarse aggregate + 1.77 on fine aggregate = 7.59 lb, the mixing water required for a yd³ of concrete with the same slump as the trial batch should be

$$\frac{7.59 \times 27}{0.815} = 251 \text{ lb}$$

The slump was satisfactory, but since the air content was too high by 0.5 percent, more water will be needed for proper slump when the air content is corrected. As indicated in Paragraph 6.3.9.2, the mixing water should be increased roughly 5 x 0.5 or about 3 lb, bringing the new estimate to 254 lb/yd³.

7.3.9.2 With the decreased mixing water, less cement will be required to provide the desired water-cement ratio of 0.5. The new cement content becomes

$$254/0.5 = 508 \text{ lb}$$

7.3.9.3 Since the concrete was found to be oversanded, the quantity of coarse aggregate per unit volume will be increased 10 percent to 0.74, in an effort to correct the condition. The amount of coarse aggregate per yd³ becomes

$$0.74 \times 27 \times 95 = 1898 \text{ lb dry}$$

or

$$1898 \times 1.03 = 1955 \text{ wet}$$

and

$$1898 \times 1.005 = 1907 \text{ lb SSD}$$

7.3.9.4 The new estimate for the weight of the concrete with 0.5 percent less air is 141.8/0.995 = 142.50 lb/ft³ or 142.50 x 27 = 3848 lb/yd³. The weight of sand, therefore, is

$$3848 - (254 + 508 + 1907) = 1179 \text{ lb SSD}$$

or

$$1179/1.007 = 1170 \text{ lb dry}$$

The adjusted basic batch weights per yd³ of concrete are:

Water, net mixing	254 lb
Cement	508 lb
Coarse aggregate, dry	1898 lb
Fine aggregate, dry	1170 lb

Admixture dosage must be reduced to provide the desired air content.

7.3.10 Adjustments of proportions determined on an absolute volume basis would follow the procedure outlined in Paragraph 7.2.10, which will not be repeated for this example.

CHAPTER 8 -- REFERENCES

8.1 -- *Recommended references*

The documents of the various standards-producing organizations referred to in this document are listed below with their serial designation, including year of adoption or revision. The documents listed were the latest effort at the time this document was revised. Since some of these documents are revised frequently, generally in minor detail only, the user of this document should check directly with the sponsoring group if it is desired to refer to the latest revision.

American Concrete Institute

116R-90	Cement and Concrete Terminology, SP-19(90)
201.2R-77 (Reapproved 1982)	Guide to Durable Concrete
207.1R-87	Mass Concrete
207.2R-90	Effect of Restraint, Volume Change, and Reinforcement on Cracking of Mass Concrete
207.4R-80(86)	Cooling and Insulating Systems for Mass Concrete
212.3R-89	Chemical Admixtures for Concrete
214-77 (Reapproved 1989)	Recommended Practice for Evaluation of Strength Test Results of Concrete
224R-90	Control of Cracking in Concrete Structures
225R-85	Guide to the Selection and Use of Hydraulic Cements
226.1R-87	Ground Granulated Blast-Furnace Slag as a Cementitious Constituent in Concrete
226.3R-87	Use of Fly Ash in Concrete
301-89	Specifications for Structural Concrete for Buildings
302.1R-89	Guide for Concrete Floor and Slab Construction
304R-89	Guide for Measuring, Mixing, Transporting, and Placing Concrete
304.3R-89	Heavyweight Concrete: Measuring, Mixing, Transporting, and Placing
318-83	Building Code Requirements for Reinforced Concrete

345-82	Standard Practice for Concrete Highway Bridge Deck Construction
ASTM	
C 29-78	Standard Test Method for Unit Weight and Voids in Aggregate
31-87a	Standard Method of Making and Curing Concrete Test Specimens in the Field
C 33-86	Standard Specification for Concrete Aggregates
C 39-86	Standard Test Method for Compressive Strength of Cylindrical Concrete Specimens
C 70-79(1985)	Standard Test Method for Surface Moisture in Fine Aggregate
C 78-84	Standard Test Method for Flexural Strength of Concrete (Using Simple Beam with Third-Point Loading)
C 94-86b	Standard Specification for Ready-Mixed Concrete
C 125-86	Standard Definitions of Terms Relating to Concrete and Concrete Aggregates
C 127-84	Standard Test Method for Specific Gravity and Absorption of Coarse Aggregate
C 128-84	Standard Test Method for Specific Gravity and Absorption of Fine Aggregate
C 136-84a	Standard Method for Sieve Analysis of Fine and Coarse Aggregates
C 138-81	Standard Test Method for Unit Weight, Yield, and Air Content (Gravimetric) of Concrete
C 143-78	Standard Test Method for Slump of Portland Cement Concrete
C 150-86	Standard Specification for Portland Cement
C 172-82	Standard Method of Sampling Freshly Mixed Concrete
C 173-78	Standard Test Method for Air Content of Freshly Mixed Concrete by the Volumetric Method
C 192-81	Standard Method of Making and Curing Concrete Test Specimens in the Laboratory
C 231-82	Standard Test Method for Air Content of Freshly Mixed Concrete by the Pressure Method
C 260-86	Standard Specification for Air-Entraining Admixtures for Concrete
C 293-79	Standard Test Method for Flexural Strength of Concrete (Using Simple Beam with Center-Point Loading)
C 494-86	Standard Specification for Chemical Admixtures for Concrete
C 496-86	Standard Test Method for Splitting Tensile Strength of Cylindrical Concrete Specimens
C 566-84	Standard Test Method for Total Moisture Content of Aggregate by Drying
C 595-86	Standard Specification for Blended Hydraulic Cements
C 618-85	Standard Specification for Fly Ash and Raw or Calcined Natural Pozzolan for Use as a Mineral Admixture in Portland Cement Concrete
C 637-84	Standard Specification for Aggregates for Radiation-Shielding Concrete
C 638-84	Standard Descriptive Nomenclature of Constituents of Aggregates for Radiation-Shielding Concrete
C 989-87a	Standard Specification for Granulated Blast-Furnace Slag for Use in Concrete and Mortars
C 1017-85	Standard Specification for Chemical Admixtures for Use in Producing Flowing Concrete
C 1064-86	Standard Test Method for Temperature of Freshly Mixed Portland-Cement Concrete
D 75-82	Standard Practice for Sampling Aggregates
D 3665-82	Standard Practice for Random Sampling of Construction Materials
E 380-84	Standard for Metric Practice

The above publications may be obtained from the following organizations:

American Concrete Institute
P.O. Box 19150
Detroit, MI 48219-0150

ASTM
1916 Race Street
Philadelphia, PA 19103

8.2 -- *Cited references*
1. "Silica Fume in Concrete," ACI Committee 226 Preliminary Report, ACI Materials Journal, *Proceedings* V. 84, Mar.-Apr. 1987, pp. 158-166.

8.3 -- *Additional references*
1. "Standard Practice for Concrete," *Engineer Manual* No. EM 1110-2-2000, Office, Chief of Engineers, U.S. Army Corps of Engineers, Washington, D.C., June 1974.
2. Gaynor, Richard D., "High-Strength Air-Entrained Concrete," *Joint Research Laboratory Publication* No. 17, National Ready Mixed Concrete Association/National Sand and Gravel Association, Silver Spring, 1968, 19 pp.
3. *Proportioning Concrete Mixes*, SP-46, American Concrete Institute, Detroit, 1974, 223 pp.

4. Townsend, Charles L., "Control of Temperature Cracking in Mass Concrete," *Causes, Mechanism, and Control of Cracking in Concrete*, SP-20, American Concrete Institute, Detroit, 1968, pp. 119-139.

5. Townsend, C. L., "Control of Cracking in Mass Concrete Structures," *Engineering Monograph* No. 34, U.S. Bureau of Reclamation, Denver, 1965.

6. Fuller, William B., and Thompson, Sanford E., "The Laws of Proportioning Concrete," *Transactions*, ASCE, V. 59, Dec. 1907, pp. 67-143.

7. Powers, Treval C., *The Properties of Fresh Concrete*, John Wiley & Sons, New York, 1968, pp. 246-256.

8. *Concrete Manual*, 8th Edition, U.S. Bureau of Reclamation, Denver, 1975, 627 pp.

9. Abrams, Duff A., "Design of Concrete Mixtures," *Bulletin* No. 1, Structural Materials Research Laboratory, Lewis Institute, Chicago, 1918, 20 pp.

10. Edwards, L. N., "Proportioning the Materials of Mortars and Concretes by Surface Areas of Aggregates," *Proceedings*, ASTM, V. 18, Part 2, 1918, p. 235.

11. Young, R. B., "Some Theoretical Studies on Proportioning Concrete by the Method of Surface Area Aggregate," *Proceedings*, ASTM, V. 19, Part 2, p. 1919.

12. Talbot, A. N., "A Proposed Method of Estimating the Density and Strength of Concrete and of Proportioning the Materials by Experimental and Analytical Consideration of the Voids in Mortar and Concrete," *Proceedings*, ASTM, V. 21, 1921, p. 940.

13. Weymouth, C. A. G., "A Study of Fine Aggregate in Freshly Mixed Mortars and Concretes," *Proceedings*, ASTM, V. 38, Part 2, 1938, pp. 354-372.

14. Dunagan, W. M., "The Application of Some of the Newer Concepts to the Design of Concrete Mixes," ACI Journal, *Proceedings* V. 36, No. 6, June 1940, pp. 649-684.

15. Goldbeck, A. T., and Gray, J. E., "A Method of Proportioning Concrete for Strength, Workability, and Durability," *Bulletin* No. 11, National Crushed Stone Association, Washington, D.C., Dec. 1942, 30 pp. (Revised 1953 and 1956).

16. Swayze, Myron A., and Gruenwald, Ernst, "Concrete Mix Design--A Modification of Fineness Modulus Method,"

ACI Journal, *Proceedings* V. 43, No. 7, Mar. 1947, pp. 829-844.

17. Walker, Stanton, and Bartel, Fred F., Discussion of "Concrete Mix Design--A Modification of the Fineness Modulus Method" by Myron A. Swayze and Ernst Gruenwald, ACI Journal, *Proceedings* V. 43, Part 2, Dec. 1947, pp. 844-1-844-17.

18. Henrie, James O., "Properties of Nuclear Shielding Concrete," ACI Journal, *Proceedings* V. 56, No. 1, July 1959, pp. 37-46.

19. Mather, Katharine, "High Strength, High Density Concrete," ACI Journal, *Proceedings* V. 62, No. 8, Aug. 1965, pp. 951-960.

20. Clendenning, T. G.; Kellam, B.; and MacInnis, C., "Hydrogen Evolution from Ferrophosphorous Aggregate in Portland Cement Concrete," ACI Journal, *Proceedings* V. 65, No. 12, Dec. 1968, pp. 1021-1028.

21. Popovics, Sandor, "Estimating Proportions for Structural Concrete Mixtures," ACI Journal, *Proceedings* V. 65, No. 2, Feb. 1968, pp. 143-150.

22. Davis, H. S., "Aggregates for Radiation Shielding Concrete," *Materials Research and Standards*, V. 7, No. 11, Nov. 1967, pp. 494-501.

23. *Concrete for Nuclear Reactors*, SP-34, American Concrete Institute, Detroit, 1972, 1736 pp.

24. Tynes, W. O., "Effect of Fineness of Continuously Graded Coarse Aggregate on Properties of Concrete," *Technical Report* No. 6-819, U.S. Army Engineer Waterways Experiment Station, Vicksburg, Apr. 1968, 28 pp.

25. *Handbook for Concrete and Cement*, CRD-C 3, U.S. Army Engineer Waterways Experiment Station, Vicksburg, 1949 (plus quarterly supplements).

26. Hansen, Kenneth, "Cost of Mass Concrete in Dams," *Publication* No. MS260W, Portland Cement Association, Skokie, 1973, 4 pp.

27. Canon, Robert W., "Proportioning Fly Ash Concrete Mixes for Strength and Economy," ACI Journal, *Proceedings* V. 65, No. 11, Nov. 1968, pp 969-979.

28. Butler, W. B., "Economical Binder Proportioning with Cement Replacement Materials," *Cement, Concrete, and Aggregates*, CCAGDP, V. 10, No. 1, Summer 1988, pp. 45-47.

APPENDIX 1 -- METRIC (SI) SYSTEM ADAPTATION

A1.1 Procedures outlined in this standard practice have been presented using inch-pound units of measurement. The principles are equally applicable in SI system with proper adaptation of units. This Appendix provides all of the information necessary to apply the proportioning procedure using SI measurements. Table A1.1 gives relevant conversion factors. A numerical example is presented in Appendix 2.

TABLE A1.1—CONVERSION FACTORS, in.-lb TO SI UNITS*

Quantity	in.-lb unit	SI† unit	Conversion factor (Ratio: in.-lb/SI)
Length	inch (in.)	millimeter (mm)	25.40
Volume	cubic foot (ft³)	cubic meter (m³)	0.02832
	cubic yard (yd³)	cubic meter (m³)	0.7646
Mass	pound (lb)	kilogram (kg)	0.4536
Stress	pounds per square inch (psi)	megapascal (MPa)	6.895 x 10⁻²
Density	pounds per cubic foot (lb/ft³)	kilograms per cubic meter (kg/m³)	16.02
	pounds per cubic yard (lb/yd³)	kilograms per cubic meter (kg/m³)	0.5933
Temperature	degrees Fahrenheit (F)	degrees Celsius (C)	‡

*Gives names (and abbreviations) of measurement units in the inch-pound system as used in the body of this report and in the SI (metric) system, along with multipliers for converting the former to the latter. From ASTM E 380.
†Systéme International d'Unites
‡C = (F − 32)/1.8

A1.2 For convenience of reference, numbering of subsequent paragraphs in this Appendix corresponds to the body of the report except that the designation "A1" is prefixed. All tables have been converted and reproduced. Descriptive portions are included only where use of the SI system requires a change in procedure or formula. To the extent practicable, conversions to metric units have been made in such a way that values are realistic in terms of usual practice and significance of numbers. For example, aggregate and sieve sizes in the metric tables are ones commonly used in Europe. Thus, there is not always a precise mathematical correspondence between inch-pound and SI values in corresponding tables.

A1.3 *Steps in calculating proportions* -- Except as discussed below, the methods for arriving at quantities of ingredients for a unit volume of concrete are essentially the same when SI units are employed as when inch-pound units are employed. The main difference is that the unit volume of concrete becomes the cubic meter and numerical values must be taken from the proper "A1" table instead of the one referred to in the text.

A1.5.3.1 *Step 1. Choice of slump* -- See Table A1.5.3.1.

TABLE A1.5.3.1 — RECOMMENDED SLUMPS FOR VARIOUS TYPES OF CONSTRUCTION (SI)

Types of construction	Slump. mm	
	Maximum*	Minimum
Reinforced foundation walls and footings	75	25
Plain footings, caissons, and substructure walls	75	25
Beams and reinforced walls	100	25
Building columns	100	25
Pavements and slabs	75	25
Mass concrete	75	25

*May be increased 25 mm for methods of consolidation other than vibration.

A1.5.3.2 *Step 2. Choice of nominal maximum size of aggregate.*

A1.5.3.3 *Step 3. Estimation of mixing water and air content* -- See Table A1.5.3.3.

A1.5.3.4 *Step 4. Selection of water-cement ratio* -- See Table A1.5.3.4.

A1.5.3.5 *Step 5. Calculation of cement content.*

A1.5.3.6 *Step 6. Estimation of coarse aggregate content* -- The dry mass of coarse aggregate required for a cubic meter of concrete is equal to the value from Table A1.5.3.6 multiplied by the dry-rodded unit mass of the aggregate in kilograms per cubic meter.

A1.5.3.7 *Step 7. Estimation of fine aggregate content* -- In the SI, the formula for calculation of fresh concrete mass per cubic meter is:

$$U_M = 10G_a(100 - A) + C_M(1 - G_a/G_c) - W_M(G_a - 1)$$

where

U_M = unit mass of fresh concrete, kg/m³
G_a = weighted average specific gravity of combined fine and coarse aggregate, bulk, SSD
G_c = specific gravity of cement (generally 3.15)
A = air content, percent
W_M = mixing water requirement, kg/m³
C_M = cement requirement, kg/m³

A1.5.3.9 *Step 9. Trial batch adjustments* -- The following "rules of thumb" may be used to arrive at closer approximations of unit batch quantities based on results for a trial batch:

A1.5.3.9.1 The estimated mixing water to produce the same slump as the trial batch will be equal to the net amount of mixing water used divided by the yield of the trial batch in m³. If slump of the trial batch was not correct, increase or decrease the re-estimated water content by 2 kg/m³ of concrete for each increase or decrease of 10 mm in slump desired.

A1.5.3.9.2 To adjust for the effect of

TABLE A1.5.3.3 — APPROXIMATE MIXING WATER AND AIR CONTENT REQUIREMENTS FOR DIFFERENT SLUMPS AND NOMINAL MAXIMUM SIZES OF AGGREGATES (SI)

Slump, mm	Water, Kg/m³ of concrete for indicated nominal maximum sizes of aggregate							
	9.5*	12.5*	19*	25*	37.5*	50†*	75†‡	150†‡
Non-air-entrained concrete								
25 to 50	207	199	190	179	166	154	130	113
75 to 100	228	216	205	193	181	169	145	124
150 to 175	243	228	216	202	190	178	160	—
Approximate amount of entrapped air in non-air-entrained concrete, percent	3	2.5	2	1.5	1	0.5	0.3	0.2
Air-entrained concrete								
25 to 50	181	175	168	160	150	142	122	107
75 to 100	202	193	184	175	165	157	133	119
150 to 175	216	205	197	184	174	166	154	—
Recommended average§ total air content, percent for level of exposure:								
Mild exposure	4.5	4.0	3.5	3.0	2.5	2.0	1.5**††	1.0**††
Moderate exposure	6.0	5.5	5.0	4.5	4.5	4.0	3.5**††	3.0**††
Extreme exposure‡‡	7.5	7.0	6.0	6.0	5.5	5.0	4.5**††	4.0**††

*The quantities of mixing water given for air-entrained concrete are based on typical total air content requirements as shown for "moderate exposure" in the Table above. These quantities of mixing water are for use in computing cement contents for trial batches at 20 to 25 C. They are maximum for reasonably well-shaped angular aggregates graded within limits of accepted specifications. Rounded coarse aggregate will generally require 18 kg less water for non-air-entrained and 15 kg less for air-entrained concretes. The use of water-reducing chemcial admixtures, ASTM C 494, may also reduce mixing water by 5 percent or more. The volume of the liquid admixtures is included as part of the total volume of the mixing water.

†The slump values for concrete containing aggregate larger than 40 mm are based on slump tests made after removal of particles larger than 40 mm by wet-screening.

‡These quantities of mixing water are for use in computing cement factors for trial batches when 75 mm or 150 mm normal maximum size aggregate is used. They are average for reasonably well-shaped coarse aggregates, well-graded from coarse to fine.

§Additional recommendations for air-content and necessary tolerances on air content for control in the field are given in a number of ACI documents, including ACI 201, 345, 318, 301, and 302. ASTM C 94 for ready-mixed concrete also gives air content limits. The requirements in other documents may not always agree exactly so in proportioning concrete consideration must be given to selecting an air content that will meet the needs of the job and also meet the applicable specifications.

**For concrete containing large aggregates which will be wet-screened over the 40 mm sieve prior to testing for air content, the percentage of air expected in the 40 mm minus material should be as tabulated in the 40 mm column. However, initial proportioning calculations should include the air content as a percent of the whole.

††When using large aggregate in low cement factor concrete, air entrainment need not be detrimental to strength. In most cases mixing water requirement is reduced sufficiently to improve the water-cement ratio and to thus compensate for the strength reducing effect of entrained air concrete. Generally, therefore, for these large nominal maximum sizes of aggregate, air contents recommended for extreme exposure should be considered even though there may be little or no exposure to moisture and freezing.

‡‡These values are based on the criteria that 9 percent air is needed in the mortar phase of the concrete. If the mortar volume will be substantially different from that determined in this recommended practice, it may be desirable to calculate the needed air content by taking 9 percent of the actual mortar volume.

TABLE A1.5.3.4(a) — RELATIONSHIPS BETWEEN WATER-CEMENT RATIO AND COMPRESSIVE STRENGTH OF CONCRETE (SI)

Compressive strength at 28 days, MPa*	Water-cement ratio, by mass	
	Non-air-entrained concrete	Air-entrained concrete
40	0.42	—
35	0.47	0.39
30	0.54	0.45
25	0.61	0.52
20	0.69	0.60
15	0.79	0.70

*Values are estimated average strengths for concrete containing not more than 2 percent air for non-air-entrained concrete and 6 percent total air content for air-entrained concrete. For a constant water-cement ratio, the strength of concrete is reduced as the air content is increased.

Strength is based on 152 × 305 mm cylinders moist-cured for 28 days in accordance with the sections on "Initial Curing" and "Curing of Cylinders for Checking the Adequacy of Laboratory Mixture Proportions for Strength or as the Basis for Acceptance or for Quality Control" of ASTM Method C 31 for Making and Curing Concrete Specimens in the Field. These are cylinders cured moist at 23 ± 1.7 C prior to testing.

The relationship in this Table assumes a nominal maximum aggregate size of about 19 to 25 mm. For a given source of aggregate, strength produced at a given water-cement ratio will increase as nominal maximum size of aggregate decreases; see Sections 3.4 and 5.3.2.

incorrect air content in a trial batch of air-entrained concrete on slump, reduce or increase the mixing water content of A1.5.3.9.1 by 3 kg/m³ of concrete for each 1 percent by which the air content is to be increased or decreased from that of the trial batch.

A1.5.3.9.3 The re-estimated unit mass of the fresh concrete for adjustment of trial batch proportions is equal to the unit mass in kg/m³ measured on the trial batch, reduced or increased by the percentage increase or decrease in air content of the adjusted batch from the first trial batch.

TABLE A1.5.3.4(b) — MAXIMUM PERMISSIBLE WATER-CEMENT RATIOS FOR CONCRETE IN SEVERE EXPOSURES (SI)*

Type of structure	Structure wet continuously or frequently and exposed to freezing and thawing†	Structure exposed to sea water or sulfates
Thin sections (railings, curbs, sills, ledges, ornamental work) and sections with less than 5 mm cover over steel	0.45	0.40‡
All other structures	0.50	0.45‡

*Based on ACI 201.2R.

†Concrete should also be air-entrained.

‡If sulfate resisting cement (Type II or Type V of ASTM C 150) is used, permissible water-cement ratio may be increased by 0.05.

TABLE A1.5.3.6 — VOLUME OF COARSE AGGREGATE PER UNIT OF VOLUME OF CONCRETE (SI)

Nominal maximum size of aggregate, mm	Volume of dry-rodded coarse aggregate* per unit volume of concrete for different fineness moduli† of fine aggregate			
	2.40	2.60	2.80	3.00
9.5	0.50	0.48	0.46	0.44
12.5	0.59	0.57	0.55	0.53
19	0.66	0.64	0.62	0.60
25	0.71	0.69	0.67	0.65
37.5	0.75	0.73	0.71	0.69
50	0.78	0.76	0.74	0.72
75	0.82	0.80	0.78	0.76
150	0.87	0.85	0.83	0.81

*Volumes are based on aggregates in dry-rodded condition as described in ASTM C 29.

These volumes are selected from empirical relationships to produce concrete with a degree of workability suitable for usual reinforced construction. For less workable concrete such as required for concrete pavement construction they may be increased about 10 percent. For more workable concrete, such as may sometimes be required when placement is to be by pumping, they may be reduced up to 10 percent.

†See ASTM Method 136 for calculation of fineness modulus.

TABLE A1.5.3.7.1 — FIRST ESTIMATE OF MASS OF FRESH CONCRETE (SI)

Nominal maximum size of aggregate, mm	First estimate of concrete unit mass, kg/m³*	
	Non-air-entrained concrete	Air-entrained concrete
9.5	2280	2200
12.5	2310	2230
19	2345	2275
25	2380	2290
37.5	2410	2350
50	2445	2345
75	2490	2405
150	2530	2435

*Values calculated by Eq. (A1.5.3.7) for concrete of medium richness (330 kg of cement per m³) and medium slump with aggregate specific gravity of 2.7. Water requirements based on values for 75 to 100 mm slump in Table A1.5.3.3. If desired, the estimate of unit mass may be refined as follows if necessary information is available: for each 5 kg difference in mixing water from the Table A1.5.3.3 values for 75 to 100 mm slump, correct the mass per m³ 8 kg in the opposite direction; for each 20 kg difference in cement content from 330 kg, correct the mass per m³ 3 kg in the same direction; for each 0.1 by which aggregate specific gravity deviates from 2.7, correct the concrete mass 60 kg in the same direction. For air-entrained concrete the air content for severe exposure from Table A.1.5.3.3 was used. The mass can be increased 1 percent for each percent reduction in air content from that amount.

APPENDIX 2 -- EXAMPLE PROBLEM IN METRIC (SI) SYSTEM

A2.1 *Example 1* -- Example 1 presented in Section 6.2 will be solved here using metric units of measure. Required average strength will be 24 MPa with slump of 75 to 100 mm. The coarse aggregate has a nominal maximum size of 37.5 mm and dry-rodded mass of 1600 kg/m³. As stated in Section 6.1, other properties of the ingredients are: cement -- Type I with specific gravity of 3.15; coarse aggregate -- bulk specific gravity 2.68 and absorption 0.5 percent; fine aggregate -- bulk specific gravity 2.64, absorption 0.7 percent, and fineness modulus 2.8.

A2.2 All steps of Section 5.3 should be followed in sequence to avoid confusion, even though they sometimes merely restate information already given.

A2.2.1 *Step 1* -- The slump is required to be 75 to 100 mm.

A2.2.2 *Step 2* -- The aggregate to be used has a nominal maximum size of 37.5 mm.

A2.2.3 *Step 3* -- The concrete will be non-air-entrained since the structure is not exposed to severe weathering. From Table A1.5.3.3, the estimated mixing water for a slump of 75 to 100 mm in non-air-entrained concrete made with 37.5 mm aggregate is found to be 181 kg/m³.

A2.2.4 *Step 4* -- The water-cement ratio for non-air-entrained concrete with a strength of 24 MPa is found from Table A1.5.3.4(a) to be 0.62.

A2.2.5 *Step 5* -- From the information developed in Steps 3 and 4, the required cement content is found to be 181/0.62 = 292 kg/m³.

A2.2.6 *Step 6* -- The quantity of coarse aggregate is estimated from Table A 1.5.3.6. For a fine aggregate having a fineness modulus of 2.8 and a 37.5 mm nominal maximum size of coarse aggregate, the table indicates that 0.71 m³ of coarse aggregate, on a dry-rodded basis, may be used in each cubic meter of concrete. The required dry mass is, therefore, 0.71 x 1600 = 1136 kg.

A2.2.7 *Step 7* -- With the quantities of water, cement and coarse aggregate established, the remaining material comprising the cubic meter of concrete must consist of fine aggregate and whatever air will be entrapped. The required fine aggregate may be determined on the basis of either mass or absolute volume as shown below:

A2.2.7.1 *Mass basis* -- From Table A1.5.3.7.1, the mass of a cubic meter of non-air-entrained concrete made with aggregate having a nominal maximum size of 37.5 mm is estimated to be 2410 kg. (For a first trial batch, exact adjustments of this value for usual differences in slump, cement factor, and aggregate specific gravity are not critical.) Masses already known are:

Water (net mixing)	181 kg
Cement	292 kg
Coarse aggregate	1136 kg
Total	1609 kg

The mass of fine aggregate, therefore, is estimated to be

$$2410 - 1609 = 801 \text{ kg}$$

A2.2.7.2 *Absolute volume basis* -- With the quantities of cement, water, and coarse aggregate established, and the approximate entrapped air content (as opposed to purposely entrained air) of 1 percent determined from Table A1.5.3.3, the sand content can be calculated as follows:

$$\text{Volume of water} = \frac{181}{1000} = 0.181 \text{ m}^3$$

$$\text{Solid volume of cement} = \frac{292}{3.15 \times 1000} = 0.093 \text{ m}^3$$

Solid volume
of coarse = $\dfrac{1136}{2.68 \times 1000}$ 0.424 m³
aggregate

Volume of entrapped
air = 0.01 x 1.000   0.010 m³

Total solid volume
of ingredients except
fine aggregate   0.708 m³

Solid volume of
fine aggregate
required = 1.000 - 0.705   0.292 m³

Required weight
of dry = 0.292 x 2.64
fine aggregate   x 1000   771 kg

A2.2.7.3 Batch masses per cubic meter of concrete calculated on the two bases are compared below:

	Based on estimated concrete mass, kg	Based on absolute volume of ingredients, kg
Water (net mixing)	181	181
Cement	292	292
Coarse aggregate (dry)	1136	1136
Sand (dry)	801	771

A2.2.8 *Step 8* -- Tests indicate total moisture of 2 percent in the coarse aggregate and 6 percent in the fine aggregate. If the trial batch proportions based on assumed concrete mass are used, the adjusted aggregate masses become

Coarse aggregate (wet) = 1136(1.02) = 1159 kg
Fine aggregates (wet) = 801(1.06) = 849 kg

Absorbed water does not become part of the mixing water and must be excluded from the adjustment in added water. Thus, surface water contributed by the coarse aggregate amounts to 2 - 0.5 = 1.5 percent; by the fine aggregate 6 - 0.7 = 5.3 percent. The estimated requirement for added water, therefore, becomes

181 - 1136(0.015) - 801(0.053) = 122 kg

The estimated batch masses for a cubic meter of concrete are:

Water (to be added)	122 kg
Cement	292 kg
Coarse aggregate (wet)	1159 kg

Fine aggregate (wet)	849 kg
Total	2422 kg

A2.2.9 *Step 9* -- For the laboratory trial batch, it is found convenient to scale the masses down to produce 0.02 m³ of concrete. Although the calculated quantity of water to be added was 2.44 kg, the amount actually used in an effort to obtain the desired 75 to 100 mm slump is 2.70 kg. The batch as mixed, therefore, consists of

Water (added)	2.70 kg
Cement	5.84 kg
Coarse aggregate (wet)	23.18 kg
Fine aggregate (wet)	16.98 kg
Total	48.70 kg

The concrete has a measured slump of 50 mm and unit mass of 2390 kg/m³. It is judged to be satisfactory from the standpoint of workability and finishing properties. To provide proper yield and other characteristics for future batches, the following adjustments are made:

A2.2.9.1 Since the yield of the trial batch was

$$48.70/2390 = 0.0204 \text{ m}^3$$

and the mixing water content was 2.70 (added) + 0.34 (on coarse aggregate) + 0.84 (on fine aggregate) = 3.88 kg, the mixing water required for a cubic meter of concrete with the same slump as the trial batch should be

$$3.88/0.0204 = 190 \text{ kg}$$

As indicated in A1.5.3.9.1, this amount must be increased another 8 kg to raise the slump from the measured 50 mm to the desired 75 to 100 mm range, bringing the total mixing water to 198 kg.

A2.2.9.2 With the increased mixing water, additional cement will be required to provide the desired water-cement ratio of 0.62. The new cement content becomes

$$198/0.62 = 319 \text{ kg}$$

A2.2.9.3 Since workability was found to be satisfactory, the quantity of coarse aggregate per unit volume of concrete will be maintained the same as in the trial batch. The amount of coarse aggregate per cubic meter becomes

$$\frac{23.18}{0.0204} = 1136 \ kg \ wet$$

which is

$$\frac{1136}{1.02} = 1114 \; kg \; dry$$

$$\frac{23.18}{0.0202} = 1153 \; kg \; wet$$

and

$$1114 \times 1.005 = 1120 \; kg \; SSD*$$

A2.2.9.4 The new estimate for the mass of a cubic meter of concrete is the measured unit mass of 2390 kg/m³. The amount of fine aggregate required is, therefore

$$2390 - (198 + 319 + 1120) = 753 \; kg \; SSD*$$

or

$$753/1.007 = 748 \; kg \; dry$$

The adjusted basic batch masses per cubic meter of concrete are

Water (net mixing)	198 kg
Cement	319 kg
Coarse aggregate (dry)	1114 kg
Fine aggregate (dry)	748 kg

A2.2.10 Adjustments of proportions determined on an absolute volume basis follow a procedure similar to that just outlined. The steps will be given without detailed explanation:

A2.2.10.1 Quantities used in the nominal 0.02 m³ batch are

Water (added)	2.70 kg
Cement	5.84 kg
Coarse aggregate (wet)	23.18 kg
Fine aggregate (wet)	16.34 kg
Total	48.08 kg

Measured slump 50 mm; unit mass 2390 kg/m³; yield 48.08/2390 = 0.0201 m³; workability o.k.

A2.2.10.2 Re-estimated water for same slump as trial batch:

$$\frac{2.70 + 0.34 + 0.81}{0.0201} = 192 \; kg$$

Mixing water required for slump of 75 to 100 mm:

$$192 + 8 = 200 \; kg$$

A2.2.10.3 Adjusted cement content for increased water:

$$200/0.62 = 323 \; kg$$

A2.2.10.4 Adjusted coarse aggregate requirement:

---
* Saturated-surface-dry.

$$\frac{1163}{0.0202} = 1153 \; kg \; wet$$

or

$$1163/1.02 = 1130 \; kg \; dry$$

A2.2.10.5 The volume of ingredients other than air in the original trial batch was

Water	$\dfrac{3.85}{1000}$	$= 0.0039 \; m^3$
Cement	$\dfrac{5.84}{3.15 \times 1000}$	$= 0.0019 \; m^3$
Coarse aggregate	$\dfrac{22.72}{2.68 \times 1000}$	$= 0.0085 \; m^3$
Fine aggregate	$\dfrac{15.42}{2.64 \times 1000}$	$= \underline{0.0058 \; m^3}$

Total	0.0201 m³

Since the yield was also 0.0201 m³, there was no air in the concrete detectable within the precision of the unit mass test and significant figures of the calculations. With the proportions of all components except fine aggregate established, the determination of adjusted cubic meter batch quantities can be completed as follows:

Volume of water	=	$\dfrac{200}{1000}$	= 0.200 m³
Volume of cement	=	$\dfrac{323}{3.15 \times 1000}$	= 0.103 m³
Allowance for volume of cement			= 0.000 m³
Volume of coarse aggregate	=	$\dfrac{1130}{2.68 \times 1000}$	= $\underline{0.422 \; m^3}$
Total volume exclusive of fine aggregate			= 0.725 m³
Volume of fine aggregate required	=	1.000 - 0.725	= 0.275 m³
Mass of fine aggregate (dry basis)	=	0.275 × 2.64 × 1000	= 726 kg

The adjusted basic batch weights per cubic meter of concrete, then, are:

Water (net mixing)	200 kg

Cement	323 kg
Coarse aggregate (dry)	1130 kg
Fine aggregate (dry)	726 kg

These differ only slightly from those given in Paragraph A2.2.9.4 for the method of assumed concrete weight. Further trials or experience might indicate small additional adjustments for either method.

APPENDIX 3 -- LABORATORY TESTS

A.3.1 Selection of concrete mix proportions can be accomplished effectively from results of laboratory tests which determine basic physical properties of materials to be used, establish relationships between water-cement ratio or water to cement and pozzolan ratio, air content, cement content, and strength, and which furnish information on the workability characteristics of various combinations of ingredient materials. The extent of investigation desirable for any given job will depend on its size and importance and on the service conditions involved. Details of the laboratory program will also vary, depending on facilities available and on individual preferences.

A3.2 *Properties of cement*

A3.2.1 Physical and chemical characteristics of cement influence the properties of hardened concrete. However, the only property of cement used directly in computation of concrete mix proportions is specific gravity. The specific gravity of portland cements of the types covered by ASTM C 150 and C 175 may usually be assumed to be 3.15 without introducing appreciable error in mix computations. For other types such as the blended hydraulic cements of ASTM C 595, slag cement in C 989 or pozzolan covered in C 618, the specific gravity for use in volume calculations should be determined by test.

A3.2.2 A sample of cement should be obtained from the mill which will supply the job, or preferably from the concrete supplier. The sample should be ample for tests contemplated with a liberal margin for additional tests that might later be considered desirable. Cement samples should be shipped in airtight containers, or at least in moisture-proof packages. Pozzolans should also be carefully sampled.

A3.3 *Properties of aggregate*

A3.3.1 Sieve analysis, specific gravity, absorption, and moisture content of both fine and coarse aggregate and dry-rodded unit weight of coarse aggregate are physical properties useful for mix computations. Other tests which may be desirable for large or special types of work include petrographic examination and tests for chemical reactivity, soundness, durability, resistance to abrasion, and various deleterious substances. Such tests yield information of value in judging the long-range serviceability of concrete.

A3.3.2 Aggregate gradation as measured by the sieve analysis is a major factor in determining unit water requirement, proportions of coarse aggregate and sand, and cement content for satisfactory workability. Numerous "ideal" aggregate grading curves have been proposed, and these, tempered by practical considerations, have formed the basis for typical sieve analysis requirements in concrete standards. ASTM C 33 provides a selection of sizes and gradings suitable for most concrete. Additional workability realized by use of air-entrainment permits, to some extent, the use of less restrictive aggregate gradations.

A3.3.3 Samples for concrete mix tests should be representative of aggregate available for use in the work. For laboratory tests, the coarse aggregates should be separated into required size fractions and reconstituted at the time of mixing to assure representative grading for the small test batches. Under some conditions, for work of important magnitude, laboratory investigation may involve efforts to overcome grading deficiencies of the available aggregates. Undesirable sand grading may be corrected by (1) separation of the sand into two or more size fractions and recombining in suitable proportions; (2) increasing or decreasing the quantity of certain sizes to balance the grading; or (3) reducing excess coarse material by grinding or crushing. Undesirable coarse-aggregate gradings may be corrected by: (1) crushing excess coarser fractions; (2) wasting sizes that occur in excess; (3) supplementing deficient sizes from other sources; or (4) a combination of these methods. Whatever grading adjustments are made in the laboratory should be practical and economically justified from the standpoint of job operation. Usually, required aggregate grading should be consistent with that of economically available materials.

A3.4 *Trial batch series*

A3.4.1 The tabulated relationships in the body of this report may be used to make rough estimates of batch quantities for a trial mix. However, they are too generalized to apply with a high degree of accuracy to a specific set of materials. If facilities are available, therefore, it is advisable to make a series of concrete tests to establish quantitative relationships for the materials to be used. An illustration of such a test program is shown in Table A3.4.1.

A3.4.2 First, a batch of medium cement content and usable consistency is proportioned by the described methods. In preparing Mix No. 1, an amount of water is used which will produce the desired slump even if this differs from the estimated requirement. The fresh concrete is tested for slump and unit weight and observed closely for workability and finishing characteristics. In the example, the yield is too high and the concrete is judged to contain an excess of fine aggregate.

A3.4.3 Mix No. 2 is prepared, adjusted to correct the errors in Mix No. 1, and the testing and evaluation repeated. In this case, the desired properties are achieved within close tolerances and cylinders are molded to check the compressive strength. The information derived so far can now be used to select proportions for a series of additional mixes, No. 3 to 6, with cement contents above and below that of Mix No. 2, encompassing the range likely to be needed. Reasonable

TABLE A3.4.1 — TYPICAL TEST PROGRAM TO ESTABLISH CONCRETE-MAKING PROPERTIES OF LOCAL MATERIALS

| | Cubic yard batch quantities, lb | | | | | | Concrete characteristics | | | | |
| Mix No. | Cement | Sand | Coarse Aggregate | Water | | Total used | Slump in. | Unit wt., lb per cu ft | Yield cu ft | 28-day Compressive strength, psi | Work-ability |
				Estimated	Used						
1	500	1375	1810	325	350	4035	4	147.0	27.45	—	Oversanded
2	500	1250	1875	345	340	3965	3	147.0	26.97	3350	o.k.
3	400	1335	1875	345	345	3955	4.5	145.5	27.18	2130	o.k.
4	450	1290	1875	345	345	3960	4	146.2	27.09	2610	o.k.
5	550	1210	1875	345	345	3980	3	147.5	26.98	3800	o.k.
6	600	1165	1875	345	345	3985	3.5	148.3	26.87	4360	o.k.

refinement in these batch weights can be achieved with the help of corrections given in the notes to Table 6.3.7.1.

A3.4.4 Mix No. 2 to 6 provide the background, including the relationship of strength to water-cement ratio for theparticular combination of ingredients, needed to select proportions for a range of specified requirements.

A3.4.5 In laboratory tests, it seldom will be found, even by experienced operators, that desired adjustments will develop as smoothly as indicated in Table A3.4.1. Furthermore, it should not be expected that field results will check exactly with laboratory results. An adjustment of the selected trial mix on the job is usually necessary. Closer agreement between laboratory and field will be assured if machine mixing is employed in the laboratory. This is especially desirable if air-entraining agents are used since the type of mixer influences the amount of air entrained. Before mixing the first batch, the laboratory mixer should be "buttered" or the mix "overmortared" as described in ASTM C 192. Similarly, any processing of materials in the laboratory should simulate as closely as practicable corresponding treatment in the field.

A3.4.6 The series of tests illustrated in Table A3.4.1 may be expanded as the size and special requirements of the work warrant. Variables that may require investigation include: alterative aggregate sources; maximum sizes and gradings; different types and brands of cement; pozzolans; admixtures; and considerations of concrete durability, volume change, temperature rise, and thermal properties.

A3.5 *Test methods*

A3.5.1 In conducting laboratory tests to provide information for selecting concrete proportions, the latest revisions of the following methods should be used:

A3.5.1.1 For tests of ingredients:

Sampling hydraulic cement--ASTM C 183

Specific gravity of hydraulic cement--ASTM C 188

Sampling stone, slag, gravel, sand, and stone block for use as highway materials--ASTM D 75

Sieve or screen analysis of fine and coarse aggregates--ASTM C 136

Specific gravity and absorption of coarse aggregates--ASTM C 127

Specific gravity and absorption of fine aggregates--ASTM C 128

Surface moisture in fine aggregate--ASTM C 70

Total moisture content of aggregate by drying--ASTM C

Unit weight of aggregate--ASTM C 29

Voids in aggregate for concrete--ASTM C 29

Fineness modulus--Terms relating to concrete and concrete aggregates, ASTM C 125

A3.5.1.2 For tests of concrete:

Sampling fresh concrete--ASTM C 172

Air content of freshly mixed concrete by the volumetric method--ASTM C 173

Air content of freshly mixed concrete by the pressure method--ASTM C 231

Slump of portland cement concrete--ASTM C 143

Weight per cubic foot, yield, and air content (gravimetric) of concrete--ASTM C 138

Concrete compression and flexure test specimens, making and curing in the laboratory--ASTM C 192

Compressive strength of molded concrete cylinders--ASTM C 39

TABLE A3.6.1 — CONCRETE MIXES FOR SMALL JOBS

Procedure: Select the proper nominal maximum size of aggregate (see Section 5.3.2). Use Mix B, adding just enough water to produce a workable consistency. If the concrete appears to be undersanded, change to Mix A and, if it appears oversanded, change to Mix C.

| Nominal maximum size of aggregate, in. | Approximate weights of solid ingredients per cu ft of concrete, lb | | | | | |
| | Mix designation | Cement | Sand* | | Coarse aggregate | |
			Air-entrained concrete†	Concrete without air	Gravel or crushed stone	Iron blast furnace slag
½	A	25	48	51	54	47
	B	25	46	49	56	49
	C	25	44	47	58	51
¾	A	23	45	49	62	54
	B	23	43	47	64	56
	C	23	41	45	66	58
1	A	22	41	45	70	61
	B	22	39	43	72	63
	C	22	37	41	74	65
1½	A	20	41	45	75	65
	B	20	39	43	77	67
	C	20	37	41	79	69
2	A	19	40	45	79	69
	B	19	38	43	81	71
	C	19	36	41	83	72

*Weights are for dry sand. If damp sand is used, increase tabulated weight of sand 2 lb and, if very wet sand is used, 4 lb.

†Air-entrained concrete should be used in all structures which will be exposed to alternate cycles of freezing and thawing. Air-entrainment can be obtained by the use of an air-entraining cement or by adding an air-entraining admixture. If an admixture is used, the amount recommended by the manufacturer will, in most cases, produce the desired air content.

Flexural strength of concrete (using simple beam with third-point loading)--ASTM C 78

Flexural strength of concrete (using simple beam with center point loading--ASTM C 293

Splitting tensile strength of molded concrete cylinders--ASTM C 496

A3.6 *Mixes for small jobs*

A3.6.1 For small jobs where time and personnel are not available to determine proportions in accordance with the recommended procedure, mixes in Table A3.6.1 will usually provide concrete that is amply strong and durable if the amount of water added at the mixer is never large enough to make the concrete overwet. These mixes have been predetermined in conformity with the recommended procedure by assuming conditions applicable to the average small job, and for aggregate of medium specific gravity.

Three mixes are given for each nominal maximum size of coarse aggregate. For the selected size of coarse aggregate, Mix B is intended for initial use. If this mix proves to be oversanded, change to Mix C; if it is undersanded, change to Mix A. It should be noted that the mixes listed in the table are based on dry or surface-dry sand. If the fine aggregate is moist or wet, make the corrections in batch weight prescribed in the footnote.

A3.6.2 The approximate cement content per cubic foot of concrete listed in the table will be helpful in estimating cement requirements for the job. These requirements are based on concrete that has just enough water in it to permit ready working into forms without objectionable segregation. Concrete should slide, not run, off a shovel.

APPENDIX 4 -- HEAVYWEIGHT CONCRETE MIX PROPORTIONING

A4.1 Concrete of normal placeability can be proportioned for densities as high as 350 lb per cu ft by using heavy aggregates such as iron ore, iron or steel shot, barite, and iron or steel punchings. Although each of the materials has its own special characteristics, they can be processed to meet the standard requirements for grading, soundness cleanliness, etc. The selection of the aggregate should depend on its intended use. In the case of radiation shielding, determination should be made of trace elements within the material which may become reactive when subjected to radiation. In the selection of materials and proportioning of heavyweight concrete, the data needed and procedures used are similar to those required for normal weight concrete.

Aggregate density and composition for heavyweight concrete should meet requirements of ASTM C 637 and C 638. The following items should be considered.

A4.1.1 Typical materials used as heavy aggregates are listed in Table A4.1.1.

A4.1.2 If the concrete in service is to be exposed to a hot, dry environment resulting in loss of weight, it should be proportioned so that the fresh unit weight is higher than the required dry unit weight by the amount of the anticipated loss determined by performing an oven dry unit weight on concrete cylinders as follows. Three cylinders are cast and the wet unit weight determined in accordance with ASTM C 138. After 72 hours of standard curing, the cylinders are oven dried to a constant weight at 211 to 230 F and the average unit weight determined. The amount of water lost is determined by subtracting the oven dry unit weight from the wet unit weight. This difference is added to the required dry unit weight when calculating mixture proportions to allow for this loss. Normally, a freshly mixed unit weight is 8 to 10 lb per cu ft higher than the oven dry unit weight[2].

A4.1.3 If entrained air is required to resist conditions of exposure, allowance must be made for the loss in weight due to the space occupied by the air. To compensate for the loss of entrained air as a result of vibration, the concrete mixture should be proportioned with a higher air content to anticipate this loss.

A4.2 Handling of heavyweight aggregates should be in accordance with ACI 304.3R. (See also ASTM C 637 and C 638.) Proportioning of heavyweight concrete to be placed by conventional means can be accomplished in accordance with ACI 211.1 Sections 5.2 through 5.3.7 and the absolute volume method in Section 5.3.7.2. Typical proportions are shown in Table 2 of ACI 304.3R.

A4.3 *Preplaced heavyweight concrete* -- Heavyweight preplaced-aggregate concrete should be proportioned in the same manner as normal weight preplaced-aggregate concrete. (Refer to ACI 304, Table 7.3.2 -- Gradation limits for fine and coarse aggregate for preplaced aggregate concrete.) Example mixture proportions for the preplaced-aggregate method are shown in ACI 304.3R, Table 2 -- Typical proportions for high density concrete, and typical grout proportions can be found in ACI 304.3R, Table 3 -- Typical grout proportions.

A4.4 *Example* -- Concrete is required for counterweights on a lift bridge that will not be subjected to freezing and

TABLE A4.1.1—TYPICAL HEAVYWEIGHT AGGREGATES

Material	Description	Specific gravity	Concrete, unit wt (lb/cu ft)
Limonite Goethite	Hydrous iron ores	3.4-3.8	180-195
Barite	Barium sulfate	4.0-4.4	205-225
Ilmenite Hematite Magnetite	Iron ores	4.2-5.0	215-240
Steel/iron	Shot, pellets, punchings, etc.	6.5-7.5	310-350

Note: Ferrophosphorous and ferrosilicon (heavyweight slags) materials should be used only after thorough investigation. Hydrogen gas evolution in heavyweight concrete containing these aggregates has been known to result from a reaction with the cement.

thawing conditions. An average 28 day compressive strength of 4500 psi will be required. Placement conditions permit a slump of 2 to 3 in. at point of placement and a nominal maximum size aggregate of 1 in. The design of the counterweight requires* an oven dry unit weight of 225 lb per cu ft. An investigation of economically available materials has indicated the following:

Cement	ASTM C 150 Type I (non-air-entraining)
Fine aggregate	Specular hematite
Coarse aggregate	Ilmenite

Table A4.1.1 indicates that this combination of materials may result in an oven dry unit weight of 215 to 240 lb per cu ft. The following properties of the aggregates have been obtained from laboratory tests.

	Fine aggregate	Coarse aggregate
Fineness modulus	2.30	--
Specific gravity (Bulk SSD)	4.95	4.61
Absorption (percent)	0.05	0.08
Dry rodded weight	--	165 lb per cu ft
Nominal maximum size	--	1 in.

Employing the sequence outlined in Section 5 of this standard practice, the quantities of ingredients per cubic yard of concrete are calculated as follows:

A4.4.1 *Step 1* -- As indicated, the desired slump is 2 to 3 in. at point of placement.

A4.4.2 *Step 2* -- The available aggregate sources have been indicated as suitable, and the course aggregate will be a well-graded and well-shaped crushed ilmenite with a nominal maximum size of 1 in. The fine aggregate will be hematite.

A4.4.3 *Step 3* -- By interpolation in Table 6.3.3, non-air-entrained concrete with a 2 to 3 in. slump and a 1 in. nominal maximum size aggregate requires a water content of approximately 310 lb per cu yd. The estimated entrapped air is 1.5 percent. (Non-air-entrained concrete will be used because (1) the concrete is not to be exposed to severe weather, and (2) a high air content could reduce the dry unit weight of the concrete.)

Note: Values given in Table 6.3.3 for water requirement are based on the use of well-shaped crushed coarse aggregates. Void content of compacted dry fine or coarse aggregate can be used as an indicator of angularity. Void contents of compacted 1 in. coarse aggregate of significantly more than 40 percent indicate angular material that will probably require more water than that listed in Table 5.3.3. Conversely, rounded aggregates with voids below 35 percent will probably need less water.

---

* Oven dry is specified and is considered a more conservative value than that of the air dry.

A4.4.4 *Step 4* -- From Table 6.3.4(a) the water-cement ratio needed to produce a strength of 4500 psi in non-air-entrained concrete is found to be approximately 0.52.

A4.4.5 *Step 5* -- From the information derived in Steps 3 and 4, the required cement content is calculated to be 310/0.52 = 596 lb per cu yd.

A4.4.6 *Step 6* -- The quantity of coarse aggregate is estimated by extrapolation from Table 6.3.6. For a fine aggregate having a fineness modulus of 2.30 and a 1 in. nominal maximum size aggregate, the table indicates that 0.72 cu ft of coarse aggregate, on a dry-rodded basis, may be used in each cubic foot of concrete. For a cubic yard, therefore, the coarse aggregate will be 27 x 0.72 = 19.44 cu ft, and since the dry-rodded unit weight of coarse aggregate is 165 lb per cu ft, the dry weight of coarse aggregate to be used in a cubic yard of concrete will be 19.44 x 165 = 3208 lb. The angularity of the coarse aggregate is compensated for in the ACI proportioning method through the use of the dry-rodded unit weight; however, the use of an extremely angular fine aggregate may require a higher proportion of fine aggregate, an increased cement content, or the use of air entrainment to produce the required workability. The use of entrained air reduces the unit weight of the concrete, but in some instances is necessary for durability.

A4.4.7 *Step 7* -- For heavyweight concrete, the required fine aggregate should be determined on the absolute volume basis. With the quantities of cement, water, air, and coarse aggregate established, the fine aggregate content can be calculated as follows:

$$\text{Volume of water} = \frac{310 \text{ lb}}{62.4 \text{ lb per cu ft}} = 4.97 \text{ cu ft}$$

$$\text{Volume of air} = 0.015 \times 27 \text{ cu ft} = 0.40 \text{ cu ft}$$

$$\text{Solid volume of cement} = \frac{596 \text{ lb}}{3.15 \times 62.4 \text{ lb per cu ft}} = 3.03 \text{ cu ft}$$

$$\text{Solid volume of coarse aggregate} = \frac{3208 \text{ lb}}{4.61 \times 62.4 \text{ lb per cu ft}} = 11.15 \text{ cu ft}$$

Total volume of all ingredients except fine aggregate = 19.55 cu ft

$$\text{Solid volume of fine aggregate} = 27 \text{ cu ft} - 19.55 \text{ cu ft} = 7.45 \text{ cu ft}$$

$$\text{Required weight of fine aggregate} = 7.45 \text{ cu ft} \times 4.95 \times 62.4 \text{ lb per cu ft} = 2301 \text{ lb}$$

The actual test results indicated the concrete possessed the following properties:

Unit weight (freshly mixed)	235.7 lb per cu ft
Oven dry unit weight	228.2 lb per cu ft
Air content	2.8 percent

Slump	2½ in.
Strength	5000 psi at 28 days

Note: Oven dry unit weight of the concrete having a combination of hematite and ilmenite aggregates was 7.5 lb per cu ft less than the freshly mixed unit weight.

APPENDIX 5 -- MASS CONCRETE MIX PROPORTIONING

A5.1 *Introduction* -- Mass concrete is defined as "any volume of concrete with dimensions large enough to require that measures be taken to cope with generation of heat of hydration from the cement and attendant volume change to minimize cracking."[A5.9] The purpose of the mass concrete proportioning procedure is to combine the available cementitious materials, water, fine and coarse aggregate, and admixtures such that the resulting mixture will not exceed some established allowable temperature rise, and yet meet requirements for strength and durability. In some instances, two mixtures may be required -- an interior mass concrete and an exterior concrete for resistance to the various conditions of exposure. Accordingly, concrete technologists and designers during the design stage should consider the effects of temperature on the properties of concrete. A 6-in. wall, for example, will dissipate the generated heat quite readily, but as the thickness and size of the placement increase, a point is reached, whereby, the rate of heat generated far exceeds the rate of heat dissipated. This phenomenon produces a temperature rise within the concrete and may cause sufficient temperature differential between the interior and exterior of the mass or between peak and ultimate stable temperature to induce tensile stresses. The temperature differential between interior and exterior of the concrete generated by decreases in ambient air temperature conditions may cause cracking at exposed surfaces. Furthermore, as the concrete reaches its peak temperature and subsequent cooling takes place, tensile stresses are induced by the cooling if the change in volume is restrained by the foundation or connections to other parts of the structure.

The tensile stress developed by these conditions can be expressed by the equation $S = REeT$; where R is the restraint factor, E is the modulus of elasticity, e is the thermal coefficient of expansion, and T is the temperature difference between the interior and exterior of the concrete or between the concrete at maximum temperature and at ambient air temperature. Detailed discussions on this subject of mass concrete can be found in References A5.1, A5.2, A5.3, A5.5 and A5.14.

Thermal cracking of bridge piers, foundations, floor slabs, beams, columns, and other massive structures (locks and dams) can or may reduce the service life of a structure by promoting early deterioration or excessive maintenance. Furthermore, it should be recognized that the selection of proper mixture proportions is only one means of controlling temperature rise, and that other aspects of the concrete work should be studied and incorporated into the design and construction requirements. For additional information on heat problems and solutions, consult References A5.2 and A5.14.

A5.2 *Mass concrete properties* -- During the design stage of a proposed project, desired specified compressive strength with adequate safety factors for various portions of the structure are normally first established. The engineer will then expand on the other desired properties required of the concrete.

The proportioning of ingredients such that a mass concrete mixture will have the desired properties requires an evaluation of the materials to be used. If adequate data are not available from recent construction projects using the proposed materials, representative samples of all materials proposed for use in the concrete must be tested to determine their properties and conformance with applicable specifications.

A5.3 *Properties of material related to heat generation --*

A5.3.1 *Cementitious materials* -- Cementitious material for mass concrete work may consist of portland cement or blended hydraulic cements as specified in ASTM C 150 and ASTM C 595, respectively, or a combination of portland cement and pozzolan. Pozzolans are specified in ASTM C 618.

A5.3.1.1 *Portland cement* -- The hydration of portland cement is exothermic; that is, heat is generated during the reaction of cement and water. The quantity of heat produced is a function of the chemical composition of the cement as shown in Fig. A5.3 and the initial temperature.

Type II cement is most commonly used in mass concrete, since it is a moderate heat cement and generally has favorable properties for most types of construction. When used with a pozzolanic admixture, which will be discussed later, the heat generated by a combination of Type II and pozzolan is comparative with that of Type IV. In addition, Type II is more readily available than Type IV. Optional heat of hydration requirements may be specified for Type II cement by limitations on the chemical compounds or actual heat of hydration at 7 days.

Low initial concrete placing temperature, commonly used in mass concrete work, will generally decrease the rate of cement hydration and initial heat generated. Correspondingly, strength development in the first few days may also be reduced.

The fineness of the cement also affects the rate of heat of hydration; however, it has little effect on the initial heat

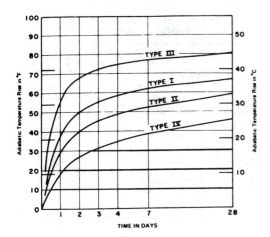

Cement Type	Fineness ASTM C 115 cm²/gm	28-Day Heat of Hydration Calories per gm
I	1790	87
II	1890	76
III	2030	105
IV	1910	60

Fig. A5.3—Temperature rise of mass concrete containing 376 pcy (223 kg/m³) of cement.

generated. Fine-ground cements will produce heat more rapidly during the early ages than a coarse-ground cement, all other cement properties being equal.

A5.3.1.2 *Blended hydraulic cements* -- Blended hydraulic cements conforming to the requirements of ASTM C 595, if available and economical, may be used effectively in mass concrete. These cements are composed of a blend of portland cement and blast-furnace slag or pozzolan. The suffix (MH) or (LH) may be used with the designated type of blended cement to specify moderate heat or low heat requirements where applicable.

A5.3.1.3 *Pozzolans* -- Major economic and temperature rise benefits have been derived from the use of pozzolans. Pozzolan is defined as "a siliceous or siliceous and aluminous material which in itself possesses little or no cementitious value, but will, in finely divided form and in the presence of moisture, chemically react with calcium hydroxide at ordinary temperatures to form compounds possessing cementitious properties."[A5.9] Pozzolans include some diatomaceous earths, opaline cherts and shales, tuffs and volcanic ashes or pumicites, any of which may or may not be processed by calcination, and other various materials requiring calcination to induce satisfactory properties, such as some clays and shales. Fly ash, the finely divided residue that results from the combustion of ground or powdered coal and is transported from the combustion chamber by exhaust gases is also a pozzolan.

Utilization of pozzolans in mass concrete provides a partial replacement of cement with a material which generates considerably less heat at early ages. The early age heat contribution of a pozzolan may conservatively be estimated to range between 15 to 50 percent of that of an equivalent weight of cement.

The effects of pozzolan on the properties of freshly mixed concrete vary with the type and fineness; the chemical, mineralogical and physical characteristics of the pozzolan; the fineness and composition of the cement; the ratio of cement to pozzolan; and the weight of cement plus pozzolan used per unit volume of concrete. For example, it has been reported that some pozzolans may reduce water requirements by as much as 7 percent with a reduction of air-entraining admixture needs by up to about 20 percent. Since certain other pozzolans may require as much as 15 percent additional water and over 60 percent more air-entraining admixture, it is important to evaluate the pozzolan intended for use prior to the start of proportioning.

The proportion of cement to pozzolan depends upon the strength desired at a given age, heat considerations, the chemical and physical characteristics of both cement and pozzolan and the cost of the respective materials. Typical quantities of various types of pozzolan and other materials blended with portland cement to reduce heat generation are shown in Table A5.1.

A5.3.2 *Aggregates* -- The nominal maximum size aggregates recommended for use under various placing conditions are shown in Table A5.2. A nominal maximum size aggregate up to 6 in. (150 mm) should be considered, if large size aggregate is available, economical, and placing conditions permit. Because the larger aggregate provides less surface area to be coated by cement paste, a reduction in the quantity of cement and water can be realized for the same water-cement ratio. This relationship is reflected in Table 6.3.3. Typical gradations for individual size fractions of coarse aggregate are shown in Table A5.3. Gradings and other physical properties of fine aggregate should comply with the requirements of ASTM C 33.

A5.3.2.1 *Coarse aggregate combination* -- Upon determining the nominal maximum size, the individual aggregate size groups available should be combined to produce a gradation approaching maximum density and minimum voids. This results in the maximum amount of mortar available for placeability, workability, and finishability. The dry rodded unit weight method is generally applicable for combining size groups up to a nominal maximum size of 1½ in. (37.5 mm); however, this method is impractical for combining size groups of 3 in. (75 mm) or 6 in. (150 mm) nominal maximum size. Eq. (A5.3) gives an approximate percentage of material passing each sieve size required for a given aggregate type. This equation was developed from work by Fuller and Thompson (Reference A5.13) on the packing characteristics of particulate material. The parabolic curve generated from the equation approximates the ideal gradation for maximum density and minimum voids according to the particle shape of the aggregate. Combining the individual coarse aggregate size groups to approximate the ideal curve is the recommended procedure for use with 6 in. (150 mm) and 3 in. (75 mm) nominal maximum size aggregate mixtures in place of the dry rodded unit weight method.

$$P = \frac{d^x - 0.1875^x}{D^x - 0.1875^x} (100)$$

where

P = cumulative percent passing the d-size sieve
d = sieve opening, in. (mm)
D = nominal maximum size aggregate, in. (mm)
x = exponent (0.5 for rounded and 0.8 for crushed aggregate)

Based on the above equation, the ideal combined gradings for 6 in. and 3 in. (150 and 75 mm) crushed and rounded aggregates are shown in Table A5.4. An acceptable grading for an aggregate that is partially crushed or partially rounded may be interpolated from the gradations in Table A5.4. Using the individual gradation of each size group, 6 in. to 3 in. (150 mm to 75 mm), 3 in. to 1½ in. (75 mm to 37.5 mm)

TABLE A5.1 — TYPICAL QUANTITIES OF POZZOLANS AND OTHER MATERIALS*

Material or class of material	Percent of total cementing material by absolute volume	
	Unexposed concrete†	Exposed concrete‡
Pozzolans (ASTM C618):		
Class F	35	25
Class N, all types except uncalcined diatomite	30	20
Class N, uncalcined diatomite	20	20
Other materials:		
Slag or natural cement	35	25

*Other quantities of pozzolan or other materials may be used if verified to be acceptable by laboratory mixture evaluations or previous experience. No typical quantities have been established for Class C pozzolan.
†Unexposed concrete for massive structures (i.e., gravity dams, spillways, lock walls, and similar massive structures).
‡Exposed concrete for massive structures (see previous note), and exposed structural concrete (i.e., floodwalls, building foundations, pavements, and similar moderate-size structures).

TABLE A5.2 — NOMINAL MAXIMUM SIZE OF AGGREGATE RECOMMENDED FOR VARIOUS TYPES OF CONSTRUCTION

Features	Nominal maximum size, in. (mm)
Sections over 7½ in. (190 mm) wide, and in which the clear distance between reinforcement bars is at least 2¼ in. (57 mm)	1½(37.5)
Unreinforced sections over 12 in. (300 mm) wide and reinforced sections over 18 in (457 mm) wide, in which the clear distance between reinforcement bars is over 6 in. (150 mm) and under 10 in. (250 mm)	3(75)
Massive sections in which the clear distance between reinforcement bars is at least 10 in. (250 mm) and for which suitable provision is made for placing concrete containing the larger sizes of aggregate without producing rock pockets or other undesirable conditions.	6(150)

TABLE A5.3 — TYPICAL COARSE AGGREGATE GRADATION LIMITS

	Size separation			
	Percent by weight passing individual sieves			
	No. 4 to ¾ in.	¾ in. to 1½ in.	1½ in. to 3 in.	3 in. to 6 in.
Sieve size in. (mm)	(4.75 mm to 19 mm)	(19 mm to 37.5 mm)	(37.5 mm to 75 mm)	(75 mm to 150 mm)
7(177)				100
6(150)				90-100
4(100)			100	20-55
3(75)			90-100	0-15
2(50)		100	20-55	0-5
1-1/2(37.5)		90-100	0-10	
1(25)	100	20-55	0-5	
3/4(19)	90-100	0-15		
3/8(9.5)	20-55	0-5		
No. 4(4.75)	0-10			
No. 8(2.36)	0-5			

TABLE A5.4—IDEALIZED COMBINED GRADING FOR 6 IN. (150 mm) AND 3 IN. (75 mm) NOMINAL MAXIMUM SIZE AGGREGATE FROM EQ. (A5.3)

	6 in. (150 mm)		3 in. (75 mm)	
	Percent passing		Percent passing	
Sieve size — in. (mm)	Crushed	Rounded	Crushed	Rounded
6(150)	100	100	—	—
5(125)	85	89	—	—
4(100)	70	78	—	—
3(75)	54	64	100	100
2(50)	38	49	69	75
1-1/2(37.5)	28	39	52	61
1(25)	19	28	34	44
3/4(19)	13	21	25	33
3/8(9.5)	5	9	9	14

1½ in. to ¾ in. (37.5 mm to 19 mm), and ¾ in. to No. 4 (19 mm to 4.75 mm), a trial and error method of selecting the percentage of each size group will be necessary to produce a combined grading of the total coarse aggregate approximating the idealized gradation. Selection of the percentage of each size group can usually be done such that the combined grading is generally within 2 or 3 percent of the ideal grading if the individual size group gradings are within the limits of Table A5.3. Where grading limits other than those of Table A5.3 may be used, more tolerance may be required on certain sieve sizes. Furthermore, natural aggregates in some areas may be deficient of certain sizes and, in such cases, modification of the idealized grading to permit use of this aggregate is recommended.

A5.3.2.2 *Coarse aggregate content* -- The proportion of fine aggregate for mass concrete depends on the final combined grading of coarse aggregate, particle shape, fineness modulus of the fine aggregate, and the quantity of cementitious material. Coarse aggregate amount can be found using the b/b_o method, Table 5.3.6 of ACI 211.1, if the ASTM C29 bulk unit weight has been determined. For large 3 in. (75 mm) and 6 in. (150 mm) nominal maximum size aggregate Table A5.5 approximates the amount of coarse aggregate as a percent of the total aggregate volume for different moduli of fine aggregate and nominal maximum sizes of coarse aggregate. The table is only applicable for 3 in. (75 mm) and 6 in. (150 mm) nominal maximum size aggregate.

A5.3.3 *Admixtures* -- When proportioning mass concrete use of admixtures should always be considered. The two most commonly used admixtures in mass concrete are air-entraining and water-reducing admixtures.

A5.3.3.1 *Air entrainment* -- Air entrainment in mass concrete is necessary if for no other reason than to increase workability of lean concrete mixtures. The use of air entrainment in mass concrete, as in other concrete, permits a marked improvement in durability, improvement in plasticity and workability, and reduction in segregation and bleeding. The effect of air entrainment on the strength of mass concrete is minimized due to the reduction in the quantity of paste in concrete which contains 3 in. (75 mm) and 6 in. (150 mm) nominal maximum size aggregate. However, such effects should be considered in the design of mass concrete having 1½ in. (37.5 mm) or ¾ in. (19 mm) nominal maximum size aggregate. In lean mixtures strengths are not reduced as much when air entrainment is used; in some

TABLE A5.5 — APPROXIMATE COARSE AGGREGATE CONTENT WHEN USING NATURAL (*N*) OR MANUFACTURE (*M*) FINE AGGREGATE (Percent of total aggregate by absolute volume)

Nominal maximum size and type coarse aggregate	Sand type:	Fineness modulus							
		2.40		2.60		2.80		3.00	
		N	M	N	M	N	M	N	M
6 in. (150 mm) crushed		80	78	79	77	78	76	77	75
6 in. (150 mm) rounded		82	80	81	79	80	78	79	77
3 in. (75 mm) crushed		75	73	74	72	73	71	72	70
3 in. (75 mm) rounded		77	75	76	74	75	73	74	72

Note: For concrete containing 5½ percent air content and a slump of 2 in. (50 mm), both measured on the minus 1½ in. (37.5 mm) portion. The coarse aggregate contents given above may be increased approximately 1 or 2 percent if good control procedures are followed. The coarse aggregate content in the table pertains primarily to the particle shape in the minus 1½ in. (37.5 mm) portion.

TABLE A5.6—APPROXIMATE MORTAR AND AIR CONTENT FOR VARIOUS NOMINAL MAXIMUM SIZE AGGREGATES [1½ in. (37.5 mm) slump and air content of 5 to 6 percent in minus 1½ in. (37.5 mm) portion]

Nominal maximum size and type coarse aggregate	Mortar content cu ft/cu yd ± 0.2 (m 3/m 3 + 0.01)	Air content Total mixture, percent
6 in. (150 mm) crushed	10.5 (0.39)	3.0-4.0
6 in. (150 mm) rounded	10.0 (0.37)	3.0-4.0
3 in. (75 mm) crushed	12.0 (0.44)	3.5-4.5
3 in. (75 mm) rounded	11.5 (0.43)	3.5-4.5

TABLE A5.7 — APPROXIMATE COMPRESSIVE STRENGTHS OF AIR-ENTRAINED CONCRETE FOR VARIOUS WATER-CEMENT RATIOS [Based on the use of 6 × 12-in. (152 × 305-mm) cylinders.]

Water-cement ratio by weight*	Approximate 28-day compressive strength, psi (MPa) (f_c')†	
	Natural aggregate	Crushed aggregate
0.40	4500 (31.0)	5000 (34.5)
0.50	3400 (23.4)	3800 (26.2)
0.60	2700 (18.6)	3100 (21.4)
0.70	2100 (14.5)	2500 (17.2)
0.80	1600 (11.0)	1900 (13.1)

*These W/C ratios may be converted to W/(C + P) ratios by the use of the equation in Section 5.3.4
†90 days when using pozzolan.

TABLE A5.8 — MAXIMUM PERMISSIBLE WATER-CEMENT RATIOS FOR MASSIVE SECTIONS

Location of structure	Water-cement ratios, by weight	
	Severe or moderate climate	Mild climate, little snow or frost
At the waterline in hydraulic or waterfront structures where intermittent saturation is possible	0.50	0.55
Unexposed portions of massive structure	No limit*	No limit
Ordinary exposed structures	0.50	0.55
Complete continuous submergence in water	0.58	0.58
Concrete deposited in water	0.45	0.45
Exposure to strong sulfate groundwater or other corrosive liquid, salt or sea water	0.45	0.45
Concrete subjected to high velocity flow of water (>40 f/s) (>12 m/s)	0.45	0.45

Note 1. These W/C ratios may be converted to W/(C + P) ratios by use of equation in Section 5.3.4.
*Limit should be based on the minimum required for workability or Table A5.7 for strength.

cases strengths may increase due to the reduction in mixing water requirements with air entrainment. Air contents should be in accordance with those recommended in Table A5.6.

A5.3.3.2 *Water-reducing admixture* -- Water-reducing admixtures meeting the requirements of ASTM C 494 have been found effective in mass concrete mixtures. The water reduction permits a corresponding reduction in the cement content while maintaining a constant water-cement ratio. The amount of water reduction will vary with different concretes; however, 5 to 8 percent is normal. In addition, certain types of water-reducing admixture tend to improve the mobility of concrete and its response to vibration, particularly in large aggregate mixtures.

A5.4 *Strength and durability* -- The procedure for proportioning mass concrete is used primarily for controlling the generation of heat and temperature rise, while satisfying the requirements for strength and durability. The strength and durability properties are primarily governed by the water-cement ratio. The water-cement ratio is the ratio, by

TABLE A5.9 — QUANTITIES OF MATERIALS SUGGESTED
FOR CONCRETE PROPORTIONING TRIAL MIXTURES

| Nominal maximum size aggregate in mixture in. (mm) | Fine aggregate | Quantities of aggregates, lb (kg) | | | | | Cement, lb. (kg) |
| | | Coarse aggregates | | | | | |
		No. 4 to ¾ in. (4.75 mm to 19 mm)	¾ in. to 1½ in. (19 mm to 37.5 mm)	1½ in. to 3 in. (37.5 to 75 mm)	3 in. to 6 in. (75 mm to 150 mm)		
¾ (19)	1200 (544)	1200 (544)	—	—	—		400 (181)
1½ (37.5)	1000 (454)	1000 (454)	1000 (454)	—	—		400 (181)
3 (75)	2000 (907)	1500 (680)	1000 (454)	2000 (907)	—		500 (227)
6 (150)	3000 (1361)	2000 (907)	1500 (680)	2500 (1134)	3000 (1361)		700 (318)

Note 1. The actual quantity of materials required depends upon the laboratory equipment, availability of materials, and extent of the testing program.
Note 2. If a pozzolan or fly ash is to be used in the concrete, the quantity furnished should be 35 percent of the weight of the cement.
Note 3. One gal. (3.8) of a proposed air-entraining admixture or chemical admixture will be sufficient.

weight, of amount of water, exclusive of that absorbed by the aggregates, to the amount of cement in a concrete or mortar mixture. Unless previous water-cement ratio-compressive strength data are available, the approximate compressive strength of concrete tested in 6 x 12-in. (152 x 305-mm) cylinders for various water-cement ratios can be estimated from Table A5.7. The recommended maximum permissible water-cement ratio for concrete subject to various conditions of exposure are shown in Table A5.8. The water-cement ratio determined by calculation should be verified by trial batches to ensure that the specified properties of the concrete are met. Results may show that strength or durability rather than heat generation govern the propor-tions. When this situation occurs alterative measures to control heat will be necessary. For example, in gravity dam construction an exterior-facing mix may be used which con-tains additional cement to provide the required durability. Other measures may include a reduction in the initial temp-erature of concrete at placement or a limitation on the size of the placement. If compressive strengths are given for full mass mixture containing aggregate larger than 1½ in. (75 mm), approximate relationships between strength of the full mass mixture and wet screened 6 x 12-in. (152 x 305-mm) cylinder are available from sources such as Reference A5.6.

A5.5 *Placement and workability* -- Experience has demonstrated that large aggregate mixtures, 3 in. (75 mm) and 6 in. (150 mm) nominal maximum size aggregate, require a minimum mortar content for suitable placing and workability properties. Table A5.6 reflects the total absolute volume of mortar (cement, pozzolan, water, air, and fine aggregate) which is suggested for use in mixtures containing large aggregate sizes. These values should be compared with those determined during the proportioning procedure and appropriate adjustments made by either increasing or decreasing the trial mixture mortar contents for improved workability.

A5.6 *Procedure* -- Upon determining the properties of the materials and knowing the properties of the concrete, the proportioning procedure follows a series of straight-forward steps outlined in A5.6.1 to A5.6.12. Proportions should be determined for the anticipated maximum placing temperature due to the influence on the rate of cement hydration and heat generated. With the use of 3 in. (75 mm)

or 6 in. (150 mm) nominal maximum size aggregate, the pro-cedure may be somewhat different from ACI 211. 1, mainly because of the difficulty in determining the density of the large aggregate by the dry rodded unit weight method. For nominal maximum size aggregate 1½ in. (37.5 mm) or less, proportioning in accordance with ACI 211.1 may be used.

A5.6.1 *Step 1* -- Determine all requirements relating to the properties of the concrete including:

1. Nominal maximum size of aggregates that can be used.
2. Slump range.
3. Water-cement ratio limitations.
4. Expected maximum placing temperature.
5. Air content range.
6. Specified strengths and test ages.
7. Expected exposure conditions.
8. Expected water velocities, when concrete is to be subjected to flowing water.
9. Aggregate quality requirements.
10. Cement and/or pozzolan properties.

A5.6.2 *Step 2* -- Determine the essential properties of materials if sufficient information is not available. Representative samples of all materials to be incorporated in the concrete should be obtained in sufficient quantities to provide verification tests by trial batching. The suggested quantities of materials necessary to complete the required tests are shown in Table A5.9. If pozzolan is economically available, or required by the specification, the percentage as suggested in Table A5.1 should be used as a starting point in the trial mixes.

From the material submitted for the test program, determine the following properties:

1. Sieve analysis of all aggregates.
2. Bulk specific gravity of aggregates.
3. Absorption of aggregates.
4. Particle shape of coarse aggregates.
5. Fineness modulus of fine aggregate.
6. Specific gravity of portland cement, and/or pozzolans and blended cement.
7. Physical and chemical properties of portland cement and/or pozzolans and blended cement including heat of hydration at 7 days.

A complete record of the above properties should be made available for field use; this information will assist in adjusting the mixture should any of the properties of the materials used in the field change from the properties of the materials used in the laboratory trial mix program.

A5.6.3 *Step 3* -- Selection of W/C ratio. If the water-cement ratio is not given in the project document, select from Table A5.8 the maximum permissible water-cement (W/C) ratio for the particular exposure conditions. Compare this W/C ratio with the maximum permissible W/C ratio required in Table A5.7 to obtain the average strength which includes the specified strength plus an allowance for anticipated variation and use the lowest W/C ratio. The W/C ratio should be reduced 0.02 to assure that the maximum permissible W/C ratio is not exceeded during field adjustments. This W/C ratio, if required, can be converted to a water-cement plus pozzolan ratio by the use of Eq. (6.3.4.1).

A5.6.4 *Step 4* -- Estimate of mixing water requirement. Estimate the water requirement from Table 6.3.3 for the specified slump and nominal maximum size aggregate. Initial placing temperature may affect this water requirement; for additional information consult Reference A5.6.

A5.6.5 *Step 5* -- Selection of air content. Select a total air content of the mixture as recommended in Table A5.6. An accurate measure of air content can be made during future adjustment of the mixture by use of Eq. (A5.6).

$$A = \frac{a}{1 + r\left(1 - \dfrac{a}{100}\right)} \qquad (A5.6)$$

where

A = air content of total mixture, expressed as a percent
a = air content of minus 1½ in. (37.5 mm) fraction of mixture, expressed as a percent
r = ratio of the absolute volume of plus 1½ in. (37.5 mm) aggregate to the absolute volume of all other materials in the mixture except air. If 100 percent of the aggregate passes the 1½ in. (37.5 mm) sieve, r = 0, and $A = a$

A5.6.6 *Step 6* -- Compute the required weight of cement from the selected W/C (A5.6.3) and water requirement (A5.6.4).

A5.6.7 *Step 7* -- Determine the absolute volume for the cementitious materials, water content, and air content from information obtained in Steps 4, 5, and 6. Compute individual absolute volumes of cement and pozzolan.

$$V_{c+p} = \frac{C_w}{G_c(62.4)} \text{ cu ft or } \frac{C_w}{G_c(1000)} \text{ m}^3 \quad (A5.6A)$$

$$V_c = V_{c+p}(1 - F_v) \qquad (A5.6B)$$

$$V_p = V_{c+p}(F_v) \qquad (A5.6C)$$

where

C_w = weight of the equivalent portland cement as determined from Step 6

G_c = specific gravity of portland cement

V_c = volume of cement (cu ft) (m³)

V_p = volume of pozzolan (cu ft) (m³)

V_{c+p} = volume of cement and pozzolan (cu ft) (m³)

F_v = percent pozzolan by absolute volume of the total absolute volume of cement plus pozzolan expressed as a decimal factor

A5.6.8 *Step 8* -- Select percent of coarse aggregate. From Table A5.5, and based on the fineness modulus of the fine aggregate as well as the nominal maximum size and type of coarse aggregate, determine the coarse aggregate percentage of the total volume of aggregate.

A5.6.9 *Step 9* -- Determine the absolute volume of the total aggregate by subtracting from the unit volume the absolute volumes of each material as computed in Step 7. Based on the amount of coarse aggregate selected in Step 8, determine the absolute volume of the coarse aggregate. The remainder of the absolute volume represents the quantity of fine aggregate in the mix.

A5.6.10 *Step 10* -- Establish the desired combination of the separate coarse aggregates size groups. Using the individual coarse aggregates gradings, combine all coarse aggregate to a uniform grading approximating the gradings shown in Table A5.4 for 6 in. (150 mm) nominal maximum size aggregate (NMSA) or 3 in. (75 mm) NMSA. The percentage of each size group should be rounded to the nearest whole percent.

A5.6.11 *Step 11* -- Convert all absolute volumes to weight per unit volume of all ingredients in the mixture.

A5.6.12 *Step 12* -- Check the mortar content. From the absolute volumes computed earlier, compute the mortar content and compare the results with values given in Table A5.6. Values in Table A5.6 will provide an indication of the workability of the mixture as determined by past field performance. Table A5.6 can be used as an aid in making laboratory adjustments of the mixture.

A5.7 *Example problem* -- Concrete is required for a heavy bridge pier that will be exposed to fresh water in a severe climate. The design compressive strength is 3000 psi (20.7 MPa) at 28 days. Placement conditions permit the use of a large nominal maximum size aggregate, and 6 in. (150 mm) nominal maximum size crushed stone is available. Laboratory tests indicate that 6, 3, 1½, and ¾ in. (150, 75, 37.5, and 19 mm) size groups of crushed stone have bulk specific gravities (saturated-surface-dry, S.S.D. basis) of 2.72, 2.70, 2.70, and 2.68, respectively; the natural fine aggregate available has a bulk specific gravity of 2.64 with a fineness modulus of 2.80. A Class F (fly ash) pozzolan is available and should be used to reduce the generation of heat in the concrete. The pozzolan has a specific gravity of 2.45, and Type II portland cement is available.

A5.7.1 *Step 1* -- Determine desired properties. The following properties have been specified upon review of the project documents and consultation with the engineer:

1. A 6 in. (150 mm) nominal maximum size crushed stone aggregate is available and economically feasible to use.
2. Slump range of the concrete will be 1 to 2 in. (25 to 50 mm) as measured in the minus 1½ in. (37.5 mm) portion.
3. Maximum permissible *W/C* ratio by weight required to be 0.50 for durability purposes.
4. Project documents require the concrete to be placed at 65 F (18 C) or below.
5. The concrete is required to be air entrained within a range of 1½ percent of 5 percent when tested on the minus 1½ in. (37.5 mm) material.
6. Assuming a standard deviation of 500 psi (3.45 MPa), considered good overall general construction control, and 80 percent of the tests above design strength, an average compressive strength of no less than 3400 psi (23.4 MPa) at 28 days (90 days with pozzolan) is required in accordance with ACI 214-77.
7. The concrete will be subjected to severe exposure conditions.
8. Water velocities around the concrete will not exceed 40 ft/sec (12 m/s).
9. Aggregates meeting the requirements of the project specifications are available.
10. The project specifications require the use of portland cement Type II and permit the use of pozzolan.

A5.7.2 *Step 2* -- Determine properties of the materials.

1. The coarse aggregates have the following sieve analyses:

	Percent by weight passing individual sieves			
	No. 4 to ¾ in.	¾ in. to 1½ in.	1½ in. to 3 in.	3in. to 6 in.
Sieve size in. (mm)	(4.75 mm to 19 mm)	(19 mm to 37.5 mm)	(37.5 mm to 75 mm)	(75 mm to 150 mm)
7 (175)				100
6 (150)				98
5 (125)				60
4 (100)			100	30
3 (75)			92	10
2 (50)		100	30	2
1½ (37.5)		94	6	
1 (25)	100	36	4	
¾ (19)	92	4		
⅜ (9.5)	30	2		
No. 4 (4.75)	2			

2. The bulk specific gravities (saturated-surface-dry, S.S.D. basis) of the coarse and fine (sand) aggregates are determined to be:

Size group	Specific gravity
6 in. to 3 in. (150 to 75 mm)	2.72
3 in. to 1½ in. (75 to 37.5 mm)	2.70
1½ in. to ¾ in. (37.5 to 19 mm)	2.70
¾ in. to No. 4 (19 to 4.75 mm)	2.68
Fine aggregate	2.64

3. The absorptions of the coarse and fine aggregates are as follows:

Size group	Absorption (percent)
6 in. to 3 in. (150 to 75 mm)	0.5
3 in. to 1½ in. (75 to 37.5 mm)	0.75
1½ in. to ¾ in. (37.5 to 19 mm)	1.0
¾ in. to No. 4 (19 to 4.75 mm)	2.0
Fine aggregate	3.2

4. The coarse and fine aggregate are totally crushed and natural, respectively.
5. The fineness modulus of the fine aggregate is 2.80.
6. Specific gravities of the portland cement and pozzolan are 3.15 and 2.45, respectively.
7. Physical and chemical tests of the portland cement and pozzolan verify compliance with the requirements of the project specifications.

A5.7.3 *Step 3* -- Selection of *W/C* ratio. From Table A5.8, the exposure conditions permit a maximum permissible *W/C* ratio of 0.50 and Table A5.7 recommends a maximum *W/C* ratio of 0.57 to obtain the desired average strength of 3400 psi (23.44 MPa). Since the exposure conditions require the lower *W/C* ratio, the designed *W/C* ratio will be 0.48 or 0.02 less than that permitted to allow for field adjustments.

Since a fly ash pozzolan is available and the quantity of concrete in the project justifies its use economically, 25 percent by volume will be used according to Table A5.1.

A5.7.4 *Step 4* -- Estimate of mixing water requirement. From Table 6.3.3 the estimated water content is 180 lb/cu yd (107 kg/m³) based on the use of a 6 in. (150 mm) crushed stone (NMSA) and a slump of 1 to 2 in. (25 to 50 mm).

A5.7.5 *Step 5* -- Selection of air content. A total air content of 3.2 percent is selected which is within the range recommended in Table A5.6. During later adjustments, after all ingredients are determined, a more accurate total air content can be derived by the use of Eq. (A5.6).

A5.7.6 *Step 6* -- Determine weight of cement from selected *W/C* ratio and water demand.

from Step 3 *W/C* = 0.48

therefore: weight of cement in a total portland cement mixture equals

PROPORTIONS FOR NORMAL, HEAVYWEIGHT, AND MASS CONCRETE   211.1-37

	Grading of individual size groups percent passing				Combined grading computations Trial and error selection Size group percentages and gradings				Combined grading percent passing	Idealize* grading percent passing
Sieve size in. (mm)					45 percent	25 percent	15 percent	15 percent		
	6 in. to 3 in. (150 mm to 75 mm)	3 in. to 1½ in. (75 mm to 37.5 mm)	1½ in. to ¾ in. (37.5 mm to 19 mm)	¾ in. to No. 4 (19 mm to 4.75 mm)	6 in. to 3 in. (150 mm to 75 mm)	3 in. to 1½ in. (75 mm to 37.5 mm)	1½ in. to ¾ in. (37.5 mm to 19 mm)	¾ in. to No. 4 (19 mm to 4.75 mm)		
7 (175)	100				45	25	15	15	100	
6 (150)	98				44	25	15	15	99	100
4 (100)	30	100			14	25	15	15	69	70
3 (75)	10	92			4	23	15	15	57	54
2 (50)	2	30	100		1	8	15	15	39	38
1½ (37.5)		6	94			2	14	15	31	28
1 (25)		4	36	100		1	5	15	21	21
¾ (19)			4	92			1	14	15	15
⅜ (9.5)			2	30			0	5	5	5
No.4(4.75)				2				0	0	0

*From Table A5.4 for 6 in. (150 mm) nominal maximum size crushed material.

$$\frac{180}{0.48} = 375 \; lb/cu \; yd \; or \; (222 \; kg/m^3)$$

$$V_w = \frac{180}{62.4} = \underline{2.88 \, cu \, ft} \, or \left(\frac{107}{1000} = \underline{0.107 \, m^3/m^3}\right)$$

A5.7.7 *Step 7* -- Determine absolute volume per cubic yard (cubic meter) for the cementitious materials, water content and air content. As recommended in Table A5.1, 25 percent pozzolan by volume will be used. Using Eq. (A5.6.7A), (B), and (C), the absolute volume of cementitious material can be determined.

$$V_A = 0.032\,(27) = \underline{0.86 \, cu \, ft/cu \, yd} \, or$$
$$\left(0.032\,(1.0) = \underline{0.032 \, m^3/m^3}\right)$$

$$V_{c+p} = \frac{C_w}{G_c\,(62.4)} = \frac{375}{3.15\,(62.4)} = \underline{1.91 \, cu \, ft/cu \, yd} \, or$$
$$\left(\frac{222}{3.15\,(1000)} = \underline{0.070 \, m^3/m^3}\right)$$

A5.7.8 *Step 8* -- For a natural fine aggregate with an F.M. of 2.80 and a 6-in. (152 mm) (NMSA) crushed stone, the volume of coarse aggregate to be used in the trial batch is 78 percent--see Table A5.5.

A5.7.9 *Step 9* -- Determine the absolute volume of fine and coarse aggregates.

$$V_c = V_{c+p}\,(1 - F_v) = 1.91\,(1 - 0.25) = \underline{1.43 \, cu \, ft/cu \, yd}$$
$$or \left(0.070\,(1 - 0.25) = \underline{0.052 \, m^3/m^3}\right)$$

27 - V_w - V_A - V_{c+p} = Vol of aggregate/cu yd or
(1.0 - V_w - V_A - V_{c+p} = Vol of aggregate/m³)
27 - 2.88 - 0.86 - 1.91 = 21.35 cu ft/cu yd or (0.79m³/m³)

Vol of coarse aggregate	= 21.35 (0.78) cu ft/cu yd or [0.79(0.78) m³/m³] = 16.65 cu ft/cu yd or (0.62 m³/m³)
Vol of fine aggregate	= 21.35(0.22) cu ft/cu yd or [0.79(0.22) m³/m³] = 4.70 cu ft/cu yd or (0.17m³/m³)

$$V_p = V_{c+p}\,(F_v) = 1.91\,(0.25) = \underline{0.48 \, cu \, ft/cu \, yd} \, or$$
$$\left(0.070\,(0.25) = \underline{0.018 \, m^3/m^3}\right)$$

A5.7.10 *Step 10* -- Combine the various size groups of coarse aggregate. The existing coarse aggregate gradings were combined by trial-and-error computations, resulting in the following percentages of each size group:

No. 4 to ¾ in.	(4.75 to 19 mm)	15 percent
¾ in. to 1½ in.	(19 to 75 mm)	15 percent
1½ in. to 3 in.	(75 to 150 mm)	25 percent
3 in. to 6 in.	(150 to 300 mm)	45 percent

A5.7.11 *Step 11* -- Convert all absolute volumes to weight per unit volume.

Material	Absolute volume × specific gravity × 62.4	lb/cu yd (kg/m³)
Portland cement	1.43(3.15)62.4	281(167)
Pozzolan	0.48(2.45)62.4	73 (43)
Water	2.88(1.00)62.4	180(107)
Air	0.86	—
Fine aggregate	4.70(2.64)62.4	774(459)S.S.D.*
Coarse aggregate No. 4-¾ in.		
(4.75 –19 mm)	16.65(0.15)(2.68)62.4	418(248)S.S.D.*
¾–1½ in.		
(19mm–75 mm)	16.65(0.15)(2.70)62.4	421(250)S.S.D.*
1½–3 in.		
(75mm–150 mm)	16.65(0.25)(2.70)62.4	701(416)S.S.D.*
3–6 in.		
(150–300 mm)	16.65(0.45)(2.72)62.4	1272(755)S.S.D.*

*Weights based on aggregates in a saturated-surface-dry condition.

A5.7.12 *Step 12* -- Check mortar content and compare with Table A5.6.

$$Mortar\ content = V_c + V_p + V_w + V_s + V_A$$
$$= 1.43 + 0.48 + 2.88 + 4.70 + 0.86$$
$$= 10.35\ cu\ ft/cu\ yd\ (0.383\ m^3/m^3)$$

From Table A5.6 the mortar content is estimated to be 10.5 cu ft/cu yd (0.39 m³/m³) which is within the ± 0.2 cu ft (± 0.01 m³) of the actual value.

A5.7.13 *Trial batch* -- From the above information the absolute volume and weight per cubic yard of each ingredient computes as follows:

Material	Absolute volume ft³/yd³(m³/m³)	Weight lb/yd³(kg/m³)
Portland cement	1.43(0.052)	281 (167)
Pozzolan	0.48(0.018)	73 (43)
Water	2.88(0.107)	180 (107)
Air	0.86(0.032)	—
Fine aggregate No. 4-¾ in.	4.70(0.174)	774 (459)S.S.D.*
(4.75 –19 mm)	2.50(0.093)	418 (248)S.S.D.*
¾–1½ in.		
(19mm–75 mm)	2.50(0.093)	421 (250)S.S.D.*
1½–3 in.		
(75mm–150 mm)	4.16(0.154)	701 (416)S.S.D.*
3–6 in.		
(150–300 mm)	7.49(0.277)	1272 (755)S.S.D.*
Total	27.00(1.000)	4120(2444)

*Weights are based on aggregate in a saturated-surface-dry condition.

The weights above should be reduced proportionately to facilitate the preparation of trial batches which in turn should be evaluated for proper moisture correction, slump, air content, and general workability. After the necessary adjustments, trial mixtures for strength verification and other desired properties of concrete should be made. Reference 2 will provide guidance in estimating the heat generated by the trial mixture and in determining whether or not other temperature control measures are needed.

A5.8 *References*

A5.1 Townsend, Charles L., "Control of Temperature Cracking in Mass Concrete," *Causes, Mechanism, and Control of Cracking in Concrete*, SP-20, American Concrete Institute, Detroit, 1968, pp. 119-139.

A5.2 ACI Committee 207, "Effect of Restraint, Volume Change, and Reinforcement on Cracking of Massive Concrete," ACI Journal, *Proceedings* V. 70, No. 7, July 1973, pp. 445-470. Also, *ACI Manual of Concrete Practice*, Part 1.

A5.3 Townsend, C. L., "Control of Cracking in Mass Concrete Structures," *Engineering Monograph* No. 34, U.S. Bureau of Reclamation, Denver, 1965.

A5.4 ACI Committee 207, "Mass Concrete for Dams and Other Massive Structures," ACI Journal, *Proceedings* V. 67, No. 4, Apr. 1970, pp. 273-309. Also, ACI Manual of Concrete Practice, Part 1.

A5.5 ACI Committee 224, "Control of Cracking in Concrete Structures," ACI Journal, *Proceedings* V. 69, No. 12, Dec. 1972, pp. 717-753.

A5.6 *Concrete Manual*, 8th Edition, U.S. Bureau of Reclamation, Denver, 1975, 627 pp.

A5.7 *Proportioning Concrete Mixes*, SP-46, American Concrete Institute, Detroit, 1974, 223 pp.

A5.8 Tynes, W. O., "Effect of Fineness of Continuously Graded Coarse Aggregate on Properties of Concrete," *Technical Report* No. 6-819, U.S. Army Engineer Waterways Experiment Station, Vicksburg, Apr. 1968, 28 pp.

A5.9 ACI Committee 116, *Cement and Concrete Terminology*, 2nd Edition, SP-19(78), American Concrete Institute, Detroit, 1978, 50 pp.

A5.10 *Handbook for Concrete and Cement*, CRD-C 3, U.S. Army Engineer Waterways Experiment Station, Vicksburg, 1949 (with quarterly supplements).

A5.11 "Standard Practice for Concrete," EM 1110-2-2000 Office, Chief of Engineers, U.S. Army Corps of Engineers, Washington, D.C., June 1974.

A5.12 Hansen, Kenneth, "Cost of Mass Concrete in Dams," *Publication* No. MS260W, Portland Cement Association, Skokie, 1973, 4 pp.

A5.13 Powers, Treval C., *The Properties of Fresh Concrete*, John Wiley and Sons, New York, 1968, pp. 246-256.

A5.14 ACI Committee 207, "Cooling and Insulating Systems for Mass Concrete," (ACI 207.4R-80) *Concrete International--Design and Construction*, V.2, No. 5, May 1980, pp. 45-64.

GLULAM GARAGE DOOR HEADERS

DESIGN EXAMPLE

The 16-foot 3-inch beam span in Figure 3 supports roof trusses on a 28-foot-wide house with 2-foot overhangs and a 25 psf design snow load. According to the data in Table 1 (Pages 12-13), four different sizes of glulam beams could be selected: 3-1/8 by 13-1/2 inches, 3-1/2 by 12 inches, 5-1/8 by 10-1/2 inches and 5-1/2 by 10-1/2 inches, all suitable to carry the required design loads with the final choice being based on local availability, cost competitiveness and design preference.

FIGURE 3.

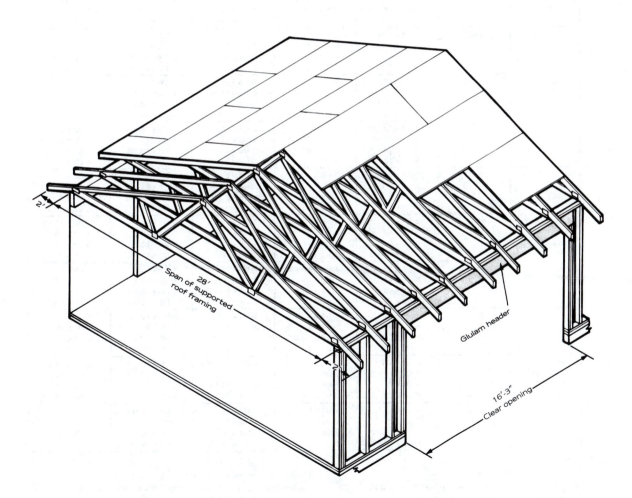

Courtesy of APA—The Engineered Wood Association.

TABLE 1A: 24F *WESTERN SPECIES* GLULAM GARAGE DOOR HEADERS

	Clear Door Opening (ft.)	Span of supported roof trusses (ft.)				
		24	28	32	36	40
		Glulam Size (in.)				
Non-Snow Load (125%) 10 psf Dead 20 psf Live	9'-3"	3-1/8 x 7-1/2 3-1/2 x 7-1/2 5-1/8 x 6 5-1/2 x 6	3-1/8 x 7-1/2 3-1/2 x 7-1/2 5-1/8 x 6 5-1/2 x 6	3-1/8 x 7-1/2 3-1/2 x 7-1/2 5-1/8 x 6 5-1/2 x 6	3-1/8 x 7-1/2 3-1/2 x 7-1/2 5-1/8 x 6 5-1/2 x 6	3-1/8 x 7-1/2 3-1/2 x 7-1/2 5-1/8 x 7-1/2 5-1/2 x 7-1/2
	16'-3"	3-1/8 x 12 3-1/2 x 12 5-1/8 x 10-1/2 5-1/2 x 10-1/2	3-1/8 x 12 3-1/2 x 12 5-1/8 x 10-1/2 5-1/2 x 10-1/2	3-1/8 x 12 3-1/2 x 12 5-1/8 x 10-1/2 5-1/2 x 10-1/2	3-1/8 x 13-1/2 3-1/2 x 12 5-1/8 x 10-1/2 5-1/2 x 10-1/2	3-1/8 x 13-1/2 3-1/2 x 13-1/2 5-1/8 x 12 5-1/2 x 12
	18'-3"	3-1/8 x 13-1/2 3-1/2 x 12 5-1/8 x 10-1/2 5-1/2 x 10-1/2	3-1/8 x 13-1/2 3-1/2 x 13-1/2 5-1/8 x 12 5-1/2 x 12	3-1/8 x 13-1/2 3-1/2 x 13-1/2 5-1/8 x 12 5-1/2 x 12	3-1/8 x 15 3-1/2 x 13-1/2 5-1/8 x 12 5-1/2 x 12	3-1/8 x 15 3-1/2 x 15 5-1/8 x 13-1/2 5-1/2 x 12
Snow Load (115%) 10 psf Dead 25 psf Live	9'-3"	3-1/8 x 7-1/2 3-1/2 x 7-1/2 5-1/8 x 6 5-1/2 x 6	3-1/8 x 7-1/2 3-1/2 x 7-1/2 5-1/8 x 6 5-1/2 x 6	3-1/8 x 9 3-1/2 x 7-1/2 5-1/8 x 7-1/2 5-1/2 x 6	3-1/8 x 9 3-1/2 x 9 5-1/8 x 7-1/2 5-1/2 x 7-1/2	3-1/8 x 9 3-1/2 x 9 5-1/8 x 7-1/2 5-1/2 x 7-1/2
	16'-3"	3-1/8 x 12 3-1/2 x 12 5-1/8 x 10-1/2 5-1/2 x 10-1/2	3-1/8 x 13-1/2 3-1/2 x 12 5-1/8 x 10-1/2 5-1/2 x 10-1/2	3-1/8 x 13-1/2 3-1/2 x 13-1/2 5-1/8 x 12 5-1/2 x 10-1/2	3-1/8 x 15 3-1/2 x 13-1/2 5-1/8 x 12 5-1/2 x 12	3-1/8 x 15 3-1/2 x 15 5-1/8 x 12 5-1/2 x 12
	18'-3"	3-1/8 x 13-1/2 3-1/2 x 13-1/2 5-1/8 x 12 5-1/2 x 12	3-1/8 x 15 3-1/2 x 13-1/2 5-1/8 x 12 5-1/2 x 12	3-1/8 x 15 3-1/2 x 15 5-1/8 x 12 5-1/2 x 12	3-1/8 x 16-1/2 3-1/2 x 15 5-1/8 x 13-1/2 5-1/2 x 13-1/2	3-1/8 x 16-1/2 3-1/2 x 16-1/2 5-1/8 x 13-1/2 5-1/2 x 13-1/2
Snow Load (115%) 10 psf Dead 30 psf Live	9'-3"	3-1/8 x 7-1/2 3-1/2 x 7-1/2 5-1/8 x 6 5-1/2 x 6	3-1/8 x 9 3-1/2 x 7-1/2 5-1/8 x 7-1/2 5-1/2 x 6	3-1/8 x 9 3-1/2 x 9 5-1/8 x 7-1/2 5-1/2 x 7-1/2	3-1/8 x 9 3-1/2 x 9 5-1/8 x 7-1/2 5-1/2 x 7-1/2	3-1/8 x 9 3-1/2 x 9 5-1/8 x 7-1/2 5-1/2 x 7-1/2
	16'-3"	3-1/8 x 13-1/2 3-1/2 x 12 5-1/8 x 10-1/2 5-1/2 x 10-1/2	3-1/8 x 13-1/2 3-1/2 x 13-1/2 5-1/8 x 12 5-1/2 x 10-1/2	3-1/8 x 15 3-1/2 x 13-1/2 5-1/8 x 12 5-1/2 x 12	3-1/8 x 15 3-1/2 x 15 5-1/8 x 12 5-1/2 x 12	3-1/8 x 16-1/2 3-1/2 x 15 5-1/8 x 13-1/2 5-1/2 x 12
	18'-3"	3-1/8 x 15 3-1/2 x 13-1/2 5-1/8 x 12 5-1/2 x 12	3-1/8 x 16-1/2 3-1/2 x 15 5-1/8 x 13-1/2 5-1/2 x 12	3-1/8 x 16-1/2 3-1/2 x 16-1/2 5-1/8 x 13-1/2 5-1/2 x 13-1/2	3-1/8 x 18 3-1/2 x 16-1/2 5-1/8 x 13-1/2 5-1/2 x 13-1/2	3-1/8 x 18 3-1/2 x 18 5-1/8 x 15 5-1/2 x 13-1/2
Snow Load (115%) 10 psf Dead 40 psf Live	9'-3"	3-1/8 x 9 3-1/2 x 9 5-1/8 x 7-1/2 5-1/2 x 7-1/2	3-1/8 x 9 3-1/2 x 9 5-1/8 x 7-1/2 5-1/2 x 7-1/2	3-1/8 x 9 3-1/2 x 9 5-1/8 x 7-1/2 5-1/2 x 7-1/2	3-1/8 x 10-1/2 3-1/2 x 9 5-1/8 x 7-1/2 5-1/2 x 7-1/2	3-1/8 x 12 3-1/2 x 10-1/2 5-1/8 x 9 5-1/2 x 9
	16'-3"	3-1/8 x 15 3-1/2 x 13-1/2 5-1/8 x 12 5-1/2 x 12	3-1/8 x 15 3-1/2 x 15 5-1/8 x 12 5-1/2 x 12	3-1/8 x 16-1/2 3-1/2 x 15 5-1/8 x 13-1/2 5-1/2 x 12	3-1/8 x 18 3-1/2 x 16-1/2 5-1/8 x 13-1/2 5-1/2 x 13-1/2	3-1/8 x 19-1/2 3-1/2 x 18 5-1/8 x 15 5-1/2 x 13-1/2
	18'-3"	3-1/8 x 16-1/2 3-1/2 x 15 5-1/8 x 13-1/2 5-1/2 x 13-1/2	3-1/8 x 18 3-1/2 x 16-1/2 5-1/8 x 13-1/2 5-1/2 x 13-1/2	3-1/8 x 18 3-1/2 x 18 5-1/8 x 15 5-1/2 x 13-1/2	3-1/8 x 19-1/2 3-1/2 x 18 5-1/8 x 15 5-1/2 x 15	3-1/8 x 21 3-1/2 x 19-1/2 5-1/8 x 16-1/2 5-1/2 x 15

Notes:

(1) Service condition = dry.

(2) Maximum deflection under live load = span/240.

(3) Maximum deflection under total load = span/180.

(4) 2-ft roof overhangs.

(5) Beam weight = 35 pcf.

(6) Design properties at normal load duration and dry-use service conditions –
F_b = 2400 psi, f_v = 165 psi, E = 1.8 x 10^6 psi.

TABLE 1B: 24F *SOUTHERN PINE* GLULAM GARAGE DOOR HEADERS

	Clear Door Opening (ft.)	Span of supported roof trusses (ft.)				
		24	28	32	36	40
		Glulam Size (in.)				
Non-Snow Load (125%) 10 psf Dead 20 psf Live	9'-3"	3 x 6-7/8 / 3-1/8 x 6-7/8 / 5 x 5-1/2 / 5-1/8 x 5-1/2	3 x 6-7/8 / 3-1/8 x 6-7/8 / 5 x 6-7/8 / 5-1/8 x 6-7/8	3 x 6-7/8 / 3-1/8 x 6-7/8 / 5 x 6-7/8 / 5-1/8 x 6-7/8	3 x 8-1/4 / 3-1/8 x 8-1/4 / 5 x 6-7/8 / 5-1/8 x 6-7/8	3 x 8-1/4 / 3-1/8 x 8-1/4 / 5 x 6-7/8 / 5-1/8 x 6-7/8
	16'-3"	3 x 12-3/8 / 3-1/8 x 11 / 5 x 9-5/8 / 5-1/8 x 9-5/8	3 x 12-3/8 / 3-1/8 x 12-3/8 / 5 x 11 / 5-1/8 x 11	3 x 12-3/8 / 3-1/8 x 12-3/8 / 5 x 11 / 5-1/8 x 11	3 x 13-3/4 / 3-1/8 x 13-3/4 / 5 x 11 / 5-1/8 x 11	3 x 13-3/4 / 3-1/8 x 13-3/4 / 5 x 11 / 5-1/8 x 11
	18'-3"	3 x 13-3/4 / 3-1/8 x 12-3/8 / 5 x 11 / 5-1/8 x 11	3 x 13-3/4 / 3-1/8 x 13-3/4 / 5 x 12-3/8 / 5-1/8 x 11	3 x 13-3/4 / 3-1/8 x 13-3/4 / 5 x 12-3/8 / 5-1/8 x 12-3/8	3 x 15-1/8 / 3-1/8 x 15-1/8 / 5 x 12-3/8 / 5-1/8 x 12-3/8	3 x 15-1/8 / 3-1/8 x 15-1/8 / 5 x 12-3/8 / 5-1/8 x 12-3/8
Snow Load (115%) 10 psf Dead 25 psf Live	9'-3"	3 x 6-7/8 / 3-1/8 x 6-7/8 / 5 x 6-7/8 / 5-1/8 x 6-7/8	3 x 8-1/4 / 3-1/8 x 8-1/4 / 5 x 6-7/8 / 5-1/8 x 6-7/8	3 x 8-1/4 / 3-1/8 x 8-1/4 / 5 x 6-7/8 / 5-1/8 x 6-7/8	3 x 8-1/4 / 3-1/8 x 8-1/4 / 5 x 6-7/8 / 5-1/8 x 6-7/8	3 x 9-5/8 / 3-1/8 x 9-5/8 / 5 x 6-7/8 / 5-1/8 x 6-7/8
	16'-3"	3 x 12-3/8 / 3-1/8 x 12-3/8 / 5 x 11 / 5-1/8 x 11	3 x 13-3/4 / 3-1/8 x 13-3/4 / 5 x 11 / 5-1/8 x 11	3 x 13-3/4 / 3-1/8 x 13-3/4 / 5 x 11 / 5-1/8 x 11	3 x 15-1/8 / 3-1/8 x 15-1/8 / 5 x 12-3/8 / 5-1/8 x 12-3/8	3 x 15-1/8 / 3-1/8 x 15-1/8 / 5 x 12-3/8 / 5-1/8 x 12-3/8
	18'-3"	3 x 13-3/4 / 3-1/8 x 13-3/4 / 5 x 12-3/8 / 5-1/8 x 12-3/8	3 x 15-1/8 / 3-1/8 x 15-1/8 / 5 x 12-3/8 / 5-1/8 x 12-3/8	3 x 16-1/2 / 3-1/8 x 15-1/8 / 5 x 12-3/8 / 5-1/8 x 12-3/8	3 x 16-1/2 / 3-1/8 x 16-1/2 / 5 x 13-3/4 / 5-1/8 x 13-3/4	3 x 17-7/8 / 3-1/8 x 16-1/2 / 5 x 13-3/4 / 5-1/8 x 13-3/4
Snow Load (115%) 10 psf Dead 30 psf Live	9'-3"	3 x 8-1/4 / 3-1/8 x 8-1/4 / 5 x 6-7/8 / 5-1/8 x 6-7/8	3 x 8-1/4 / 3-1/8 x 8-1/4 / 5 x 6-7/8 / 5-1/8 x 6-7/8	3 x 8-1/4 / 3-1/8 x 8-1/4 / 5 x 6-7/8 / 5-1/8 x 6-7/8	3 x 9-5/8 / 3-1/8 x 9-5/8 / 5 x 6-7/8 / 5-1/8 x 6-7/8	3 x 9-5/8 / 3-1/8 x 9-5/8 / 5 x 8-1/4 / 5-1/8 x 8-1/4
	16'-3"	3 x 13-3/4 / 3-1/8 x 13-3/4 / 5 x 11 / 5-1/8 x 11	3 x 13-3/4 / 3-1/8 x 13-3/4 / 5 x 11 / 5-1/8 x 11	3 x 15-1/8 / 3-1/8 x 15-1/8 / 5 x 12-3/8 / 5-1/8 x 12-3/8	3 x 16-1/2 / 3-1/8 x 15-1/8 / 5 x 13-3/4 / 5-1/8 x 13-3/4	3 x 16-1/2 / 3-1/8 x 16-1/2 / 5 x 13-3/4 / 5-1/8 x 12-3/8
	18'-3"	3 x 15-1/8 / 3-1/8 x 15-1/8 / 5 x 12-3/8 / 5-1/8 x 12-3/8	3 x 16-1/2 / 3-1/8 x 15-1/8 / 5 x 12-3/8 / 5-1/8 x 12-3/8	3 x 16-1/2 / 3-1/8 x 16-1/2 / 5 x 13-3/4 / 5-1/8 x 13-3/4	3 x 17-7/8 / 3-1/8 x 17-7/8 / 5 x 13-3/4 / 5-1/8 x 13-3/4	3 x 19-1/4 / 3-1/8 x 17-7/8 / 5 x 15-1/8 / 5-1/8 x 15-1/8
Snow Load (115%) 10 psf Dead 40 psf Live	9'-3"	3 x 8-1/4 / 3-1/8 x 8-1/4 / 5 x 6-7/8 / 5-1/8 x 6-7/8	3 x 9-5/8 / 3-1/8 x 9-5/8 / 5 x 6-7/8 / 5-1/8 x 6-7/8	3 x 9-5/8 / 3-1/8 x 9-5/8 / 5 x 8-1/4 / 5-1/8 x 8-1/4	3 x 11 / 3-1/8 x 9-5/8 / 5 x 8-1/4 / 5-1/8 x 8-1/4	3 x 11 / 3-1/8 x 11 / 5 x 8-1/4 / 5-1/8 x 8-1/4
	16'-3"	3 x 15-1/8 / 3-1/8 x 15-1/8 / 5 x 12-3/8 / 5-1/8 x 12-3/8	3 x 16-1/2 / 3-1/8 x 15-1/8 / 5 x 12-3/8 / 5-1/8 x 12-3/8	3 x 16-1/2 / 3-1/8 x 16-1/2 / 5 x 13-3/4 / 5-1/8 x 13-3/4	3 x 17-7/8 / 3-1/8 x 17-7/8 / 5 x 13-3/4 / 5-1/8 x 13-3/4	3 x 19-1/4 / 3-1/8 x 17-7/8 / 5 x 15-1/8 / 5-1/8 x 13-3/4
	18'-3"	3 x 16-1/2 / 3-1/8 x 16-1/2 / 5 x 13-3/4 / 5-1/8 x 13-3/4	3 x 17-7/8 / 3-1/8 x 17-7/8 / 5 x 13-3/4 / 5-1/8 x 13-3/4	3 x 19-1/4 / 3-1/8 x 17-7/8 / 5 x 15-1/8 / 5-1/8 x 15-1/8	3 x 19-1/4 / 3-1/8 x 19-1/4 / 5 x 15-1/8 / 5-1/8 x 15-1/8	3 x 20-5/8 / 3-1/8 x 20-5/8 / 5 x 16-1/2 / 5-1/8 x 16-1/2

Notes:

(1) Service condition = dry.

(2) Maximum deflection under live load = span/240.

(3) Maximum deflection under total load = span/180.

(4) 2-ft roof overhangs.

(5) Beam weight = 36 pcf.

(6) Design properties at normal load duration and dry-use service conditions –
F_b = 2400 psi, f_v = 200 psi, E = 1.8×10^6 psi.

SUBSTITUTING GLULAMS FOR STEEL OR SOLID-SAWN LUMBER BEAMS

Substitution of *APA EWS* Glulams for solid-sawn beams is simple. Suppose the plans show a solid-sawn 4x14 Select Structural Douglas-fir beam spanning 12 feet and supporting the first floor over a basement in a 24-foot-wide house.

Table 3 shows that either a 3-1/8" x 12" or 2-1/2" x 12" 24F *APA EWS* Glulam can be substituted.

To check the substitution of a 3-1/8" x 12" glulam, calculate:

Load to beam —
  (10 + 40)(12) = 120 plf dead
  load + 480 plf live load = 600 plf

Table 2 shows that a 3-1/8" x 12" *APA EWS* western species glulam will support loads up to a total of 825 plf on a 12-foot span.

Tables 3-4 show glulam equivalents for 4x solid-sawn floor beams. Tables 5-8 show glulam equivalents for 4x solid-sawn roof beams. Tables 9-10 show glulam equivalents for steel floor beams.

TABLE 2
ALLOWABLE LOADS FOR SIMPLE SPAN *WESTERN SPECIES* GLUED LAMINATED FLOOR BEAMS (plf)

(Load Duration Factor = 1.00)

F_b = 2,400 psi, E = 1,800,000 psi, F_v = 165 psi

3-1/8-INCH WIDTH　　　　　　　　　　　　　　　　　　　　　SPAN (ft)

Depth (in.)	8	10	12	14	16	18	20	22	24	26	28	30	32	34	36	38	40	42	44	46	48
6	366	187	109	68	—	—	—	—	—	—	—	—	—	—	—	—	—	—	—	—	—
7-1/2	715	366	212	133	89	63	—	—	—	—	—	—	—	—	—	—	—	—	—	—	—
9	952	633	366	231	154	109	79	59	—	—	—	—	—	—	—	—	—	—	—	—	—
10-1/2	1155	875	582	366	245	172	126	94	73	57	—	—	—	—	—	—	—	—	—	—	—
12	1375	1031	**825**	547	366	257	187	141	109	85	68	56	—	—	—	—	—	—	—	—	—
13-1/2	1614	1198	952	775	521	366	267	201	154	122	97	79	65	54	—	—	—	—	—	—	—
15	1875	1375	1086	897	715	502	366	275	212	167	133	109	89	75	63	53	—	—	—	—	—
16-1/2	2161	1565	1226	1008	856	669	487	366	282	222	178	144	119	99	84	71	61	53	—	—	—
18	2475	1768	1375	1125	952	825	633	475	366	288	231	187	154	129	109	92	79	68	59	52	—
19-1/2	2822	1986	1532	1247	1051	909	792	604	466	366	293	238	196	164	138	117	101	87	76	66	58
21	3208	2221	1699	1375	1155	996	875	751	582	457	366	298	245	205	172	147	126	109	94	83	73
22-1/2	3640	2475	1875	1509	1263	1086	952	848	713	563	450	366	302	252	212	180	154	133	116	102	89
24	4125	2750	2062	1650	1375	1179	1031	917	806	681	547	444	366	305	257	219	187	162	141	123	109
25-1/2	4675	3049	2262	1798	1492	1275	1113	988	888	765	654	533	439	366	309	262	225	194	169	148	130
27	5304	3375	2475	1954	1614	1375	1198	1061	952	852	729	631	521	435	366	311	267	231	201	176	154

Table excerpted from *AWS Data File: Glued Laminated Beam Design Tables*, Form No. EWS S475.

TABLE 3
24F GLULAM EQUIVALENTS FOR 4x_ *DOUGLAS FIR-LARCH* LUMBER
FLOOR BEAMS

Designed According to the 1991 NDS
(Load Duration Factor = 1.00)

Span (ft)	Glulam Species	4 x 8 Douglas Fir Select Struc.	4 x 8 Douglas Fir No. 1	4 x 10 Douglas Fir Select Struc.	4 x 10 Douglas Fir No. 1	4 x 12 Douglas Fir Select Struc.	4 x 12 Douglas Fir No. 1	4 x 14 Douglas Fir Select Struc.	4 x 14 Douglas Fir No. 1
		24F Glulam Equivalent (in.)							
10	Western Species	2-1/2 x 9 3-1/8 x 7-1/2	2-1/2 x 7-1/2 3-1/8 x 7-1/2	2-1/2 x 9 3-1/8 x 9	2-1/2 x 9 3-1/8 x 9	2-1/2 x 10-1/2 3-1/8 x 9	2-1/2 x 10-1/2 3-1/8 x 9	2-1/2 x 12 3-1/8 x 10-1/2	2-1/2 x 10-1/2 3-1/8 x 10-1/2
	Southern Pine	2-1/2 x 8-1/4 3 x 8-1/4	2-1/2 x 8-1/4 3 x 6-7/8	2-1/2 x 9-5/8 3 x 9-5/8	2-1/2 x 9-5/8 3 x 8-1/4	2-1/2 x 9-5/8 3 x 9-5/8	2-1/2 x 9-5/8 3 x 9-5/8	2-1/2 x 11 3 x 11	2-1/2 x 11 3 x 9-5/8
12	Western Species	2-1/2 x 9 3-1/8 x 9	2-1/2 x 9 3-1/8 x 7-1/2	2-1/2 x 10-1/2 3-1/8 x 10-1/2	2-1/2 x 9 3-1/8 x 9	2-1/2 x 12 3-1/8 x 10-1/2	2-1/2 x 10-1/2 3-1/8 x 10-1/2	**2-1/2 x 12** **3-1/8 x 12**	2-1/2 x 12 3-1/8 x 10-1/2
	Southern Pine	2-1/2 x 8-1/4 3 x 8-1/4	2-1/2 x 8-1/4 3 x 8-1/4	2-1/2 x 11 3-1/8 x 10-1/2	2-1/2 x 9-5/8 3 x 9-5/8	2-1/2 x 11 3 x 11	2-1/2 x 11 3 x 9-5/8	2-1/2 x 12-3/8 3 x 11	2-1/2 x 11 3 x 11
14	Western Species	2-1/2 x 9 3-1/8 x 9	2-1/2 x 9 3-1/8 x 7-1/2	2-1/2 x 12 3-1/8 x 10-1/2	2-1/2 x 10-1/2 3-1/8 x 9	2-1/2 x 12 3-1/8 x 12	2-1/2 x 10-1/2 3-1/8 x 10-1/2	2-1/2 x 13-1/2 3-1/8 x 12	2-1/2 x 12 3-1/8 x 10-1/2
	Southern Pine	2-1/2 x 8-1/4 3 x 8-1/4	2-1/2 x 8-1/4 3 x 8-1/4	2-1/2 x 11 3 x 11	2-1/2 x 9-5/8 3 x 9-5/8	2-1/2 x 12-3/8 3 x 11	2-1/2 x 11 3 x 11	2-1/2 x 13-3/4 3 x 12-3/8	2-1/2 x 12-3/8 3 x 11
16	Western Species	2-1/2 x 9 3-1/8 x 9	2-1/2 x 9 3-1/8 x 7-1/2	2-1/2 x 12 3-1/8 x 10-1/2	2-1/2 x 10-1/2 3-1/8 x 10-1/2	2-1/2 x 13-1/2 3-1/8 x 12	2-1/2 x 12 3-1/8 x 10-1/2	2-1/2 x 13-1/2 3-1/8 x 13-1/2	2-1/2 x 12 3-1/8 x 12
	Southern Pine	2-1/2 x 8-1/4 3 x 8-1/4	2-1/2 x 8-1/4 3 x 8-1/4	2-1/2 x 11 3 x 11	2-1/2 x 11 3 x 9-5/8	2-1/2 x 12-3/8 3 x 12-3/8	2-1/2 x 11 3 x 11	2-1/2 x 13-3/4 3 x 12-3/8	2-1/2 x 12-3/8 3 x 11
18	Western Species	2-1/2 x 9 3-1/8 x 9	2-1/2 x 9 3-1/8 x 7-1/2	2-1/2 x 10-1/2 3-1/8 x 10-1/2	2-1/2 x 10-1/2 3-1/8 x 10-1/2	2-1/2 x 13-1/2 3-1/8 x 12	2-1/2 x 12 3-1/8 x 10-1/2	2-1/2 x 15 3-1/8 x 13-1/2	2-1/2 x 13-1/2 3-1/8 x 12
	Southern Pine	2-1/2 x 8-1/4 3 x 8-1/4	2-1/2 x 8-1/4 3 x 8-1/4	2-1/2 x 11 3 x 11	2-1/2 x 11 3 x 9-5/8	2-1/2 x 13-3/4 3 x 12-3/8	2-1/2 x 11 3 x 11	2-1/2 x 13-3/4 3 x 13-3/4	2-1/2 x 12-3/8 3 x 12-3/8
20	Western Species	2-1/2 x 9 3-1/8 x 9	2-1/2 x 9 3-1/8 x 7-1/2	2-1/2 x 10-1/2 3-1/8 x 10-1/2	2-1/2 x 10-1/2 3-1/8 x 10-1/2	2-1/2 x 13-1/2 3-1/8 x 12	2-1/2 x 12 3-1/8 x 12	2-1/2 x 15 3-1/8 x 13-1/2	2-1/2 x 13-1/2 3-1/8 x 12
	Southern Pine	2-1/2 x 8-1/4 3 x 8-1/4	2-1/2 x 8-1/4 3 x 8-1/4	2-1/2 x 11 3 x 11	2-1/2 x 11 3 x 9-5/8	2-1/2 x 13-3/4 3 x 12-3/8	2-1/2 x 12-3/8 3 x 11	2-1/2 x 15-1/8 3 x 13-3/4	2-1/2 x 13-3/4 3 x 12-3/8

Notes:

(1) Span = uniformly loaded simply supported beam.

(2) Maximum deflection = L/360 under live load, based on live/total load = 0.8.

(3) Service condition = dry.

(4) Beam weights for sawn and glulam members are assumed to be the same.

(5) Volume factors for glulam members and size factors for sawn lumber members are in accordance with 1991 NDS.

(6) Minimum glulam sizes considered in the table are: 2-1/2 x 6 and 3-1/8 x 6 (*western species*), and 2-1/2 x 5-1/2 and 3 x 5-1/2 (*southern pine*).

(7) Design properties at normal load duration and dry-use service conditions -
Select Structural sawn lumber members: F_b = 1450 psi, F_v = 95 psi, E = 1.9 x 10^6 psi.
No. 1 sawn lumber members: F_b 1000 psi, F_v = 95 psi, E = 1.7 x 10^6 psi.
Glulam members: F_b = 2400 psi, F_v = 165 psi (*western species*) or 200 psi (*southern pine*), E = 1.8 x 10^6 psi.

TABLE 4
24F GLULAM EQUIVALENTS FOR 4x_ *SOUTHERN PINE* LUMBER
FLOOR BEAMS

Designed According to the 1991 NDS
(Load Duration Factor = 1.00)

Span (ft)	Glulam Species	4 x 6 Southern Pine		4 x 8 Southern Pine		4 x 10 Southern Pine		4 x 12 Southern Pine	
		Select Struc.	No. 1	Select Struc.	No. 1	Select Struc.	No. 1	Select Struc.	No. 1
		24F Glulam Equivalent (in.)							
10	Western Species	2-1/2 x 7-1/2 3-1/8 x 6	2-1/2 x 7-1/2 3-1/8 x 6	2-1/2 x 9 3-1/8 x 7-1/2	2-1/2 x 9 3-1/8 x 7-1/2	2-1/2 x 9 3-1/8 x 9	2-1/2 x 9 3-1/8 x 9	2-1/2 x 10-1/2 3-1/8 x 9	2-1/2 x 10-1/2 3-1/8 x 9
	Southern Pine	2-1/2 x 6-7/8 3 x 6-7/8	2-1/2 x 6-7/8 3 x 6-7/8	2-1/2 x 8-1/4 3 x 8-1/4	2-1/2 x 8-1/4 3 x 8-1/4	2-1/2 x 9-5/8 3 x 8-1/4	2-1/2 x 9-5/8 3 x 8-1/4	2-1/2 x 9-5/8 3 x 9-5/8	2-1/2 x 9-5/8 3 x 9-5/8
12	Western Species	2-1/2 x 7-1/2 3-1/8 x 6	2-1/2 x 7-1/2 3-1/8 x 6	2-1/2 x 9 3-1/8 x 9	2-1/2 x 9 3-1/8 x 7-1/2	2-1/2 x 10-1/2 3-1/8 x 9	2-1/2 x 10-1/2 3-1/8 x 9	2-1/2 x 10-1/2 3-1/8 x 10-1/2	2-1/2 x 10-1/2 3-1/8 x 10-1/2
	Southern Pine	2-1/2 x 6-7/8 3 x 6-7/8	2-1/2 x 6-7/8 3 x 6-7/8	2-1/2 x 8-1/4 3 x 8-1/4	2-1/2 x 8-1/4 3 x 8-1/4	2-1/2 x 11 3 x 9-5/8	2-1/2 x 9-5/8 3 x 9-5/8	2-1/2 x 11 3 x 11	2-1/2 x 11 3 x 11
14	Western Species	2-1/2 x 7-1/2 3-1/8 x 6	2-1/2 x 6 3-1/8 x 6	2-1/2 x 9 3-1/8 x 9	2-1/2 x 9 3-1/8 x 7-1/2	2-1/2 x 10-1/2 3-1/8 x 10-1/2	2-1/2 x 10-1/2 3-1/8 x 10-1/2	2-1/2 x 12 3-1/8 x 12	2-1/2 x 12 3-1/8 x 10-1/2
	Southern Pine	2-1/2 x 6-7/8 3 x 6-7/8	2-1/2 x 6-7/8 3 x 6-7/8	2-1/2 x 8-1/4 3 x 8-1/4	2-1/2 x 8-1/4 3 x 8-1/4	2-1/2 x 11 3 x 11	2-1/2 x 11 3 x 9-5/8	2-1/2 x 12-3/8 3 x 11	2-1/2 x 12-3/8 3 x 11
16	Western Species	2-1/2 x 7-1/2 3-1/8 x 6	2-1/2 x 6 3-1/8 x 6	2-1/2 x 9 3-1/8 x 7-1/2	2-1/2 x 9 3-1/8 x 7-1/2	2-1/2 x 10-1/2 3-1/8 x 10-1/2	2-1/2 x 10-1/2 3-1/8 x 10-1/2	2-1/2 x 13-1/2 3-1/8 x 12	2-1/2 x 12 3-1/8 x 12
	Southern Pine	2-1/2 x 6-7/8 3 x 6-7/8	2-1/2 x 6-7/8 3 x 6-7/8	2-1/2 x 8-1/4 3 x 8-1/4	2-1/2 x 8-1/4 3 x 8-1/4	2-1/2 x 11 3 x 11	2-1/2 x 11 3 x 9-5/8	2-1/2 x 13-3/4 3 x 12-3/8	2-1/2 x 12-3/8 3 x 11
18	Western Species	2-1/2 x 7-1/2 3-1/8 x 6	2-1/2 x 6 3-1/8 x 6	2-1/2 x 9 3-1/8 x 7-1/2	2-1/2 x 9 3-1/8 x 7-1/2	2-1/2 x 10-1/2 3-1/8 x 10-1/2	2-1/2 x 10-1/2 3-1/8 x 10-1/2	2-1/2 x 13-1/2 3-1/8 x 12	2-1/2 x 13-1/2 3-1/8 x 12
	Southern Pine	2-1/2 x 6-7/8 3 x 6-7/8	2-1/2 x 6-7/8 3 x 6-7/8	2-1/2 x 8-1/4 3 x 8-1/4	2-1/2 x 8-1/4 3 x 8-1/4	2-1/2 x 11 3 x 11	2-1/2 x 11 3 x 9-5/8	2-1/2 x 13-3/4 3 x 12-3/8	2-1/2 x 12-3/8 3 x 12-3/8
20	Western Species	2-1/2 x 7-1/2 3-1/8 x 6	2-1/2 x 6 3-1/8 x 6	2-1/2 x 9 3-1/8 x 7-1/2	2-1/2 x 9 3-1/8 x 7-1/2	2-1/2 x 10-1/2 3-1/8 x 10-1/2	2-1/2 x 10-1/2 3-1/8 x 10-1/2	2-1/2 x 13-1/2 3-1/8 x 12	2-1/2 x 13-1/2 3-1/8 x 12
	Southern Pine	2-1/2 x 6-7/8 3 x 6-7/8	2-1/2 x 6-7/8 3 x 6-7/8	2-1/2 x 8-1/4 3 x 8-1/4	2-1/2 x 8-1/4 3 x 8-1/4	2-1/2 x 11 3 x 11	2-1/2 x 11 3 x 9-5/8	2-1/2 x 13-3/4 3 x 12-3/8	2-1/2 x 12-3/8 3 x 12-3/8

Notes:

(1) Span = uniformly loaded simply supported beam.

(2) Maximum deflection = L/360 under live load, based on live/total load = 0.8.

(3) Service condition = dry.

(4) Beam weights for sawn and glulam members are assumed to be the same.

(5) Volume factors for glulam members and size factors for sawn lumber members are in accordance with 1991 NDS.

(6) Minimum glulam sizes considered in the table are: 2-1/2 x 6 and 3-1/8 x 6 (*western species*), and 2-1/2 x 5-1/2 and 3 x 5-1/2 (*southern pine*).

(7) Design properties at normal load duration and dry-use service conditions -
Select Structural sawn lumber members: F_b = 2300 (8"),1900 (12") psi, F_v = 90 psi, E = 1.8 x 10^6 psi.
No. 1 sawn lumber members: F_b 1650 (6"), 1500 (8"), 1300 (10"), 1250 (12") psi, F_v = 90 psi, E = 1.7 x 10^6 psi.
Glulam members: F_b = 2400 psi, F_v = 165 psi (*western species*) or 200 psi (*southern pine*), E = 1.8 x 10^6 psi.

TABLE 5
24F GLULAM EQUIVALENTS FOR 4x_ *DOUGLAS FIR-LARCH* LUMBER
ROOF BEAMS – SNOW LOADS

Designed According to the 1991 NDS
(Load Duration Factor = 1.15)

Span (ft)	Glulam Species	4 x 8 Douglas Fir		4 x 10 Douglas Fir		4 x 12 Douglas Fir		4 x 14 Douglas Fir	
		Select Struc.	No. 1	Select Struc.	No. 1	Select Struc.	No. 1	Select Struc.	No. 1
		24F Glulam Equivalent (in.)							
10	Western Species	2-1/2 x 7-1/2 3-1/8 x 7-1/2	2-1/2 x 7-1/2 3-1/8 x 7-1/2	2-1/2 x 9 3-1/8 x 9	2-1/2 x 9 3-1/8 x 7-1/2	2-1/2 x 10-1/2 3-1/8 x 9	2-1/2 x 9 3-1/8 x 9	2-1/2 x 12 3-1/8 x 10-1/2	2-1/2 x 10-1/2 3-1/8 x 10-1/2
	Southern Pine	2-1/2 x 8-1/4 3 x 6-7/8	2-1/2 x 6-7/8 3 x 6-7/8	2-1/2 x 9-5/8 3 x 8-1/4	2-1/2 x 8-1/4 3 x 8-1/4	2-1/2 x 9-5/8 3 x 9-5/8	2-1/2 x 9-5/8 3 x 8-1/4	2-1/2 x 11 3 x 11	2-1/2 x 11 3 x 9-5/8
12	Western Species	2-1/2 x 9 3-1/8 x 7-1/2	2-1/2 x 7-1/2 3-1/8 x 7-1/2	2-1/2 x 10-1/2 3-1/8 x 9	2-1/2 x 9 3-1/8 x 7-1/2	2-1/2 x 10-1/2 3-1/8 x 10-1/2	2-1/2 x 9 3-1/8 x 9	2-1/2 x 12 3-1/8 x 10-1/2	2-1/2 x 10-1/2 3-1/8 x 10-1/2
	Southern Pine	2-1/2 x 8-1/4 3 x 8-1/4	2-1/2 x 8-1/4 3 x 6-7/8	2-1/2 x 9-5/8 3 x 9-5/8	2-1/2 x 8-1/4 3 x 8-1/4	2-1/2 x 11 3 x 9-5/8	2-1/2 x 9-5/8 3 x 8-1/4	2-1/2 x 12-3/8 3 x 11	2-1/2 x 11 3 x 9-5/8
14	Western Species	2-1/2 x 9 3-1/8 x 9	2-1/2 x 7-1/2 3-1/8 x 7-1/2	2-1/2 x 10-1/2 3-1/8 x 9	2-1/2 x 9 3-1/8 x 9	2-1.2 x 12 3-1/8 x 10-1/2	2-1/2 x 10-1/2 3-1/8 x 9	2-1/2 x 13-1/2 3-1/8 x 12	2-1/2 x 10-1/2 3-1/8 x 10-1/2
	Southern Pine	2-1/2 x 8-1/4 3 x 8-1/4	2-1/2 x 8-1/4 3 x 6-7/8	2-1/2 x 9-5/8 3 x 9-5/8	2-1/2 x 9-5/8 3 x 8-1/4	2-1/2 x 11 3 x 11	2-1/2 x 9-5/8 3 x 9-5/8	2-1/2 x 12-3/8 3 x 12-3/8	2-1/2 x 11 3 x 9-5/8
16	Western Species	2-1/2 x 9 3-1/8 x 9	2-1/2 x 9 3-1/8 x 7-1/2	2-1/2 x 10-1/2 3-1/8 x 10-1/2	2-1/2 x 9 3-1/8 x 9	2-1/2 x 12 3-1/8 x 10-1/2	2-1/2 x 10-1/2 3-1/8 x 9	2-1/2 x 13-1/2 3-1/8 x 12	2-1/2 x 10-1/2 3-1/8 x 10-1/2
	Southern Pine	2-1/2 x 8-1/4 3 x 8-1/4	2-1/2 x 8-1/4 3 x 8-1/4	2-1/2 x 11 3 x 9-5/8	2-1/2 x 9-5/8 3 x 8-1/4	2-1/2 x 11 3 x 11	2-1/2 x 9-5/8 3 x 9-5/8	2-1/2 x 12-3/8 3 x 12-3/8	2-1/2 x 11 3 x 11
18	Western Species	2-1/2 x 9 3-1/8 x 9	2-1/2 x 9 3-1/8 x 7-1/2	2-1/2 x 10-1/2 3-1/8 x 10-1/2	2-1/2 x 10-1/2 3-1/8 x 9	2-1/2 x 12 3-1/8 x 12	2-1/2 x 10-1/2 3-1/8 x 10-1/2	2-1/2 x 13-1/2 3-1/8 x 12	2-1/2 x 12 3-1/8 x 10-1/2
	Southern Pine	2-1/2 x 8-1/4 3 x 8-1/4	2-1/2 x 8-1/4 3 x 8-1/4	2-1/2 x 11 3 x 9-5/8	2-1/2 x 9-5/8 3 x 9-5/8	2-1/2 x 12-3/8 3 x 11	2-1/2 x 11 3 x 9-5/8	2-1/2 x 12-3/8 3 x 12-3/8	2-1/2 x 11 3 x 11
20	Western Species	2-1/2 x 9 3-1/8 x 9	2-1/2 x 9 3-1/8 x 7-1/2	2-1/2 x 12 3-1/8 x 10-1/2	2-1/2 x 10-1/2 3-1/8 x 9	2-1/2 x 12 3-1/8 x 12	2-1/2 x 10-1/2 3-1/8 x 10-1/2	2-1/2 x 13-1/2 3-1/8 x 12	2-1/2 x 12 3-1/8 x 10-1/2
	Southern Pine	2-1/2 x 8-1/4 3 x 8-1/4	2-1/2 x 8-1/4 3 x 8-1/4	2-1/2 x 11 3 x 11	2-1/2 x 9-5/8 3 x 9-5/8	2-1/2 x 12-3/8 3 x 12-3/8	2-1/2 x 11 3 x 11	2-1/2 x 13-3/4 3 x 12-3/8	2-1/2 x 12-3/8 3 x 11

Notes:

(1) Span = uniformly loaded simply supported beam.

(2) Maximum deflection = L/180 under total load. Deflection under live load must be verified when live/total load > 3/4.

(3) Service condition = dry.

(4) Beam weights for sawn and glulam members are assumed to be the same.

(5) Volume factors for glulam members and size factors for sawn lumber members are in accordance with 1991 NDS.

(6) Minimum glulam sizes considered in the table are: 2-1/2 x 6 and 3-1/8 x 6 (*western species*), and 2-1/2 x 5-1/2 and 3 x 5-1/2 (*southern pine*).

(7) Design properties at normal load duration and dry-use service conditions -
Select Structural sawn lumber members: F_b = 1450 psi, F_v = 95 psi, E = 1.9 x 10^6 psi.
No. 1 sawn lumber members: F_b 1000 psi, F_v = 95 psi, E = 1.7 x 10^6 psi.
Glulam members: F_b = 2400 psi, F_v = 165 psi (*western species*) or 200 psi (*southern pine*), E = 1.8 x 10^6 psi.

Table excerpted from *AWS Data File: Substitution of Glued Laminated Beams for Steel or Solid Sawn Lumber*, Form No. EWS S570.

TABLE 6
24F GLULAM EQUIVALENTS FOR 4x_ *SOUTHERN PINE* LUMBER
ROOF BEAMS – SNOW LOADS

Designed According to the 1991 NDS
(Load Duration Factor = 1.15)

Span (ft)	Glulam Species	4 x 6 Southern Pine		4 x 8 Southern Pine		4 x 10 Southern Pine		4 x 12 Southern Pine	
		Select Struc.	No. 1	Select Struc.	No. 1	Select Struc.	No. 1	Select Struc.	No. 1
		24F Glulam Equivalent (in.)							
10	Western Species	2-1/2 x 7-1/2 3-1/8 x 6	2-1/2 x 6 3-1/8 x 6	2-1/2 x 7-1/2 3-1/8 x 7-1/2	2-1/2 x 7-1/2 3-1/8 x 7-1/2	2-1/2 x 9 3-1/8 x 7-1/2	2-1/2 x 9 3-1/8 x 7-1/2	2-1/2 x 10-1/2 3-1/8 x 9	2-1/2 x 10-1/2 3-1/8 x 9
	Southern Pine	2-1/2 x 6-7/8 3 x 6-7/8	2-1/2 x 6-7/8 3 x 5-1/2	2-1/2 x 8-1/4 3 x 6-7/8	2-1/2 x 8-1/4 3 x 6-7/8	2-1/2 x 9-5/8 3 x 8-1/4	2-1/2 x 9-5/8 3 x 8-1/4	2-1/2 x 9-5/8 3 x 9-5/8	2-1/2 x 9-5/8 3 x 9-5/8
12	Western Species	2-1/2 x 7-1/2 3-1/8 x 6	2-1/2 x 7-1/2 3-1/8 x 6	2-1/2 x 9 3-1/8 x 7-1/2	2-1/2 x 7-1/2 3-1/8 x 7-1/2	2-1/2 x 9 3-1/8 x 9	2-1/2 x 9 3-1/8 x 9	2-1/2 x 10-1/2 3-1/8 x 9	2-1/2 x 10-1/2 3-1/8 x 9
	Southern Pine	2-1/2 x 6-7/8 3 x 6-7/8	2-1/2 x 6-7/8 3 x 6-7/8	2-1/2 x 8-1/4 3 x 8-1/4	2-1/2 x 8-1/4 3 x 8-1/4	2-1/2 x 9-5/8 3 x 8-1/4	2-1/2 x 9-5/8 3 x 8-1/4	2-1/2 x 11 3 x 9-5/8	2-1/2 x 11 3 x 9-5/8
14	Western Species	2-1/2 x 7-1/2 3-1/8 x 6	2-1/2 x 6 3-1/8 x 6	2-1/2 x 9 3-1/8 x 9	2-1/2 x 9 3-1/8 x 7-1/2	2-1/2 x 10-1/2 3-1/8 x 9	2-1/2 x 9 3-1/8 x 9	2-1/2 x 12 3-1/8 x 10-1/2	2-1/2 x 10-1/2 3-1/8 x 10-1/2
	Southern Pine	2-1/2 x 6-7/8 3 x 6-7/8	2-1/2 x 6-7/8 3 x 6-7/8	2-1/2 x 8-1/4 3 x 8-1/4	2-1/2 x 8-1/4 3 x 8-1/4	2-1/2 x 9-5/8 3 x 9-5/8	2-1/2 x 9-5/8 3 x 9-5/8	2-1/2 x 11 3 x 11	2-1/2 x 11 3 x 9-5/8
16	Western Species	2-1/2 x 7-1/2 3-1/8 x 6	2-1/2 x 6 3-1/8 x 6	2-1/2 x 9 3-1/8 x 9	2-1/2 x 9 3-1/8 x 7-1/2	2-1/2 x 10-1/2 3-1/8 x 10-1/2	2-1/2 x 10-1/2 3-1/8 x 9	2-1/2 x 12 3-1/8 x 10-1/2	2-1/2 x 10-1/2 3-1/8 x 10-1/2
	Southern Pine	2-1/2 x 6-7/8 3 x 6-7/8	2-1/2 x 6-7/8 3 x 6-7/8	2-1/2 x 8-1/4 3 x 8-1/4	2-1/2 x 8-1/4 3 x 8-1/4	2-1/2 x 11 3 x 11	2-1/2 x 9-5/8 3 x 9-5/8	2-1/2 x 12-3/8 3 x 11	2-1/2 x 11 3 x 11
18	Western Species	2-1/2 x 7-1/2 3-1/8 x 6	2-1/2 x 6 3-1/8 x 6	2-1/2 x 9 3-1/8 x 7-1/2	2-1/2 x 9 3-1/8 x 7-1/2	2-1/2 x 10-1/2 3-1/8 x 10-1/2	2-1/2 x 10-1/2 3-1/8 x 9	2-1/2 x 13-1/2 3-1/8 x 12	2-1/2 x 12 3-1/8 x 10-1/2
	Southern Pine	2-1/2 x 6-7/8 3 x 6-7/8	2-1/2 x 6-7/8 3 x 6-7/8	2-1/2 x 8-1/4 3 x 8-1/4	2-1/2 x 8-1/4 3 x 8-1/4	2-1/2 x 11 3 x 11	2-1/2 x 9-5/8 3 x 9-5/8	2-1/2 x 12-3/8 3 x 12-3/8	2-1/2 x 11 3 x 11
20	Western Species	2-1/2 x 7-1/2 3-1/8 x 6	2-1/2 x 6 3-1/8 x 6	2-1/2 x 9 3-1/8 x 7-1/2	2-1/2 x 9 3-1/8 x 7-1/2	2-1/2 x 10-1/2 3-1/8 x 10-1/2	2-1/2 x 10-1/2 3-1/8 x 10-1/2	2-1/2 x 13-1/2 3-1/8 x 12	2-1/2 x 12 3-1/8 x 10-1/2
	Southern Pine	2-1/2 x 6-7/8 3 x 6-7/8	2-1/2 x 6-7/8 3 x 6-7/8	2-1/2 x 8-1/4 3 x 8-1/4	2-1/2 x 8-1/4 3 x 8-1/4	2-1/2 x 11 3 x 11	2-1/2 x 11 3 x 9-5/8	2-1/2 x 13-3/4 3 x 12-3/8	2-1/2 x 12-3/8 3 x 11

Notes:

(1) Span = uniformly loaded simply supported beam.

(2) Maximum deflection = L/180 under total load. Deflection under live load must be verified when live/total load > 3/4.

(3) Service condition = dry.

(4) Beam weights for sawn and glulam members are assumed to be the same.

(5) Volume factors for glulam members and size factors for sawn lumber members are in accordance with 1991 NDS.

(6) Minimum glulam sizes considered in the table are: 2-1/2 x 6 and 3-1/8 x 6 (*western species*), and 2-1/2 x 5-1/2 and 3 x 5-1/2 (*southern pine*).

(7) Design properties at normal load duration and dry-use service conditions -
Select Structural sawn lumber members: F_b = 2300 (8"), 2050 (10"), 1900 (12") psi, F_v = 90 psi, E = 1.8 x 10^6 psi.
No. 1 sawn lumber members: F_b 1650 (6"), 1500 (8"), 1300 (10"), 1250 (12") psi, F_v = 90 psi, E = 1.7 x 10^6 psi.
Glulam members: F_b = 2400 psi, F_v = 165 psi (*western species*) or 200 psi (*southern pine*), E = 1.8 x 10^6 psi.

Table excerpted from *AWS Data File: Substitution of Glued Laminated Beams for Steel or Solid Sawn Lumber*, Form No. EWS S570.

TABLE 7
24F GLULAM EQUIVALENTS FOR 4x_ *DOUGLAS FIR-LARCH* LUMBER
ROOF BEAMS – NON-SNOW LOADS

Designed According to the 1991 NDS
(Load Duration Factor = 1.25)

Span (ft)	Glulam Species	4 x 8 Douglas Fir		4 x 10 Douglas Fir		4 x 12 Douglas Fir		4 x 14 Douglas Fir	
		Select Struc.	No. 1	Select Struc.	No. 1	Select Struc.	No. 1	Select Struc.	No. 1
		24F Glulam Equivalent (in.)							
10	Western Species	2-1/2 x 7-1/2 / 3-1/8 x 7-1/2	2-1/2 x 7-1/2 / 3-1/8 x 7-1/2	2-1/2 x 9 / 3-1/8 x 9	2-1/2 x 9 / 3-1/8 x 7-1/2	2-1/2 x 10-1/2 / 3-1/8 x 9	2-1/2 x 9 / 3-1/8 x 9	2-1/2 x 12 / 3-1/8 x 10-1/2	2-1/2 x 10-1/2 / 3-1/8 x 10-1/2
	Southern Pine	2-1/2 x 8-1/4 / 3 x 8-1/4	2-1/2 x 6-7/8 / 3 x 6-7/8	2-1/2 x 9-5/8 / 3 x 8-1/4	2-1/2 x 8-1/4 / 3 x 8-1/4	2-1/2 x 9-5/8 / 3 x 9-5/8	2-1/2 x 9-5/8 / 3 x 8-1/4	2-1/2 x 11 / 3 x 11	2-1/2 x 11 / 3 x 9-5/8
12	Western Species	2-1/2 x 9 / 3-1/8 x 7-1/2	2-1/2 x 7-1/2 / 3-1/8 x 7-1/2	2-1/2 x 10-1/2 / 3-1/8 x 9	2-1/2 x 9 / 3-1/8 x 9	2-1/2 x 10-1/2 / 3-1/8 x 10-1/2	2-1/2 x 9 / 3-1/8 x 9	2-1/2 x 12 / 3-1/8 x 10-1/2	2-1/2 x 10-1/2 / 3-1/8 x 10-1/2
	Southern Pine	2-1/2 x 8-1/4 / 3 x 8-1/4	2-1/2 x 8-1/4 / 3 x 6-7/8	2-1/2 x 9-5/8 / 3 x 9-5/8	2-1/2 x 8-1/4 / 3 x 8-1/4	2-1/2 x 11 / 3 x 9-5/8	2-1/2 x 9-5/8 / 3 x 9-5/8	2-1/2 x 12-3/8 / 3 x 11	2-1/2 x 11 / 3 x 9-5/8
14	Western Species	2-1/2 x 9 / 3-1/8 x 9	2-1/2 x 7-1/2 / 3-1/8 x 7-1/2	2-1/2 x 10-1/2 / 3-1/8 x 9	2-1/2 x 9 / 3-1/8 x 9	2-1/2 x 12 / 3-1/8 x 10-1/2	2-1/2 x 10-1/2 / 3-1/8 x 9	2-1/2 x 13-1/2 / 3-1/8 x 12	2-1/2 x 10-1/2 / 3-1/8 x 10-1/2
	Southern Pine	2-1/2 x 8-1/4 / 3 x 8-1/4	2-1/2 x 8-1/4 / 3 x 8-1/4	2-1/2 x 11 / 3 x 9-5/8	2-1/2 x 9-5/8 / 3 x 8-1/4	2-1/2 x 11 / 3 x 11	2-1/2 x 9-5/8 / 3 x 9-5/8	2-1/2 x 12-3/8 / 3 x 12-3/8	2-1/2 x 11 / 3 x 9-5/8
16	Western Species	2-1/2 x 9 / 3-1/8 x 9	2-1/2 x 9 / 3-1/8 x 7-1/2	2-1/2 x 10-1/2 / 3-1/8 x 10-1/2	2-1/2 x 9 / 3-1/8 x 9	2-1/2 x 12 / 3-1/8 x 10-1/2	2-1/2 x 10-1/2 / 3-1/8 x 10-1/2	2-1/2 x 13-1/2 / 3-1/8 x 12	2-1/2 x 12 / 3-1/8 x 10-1/2
	Southern Pine	2-1/2 x 8-1/4 / 3 x 8-1/4	2-1/2 x 8-1/4 / 3 x 8-1/4	2-1/2 x 11 / 3 x 9-5/8	2-1/2 x 9-5/8 / 3 x 9-5/8	2-1/2 x 12-3/8 / 3 x 11	2-1/2 x 11 / 3 x 9-5/8	2-1/2 x 12-3/8 / 3 x 12-3/8	2-1/2 x 11 / 3 x 11
18	Western Species	2-1/2 x 9 / 3-1/8 x 9	2-1/2 x 9 / 3-1/8 x 7-1/2	2-1/2 x 12 / 3-1/8 x 10-1/2	2-1/2 x 10-1/2 / 3-1/8 x 9	2-1/2 x 12 / 3-1/8 x 12	2-1/2 x 12 / 3-1/8 x 10-1/2	2-1/2 x 13-1/2 / 3-1/8 x 12	2-1/2 x 12 / 3-1/8 x 10-1/2
	Southern Pine	2-1/2 x 8-1/4 / 3 x 8-1/4	2-1/2 x 8-1/4 / 3 x 8-1/4	2-1/2 x 11 / 3 x 11	2-1/2 x 9-5/8 / 3 x 9-5/8	2-1/2 x 12-3/8 / 3 x 11	2-1/2 x 11 / 3 x 11	2-1/2 x 13-3/4 / 3 x 12-3/8	2-1/2 x 12-3/8 / 3 x 11
20	Western Species	2-1/2 x 9 / 3-1/8 x 9	2-1/2 x 9 / 3-1/8 x 7-1/2	2-1/2 x 12 / 3-1/8 x 10-1/2	2-1/2 x 10-1/2 / 3-1/8 x 9	2-1/2 x 13-1/2 / 3-1/8 x 12	2-1/2 x 12 / 3-1/8 x 10-1/2	2-1/2 x 13-1/2 / 3-1/8 x 13-1/2	2-1/2 x 12 / 3-1/8 x 12
	Southern Pine	2-1/2 x 8-1/4 / 3 x 8-1/4	2-1/2 x 8-1/4 / 3 x 8-1/4	2-1/2 x 11 / 3 x 11	2-1/2 x 9-5/8 / 3 x 9-5/8	2-1/2 x 12-3/8 / 3 x 12-3/8	2-1/2 x 11 / 3 x 11	2-1/2 x 13-3/4 / 3 x 12-3/8	2-1/2 x 12-3/8 / 3 x 11

Notes:

(1) Span = uniformly loaded simply supported beam.

(2) Maximum deflection = L/180 under total load. Deflection under live load must be verified when live/total load > 3/4.

(3) Service condition = dry.

(4) Beam weights for sawn and glulam members are assumed to be the same.

(5) Volume factors for glulam members and size factors for sawn lumber members are in accordance with 1991 NDS.

(6) Minimum glulam sizes considered in the table are: 2-1/2 x 6 and 3-1/8 x 6 (*western species*), and 2-1/2 x 5-1/2 and 3 x 5-1/2 (*southern pine*).

(7) Design properties at normal load duration and dry-use service conditions -
Select Structural sawn lumber members: F_b = 1450 psi, F_v = 95 psi, E = 1.9 x 10⁶ psi.
No. 1 sawn lumber members: F_b 1000 psi, F_v = 95 psi, E = 1.7 x 10⁶ psi.
Glulam members: F_b = 2400 psi, F_v = 165 psi (*western species*) or 200 psi (*southern pine*), E = 1.8 x 10⁶ psi.

Table excerpted from *AWS Data File: Substitution of Glued Laminated Beams for Steel or Solid Sawn Lumber*, Form No. EWS S570.

TABLE 8
24F GLULAM EQUIVALENTS FOR 4x_ *SOUTHERN PINE* LUMBER
ROOF BEAMS – NON-SNOW LOADS

Designed According to the 1991 NDS
(Load Duration Factor = 1.25)

Span (ft)	Glulam Species	4 x 6 Southern Pine		4 x 8 Southern Pine		4 x 10 Southern Pine		4 x 12 Southern Pine	
		Select Struc.	No. 1	Select Struc.	No. 1	Select Struc.	No. 1	Select Struc.	No. 1
		24F Glulam Equivalent (in.)							
10	Western Species	2-1/2 x 7-1/2 3-1/8 x 6	2-1/2 x 7-1/2 3-1/8 x 6	2-1/2 x 7-1/2 3-1/8 x 7-1/2	2-1/2 x 7-1/2 3-1/8 x 7-1/2	2-1/2 x 9 3-1/8 x 7-1/2	2-1/2 x 9 3-1/8 x 7-1/2	2-1/2 x 10-1/2 3-1/8 x 9	2-1/2 x 10-1/2 3-1/8 x 9
	Southern Pine	2-1/2 x 6-7/8 3 x 6-7/8	2-1/2 x 6-7/8 3 x 6-7/8	2-1/2 x 8-1/4 3 x 6-7/8	2-1/2 x 8-1/4 3 x 6-7/8	2-1/2 x 9-5/8 3 x 8-1/4	2-1/2 x 9-5/8 3 x 8-1/4	2-1/2 x 9-5/8 3 x 9-5/8	2-1/2 x 9-5/8 3 x 9-5/8
12	Western Species	2-1/2 x 7-1/2 3-1/8 x 6	2-1/2 x 7-1/2 3-1/8 x 6	2-1/2 x 9 3-1/8 x 9	2-1/2 x 9 3-1/8 x 7-1/2	2-1/2 x 9 3-1/8 x 9	2-1/2 x 9 3-1/8 x 9	2-1/2 x 10-1/2 3-1/8 x 9	2-1/2 x 10-1/2 3-1/8 x 9
	Southern Pine	2-1/2 x 6-7/8 3 x 6-7/8	2-1/2 x 6-7/8 3 x 6-7/8	2-1/2 x 8-1/4 3 x 8-1/4	2-1/2 x 8-1/4 3 x 8-1/4	2-1/2 x 9-5/8 3 x 9-5/8	2-1/2 x 9-5/8 3 x 8-1/4	2-1/2 x 11 3 x 9-5/8	2-1/2 x 11 3 x 9-5/8
14	Western Species	2-1/2 x 6-7/8 3-1/8 x 6	2-1/2 x 6 3-1/8 x 6	2-1/2 x 9 3-1/8 x 9	2-1/2 x 9 3-1/8 x 7-1/2	2-1/2 x 10-1/2 3-1/8 x 10-1/2	2-1/2 x 10-1/2 3-1/8 x 9	2-1/2 x 12 3-1/8 x 10-1/2	2-1/2 x 10-1/2 3-1/8 x 10-1/2
	Southern Pine	2-1/2 x 6-7/8 3 x 6-7/8	2-1/2 x 6-7/8 3 x 6-7/8	2-1/2 x 8-1/4 3 x 8-1/4	2-1/2 x 8-1/4 3 x 8-1/4	2-1/2 x 11 3 x 9-5/8	2-1/2 x 9-5/8 3 x 9-5/8	2-1/2 x 11 3 x 11	2-1/2 x 11 3 x 9-5/8
16	Western Species	2-1/2 x 7-1/2 3-1/8 x 6	2-1/2 x 6 3-1/8 x 6	2-1/2 x 9 3-1/8 x 9	2-1/2 x 9 3-1/8 x 7-1/2	2-1/2 x 10-1/2 3-1/8 x 10-1/2	2-1/2 x 10-1/2 3-1/8 x 9	2-1/2 x 12 3-1/8 x 12	2-1/2 x 12 3-1/8 x 10-1/2
	Southern Pine	2-1/2 x 6-7/8 3 x 6-7/8	2-1/2 x 6-7/8 3 x 6-7/8	2-1/2 x 8-1/4 3 x 8-1/4	2-1/2 x 8-1/4 3 x 8-1/4	2-1/2 x 11 3 x 11	2-1/2 x 9-5/8 3 x 9-5/8	2-1/2 x 12-3/8 3 x 11	2-1/2 x 11 3 x 11
18	Western Species	2-1/2 x 7-1/2 3-1/8 x 6	2-1/2 x 6 3-1/8 x 6	2-1/2 x 9 3-1/8 x 7-1/2	2-1/2 x 9 3-1/8 x 7-1/2	2-1/2 x 10-1/2 3-1/8 x 10-1/2	2-1/2 x 10-1/2 3-1/8 x 10-1/2	2-1/2 x 13-1/2 3-1/8 x 12	2-1/2 x 12 3-1/8 x 10-1/2
	Southern Pine	2-1/2 x 6-7/8 3 x 6-7/8	2-1/2 x 6-7/8 3 x 6-7/8	2-1/2 x 8-1/4 3 x 8-1/4	2-1/2 x 8-1/4 3 x 8-1/4	2-1/2 x 11 3 x 11	2-1/2 x 11 3 x 9-5/8	2-1/2 x 13-3/4 3 x 12-3/8	2-1/2 x 12-3/8 3 x 11
20	Western Species	2-1/2 x 7-1/2 3-1/8 x 6	2-1/2 x 6 3-1/8 x 6	2-1/2 x 9 3-1/8 x 7-1/2	2-1/2 x 9 3-1/8 x 7-1/2	2-1/2 x 10-1/2 3-1/8 x 10-1/2	2-1/2 x 10-1/2 3-1/8 x 10-1/2	2-1/2 x 13-1/2 3-1/8 x 12	2-1/2 x 12 3-1/8 x 12
	Southern Pine	2-1/2 x 6-7/8 3 x 6-7/8	2-1/2 x 6-7/8 3 x 6-7/8	2-1/2 x 8-1/4 3 x 8-1/4	2-1/2 x 8-1/4 3 x 8-1/4	2-1/2 x 11 3 x 11	2-1/2 x 11 3 x 9-5/8	2-1/2 x 13-3/4 3 x 12-3/8	2-1/2 x 12-3/8 3 x 11

Notes

(1) Span = uniformly loaded simply supported beam.

(2) Maximum deflection = L/180 under total load. Deflection under live load must be verified when live/total load > 3/4.

(3) Service condition = dry.

(4) Beam weights for sawn and glulam members are assumed to be the same.

(5) Volume factors for glulam members and size factors for sawn lumber members are in accordance with 1991 NDS.

(6) Minimum glulam sizes considered in the table are: 2-1/2 x 6 and 3-1/8 x 6 (*western species*), and 2-1/2 x 5-1/2 and 3 x 5-1/2 (*southern pine*).

(7) Design properties at normal load duration and dry-use service conditions -
Select Structural sawn lumber members: F_b = 2300 (8″), 2050 (10″), 1900 (12″) psi, F_v = 90 psi, E = 1.8 x 10^6 psi.
No. 1 sawn lumber members: F_b 1650 (6″), 1500 (8″), 1300 (10″), 1250 (12″) psi, F_v = 90 psi, E = 1.7 x 10^6 psi.
Glulam members: F_b = 2400 psi, F_v = 165 psi (*western species*) or 200 psi (*southern pine*), E = 1.8 x 10^6 psi.

Table excerpted from *AWS Data File: Substitution of Glued Laminated Beams for Steel or Solid Sawn Lumber*, Form No. EWS S570.

TABLE 9
24F *WESTERN SPECIES* GLULAM EQUIVALENTS FOR STEEL FLOOR BEAMS

(Load Duration Factor for Glulam = 1.00)

Span (ft)	W6x9	W8x10	W12x14	W12x16	W12x19	W10x22
	24F *Western Species* Glulam Equivalent (in.)					
12	3-1/8 x 10-1/2 5-1/8 x 9	3-1/8 x 13-1/2 5-1/8 x 10-1/2	3-1/8 x 21 5-1/8 x 15	3-1/8 x 24 5-1/8 x 16-1/2	3-1/8 x 27 5-1/8 x 19-1/2	3-1/8 x 28-1/2 5-1/8 x 21
16	3-1/8 x 10-1/2 5-1/8 x 9	3-1/8 x 13-1/2 5-1/8 x 12	3-1/8 x 18 5-1/8 x 15	3-1/8 x 21 5-1/8 x 15	3-1/8 x 24 5-1/8 x 16-1/2	3-1/8 x 25-1/2 5-1/8 x 18
20	3-1/8 x 10-1/2 5-1/8 x 9	3-1/8 x 13-1/2 5-1/8 x 12	3-1/8 x 18 5-1/8 x 15	3-1/8 x 19-1/2 5-1/8 x 16-1/2	3-1/8 x 21 5-1/8 x 18	3-1/8 x 19-1/2 5-1/8 x 16-1/2
24	3-1/8 x 10-1/2 5-1/8 x 9	3-1/8 x 13-1/2 5-1/8 x 12	3-1/8 x 18 5-1/8 x 16-1/2	3-1/8 x 19-1/2 5-1/8 x 16-1/2	3-1/8 x 21 5-1/8 x 18	3-1/8 x 19-1/2 5-1/8 x 16-1/2
28	3-1/8 x 10-1/2 5-1/8 x 9	3-1/8 x 13-1/2 5-1/8 x 12	3-1/8 x 18 5-1/8 x 16-1/2	3-1/8 x 19-1/2 5-1/8 x 16-1/2	3-1/8 x 21 5-1/8 x 18	3-1/8 x 19-1/2 5-1/8 x 16-1/2
32	3-1/8 x 10-1/2 5-1/8 x 9	3-1/8 x 13-1/2 5-1/8 x 12	3-1/8 x 18 5-1/8 x 16-1/2	3-1/8 x 19-1/2 5-1/8 x 16-1/2	3-1/8 x 21 5-1/8 x 18	3-1/8 x 19-1/2 5-1/8 x 16-1/2
36	3-1/8 x 10-1/2 5-1/8 x 9	3-1/8 x 13-1/2 5-1/8 x 12	3-1/8 x 18 5-1/8 x 16-1/2	3-1/8 x 19-1/2 5-1/8 x 16-1/2	3-1/8 x 21 5-1/8 x 18	3-1/8 x 19-1/2 5-1/8 x 16-1/2
40	3-1/8 x 10-1/2 5-1/8 x 9	3-1/8 x 13-1/2 5-1/8 x 12	3-1/8 x 18 5-1/8 x 16-1/2	3-1/8 x 19-1/2 5-1/8 x 16-1/2	3-1/8 x 21 5-1/8 x 18	3-1/8 x 19-1/2 5-1/8 x 16-1/2

Notes:

(1) Span = uniformly loaded simply supported beam.

(2) Maximum deflection = L/360 under live load, based on live/total load = 0.8.

(3) Service condition for glulam members = dry.

(4) Beam weights for steel and glulam members (assumed 35 pcf) are included.

(5) Volume factors for glulam members are in accordance with 1991 NDS.

(6) Minimum glulam sizes considered in the table are: 3-1/8 x 6 and 5-1/8 x 6.

(7) Design properties for steel members: F_b = 0.66 x 36 ksi, F_v = 0.4 x 36 ksi, E = 29 x 10^6 psi.

(8) Design properties for glulam members at normal load duration and dry-use service conditions: F_b = 2400 psi, F_v = 165 psi, E = 1.8 x 10^6 psi.

TABLE 10
24F *SOUTHERN PINE* GLULAM EQUIVALENTS FOR STEEL FLOOR BEAMS
(Load Duration Factor for Glulam = 1.00)

Span (ft)	W6x9	W8x10	W12x14	W12x16	W12x19	W10x22
	24F *Southern Pine* Glulam Equivalent (in.)					
12	3 x 11	3 x 13-3/4	3 x 19-1/4	3 x 20-5/8	3 x 24-3/4	3 x 26-1/8
	5 x 9-5/8	5 x 11	5 x 13-3/4	5 x 15-1/8	5 x 16-1/2	5 x 17-7/8
16	3 x 11	3 x 13-3/4	3 x 17-7/8	3 x 19-1/4	3 x 22	3 x 23-3/8
	5 x 9-5/8	5 x 11	5 x 15-1/8	5 x 15-1/8	5 x 16-1/2	5 x 17-7/8
20	3 x 11	3 x 13-3/4	3 x 17-7/8	3 x 19-1/4	3 x 20-5/8	3 x 20-5/8
	5 x 9-5/8	5 x 11	5 x 15-1/8	5 x 16-1/2	5 x 17-7/8	5 x 17-7/8
24	3 x 11	3 x 13-3/4	3 x 17-7/8	3 x 19-1/4	3 x 20-5/8	3 x 20-5/8
	5 x 9-5/8	5 x 11	5 x 16-1/2	5 x 16-1/2	5 x 17-7/8	5 x 17-7/8
28	3 x 11	3 x 13-3/4	3 x 17-7/8	3 x 19-1/4	3 x 20-5/8	3 x 20-5/8
	5 x 9-5/8	5 x 11	5 x 16-1/2	5 x 16-1/2	5 x 17-7/8	5 x 17-7/8
32	3 x 11	3 x 13-3/4	3 x 17-7/8	3 x 19-1/4	3 x 20-5/8	3 x 20-5/8
	5 x 9-5/8	5 x 11	5 x 16-1/2	5 x 16-1/2	5 x 17-7/8	5 x 17-7/8
36	3 x 11	3 x 13-3/4	3 x 17-7/8	3 x 19-1/4	3 x 20-5/8	3 x 20-5/8
	5 x 9-5/8	5 x 11	5 x 16-1/2	5 x 16-1/2	5 x 17-7/8	5 x 17-7/8
40	3 x 11	3 x 13-3/4	3 x 17-7/8	3 x 19-1/4	3 x 20-5/8	3 x 19-1/4
	5 x 9-5/8	5 x 12-3/8	5 x 16-1/2	5 x 16-1/2	5 x 17-7/8	5 x 17-7/8

Notes:

(1) Span = uniformly loaded simply supported beam.

(2) Maximum deflection = L/360 under live load, based on live/total load = 0.8.

(3) Service condition for glulam members = dry.

(4) Beam weights for steel and glulam members (assumed 36 pcf) are included.

(5) Volume factors for glulam members are in accordance with 1991 NDS.

(6) Minimum glulam sizes considered in the table are: 3-1/8 x 6 and 5-1/8 x 6.

(7) Design properties for steel members: F_b = 0.66 x 36 ksi, F_v = 0.4 x 36 ksi, E = 29 x 10^6 psi.

(8) Design properties for glulam members at normal load duration and dry-use service conditions: F_b = 2400 psi, F_v = 200 psi, E = 1.8 x 10^6 psi.

▪ Index